7/22/2013

France
The Dark Years
1940–1944

France
The Dark Years
1940–1944

Julian Jackson

OXFORD

UNIVERSITY PRESS

Great Clarendon Street, Oxford OX2 6DP

Oxford University Press is a department of the University of Oxford.
It furthers the University's objective of excellence in research, scholarship,
and education by publishing worldwide in

Oxford New York

Auckland Bangkok Buenos Aires Cape Town Chennai
Dar es Salaam Delhi Hong Kong Istanbul Karachi Kolkata
Kuala Lumpur Madrid Melbourne Mexico City Mumbai Nairobi
São Paulo Shanghai Taipei Tokyo Toronto

Oxford is a registered trade mark of Oxford University Press
in the UK and certain other countries

Published in the United States
by Oxford University Press Inc., New York

British Library Cataloguing in Publication Data

Data available

Library of Congress Cataloging in Publication Data

Data available

ISBN 0-19-820706-9 (hbk)
ISBN 0-19-925457-5 (pbk)

10 9 8 7 6 5 4 3 2 1

Typeset by SNP Best-set Typesetter Ltd., Hong Kong
Printed in Great Britain
on acid-free paper by
Biddles Ltd,
Guildford and Kings Lynn

To the Memory of My Mother

Preface

This book is inspired by the conviction that the time is ripe for a new history of France during the German Occupation. The last general history of this subject, by the French historian Jean-Pierre Azéma, appeared in 1973, but in the twenty-seven years since then a huge amount of research has taken place. My ambition in writing this study is to offer a new interpretative synthesis which takes account of the massive quantity of new work. What this means, therefore, is that this book could not have been written without the pioneering archival work of innumerable other historians. I hope that I have made my debts to them clear in the footnotes, but I would like to take the opportunity in this preface to mention by name some of those historians whose work has been of particular inspiration and stimulation to me: Philippe Burrin, Luc Capdevila, Daniel Cordier, Jean-Louis Crémieux-Brilhac, Laurent Douzou, Jean-Marie Guillon, Stanley Hoffmann, Roderick Kedward, Pierre Laborie, François Marcot, Robert Paxton, Denis Peschanski, Henry Rousso, Gisèle Sapiro, John Sweets, Olivier Wieviorka.

It can be seen that the majority of names on this list are French, and this fact perhaps needs underlining given the seemingly ineradicable belief outside France (and indeed sometimes in France as well) that the French are still unwilling to 'face up' to their past. While writing this book I lost count of the number of people who wanted to tell me about France's voluntary amnesia about the Occupation and her predeliction for believing in heroic legends about the Resistance. The problem with such comments is not only the unwarranted condescension which underlies them—the assumption is that 'we', the British, would have faced up to things much better in similar circumstances—but also the fact that they are so patently false. It is true that the first important studies of the Vichy regime came from outside France, but French historians caught up long ago. Far from being years which French historians avoid, the Vichy period is probably at present the most intensively researched in French history even if it is difficult to say how far, and in what ways, the findings of the scholarly community have penetrated to the wider public. If anything, however, popular views of the Occupation in France have become excessively fixated on collaboration and anti-semitism while the most recent scholarly research has tended to focus again on the Resistance after some years of neglect. One of my aims in this book is also to bring the Resistance back into the picture while not in any way underplaying the bleaker aspects of the period.

I am most grateful to Tony Morris, formerly of OUP, for having encouraged me to write this book and supporting it so enthusiastically. When I told him that I wanted to write a short book about Vichy, he told me that I should think about writing something more ambitious. I am glad that I followed his advice, but if readers find this book too long, he must share part of the blame. Thanks also to Ruth Parr, Tony Morris's successor at OUP, for continuing to back a project that was not originally her own, to Michael Watson for seeing it through the production process, and to Rowena Anketell for her extraordinarily efficient copy-editing. Much of the research for this book was carried out in the library of the Institut d'histoire du temps présent, and I am especially grateful for the helpfulness of the librarian Jean Astruc. I would also like to thank the staff of the BDIC library at Nanterre. One beneficial side-effect of the last stages of my research was that I even came to appreciate, if not to love, the new Bibliothèque de France: perhaps affection will come with time. I would also like to record my thanks to David Eastwood, my head of Department, who has given my work on this book such support, and has managed in our Department to preserve such a civilized and good humoured working atmosphere even in this unpleasant period of Blairo-Thatcherite permanent revolution in British universities.

I would also like to thank Frank Cherbé for his encouragement and for providing me with huge amounts of material about the reporting of the Papon trial in France. Eleanor Breuning was kind enough to help me proof read the entire text: her heroic efforts saved me from numerous solecisms. Three people kindly read the manuscript at earlier stages. Patrick Higgins read quite a lot of an early draft. His careful reading showed me how much more work there was to be done. But my debt to Patrick is much deeper than that. I have learnt so much from him in our twenty years of friendship, and one day I hope I will know half as much history as he does. Roderick Kedward read the whole of the finished manuscript and made numerous helpful suggestions. His encouragement has been very important to me, and the stimulus which his work and inspiration has given to the study of Vichy and the French Resistance in Britain is quite incalculable. Kevin Passmore read the manuscript at too late a stage to be able to make many detailed comments, but I tried to take on board those suggestions which he did permit himself to make. More generally, however, he has taught me a huge amount about inter-war French politics both in his writing and in our many conversations. Having him as a colleague in a university close to my own has been very important.

Finally, and most importantly, I would like to thank Douglas who has lived in closer proximity to this book than he would probably have liked at times. Unfortunately there are few activities that render one more self-centred and selfish than writing a book. I shall try harder to overcome this next time, but in the meantime I can only record my heartfelt gratitude for everything that 1 owe him.

Swansea, July 2000

Contents

List of Maps and Figure

Abbreviations

The numbers in brackets refer to the page in the text where it first appears with an English translation or explanation.

ACA	Assemblée des cardinales et archevêques [268]	CDLR	Ceux de la Résistance [413]
ACJF	Association catholique de la jeunesse française [270]	CEES	Comité d'études éonomiques et sociales [297]
ADMP	Association pour défendre la mémoire du Maréchal Pétain [609]	CF	Croix de feu [72]
		CFA	Comité franco-allemand [88]
		CFL	Corps franc de la Libération [540]
AI	Action immédiate [502]	CFLN	Comité français de la Libération nationale [459]
AMGOT	Allied Military Government of Occupied Territories [527]	CFTC	Confédération française des travailleurs chrétiens [270]
ANAPF	Alliance nationale pour l'accroissement de la population Française [31]	CGE	Comité général d'études [434]
		CGQ J	Commissariat général aux questions juives [357]
ANOD	Association nationale pour l'organisation de la démocratie [51]	CGT	Confédération générale du travail [46]
AO	Action ouvrière [411]	CGTU	Confédération générale du travail unitaire [66]
AS	Armée secrète [436]		
ATP	Arts et traditions populaires [30]	CIMADE	Comité intermouvement auprès des évacués [377]
BCRA	Bureau central de renseignements et d'action [432]	CLL	Comité local de Libération [538]
BCRAM	Bureau central de renseignements et d'action militaire [400]	CMN	Comité national militaire (of FTP) [423]
		CMR	Comité médical de la Résistance [499]
BIP	Bureau d'information et de presse [434]	CND	Confrérie Notre Dame [400]
		CNE	Comité national des écrivains [499]
BS	Brigades spéciales [158]		
CAD	Centre d'action et de documentation [200]	CNIE	Commission nationale interprofessionnelle d'épuration [590]
CAS	Comité d'action socialiste [419]	CNR	Conseil national de la Résistance [456]
CCDM	Comité central des mouvements de Résistance [465]	CNU	Comité national de l'urbanisme [348]
CDJC	Centre de documentation juive contemporaine [14]	CO	Comité d'organisation [162]
		COIC	Comité d'organisation du cinéma [318]
CDL	Comité départemental de Libération [518]	COMAC	Commission d'action militaire [521]
CDLL	Ceux de la Libération [413]		

COSI   Comité ouvrier de secours immédiat [297]
CPL   Comité parisien de Libération [519]
CRI   Commissariat technique à la reconstruction immobilière [347]
CRIF   Conseil représentatif des Israélites de France [613]
CRS   Compagnie republicaine de securité [260]
CSAR   Comité secret d'action révolutionnaire [77]
CSC   Comité syndical de coordination [296]
CSEIC   Conseil supérieur de l'économie industrielle et commerciale [163]
CSP   Centre syndical du propagande [197]
CVR   Combattant volontaire de la Résistance [477]
DGEN   Délégation général à l'équipement national [162]
DGREFA Délégation générale aux relations économiques franco-allemandes [186]
DGSS   Direction générale des services spéciales [464]
DMN   Délégué militaire national [521]
DMR   Délégué militaire de région [520]
DMZ   Délégué militaire de zone [520]
EMFFI   État-Major des forces françaises de l'intérieur [547]
EIF   Éclaireurs israélites de France [160]
ENA   École nationale d'administration [595]
ERC   Emergency Rescue Committee [300]
FFI   Forces françaises de l'intérieur [505]
FN   Front national [444]
FNC   Fédération nationale catholique [68]
FNSP   Fondation nationale des sciences politiques (11)

FRN   Front national révolutionnaire [220]
FST   Front social du travail [197]
FTP   Franc-Tireurs et partisans [368]
GMR   Groupes mobiles de réserve [260]
GPRF   Gouvernement provisoire de la République française [543]
GTE   Groupement de travailleurs étrangers [150]
IEQ J   Institut d'études des questions juives [200]
IEQJER Institut d'étude des questions juives et ethno-raciales [358]
IHTP   Institut d'histoire du temps présent [7]
INED   Institut national d'études démographiques [597]
JEC   Jeunesse étudiante chrétienne [414]
JFOM   Jeunesse de France et d'Outremer [160]
LVF   Légion de volontaires français [194]
MBF   Militärbefehlshaber in Frankreich [170]
MLN   Mouvement de Libération nationale [470]
MNCR   Mouvement national contre le racisme [369]
MNRPDG Mouvement national de résistance des prisonniers de guerre [511]
MOI   Main d'oeuvre immigrée [365]
MRP   Mouvement républicain populaire [514]
MSR   Mouvement social révolutionnaire [192]
MUR   Mouvements unis de la Résistance [436]
NAP   Noyautage des administrations publiques [411]
NRF   Nouvelle revue française [38]
OCM   Organisation civile et militaire [413]
OCPRI   Office central de répartition des produits industriels [162]
OFI   Office central d'information [253]

OG   Operational Group [548]
OJC   Organisation juive de combat [368]
ORA   Organisation de Résistance de l'armée [505]
OS   Organisation spéciale [423]
OSE   Oeuvre de secours aux enfants [370]
OSS   Office of Strategic Services [408]
PCF   Parti communiste français [66]
PPF   Parti populaire français [78]
PQ J   Police aux questions juives [260]
PDP   Parti démocrate populaire [70]
PKWN   Polski Komitet Wyzwolenia Narodowego [494]
PNB   Parti national breton [248]
POWN   Polska organizacja walki o niepodlogosc [494]
PSF   Parti social français [74]
RNP   Rassemblement national populaire [193]
RPF   Rassemblement du peuple français [603]
SAP   Section d'atterrisage et de parachutage [548]
SAS   Special Air Services [548]
SCAP   Service du contrôle des administrateurs provisoires [356]
SD   Sicherheitsdienst [170]
SEC   Service d'enquête et de contrôle [260]
SFIO   Section française de l'internationale ouvrière [197]
SGJ   Secrétariat général à la jeunesse [149]
SNM   Service national du maquis [453]
SOAM   Service des opérations aériennes et maritimes [435]

SOE   Special Operations Executive [400]
SOL   Service d'ordre légionnaire [230]
SPAC   Service de police anti-communiste [260]
SRMAN   Service de répression des menées antinationales [261]
SSS   Service des sociétés secrètes [260]
STO   Service du travail obligatoire [228]
TA   Travail allemand [494]
UDSR   Union démocratique et sociale de la Résistance [594]
UFF   Union des femmes françaises [508]
UGIF   Union générale des Israélites de France [357]
UNE   Union nacional española [495]
UNR   Union nationale de la Résistance [470]
UNSA   Union nationale des syndicats agricoles (290)
WT   Wireless Transmission [435]

Abbreviations used in footnotes

EHQ   *European History Quarterly*
FHS   *French Historical Studies*
GMCC   *Guerres mondiales et conflits contemporains*
HJ   *Historical Journal*
JCH   *Journal of Contemporary History*
JMH   *Journal of Modern History*
MS   *Mouvement social*
RHDGM   *Revue d'histoire de la Deuxième Guerre mondiale*
RHMC   *Revue d'histoire moderne et contemporaine*
VEF   J-P. Azéma and F. Bédarida, *Le Régime de Vichy et les Français* (1993)
VSRH   *Vingtième siècle, revue d'histoire*

Map 1 French *départements*

A Unoccupied Zone
B Occupied Zone
C Zone attached to German command in Brussels
D 'Reserved' or 'Forbidden' Zone
E Annexed Zone
F Coastal Zone (from Oct. 1941)
G Italian Zone from June 1940–Nov. 1942
H Italian Zone after
   Nov. 1942

Map 2 Occupied France

Introduction: Historians and the Occupation

In France, the period between 1940 and 1944 is known as the 'Dark Years'. The prosecutor at the post-war trial of Marshal Pétain, André Mornet, entitled his memoirs 'Four Years to Erase from our History'.[1] There was a lot to erase. In 1940, after a battle lasting only six weeks, France suffered a catastrophic military defeat. An armistice was signed with Germany, and half of France, including Paris, was occupied by German troops. In the other half, a supposedly independent French government, headed by Marshal Pétain, installed itself in the spa town of Vichy. The Vichy government liquidated France's democratic institutions, persecuted Freemasons, Jews, and Communists, and embarked on a policy of collaboration with Germany. Eventually 650,000 civilian French workers were compulsorily drafted to work in German factories; 75,000 Jews from France perished in Auschwitz; 30,000 French civilians were shot as hostages or members of the Resistance; another 60,000 were deported to German concentration camps.

André Mornet's desire to erase these years from history was widely shared. De Gaulle tried to do the same. In August 1944, his provisional government issued an ordinance declaring that all Vichy's legislation was null and void: history would resume where it had stopped in 1940. When de Gaulle was asked in liberated Paris to announce the restoration of the French Republic, he refused—on the grounds that it had never ceased to exist. This legal fiction became the foundation of a heroic reinterpretation of the Dark Years. According to this reinterpretation, most of the horrors inflicted on France had been the work of the Germans alone; de Gaulle and the Resistance had incarnated the real France; and the mass of the French people, apart from a handful of traitors, had been solidly behind them, whether in thought or in deed. Even Mornet contradicted the title to his own memoirs, by stating in the epigraph that the Resistance had made the period between 1940 and 1944 'years to inscribe in our history'. This Resistance myth reached its apogee in the 1960s when de Gaulle was president

---

[1] *Quatre ans à rayer de notre histoire* (1949).

of the Fifth Republic. In 1964, the remains of Jean Moulin, who had been de Gaulle's envoy to the Resistance, were transferred to the Panthéon where France's national heroes are buried.

The heroic myth ignored too many inconvenient realities to survive for ever— during the Occupation Mornet himself offered his legal services to the prosecution at the Riom trial where Vichy had put its political enemies in the dock—and it started to crumble in the 1970s. A catalyst in this process was Marcel Ophuls's documentary film *The Sorrow and the Pity*. Arguably one of the most important historical documentaries ever made, Ophuls's three-hour film, released in 1971, was a craftily constructed work which presented the French population during the Occupation in an unprecedentedly unfavourable light, depicting them as predominantly selfish and *attentiste*. Ophuls delighted in capturing on screen people's attempts to rewrite their past. The film had been made for television, but it was so iconoclastic that the authorities refused to broadcast it, and it was not televised in France until 1981. *The Sorrow and the Pity* was part of the 1968 mood of youth rebellion: de Gaulle was president, and it was his version of the past that was being challenged. A second film with a great impact was Louis Malle's *Lacombe Lucien* (1974), the story of an adolescent peasant boy who becomes a collaborator by chance not conviction. Returning on his bicycle from an attempt to join the Resistance, he has a puncture, stumbles upon some Germans, and ends up working for them instead. The film depicts an amoral world without heroes where destiny is arbitrary.[2]

From the 1970s, the French were increasingly reminded in films, books, and newspapers that millions of people had revered Marshal Pétain; that Vichy laws, not German ones, had represented the 'true' France and discriminated against French Jews and French Freemasons; that French policemen, not German ones, had arrested Jews and Communists; that the resisters had been a small minority; and that most people had been *attentistes* not heroes. The myth was turned on its head. Films now treated the Resistance in a debunking mode: Vichy, not de Gaulle or the Resistance, now seemed to represent the 'true' France.

This vision of the Occupation is no more satisfactory than the Gaullist one. Pétain was certainly popular, but his regime less so. Jews were persecuted by the French government, but a larger proportion of Jews survived the Holocaust in France than in most other occupied countries. Opinion was *attentiste*, but *attentisme* covered a multitude of positions. There was a Resistance myth which needed to be punctured, but that does not mean that the Resistance was a myth.

Redressing the balance does not, however, involve returning to the old mythology. The history of the Occupation should be written not in black and white, but in shades of grey. Vichy may have been a reactionary and authoritarian regime, but it enjoyed heterogeneous support, even from people who had backed the left-wing Popular Front in the 1930s. At different times, and to

---

[2] For the post-war memory and representation of the Occupation, see H. Rousso, *The Vichy Syndrome* (1991).

differing degrees, Vichy attracted people as varied as the architect Le Corbusier, the journalist Hubert Beuve-Méry, the future president François Mitterrand, the economist François Perroux, the theatre director Jean Vilar. These are not marginal figures in France's twentieth-century history, and Vichy was the beginning of their careers not the end. Mitterrand's importance hardly needs emphasis; Beuve-Méry, founder of *Le Monde*, was the most powerful newspaper editor in France from 1945 until 1969; Perroux was the most distinguished French economist of the twentieth century, the French Keynes as his obituaries put it; Vilar was the founder of the Avignon festival, a pioneer of the democratization of theatre in post-war France. Mentioning these names is not intended to discredit the individuals concerned, but to emphasize the complexity of Vichy. Some of the people in this list eventually ended up in the Resistance, but this did not necessarily mean that they repudiated the values which had led them to Vichy. The Resistance was never monolithic, and the lines dividing it from Vichy were not always well defined.

Ambiguities

The ambiguities of the period can be illustrated by five short quotations. The first is from Henri Frenay, one of the earliest resisters. It comes from the manifesto of the Resistance movement he began to organize in the autumn of 1940:

> We are passionately attached to the work of Marshal Pétain. We subscribe to the body of great reforms which have been undertaken. We are animated by the desire that they turn out to be durable and that other reforms will complete those already undertaken. It is with this aim in mind that we form part of the movement of National Liberation . . . All those who serve in our ranks, like those who are already there, will be authentic Frenchmen. The Jews will serve in our ranks if they have really fought in one of the two wars.[3]

The second quotation comes from a letter written in June 1940 by François Valentin who shortly afterwards became leader of the Légion des Combattants, an organization created by Vichy to drum up support for Pétain.

> I consider the attitude of the Pétain government to be mad. We are beaten. Alas, this is true. But it is no reason to accept as definitive what, with an exercise of will, need not be more than an accident. To treat with the enemy is to submit! It is to reinforce Germany against England, our last hope: it is to dishonour ourselves in furnishing arms to our enemy against our ally. We must hope and therefore hold out . . . If the possibility offers itself for me to leave for England, I will not let it slip through my hands.[4]

---

[3] In D. Cordier, *Jean Moulin: L'Inconnu du Panthéon*, i. *Une ambition pour la République* (1989), 25–8.
[4] Valentin writing to his wife on 23 June 1940, cited in J.-P. Cointet, *La Légion française des combattants 1940–1944: La Tentation du fascisme* (1995), 71.

The third quotation comes from the journal of the Catholic philosopher Emmanuel Mounier who was, when he penned these words in October 1940, a qualified supporter of the Vichy regime. He is commenting on Vichy's Statute discriminating against Jews:

> This evening appeared the shameful Jewish Statute, much more severe than anything which had been expected . . . I feel myself aged as if by an illness.[5]

The fourth quotation comes from Maurice Ripoche, founder of the Resistance organization Ceux de la Résistance:

> We need to get rid of talkative politicians and Jews without fatherland.[6]

The final quotation comes from a study published in 1942 by the Resistance movement OCM:

> The Jewish minority, concentrated in some big centres and represented in political, intellectual, and financial milieux is active and very much in evidence . . . Anti-semitism . . . remains universal even in liberal countries. This suggests that it is based on a reality.[7]

A pro-Pétainist resister; a pro-British and anti-German Pétainist; a pro-Jewish Pétainist; two anti-Semitic resisters: these are not the categories we might expect. They reveal the complexity of reactions to the Occupation and the extent to which antagonists might share as many assumptions with their enemies as with those on their own side. People who made different choices often did so in defence of similar values.

Péguy's Frances

One common point of reference for resisters, Vichy conservatives, and Paris-based fascists alike was the writer Charles Péguy. On the day Marshal Pétain announced he was seeking an armistice, the Christian Democrat activist Edmond Michelet distributed in the streets of his town a tract containing six quotations from Péguy. One of these read: 'In wartime he who does not surrender is my man, whoever he is, wherever he comes from, and whatever his party . . . And he who surrenders is my enemy whoever he is, wherever he comes from, and whatever his party.'[8] Michelet was the first of many resisters to quote Péguy. His name was often invoked by resisters opposed to Vichy's anti-Semitic laws.[9] De

---

[5] Cordier, *Jean Moulin: L'Inconnu du Panthéon*, iii. *De Gaulle capitale de la Résistance* (1993), 214.

[6] Quoted ibid. 219.

[7] A. Calmette, *L' "O.C.M."—Organisation civile et militaire. Histoire d'un mouvement de résistance* (1961), 53.

[8] H. Noguères, *Histoire de la Résistance en France*, i (1967), 455–6; H. R. Kedward, *Resistance in Vichy France* (1983), 25–7.

[9] e.g. the second issue of the resistance paper *La France continue* in Oct. 1941, and the sixth issue of the resistance journal *Cahiers du témoignage chrétien*. See also *Péguy-Péri* published by the underground Resistance publishing house Éditions de Minuit in 1944. For the uses and abuses of Péguy's name under the Occupation, see J. Bastaire, *Péguy contre Pétain: L'Appel du 18 juin* (2000).

Gaulle himself was steeped in Péguy's writing; he quoted him in a speech on 18 June 1942.[10]

Vichy was also eager to claim the patronage of Péguy. There was even talk of instituting a national holiday to commemorate him.[11] Péguy was cited as an inspiration behind the regime's conservative counter-revolution, christened the National Revolution.[12] One of Péguy's sons, Pierre, wrote a book to support this interpretation.[13] But Péguy was also praised by hardline 'collaborationists' who believed that Vichy's reforms were insufficiently radical and wanted a fascist regime in France. One of this group, the novelist Robert Brasillach, saw Péguy as 'the inspirer of the new France, in brief a French National Socialist'. He regretted only that Péguy had not been a racist,[14] but in 1941 Péguy's other son, Marcel, published *Le Destin de Charles Péguy* which claimed: 'My father is above all a racist . . . His thought could be summed up as: a country, a race, a leader.'[15]

It is not unusual for historical figures to undergo a posthumous annexation which pays little respect to the reality of their lives—Joan of Arc was also invoked by all sides under the Occupation—but Péguy's writing genuinely lent itself to contradictory interpretation. As a young Socialist at the turn of the century, he was an ardent defender of the innocence of Alfred Dreyfus, seeing the Dreyfusard cause as a spiritual crusade to defend the purity of the Republican tradition. By 1904, however, he had come to deplore the way Dreyfusism had been appropriated by careerist politicians. As he put it in a famous aphorism: 'Everything begins as *mystique* and ends as *politique*.' In 1905, in the shadow of Franco-German rivalry, Péguy's book *Notre patrie* celebrated patriotism, and distanced him from the internationalism of the Socialists with whom he had fought for Dreyfus. In 1910, his poem *Le Mystère de la charité de Jeanne d'Arc* announced his conversion to Catholicism. He died at the battle of the Marne in 1914, after which he became the object of a patriotic cult.[16]

The essential point about Péguy, however, is not that his life was a series of renunciations and repudiations. Rather it was one of accumulations and accretions. He was not, as he saw it, *first* Socialist, Republican, and pro-Jewish and *then* Catholic and patriotic: he was all these things at the same time. This made Péguy an awkward member of any camp he joined. He was a Republican who despised political parties; a Catholic who attacked the institutional Church; a defender of French rootedness who wrote in passionate praise of Judaism. Above

---

[10] On de Gaulle and Péguy see the articles in *Études gaulliennes*, 13/41 (1983).

[11] S. Laurent, 'Daniel Halévy 1872–1962: Face à l'histoire et à la politique' (Masters thesis, Institut d'études politiques, Paris, 1993), 171.

[12] D. Halévy, *Péguy* (1941); P. Donceur, *Péguy, la Révolution et le sacré* (1943); R. Vallery-Radot, *Sources d'une doctrine nationale: De Joseph de Maistre à Charles Péguy* (1942).

[13] *Péguy présenté aux jeunes* (1941).

[14] D. Carroll, *French Literary Fascism: Nationalism, Anti-Semitism and the Ideology of Culture* (1995), 47.

[15] pp. vi, viii.

[16] G. Leroy, *Péguy entre l'ordre et la révolution* (1981) is the best study of Péguy.

all, Péguy was a moralist and a prophet. If there is a thread running through his writing, it is to be found in his deep immersion in French history, his suspicion of the 'modern', and his cult of the traditions of the French countryside and artisan labour. Claiming to despise intellectuals who dealt only in abstractions—one of his key words is *charnel*—Péguy was as involved in the physical production of the journal he published as he was in writing for it. Péguy's fundamental belief was that all the traditions he celebrated—the Catholic, the Socialist (his socialism was never Marxist), the Republican, the Jewish—are part of the rich soil of France's history. There is no writer more French than Péguy, but he was at the confluence of many different Frances.

Vichy conservatives admired Péguy's obsession with rootedness and tradition; de Gaulle his passionate patriotism; Catholic resisters his concern for spiritual values; Republican resisters his defence of the purest Republican ideal; fascists his furious intransigence. These strands cannot be easily separated out, and this is what makes Péguy such a perfect emblem for France's history between 1940 and 1944.

Over the past twenty-five years, that tortured history has been the subject of intensive historical research. Nothing could be less true than the journalistic cliché, particularly common among the British, that France has failed to 'confront' her wartime past. Thus before the recent trial of the Vichy functionary Maurice Papon for crimes against humanity, *The Times* informed its readers that the event 'set the stage for a painful and overdue examination of France's wartime past'.[17] The re-examination may be painful, but it is not overdue. If one goes into any bookshop in France, there is frequently a whole table displaying recent works on the Occupation, and usually those concentrating on its most unsavoury aspects. Such books can literally be bought on station platforms. The flood of writing on the Occupation seems unstoppable: it is now the most intensively researched period of French history.

1945–1965: The Resistance writes its History

The writing of the history of the Occupation began even while German soldiers were still present in France. In October 1944, de Gaulle's government set up a historical committee to study the occupation and liberation of France. This became the Comité d'histoire de la Deuxième Guerre mondiale, headed by the historian Henri Michel. The Comité set about building an archive of material relating to the war, and it founded a journal, the *Revue d'histoire de la Deuxième Guerre mondiale*, which published the first scholarly articles on the period, and has done so ever since. The Comité had a team of departmental correspondents—156 of them by 1979—many of them secondary school teachers, who collected local information on the Occupation and conducted some 2,000

---

[17] 19 Sept. 1996.

interviews with resisters. In 1980, it was subsumed into the Institut d'histoire du temps présent (IHTP) which is devoted to the study of contemporary history in general, but still concentrates primarily on the Occupation.[18]

In the first twenty years after 1945, historical writing centred mainly on the Resistance. When Michel published a critical bibliography of the Resistance in 1964, he listed 1,200 items.[19] Many of them were the work of former resisters who wanted to tell their stories. Memoirs were also produced by members of de Gaulle's London-based Free French,[20] and by some Resistance leaders who had remained in France.[21] Very different pictures emerged depending whether the writer had been based in London or France. Colonel Passy, head of de Gaulle's intelligence service, described the Resistance in France as 'an abundant desire to do well, brave thoughts and exalted imagination which translated into disorganised actions without real effectiveness'.[22] De Gaulle's own memoirs which appeared between 1954 and 1959 said a lot about his conflicts with his Anglo-Saxon allies but treated the Resistance with a mixture of glacial respect and Olympian disdain, as a piece in the larger Gaullist enterprise to rescue French honour.

A number of histories began to appear, starting in 1951 with a study of the small movement Résistance,[23] and continuing into the 1960s with histories of larger movements[24] and of Resistance institutions.[25] Most of these appeared with the encouragement of Michel's Comité, in a series called 'Esprit de la Résistance', whose self-proclaimed objective was to be 'the edification of our citizens and the re-establishment of a truth which puts each person in their just place, the formation of the young in France'.[26] Although the authors had usually been involved in the Resistance, these were scholarly works based considerably on oral evidence. As Lucien Febvre wrote in the preface to one study, the Resistance generation had to provide its own account of its history.[27] The Comité even set about producing a chronology, *département* by *département*, of every single act of resistance recorded on over 150,000 index cards. This was not just historical

---

[18] H. Michel, 'Le Comité d'histoire de la Deuxième Guerre mondiale', *RHDGM* 124 (1981), 2–17.

[19] *Bibliographie critique de la Résistance* (1964). In fact, many of the items listed are more concerned with Vichy than the Resistance.

[20] Colonel Passy (A. Dewavrin), *2ᵉ Bureau Londres* (1947); id., *10 Duke Street Londres* (1948); id., *Missions secrètes en France* (1951); J. Soustelle, *Envers et contre tout*, 2 vols. (1947–50).

[21] G. de Bénouville, *Le Sacrifice du matin* (1946); Y. Farge, *Rebelles, soldats et citoyens* (1946); A. Humbert, *Notre guerre* (1946); C. Pineau, *La Simple Vérité* (1961).

[22] *10 Duke Street*, 105.

[23] F. Bruneau, *Essai d'historique du mouvement né autour du journal clandestin Résistance* (1951).

[24] M. Granet and H. Michel, *Combat: Histoire d'un mouvement de Résistance* (1957); M. Granet, *Défense de la France* (1960); A. Calmette, *L' "O.C.M."*; M. Granet, *Ceux de la Résistance* (1964).

[25] R. Hostache, *Le Conseil national de la Résistance* (1958).

[26] G. Bidault in the preface to H. Michel and B. Mirkine-Guetzévitch, *Les Idées politiques et sociales de la Résistance* (1954), p. vi.

[27] Avant-propos to Michel and Mirkine-Guetzévitch, *Les Idées*, p. x; repeated by Michel himself, in Granet and Michel, *Combat*, 3–4.

positivism gone mad, but also an act of piety: the Comité saw its role as trans-mitting part of the national heritage to future generations.[28]

The dominant figure of this historiography was Henri Michel (1907–86) whose prolific output included the first short general history of the Resistance in 1950, the first doctoral thesis devoted to it, and the first scholarly study of a single resistance movement.[29] Before 1940, Michel had been a history teacher and Socialist activist in Toulon. He participated in the Resistance of the Var *département*, representing the Socialists on the Departmental Liberation Com-mittee. He was both a scholar and an effective popularizer, inspired by a sense of duty to the memory of the Resistance. It was, he wrote, 'one of the most magnificent episodes in the history of France' despite the fact that 'moving from *mystique* to *politique*, it became loaded, in spite of itself, with impurities'.[30] Michel, while not ignoring conflicts between France and London, sometimes let piety get the better of him. Thus in his biography of Jean Moulin, Michel wrote of the conflict between Moulin and another leading Gaullist resister, Pierre Brossolette: 'It is, in my view, unnecessary to linger over this episode. Jean Moulin and Pierre Brossolette both died heroically as victims of the Gestapo and our memory of them cannot be dissociated from the same feeling of respect and admiration.'[31] This biography appeared in 1964, the year in which de Gaulle's decision to transfer Moulin's remains to the Panthéon signified that he had been selected as the emblematic hero of the Resistance, the man who had unified it and rallied it to de Gaulle.

This Gaullist consensus was rejected by the Communists who proclaimed their predominant role in the Resistance.[32] The Party downplayed the impact of de Gaulle's BBC speech of 18 June 1940 and claimed that its own Appeal of 10 July had been more important. Non-Communist historians, however, argued that the Party had not started to resist until Hitler invaded the Soviet Union in June 1941. One respect in which Gaullist and Communist interpretations did converge was in emphasizing the centrality of resistance, whether Gaullist or Communist. Between these Gaullist and Communist monoliths, there was little room for dissenting voices, although one or two squeezed through in the memoirs of resisters like Emmanuel d'Astier de la Vigerie and Georges Bidault. But these did not substantially affect the overall picture. D'Astier had a reputa-tion for irreverence and Bidault was known to have personal grudges against de Gaulle whose Algerian policy he opposed.[33]

This concentration on the Resistance meant that the history of Vichy was

---

[28] Michel, 'Le Comité', 9; id., 'Pour une chronologie de la Résistance', *Revue historique*, 224 (1960), 111–22.

[29] Id., *Histoire de la Résistance en France* (1951); id., *Les Courants de pensée de la Résistance* (1962); Granet and Michel, *Combat*.

[30] *Histoire de la Résistance* (1969 edn.), 118, 125.

[31] *Jean Moulin: L'Unificateur* (1964), 159.

[32] Institut Maurice Thorez, *Le Parti français communiste dans la Résistance* (1967); J. Duclos, *Mémoires: Dans la bataille clandestine* (1970); C. Tillon, *Les FTP* (1962); F. Grenier, *C'était ainsi* (1959).

[33] E. Astier de la Vigerie, *Sept fois sept jours* (1961); G. Bidault, *D'une Résistance à l'autre* (1965).

largely ignored. The *Revue d'histoire de la Deuxième Guerre mondiale* did not devote an issue to the Occupation and Vichy before 1964. Most writing on Vichy took the form of exculpatory memoirs written by the regime's former supporters.[34] The start of the Cold War provided a more sympathetic audience for these accounts than they would have received in 1945. In 1957 Laval's daughter produced a three-volume collection of testimonies by former collaborators of her father. Although much of the documentation was useful, the interpretations were tendentious, and produced an angry rebuttal by historians on the Comité.[35]

The first history of Vichy came not from an academic historian, but from the writer Robert Aron in 1954. In the 1930s, Aron was one of that generation of young intellectuals disgusted by what they considered to be the impotence of the Third Republic. Aron himself had belonged to a group called Ordre nouveau, whose members included Jean Jardin, later a close adviser to Laval in 1942. Thanks to his relationship with Jardin, Aron evaded anti-Semitic persecution and escaped to North Africa where he supported General Giraud, the conservative general whom the Americans sponsored as a counterweight to de Gaulle. Aron was well connected in the worlds of politics and business, and his history of Vichy was based to a considerable extent on personal information (and also on the records of the post-war trials). Writing with no nostalgia for the Third Republic, Aron produced a subtly apologetic account of Vichy which argued that the regime had acted as a 'shield' between the French and the Germans, doing its best to resist German pressure for collaboration. When this did not succeed, the fault lay with Laval not Pétain.[36] Aron's distinction between a Vichy of Pétain and a Vichy of Laval received the imprimatur in 1956 of the respected political scientist André Siegfried.[37]

For all its faults, Aron's book had the merit of viewing Vichy as more than simply a tool of Germany. He reinserted it into French history as worthy of study in itself. Although Aron's interpretation of Vichy was clearly not Gaullist, it did not necessarily subvert the Gaullist myth. By suggesting that Vichy had tried to resist in its own way, Aron, like the Gaullists and Communists, limited the number of real 'traitors' to a handful. He too agreed that the 'real' France was about resistance; he merely wanted to include Vichy in it.

1970s: Enter the Vichy Regime

The professional historians at last turned their attention to Vichy in the late 1960s. From this point one can discern three distinct phases in the study of

---

[34] H. du Moulin de Labarthète, *Le Temps des Illusions: Souvenirs (juillet 1940–avril 1942)* (1946); M. Peyrouton, *Du service public à la prison commune* (1950); Y. Bouthillier, *Le Drame de Vichy*, 2 vols. (1950–1); J. Barthélemy, *Mémoires, ministre de la justice: Vichy (1941–1943)* (1989 edn.).

[35] *La Vie des Français sous l'occupation* (1957); P. Arnoult et al., *La France sous l'Occupation* (1959).

[36] *Histoire de Vichy 1940–1944* (1954).

[37] Siegfried, 'Le Vichy de Pétain, le Vichy de Laval', *Revue française de science politique*, 6/4 (1956), 737–49.

Vichy. The first concentrated primarily on the nature of the regime; the second on public opinion and the reactions of different social groups; the third on the interactions between regime and society.

The first phase was inaugurated by the publication in 1972 of Robert Paxton's *Vichy France: Old Guard and New Order, 1940–1944* (translated into French a year later). Paxton, who taught at Columbia University, had already established his scholarly credentials with a study of the army under Vichy.[38] But his second book caused outrage in some quarters in France, not least at the presumption of a 41-year-old American lecturing the French about their past. Henri Michel, who reviewed the book favourably, wondered if the moral passion underlying Paxton's scholarship was not inspired by a degree of anti-Frenchness. Answering this point in the preface to a 1982 edition of his book, Paxton observed that, writing at the time of the Vietnam war, his target was 'nationalist conformism of any kind'.[39] Paxton has since become the inspiration for a generation of younger French historians—recently his book was described in France as the 'Copernican revolution' in the study of Vichy[40]—and he has become the most celebrated Vichy historian. His book, even after twenty-five years, remains the best study of the regime.

Paxton's interpretation had three main strands. First, he showed that the leaders of the Vichy regime had consistently sought to collaborate with Germany. Making extensive use of German archives, Paxton rejected the distinction between a collaborating and pro-German Vichy of Laval and a patriotic and anti-German one of Pétain. For Paxton, there was no Pétainist double game. Secondly, Paxton argued that Vichy had a domestic project for the political regeneration of French society. Where it had been customary to view Vichy as a victim of circumstances and blame its most unsavoury policies on the Germans, Paxton distinguished between policies which were imposed by the Germans and those which were not. For example, he showed incontrovertibly that Vichy had its own anti-Semitic agenda. Thirdly, Paxton demonstrated the complexity and incoherence of Vichy's domestic policies. Instead of seeing Vichy as an exclusively reactionary regime, Paxton showed that it contained modernizers as well as conservatives: the subtitle of his book was 'Old Guard and New Order'. Thus Paxton reinserted Vichy into a longer historical context, drawing out continuities with France's past and future. Vichy could no longer be viewed as an aberration or parenthesis in French history.

It would be wrong to see Paxton's interpretation as novel in all respects. The impact of his book has overshadowed other studies which anticipated many of his conclusions. There was, for example, the Franco-American historian Stanley

---

[38] *Parades and Politics at Vichy: The French Officer Corps under Marshal Pétain* (Princeton, 1966).

[39] Rousso, *Vichy Syndrome*, 251–6. For the critical reception of Paxton in France, see J. Sweets, '*Chaque livre un événement*: Robert Paxton and the French, from *briseur de glace* to *iconoclaste tranquille*', in S. Fishman et al. (eds.), *France at War: Vichy and the Historians* (Oxford, 2000), 21–34.

[40] J.-P. Azéma and F. Bédarida, 'Vichy et ses historiens', *Esprit*, 181 (1992), 43–51: 47.

Hoffmann, who had passed his adolescence in occupied France. Hoffmann was the author of two brilliant articles, which remain among the most important pieces ever written on the regime. In the first, he interpreted Vichy not as a simple revenge of the reactionary right but a 'pluralist dictatorship' where different political factions competed for influence. In the second, he analysed the different strands of collaboration.[41] Although Hoffmann argued that there were several Vichys and several kinds of collaboration, the distinction was not between a 'good' one and a 'bad' one, between Pétain and Laval. While emphasizing the diversity of Vichy, Hoffmann argued for an internal logic running through the history of the regime from the beginning to the end.

Another pioneering work, appearing in French translation in 1968, was *La France dans l'Europe de Hitler* by the German historian Eberhard Jäckel.[42] From the German archives Jäckel showed that Vichy had actively sought collaboration, and that this policy had been carried out even when Laval was not in power. Vichy's domestic policies came under scrutiny in 1970 when the august Fondation nationale des sciences politiques organized a colloquium on Vichy, assembling survivors from the period and historians of it.[43] Although confining itself to the study of policy and institutions, this colloquium provided new information on Vichy policy, and addressed the issue of continuity between Vichy and the years surrounding it.

These studies had nibbled away at Aron's interpretation, but it was Paxton's study which made the impact.[44] His book was written with a moral passion which was all the more effective for being restrained in its expression. More importantly, no one had offered such a trenchantly comprehensive synthesis. Hoffmann's articles constructed the conceptual framework around which a history of Vichy might be written, but he had not himself written that history; Jäckel had not addressed domestic policy; the 1970 colloquium had not covered foreign policy, and thus it sidestepped the relationship between Vichy's internal reforms and collaboration.

It is not enough to write a good history book (which Paxton certainly did); it helps to write it at the right time. Paxton's book appeared when the Gaullist myth was losing its credibility, and people wanted to hear what he was saying. Jäckel's book, although narrower in focus than Paxton's, was hardly less important. Appearing in French in 1968, it sold 3,000 copies in its first ten years; Paxton's sold over 58,000 in its first twelve years.[45]

[41] 'The Vichy Circle of French Conservatives' (1956) and 'Self-Ensnared: Collaboration with Nazi Germany' (1968), both repr. in S. Hoffmann, *Decline or Renewal? France since the 1930s* (New York, 1974), 3–25 and 26–44.
[42] (1st pub. in Ger., 1966.)
[43] Fondation nationale des sciences politiques, *Le Gouvernement de Vichy 1940–1942* (1972).
[44] Other important pioneering studies which deserve not to be forgotten were A. Hytier, *Two Years of French Foreign Policy: Vichy 1940–1942* (Geneva, 1958); H. Michel, *Vichy, année 1940* (1966); G. Warner, *Pierre Laval and the Eclipse of France* (1968); Y. Durand, *Vichy* (1972).
[45] Rousso, *Vichy Syndrome*, 276.

Subsequent work on the regime has extended or refined Paxton's interpreta-tions, but not challenged them substantially.[46] In 1982, the doyen of French diplomatic historians, Jean-Baptiste Duroselle, produced a study of foreign policy based on newly opened French archives. He identified more internal debate in the making of French foreign policy, but did not fundamentally differ from Paxton except on details.[47] Studies of economic policy-making in France by the American historian Richard Kuisel and the French historian Michel Margairaz have underlined even more emphatically than Paxton the continuities between Vichy and what came before and after: their account of the modern-ization of the French economy gives a central role to the Vichy period.[48]

There have been some rearguard actions against Paxton's interpretation. Michèle Cointet has tried to salvage the existence at Vichy of a liberal tradition by studying the regime's attempt to set up a consultative body called the Conseil national.[49] But if the Conseil's history is worth writing, it should not be given excessive centrality: it had no power. In 1989, there was a boldly apologetic biography of the Vichy leader Admiral Darlan. But despite the authors' best endeavours, the new documentation they unearthed only further undermined the case they wished to prove.[50] The consensus existing in the historical profes-sion today is best demonstrated by the fact that when in 1990 Francis-Georges Dreyfus provided a *réchauffé* version of the Aron thesis, his efforts excited indif-ference more than outrage.[51]

The 1980s: From Regime to Society

The second phase in the historiography of Vichy was a move at the end of the 1970s, from a study of the regime to a study of those who lived under it, from politics to society.[52] Inasmuch as Paxton discussed this subject, his view was that the Resistance was a tiny minority, and that most people, whatever their private views of the Germans, were 'functional collaborators'. Just as the German archives had allowed Paxton to challenge previous orthodoxy, it was the opening up of prefects' reports, and other contemporary reports on public opinion, which allowed his judgement of the attitudes of the French population to be contested.

---

[46] Paxton's interpretation was followed by the main French textbook on the period, J.-P. Azéma, *De Munich à la Libération* (1979).

[47] *L'Abîme 1939–1945* (1982).

[48] Margairaz, *L'État, les finances et l'économie: Histoire d'une conversion 1932–1952* (1991); Kuisel, *Capitalism and the State in Modern France* (Cambridge, 1981).

[49] *Le Conseil national de Vichy 1940–1944* (1989).

[50] H. Coutau-Bégarie and C. Huan, *Darlan* (1989); see the critique by Paxton, 'Un amiral entre deux blocs', *VSRH* 36 (1992), 3–19.

[51] *Histoire de Vichy* (1990). See H. Rousso, 'Quand Vichy est soumis à la "révision"', *L'Histoire*, 139 (1990), 82–4, and 141 (1991), 64–5.

[52] A pioneer was M. Baudot, *L'Opinion publique sous l'occupation* (1961), on the Eure *département*.

Prefects are the agents of the government in the *départements*. Each *département* has a prefect at its head, and one of his duties is to provide the government with regular bulletins on public opinion. Obviously this source needs to be used carefully, not least because prefects' reports were coloured by their author's own ideological assumptions, and their *déformation professionnelle* inclined them to present a picture corresponding to the desires of their superiors. But these biases can be detected, and under Vichy the prefects were soon reporting what their superiors did not wish to hear. Using such sources, Pierre Laborie for the *département* of the Lot in the south-west, and John Sweets for the city of Clermont Ferrand, reached remarkably similar conclusions about public opinion.[53] They found almost universal hostility to the Germans from early on, and a fairly rapid disenchantment with Vichy. If the French were *attentiste*, it was not out of sympathy with the occupier. A proliferation of regional studies has largely confirmed these interpretations.

More importantly, such studies have challenged overly simplistic categorizations of opinion. The dichotomy between 'resistance' and 'collaboration' is too crude to accommodate the multiplicity of responses to the regime. Laborie has plotted the confusion, changeability, and complexity of public opinion.[54] These general studies of public opinion have been buttressed by studies of particular social and political groups: committed collaborators,[55] workers,[56] industrialists,[57] prisoners of war,[58] women,[59] the young.[60] The best indication of the transformation of research agendas was the publication twenty years after the 1970 colloquium on the regime of another huge colloquium organized in 1990 by the IHTP on the theme of 'Vichy and the French people'.[61]

The third phase in the historiography of Vichy from the mid-1980s has concerned the interaction between regime and people: the study of social and cultural organizations, some established or encouraged by the regime, others independent of it, which mediated between State and society. This has opened

[53] Laborie, *Résistants, Vichyssois et autres: L'Évolution de l'opinion et des comportements dans le Lot 1939 à 1944* (1980); Sweets, *Choices in Vichy France* (New York, 1986).
[54] *L'Opinion publique sous Vichy* (1990).
[55] P. Ory, *Les Collaborateurs 1940–1945* (1976); B. Gordon, *Collaborationism in France during the Second World War* (1980).
[56] 'Syndicalismes sous Vichy', special issue of *MS* 158 (Jan./Mar. 1993), ed. J.-L. Robert; D. Peschanski and J.-L. Robert, *Les Ouvriers en France pendant la Deuxième Guerre mondiale* (1992).
[57] R. de Rochebrune and J.-C. Hazera, *Les Patrons sous l'Occupation* (1995); A. Beltram, R. Frank, and H. Rousso, *La Vie des entreprises sous l'Occupation* (1994).
[58] Y. Durand, *La Captivité: Histoire des prisonniers de guerre français 1939–1945* (1980).
[59] S. Fishman, *We will wait: Wives of French Prisoners of War, 1940–1945* (1991); H. Diamond, *Women and the Second World War in France 1939–1948: Choices and Constraints* (1999), 82–6.
[60] W. Halls, *The Youth of Vichy France* (Oxford, 1981) (a pioneering book but more about the policies of the regime than the responses of those who lived under it); P. Giolitto, *Histoire de la jeunesse sous Vichy* (1991).
[61] See *VEF*; see also P. Burrin, *La France à l'heure allemande* (1995).

up new areas of research into cinema,[62] theatre,[63] art,[64] propaganda,[65] icono-graphical representations,[66] labour organizations,[67] and so on. These studies revealed all kinds of intermediate positions between support for the regime and opposition to it: especially in the cultural sphere, the regime was seen to permit a surprising degree of latitude. Again, these new research agendas were discussed at another important colloquium of the IHTP in 1987 devoted to 'cultural life under Vichy'.[68]

If one wanted to summarize the periodization which this historiographical survey has suggested, it would run as follows: A benevolent interpretation of the Vichy regime and the conduct of the French who lived under it (Aron: the mid-1950s to the mid-1960s) was replaced by a more critical one (Paxton: the mid-1970s to the mid-1980s); and this was subsequently modified by a more nuanced account of the social and political attitudes of the French population (Laborie: mid-1980s onwards).

Le Grand Absent: The Jews

These historiographical stages emerge particularly clearly in the way the historiography has treated one specific issue: Vichy and the Jews. Until the end of the 1960s the fate of the Jews and Vichy's policy towards them was largely ignored: Michel's 1964 bibliography lists only a handful of books about the Jews. The 1970 colloquium hardly mentioned the issue at all. It is not true that nothing was written about the Jews during this period. On the contrary, a very impor-tant body of work was produced by the Centre de documentation juive con-temporaine (CDJC) founded during the war by Isaac Schneersohn. Born into a Polish Hasidic family, Schneersohn had arrived in France in 1920 where he had become a successful businessman. His original idea for what became the CDJC was to gather documentation in order to help Jews obtain restitution of their property after the war. Thanks to an audacious initiative by Schneersohn's young helper Léon Poliakov after the Liberation, the CDJC obtained the papers of the SS in France. This important body of archives allowed the CDJC to become a major research centre. In 1945, it founded *Le Monde juif*, the first journal in the world devoted to the exclusive study of the Holocaust.[69] Historians attached to

---

[62] J.-P. Bertin-Maghit, *Le Cinéma sous l'Occupation* (1989); F. Garçon, *De Blum à Pétain: Cinéma et société française 1936–1944* (1984).

[63] S. Added, *Le Théâtre dans les années Vichy 1940–1944* (1992).

[64] L. Bertrand-Dorléac, *L'Art de la défaite 1940–1944* (1993); M. Cone, *Artists under Vichy: A Case of Prejudice and Persecution* (Princeton, 1992).

[65] L. Gervereau and D. Peschanski, *La Propagande sous Vichy 1940–1944* (1990).

[66] C. Faure, *Le Projet culturel de Vichy: Folklore et Révolution nationale 1940–1944* (1989).

[67] J.-P. Le Crom, *Syndicats, nous voilà! Vichy et le corporatisme* (1995).

[68] J.-P. Rioux (ed.), *La Vie culturelle sous Vichy* (Brussels, 1990).

[69] See A. Wieviorka, *Déportation et génocide: Entre la mémoire et l'oubli* (1995 edn.), 412–30; A. Kaspi, 'Le Centre de documentation juive contemporaine', *RHMC* 23 (1976), 305–11; R. Poznanski,

the CDJC published pioneering works in the 1940s and 1950s on the Jews in occupied France during the war: on Jewish resistance,[70] on internment camps for Jews in occupied France,[71] and on Vichy institutions dealing with the Jews.[72]

The CDJC's work was entirely on the margins of official French historiography and went unnoticed by the wider public, another example of how the reception of historical writing is as much a product of the time it is written as of its 'objective' quality. The neglect was both a result of the Jacobin tendency of French historiography—a reluctance to treat specific groups apart from their identity as French citizens[73]—and also a reluctance by French Jews themselves to confront the horrors of the period. Many Jews after the war wanted to fit back into French society and preferred to accept the idea that responsibility for their persecution rested with the Germans.

This perspective changed in the 1970s partly because the Arab–Israeli war developed a clearer sense of identity among France's Jewish population, partly as a result of the challenging of myths in the wake of *The Sorrow and the Pity* (the film did not duck French persecution of the Jews). Among historians, Robert Paxton was again a pioneer, co-authoring in 1981 a merciless account of Vichy's policy towards the Jews, which showed how Vichy's discriminatory laws were passed independently of German pressure and argued that until 1942 the attitude of the French population towards the Jews was one of indifference verging on hostility.[74] At the same time the French Jewish lawyer and historian Serge Klarsfeld reached similar conclusions about Vichy policy.[75] Klarsfeld, whose father died in Auschwitz, has sought to pay homage to the victims and make the guilty pay. One of Klarsfeld's achievements has been to reconstitute painstakingly the names of all the Jewish victims of the Holocaust from France.[76] It was his efforts during the 1980s which pressurized the French government to try those surviving executants of Vichy's Jewish policy who had escaped punishment at the Liberation. Throughout the 1980s, huge numbers of books appeared on the Jews and Vichy, and on Vichy's wider policy of persecution: its concentration camps, its treatment of foreigners, gypsies, Communists, and Jews.[77] Where historians once distinguished the early years of the regime from the police state of 1944, they now emphasized the continuity of Vichy repression: persecution was there from the start and the radicalization merely a matter of degree.[78]

'La Création du Centre de documentation juive contemporaine', *VSRH* 63 (1999), 51–64; L. Poliakov, *L'Auberge des musiciens* (1980), 164–5.

[70] D. Knout, *Contribution à l'histoire de la Résistance juive en France* (1947).
[71] J. Weill, *Contribution à l'histoire des camps d'internement dans l'Anti-France* (1946).
[72] J. Billig, *Le Commissariat général aux questions juives* (1955–60).
[73] Wieviorka, *Déportation*, 431.
[74] M. Marrus and R. Paxton, *Vichy France and the Jews* (New York, 1981).
[75] *Vichy-Auschwitz: Le Rôle de Vichy dans la solution finale en France*, 2 vols. (1983–5).
[76] *Mémorial de la déportation des Juifs de France* (1978).
[77] e.g. A. Grynberg, *Les Camps de la honte: Les Internés juifs des camps français* (1991).
[78] D. Peschanski, *Vichy 1940–1944: Contrôle et exclusion* (Brussels, 1997).

To the extent that professional historians did discuss the fate of the Jews in occupied France they took the view that the Vichy regime had done its best to protect them from the Germans. This was the line followed by Raul Hilberg's pioneering study of the Holocaust in 1961, *The Destruction of the European Jews*.[79]

Recently, however, historians have begun to refine their account of the attitude of the population towards the Jews while not questioning the culpability of the regime. They have had to confront the paradox that despite Vichy's anti-Semitism, a comparatively high proportion of Jews in France survived the war. For Paxton the explanation lies in the vagaries of German policy, but for Klarsfeld, who always distinguished between the regime and the population, it lies in the reactions of the French people. He is not the only French Jewish historian (and survivor) of the period to offer this less negative perspective which has been adopted by other recent historical writing on the subject. But this has not yet penetrated to the wider public which still resists the view that the Occupation might after all have contained heroes.[80] It is interesting, however, that Louis Malle's second film on the Occupation, *Au revoir les enfants* (1987), the story of three Jewish boys given refuge in a Catholic school, paints a less bleak picture than that presented in *Lacombe Lucien*, even if the film ends with the boys' arrest.

1990s: The Resistance Returns

What happened to the history of the Resistance during these years of obsession with Vichy?[81] It was inevitable that in the 1970s the Gaullist orthodoxy on the Resistance would face a battering similar to that received by the orthodoxy on Vichy. The first challenge came from the memoirs of two leading resisters, Henri Frenay and Claude Bourdet.[82] Presenting a view of the Resistance from France not London, they were acerbic about de Gaulle's historical annexation of the Resistance. A primarily metropolitan perspective also emerged from the five-volume history of the Resistance by Henri Noguères which appeared between 1967 and 1981.[83] Noguères had himself been a local Resistance leader of

---

[79] M. Marrus, 'Vichy France and the Jews: After Fifteen Years', in Fishman et al. (eds.), *France at War*, 35–47: 36–8.

[80] A. Rayski, *Le Choix de juifs sous Vichy: Entre soumission et résistance* (1992); S. Zuccotti, *The Holocaust, the French and the Jews* (Lincoln, Nebr., 1993); R. Poznanski, *Être Juif en France pendant la Deuxième Guerre mondiale* (1994); A. Cohen, *Persécutions et sauvetages: Juifs et Français sous l'occupation et sous Vichy* (1993).

[81] F. Bédarida, 'L'Histoire de la Résistance: Lectures d'hier, chantiers de demain', *VSRH* 11 (1986), 75–89; H. Rousso, 'La Résistance entre la légende et l'oubli', *L'Histoire*, 41 (1982), 99–111; J.-P. Azéma and F. Bédarida, 'L'Historisation de la Résistance', *Esprit*, 198 (1994), 19–35; P. Laborie, 'Historiens sous haute surveillance', *Esprit*, 198 (1994), 36–50.

[82] Frenay, *La Nuit finira* (1973); Bourdet, *L'Aventure incertaine: De la Résistance à la restauration* (1975).

[83] H. Noguères (with M. Degliame-Fouché), *Histoire de la Résistance en France de 1940 à 1945*, 5 vols. (1967–81).

Socialist sympathies. His books, written in conjunction with another former resister, the Communist Marcel Degliame-Fouché, provided a month-by-month account of the Resistance, built out of the testimonies of leading resisters. The result is an informative chronicle, not an interpretative history. Indeed on the vexed question of Communist participation in the Resistance, the first two volumes appeared with a dissenting appendix by a third contributor, Jean-Louis Vigier, who left the project after this point.

Noguères was not a professional historian, and the most striking fact about the historiography of the Resistance from about 1970 is that it no longer engaged the attention of French historians to the same degree as Vichy. It is not true that the writing of resistance history ceased after 1970. Of the 7,000 books and articles devoted to the period in the thirty years since Michel's 1964 bibliography, some 1,500 at least were devoted to the Resistance.[84] More books on Resistance movements were published in the 1970s, but these studies, which concentrated on organizations, followed the model of the earlier works of the 1960s without offering new interpretative agendas.[85] By 1992, the review *Esprit* could comment that the Resistance had become 'a blank . . . a taboo' in historical research.[86]

It was symptomatic of this neglect of the Resistance by French historians that the most important work to appear in the 1970s was by a British historian, H. Roderick Kedward's *Resistance in Vichy France* (1978), which studied the southern Resistance up to the end of 1942.[87] Unlike previous historians of Resistance, he was more interested in individuals and motivations than in structures and organizations, in tentative beginnings as much as outcomes. In that sense his book is informed by the anti-institutional spirit of 1960s radicalism. Kedward, who betrayed real warmth for his subject, teased out continuities between past and present and located the Resistance in the society around it. But the lack of mainstream interest in the Resistance meant that Kedward's book had to wait eleven years (1989) for a French translation. Paxton, who had waited only one year, wrote the right book at the right time, Kedward the right one at the wrong time.

No less revealing of the neglect of the Resistance by professional French historians was the fact that the major contribution to the history of the Resistance in the 1980s came from Daniel Cordier, a former resister outside the historical establishment. During the war, Cordier had run Jean Moulin's secretariat, and he possessed an archive of telegrams and correspondence between the Resistance and the Free French. As Cordier tells his story, at the Liberation he had put the

---

[84] J.-M. Guillon, 'La Résistance, 50 ans et 2000 titres après', in id. and P. Laborie, *Mémoire et histoire: La Résistance* (Toulouse, 1995), 27–43.

[85] R. Bédarida, *Les Armes de l'esprit: Témoignage chrétien 1941–1944* (1977); J. Sweets, *The Politics of Resistance in France: 1940–44: A History of the Mouvements Unis de la Résistance* (De Kalb, 1976); D. Veillon, *Le Franc-Tireur, un journal clandestin un mouvement de résistance, 1940–1944* (1977).

[86] E. Conan and D. Lindenberg, 'Que faire de Vichy', *Esprit*, 181 (1992), 5–15: 13.

[87] *Resistance in Vichy France* (Oxford, 1978).

past behind him, and started a thirty-year career as a dealer in modern art, avoiding contact with Resistance circles. In 1977, however, he was invited to appear in a television debate on Moulin, and found himself sharing a platform with Henri Frenay who put the case that Moulin had been a crypto-Communist. To disprove this allegation, Cordier returned to his archives. What started as a desire to refute Frenay blossomed into the ambition to write a full biography of Moulin.[88]

Despite being an actor from the period he was studying, Cordier writes as a historian, confronting the fallibility of memory and the unreliability of anecdotes with the authority of archival evidence. His biography of Moulin runs to over 4,000 pages.[89] Cordier has provided the most fully documented and finely analysed account of the high politics of the Resistance, especially the relationship between London and the Resistance. But Cordier's work originated as an act of piety—almost an act of love—and despite his aspiration towards scientific rigour, he sometimes falls into the role of defence counsel for Moulin. His approach to the Resistance is insufficiently open-ended, transforming Moulin almost into a historical necessity.

Cordier's enterprise is a very personal one, but since the late 1980s there has been a revival of interest in the Resistance among historians. There are three reasons for this. First, the gradual de-Stalinization of the French Communist Party paved the way for an opening up of the Party's historiography. In 1968 a French Communist historian admitted for the first time the existence of a secret protocol attached to the Nazi-Soviet Pact. Such early revisionism was faltering, and when the Party historian Roger Bourderon started a timid critique of Communist historiography in 1979, he was called to order. A turning point came in 1983 with a conference on 'the Communist Party between 1939 and 1941' attended by both non-Communist and Communist historians. Their interpretations remained different, but the occasion was at least a dialogue, suggesting it might soon be possible to move beyond the single, and sterile, question whether or not the Communists had started to resist before June 1941.[90]

Secondly, the more complex account of the relationship between Vichy and public opinion which emerged in the 1980s reopened the problem of the relationship between the Resistance and the French population. Henri Michel had once written: 'the Resistance always comprised a minority . . . and the majority of *attentistes* . . . could not pardon it for having been right and having saved

---

[88] Cordier, 'De l'acteur à l'historien: Un itinéraire et une méthode', *Bulletin de l'IHTP*, 35 (1989), 23–36.

[89] Originally Cordier projected seven volumes. Three of these appeared between 1989 and 1993 under the general title of *Jean Moulin: L'Inconnu du Panthéon*. In 1999, he produced a single book, *Jean Moulin: La République des Catacombes*, with a different publisher, which summarized the contents of the first three volumes, and then covered the rest of the ground which had originally been projected for the four subsequent volumes. One assumes that the project is now complete.

[90] J.-P. Azéma, A. Prost, J.-P. Rioux (eds.), *Le Parti communiste français des années sombres 1938–1941* (1986); eid., *Les Communistes français de Munich à Chateaubriant (1938–1941)* (1987).

them'.[91] But the new research into public opinion, viewing *attentisme* in more complex terms, opened the way towards less Manichaean interpretations of the relationship between population and Resistance. Such re-evaluation was easier to undertake if one had not been personally involved in the period, and this provides a third reason for the renewed interest in Resistance in the late 1980s: the prospect that the Resistance generation was coming to the end of its life.

Because many resisters had been extremely young, Resistance historiography was, until the 1980s, dominated by writers personally marked by the experience. The doyen of Resistance historians, Henri Michel, had begun to develop an almost proprietary approach to the subject, and was not always welcoming to younger scholars who wanted to work on it. Younger historians in general felt the inhibiting presence over their shoulder of the vigilant Resistance generation.[92] The prickliness of many former resisters emerged at the colloquium where Cordier first presented his research. He received a hostile reception from many historic resisters, and the wartime squabbles between London and Paris were fought out again in 1983. When one of the resisters present said that Cordier's lecture made him feel as if resisters were being judged by administrators, he sounded exactly like Henri Frenay complaining in 1942 about the bureaucratization of the Resistance by Moulin.[93] At a colloquium on the Resistance held at Toulouse in 1986 two former resisters almost came to blows over what had really happened in Toulouse in 1944. But they were united in preferring to rehearse these old feuds than to engage with the questions of a young female historian about the attitude of the resistance towards gender. Her observations were treated with outrage, and allowed the old rivals of 1944 to close ranks by repeating well-worn pieties about the noble role of women in the Resistance.[94]

But this is changing. Three Resistance movements have recently had important theses devoted to them.[95] These studies are exemplary in their attempt to combine a social analysis with a political one; they are nuanced, archivally based, and sophisticated in their use of oral material. But the most significant fact is that the authors are part of the first genuine post-Resistance generation of Resistance historians. The history of the Resistance, unlike that of Vichy, is beginning (again). It is no longer the 'taboo' noted by *Esprit* in 1992. What new approaches are emerging in the history of the Resistance? There is, first, a greater emphasis on the diversity of resistance, and on the experience of non-dominant groups such as immigrants and women.[96] Secondly, there is an attempt to

[91] Michel and Mirkine-Guetzévitch, *Les Idées*, 37.

[92] Laborie, 'Historiens sous haute surveillance', 41–2.

[93] See the debate at the conference at which Cordier first presented his interpretation of Moulin, D. Cordier et al., *Jean Moulin et le Conseil national de la Résistance* (1983), 35–58.

[94] R. Trempé (ed.), *La Libération dans le midi de la France* (Toulouse, 1986), 175–82.

[95] O. Wieviorka, *Une certaine idée de la résistance: Défense de la France 1940–1949* (1995); L. Douzou, *La Désobéissance: Histoire d'un mouvement et d' un journal clandestins: Libération-Sud (1940–1944)* (1995); A. Aglan, *La Résistance sacrifiée: Le Mouvement Libération-Nord* (1999).

[96] S. Courtois, D. Peschanski, A. Rayski, *Le Sang de l'étranger: Les Immigrés de la MOI dans la*

conceptualize resistance history in the light of insights from other disciplines such as anthropology, and to offer a more comparative dimension.[97] Thirdly, more attention is being directed towards the interaction between 'the Resistance' narrowly defined and the social context which was the condition of its survival, between 'Resistance as organization' and 'Resistance as movement' in the words of François Marcot. Between 1993 and 1997, major colloquia on the Resistance were organized in six different French universities.[98] The presiding theme of each occasion was the study of the Resistance in its social environment. This is also a major theme of Jean-Marie Guillon's (unpublished) monumental thesis on the Resistance in the Var, of François Marcot's work on the Jura, and of Roderick Kedward's most recent book which continues where his first one left off, and studies the southern Maquis from 1943.[99] In short, we are moving towards a social history of the Resistance.[100]

The future of the history of the Resistance needs to embrace its full diversity—Gaullist and non-Gaullist, Communist and non-Communist, North and South, men and women, French and immigrants—but also to reconnect the history of the Resistance to the society around it, to the French past, and to the Vichy regime. As our opening quotations have shown, the history of France in this period cannot be understood in separate compartments like 'the Vichy regime', 'the Resistance', or 'collaboration': these existed in dynamic relation to each other, and the history of France in this period must be conceived as a whole. There are strands, but they make up one history.

Résistance (1989); M. Weitz, *Sisters in the Resistance: How Women fought to free France 1940–1945* (1995); P. Schwartz, 'Women, Resistance and Communism in France 1939–1945' (unpublished Ph.D. thesis, New York, 1998).

[97] H. R. Kedward, 'Resiting French Resistance', *Transactions of the Royal Historical Society* (1999), 271–82: 273–4.

[98] Guillon and Laborie, *Mémoire et histoire*; J. Sainclivier and C. Bougeard, *La Résistance et les Français: Enjeux stratégiques et environnement social* (Rennes, 1995); R. Frank and J. Gotovitch, *La Résistance et les Européens du Nord*, 2 vols. (1994–6); F. Marcot (ed.), *La Résistance et les Français: Lutte armée et maquis* (1996); L. Douzou et al. (eds.), *La Résistance et les Français: Villes, centres et logiques de décision* (1995); J.-M. Guillon and R. Mencherini, *La Résistance et les Européens du sud* (1999).

[99] Guillon, 'La Résistance dans le Var: Essai d'histoire politique' (Doctorat d'État, Aix, 1989); Marcot, 'Résistance et population 1940–1944' (Mémoire pour l'habilitation à diriger des recherches, Université Franche-Comté, 1990); Kedward, *In Search of the Maquis: Rural Resistance in Southern France* (Oxford, 1993).

[100] See the articles collected in 'Pour une histoire sociale de la Résistance', *MS* 180 (1997).

Part I

Anticipations

Introduction to Part I

In January 1945, the lifelong anti-Republican polemicist Charles Maurras was found guilty of collaboration with Germany. 'The revenge of Dreyfus' was Maurras's comment on the verdict. Maurras had a famously long memory, but there were certainly echoes of the Dreyfus Affair during the Occupation. The last head of Vichy's anti-Semitic Commissariat for Jewish Affairs was Charles Mercier Du Paty de Clam, a descendant of the Paty de Clam who had arrested Dreyfus in 1894. In 1944, Vichy's semi-official police, the Milice, had assassinated the 81-year-old Victor Basch whose crime, apart from being a Jew, was to have been an ardent Dreyfusard and former president of the League of the Rights of Man, founded during the Dreyfus Affair. Thus the conflicts of occupied France can be seen as a continuation of what have been called the 'Franco-French wars'—between those who accepted the legacy of the Revolution and those who did not. As the historian René Rémond says about 1940: 'those who had never accepted 1789 finally took their revenge'.[1]

Some historians push the idea of the 'two Frances' even further back—to the division in the seventeenth century between a maritime, liberal, and Protestant France and a rural, authoritarian, and Catholic one.[2] During the Occupation the economist Charles Rist, himself a Protestant who abhorred Vichy, compared the regime's supporters to the Catholic League of the sixteenth century: 'Replace the Italo-Germany of Hitler–Mussolini by the Spain of Philip II and you have France's situation under Charles IX.' Rist also saw parallels between the behaviour of French conservatives in 1940 and 1870.[3]

One approach to the problem of finding a 'pedigree' for Vichy is offered by the Israeli historian Zeev Sternhell, author of a trilogy of books on fascism in France. Sternhell has argued that, far from being an alien graft on to French political culture, fascism's origins as a coalescence of the anti-liberal right and anti-liberal left date back to late nineteenth-century France. He goes on to argue that in the 1930s, fascist ideology, or at least a fascist sensibility, was permeating French politics, and that the Occupation can only be understood in this

---

[1] See 'Les Guerres franco-françaises', *VSRH* 5 (1985), esp. H. Rousso, 'Vichy, le grand fossé', 55–80.
[2] E. W. Fox, *History in Geographic Perspective: The Other France* (New York, 1971).
[3] *Une saison gâtée: Journal de guerre et de l'occupation* (1983), 108, 347.

light.[4] Sternhell has been criticized for being too imprecise in his definition of fascism, enrolling any critic of liberal democracy under the banner of fascism. Nonetheless his work does reveal, more than previous historians had done, the existence of strong anti-liberal currents in French political culture, especially in the 1930s. The British historian Tony Judt, analysing the influence of communism on French intellectuals after 1945, has also emphasized the weaknesses of liberal ideas in France. Judt notes that several Communist intellectuals had started in the 1930s as ultra-conservatives: he explains their conversion by their consistent antipathy to liberal democracy.[5]

To understand the history of occupied France, then, it is necessary to start before 1940. But the heterogeneity of support upon which the Vichy regime drew, at least initially, suggests that it is misleading to draw neat boundaries between 'two Frances'—between supporters and opponents of liberal democracy. Vichy also drew upon political and cultural values shared between liberals and non-liberals, Republicans and anti-Republicans. Vichy emerged not only from what divided the French but also what united them: pacifism, fear of population decline, loss of confidence in national identity, anti-Semitism, discontent with existing political institutions, ambivalence about modernity. The existence of this common ground also complicated the early history of the Resistance. It may well be, as Robert Paxton argues, 'that there come cruel times when to save a nation's deepest values one must disobey the State', but it was not necessarily clear, in 1940, what those values were, or that Vichy was in all respects opposed to them.[6]

Although it was France's defeat by Germany which caused these 'cruel times' and exposed the prevalence of anti-liberal currents in French political culture, it is also necessary to relate the collapse of French democracy to longer-term social developments which undermined the foundations on which French political stability had been built at the end of the nineteenth century. In trying to explain the terrible events which occurred in Germany in the twentieth century, historians have often argued that the causes were rooted in the peculiarities of Germany's social and political development at the end of the nineteenth century. The problem with this idea of a German 'special way' (*Sonderweg*) is that it implies the existence of a 'normal' process of development from which Germany can be said to have deviated.[7] The truth is that every country has its own *Sonderweg*. In the case of France, the 'peculiarity' lay in the gradualness of industrialization, resulting in the development of a dual economy where a highly concentrated industrial sector coexisted with a large class of peasants and small producers (the *classes moyennes*). Political stability was preserved by an implicit

[4] *Ni droite ni gauche: L'Idéologie fasciste en France* (1983).
[5] *Past Imperfect: French Intellectuals, 1944–1956* (1992).
[6] *Vichy France*, 383.
[7] G. Eley and D. Blackbourn, *The Peculiarities of German History: Bourgeois Society and Politics in Nineteenth Century Germany* (Oxford, 1984).

coalition of interest between bourgeois elites, on the one hand, and peasants and small producers, on the other. This 'Republican synthesis', as Stanley Hoffmann has dubbed it, guaranteed the defence of property and provided an education system which offered the possibility of social promotion to the children of the *classes moyennes*. In addition it relegated the working class to the political and social margins.[8]

The term 'synthesis' is misleading if it implies that the situation was ever static. Even when the Republican consensus was working relatively well, it contained tensions and contradictions. The economic relationship between big business and small producers was never entirely harmonious despite their common opposition to organized labour. Another fault-line was religion: the division between Catholics and anticlericals. In the 1890s it had looked briefly as if this issue would be resolved when Catholics and Republicans seemed ready to bury the hatchet in the interests of social defence during the so-called *ralliement*—the 'rallying' of the Church to the Republic. But the Dreyfus Affair at the turn of the century reopened the religious divide. By creating the political parties which would dominate France for the next forty years, the Dreyfus Affair built religious conflict structurally into French politics. Religion was not an epiphenomenal issue: Catholic and lay associations had networks of patronage and social organization extending into almost every crevice of French associational life.[9]

At the epicentre of these contradictions was the Radical Party, the pre-eminent force in French politics since 1900. As the party committed above all to anticlericalism, the Radicals instinctively looked to alliances with the Socialists, on their left, or anticlerical conservatives, on their right. But as the party which represented above all small producers, they were suspicious both of the Socialists and of those conservatives linked to big business. The conservatives most sympathetic to small production were not necessarily those who opposed the Church. In other words, the two fault-lines within the Republican synthesis did not necessarily overlap. As long as the working class could be successfully marginalized, these contradictions were not important enough to threaten the stability of the Republic. But even before 1914 the containment of the working class was becoming increasingly difficult as industrial conflict intensified. After the war it became impossible.

The aim of Part I of this book, then, is to situate the Occupation within this longer-term context. The intention is not to provide a full history of inter-war France, but to explore some aspects of that history in the light of 1940. Chapter I examines the cultural legacy of the Great War, suggesting that it provided a

[8] Hoffman, 'The Paradoxes of the French Political Community', in id. (ed.), *The Paradoxes of the French Political Community* (New York, 1963); S. Elwitt, *The Third Republic Defended: Bourgeois Reform in France* (Baton Rouge, La., 1986); G. Noiriel, *Les Origines républicaines de Vichy* (1999), 45–98.

[9] The argument of this paragraph owes a lot to K. Passmore, 'The French Third Republic: Stalemate Society or Cradle of Fascism?', *French History*, 7/4 (1993), 417–49.

repository of themes, transcending left and right, which in many respects anticipated Vichy. The war is an obvious place to start because, after all, the Vichy regime was headed by the popular hero of that war. It is striking how much Vichy's National Revolution owed to the rhetoric of the Great War: the exaltation of national unity, the celebration of the Soldier-Peasant and the nurturing Mother, the cult of the military leader, and the suspicion of politicians.

Chapter 2 surveys the long history of dissatisfaction with the Third Republic and its institutions. Some of this dissatisfaction originated within the Republican mainstream from as early as the 1890s; some came from arch-conservatives; some came from the post-war generation for whom the heroic early years of the Republic were ancient history. The point of this chapter is to show that if Vichy's renunciation of the Republic was partly a victory of reactionary conservatism, it also represented much of what was best and brightest in French politics.

Political boundaries must not, however, be blurred entirely, and Chapter 3 examines how the Great War and the Depression of the 1930s exacerbated class tensions and threatened the social bases of the Republican consensus. To the extent that there was a civil war in France between 1940 and 1944, it had started several years earlier. Chapter 4 examines some aspects of the relationship between France and Germany in the inter-war years, and discusses French responses to the German problem. What came to be called 'collaboration' had a long prehistory, and this complicated responses to defeat in 1940. Chapter 5 shows how many of the themes discussed in the previous chapters culminated in the last peacetime government of the Third Republic after April 1938, and examines how that government anticipated the Vichy regime which followed it.

These five chapters are all intended to suggest anticipations of the future, but not a teleology. Thus Chapter 6 will restore the notion of discontinuity by examining the impact of the defeat of May 1940. Without defeat there would have been no Vichy regime, but without the trends examined in the previous chapters, the Vichy regime would not have taken the form that it did.

1

The Shadow of War:
Cultural Anxieties and
Modern Nightmares

The first French film to hit the screens after the Fall of France was Marcel Pagnol's *La Fille du puisatier* (The Well-Finder's Daughter). The film tells the story of a peasant girl, Patricia, made pregnant by Jacques, a dashing airman from a bourgeois family in the local town. He is called away for military manoeuvres, and his parents refuse to take responsibility for his behaviour. Patricia's father, shamed by her conduct, casts her out, and she takes refuge in her aunt's house where she gives birth to a baby boy. Eventually, succumbing to the desire to see his grandson, her father relents. Meanwhile Jacques is reported killed in the war and his distraught parents feel remorse and wish to acknowledge their grandchild. The two families are reconciled. Then it is suddenly revealed that the airman is not dead after all. He returns and asks for Patricia's hand in marriage. She expresses the hope that once they are married, he will leave the city to live on the land: 'I would be happy in a farm of our own on land which we were bringing to life. I would do the dishes and the cleaning—and each day at sunset I would go to the end of the path and await the return of my man coming back from the field.'

The film celebrates the virtues of motherhood, of the countryside, and of the peasantry. These were quintessential Vichy themes. So also was the idea that misfortune can lead to reconciliation and resurrection. The film's most famous scene occurs when the two reconciled families listen, together with the rest of the village, to Marshal Pétain's speech of 17 June announcing the need for an armistice. For such reasons *La Fille du puisatier* has often been seen as the first 'Vichy film'. This would be true except that most of the filming had taken place before the defeat, and the scene containing Pétain's speech was added quite late. Indeed, it has been alleged that when the film was shown after the Liberation, this scene was substituted with a similar one of the family listening to General de Gaulle. There is no truth in this, but it is true that there was nothing specifically Vichyist about the film. It is in the spirit of all Pagnol's films during the

1930s.[1] Being as much the last film of the Third Republic as the first film of Vichy, *La Fille du puisatier* suggests that there is no simple cultural caesura between the two regimes: Pagnol speaks as convincingly to the France of the Third Republic as to the France of Vichy.

Verdun: The Soldier-Peasant

The French cult of the peasant—such a recurrent theme of Pagnol's films—was strongly reinforced by the Great War, in particular the battle of Verdun. In the French collective imagination, the Great War is Verdun. On the Allied side the French fought alone, and Pétain, the general in charge, organized a rotation system so that no one served continuously at Verdun for more than a few weeks. As a result, most French soldiers fought there. For 300 days and nights raged a battle which concentrated all the horror of the war. Henri de Montherlant wrote: 'If all the men who died here got up, there would be no place for them to stand since they were killed in successive layers.'[2] The most chilling aspect for those arriving at Verdun for the first time was the haunted faces of the men whom they was relieving. As Antoine Prost puts it: 'Like Auschwitz, Verdun marks a transgression of the limits of the human condition.'[3] But unlike the Somme and Passchendaele where, for the British, a certain idea of heroism died in the mud, Verdun came to symbolize the glory of the war as well as its horror. This was not glory as conceived in 1914—soldiers charging with their bayonets gleaming in the sun—but the noble tenacity of the French peasant doggedly defending the soil of France, as he would his farm and family. French commentators claimed that the battle illustrated the virtues of the French peasant: the endurance of the Auvergnat, the abnegation of the Breton, the toughness of the mountain dwellers of the Pyrenees and Alps.[4] Verdun was represented as the 'shield' of France, the victory of the 'soldier-peasant' over German steel.[5]

Although hardly a convincing explanation of why France won the war, as an explanation of the victory of Verdun, it was not entirely false. At Verdun, there were no proper lines of trenches, only jagged 'lines' of craters offering little protection. It was a battle of isolated groups of men, without orders, desperately clinging on to a crater or struggling from shell hole to shell hole. If the battle of the Marne was a victory of planning, Verdun was genuinely the battle of the ordinary soldier—the *poilu*—a battle over which the high command exercised little control: it was a victory of endurance. As the historian Gabriel Hanotoux

---

[1] See the four film adaptations he made of novels by Jean Giono: *Joffroi, Regain, Angèle, La Femme du boulanger.*

[2] A. Ducasse et al., *Vie et mort des Français 1914–1918* (1960), 167.

[3] 'Verdun', in P. Nora (ed.), *Les Lieux de mémoire*, pt ii. *La Nation*, vol. iii (1986), 111–41.

[4] P. Barral, *Les Agrariens français de Méline à Pisani* (1968), 180.

[5] P. Servent, *Le Mythe Pétain: Verdun ou les tranchées de la mémoire* (1992), 109–34.

wrote in 1920: 'This was a war fought by men of the land . . . It is by the land, with the land, with men of the land, that France defends herself . . . This peasant, this Frenchman of the war, has become suddenly the archetypal Frenchman, the Frenchman of the peace.'[6] 'The peasant', said Pétain in 1935, 'accomplishes his military duty with the same tranquil assurance as he does his duty as a farmer . . . In the most sombre moments of the war, it was the determined and serene gaze of the French peasant which bolstered my confidence.'[7] Since the late nineteenth century, conservative writers had deplored the exodus from the countryside and celebrated France's perfect balance of agriculture and industry.[8] But Verdun, the nightmare battle at the heart of this most modern of wars, gave new resonance to rural representations of French identity.

Ruralism was an important theme in the literature and painting of the 1920s. There was a vogue for regionalist and rustic novels such as Henri Pourrat's Auvergne novel sequence *Gaspard des montagnes*, published between 1925 and 1931. The solid virtues which Pourrat ascribed to his hero from the Auvergne mountains, he later rediscovered in Marshal Pétain to whom he devoted a work of hagiography in 1942.[9] In 1938, three out of the four main French literary prizes—Femina, Renaudot, and Interallié—went to rustic novels.[10] After the war, there was a craze for the peaceable paintings of Utrillo, whose career had hitherto been undistinguished. In the words of the regionalist writer André Chamson: 'Utrillo's work depicts the resurgence of an almost abolished world . . . A world which orders itself entirely around the church and the small village hall.'[11]

Regionalism and ruralism influenced the post-war reconstruction of France. The art historian Paul Léon, who was in charge of architecture at the Ministry of Fine Arts, turned regionalism into the official doctrine of reconstruction. 'Born without architects', he wrote, 'peasant architecture developed freely in our provinces like the natural product of the soil.' In rebuilding France it was necessary to guard against 'outside intrusions'. In architectural history, 1923 may be famous as the year of publication of Corbusier's *Vers une architecture*, but more important at the time was the appearance of the first volume of Charles Letrosne's *Murs et toits pour les pays de chez nous* which became the manual of architectural regionalism.[12] Regionalism went hand in hand with a celebration of France's medieval heritage, a theme which had acquired poignancy after the destruction of Reims cathedral by German artillery. The mutilated cathedral was

[6] G. de Puygène, *Chauvin, le soldat-laboureur: Contribution à l'étude des nationalismes* (1993), 236–9.

[7] Barral, *Les Agrariens*, 181.

[8] The classic of the genre is Jules Méline's *Le Retour à la terre* (1st pub. 1905; reissued 1919).

[9] *Le Chef français* (Marseilles, 1942).

[10] G. Sapiro, 'Complicités et anathèmes en temps de crise: modes de survie du champ littéraire et des ses institutions 1940–1953' (Doctoral thesis, École des hautes études en sciences sociales, 1994), 200.

[11] R. Golan, *Modernity and Nostalgia: Art and Politics in France between the Wars* (1995), 44–5, 49.

[12] Ibid. 27. See P. Léon, *Art et artistes d'aujourd'hui* (1925); C. Ellis, 'French Re-Connection', *Architectural Review*, 192 (Jan. 1993), 70–3.

depicted on innumerable cards and posters. After the war there was a neo-medieval revival in French church architecture.[13]

At the two world fairs held in Paris during the inter-war years—the Arts Décoratifs Exhibition of 1925 and the International Exhibition of 1937—regionalism was prominent in the French entries. This had not been true of previous fairs in 1889 and 1900 where it played almost no part. The 1925 Exhibition is remembered today for Le Corbusier's Pavillon de l'Esprit Nouveau which was one of the programmatic statements of modernism, but the Pavillon was hidden behind the Grand Palais, and pride of place was given to the regional pavilions and the miniature French village.[14] In 1937 regionalism was even more pronounced. The exhibition organizer declared: 'I have chosen a watchword: regionalism. Never have the provinces been invited to participate so directly in an international event.' At the heart of the exhibition, there was a regional centre depicting the life of twenty-seven French regions, and a rural centre containing a model village.[15]

Regionalism transcended political boundaries. In 1937 France was governed by a Socialist Popular Front government which backed the regionalist emphasis of the exhibition. The same government also set up France's first museum devoted to folklore, the Musée des Arts et Traditions Populaires (ATP). The Rural Centre had performances by folklore groups (most of whom in fact came from Paris) and demonstrations by lacemakers and rural artisans. But regionalism did not necessarily mean nostalgia. The Rural Centre promoted the idea of rural modernization. It tried to avoid pastiche by portraying a model village with electricity and running water. The right complained because the village did not contain a church. Thus there were different readings of regionalism, but agrarian spokesmen were united in praising the fact that the exhibition had 'for the first time in France placed rural France on almost the same level as that reserved for the rest of the country'.[16]

Dénatalité: The Disappearance of France

Not only was the peasantry a central representation of French identity, it was also viewed as central to the survival of the French nation: the land represented fertility and the peasantry incarnated the virtues of family. In November 1920, soon after the burial of the Unknown Soldier—by implication an Unknown Soldier-Peasant—there was a barrage of publicity for the presentation of the Cognacq-Jay prizes for the largest families in France. Much was made of

---

[13] Golan, *Modernity and Nostalgia*, 23–30.

[14] Ibid. 58–60.

[15] S. Peer, *France on Display: Peasants, Provincials and Folklore in the 1937 Paris World's Fair* (Albany, NY, 1998).

[16] Id., 'Peasants in Paris: Representations of Rural France in the 1937 International Exposition', in S. Ungar and T. Conley (eds.), *Identity Papers: Contested Nationhood in Twentieth Century France* (Minneapolis, 1996), 21.

the rural origins of the winning families.[17] Having defended France with its blood, the peasantry would now repopulate her.

The rural exodus was deplored especially for its impact on birth rates. Family size was larger in the country than the towns. The regeneration of the nation had to come from the countryside. This was the theme of one of Pagnol's most lyrical films of 1930s, *Regain*, which depicts the death and rebirth of a village whose last surviving inhabitant finds a woman and sets up house with her. Having become almost a savage, he is gradually domesticated, and in the last scene, as they are sowing their fields, she announces, to the strains of a stirring soundtrack by Arthur Honegger, that she is pregnant.

After 1918, concern about French population size started to become a national obsession. Despite a superficial climate of nationalist triumphalism, France's post-war mood was one of pessimism and uncertainty, reflected in Paul Valéry's remark in 1919 that the war had demonstrated the mortality of civilizations: 'a civilization is just as fragile as a life'.[18] Even the fervently nationalistic writer Maurice Barrès, whose chauvinistic war journalism ran to fourteen volumes, was haunted by doubts about the consequences of the war. In optimistic vein, he celebrated how the war had thickened the texture of French patriotism, creating a spiritual community between the living and the dead; in pessimistic vein, he wondered if France could ever recover from so many deaths.[19] Such cultural pessimism, reflected in works like Spengler's *The Decline of the West* (1918), was widespread in post-war Europe, but only in France did it focus so obsessively on population.

The obsession was not surprising since no other great power had suffered a higher proportion of deaths in the war: 1.3 million Frenchmen had been killed. Such figures were especially alarming in a country where preoccupation about the population long pre-dated the war. Once the most populous state in Europe, France's birth rate had started to decline at the beginning of the nineteenth century. This came to be conceived as a problem in the aftermath of the Franco-Prussian war, especially during the 1890s, when for four years the number of deaths exceeded births. Between 1871 and 1911, France's population increased by only 8.6 per cent, Germany's by 60 per cent, and Great Britain's by 54 per cent. *Dénatalité* became the most palpable evidence of French national decline.

The year 1896 saw the foundation of the National Alliance for the Growth of the French Population (ANAPF). Philanthropists established prizes for the parents of large families. The Cognacq-Jay prize offered 25,000 francs to ninety fathers of ten or more living children. Émile Zola, always a barometer of contemporary anxieties, treated depopulation in his novel *Fécondité* (1899). It tells the story of a country couple living in harmony and prosperity with a family of

---

[17] Puygène, *Chauvin*, 238.
[18] 'Regards sur le monde actuel', in *Œuvres*, ii. (1960), 913–1158: 927–8, 995.
[19] M. Baumont, 'Maurice Barrès et les morts de la guerre de 1914–1918', *L'Information historique*, 1 (1969), 30–5.

twelve children, while the other characters, living in the city, with only small families, all come to tragic ends. The moral was not only that large families are desirable, but that the countryside is fecund and the city sterile.[20]

On the eve of the war, the ANAPF had 2,900 members; 241 *députés* had joined the natalist group in the Chamber.[21] But at this stage the ANAPF remained only an elite pressure group. Its effectiveness was hindered by uncertainty whether it should concentrate on reducing infant mortality or promoting incentives for large families. Natalist propaganda was also resisted in syndicalist circles where Malthusian ideas (the restriction of family size) had an audience: why bring up children to be factory labour or cannon fodder?[22] Malthusianism chimed in with fears whether the drive for 'quantity' would lead to a decline in 'quality'. Late nineteenth-century worries about population size fitted into a wider obsession with decadence and racial degeneration spawned by the social consequences of urbanization and industrialization. The three great scourges of the day were believed to be syphilis, TB, and alcoholism.[23] The National League against Alcoholism had been founded the year before the ANAPF. In 1915 it got the government to outlaw the production and sale of absinthe.[24]

In many countries, concerns about racial degeneration had encouraged the development of eugenics. Since eugenicists in America and Britain advocated the restriction of births, even sterilization, their objectives potentially contradicted those of the natalists. But in France, where the Eugenics Society was founded in 1912, most eugenicists subscribed to the neo-Lamarckian theory of the inheritance of acquired characteristics. This meant that the dominant strand in eugenics was not 'negative'—restriction of births—but 'positive'—measures to improve social hygiene. Not until the 1930s did the competing claims of 'quantity' and 'quality' diverge in the face of concern about immigration.[25]

After the war, natalists were no longer crying in the wilderness. Clemenceau announced during the debate on the Versailles Treaty: 'If France gives up large families, one can put all the clauses one wishes in the treaty . . . France will be lost because there will be no more French.' The ANAPF's membership increased to 40,000 by the end of the decade. In 1920 parliament created a Conseil supérieur de natalité to advise on increasing the birth rate. Its vice-president,

[20] S. Pedersen, *Family Dependence and the Origins of the Welfare State* (Cambridge, 1993), 26–9.

[21] R. Tomlinson, 'The Politics of *dénatalité* during the French Third Republic 1890–1940' (unpublished Ph.D., Cambridge, 1983); 'The Disappearance of France, 1896–1940: French Politics and the Birthrate', *Historical Journal*, 28 (1985), 405–15; P. Ogden and M.-M. Huss, 'Demography and Pro-Natalism in France in the 19th and 20th Centuries', *Journal of Historical Geography*, 8/3 (1982), 283–98.

[22] F. Ronsin, *La Grève des ventres: Propagande néo-malthusienne et baisse de la natalité en France 19ᵉ–20ᵉ siècles* (1980).

[23] R. Nye, *Crime, Madness and Politics in Modern France* (Princeton, 1984).

[24] P. Prestwich, *Drink and the Politics of Social Reform: Anti-Alcoholism in France since 1870* (Palo Alto, Calif., 1988).

[25] W. Schneider, *Quality and Quantity: The Quest for Biological Regeneration in Twentieth Century France* (Cambridge, 1990); 'Towards the Improvement of the Human race', *JMH* 54 (1982), 268–91; A. Carol, *Histoire de l'eugénisme en France* (1995).

Fernand Boverat, was one of the ANAPF's most energetic leaders. The ANAPF launched the idea of Mothers' Day where deserving mothers were rewarded by the attribution of medals: gold for those with over ten children. This event was launched with great publicity in 1920, and in 1926 it was made official by the government. But Mothers' Day never caught on and, until resuscitated by Vichy in 1941, it largely went unnoticed.[26] The main success of the natalist lobby was the 1920 law increasing penalties for abortion, and prohibiting the sale of contraceptive devices or the dissemination of birth control information.

After 1918, natalism was not confined to conservatives. Malthusianism lost ground even in syndicalist circles.[27] Only fifty-five *députés* voted against the 1920 abortion laws. Left and right differed not over the desirability of natalism, but over how to promote it. Some conservatives wanted to grant extra votes to parents of large families in proportion to the number of children they had. A proposal to implement this 'family vote' was only narrowly defeated in parliament in 1923. The original inspiration behind the family vote was to strengthen family ties, and only incidentally to increase family size. But if 'familialism' and natalism were distinct in origin, after the war they increasingly converged. The family vote became one of the major themes of the ANAPF's propaganda, although the urgent need to increase births meant that French culture maintained considerable tolerance towards illegitimacy.[28]

Proponents of the family vote were not in favour of female suffrage. A female suffrage bill was narrowly defeated in the Senate in 1922, and although it was periodically resuscitated, it never again came close to becoming law. The opposition came partly from anticlericals suspicious about the influence of the Church over women.[29] But conservative natalists also opposed a measure liable to distract women from their natural role as mothers. Boverat claimed that in countries where women had the vote, the birth rate had declined.[30] The emphasis which French eugenicists put on childcare also gave a scientific legitimation to the idea that women must devote themselves fully to motherhood.

Old Mother or New Woman?

During the war, the major contribution of women to the victory had been in the factories, but official propaganda preferred to portray women allegorically, as 'Marianne' and 'Victory', or as nurses, wives, and mothers. There was a vogue

[26] A. Reggiani, 'Procreating France: The Politics of Demography', *FHS* 19/3 (1996), 725–54; F. Thébaud, 'Le Mouvement nataliste dans la France de l'entre-deux-guerres', *RHMC* 32 (1985); M.-M. Huss, 'Pro-Natalism in the Inter-War Period in France', *JCH* 25 (1990), 39–68; Tomlinson, 'Politics of *dénatalité*', 132 ff.

[27] J.-L. Robert, 'La CGT et la famille ouvrière 1914–1918', *MS* 116 (1981), 47–66.

[28] See e.g., Pagnol's films, *Regain, Angèle, La Fille du puisatier.*

[29] P. Smith, *Feminism and the Third Republic: Women's Political and Social Rights in France* (Oxford, 1996).

[30] Tomlinson, 'Politics of *dénatalité*', 167.

for postcards celebrating motherhood and reminding the *poilu* of his second duty to the country. On one card, a returning soldier, greeted by his wife with the words 'now you can rest', replies 'impossible: preparing the class of 1936'; in another, a soldier is congratulated on having given a good thrust of his bayonet, from which three babies dangle. These cards remained popular during the inter-war years, contrasting with similarly humorous cards in Britain where babies were portrayed negatively as the end of romantic bliss.[31]

The reaffirmation of woman's maternal destiny was fuelled by male anxieties over the blurring of traditional gender boundaries during the war.[32] Women wore shorter skirts and shorter hair; they seemed bolder and threatening. The more 'masculine' women threatened the sexual identity of the returning males, all the more so because the nature of the combat had sapped masculine self-esteem. Far from being heroes, charging with bayonets at the ready, the *poilus* spent much of the war trapped in mud, waiting for shells to rain upon them: the experience was one of passivity and emasculation. The novelist Drieu la Rochelle wrote of his own experience of the war: 'I was reduced to making vain gestures . . . I felt the Man in me had died.'[33]

Masculine insecurity was heightened by soldiers' fear of female infidelity. One celebrated treatment of this theme was *Le Diable au corps* (1923) by the young prodigy Roland Radiguet. The novel is the story of an adolescent who has an affair with the wife of a soldier at the front. This amoral adventure of sexual initiation was the nightmare haunting the imagination of many soldiers. Radiguet sent his novel to the war novelist Raymond Dorgelès who was appalled by its cynicism. Dorgelès had himself been the victim of such an affair and the theme of sexual infidelity runs through his writing. In his post-war novel *Le Réveil des morts*, the hero marries a war widow and gradually realizes their affair had started while her husband was alive at the front. He comes to identify with the dead husband and reject the perfidious wife. In this book, another kind of female treason makes its appearance: women in the occupied part of the country, who fraternize, even sleep, with German soldiers. But as one character says: 'women will be women'.[34] Resentment of women was also stoked by anti-war writers who accused them of manufacturing the shells which killed the soldiers.

After 1918, the 'new woman' came to symbolize the *poilu's* sense of estrangement from the post-war world.[35] No one was more conservative than the *poilu*

---

[31] M.-M. Huss, 'Pro-Natalism and the Popular Ideology of the Child in Inter-War France: The Evidence of the Picture Postcard', in R. Wall and J. Winter (eds.), *The Upheaval of War: Family, Work and Welfare in Europe 1914–1918* (Cambridge, 1988), 329–67.

[32] M.-M. Huss, 'Virilité et religion dans la France de 1914–1918: Le Catéchisme du poilu', in M. Cornick (ed.), *Beliefs and Identity in Modern France* (1990), 114–45.

[33] *La Comédie de Charleroi* (1934), 72.   [34] *Le Réveil des morts* (1948 edn.), 70.

[35] In general, see M. Roberts, *Civilization without Sexes: Reconstructing Gender in Postwar France, 1917–1927* (Chicago, 1994); and id., 'Samson and Delilah Revisited: The Politics of Women's Fashion in 1920s France', *American Historical Review*, 98 (1993), 657–84.

with his fund of nostalgic images of a world that was ending—the world depicted in the famous song 'Madelon'. When the novelist Georges Duhamel wrote of the loyal wife 'who maintains a radiant home . . . and spins at her wheel behind the door, awaiting our return', he was describing a world in which the *poilu* desperately wanted to believe.[36] In André Lamandé's novel *Les Lions en croix* (1923), the woman's betrayal of the hero during the war mirrors the betrayal of all the hopes of the veterans after the war: his life becomes an obsession to find her and exorcize her memory.

Post-war anxieties about women were epitomized in the reactions to Victor Margueritte's novel *La Garçonne* which was the *succès de scandale* of the 1920s, causing Margueritte to be stripped of his Légion d'honneur. Selling a million copies by the end of the decade, the novel also spawned a doll, a perfume, a play, and a film. It tells the story of a girl of bourgeois origins who discovers that her fiancé has not been faithful. She breaks off the engagement and throws herself into a life of frenzied independence, taking male lovers, experimenting with lesbianism, cutting her hair short, smoking, taking opium. What shocked the book's readers was that these adventures happened to a middle-class girl, not a member of the *demi-monde*. In fact the denouement is eminently moral. The heroine's pursuit of pleasure brings her no satisfaction, and ultimately she discovers fulfilment by marrying and caring for a war veteran.[37]

The heroine of *La Garçonne* had wanted to bear a child, but discovered she was sterile. Eventually her sterility turns out to be a symbolic reflection of the aridness of her life, since in the book's sequel, *Le Compagnon* (1923), she succeeds in having children once she is married. In Clement Vautel's satire *Madame ne veut pas d'enfant* (1924; Madame Doesn't Want a Child), the hero's wife will not have children for fear of spoiling her figure and ending her life of pleasure. Her parents are Esperanto-speaking vegetarians, and ardent Malthusians. She dances the foxtrot with blacks, listens to jazz, eats new-fangled dishes like lobster *à l'Americaine*, and furnishes her flat with cubist paintings and modern furniture. In desperation, the hero finds a mistress who serves him traditional *pot-au-feu* in a flat which is an oasis of French bourgeois calm, furnished in *faux* Henri III style. His wife finds out, but the mistress tells her how to recover her husband: offer him a baby. The wife discovers the joys of motherhood and is congratulated by the doctor who warns that if more women do not follow her example France will disappear 'unless the barbarians come to make children by our pretty girls'.[38]

[36] Roberts, *Civilization without Sexes*, 10.

[37] Id., ' "This Civilization no longer has Sexes": *La Garçonne* and Cultural Crisis in France after World War I', *Gender and History*, 4/1 (1982), 49–69; A.-M. Sohn, '*La Garçonne* face à l'opinion publique: Type littéraire ou type social des années 20?', *MS* 80 (1972), 3–27.

[38] C. Vautel, *Madame ne veut pas d'enfant* (1924); Roberts, *Civilization without Sexes*, 131–7.

America: Scenes of the Future

In Vautel's heavy-handed satire, the wife's predilection for things American demonstrates her repudiation of a woman's traditional role. This was one example of France's growing obsession with America after the war. Generally the French attitude to America before 1914 was one of mild condescension.[39] When America joined the war, it took time to appreciate that she might have an independent policy, contrary to French interests. France was made brutally aware of her diminished influence at the Paris conference when English was for the first time treated as a diplomatic language equal to French.

American cultural power was reflected in the displacement of France by America as the dominant force in world cinema.[40] In 1910, French cinema enjoyed the supremacy of Hollywood today. This position, already under threat before 1914, was finally destroyed by the war. French studios closed in 1914, expecting a short war. When they reopened a year later, the first Keystone films had arrived in France, and Chaplin was about to become a cult. During the 1920s, it was feared that America was destroying the French film industry. In 1928, the government imposed a quota on foreign film imports. This was largely ineffective, and one politician in 1930 deplored the fact that 'Joan of Arc might be played by a young Californian, and a native of Illinois with the features of his region might play Napoleon'.[41]

Publicists and politicians visited the States and wrote their impressions. Even strip cartoon characters crossed the Atlantic: the Breton maid Bécassine in 1921; Tintin in 1931. Three books that played a significant role in forming views appeared in 1927: André Siegfried's *Les États Unis aujourd'hui*, André Tardieu's *Notes sur l'Amérique*, and Lucien Romier's revealingly titled *Qui sera le maître: Europe ou Amérique?* Siegfried wondered whether 'traditionalist France' had any future: 'What is at stake in essence is France's individuality itself, the original character of a whole civilisation.'[42] Romier contrasted European harmony and individualism with American excess and uniformity.

These authors were at least open to the idea that America also had something to offer Europe. This was not true of the most celebrated anti-American tract of the decade, Georges Duhamel's *Scènes de la vie future* (1930). Previously best known for his war book *Civilisation*, recounting his experiences as a doctor, Duhamel came from the progressive and pacifist left, committed to a vision of European humanism. The war had represented one threat to this; America represented another, hardly less pernicious. One was a nightmare that had occurred;

[39] M. Winock, 'L'Anti-Américanisme français', in id., *Nationalisme, antisémitisme en France* (1990), 50–76; D. Strauss, *Menace in the West: The Rise of French Anti-Americanism in Modern Times* (Westport, Conn., 1978).

[40] R. Abel, *French Cinema: The First Wave 1915–1929* (Princeton, 1984); P. Monaco, *Cinema and Society: France and Germany in the 1920s* (New York, 1976).

[41] Strauss, *Menace in the West*, 150.

[42] Quoted in Peer, *France on Display*, 18.

the other a nightmare that loomed. Duhamel attacked every aspect of American life: cinema was an entertainment of submissive helots; jazz was barbaric; American food tasted industrial; baseball was a savage game without elegance. In short, Americans were obsessed by work and health, enslaved to machines, tyrannized by moral conformism, and brainwashed by advertising. How different was France with her little local bistros, her sense of harmony, her innumerable cheeses.

Duhamel's contrast between French humanism and rootedness, on one hand, and a society of deracinated nomads, on the other, was the theme of another tirade, *Le Cancer américain* (The American Cancer) published a year later by Robert Aron and Armand Dandieu. In the 1930s, after America had been hit by the Depression, American values seemed less threatening, but this only confirmed that France had been right to avoid excessive industrialization and mass production. The moral was noted by one organizer of the 1937 Exhibition: 'the world is at present suffering from exaggerated standardisation in that quality is being sacrificed to cheapness, and good taste to mass production'. It was time to return to the 'glorious tradition of France's artisans'.[43]

Le Rappel à l'ordre: The New Classicism

The critique of America did not so much describe a reality—Duhamel only spent six weeks in America—as invent a foil. Expressing a sense of the fragility of European culture, it was also a means of defining the essence of Frenchness: quality, moderation (*mesure*), and harmony.

The idea of *mesure* was central to the revival of classicism in the arts after the war.[44] This revival, dubbed the *rappel à l'ordre*, was a repudiation of the supposed excesses of the pre-war avant-garde, notably cubism.[45] Already before 1914, cubist painters had been accused of being Germanic: cubism was sometimes spelt by its detractors with a 'k' to emphasize the point. The war placed the avant-garde on the defensive: pre-war cubists retreated from experimentation. Robert Delaunay, who had previously had important links to the German avant-garde, now castigated 'cubist hoaxes' imposed on the French by 'foreign mystificators'— a barely concealed reference to Picasso. Picasso himself, although not entirely abandoning cubism, also returned to representational portraiture, and embarked upon some Ingres-like drawings. These explicit classical references echoed wartime propaganda depicting France as the defender of Mediterranean classical purity against Germanic gothicism, *civilisation* against *Kultur*. Classicism was the presiding reference of the new artistic climate: it became fashionable to paint

---

[43] Peer, *France on Display*, 67.

[44] See in general C. Prochasson and A. Ramusssen, *Au Nom de la patrie: Les Intellectuels et la Première Guerre mondiale (1910–1919)* (1996), 271–8.

[45] K. Silver, *Esprit de Corps: The Art of the Parisian Avant-Garde and the First World War, 1914–1925* (1989); A. Lantenois, 'Analyse critique d'une formule "retour à l'ordre"', *VSRH* 45 (1995), 40–53.

Harlequins. Between 1921 and 1924, Picasso produced a whole series of neoclassical works; Braque painted a homage to Corot which was praised by one critic for a 'sense of proportion and severe grace which are born only in France'.[46]

No painting style is of course intrinsically progressive or reactionary, but the contemporary debate about the avant-garde was cast in such terms. The critic Bessières, who had been the first to use the term *rappel à l'ordre*, argued in 1920 for the need to aspire to the order and certainty represented by Raphael. Symbolic of the new post-war mood was the publication at the end of 1918 of *Après le cubisme* by Amédée Ozenfant and Charles-Edouard Jeanneret (the future Le Corbusier). They characterized cubism as 'the troubled art of a troubled and self-indulgent epoch, the final flowering of romantic individualism which should now give way to a more intellectual art emphasising line over colour, structure over decoration.'[47]

The new cultural climate saw a negative revaluation of impressionism. 'Down with Renoir', proclaimed Jean Cocteau in 1919. Cocteau, in a bid to become the cultural impresario of the decade, wrote a collection of essays called *Le Rappel à l'ordre* which defined the new cultural agenda. The first essay, with the 'Gallo-Latin' title of 'The Cock and the Harlequin', called for a 'French music of France'. This was an attack on Debussy for being too mistily foreign ('Debussy translates Monet into Russian'), and a defence of Erik Satie for his French clarity: 'Satie speaks of Ingres'. Cocteau became the spokesman of the post-war generation of French composers known as 'Les Six' who represented a reaction against Debussyan impressionism, and sought, to quote Darius Milhaud on Satie, a 'French music freed of any foreign influence'.[48] Standing apart was Stravinsky, but his own return to classicism in this period was favourably noted by Cocteau. He commented that Stravinsky was putting his 'eastern romanticism . . . in the service of Latin order'.

Cocteau represented the fashionable literary world of the Paris right bank. Very different was the austere seriousness of the left-bank literary periodical, the *Nouvelle revue française* (*NRF*) which entered after the war into its period of cultural dominance. Any writer who wished to be taken seriously aspired to publish in the *NRF*. Although attacked by conservatives as a cradle of immorality, the *NRF* was itself concerned to rediscover artistic order in the turmoil of post-war society. In 1919 its editor Jacques Rivière wrote that the age of romanticism was over; he predicted a 'classical renaissance'. A similar idea was expressed by one of the newest *NRF* recruits, the young novelist Marcel Arland who in 1924 wrote a celebrated article diagnosing a 'new mal du siècle' against which it was necessary to set a 'new harmony'. Arland dramatized this dilemma in his 1930 novel *L'Ordre* whose hero, ambitious for literary success and spiritual values, dies a wreck eaten up by drugs and alcohol, a victim of his obsession with self.

---

[46] Silver, *Esprit de Corps*, 237.   [47] Ibid. 227–31.
[48] R. Shattuck, *The Banquet Years: The Avant-garde in France* (1959), 189.

Modernist Nightmares: Morand and Céline

This oscillation between 'order' and 'anxiety' was the theme taken up by another *NRF* contributor, the critic Benjamin Crémieux, in a 1930 survey of the literature of the post-war decade.[49] The anxiety took several forms: the iconoclastic irreverence of Dada and surrealism; the literature of exoticism and escapism (Paul Morand, Pierre Macorlan); the flight into morbid introspection (Pierre Drieu la Rochelle); the search for certainty in Catholicism (Julien Green, François Mauriac, Georges Bernanos).

Of all these writers it is Paul Morand (1888–1976) who is most identified with the decade of the 1920s and best illustrates its cultural ambivalence. Morand leapt to fame after the publication of his first collection of stories *Tendres stocks* in 1921. These stories are often viewed as the embodiment of the spirit of the 1920s, and Morand posed as the chronicler of his age by grouping four of his novels between 1925 and 1930 under the collective title *Chroniques du XXème siècle*. He was widely read: *Ouvert la nuit* (1922), his second collection of stories, was in its 135th edition by 1931.

Morand's father was a successful dramatist who had written the translation of Hamlet so famously performed by Sarah Bernhardt. In 1912 Morand entered the diplomatic service, moving easily in the beau monde of London and Paris. During the 1920s, he travelled widely, and in 1927 he married a Romanian princess. It is this cosmopolitan politico-artistic milieu which forms the subject of Morand's writing. It is a world of wagons-lits, parties in London, cafés in Vienna, hotels in Istanbul, a world of social flux and disintegrating boundaries, peopled by arrivistes, fallen aristocrats, and victims of history. Reflecting the fragmented and turbulent 1920s, Morand's style, much admired by the surrealists, is allusive and elliptical, his descriptions fizzing with unexpected images. The tone is always knowing, detached, and cynical.

But the veneer of worldliness, cosmopolitanism, and stylistic virtuosity is misleading. The smart chronicler is prey to social and cultural anxieties, and more nostalgic for the stable past than at first appears. One theme of Morand's writing is the modern woman. The first collections of stories contain six portraits of women, mostly 'modern' women, who are threatening and inaccessible. A favourite theme is female homosexuality. In the story *La Nuit de Babylone* a man is seen in a car between two women who are kissing each other across him. He is worrying that his mistress had been seduced by another woman. In the story *Madame Fredda* the protagonist is a conservative journalist who looks back nostalgically on the past. He meets a Dutch woman, who makes it clear that she wants to sleep with a Frenchman. She is a modern woman, lacking modesty or inhibitions.

---

[49] B. Crémieux, *Inquiétude et reconstruction: Essai sur la littérature de l'après guerre* (1931); D. Nasaw, 'From Inquiétude to Reconstruction' *JCH* 11 (1976), 149–72; J.-P. Maxence, *Histoire de dix ans 1927–1937* (1939), 64–75.

Another of Morand's themes is race. The protagonist of *Madame Fredda* is not convinced that France has won the war since Paris has been 'surrounded and captured' not by the Germans but by an influx of foreigners. The body of France is described as suffering from 'periodic eczema of Italian emigration; suspect spots of Romanian origin; colonies of American boils; levantine pus'. Morand was prone from his earliest writing to racial stereotyping, especially of Jews and blacks. His bedside reading on a 1927 visit to the West Indies was Gobineau's *Essai sur l'inégalité des races*. In the story *Baton rouge* a black singer, clearly modelled on Josephine Baker, is suddenly, in the middle of a triumphal Parisian tour, 'repossessed by ancestral fears and superstitions'. Racial mixing and modern women were symbols of threatening modernity. America was another. In *New York* (1930) Morand writes: 'Once I wanted Paris to . . . resemble New York. Today I no longer want this . . . I wrote a few years ago that France had no other chance than to become American or Bolshevik, but now I believe that we must avoid these two precipices with all our strength . . . The genius of Paris is precisely that of a meticulous peasant.'[50]

Traditional Paris was also a preoccupation of the writer Louis-Ferdinand Destouches, better known under his pseudonym, Céline. On the face of it, no one could have been more different from the sophisticated and urbane Morand than the asocial and eccentric Céline whose first novel, *Voyage to the End of the Night*, erupted on to France's literary scene in 1932. When the book appeared, its 38-year-old author was an unknown figure, earning his living as a doctor. Céline had been brought up in central Paris where his mother had a lace shop in the Passage Choiseul, one of those nineteenth-century covered passages of small shops, where time seems to have stopped. This world of Parisian *petit commerce*, precariously surviving into the twentieth century in the face of the combined forces of capital and labour, was the subject of Céline's second novel, *Mort à crédit* (1936).

The defining moment of Céline's life was the war, in which he played a briefly heroic role before being invalided out in October 1914. After the war he trained as a doctor and then worked for the League of Nations as an expert on hygiene and social medicine. In this capacity he visited America to study conditions in the Ford factory at Detroit. Leaving the League he became a doctor in the working-class Paris suburb of Clichy. Many of these events were incorporated into *Voyage to the End of the Night*. It begins with the war where its picaresque hero, Bardamu, discovers a universe of futility and horror. His only concern is to avoid getting killed, and it is a matter of complete indifference to him whether the Germans or French win providing he remains alive. Much of the war he spends convalescing from his wounds, marvelling at the propaganda lies which keep the conflict going: 'the mania for telling lies and believing them is as con-

---

[50] Morand, *Nouvelles complètes*, i (1991); P. McCarthy, 'The Evils of Modernity', *Times Literary Supplement*, 27 Nov. 1992; M. Collomb, *La Littérature Art Déco* (1987); A. Loselle, 'The Historical Nullification of Paul Morand's Gendered Eugenics', in M. Hawthorne and R. Golsan (eds.), *Gender and Fascism in Modern France* (Hanover, NH, 1997), 101–18.

tagious as the itch'. Next Bardamu goes to Africa where he encounters the corruption and brutality of colonialism. Escaping Africa, he heads for America. His
'isolation in the American anthill' turns out to be even more soul-destroying
than his loneliness in Africa. He sinks into a 'terrifying, sickly sweet torpor'.
Having got a job in the Ford factory, where he is told that 'all we need is chim-
panzees', he becomes reduced to the status of an automaton, crushed by the din
of the factory: 'you give in to noise as you give in to war'. Eventually he returns
to Paris, and sets up as a doctor in a suburb of unbelievable squalor.

This brief summary is enough to make clear that Céline's vision is one of
unrelieved pessimism although the story is told with a sardonic black humour.
His novel was also shocking for its stylistic unorthodoxy, using popular language
and slang instead of formally correct usage. *Voyage to the End of the Night* was
admired more by the left than the right: Sartre used a quotation from Céline as
the epigraph to his first novel *Nausea*. Trotsky, however, was quick to see that
there was nothing for Socialists in Céline's coruscating social criticism: his
nihilism offers no prospect that the human condition can ever be improved. The
book is a howl of rage against the world born out of the catastrophe of war:
'While the war was still on, the seeds of our hateful peace were being sown. A
hysterical bitch, you could see what she'd be like just by watching her cavorting
in the dance hall of the Olympia. In that long cellar room, you could see her
squinting out of a hundred mirrors, stamping her feet in the dust and despair
to the music of a Negro-Judaeo-Saxon band.'

Of the world before the catastrophe, there is only a glimpse. The novel opens
with a few moments of innocence when Bardamu is still a 'virgin in horror'. He
and a friend are sitting at the terrace of a café in the Place Clichy in Montmartre
in August 1914. A few hours later they have joined the army and there is no
turning back: 'They'd quietly shut the gate behind us civilians. We were caught
like rats.' The choice of the Place Clichy to open the novel is highly significant.
In the inter-war years Montmartre functioned in the French literary imagination as a trope of immobility, security, and tradition with its picturesque village-
style squares, its vineyard, and its associations with the late nineteenth century.
Montmartre was Utrillo's Paris: it was the antithesis of the cosmopolitan, gleaming chrome bars of Montparnasse, the centre of artistic life in the post-war years.
Although in *Voyage to the End of the Night* the war forms the barrier between
'before' and 'after', in *Mort à crédit* Céline pushes his diagnosis of the evils of
the modern world even further back—to the Exhibition of 1900 where the petty
bourgeois parents of the narrator are confronted with the sense that the world
is passing them by. It was no coincidence that Céline took as his pseudonym the
name of his grandmother, who had lived almost her entire life in the nineteenth
century.[51]

---

[51] The literature on Céline is immense. The best biography is F. Gibault, *Céline*, 3 vols. (1977–85).
For the importance of Montmartre in *Voyage au bout de la nuit*, see N. Hewitt, *The Golden Age of Louis-
Ferdinand Céline* (1987), 70–4.

It would clearly be absurd to take a figure as strange and original as Céline as representative of his age, or read *Voyage to the End of the Night* as a novel 'about' the 1920s. But equally it would be wrong to overlook the degree to which the novel mirrors the cultural preoccupations of the decade. Like Morand, but to an infinitely more extreme degree, Céline is haunted by the evils of modernity. Their pessimism deepened in the 1930s, and found an outlet in anti-Semitism. Céline wrote two anti-Semitic pamphlets which are almost deranged in their violence. Morand's book *France la Doulce* (1934) bemoaned the supposed stranglehold of the Jews over the French film industry. For this reason alone it is not surprising that both Céline and Morand found compensations in the defeat of France in 1940. When Pétain signed the Armistice Morand was in London, attached to the French Embassy. He returned to France to offer his services to the new regime. In 1942 he was in Pierre Laval's *cabinet* before being sent to the French Embassy in Bucharest. He ended the war in the Embassy at Berne, and wisely preferred to stay in Switzerland than return to a country where he was now a blacklisted writer.

Céline, however, had no truck with the *bien-pensant* tone of the Vichy regime. He spent the war in Paris where he was involved in the fringes of the ultra-collaborationist world, and wrote a third anti-Semitic pamphlet. In August 1944, he fled to Germany with the hard-core collaborators who took refuge in the town of Sigmaringen where the Vichy regime lived out its final days. In the futility of Sigmaringen Céline found a subject whose grotesque absurdity matched anything he had so far created in his fiction. Finally, having followed the collaborationist adventure to its extreme end, he escaped across war-torn Germany to take refuge in Denmark. There was nothing inevitable of course about the trajectories of these two anti-modern literary modernists, Morand and Céline, but the choices they made in 1940 must be understood partly in terms of the cultural anxieties and upheavals of the post-war decade.

2

Rethinking the
Republic: 1890–1934

The Vichy regime styled itself the 'État français' (French State). This did not define what it was, but it signalled clearly what it was not: the Third Republic, founded in 1875, was dead. The busts of Marianne, symbol of the Republic, were replaced in town halls by statues of Pétain; 'Liberty, Equality, Fraternity' gave way to 'Work, Family, *patrie*'.

It was not only Vichy which rejected the Republic in 1940. Many early resisters felt little loyalty to it either. De Gaulle initially refused to identify himself with the defunct regime or with republicanism in general. For a year, the broadcasts of his Free French movement were introduced by the slogan 'Honour and *patrie*' not 'Liberty, Equality, Fraternity'. The Republic had few friends in 1940.

This was not altogether surprising in light of the defeat of 1940. The Second Empire, which had triumphed in the plebiscite of May 1870, collapsed four months later in the defeat of Sedan. But, unlike the Empire, or the Weimar Republic, the French Third Republic had put down deep roots in French society. It had been in existence for sixty-five years. It symbols—the tricolour, the Marseillaise, Bastille Day—were intimately bound up with French national identity. How could this heritage be so totally repudiated in 1940? One reason was the polarization of French politics after February 1934 when anti-parliamentary riots took place in Paris. That polarization, which forms the immediate background to 1940, will be considered in the next chapter. But there was a longer tradition of disaffection from the Republic which stretched back beyond 1934. One historian has even asserted, with some exaggeration, that the Republic was 'culturally dead' in 1900.[1]

Critics of the Republic could be found not only among the doctrinaire anti-Republicans like Charles Maurras, but also within the Republican consensus. Vichy was the victory not only of the Republic's enemies, but also of those of

---

[1] D. Lindenberg, *Les Années souterraines 1937–1947* (1990), 15.

its friends who despaired of reforming it. In short, the capitulation of France's elites to anti-Republican values in 1940 had a long prehistory.

Before 1914: 'La Fin des notables?'

Almost as soon as the liberal conservative Orleanists had accepted the Republic in the 1870s, they wondered if they had made a mistake. The crisis of the Republic was almost as old as the Republic itself. The Constitution of 1875, in which the influence of the Lower House—the Chamber of *députés*—was counterbalanced by a President and Senate, had embodied the Orleanist ideal of checks and balances. In practice, however, from the early 1880s, the Chamber emerged as supreme: the President became a mere cipher. This was not the Republic in which the Orleanist liberals had believed, and they started to discuss how the situation could be remedied.[2] Most of the proposals to reform the Republic in the inter-war years can be traced back to the 1890s—to the writings, for example, of the liberal conservative parliamentarian, journalist, publicist, and academic Charles Benoist (1861–1936). Author of books like *La Crise de l'État moderne* (1895) and *L'Organisation de la démocratie* (1900), Benoist argued that the dominance of the democratically elected Chamber over the Senate and Presidency had betrayed the spirit of the constitution. The democratization of politics was creating a chasm between France's political institutions and her bourgeois elites, between her political leaders and those social groups which had professional competence and social standing—*les compétences*, as they were described.

Benoist's ideas appealed not only to those liberal conservatives nostalgic for a world they had lost, but also to new republican elites which had come through the Paris Bar or the École libre des sciences politiques (Sciences Po). Such people dominated the higher reaches of the administration, staffed ministerial *cabinets*, and sometimes entered politics. But they had little in common with the average *député* or with the rural notables and lay schoolteachers who were the ballast of the regime in the provinces. This cultural chasm between republican elites and the parliamentary rank and file deepened after the turn of the century when the Dreyfus Affair brought to power the Radical Party, representing the petite bourgeoisie of provincial France. Benoist's worst fears were realized: the Radicals heralded the advent of the professional politician. In 1906, parliamentary pay was raised from 9,000 francs (where it had been since 1875) to 15,000 francs. From this period dated the stereotype of the *député* as a provincial windbag, usually from the Midi, good for nothing except electioneering and intrigue: the Republic of 'country vets' had replaced the Republic of *compétences*.[3] To remedy this

[2] A. Pitt, 'The Evolution of Liberal Thought under the Third French Republic c.1860–c.1940' (unpublished Cambridge Ph.D. thesis, 1995).

[3] G. Le Béguec, 'L'Entrée au Palais Bourbon: Les Filières privilégiés d'accès à la fonction parlementaire, 1919–1939' (unpublished thesis, University of Paris-X, 1989), 160–76; id., 'Charles Benoist ou les métamorphoses de l'esprit modéré', *Contrepoint*, 22–3 (1976), 74–95.

situation, Benoist and other centre-right critics of the system proposed a whole battery of reforms: proportional representation, shorter parliamentary sessions, restriction of the right of *députés* to initiate financial legislation, reinforcement of the authority of the President of the Republic.

Criticism of the parliamentary Republic did not only come from the centre-right. There was also a centre-left critique exemplified by Robert de Jouvenel's *La République de camarades* (1914), a savage attack on parliamentarians as a caste. De Jouvenel was one of a group of progressive Radicals arguing for a republic technically equipped to deal with the problems of the modern world. This critique, which could be described as proto-technocratic, overlapped with the 'Orleanist' one only in requiring the Republic to be reconnected with those social groups who had professional expertise and authority.

Such critics of the Republic argued from within the Republican consensus: they wanted the Republic to work better. This distinguished them from the uncompromising anti-Republicanism of Charles Maurras's movement, Action française. Maurras came to prominence in 1898 when he wrote an article defending the 'patriotic forgery' of the officer who had fabricated a document to incriminate Dreyfus. Apart from a genius for such provocations, Maurras's real achievement was to synthesize royalism, nationalism, and Catholicism into a single doctrine which he called 'integral nationalism'. Convinced of France's decadence, he believed that the solutions must be political; his slogan was 'politique d'abord'. The keystone of his doctrine was the ideal of classical order. For Maurras, who came from Provence, started as a literary critic, and liked to think of himself as a poet, France represented the continuation of Mediterranean classical civilization, and the antithesis of the cultural values of her hereditary foe Germany. France's enemies were individualism and romanticism—whether in literature, politics (the French Revolution), or religion (Protestantism).

Maurras's model was the pre-revolutionary *ancien régime*. The antidote to romantic disintegration was the restoration of the monarchy and the authority of the Catholic Church (although Maurras was himself a non-believer). Maurras distinguished between what he called the 'pays légal'—the formal structure of Republican institutions—and the 'pays réel'—the true France of community, family, region, and workplace. Maurras also wanted to exclude from influence what he called the four 'confederated' states sapping France's unity: Protestants, Freemasons, Jews, and *métèques* (half-breeds). Nonetheless Maurras claimed not to be a racist—racism was German—and he justified the exclusion of the Jews on grounds not of race but cultural inassimilability.

Action française did not fight elections before 1918. Its influence derived from the construction of an intellectual counterculture based upon its newspapers, its institute, and its publishing house. As Maurras used to put it about his activities at this time: 'we were working with 1950 in mind'.[4] Although not all Maurras's followers subscribed to every detail of his system—many were

---

[4] Quoted by M. Winock in *Le Siècle des intellectuels* (1999 edn.), 95.

monarchists only in the most perfunctory sense—intellectually he reinvigorated a monarchical tradition living on nostalgia and sentiment. As he wrote in his *Enquête sur la monarchie*: 'The necessity of monarchy is demonstrated like a theorem. Once the wish to defend our French homeland is admitted as a postulate, everything unfolds, everything follows ineluctably.'[5] Maurras made it intelligent to be monarchist, or at least anti-Republican. He had a considerable following among students of the Latin Quarter.

Once Maurras had worked out his doctrine, he had nothing new to say. But he went on saying it for forty years, as if the deafness afflicting him since childhood cut him off from the sounds of the modern world, immuring him in his certainties. This bestowed an aspect of impregnability and granite-like coherence on his thought. The conservative novelist Paul Bourget once declared that Action française, along with the British House of Lords, the Papacy, and the Prussian General Staff, was one of the four European fortresses against revolution.[6]

One surprising initiative taken by Action française was the attempt to build bridges to the working class through the 'Cercle Proudhon', an economic and social study group, created in 1911 by Georges Valois. Unusual among Action française members in displaying an interest in social problems, Valois hoped to win syndicalist leaders to the monarchist cause. Although attracting few workers, Valois did win over some syndicalist intellectuals. Even if the Cercle Proudhon proved abortive, it demonstrated that there was some common ground between the ultra-conservative critique of the Republic and the syndicalist one. Both deplored the individualistic Republican ideal of the abstract citizen. Against Republican individualism, Maurrasianism celebrated the 'organic' communities of the *ancien régime*, and the syndicalists the community of the workplace.

Syndicalism was rooted in the Proudhonian ideal of the moral dignity of labour. As a producer in control of his labour, an individual obtained real freedom as opposed to the formal freedom of the Republican citizen-voter. Syndicalists believed in the self-sufficiency of labour to protect working-class interests, and were suspicious of all politicians, even Socialist ones. Syndicalism was successful in France because the working class received so little from the Republic that it made sense to opt out of formal politics entirely. The syndicalist utopia was a decentralized society of producers where the State would lose its *raison d'être* and disappear. This vision was plausible in France where artisans and small-scale industry were numerous. Since 1906, the French trade-union federation, the CGT, had been committed to the most revolutionary version of syndicalism, believing its objectives could be achieved through direct action: the general strike. Although the number of syndicalists genuinely committed to revolution was diminishing before the war, the broader syndicalist vision, especially the distrust of politics, remained influential. It appealed to those on the left who felt that politicians had betrayed the idealism of the Dreyfus Affair.

---

[5] (1909 edn.), 116.   [6] G. Sapiro, *La Guerre des écrivains 1940–1953* (1999), 44.

No one better exemplified the mood of post-Dreyfusard disillusion than the writer Daniel Halévy. Halévy is particularly interesting because he stands at the confluence of many of the intellectual currents described above: his entire career is emblematic of the drift away from Republican values by a part of France's elite. He was born into a grand Parisian *haut-bourgeois* family, son of the librettist Ludovic Halévy. This was a deeply Orleanist milieu—'you belong to one of the most noble families of the old Orleanist Republican tradition' wrote Péguy— and when in 1930 Halévy published his classic book *La Fin des notables*, an elegiac history of the passing of the Orleanist era in the 1870s, he was casting a nostalgic eye upon the world of his childhood.

The turning point of Halévy's life was the Dreyfus Affair. Convinced of Dreyfus's innocence, he collaborated closely with Péguy on the *Cahiers de la quinzaine*. Although much of his later life was spent memorializing Péguy, the hero of his youth, their actual relations cooled after Halévy wrote his *Apologie pour notre passé* (1910) questioning whether the Dreyfusards had not been duped. It was this book which gave rise to Péguy's famous *Notre jeunesse* which defended the battles of their youth, while sharing the same sense of betrayal.

At the time of the Affair Halévy defined himself as a Socialist, and he was involved in the Universités populaires where intellectuals sought to bring culture to the people. The 'people' in whom Halévy believed were sturdy independent artisans not the modern proletariat. His other idol, after Péguy, was Proudhon. 'Proudhon's socialism', wrote Halévy, 'respects natural groups, the family . . . the old artisanal France which Péguy had known and which he defended.' Halévy's 'people' also included the peasantry. An intrepid walker, he wrote four books recounting his visits to the countryside and his observations on the peasantry. In the first of these, in 1907, he was a young man of the left looking for pio-neers of peasant syndicalism; by the last, in 1934, he was writing an elegy for a disappearing world, which represented the only barrier against modern unifor-mity and proletarian levelling.

By the 1930s, Halévy was a pessimistic conservative, displaying even a cau-tious admiration of Maurras. He became a formidable anti-Republican polemi-cist. In books like *Décadence de la liberté* (1931) and *La République des comités* (1934), which are contemporaneous with his historical evocations of the last days of Orleanism, he denounced a political system dominated by professional politicians operating through Masonic committees. The link between Halévy's nostalgia for the 'Republic of Notables' and his cult of the independent artisan and peasant, between his Orleanism and his Proudhonism, is the idea that both incarnated a real France from which the Republic had cut itself off. By 1940, he was ready to welcome the Vichy regime as the last chance to preserve that France.[7]

---

[7] Halévy, *Décadence de la liberté* (1931); id., *Visites aux paysans du Centre*; id., *La République des comités: Essai d'histoire contemporaine* (1934). On Halévy see A. Silvera, *Daniel Halévy and his Times: A Gentleman*

The 1920s: The Maurrassian Moment

Halévy's journey from Dreyfus to Vichy, with Péguy and Proudhon as its central threads, started well before 1918, but it was certainly accelerated by the upheaval of the Great War. The consequences of the war for republicanism were, however, more ambiguous than this single example suggests. After all, the Republic had proved effective enough to win the war. While Willhelmine Germany had succumbed to defeat under the military dictatorship of Hindenburg, in France the war was won under the leadership of the intransigently Republican Georges Clemenceau, a leader whom even Maurras could admire. Did this mean that anti-Republicans were now ready to swallow their historic objections to the Republic?

Even after 1918, there were conservative families for whom the Republic remained the incarnation of evil. Indeed in the Vendée there are still families today who will not receive descendants of people who bought *biens nationaux* during the Revolution.[8] During the inter-war years, the family of the future historian Philippe Ariès left Paris on 14 July to avoid being present in the capital on this revolutionary day.[9] In 1919, the government was worried enough about the susceptibilities of anti-Republicans to abandon its idea of burying the Unknown Soldier in the Panthéon because the building was too identified with the Republic.[10] Instead he was buried under the Arc de Triomphe.

Nonetheless the war did give the iconography of the Republic greater legitimacy than it had enjoyed before 1914. The victory parade of 14 July 1919, with Foch and Joffre at its head, displaced the central axis of the Bastille Day celebrations from the poor quarters of eastern Paris to the Champs-Élysées in the west: 14 July 1919 celebrated not the victory of republicanism over reaction but France's victory over Germany.[11] Similarly the Marseillaise received its apotheosis during the war, sung on the Marne as it had been at Valmy: in 1917 it was the monarchist Louis de Joantho who published a book entitled *Triomphe de la Marseillaise*.[12]

These developments can be read in two ways: after 1918, the symbols of Republicanism were less contested than they had ever been before, but the meanings attached to them became less precise.[13] Clemenceau may have triumphantly

Commoner in the Third Republic (1966); S. Laurent, 'Daniel Halévy 1872–1962'; P. Guiral, 'Daniel Halévy: Esquisse d'un itinéraire', *Contrepoint*, 20 (1976), 79–95.

[8] J. Laurent, *Histoire egoïste* (1978 edn.), 33.

[9] P. Ariès, *Un historien de dimanche* (1980), 22.

[10] G. Bonnefous, *Histoire politique de la Troisième République*, iii. *L'Après-Guerre, 1919–1924* (1968), 171–4; A. Becker, 'Du 14 juillet 1919 au 11 novembre 1920: Mort où est ta victoire?', *VSRH* 49 (1996), 31–44.

[11] C. Amalvi, 'Le 14-juillet', in Nora (ed.), *Les Lieux de mémoire*, pt. i. *La République*, 412–72: 461.

[12] M. Vovelle, 'La Marseillaise', in Nora (ed.), *Les Lieux de mémoire*, pt. i. *La République*, 85–136.

[13] On the lack of enthusiasm for this iconography as reflected in the 1920 celebration see G. Guy-Grand, *L'Avenir de la démocratie* (1928).

reasserted the primacy of Republican government over military power, but the military had also emerged from the war with unprecedented prestige. In 1914–15 the cult of Joffre had reached unbelievable proportions, to be equalled in the twentieth century only by that of Pétain after 1940. Pétain and Foch had also emerged from the war with titanic reputations. The funerals of Foch in 1929 and Joffre in 1931 were massive occasions on a scale not witnessed since that of Victor Hugo in 1885. In short, although it is often pointed out that after 1918 the French people hated war, it is less often noted that this was not the same thing as hating generals.

All this helps to explain the paradox that while the republican consensus had never seemed wider than after 1919, the early 1920s represented the apogee of influence of Action française.[14] Because Action française was not a conventional electoral movement, it is difficult to quantify its influence, but undoubtedly Maurras's prestige had never been higher. His nationalistic Germanophobia had fitted into the wartime 'Sacred Union'. During and after the war Maurras enjoyed a friendly correspondence with the respectable conservative politician Poincaré; André Malraux in 1923 called Maurras 'one of the great intellectual forces of today'. In the mid-1920s, the paper's circulation was about 100,000, and Action française historians like Pierre Gaxotte and Jacques Bainville were best-selling authors. Action française was well represented in the Académie française to which Maurras himself was elected in 1938. Maurras's defence of classicism chimed in with the post-war classical revival. In his book *Défense de l'occident* (1927) the young Maurrassian Henri Massis extended this into a defence not just of French values but of the entire tradition of western civilization. The writer Jacques Laurent, who joined Action française in the 1920s, wrote subsequently that he was not just joining a party but opting for civilization itself. One of Massis's favourite targets was André Gide and the literary individualism of the *NRF*.[15]

It is generally argued that Action française's influence began to decline after 1926 when it was condemned by the Vatican as part of a papal policy to reconcile Catholicism with democracy in France. The Vatican decision affected *Action française's* readership in conservative Catholic circles. At the same time, younger members of the movement felt that Maurras was more talk than action—'Inaction française' was their term—and they started to look to more radical movements of the right. But the long-term effects of Maurras's post-war influence should not be underestimated for two reasons. First, the Maurrassian counter-culture, comparable in its influence on the right to that of communism on the left thirty years later, inoculated many young right-wing intellectuals against the attraction of republicanism. Action française was often the apprenticeship in a

[14] P. Nora, 'Les Deux Apogées de l'Action française', *Annales ESC* (1964), 127–41; S. Wilson, 'The Action française in French Intellectual Life', *HJ* 12 (1969), 328–50; V. Nguyen, 'Situation des études maurassiennnes: Contribution à l'étude de la presse et des mentalités', *RHMC* (1971), 503–38.
[15] Sapiro, *La Guerre des écrivains*, 142–52.

journey towards different varieties of extremist politics, fascism in some cases (Robert Brasillach, Lucien Rebatet), communism in others (Claude Roy, Claude Morgan, and Roger Vailland). As one commentator wrote in 1935: 'beyond its real, visible and measurable strength, Action française also disposes of the strength provided by all those who have left it'.[16] When Claude Roy joined the Communist Party during the Occupation he was struck by how many former Action française intellectuals he encountered.[17]

Secondly, the new 'respectability' which drove Maurras's younger disciples to more exciting shores made him more acceptable to elements of the Republican centre. Although Maurras was a counter-revolutionary and reactionary thinker, Maurrassianism spread like a stain through French liberal conservatism after 1919: 1940 was not so much the victory of 'reaction' over liberal conservatism as proof of how much the latter had already conceded to the former.

This was true of Charles Benoist who announced his conversion to Action française in 1925, and became the tutor of the Royalist pretender, the Comte de Paris. Benoist did not live to participate in the Vichy regime. Someone who did was Lucien Romier who joined the government in 1941 to become one of the ministers most trusted by Pétain. In the inter-war years, Romier was one of the pillars of liberal bourgeois opinion. He was both a popular historian specializing in the wars of religion and a leading journalist who contributed regularly to *Le Figaro* and *Le Temps*, the two leading papers of moderate conservatism. Romier was alarmed at many aspects of post-war French society: depopulation, the new woman, artistic anarchy. Although seeing himself as a liberal Republican, in 1924 he wrote a pamphlet calling for an aristocracy of *fonctionnaires* to save the Republic from its crisis of authority. His book *Explication de notre temps* (1925) noted with approval that Maurras's ideas had an audience which went beyond Action française.[18]

Another liberal conservative who ended up at Vichy was Joseph Barthélemy who served as Minister of Justice from 1941 to 1943. Like Romier, Barthélemy was a regular contributor to *Le Temps* in the inter-war years. He was a highly respected jurist who wrote prolifically on constitutional matters. In 1918 his book *Le Problème de la compétence dans la démocratie* (The Problem of Competence in Democracy) confronted what many liberal conservatives believed to be the fundamental issue facing the Republic. Barthélemy had been elected to parliament on a centre-right ticket in 1918, but he was defeated in 1924, and all subsequent attempts at re-election were unsuccessful. Like Romier he was increasingly unhappy about mass culture. 'Democracy', he wrote in 1934, 'involves the advent of new social groups [*nouvelles couches*] . . . It is another world. It is the end of the notables.' Nonetheless until 1940 Barthélemy remained

---

[16] Nguyen, 'Situation', 506.

[17] C. Roy, *Moi je* (1969 edn.), 200.

[18] L. Romier, *Explication de notre temps* (1925); id., *La Crise de l'État* (1924). C. Roussel, *Lucien Romier 1885–1944: Historien, économiste, journaliste* (1979), is unenlightening.

committed to Republican institutions, wanting only to rationalize them. In his memoirs written in 1944 he commented on the 'contradictory destiny of a man who has all his life defended liberty and then makes his ministerial debut in an authoritarian regime in which liberty suffers the most complete eclipse that it had known for centuries'. This may have been a 'contradiction', but it had a logic, and did not involve a radical discontinuity with the position which Barthélemy had adopted in the inter-war years.[19]

1919–1928: Missed Opportunities?

The trajectories of such people as Romier, Barthélemy, and Benoist were all different in detail, but one step in their progressive disillusion with the Republic was the belief that an opportunity for reform had been missed after the war.

It is often suggested that the mood of politics after 1919 was nostalgia for the golden age of the *belle époque*. But in many circles the war had fuelled the call for reform. On the centre-right, several organizations were founded after 1918 to promote reform: the National Association for the Organization of Democracy (ANOD); the League for a New Democracy; the Republican Party of National Reorganization otherwise known as the IVth Republic Movement.[20] These groups shared various keywords: organization, modernization, institutional reform (a stronger executive), efficiency, technical competence. Arguing that France must apply the lessons learnt from the war, they cited the examples of Walter Rathenau who had organized the German war economy; F. W. Taylor, the American proponent of the scientific organization of labour; and the Lloyd George war cabinet.

Although the impact of these reforming groups must not be exaggerated, they attracted some bright young political figures: ANOD claimed to have the support of ninety-two *députés*. Nonetheless, little came of their hopes. The 1919 Parliament was dominated by a massive right-wing majority—the Bloc national—more interested in increasing the influence of the Church than in institutional reforms. Governments were absorbed by the intractable problems of reconstruction, reparations, inflation, and budget deficits. The reformers also lacked a charismatic leader. The only major politician to take up their ideas was the Socialist turned conservative Alexandre Millerand. But having been elected president of the Republic in 1920 he lost interest. When Millerand returned to the idea of constitutional reform in 1923, proposing a strengthening of the power of the presidency, it was because the left seemed likely to win the forthcoming elections. This gave Millerand's advocacy of constitutional reform a partisan hue, and he was forced to resign when the left returned to power in 1924.

---

[19] G. Martinez, 'Joseph Barthélemy et la crise de la démocratie liberale', *VSRH* 59 (1998), 28–47; Barthélemy, *Mémoires, ministre de la justice. Vichy (1941–1943)*.

[20] Le Béguec, 'L'Entrée', 279–401; F. Monnet, *Refaire la République: André Tardieu, une dérive réactionnaire, 1876–1945* (1993), 19–47.

Reforming themes were also popular on the left after 1919. The future Social-ist leader Léon Blum had written during the war on the need to streamline the working of government; the Radical leader Édouard Herriot published two massive tomes on the need for reform. The left in general took up the ideas of the Compagnons de l'université nouvelle, a group of young intellectuals who had served on Pétain's staff in 1917. They too were preoccupied by the in-adequacies of France's governing elites, but their solution centred on education not institutional reform. They proposed breaking down the barriers between the education of bourgeois children and the rest by creating an *école unique* where all children would receive a common education until the age of 13.[21]

Another source of reforming ideas on the left was the CGT. Here the empha-sis was not on institutional, political, or educational reforms, but on a restruc-turing of the political economy. Trade-union experience of co-operation with government and employers in organizing war production had accelerated the CGT's drift from revolutionary syndicalism. In 1918, under the influence of its leader Léon Jouhaux, the CGT produced a 'minimum programme' which demanded the nationalization of key industries and the creation of a national economic council composed of representatives of unions, consumers, employ-ers, and the State. This new reformism was not a conversion to British labourism. The CGT remained committed to the syndicalist conception of the primacy of economics over politics. The nationalized industries were not to be run by the State, but by producers (workers, technicians, managers) in co-operation with consumers and representatives of the State; the National Economic Council was to represent an integration of economic forces into decision making. The change from the pre-war period was that syndicalists now incorporated employers into their vision of reform and were ready to achieve it by gradualist means. The sus-picion of politics remained.[22]

The left-wing reformers were as unsuccessful in achieving their aims as those on the centre-right. The elections of 1924 were won by the left Cartel coalition of Radicals and Socialists, headed by Herriot, but its reforming ambitions quickly foundered. There were squabbles between the coalition partners: the Socialists, although supporting Herriot's government, would not join it because this represented too sharp a break with Marxist orthodoxy. The government wasted much time antagonizing the Church. Its main problem was the chronic financial crises which had dogged its predecessors. The Cartel coalition broke up in 1926, and the Radicals deserted the Socialists to ally with the right. The Cartel's failure was a terrible blow to left-wing opinion: it had aroused as many expec-tations as the Popular Front was to do twelve years later.

As for the CGT's ideas, these had little chance of being accepted after the failure of massive strikes that occurred in 1919 and 1920. The CGT leadership

---

[21] J. Talbott, *The Politics of Educational Reform in France* (Princeton, 1969).
[22] J. Horne, *Labour at War: France and Great Britain 1914–1918* (Oxford, 1991), 171–217.

had not wanted the strikes, but it was forced to back them. After they collapsed, the CGT's political influence was negligible for the rest of the decade, killing Jouhaux's hopes of being recognized as a partner by the government. In 1925, the Cartel did set up a national economic council, representing various economic interests, but this body was given only a limited consultative role, and paid only lip-service to syndicalist ideas.[23]

The 'Jeunes Équipes': 1928–1930

The reforming themes returned to prominence towards the end of the decade. After 1926, financial stability was restored and the economy was booming. It seemed possible to look beyond the immediate horizon of the next financial crisis. One centre of reforming ideas was the organization Redressement français, set up by the businessman Edmond Mercier in 1925.[24] As a leading figure in France's electricity industry, Mercier represented the most dynamic sector of the French economy. Impressed by a visit to America in 1925, he founded Redressement français to propagate the gospel of modernization. The organization included mainly businessmen, but also journalists and publicists, one of the most active of whom was Lucien Romier. The dominant idea was the need for economic rationalization to increase production. French businessmen were urged to renounce their congenital individualism. Modernization was essential if France was to remain a first-rank power.

The Redressement never became more than an elite pressure group but its neo-Saint-Simonian rhetoric enjoyed considerable vogue. Its politics were less clear. Its slogan was 'Enough politics, we want results', but funds were distributed to sympathetic candidates at the 1928 elections. The Redressement's study of constitutional reform was the work of Raphaël Alibert, an Action française sympathizer, but his ideas were not universally shared in the organization. Mercier himself was a Protestant, married to a niece of Dreyfus, and not drawn to traditional conservatism. Nonetheless his vision of politics was essentially elitist: government by engineers and experts.

Mercier's politics consisted of a pious hope that disinterested men of goodwill would unite around his ideas. He was encouraged by the fact that the Redressement's call to modernize France's economy coincided with an intense debate within the rising political generations about modernizing her political alignments after the post-war failures of the right and left. Such views were articulated by the journalist Jean Luchaire, whose newspaper *Notre temps*, founded in 1927, became the mouthpiece of what came to be called the 'Jeunes Équipes'. In 1928, Luchaire published a manifesto for his generation which he called *Une génération réaliste* (A Realist Generation). For Luchaire his generation

---

[23] A. Rossiter, 'Experiments with Corporatist Politics in Republican France 1916–1939' (unpublished D.Phil. thesis, Oxford, 1986).

[24] R. Kuisel, *Ernest Mercier, French Technocrat* (Berkeley and Los Angeles, 1967).

was born on 2 August 1914. Disappointed by the failure of the returning veterans to prevent a 'return to the old world', the generation was freethinking but
not anticlerical, believing that religion was no longer a political issue; it was convinced that laissez-faire was over and that France needed a more efficient state;
it was Republican but believed that the existing institutions needed reform.[25]

Some of the Jeunes Équipes joined the Radical Party where they became
known as the 'Young Radicals'. They included the brightest political figures of
their generation—Pierre Mendès France, Bertrand de Jouvenel, Pierre Cot, and
Jacques Kayser. They adopted the Party's rising star, Édouard Daladier, as their
figurehead. But the Young Radicals shared no common view. Some wanted to
recentre the Party by aligning it with centre-right. This was Luchaire's objective
although he did not formally join the Party himself. Others, like Kayser, Cot,
and de Jouvenel wanted the Party to reassert its left-wing identity, align itself
durably with moderate elements within the Socialist Party, and become a progressive, non-Marxist party of the left. This was the route favoured at this stage
by Daladier.[26]

Equally intense debates were occurring among the Socialists who interpreted
the failure of the Cartel in various ways. Those Marxists who had not wished to
participate in Herriot's government, felt vindicated by the subsequent drift of
the Radicals to the right; those who had wished to participate argued that a
Socialist presence in the government would have anchored Herriot on the left.
For some younger Socialists, these tactical questions were the starting point of a
fundamental reconsideration of the Party's commitment to Marxism. They were
influenced by the writing of the Belgian socialist Henri de Man whose 1926 book
The Psychology of Socialism was translated into French under the revealing title
Au-delà du Marxisme (1927; Beyond Marxism). De Man argued that Marxism
failed to provide a valid account of the working of modern capitalism. By rooting
socialism in materialism, it no longer offered the prospect of radical politics
because modern capitalism was capable of fulfilling the working class's material
needs.

Within the French Socialist Party, the most vigorous exponent of revisionism
was the Party's rising star, Marcel Déat. In *Perspectives socialistes* (1930), Déat
argued Socialists should look beyond the proletariat and build an alliance of anti-
capitalist forces including the petite bourgeoisie. The political corollary was that
the Socialists should abandon the commitment to Marxist purity that prevented
them participating in Radical governments.[27] This offered some common ground
with the left-wing Young Radicals. A forum for dialogue between these left-wing
reformers was offered by Georges Valois. Having left Action française, Valois had
in 1924 tried founding his own political movement, the Faisceau, inspired by

---

[25] J. Luchaire, *Une génération réaliste* (1929); see also J. Montigny, *La République réaliste* (n.d.).
[26] On the Young Radicals, S. Berstein, *Histoire du Parti radical*, ii. *Crise du radicalisme* (1982), 94–124.
[27] J. Jackson, *The Politics of Depression in France* (Cambridge, 1985), 138–43.

Mussolini. After 1926, Valois moved to the left, and he was in search of signs that the political structures were breaking up on the centre and left. Between 1928 and 1930 he published several books by members of the younger political generation including Déat's *Perspectives socialistes*, Luchaire's *Une génération réaliste*, and *L'Économie dirigée* (1928) by the Young Radical Bertrand de Jouvenel.[28] All these writers believed that liberalism had failed and that the productive forces of the economy needed to be integrated into a reformed State.

The Tardieu Moment: 1930

The prospects for change were defined by the responses of the leaders of the political parties. In October 1929, Daladier tried to tempt the Socialists into government with the offer of four ministries. For the first time, a substantial majority of the Socialist parliamentary party voted to accept, but the Party's National Committee overturned the decision. This blocked any realignment on the left and opened up a possibility on the right for the centre-right politician André Tardieu who formed a government after Daladier's failure to do so.

Tardieu, born in 1876, was one of the most flamboyantly brilliant politicians of his generation. This was an older generation than the Jeunes Équipes, and in 1919 Tardieu had not been associated with the reforming groups. But as the first war veteran to hold the premiership, Tardieu was symbolically appropriate to represent the post-war generation. Instead of the usual platitudes, his ministerial declaration of November 1929 offered a programme of economic modernization, a *politique de prospérité*. In subsequent speeches he proclaimed the end of laissez-faire and announced the need for an interventionist and technically competent State. This was in the spirit of the Redressement français with which Tardieu had links, but he also drew eclectically on the ideas of Benoist, the 1919 reformers, and the Jeunes Équipes.[29]

To carry out his programme Tardieu envisaged a political realignment around a modern centre-right incorporating elements of the Radical Party. This ambition failed because the Radical Party rejected Tardieu's invitation to join his government despite strong lobbying from Luchaire. Nevertheless Tardieu's style of government represented a sharp break with tradition. He tried to speak directly to the population over the head of parliament. Unprecedentedly he had his ministerial declaration stuck up throughout France, and he was the first politician to use the radio. All this came to nothing. Tardieu's legislative programme was whittled away by sniping in parliament: a year after it was announced, the modernization bill had not been voted. Tardieu himself aroused massive personal

---

[28] A. Douglas, *From Fascism to Libertarian Communism* (Berkeley, 1992), 150–3.
[29] Monnet, *Refaire la République*, 92–101.

antagonism until he was brought down by a financial scandal at the end of 1930.

One must be sceptical about the wilder claims made for Tardieu. Far from being an FDR *manqué* or a proto-Keynesian, he was as economically illiterate as most French politicians, and, as the Depression later demonstrated, his economic ideas were orthodox. He conceived his generous spending plans in 1929 only because of the existence of large treasury surpluses. It was largely Tardieu's style that was new. What kind of political transformation did he envisage? He has been described as a French Disraeli, stealing the ideas of his opponents to modernize the appeal of conservatism. But although Tardieu hoped to split the Radicals, he was not interested in building a French conservative party. He wanted to rally support around his personality; his model was less the Anglo-Saxon two-party model than a personalized government like Clemenceau's wartime administration.

Given that the Depression was about to change the presuppositions upon which Tardieu's politics was based, it is not true that 1930 was a turning point when politics failed to turn. The Tardieu moment testified to the existence of reforming currents within French Republicanism, but also to the blockages of French politics. In 1933, Tardieu, embittered by his failure and by the subsequent defeat of the right at the 1932 elections, launched a crusade for constitutional revision. He now believed that political realignments were not enough: the system itself required change. He wanted to introduce referenda and make it easier to dissolve parliament. Most of Tardieu's ideas (except for the referendum) had been proposed by Benoist forty years earlier and Benoist's *Les Maladies de la démocratie* was one of the texts he used.

At first Tardieu was a lone voice calling for constitutional reform. But from 1932, when the Depression hit France, politics moved into a period of great turbulence. The left won the elections of 1932, but again the Socialists refused to participate in a Radical government. Two years of ministerial instability between 1932 and 1934 led to riots in February 1934 and the arrival in power of a right-wing Government of National Unity under Gaston Doumergue. Constitutional reform was briefly at the forefront of the political agenda. Tardieu joined Doumergue's government as a minister of State. Parliament set up a commission to examine constitutional reform and decided in March 1934 to propose a simplification of the procedures to dissolve parliament. The senator Jacques Bardoux, who had been involved in some of the post-war reforming groups like ANOD, set up a Committee on the Reform of the State, whose members included Mercier and Barthélemy. But when in the autumn Doumergue submitted his own constitutional reform proposals, he was defeated. Having failed to act immediately after February 1934 when his prestige was high, Doumergue allowed the left to depict constitutional reform as a reincarnation of Bonapartism. Doumergue fell in the autumn of 1934, and Tardieu retired from politics in disgust.

The Nonconformists: Liberalism Contested 1932–1934

For Tardieu, Benoist, Bardoux, Barthélemy, and Romier on the centre-right, for Luchaire, Déat, de Jouvenel, and Valois on the centre-left, the assumption was that the nature of France's problems was essentially political or institutional and could be resolved by adjustments which were compatible with a Republican framework. But the early 1930s also saw the emergence of a generation of young intellectuals, subsequently labelled the 'nonconformists of the 1930s', whose disillusion with the Republic went deeper. Sceptical about any remedies which politics could provide, they challenged the entire philosophical presuppositions of liberal democracy.[30]

The first collective manifestation of the nonconformists occurred in December 1932 when the *NRF*, always eager to be in the vanguard, published eleven short articles defining the 'common cause of French youth . . . the first outlines of a new French Revolution'.[31] The contributors included Emmanuel Mounier (b. 1905), Robert Aron (b. 1898), Philippe Lamour (b. 1903), Georges Izard (b. 1903), Armand Dandieu (b. 1897), and Thierry Maulnier (b. 1909). They signed in the name of little-known reviews and organizations like 'Ordre Nouveau', *Esprit*, *Réaction*, and *Plans*. Despite significant differences between them, one can detect a common tone, and a sense of generational identity.

The term 'generation' loosely describes those people born between about 1895 and 1905, but within this cohort there was a division between those who had been old enough to fight in the war and those who had not: this was the abyss of four years separating Louis Aragon (b. 1897) from André Malraux (b. 1901).[32] They were a generation whose defining experience was the war or its aftermath, not the Dreyfus Affair. Some of them had been influenced by Maurras, but whereas for Maurras it still mattered to believe that Dreyfus had been guilty, for this generation it no longer did.[33]

Many right-wing intellectuals were helped to free themselves from Maurras by the neo-Thomist Catholic philosopher Jacques Maritain who had in the 1920s been close to Action française. After the papal condemnation of 1926 Maritain broke with Maurras, and his book *Primauté du spirituel* (1927) was a direct riposte to Maurras's assertion of the centrality of politics ('politique d'abord').[34] For

[30] J. Touchard, 'L'Esprit des années trente', in *Tendances politiques de la vie française de 1789 à nos jours* (1960); J. Loubet del Bayle, *Les Non-Conformistes des années trente* (1969). See also P. Andreu, *Révoltés de l'esprit: Les Revues des années trente* (1991); id., *Le Rouge et le blanc 1928–1944* (1977); R. Aron, *Fragments d'une vie* (1981).

[31] *NRF* 231 (Dec. 1932), 801–45; B. Ackermann, *Denis de Rougemont: Une biographie intellectuelle*, i (Geneva, 1996), 210–22.

[32] On the generational nuances see P. Balmand, 'Les Jeunes Intellectuels de "l'esprit des années trente": Un phénomène de génération', in J.-F. Sirinelli (ed.), *Générations intellectuelles* (1987), 49–63; also Roy, *Moi je*, 213.

[33] J. Laurent, *Histoire*, 197.

[34] P. Chenaux, 'Le Milieu Maritain', in N. Racine and M. Trebitsch (eds.), *Sociabilités intellectuelles: Lieux, milieux, réseaux* (1992), 160–71; id., *Entre Maurras et Maritain: une génération intellectuelle catholique 1920–1930* (1999).

Maritain, this was the beginning of a journey to the left that culminated in the celebrated defence of democracy he wrote in America during the war. But if Maritain's new emphasis on the 'primacy of the spiritual' liberated many young Catholic intellectuals, it did not necessarily lead them to the left. It freed them from the sterile dichotomy between support for the Republic or opposition to it, opening the way to even more radical alternatives to liberalism than those offered by Maurras.

One young intellectual influenced by Maritain was Jean-Pierre Maxence (b. 1906) who had moved from Action française towards a spiritual critique of a 'world without mystique', rejecting the materialism of both capitalism and socialism.[35] Maxence became the leading light of the 'Jeune Droite' which consisted mainly of dissidents from Action française. In 1931, he took over *Revue française*, a rather fusty conservative paper, and opened it up to young right-wing intellectuals like Thierry Maulnier and the future fascist Robert Brasillach. They believed themselves to be living through a crisis of civilization which went deeper than politics. Maulnier entitled one of his books *La Crise est dans l'homme* (1932; The Crisis is in Mankind).

Equally concerned with spiritual crisis, but to the left of Maxence, was Emmanuel Mounier, founder in October 1932 of the journal *Esprit*.[36] Mounier, who came from a modest background, had been a brilliant student, taking his philosophy *agrégation* in the same year as Sartre and Raymond Aron, and coming second overall. Nonetheless Mounier never lost the sense of being an outsider in the Parisian intellectual world, and this gives his writing a tone of moralistic self-righteousness. Perhaps it helps also to explain why he so identified with Péguy, another outsider. Mounier's ambition was to separate Catholicism from conservatism and develop a radical critique of the status quo—what he called the 'established disorder'—whether capitalist or Socialist.

Esprit attracted intellectuals of diverse origins, including several Action française dissidents. Their common link was a Catholic background of some sort; Maritain was an early sponsor of the journal. Georges Izard, a member of the group, founded a movement called the 'Third Force' to provide a political forum to defend *Esprit*'s ideas, but the association with *Esprit* was soon severed owing to Mounier's distrust of politics.

More intellectually eclectic than *Esprit* was the Ordre nouveau group whose members had backgrounds varying from Barthian Protestantism to Maurrassianism, Russian orthodoxy to Judaism.[37] The group included Robert Aron, who had previously flirted with surrealism, and his school friend Armand Dandieu,

[35] Loubet del Bayle, *Les Non-Conformistes*, 37–76; Maxence, *Histoire de dix ans.*

[36] M. Winock, *Histoire politique de la revue Esprit 1930–1950* (1975); Loubet del Bayle, *Les Non-Conformistes*, 123–57; J. Hellman, *Emmanuel Mounier and the New Catholic Left 1930–1950* (1981), 3–95.

[37] Loubet del Bayle, *Les Non-Conformistes*, 79–119; E. Lipiansky, 'L'Ordre nouveau 1930–1938', in id. and B. Rettenbach, *Ordre et démocratie: De l'Ordre nouveau au Club Jean Moulin* (1967), 1–102; Ackermann, *Denis de Rougemont*, 250–308; P. Balmand, 'Intellectuels dans l'Ordre nouveau (1933–1938): Une aristocratie de prophètes', in D. Bonnaud-Lamotte and J.-L. Rispail (eds.), *Intellectuels des années trente entre le rêve et l'action* (1989), 171–84.

who died prematurely in 1933. In 1931 Aron and Dandieu produced two books which proclaimed the guiding themes of their group. *Décadence de la nation française* denounced France's cult of rationalism and abstraction; *Le Cancer américain* used America to lambast an obsession with productivism and a neglect of the spiritual. Ordre nouveau had a strongly technocratic bent, aspiring in a mystical and Saint-Simonian way towards the rational organization of economic life.

Ordre nouveau's preoccupations overlapped with the group around the journal *Plans* founded by Philippe Lamour. The editorial board of *Plans* included the architect Le Corbusier and the syndicalist intellectual Hubert Lagardelle. *Plans* provided a mouthpiece for Ordre nouveau until the group founded its own journal in 1933. The link between technocracy and syndicalism was the idea that individualistic liberal capitalism was incapable of developing a rationally organized society.

The common element of all these groups was not so much that they opposed the Republic as that intellectually they no longer accepted it as a frame of reference. Ordre nouveau's manifesto of March 1931 declared: 'the spiritual first, and then the economic and political at its service'; the first issue of *Esprit* called for 'primacy of the spiritual'. Mounier's repugnance for politics was almost physical.[38] 'Rottenness', 'disgust', 'decadence', 'nausea', 'revulsion': these words recur repeatedly to describe Third Republic politics. The Republic was viewed as formalistic, cut off from 'real' life, a screen for the defence of materialism and individualism. Socialism and capitalism, Stalin and Ford, were rejected as two sides of the same coin, 'philosophically linked to the system of mechanistic oppression from which man suffers in the modern age'.[39]

The root of the problem was the tradition of Republican individualism which viewed man only as an abstract citizen, crushing human diversity and uprooting the individual from natural communities: 'The ideology which we combat', wrote Mounier, 'is the ideology of 1789 . . . the individual emptied of all substance and cut off from his roots . . . equality conceived as a void between neutral and interchangeable individuals.'[40] It was necessary to rediscover human beings in all their wholeness, *l'homme réel* or *l'homme concret*. The first editorial of *Plans* defined its aims as 'The expression of the real man [*l'homme réel*] . . . The blossoming of a more humane civilisation where man, dominating the tyranny of the machine created for his own good, would retrieve his place in the universe.' *L'Homme réel* was also the title of a short-lived journal of syndicalist inspiration founded in 1934 (again with the involvement of Le Corbusier). Both *Esprit* and *Ordre nouveau* described their doctrine as 'personalism'.[41] They sought communitarian alternatives to Republican anomie.[42]

---

[38] Winock, *Histoire politique*, 109–10.   [39] Andreu, *Révoltés de l'esprit*, 24.
[40] Quoted in Loubet del Bayle, *Les Non-Conformistes*, 209.
[41] Ibid. 337–55; Hellman, *Emmanuel Mounier*, 82–7.
[42] T. Judt, 'We have discovered History: Defeat, Resistance and the Intellectuals in France' *JMH* 64, suppl. (1992), 147–72.

A central inspiration of this generation was Péguy. Maxence devoted an issue of the *Cahiers* to him in 1930; he was the subject of Mounier's first book.[43] The Péguy they celebrated was the angry prophet of a more spiritual politics: 'the revolution will be moral or it will not be' was a favourite phrase.[44] Other influences were Maritain, Proudhon, Sorel, Bergson, and the Russian orthodox thinker Nicholas Berdyaev. There was also a serious revival of interest in Nietzsche.[45] To such familiar critics of individualism and rationalism was added the influence of the German phenomenologists—Heidegger, Husserl, and Jaspers—whose work percolated into France in this period and offered a powerful weapon against the traditional teaching of the French universities.[46] In the words of Raymond Aron, an early French student of these German thinkers: 'In studying phenomenology, I experienced a sort of liberation in relation to my neo-Kantian training.'[47] But Aron never succumbed to the anti-liberalism of the nonconformists and had little respect for the intellectual sophistication of Robert Aron, Dandieu, or Mounier. He also questioned whether they mattered 'outside the dining circles of the Parisian intelligentsia'.[48]

On this point Aron is probably too dismissive. Quite apart from the leading roles many of the nonconformists played in French cultural life over the next decades, there are several reasons for ascribing importance to them. First, they articulated a malaise which extended beyond the tiny readerships of their often ephemeral journals. There is an affinity between their 'disgust' and the 'nausea' in 1938 of Sartre's Roquentin, between their dissatisfaction with the 'established disorder' and the Nietzschean quest for adventure by the heroes of Malraux's early novels.[49] Malraux, viewed as a sort of French T. E. Lawrence, was very much a tutelary figure for this generation, a fellow 'brother in Nietzsche and Dostoevsky', as Drieu La Rochelle called him.[50] In Malraux's first two novels, ostensibly about the Chinese revolution, action has a metaphysical purpose not a political one: his protagonists seek not to change the world, but to transcend their sense of the futility of existence.[51] Maxence remarked that France's leaders failed to offer adventure or excitement, and ran the country like an insurance company.

---

[43] E. Mounier and G. Izard, *La Pensée de Charles Péguy* (1931).

[44] Winock, *Histoire politique*, 21–2; Maxence, *Histoire de dix ans*, 44–5; Loubet del Bayle, *Les Non-Conformistes*, 290.

[45] Lindenberg, *Les Années souterraines*, 86–97; J.-M. Besnier, *La Politique de l'impossible: L'Intellectuel entre révolte et engagement* (1988), 32–7.

[46] See the bibliography of *La Révolution nécessaire*. One of the founders of the movement, Alexandre Marc had attended the lectures of Husserl in Friburg.

[47] *Mémoires: 50 ans de réflexion politique* (1983), 68.

[48] Ibid. 101–4, 707.

[49] T. Judt, *Past Imperfect: French Intellectuals 1944–1956* (1992), 18.

[50] Maxence, *Histoire de dix ans*, 76; Andreu, *Révoltés de l'esprit*, 14; Lindenberg, *Les Années souterraines*, 91.

[51] J. Loubet del Bayle, *Politique et civilisation: Essai sur la réflexion politique de Jules Romains* (1981), 265–81.

Secondly, there were links between the nonconformists and a number of tech-nocratic reform groups that sprang up in the 1930s.[52] The most famous of these was the Centre polytechnicien d'études économiques, better known as X-Crise, a circle of *polytechniciens* set up in 1931 to discuss the problems posed by the eco-nomic crisis. X-Crise included laissez-faire liberals and socialists, but they all agreed on one thing: it was for experts to provide answers. Its leading light was the business manager Jean Coutrot. Restlessly curious and indefatigably ener-getic, Coutrot, who kept up an international correspondence with intellectuals like Aldous Huxley, was a mixture of sage and crank driven by a mystical faith in the capacity of the experts to solve the problems of the world. He set up the Centre for the Study of Human Problems whose aim was to synthesize the most recent advances in the human and social sciences, harnessing them to the quest for a modern humanism. Through the study of economics, psychology, psychobiology, eugenics, and so on it would be possible to transform man's relationship to technology and modern productive forces. The ultimate aim was to create a 'new man'.[53]

Another participant in X-Crise was the electricity industrialist Auguste Detœuf who had been a leading member of Redressement français. Some members of X-Crise—Robert Loustau (b. 1899), Robert Gibrat (b. 1904)—were in Ordre nouveau. Another link between Ordre nouveau and the wider world was Jean Jardin (b. 1904) who was an aide to Raoul Dautry, one of the great proto-technocrats of the period. Dautry (b. 1880) was a *polytechnicien* whose success in modernizing the French railways led French governments frequently to call upon his administrative expertise. In 1939, he was brought in to oversee French rearmament after the Munich agreement.

Dautry had been in the circle of the former imperial proconsul Marshal Lyautey, famous for his 1891 article on the 'Social Role of the Officer'. The leader-ship role that Lyautey ascribed to the army, Dautry conferred on public-spirited administrators dedicated to the ideals of service and efficiency. Lyautey's ideas also influenced Mercier who believed that businessmen should be the new elite. After Lyautey died in 1934, Dautry took on something of his mantle. Celebrat-ing the leadership role of elites sidestepped politics. Lyautey's own preferences had been monarchist, and Dautry's were perhaps revealed by the fact that his 1937 hymn to the idea of leadership, *Métier d'homme* (ghosted by Jardin) was dedicated to Salazar.[54]

Finally, for all their suspicion of politics, there were affinities and connections

[52] G. Brun, *Technocrates et technocratie en France* (1985).

[53] On Coutrot see O. Dard, 'Les Novations intellectuelles des anneés trente: l'Exemple de Jean Coutrot' (unpublished thesis, Institut d'études politiques, Paris, 1993); M. Beale, *The Modernist Enter-prise: French Elites and the Threat of Modernity 1900–1940* (Stanford, Calif.; 1999), 145–64; and J. Clarke, 'The Search for Joy in Work, Rationalisation and Cultural Crisis in France in the 1930s' (D.Phil. thesis, Sussex, 1998).

[54] *Métier d'homme* (1937). On Dautry see R. Baudoui, *Raoul Dautry 1888–1951: Le Technocrate de la République* (1992); Lindenberg, *Les Années souterraines*, 194–202.

between the nonconformists and the young dissidents in the Radical and Social-ist parties. In the Radical Party there were two significant defections. One was Gaston Bergery who was close in spirit to the Young Radicals although himself somewhat older (b. 1892). Bergery had been an adviser to Herriot in 1924, and from that experience he concluded that the Radicals had to align with the Social-ists. He resigned from the Party in March 1933 and formed the Front commun to rally progressive left opinion. In November 1934, the Front commun fused with Izard's Third Force to become the Front social.[55] The second Radical dis-sident was Bertrand de Jouvenel who resigned from the Party after February 1934 and started a short-lived paper called *La Lutte des jeunes* which aimed to be the mouthpiece of the new generations: its contributors included Mounier, Izard, Luchaire, and Robert Aron.[56]

In the Socialist Party, there was a split in October 1933 when twenty-eight *députés* rebelled against the Party's refusal to co-operate with the Radicals. They were expelled, and set up a breakaway party. The neo-Socialists, as they came to be called, included old right-wing Socialists who merely wished to break the taboo against participating in government, but also younger revisionists like Marcel Déat. The revisionism of de Man and Déat had been conceived during the economic growth of the 1920s, but the arrival of the economic crisis only intensified their conviction that socialism must break with Marxism. The ortho-dox Socialist answer to the Depression was that it represented the crisis of cap-italism, which freed Socialists from responsibility for devising solutions. Arguing that such an abdication of responsibility would allow fascism to develop, de Man advocated a 'Plan' of structural economic reform whose centrepiece was the nationalization of credit and key industries. In effect, he was proposing that the Socialists postpone socialism in favour of the mixed economy.

De Man's *planisme* enjoyed a considerable vogue in 1934. It was taken up by the neo-Socialists, and given publicity by *Esprit* and *Ordre nouveau*.[57] The Social-ist Party itself rejected *planisme* in 1934 as a heretical deviation from Marxism, but some younger Socialists, like Georges Lefranc, continued to argue for it from within the Party. De Man's Plan, which bore some resemblance to the CGT minimum programme of 1918, was also taken up by the CGT in 1934–5.

With all these connections to the wider world, the nonconformists' importance was not confined to Parisian dining circles. They drew upon many traditions—the Saint-Simonian cult of the modernizing elite, syndicalist dis-satisfaction with the idea of abstract citizenship, Catholic rejection of liberal indi-vidualism, de Man's Socialist revisionism—and mixed them in different ways. They were subsequently to follow different political journeys, many of them ending up at Vichy. They were a political generation bereft of political anchors, able to pass from surrealism to communism (Aragon), reformist socialism to

---

[55] P. Burrin, *La Dérive fasciste: Doriot Déat, Bergery 1933–1945* (1986), 29–38, 95–106.
[56] Andreu, *Révoltés de l'esprit*, 101–5.   [57] Hellman, *Emmanuel Mounier*, 92–3.

fascism (Déat), radicalism to fascism (Bergery), Action française to communism (Roy) with intermediate stages on the way. They all shared a suspicion, even visceral rejection, of liberal democracy. The spirit of this generation was well described by one of its members in 1932:

> We passed our adolescence in the antechamber of death. After the war, we were naked before a new world . . . without prejudice, without loyalties, without a fixed situation . . . We had hoped that a great movement of renovation would come out of the war, a new definition of the world. And we saw old men who had known neither how to avoid the killing nor make the peace take power again having learnt nothing or forgotten everything.[58]

The nonconformists claimed to transcend the traditional political divisions: 'we are neither right nor left' declared Aron and Dandieu in the preface to *La Révolution nécessaire*. There were political nuances between them. The Jeune Droite had emerged out of the orbit of Action française, *Esprit* out of left Catholicism. Ordre nouveau was more unqualified in its critique of democracy than *Esprit*, which targeted its contempt on parliamentary democracy.[59] On a left–right spectrum, Maxence should be classified on the right and Mounier on the left, with Ordre nouveau in between, but before 1934 the similarities were more evident than the differences. They shared a sense of themselves as a generation, and a generation that took itself seriously: Mounier hailed Dandieu's *La Révolution nécessaire* as the first work in French to challenge *Das Kapital*.[60]

From 1934, French politics became increasingly polarized. Even those wishing to reject political labels could no longer do so. In January 1934 *Esprit* criticized Ordre nouveau for being too sympathetic to fascism, and in April 1934 announced it was abandoning the line 'neither left nor right'; later it offered a 'fraternal salute' to the emerging Popular Front.[61] Mounier supported the Republicans in the Spanish civil war, Maxence the Nationalists. Maxence's *Revue française* folded in 1933, and its mantle was later assumed by the journal *Combat*, founded in January 1936 and edited by Thierry Maulnier. *Combat* was a formative experience for many young right-wing intellectuals of the period—Claude Roy, Jacques Laurent, Maurice Blanchot—and its tone was more violent than that of its predecessor.

If, however, it was difficult to be 'neither left nor right' after 1934, some ambiguity remained. In 1935 Mounier saw nothing reprehensible in accepting an invitation from the Institute of Fascist Culture in Rome. In 1938, in what was otherwise a very anti-Nazi article, he wrote of fascism that it was not 'absolute evil:' 'its action of harsh purification cleanses a worm-eaten structure which we have not ceased to combat in the name of other values'.[62] At the end of the

---

[58] Quoted in Balmand, 'Les Jeunes Intellectuels', 51.
[59] Loubet del Bayle, *Les Non-Conformistes*, 212.   [60] Ibid. 108.
[61] Winock, *Histoire politique*, 115–32.   [62] Burrin, *La Dérive fasciste*, 88–9.

decade, Maxence, who had chosen the other side, was able to write sympathetically of the aspirations represented by the Popular Front.[63] Nonetheless, in the second half of the decade, the sense of generational fraternity was only nostalgia: French politics had acquired the bitterness of a civil war, and political choices were unavoidable.

[63] Maxence, *Histoire de dix ans*, 235, 281, 352.

3

Class War/Civil War

In 1940, during the Phoney War, the French fascist writer Robert Brasillach published an autobiographical memoir, *Notre avant-guerre*. Its post-face is dated '6 February Year VII. National Revolution'. It was not only in retrospect that 6 February appeared to be a turning point. In 1934 itself, soon after the events of February, Jean-Pierre Maxence and Thierry Maulnier published a book dedicated to the 'dead of 6 February, first witnesses of the next Revolution'.[1]

The date 6 February 1934 marked the beginning of a French civil war lasting until 1944. The truth about that night was that a demonstration had turned ugly and the police had panicked. But since civil wars require the enemy to be demonized, the left interpreted the events of 6 February as an abortive fascist coup, the right as a massacre of fifteen innocent patriots by the Republic. The left also had its martyrs when six people were killed in a Communist counter-demonstration three days later in the place de la République: this was the bloodiest week in French politics since the Commune.

The 1920s: Defending the Bourgeois Republic

The civil war was first and foremost a class war. Its context was the Depression, but its origins went back to the First World War which had dealt a blow to the self-confidence of the French bourgeoisie. A book published in 1932 was alarmingly entitled 'The end of the rentier'.[2] Although rentier incomes were hit by wartime and post-war inflation—it has been estimated that 1,913 fortunes had halved in real value by 1929[3]—the book's title was too apocalyptic. But bourgeois civilization was about more than the defence of property. In *La Barrière et le niveau*, published in 1925, Edmond Goblot defined the bourgeoisie in terms of a style of life which involved distinguishing oneself from other classes by erecting cultural barriers. A bourgeois salon was furnished with heavy furniture in which to receive visitors; there must be servants. The bourgeoisie preserved its

---

[1] Sternhell, *Ni droite ni gauche*, 279. The book was *Demain la France*.
[2] A. Bouton, *La Fin des rentiers* (1932).
[3] C. Maier, *Recasting Bourgeois Europe* (Princeton, 1988), 40–4.

separateness when it travelled (there were three classes on trains), in the way it dressed, in the education of its children.[4]

Education was the most effective barrier, dividing those who attended the free primary school until the age of 14, from those who went to the fee-paying *lycées* which had their own primary classes. The left's advocacy of the *école unique*—amalgamating the two systems and making education free for everyone—was a fundamental assault on bourgeois privilege. The content of the syllabus was another contested issue. Traditionally the study of the classics had distinguished secondary school pupils from the others until the creation in 1902 of a modern section in the *lycée* which did not require Latin. Under the Bloc national government this reform was reversed by the Léon Bérard Law of 1923; a year later the Bérard Law was itself repealed by the Cartel. This was a debate about the defence of social capital, and it was no coincidence that in 1940 Vichy's second education minister, Georges Ripert, again abolished the modern section.

Post-war bourgeois anxiety focused on the spectre of communism.[5] At the 1919 elections, the Bolshevik threat was depicted on a notorious poster showing a hirsute brigand with a knife between his teeth. The French Communist Party (PCF) was founded in 1920, and in the next year the trade-union movement split. The new Communist union, the CGTU, abandoned the syndicalist tradition of remaining independent of politics, and created a new unionism subordinate to the Party.

In the 1920s, the Communists had little influence except in the industrial suburbs of Paris. These suburbs, which developed at the end of the nineteenth century, grew massively during the war when large-scale engineering plants burgeoned around the capital. The Renault factory at Boulogne-Billancourt had 110 workers in 1900, 4,400 by 1914, 14,600 by 1919, 20,000 by 1929.[6] What had been hardly more than villages—Saint-Ouen, Courbevoie, Puteaux, Ivry—became large agglomerations.[7] Bobigny to the north-east had a population of 3,660 in 1911, 11,412 in 1926, 17,370 in 1931. The *département* of the Seine-et-Oise (Paris's far suburb) grew by 48 per cent between 1921 and 1931, making the area around Paris one of the largest concentrations of workers in Europe.

This rapid urbanization was entirely uncontrolled. Housing conditions were appalling and public services non-existent: the Paris suburbs were the last of Céline's circles of hell. They were a tinderbox of social discontents which the Communist exploited effectively. At the elections of 1924, the Party, despite performing badly at national level, received about 25 per cent of the vote in the Seine *département* (Paris's near suburbs). The myth of the Red Belt was born, and it was on its way to becoming a reality.[8] Catholics called for the rechris-

---

[4] E. Goblot, *La Barrière et le niveau: Étude sociologique sur la bourgeoisie* (1925).
[5] S. Berstein and P. Milza, *Histoire de l'anti-communisme en France* (1987).
[6] G. Noiriel, *Workers in French Society in the 19th and 20th Centuries* (Oxford, 1990), 112.
[7] A. Fourcaut, *Bobigny, banlieue rouge* (1986); T. Stovall, *The Rise of the Paris Red Belt* (Berkeley, 1990).
[8] E. Blanc, *La Ceinture rouge* (1927).

tianization of the suburbs; Halévy in his *Pays parisiens* (1932) described them as a negation of life, a black void in which Revolution lurked.[9]

Usually the workers of the suburbs were feared without being seen, but when in 1924 the Cartel government decided to transfer the ashes of the Socialist Jean Jaurès to the Panthéon, the Communists organized a separate cortège. The panic this caused in conservative circles testifies to the nervousness of the French bourgeoisie at this time. The Communist marchers, mainly from the suburbs, were depicted as alien invaders of the city like their Communard forebears descending into Paris in 1871. One observer, who was a boy at the time, never forgot the fear on people's faces as metal blinds were pulled down to protect against revolution.[10]

In defending their social interests, conservatives were hampered by divisions in the French right dating back to the Dreyfus Affair. On the one hand, there was the centre-right Alliance démocratique, which had originally comprised those conservatives who believed that the danger to the Republic required an alliance with the anticlerical left, and on the other hand, the more right-wing Fédération républicaine which did not want the Dreyfus Affair to disrupt the defence of conservative social interests. The Fédération was not originally a confessional party, but believed that Catholics should not be penalized by discriminatory laws. In the inter-war years, however, its Catholic identity became more pronounced, as it filled the void created by the disappearance of the Action libérale populaire, a confessional party which had existed before 1914. This made it even harder to create a durable entente between the Alliance and the Fédération. Even Raymond Poincaré, the epitome of conservative moderation, a member of the Alliance, described the Fédération in the 1920s as 'men of the 16 May 1877': by this he meant that they could not be considered as true Republicans.[11] In theory, the Alliance might instead have allied with the Radical Party, and this is what many Alliance leaders wanted. The problem was that the Radicals preferred to ally with the Socialists although the petit-bourgeois nature of the Radical electorate pulled the Party to the right. Thus the Radicals tended to ally with the Socialists at elections, only to fall into the arms of the right at the first whiff of a financial crisis. This political schizophrenia contributed to political instability—although it also defused conflict by allowing the right to recover power relatively painlessly.

In addition to religious conflicts, the tension between large and small producers—the other fault-line running through the right—was exacerbated by the war which accelerated the expansion of concentrated industrial sectors like engineering, electricity, and chemicals. Some on the right were coming to see small producers as an obstacle to growth while others wished to court them as a

---

[9] Père Lhande, *Le Christ dans la banlieue* (1927); Fourcaut, *Bobigny, banlieue rouge*, 63.

[10] J. Touchard, *La Gauche en France depuis 1900* (1977), 91.

[11] Passmore, 'The French Third Republic: Stalemate Society', 425.

bulwark against communism. Even the modernizing Redressement français was divided about how to treat them. In political terms the Alliance was seen as representing more modernizing business interests; the Fédération had links to industries with higher labour costs like mining, metallurgical, and textiles; and the Radicals were pre-eminently the party of small producers. But these divisions were approximate, and no party could afford to neglect small producers entirely.[12]

Conservative politics was so fragmented that after the left won the elections of 1924 many conservatives believed their traditional parties were inadequate to defend their interests. The year 1924 saw the emergence of a number of extra-parliamentary movements calling themselves leagues. These leagues—the Jeunesses Patriotes of Pierre Taittinger, the Légion of Antoine Rédier—were inspired by a French plebiscitary tradition which went back to Boulangism and by the example of Mussolini who had taken power two years earlier.[13] Conservatives were also mobilized by the National Catholic Federation (FNC) which organized Catholic opposition to the anticlericalism of the Cartel. The FNC held large public meetings all over the country, and claimed two million members by the end of 1926. Ostensibly above politics and devoted exclusively to the defence of Catholic interests, its leaders were clearly identified with the right.[14]

This polarization of politics was accentuated by the financial instability of the early 1920s. In July 1926, the financial crisis became so acute that the Radicals panicked, and supported the return to power of the right under Raymond Poincaré. This was sufficient to restore financial confidence, and the political crisis dissipated as quickly as it had blown up. The leagues fizzled out in 1927; and the FNC was on the decline from 1929.

Fragile Consensus: 1926–1932

The extra-parliamentary bubble burst so easily because the underlying economic situation was healthy. Indeed the financial crises, by depreciating the currency, had boosted French exports. This background of economic growth explained the emergence of the Redressement français. The assumption was that growth would solve the social problem: Ford would render Marx redundant. Between 1928 and 1932, governments voted a number of important social reforms: a Social Insurance Act in 1928; the introduction of free schooling in the lower classes of secondary schools; a Family Allowance Act in 1932. Many of these reforms were introduced by Tardieu who was the politician most associated with the idea of absorbing social conflict through economic modernization.

Political polarization was also reduced by the relaxation of tension between

---

[12] K. Passmore, *From Liberalism to Fascism: The Right in a French Province* (Cambridge, 1997), 44–5.
[13] R. Soucy, *French Fascism: The First Wave* (1986).
[14] J. McMillan, 'Catholicism and Nationalism in France: The Case of the Fédération nationale catholique', in N. Atkin and F. Tallett (eds.), *Catholicism in Britain and France since 1789* (1996), 151–63.

Church and State. The conflict of 1924 had interrupted the Vatican's long-term ambition of overcoming the division between the Church and the Republic. It was the pursuit of this 'Second Ralliement' which caused the condemnation of Action française in 1926.[15] While Maurras had insisted on the 'primacy of politics', the Vatican now promoted social Catholicism, encouraging Catholics to leave the political arena and concentrate on the rechristianization of society.

The consensus of the late 1920s must not, however, be exaggerated. Tensions between small producers and large-scale industry remained acute. The Social Insurance Law, which was funded by contributions from employers and workers, alarmed small employers and reopened conflicts of interest between rationalized industrial sectors like electricity and those with higher labour costs. The Tax-payers' Federation (Fédération des contribuables) mobilized shopkeepers and small businessmen against the law. Social insurance also caused alarm in the countryside. It was in mobilizing peasant anger against it that the rural agitator Henri Dorgères leapt to prominence in 1928.[16]

Religious conflict also remained important even if the development of social Catholicism meant that the problem receded from the forefront of politics. The implications of social Catholicism for politics were complex because social Catholicism was not itself homogeneous. One strand was paternalistic and conservative, inspired by Lyautey's ideas on the social duties of elites. Among Lyautey's disciples was Robert Garric, founder in 1919 of the Équipes sociales, which aimed to prolong the fraternity of the trenches by promoting contacts between bourgeois Catholics and workers. Lyautey was also an inspiration for the Catholic scouting movement. The Dominican Marcel-Denys Forestier, founder of the Catholic 'Rover scouts' believed that scouting would combat individualism, secularism, and urban rootlessness. He edited, jointly with Garric, a Catholic periodical, *La Revue des jeunes*, which focused on social problems affecting the young. The Catholic scouting movements had 100,000 members by 1939.

A different strand of social Catholicism was represented by the Catholic Action organizations with their specialized branches for workers, peasants, and students. In contrast to the more conservative version of social Catholicism, Catholic Action aimed to generate new Catholic elites from all social classes. It infused inter-war Catholicism with extraordinary dynamism, especially among the young, but also exacerbated the fissiparousness of conservative politics: social Catholic activists were ready to challenge the authority of traditional conservative elites. This did not place Catholic Action on the 'left'. Social Catholics rejected overt links with political parties. Working through apostleship within their particular social milieu, they were open-minded about political structures.

[15] H. Paul, *The Second Ralliement: The Rapprochement between Church and State in France in the Twentieth Century* (Washington, 1967).

[16] R. Paxton, *Le Temps des chemises vertes: Révoltes paysannes et fascisme rural* (1996), 99–102; Passmore, *From Liberalism to Fascism*, 120–3.

Rejecting political anti-republicanism was not equivalent to embracing the individualist values of the Republic. Although in practice many social Catholic leaders were sympathetic to the small Christian democratic party, the PDP, founded in 1924, this was not always true of the rank and file. Social Catholics claimed to stand above class divisions, advocating a third way between socialism and capitalism. In the crisis of liberal democracy in the 1930s this did not predispose them to support Republican individualism.[17]

Shifting the centre of preoccupation from politics to society also increased the potential for secular–religious conflict as Catholics competed with lay organizations throughout society—in education, scouting, youth hostelling, leisure activities. Conservatives may have formally accepted the Republic, but they concentrated their hostility on the *instituteurs*, the State primary school teachers who were depicted as fermenters of disorder—godless, Masonic, and quasi-Communist. *Instituteurs* were also hated by Dorgères who blamed them for instilling urban ideas into impressionable young peasants.[18] The emergence of Dorgères at the end of the 1920s was a sign of the fragility of the consensus which had been reached in French politics. When the Depression arrived that consensus exploded.

The Depression

The Depression reached France later than elsewhere, but lasted longer: in 1939 industrial production was still below its 1929 levels. The Depression was prolonged in France because French governments throttled their economy with an overvalued currency by refusing to devalue the franc after the devaluations of sterling (1931) and the dollar (1933). The value of French exports fell by two-thirds between 1928 and 1933: businesses could only export by selling at uncompetitive prices.

France's attachment to a policy which condemned the economy to asphyxiation defies rational analysis. It reflected complacency that, in terms of unemployment, the social impact of the Depression was less devastating than elsewhere. Many French leaders believed that their large agricultural sector had protected France from the problems of excessive industrialization. They continued to believe in the virtue of a self-regulating gold standard and blamed the rest of the world for not playing by the rules. After the devaluation of the dollar the economist Charles Rist wrote: 'France finds herself on an isolated rock lashed by waves, but the other countries are on floating islands. In the tempest a rock, even isolated, is preferable to a floating island.'[19] This refusal to admit the reality of the outside world disguised deep anxieties. Devaluation was associated with

---

[17] K. Passmore, 'Catholicism and Nationalism: The Fédération républicaine (1927–1939)', in K. Chadwick (ed.), *Catholicism, Politics and Society in Twentieth Century France* (Liverpool, 2000), 47–72.
[18] Paxton, *Le Temps des chemises vertes*, 52–6.
[19] K. Mouré, *Managing the Franc Poincaré: Economic Understanding and Political Constraint in French Monetary Policy 1928–1936* (Cambridge, 1991), 111.

the inflation of the 1920s. Apocalyptic visions were conjured up of the final ruin of the rentiers—who were in fact profiting from the falling prices of the 1930s—and the collapse of social order. Politicians compared the defence of the franc to the defence of Verdun.[20]

The social consequences of the Depression in France were different from those in other industrialized countries. Even if official figures underestimated true unemployment, which peaked at about 1 million in 1935, this was lower than elsewhere. Owing to falling prices, the real wages of those in work increased. Workers suffered instead from employers' attempts to rationalize work practices by introducing time and motion studies or imposing piece-rate payment (the Bedaux system). Those worst affected by the Depression were peasants—agricultural prices fell by up to 60 per cent—shopkeepers, small businessmen, and artisans. Thus the Depression created the conditions for extreme social polarization: it hit the conservative electorate and stoked up working-class resentment, but, owing to relatively low levels of unemployment, the potential strength of labour was not as weakened as in other countries.[21]

For governments, the Depression meant massive budget deficits caused by falling tax revenues and rising social expenditure. The two left-wing parties which won the 1932 elections had different responses to this problem. The Radicals wanted to cut government expenditure and eliminate the budget deficit; the Socialists believed this would deepen the Depression. Logically therefore the Radicals should have governed with the right whose economic views they shared, but this was impossible immediately after winning elections on a left-wing slate. So Radical governments tried to obtain Socialist support for conservative policies. The result was deadlock: seven ministries in eighteen months.

This political paralysis caused an explosion of direct action by social groups intervening to protect their interests. There were demonstrations of State employees, peasants, shopkeepers, and small businessmen. Agricultural protests were organized by Dorgères's Defence Committees; shopkeepers mobilized behind the Taxpayers' Federation. These organizations crossed the frontier between interest-group representation and political extremism, mining a latent tradition of anti-parliamentarianism. The Taxpayers' Federation declared in February 1933: 'we will converge on this lair which is called parliament, and if necessary we will use whips and sticks'.[22]

The anti-parliamentary leagues reappeared on the scene. Two new ones appeared in 1933: the self-avowedly fascist Francistes of Marcel Bucard, a former Action française activist, and Solidarité française, run by a former colonial officer,

---

[20] J. Jackson, *The Politics of Depression in France 1932–1936* (Cambridge, 1985), 187–93; Mouré, *Managing the Franc Poincaré*, 204–17.

[21] Jackson, *Politics of Depression*, 23–7; Mouré, *Managing the Franc Poincaré*, 11–16; Passmore, *From Liberalism to Fascism*, 165–6.

[22] P. Milza, 'L'Ultra-Droite des années trente', in M. Winock (ed.), *Histoire de l'extrême droite en France* (1993), 157–89: 160.

Jean Renaud.[23] The membership of these groups was tiny. More alarming was the growing consensus, within the parliamentary right, that France's crisis had become an institutional one: that the regime was no longer working. The political deadlock was broken by the 6 February riots. The government resigned, the Radicals terminated their alliance with the left, and entered a government of National Unity headed first by Doumergue, and then successively by two other conservative politicians, Pierre-Étienne Flandin and Pierre Laval.

The 1930s Crisis: The Right's Response

The right's return to power in 1934 seemed like a replay of 1926, but there was a striking difference: 1926 had been the resolution of the crisis, 1934 was only its beginning; 1926 had been a political crisis, 1934 was a crisis of the liberal state itself. The fundamental reason for the difference was the economy: 1926 had witnessed an epiphenomenal financial crisis in a flourishing economy; in 1934 the economy was sinking deeper into depression. The right's response was deflation: cutting government expenditure to eliminate the deficit and forcing down costs to make the franc competitive again. This policy culminated in 1935 when Laval cut all government expenditure by 10 per cent, including pensions and State bonds. Deflation was as unsuccessful as it had been in Germany in 1930. Like Brüning, Doumergue and Laval resorted to emergency decree powers to force through deflationary policies: normal parliamentary procedures had failed.[24]

Another striking contrast between 1926 and 1934 was that whereas extra-parliamentary agitation had quickly abated after Poincaré's return, in 1934 it increased after Doumergue's arrival. The league overshadowing all the others was the Croix de feu (CF) which had started as a war veterans' organization in 1928. Its leader from 1931 was Colonel de la Rocque, a career officer of aristocratic background who had retired from the army. La Rocque steered the movement towards politics, and opened it up to non-veterans. In 1931 the CF created para-military organizations and in 1933 a specialized volunteer corps called the Volontaires Nationaux (VN). On 6 February 1934, a CF column 2,000 strong had marched on parliament from the Left Bank, unlike the other demonstrators who were across the river. Only a flimsy barricade protected the parliament building, but La Rocque ordered his men to disperse.

The explosion in CF membership took place after 1934. By the end of 1935 there were over 300,000 members. What made this growth different from the development of previous leagues, besides the fact that it occurred *after* the right's return to power, was the fact that the CF attacked the traditional right as well as the left. La Rocque described Doumergue's government as only a 'poultice on

[23] R. Soucy, *French Fascism: The Second Wave* (1995), 59–103; P. Milza, *Fascisme français: Passé et présent* (1987), 142–52.
[24] Jackson, *Politics of Depression*, 105–11.

a gangrenous leg'.[25] The CF demanded a limitation of the powers of parliament, the outlawing of the 'generators of disorder' (the Communists), and the implementation of corporatist economic ideas. In other respects La Rocque was studiedly vague—like the Nazi and fascist programmes which avoided specific commitments which could narrow the basis of support. The same fluidity characterized La Rocque's attitude to democracy: he claimed to support the Republic, but rejected any 'fetishism' of electoralism (the CF refused to stand in elections), and denounced political parties as 'lying, parasitical, bribed, outdated'.

The CF presented itself as a new elite, guided by a charismatic leader, ready to regenerate the nation and save it from Communists and Freemasons. How La Rocque intended to take power was unclear. He warned his followers against premature action and stressed his commitment to order, but he also made frequent references to 'H-Hour' and organized paramilitary mobilizations and parades. This sustained an atmosphere of strength and menace. Sometimes street violence occurred, but La Rocque discouraged this, preferring to give an impression of discipline. As far as membership was concerned, the CF seems to have drawn on the urban lower middle class, but also some managers and salaried engineers. One striking feature of the movement was that it professed religious neutrality, but its social doctrines attracted some social Catholics, allowing it to mobilize some of the populist anti-elitism of social Catholics. In short, it represented a revolt of rank-and-file conservatives against their leaders.

At the time, the left was convinced that the CF was a fascist movement. Until recently historians rejected this view and downplayed its challenge to democracy. The CF was portrayed as a conservative force containing little of fascism's radicalism. Its paramilitarism was dismissed by the historian René Rémond as 'Boyscouting for adults'. More recently, however, historians have questioned this orthodoxy.[26] The argument matters because those who argue that the CF was not fascist are by implication inclined to downplay the seriousness of the crisis of liberal democracy in inter-war France.

Sometimes La Rocque's 'moderation' on 6 February is used to demonstrate the CF's non-radical nature. But quite apart from the fact that neither Hitler after 1923 nor Mussolini had attempted to seize power by street violence alone, the CF's radicalization occurred after 6 February. It developed into an authoritarian-populist movement offering a major threat to liberal politics. Did this make it fascist? It is not fruitful to search for some essentialist notion of fascism. All fascist movements combined radical and reactionary elements. Certainly the

[25] Soucy, *French Fascism: The Second Wave*, 112.

[26] R. Rémond, *Les Droites en France* (1982). The case that the CF was fascist is put by R. Soucy, 'French Fascism and the Croix de Feu: A Dissenting Interpretation', *JCH* 26 (1991), 159–88; id., *French Fascism: The Second Wave*, 104–203; W. Irvine, 'Fascism in France: The Strange Case of the Croix de Feu', *JMH* 63 (1991), 271–95; and, most convincingly, K. Passmore, ' "Boyscouting for Grown-Ups?" Paramilitarism in the Croix de Feu and PSF', *FHS* 19 (1995), 527–57; id., 'The Croix de Feu: Bonapartism, National Populism or Fascism', *French History* 9/1 (1995), 93–123; id., *From Liberalism to Fascism*, 209–97.

CF was less anti-democratic than the Nazis and less violent on the streets than the Italian fascists before 1922. But even Mussolini between 1923 and 1925 was ambiguous towards the liberal state, and the dream of Liberals that he might be 'tamed' was not entirely absurd. In the conflict between the radical and moderate elements in Italy, it was ultimately the radicals who prevailed. In the CF the balance of forces between radicals and moderates may have been different, but so was the context. As Kevin Passmore reminds us, in Italy and Germany fascism developed as a response to the perceived threat of the left after the war; in France the rise of the CF pre-dated the mobilization of the left which occurred in response to the perceived threat from the right. Once the left had started to gather its forces against the CF, it became clear that the radical and anti-democratic—fascist—option would not succeed in France.[27]

In December 1935 La Rocque agreed to disarm his followers providing the left did the same and in June 1936 he did not contest a new law banning the leagues. Abandoning paramilitarism, he turned the CF into a political party, the PSF. The rise of the Popular Front showed that the left could not be beaten in the streets.

The 1930s Crisis: The Left's Response

The Popular Front was born out of the left's response to 6 February. On 12 February, a general strike in support of democracy revealed how frightened the left had been by the events of that night. What channelled this fear into a successful political movement was a reversal in the policy of the Communist Party. Before 1934, the Communists had pursued a sectarian line, attacking the Socialists and denouncing the Republic as a bourgeois regime. But Hitler's arrival in power had shown the consequences of left-wing disunity, and in 1934 Comintern drew the lesson that the left must unite if France was not to suffer the same fate. At the same time, Stalin was beginning to court France as an ally against Hitler. This made it illogical for the Communists to weaken French democracy or undermine French military strength.

During 1934 the Communists adopted the so-called Popular Front line—an attempt to build the widest possible political coalition to defend the Republic against 'fascism'. Where Communists had previously sung the Internationale and brandished the red flag, they now draped themselves in the tricolour and sang the Marseillaise. The Popular Front policy was remarkably successful: in January 1936 the Communists, Socialists, and Radicals signed a joint electoral programme. An alliance between the Communists and the Radicals was an extraordinary event, and it demonstrated the alarm caused by the antics of the CF. Support for the Popular Front was also generated by the Depression and the impact of Laval's deflation policy. The Popular Front was both a social

---

[27] *From Liberalism to Fascism*, 250.

response to the Depression and a political response to the fear of fascism. Its vast demonstrations brought huge numbers of people into the streets, showing that when it came to mass politics, the left could mobilize larger forces than the right.

In May 1936, the Popular Front won the elections. The total left vote was not much larger than in 1932, but there was a shift within the left from the Socialists to the Communists, whose vote doubled, and from the Radicals to the Socialists. The number of Communist *députés* rose from eleven to seventy-two, and the Socialists became the largest party in Parliament. Léon Blum became France's first Socialist premier at the head of a Socialist and Radical coalition government (with Communist support). His government lasted for a year after which it was brought down in a financial crisis. Blum's successor, in June 1937, was the Radical Camille Chautemps. Although in theory the Popular Front remained intact— Socialists remained in the government, and the Communists continued to support it—Chautemps's government was the start of a drift to the right by the Radicals. This culminated, in 1938, in the dislocation of the coalition that had been elected only two years earlier.

Even at the peak of its reforming zeal, Blum's government was never an experiment in socialism. Its aim was to strengthen democratic institutions and restore economic prosperity: to make capitalism work and modernize the liberal State. One sign of this was the creation of a Ministry for the National Economy to counteract the influence of the Ministry of Finances which was seen as a citadel of financial orthodoxy (Tardieu had tried something similar). The minister, Charles Spinasse, surrounded himself not with inspectors of finance, but with a new breed of economic expert, including some members of X-Crise.[28] Jean Coutrot was one of those who lent his help to the government. Blum also appointed a 'Secretary of State for the Organization of Leisure'. The holder of this new portfolio, Leo Lagrange, announced that he intended to democratize sport, culture, and leisure—promoting youth hostels, encouraging workers into museums—and show that democratic states were as ready to meet the challenge of mass politics as fascist ones.

These ambitious cultural objectives make the Popular Front one of the transforming cultural moments of the French twentieth century, drawing intellectuals into politics on a scale not seen since the Dreyfus Affair.[29] They included historic figures like Romain Rolland and André Gide, but younger ones as well: André Malraux; the Socialist *planiste* Georges Lefranc who participated in workers' education projects run by the CGT; Le Corbusier who was given the chance to show some of his projects at the Exhibition of 1937. Even Mounier showed cautious sympathy. Thus, despite its strongly Republican identity, and its manipulation of traditional Republican iconography, the Popular Front, which was sufficiently all-encompassing in its objectives to offer space for all

[28] Margairaz, *L'État, les finances et l'economie*, 245–50, 315–32.
[29] See P. Ory, *La Belle Illusion: Culture et politique sous le signe du Front populaire 1935–1938* (1994).

kinds of cultural projects, succeeded in rallying many of those 1930s nonconformists who had so little time for Republican politics. But they allowed themselves to be mobilized in spite of the Popular Front's traditional republicanism
not because of it. Or at least they were willing to give the Republic a last chance
to prove it was more than just an empty husk: the Popular Front's failure only
reinforced their conviction that it was.

The Popular Front was also a mass social movement which profoundly radicalized French politics. The electoral victory of 1936 sparked off a wave of strikes
unprecedented in French history. In June 1936 alone there were about 1.8 million
strikers, and over 12,000 strikes. Even more alarmingly, three-quarters of these
strikes turned into factory occupations; many employers were locked out of their
own premises. Under this pressure the government promised to introduce a
forty-hour week and annual holidays of two weeks' paid leave; and, in the
Matignon Agreement, employers' leaders conceded wage increases and recognition of union rights. Employers were now obliged by law to enforce collective
contracts and to accept a system of compulsory arbitration.

The strikes were less a revolutionary movement than an expression of enthusiasm at the election victory, and an attempt to hold the new government to
its promises. Once the employers had conceded reforms, the strikes died down.
But patterns of authority in the factory had been irremediably breached, and,
revolution or no revolution, the Popular Front represented a massive shift in
power towards organized labour. Between February 1936 and December 1936,
the membership of the Communist Party swelled from 90,000 to 288,000,
making it the largest party of the left. Even more remarkable was the explosion
in trade-union membership. In 1935, in the wake of a move to political unity,
the CGT and its Communist rival, the CGTU, had united to form a single
CGT. The membership of the united CGT was 785,000 in 1935; a year later, it
was 4 million.

The massive increase in union membership was not only a conjunctural effect
of the Popular Front. It was also a reflection of structural changes that had taken
place in the French economy over the last twenty years. Previously unions
had been strongest in the public sector and weakest among the proletariat of the
mass production industries—especially the aircraft and car industries. Although
these industries were the most technologically advanced sectors of the French
economy, employers had continued to exercise authority as if by divine right,
barely agreeing to recognize unions: modern techniques of production coexisted
with traditional patterns of social relations. In the Renault factory, workers arriving two minutes late would be dismissed; cloakrooms were searched for subversive material; union activists were sacked; informers were everywhere. It was
difficult for these workers to defend themselves. Recruited from immigrant
labour and from the countryside, they were socially heterogeneous in origin,
without roots in the labour movement. The old syndicalist vision was not appropriate to their situation.

It was from this new working class that the mass of trade unionists came in 1936. In the Renault factory, there had been almost no unionists in 1935; there was almost no one who was not in the union at the end of 1936. By 1937 the single largest component of the CGT was metallurgical workers: in 1935 4 per cent of them had been unionized, in 1937 71 per cent. In the unified CGT, the former CGTU and CGT leaders, respectively the *unitaires* and *confédérés*, retained their separate identities, and it was above all the *unitaires*—the Communists—who benefited from the massive influx of new members. They were more adapted to the politics of mass unionization than the former *confédéré* CGT leaders. Just as the Communists had offered a voice to the dispossessed inhabitants of the industrial suburbs in the 1920s, so in 1936, the Popular Front, in particular the Communist Party, forged a collective social identity for the new working class.

The Consequences of the Popular Front

Conservatives were wrong to believe, as many did, that June 1936 heralded a Moscow-inspired revolution, but they were correct to believe that they were living through a fundamental social transformation. The outbreak of the Spanish civil war in July fuelled their nightmares of revolution and anarchy: Spain, where the 'reds' were allegedly burning churches and massacring patriots, seemed an ominous sign of what the future held for France. Within France, the Popular Front was experienced by conservatives as an assault on bourgeois society in all its forms, the destruction of those barriers defining bourgeois distinctiveness: 'break down the barriers' was one of the slogans of the Popular Front. The massive demonstrations were an invasion of urban space by the proletarian suburbs on a scale beyond the worst nightmares of 1924; the participation of women in the strikes revived fears that traditional gender relations had been entirely destabilized, and the conservative press alleged that orgies had occurred in occupied factories; the proletarian invasion of beaches during the first paid holidays presaged an era when no social space would be sacrosanct.

In fact the Popular Front had no radical ideas on the family, and few workers could afford to go to the beaches, but the fear was what mattered. The historian Marc Bloch was not exaggerating when he wrote to Lucien Febvre in May 1940 about the impact of the Popular Front on the French bourgeoisie: 'We have not fully realized . . . the unbelievably strong, tenacious and unanimous reaction which the Popular Front provoked among such people. One must retain this date, almost equal to June [1848] as one of the great moments of the history of France.'[30]

The radicalization of the right manifested itself in many ways. The most extreme was the famous Secret Committee of Revolutionary Action (CSAR),

---

[30] Burrin, *La France à l'heure*, 42.

nicknamed the Cagoule (the Hood), founded by Eugène Deloncle, a naval engineer and former member of Action française. Its aim was to fight Communism by any means. Arms caches were prepared throughout the country and terrorist attacks carried out in 1937. The numbers in the Cagoule were small, but some money was provided by industry, and there were attempts to build links to the army. The organization's significance lay less in its size than in the dramatic radicalization which it represented, and the undoubted complicities from which it benefited. Several Cagoulard leaders were arrested in 1937, only to resurface after 1940.[31]

Ostensibly La Rocque moved in a less radical direction after 1936 when he founded the PSF. By 1937, the new party had possibly as many as one and a half million members, making it easily the largest political force in France. Because this expansion occurred after La Rocque had turned to electoral politics, it has been read as a sign of the immunity of French politics to extremism. But although La Rocque had renounced street violence and paramilitarism, he remained far from committed to democracy. His movement was still an authoritarian-populist force whose extraordinary success testifies to the dramatic polarization of politics after 1936.

Some of La Rocque's followers did believe he had become too moderate. They turned either to the Cagoule or to the new Parti populaire français (PPF), formed in June 1936 by Jacques Doriot. In the 1920s, Doriot was one of the rising stars of French communism when he acquired a reputation as a fearless street fighter. Increasingly frustrated by the sectarian policies of the Communist leadership, Doriot was expelled from the Party in 1934. Ironically, the very policy which Doriot had opposed was jettisoned by the Party only weeks after his expulsion. Although Doriot continued to call himself a Communist for the next two years, this became increasingly implausible. Doriot formed the PPF with the backing of the banker Gabriel Leroy-Ladurie. The industrialist Pierre Pucheu became one of the Party's leading figures and helped attract funds from business interests who saw Doriot as a populist figure capable of draining support from the left.

By 1937, Doriot had become violently anti-Communist. He was in favour of corporatism and an entente with Nazi Germany. The PPF adopted the fascist salute and placed a lot of emphasis on symbols such as the party flag. It also made much of its readiness to use street violence although it did not have a paramilitary section. Estimates of its membership are variable, but it probably peaked at about 70,000 in 1937.[32] It also succeeded in attracting several prominent intellectuals like the novelist Drieu la Rochelle, the critic Ramon Fernandez, and the journalist Alfred Fabre-Luce. Doriot's image of heroic, working-class virility made him attractive to self-hating middle-class fascist intellectuals. Until he

---

[31] Soucy, *French Fascism: The Second Wave*, 46–53.
[32] Burrin, *La Dérive fasciste*, 278–312; Soucy, *French Fascism: The Second Wave*, 205–78.

became rather fat, Doriot looked the part of the fascist leader (except for his glasses).

The political engagement of these right-wing intellectuals was part of a general political radicalization of intellectuals in the late 1930s. Symptomatic of this tendency was the evolution of a group of young Maurrassian intellectuals who wrote for the weekly review *Je suis partout*. Run by Maurras's former secretary Pierre Gaxotte, the other contributors included Robert Brasillach and Lucien Rebatet who had both started their literary careers in *Action française*. This group became increasingly fascinated with Nazism, and moved away from Maurras: Brasillach stopped writing for *Action française* in 1939. *Je suis partout* used the rhetoric of civil war: 'when Blum and Cot [the Popular Front Air Minister] have been shot . . . by a national government no tears will be shed over those two excrements, but champagne will be drunk by French families'.[33] *Je suis partout*'s circulation was never above 100,000, but a similar tone and similar themes were also to be found in two mass circulation right-wing papers: *Gringoire* with a circulation of 640,000 in May 1936 and *Candide* which sold about 460,000.

Perhaps the most striking illustration of political polarization was less the violence of the extremes than the blurring of the boundaries between the parliamentary right, and the extreme right. The Fédération républicaine had shifted sharply to the right, partly because conservative Catholics like Xavier Vallat and Philippe Henriot had joined it because as Catholics they felt uneasy with Action française after the papal condemnation. Both of them had been star orators of the FNC. Vallat, who had dabbled in most parties of the extreme right, did not have a republican bone in his body: he attended a Mass every 21 January in memory of Louis XVI. With such figures playing a prominent role in the Fédération, it bore little relation to the party of conservative republicanism it had been in the 1920s.[34]

That the Popular Front radicalized the right is perhaps not surprising. Less predictable was the way it caused a recomposition of the left, and paved the way for an entirely new political constellation determined by anti-Communism. Those Radicals who entered the Popular Front with misgivings felt vindicated by the *grande peur* of June 1936, and their audience in the Party increased. Radicals who had rallied to the Popular Front because they feared the threat to order posed by the right—fascism—now perceived a greater threat from the left—communism. The Radical congress of October 1936 witnessed angry opposition to the Communists; pro-Popular Front speakers were heckled, and sometimes arms were raised in what seemed like a fascist salute. If the Radical Party was not yet ready to break with the Popular Front, it had already begun the process of distancing itself from it. This journey from left to right was almost a

---

[33] P. Dioudonnat, *Je suis partout 1930–1944: Les Maurrassiens devant la tentation fasciste* (1973).

[34] See Passmore, 'Catholicism and Nationalism'; and W. Irvine, *French Conservatism in Crisis: The Republican Federation of France in the 1930s* (1979), 98–158.

tradition for the Radicals, but whereas it had previously occurred in parliament under the duress of financial crisis, this time it was underpinned by a formidable wave of anti-communism from the base of the Party.

Even more startling was the evolution towards anti-communism by many Socialists and trade unionists. There had never been any love lost between the Socialists and Communists. The Popular Front was a marriage of convenience, a negative alliance against fascism. Within the CGT, the former *confédérés* were alarmed at the degree to which the Communists were profiting from the influx of new members. René Belin, second in command of the CGT during the 1930s, founded the newspaper *Syndicats* in October 1936 to organize resistance to this alleged Communist colonization. This fault-line developing within the Popular Front ran not only between the Communists and their allies, but also through the middle of the Socialists, the former *confédérés*, and the Radicals. It crystallized not so much around domestic politics as foreign policy. So deep did it become that by 1938 Radicals and Socialists, who had in 1936 believed fascism to be the enemy, now saw the Communists as no less dangerous—if not indeed worse.

4

The German Problem

On 22 October 1940, Pierre Laval met Adolf Hitler at the railway station of the small town of Montoire-sur-le-Loir near Tours. The Montoire meeting, followed two days later by one between Hitler and Pétain, was one of the symbolic moments of Franco-German collaboration. For that policy of 'intelligence with the enemy', as it was described in 1945, Laval was executed after the war. At Montoire, however, Laval certainly did not see himself as a traitor. He was respecting one of the guiding principles of his life: the pursuit of peace. If Laval had any precedent in mind, it might well have been the meeting fourteen years earlier, on 17 September 1926, between his mentor Aristide Briand and the German Chancellor Gustav Stresemann, at another out-of-the-way location, the village of Thoiry in the Jura. At Thoiry the two men had tried to resolve the outstanding differences between France and Germany. In the end, neither meeting fulfilled the expectations aroused, but symbolically they were important moments in the twentieth-century Franco-German relationship.

Thoiry reminds us that if Franco-German 'collaboration' was above all a response to the Occupation, it drew on a longer tradition of Franco-German reconciliation, a tradition grounded both in pragmatism and idealism. In 1942, the journalist Alfred Fabre-Luce, one of the most intelligent advocates of collaboration, produced an anthology demonstrating its long pedigree in French culture.[1] The book is a rather specious piece of special pleading, but it was the genuine reflection of a lifetime commitment to Franco-German reconciliation.

One does not have to accept Fabre-Luce's annexation of even Pascal to the collaboration cause, to recognize that the road to Montoire runs back from 1940 through Munich (1938), Thoiry (1926), and Locarno (1925), even to Agadir in 1911. In that year, the Premier Joseph Caillaux had defused a dangerous crisis in Franco-German relations by negotiating an agreement giving France a sphere of influence in Morocco in return for French concessions to Germany in the Congo. Caillaux declared: 'I have saved the peace of the world.' His policy was one of rational accommodation with Germany—the beginning of what might be called the pragmatic tradition in twentieth-century French foreign policy. It

---

[1] *Anthologie de la nouvelle Europe* (1942).

was no coincidence that Fabre-Luce devoted an admiring biography to Caillaux in 1933.[2]

From Caillautism to Briandism: The Pragmatic Tradition

A myth developed that Caillaux might have prevented war in 1914, but during the July crisis he was excluded from political influence owing to a scandal involving his wife. Once Caillaux's reputation had recovered, he became the unofficial leader of a peace party in parliament. The year 1917 was one of political instability and war-weariness which boosted Caillaux's influence until the peace option was finally rejected in November when President Poincaré designated Georges Clemenceau as premier. Clemenceau was committed to war until victory; Caillaux was arrested and put on trial.

In 1918, Caillaux's voice of reconciliation was drowned by the celebrations of victory, but soon the fragility of that victory became only too apparent. During the 1920s, the rivalry between Clemenceau and Caillaux was continued by that between Poincaré and Briand. In the demonology of the left in the 1920s, Poincaré was the incarnation of narrow nationalism: as president in 1914 he had supposedly inflamed the war crisis and as premier in 1923 he had ordered the occupation of the Ruhr. He was the target of Fabre-Luce's book *La Victoire* (1924), which argued that Germany did not bear exclusive responsibility for the outbreak of war in 1914. Poincaré, who had once been photographed squinting against the light when entering a war cemetery, was dubbed by the Communists 'the man who laughs in cemeteries'. He was the villain of Jean Giraudoux's novel *Bella*, where he appears as Rebendart, a politician who takes a grim delight in the inauguration of war memorials.[3]

French policy toward Germany after Versailles was in fact nothing like the caricature portrayed by anti-Poincaré polemicists.[4] Inspired more by fear than revenge, it was muddled and inconsistent. The French were well aware that the long-term demographic and economic balance of power was favourable to Germany. Even Poincaré was more prudent than his reputation allowed, and only after considerable hesitation did he send troops into the Ruhr. Once the Germans had abandoned passive resistance and the German Chancellor Stresemann was at his mercy, Poincaré resisted the temptation to impose terms on Germany unilaterally. Instead he accepted the American proposal of a committee of experts to review reparations. In the wake of its report, an international conference was called in London in May 1924 to discuss reparations.

Poincaré's assumption that the Ruhr occupation would allow him to negotiate from strength was shattered by a financial crisis which broke at the end of

---

[2] A. Fabre-Luce, *Caillaux* (1933).

[3] For another example of anti-Poincaré polemic see V. Margueritte, *Les Criminels* (1925).

[4] For a review of the literature on this issue, see J. Jacobson, 'Strategies of French Foreign Policy after World War I', *JMH* (1983), 78–96.

1923 when foreign investors lost confidence in the franc. This made the French government dependent on American loans, and at the London conference France was in a weaker position than had seemed likely a few months earlier. Poincaré had been defeated at the elections of May 1924, and it fell to his successor, Herriot, to put France's case. Herriot was a sentimental centre-left politician, full of internationalist pieties and naively trustful of Britain. But he had the misfortune to be dealing with a new Labour government sympathetic to Germany's plight. Poincaré had dealt Herriot a weak hand, and he played it badly. He capitulated all along the line, agreeing to evacuate the Ruhr within a year and renouncing future unilateral action even if Germany defaulted on reparations.[5]

The London Conference was the turning point in inter-war international relations. The French had failed to consolidate their dominance, and a change of policy was required. The rest of the decade was a period of Franco-German reconciliation inaugurated by the Locarno Treaty of 1925 when the Germans for the first time recognized their post-Versailles borders with France.[6] Locarno was followed by the Thoiry meeting in 1926 and by a Franco-German commercial agreement in 1927.

The incarnation of the new French policy was Aristide Briand, continuously French foreign minister from 1925 to 1932. Just as it is too simple to see Poincaré as an inveterate warmonger, so it would be wrong to view Briand as a lifelong 'pilgrim of peace'. Immediately after the war, he had entirely shared the prevailing anti-German consensus, but his great quality was adaptability. Having started his career on the extreme left, Briand had become a politician so perfectly poised at the centre of the political spectrum that there was not a government into which he could not fit. The natural bent of his personality was conciliation. All his life Briand had excelled at sniffing out a Zeitgeist and giving it eloquent expression. Now the Zeitgeist coincided perfectly with his own personality: 'Briandism' was the coming together of a temperament, a moment, and a policy. The League of Nations at Geneva was the ideal forum for Briand's spellbinding lyricism; his oratory could reduce cynical diplomats to tears. The high point of Briandism was the Briand-Kellogg Pact of 1928 when fifteen countries, including France and Germany, agreed that they would never resort to war to settle their differences.

From Franco-German reconciliation, Briand moved to the idea of a European federation about which he submitted a detailed proposal to the League in May 1930. Briand's European idea never came to anything, and its failure was the beginning of the end of his influence. In fact one should not exaggerate the harmony even of the Locarno years; suspicion lay behind the smiles at the

[5] S. Schuker, *The End of French Predominance in Europe: The Financial Crisis of 1924 and the Adoption of the Dawes Plan* (Chapel Hill, NC, 1976); J. Bariéty, *Les Relations franco-allemandes après la Première Guerre mondiale* (1977).

[6] J. Jacobson, *Locarno Diplomacy: Germany and the West 1925–1929* (Princeton, 1972).

Geneva tea parties. When Briand talked of peace he meant French security; 'Europe' was a way of taming Germany. He was always a pragmatist: 'I pursue the policy imposed by our birth rate.' The optimistic rhetoric of Briandism only thinly disguised the pessimism of a country exhausted by the war, and unwilling ever to envisage such a sacrifice again. By 1928, conscription had been reduced to one year, having stood at three years at the start of the decade. In the same year, construction commenced on the defensive Maginot Line.

Briandism became the ideological frame of reference for an entire generation, apart from some carping voices on the nationalist right. Social and economic interests underpinned the idealistic rhetoric.[7] In the second half of the 1920s, Germany overtook Britain as France's first trading partner.[8] France had originally hoped that the Versailles Treaty would enable her steel industry to challenge Germany's. The treaty contained a clause opening the German market to French steel producers up to 1925. But France had not been able to supplant the German steel industry by that date, and now French steel manufacturers were keen to reach cartel arrangements with their German opposite numbers. This resulted in the forming of the Franco-German steel cartel in September 1926. Briandism was also supported by the modernizing businessmen of Redressement français who were internationalist and committed to Franco-German reconciliation.

There was also an anti-American agenda behind the pro-German theme. Quite apart from fearing American cultural influence, the French resented American intransigence on war debts. At Thoiry, Briand had suggested that Franco-German reconciliation would be a 'precondition for the possibility of avoiding American monetary supremacy'.[9] When Poincaré met Stresemann in August 1928 he talked eloquently about the cultural threat of America, and the need for Franco-German co-operation to combat it.[10]

One area where Franco-German economic co-operation overlapped with 'European' cultural defence was the film industry where international Franco-German co-productions came to dominate French cinematic output. The German company Tobis opened studios in Paris and the first film it financed was the quintessentially French *Sous les toits de Paris* (1930). This co-operation continued throughout the 1930s. In the middle of the decade, the German company UFA started to make French films in Berlin. Most French film stars of the period worked regularly in Berlin where there was a sort of French film colony: the cinematic 'collaboration' of the Occupation also had a pedigree.[11]

---

[7] E. Keeton, *Briand's Locarno Diplomacy: French Economics, Politics and Diplomacy 1925–1929* (1987).

[8] See R. Frank, 'L'Allemagne dans le commerce français, ou la tendance séculaire à l'entente franco-allemande (1910–1965)', in H. Shamir (ed.), *France and Germany in an Age of Crisis* (Leiden, 1990), 30–42.

[9] Keeton, *Briand's Locarno Diplomacy*, 214.

[10] D. Artaud, *La Question des dettes interalliées et la reconstruction de l'Europe* (Lille, 1978), 878; Jacobson, *Locarno Diplomacy*, 193–4; Keeton, *Briand's Locarno Diplomacy*, 247–8.

[11] R. Pithon, 'Cinéma français et cinéma allemand des années trente: De l'échange à l'exil', in H. Bock et al. (ed.), *Entre Locarno et Vichy: Les Relations culturelles franco-allemandes dans les années 1930* (1993), 587–99; J.-P. Jeancolas, *Quinze ans d'années trente* (1983), 21–7.

Various organizations promoting Franco-German entente were founded after 1925. The most famous of these was the Franco-German Information and Documentation Committee set up in 1926 by one of the promoters of the steel cartel, the Luxembourg industrialist Émile Mayrisch. This committee tapped into a tradition, submerged during the early 1920s, of French cultural admiration for Germany. The young Charles de Gaulle was entirely typical of the pre-1914 generation in being more steeped in German than British culture (he never learnt to speak English while his German was quite respectable); Jaurès had written his thesis on Kant and Hegel. Before the war, Romain Rolland had written a long novel cycle *Jean Christophe*, whose eponymous hero represents the Germany of Beethoven not Prussian militarism.[12] There were many French only too happy to believe that the real Germany was Madame de Staël's land of poets and dreamers.

Politically Briandism enjoyed a broad constituency, especially among Christian Democrats, Socialists, and Radicals, in particular the Young Radicals. Luchaire, mouthpiece of the Young Radicals, was a direct link between 'Caillautism' and Briandism since Caillaux was one of his political patrons. Émile Roche, a close collaborator of Caillaux, had helped him found his newspaper *Notre temps*. Luchaire was the promoter of the Sohlberg circle which encouraged cultural exchanges between the youth of France and Germany. His opposite number was a young German art teacher, Otto Abetz. The two men became very close, Abetz marrying Luchaire's French secretary in 1932.[13]

In the 1930s, Franco-German relations entered a less harmonious phase. Stresemann died in 1929 and Briand in 1932, the steel cartel collapsed in 1929 with the onset of the Depression, the Nazis broke through at the elections of 1930, and the German government in 1931 alarmed France by attempting a customs union with Austria. But if the economic, political, and diplomatic conditions underpinning Briandism began to fracture after 1930, its spirit was kept alive much longer by the pacifism that had taken hold of French society in the 1920s.

The Pacifist Consensus

Pacifism could mean many things. There was a difference between integral pacifists, for whom war was never justifiable, and people whose visceral horror of war did not rule it out in all circumstances. Until the mid-1930s, however, the two positions were to all intents and purposes identical. For most people pacifism was not an ideology, but an instinct that nothing could

---

[12] C. Digeon, *La Crise allemande de la pensée française 1870–1914* (1957), 520–30; R. Frank and L. Gervereau, *La Course au moderne: France et l'Allemagne dans l'Europe des années vingt, 1919–1933* (1992).

[13] R. Thalmann, 'Du cercle de Sohlberg au Comité France-Allemagne: Une évolution ambiguë de la coopération franco-allemande', in Bock et al. (eds.), *Entre Locarno et Vichy*, 67–84.

be worse than what they had experienced in, or heard about, the war of 1914–18.[14]

The shadow of that war was everywhere—in the hundreds of thousands of war cripples, the war widows, the ruined cities of northern France, the war memorials of every town and village of France. These memorials still have the power to move today, but this was immeasurably more true when, as the historian Raoul Girardet writes of his childhood, the monuments to the dead were still new: 'the dead remained strangely present'.[15]

Much has been written about the iconography of the war memorials, but only the most tentative conclusions can be drawn since each community's choice of memorial was subject to many influences, not least of them financial. The disputes over the memorials were more frequently inspired by long-standing Church–State conflicts—where should the memorial be situated, should it contain ostensibly religious symbolism?—than by the messages to be conveyed. The commonest memorial was a simple stele, but there were often allegorical representations (a rooster, a winged victory) or statues of *poilus*, sometimes in patriotic mode (brandishing a wreath, wielding a bayonet). Representations of mourning—a dying soldier, a grieving woman—were less common, and overtly pacifist memorials almost non-existent. But since the memorials had been mostly constructed by 1922, to the extent that they can be 'read' as a reflection of a mood, it is that of the immediate post-war period.[16]

Although the war was always present in people's minds, there was reticence in discussing it. In the preface to his 1923 novel *Les Éparges*, Maurice Genevoix noted that the public was tiring of war novels.[17] At the end of the decade this began to change. The memory of the war re-emerged in books and films, as if it was only after an interval that the horror could be faced: in 1929, the Franco-American author Jean Norton Cru published *Témoins*. Although living in America, Cru had returned to France to fight in 1914, and his book was an attempt to analyse and evaluate the authenticity of all accounts of the war written by participants in it. Of the 302 books discussed by Cru, 188 had appeared during the war itself and the remaining 114 after it. Of these post-war books, two-thirds appeared between 1919 and 1921, and then output had tailed off, falling to only two books in 1928.[18] The periodization is interesting, and confirms Genevoix's observation about the declining market for war literature. The appearance of

---

[14] N. Ingram, *The Politics of Dissent: Pacifism in France, 1919–1939* (Oxford, 1991); M. Vaisse, 'Le Pacifisme français dans les années trente', *Relations internationales*, 53 (1988), 37–52; P. de Villepin, 'Plutôt la servitude que la guerre! Le Pacifisme intégral dans les années trente', *Relations internationales*, 53 (1988), 53–67.

[15] 'L'ombre de la guerre', in P. Nora (ed.), *Essais d'ego histoire* (1987), 139–71: 139.

[16] A. Prost, *Les Anciens Combattants et la société française*, iii (1977), 35–74; id., 'Les Monuments aux morts', in Nora (ed.), *Les Lieux de mémoire*, pt. i. *La République*, 207–25; A. Becker, *Les Monuments aux morts* (1988).

[17] M. Rieuneau, *Guerre et révolution dans le roman français 1919–1939* (1974), 80.

[18] J. Norton Cru, *Témoins: Essai d'analyse et de critique des souvenirs de combattants édités en français de 1915 à 1928* (1928).

Cru's book was a sign that the floodgates of memory were opening. In the first months of 1930, nine books on the war appeared. A critic in the *NRF* noted the new vogue for war books depicting the experience of the soldiers in the most desperate terms.[19]

The impossibility of forgetting was an insistent theme of the anti-war writing of Jean Giono. Already a novelist celebrated for his writing about Provence (which fitted into the post-war regionalist mode), Giono first confronted the war in his 1931 novel *Le Grand Troupeau*. The book did not exorcize the memory. In 1934 he wrote:

> I cannot forget the war. I would like to. I might pass two or three days without thinking of it and then suddenly I see it again, I feel it again, I undergo it again. And I feel frightened . . . In the war I was afraid, I am still afraid, I tremble, I shit in my pants . . . I prefer to think about my own happiness. I do not want to sacrifice myself.

Giono, who had been gassed and almost lost his sight at Mount Kemmel in 1918, rejected war unconditionally: 'there is no glory in being French. There is only one glory: to be alive.' In 1937 he published a collection of pieces, *Refus d'obéissance*, which advocated desertion in the event of war. Arguing that war was the consequence of industrial civilization, Giono combined his pacifism with a cult of the peasantry which he saw as the main victim of the Great War.[20]

Giono inverted the notion of the soldier-peasant, turning the peasantry into the redemptive class of peace. Even if the peasantry did not conform to Giono's idealized picture of it, pacifism was widespread in the countryside. Peasant organizations and the peasant press were among the most vociferous supporters of the Munich agreement.[21] They argued that the peasants had suffered more in the war than the workers who were cosily protected in the arms factories. Pacifism was also strong among the public-sector unions, especially the 100,000 members of the primary school teachers' union the SNI.[22] Among those who wrote in its paper was Léon Emery who was probably the first person, but not the last, to utter the notorious phrase: 'rather servitude than war'.

Emery was a friend of the philosopher Émile Chartier, better known by his pseudonym Alain, whose *Mars ou la guerre jugée* (1921) was a classic anti-militarist statement. Alain's writing centred on his defence of individualism and suspicion of power. Armies were the most extreme manifestation of arbitrary power: one could not be a free man in uniform. Alain execrated Poincaré. His influence derived not only from his journalism, but also his position as teacher of philosophy in the *khâgne* class (preparation for the École normale supérieure)

---

[19] L. Mysyrowicz, *Autopsie d'une défaite* (Lausanne, 1973), 300–3.

[20] Rieuneau, *Guerre et révolution*, 282–94.

[21] Boussard, 'Le Pacifisme paysan', in Rémond and Bourdin (eds.), *La France et les français en 1938–1939*, 59–75; Mysyrowicz, *Autopsie d'une défaite*, 329–42.

[22] M. Cointet-Labrousse, 'Le Syndicat national des instituteurs, le pacifisme et l'Allemagne 1937–1939', in *Les Relations franco-allemandes 1933–1939* (1976), 137–50.

at one of the most prestigious Parisian *lycées* (his last class in 1933 was attended by the Minister of Education in person). This made Alain the formative influence on many inter-war generations of students at the École normale.[23]

Jean-François Sirinelli's study of the *normaliens* of the 1920s—what he calls the 'generation of 1905'—shows that pacifism was their dominant ideological position.[24] These were people too young to have fought in the war, but if anything they were more pacifist than those who had. Many veterans, however visceral their hatred of war, felt a grim pride in the terrible experience they had lived through: the horror had its nobility. The next generation had assimilated the horror, but mocked the honour. Indeed the moralism of the veterans was often a cause of irritation. In the words of Sartre's contemporary, the philosopher Henri Lefebvre: 'Our hatred of the war veterans knew no limits.'[25]

Rethinking Pacifism: The Impact of Hitler

It is difficult to say when pacifism acquired its greatest influence. Hitler's arrival in power certainly destroyed many Briandist illusions, but if anything the increasing likelihood of another war increased pacifist sentiment. The Nazi regime skilfully exploited the idealism that had attracted so many French intellectuals towards Franco-German rapprochement. The image of the 'good German' remained resilient despite Hitler. Abetz, not previously a Nazi, put his contacts at the service of the new regime. He was recruited by Ribbentrop's personal office, the Dienststelle Ribbentrop, which took a special interest in relations with France. In 1934, Abetz organized a meeting between Hitler and two French war veteran leaders, Jean Goy and Henri Pichot; in 1935 he was instrumental in setting up a Franco-German Committee (CFA) which published a review, *Cahiers franco-allemands*, and organized cultural and youth exchanges. The head of the CFA on the French side was the journalist Fernand de Brinon, author of the book *France–Allemagne 1918–1934*, and the first French journalist to be granted an interview with Hitler in November 1933. Luchaire's *Notre temps* continued its propaganda for reconciliation, and became effectively a mouthpiece of the CFA.[26]

In the 1930s, however, pacifists on the left started to review their position in the face of Hitler. The Popular Front had the misfortune to come to power when the internationalism of its programme began to seem threadbare. Two months before Blum took office Hitler reoccupied the Rhineland. Responding to Hitler became the most important issue facing the Popular Front. Having viewed war and fascism as equally pernicious, and seeing it as axiomatic that fascism engen-

---

[23] A. Sernin, *Alain: Un sage dans la cité* (1985).
[24] *Génération intellectuelle, khâgneux et normaliens dans l'entre-deux-guerres* (1988).
[25] J. Steel, *Paul Nizan: Un révolutionnaire conformiste* (1987), 19.
[26] F. Kupferman, 'Le Bureau Ribbentrop et les campagnes pour le rapprochement franco-allemand: 1934–1937', in *Les Relations franco-allemandes*, 87–98.

dered war, the Popular Front was confronted with the paradox that resisting fascism might require war. For the Communists, in their new ultra-patriotic incarnation, there was no dilemma: if war alone would stop Hitler, war there must be. For the ultra-pacifists, there was no dilemma either: even against Hitler war was unacceptable. But for most Socialists, Radicals, and trade unionists, the answers were not so easy. This was a period of agonizing reappraisals.

For no one were they more agonizing than Blum, who was deeply committed to peace, disarmament, and collective security. Once in power, Blum had not abandoned the prospect of reconciliation with Germany, but in September 1936 his government also initiated a major rearmament programme, although previously the Socialists had refused to vote military budgets. In 1937, Paul Faure, who had been the Party's second in command throughout the inter-war years, set up a newspaper, *Le Socialiste*, to put the pacifist case. It would be premature to describe this as the emergence of a Faurist faction within the Party, since Blum's position remained sufficiently ambiguous for Faure not to seem to be diverging from it, but there was already a difference of emphasis between the two men.

A dress rehearsal of the future conflicts on the left occurred over the Spanish civil war. Should France intervene to help the beleaguered Spanish Republic? The line between pro- and anti-interventionists passed not between the right and the left, but through the left itself: between the Communists, some Socialists, and a few Radicals favouring intervention, and many Socialists (including Faure) and most Radicals who opposed any action which might lead to European war. Blum was caught in between, his heart for intervention, his head against. In this case his head won out.[27]

From 1938, the choice between war and peace, anti-fascism and pacifism threatened to explode into open conflict on the left. It was clear that Hitler would soon move against France's ally Czechoslovakia. Blum now believed the Nazi threat to be so alarming that the Popular Front no longer corresponded to the situation, and when Chautemps's government fell in March 1938, he proposed a National Unity government stretching from the Communists to the right. This idea stood no chance of succeeding, partly because the right was now as divided as the left over foreign policy.

From Anti-Communism to Conservative Neo-Pacifism

The right's divisions were a symptom of the degree to which ideology was now overriding traditional foreign-policy alignments, and creating new configurations which anticipated 1940. Although the Briandist consensus had blurred the distinction between left and right over foreign policy, the right had remained more suspicious of Germany. When Doumergue came to power in

[27] M. Bilis, *Socialistes et pacifistes, l'intenable dilemme des socialistes français 1933–1939* (1979).

1934, his Foreign Minister, Louis Barthou, ended disarmament talks, and started to explore rapprochement with the Soviet Union. This was a traditional conservative policy: to recruit allies irrespective of ideology like Republican France in her pre-1914 alliance with Tsarist Russia. Barthou was assassinated by Croatian terrorists in October 1934, and his successor, Laval, inherited the preparations for a Franco-Soviet pact. Laval would probably not have initiated such a policy himself, but he did sign the pact in May 1935. However, when it came up for parliamentary ratification in January 1936, 164 conservative deputies voted against it, their fear of Germany now outweighed by suspicion of the Soviet Union and alarm about communism within France.

Fear of communism was exacerbated by the strikes of 1936 and the Communist campaign for intervention in Spain. Conservatives alleged that the Communists were planning to drag France into an anti-German crusade for the benefit of the Soviet Union. The evolution of conservative attitudes was demonstrated by the case of Flandin, a representative of the moderate right (Alliance démocratique), who had defended the Franco-Soviet pact in 1936. During the next two years, Flandin emerged as the most articulate spokesman of the view that Germany should be given a free hand in the east. In a major parliamentary debate on foreign policy in February 1938, shortly before the Anschluss, Flandin argued that France could no longer be the 'solitary gendarme' of Europe; the Germans needed an outlet for their 'over-industrialization and overpopulation', and France should work out with them 'new conditions' for European international relations, and not allow herself to become, as the Communists wanted, the 'soldiers of a mystique'.[28]

Flandin played a leading role in sabotaging Blum's attempt to form a National Unity government. There were some conservatives, like Paul Reynaud and Georges Mandel, whose fear of Germany outweighed their hostility to the left, but they were becoming more isolated. Blum in the end resigned himself to forming another Popular Front government, knowing that it could not survive long. This short-lived government was the last one which showed any serious signs of being ready to defend Czechoslovakia, against which the extreme right-wing press—*Je suis partout, Candide, Gringoire*—now unleashed a violent campaign. The anti-Czech camp acquired a powerful new ally in April 1938 with a sensational article by Joseph Barthélemy in *Le Temps*. Besides putting the prudential case against French involvement—no cause was worth the 'suicide' of France—he presented legal arguments supposedly demonstrating that France had no obligations to Prague.

After the fall of Blum's short-lived second government, it fell to the new government formed by Édouard Daladier to find a solution to the Czech problem. Foreign policy was entrusted to Georges Bonnet about whom historians have

---

[28] C. Micaud, *The French Right and Nazi Germany 1933–1939* (Durham, NC, 1943), 133–48; Y. Lacaze, *L'Opinion publique française et la crise de Munich* (Berne, 1991), 509–13.

had almost no good to say. He is usually depicted as shifty, ambitious, and cynical. His memoirs, mercilessly dissected by Lewis Namier after the war, were a masterpiece of mendacity. A. J. P. Taylor claimed that Bonnet was incapable even of resolution in surrender. In fact, in a government paralysed by indecision about Czechoslovakia, Bonnet was rare in knowing exactly what he wanted: to detach France from her commitments to Prague, and avoid war at any cost. Because this was not the government's official policy, Bonnet's methods were bound to be underhand (although this came naturally to him): he doctored despatches, distorted conversations, and generally used any means to achieve his ends.

What is interesting about Bonnet is that he incarnated in his person all three strands of opinion towards the German problem which have been identified in this chapter. As a member of the Caillautist wing of the Radical Party in the 1920s, he was a believer in Briandist pragmatism. As a veteran who had written a book on the psychology of the soldier,[29] he had a visceral hatred of war. As a conservative Radical who had never liked the Popular Front, he was strongly anti-Communist, and worried that rearmament would undermine financial stability and pave the way for revolution.

On 29 September 1938, Daladier flew to Munich and, jointly with Neville Chamberlain, signed an agreement giving Hitler most of what he had wanted in Czechoslovakia.[30] Daladier had fewer illusions than Chamberlain that he had brought 'peace for our time', but in view of the state of French rearmament, he felt that he had no choice. As his plane, returning from Munich, approached the airport of Le Bourget, Daladier saw a crowd waiting for him. He was convinced that they had come to boo. When he saw that they were there to cheer, he remarked to an aide: 'the fools'. In parliament, the Munich agreement was supported by a massive majority: 537 in favour and 75 against (the 73 Communists, the conservative Henri de Kérillis, and 1 Socialist).

Despite this seeming unanimity, many of those who voted for Munich had reservations about it. French opinion fell into four camps. In a distinct minority was the nationalist right, represented in the press by Émile Buré on L'Ordre, Henri de Kérillis in L'Époque, Pertinax (André Géraud) in L'Europe nouvelle. In parliament, although de Kérillis was the only conservative to vote against Munich, there were others, like Paul Reynaud and Georges Mandel, who shared similar views. As de Kérillis expressed their position: 'the regime of the Soviet Union is as repugnant to me as to all of you. But I do not allow the bourgeois in me to speak louder than the patriot.'[31]

Secondly, also opposed to Munich, was the anti-fascist left represented primarily by the Communist Party. Although the Communists were isolated on

[29] L'Âme du Soldat (1917).
[30] Y. Lacaze, La France et Munich, étude d'un processus décisionnel en matière de relations internationales (Berne, 1992).
[31] Micaud, The French Right, 201.

the left in voting against Munich, their views were shared by some in the Socialist Party (Jean Zyromski), some Radicals (Jean Zay, Cot), and some non-Communist trade unionists (Léon Jouhaux).

Thirdly, the largest group consisted of conservative neo-pacifists stretching from the extreme right to a large section of the Radical Party. Their position was based on realism and ideology. Realism meant that France was too diminished—her birth rate too low, her economy too weak, her armaments too limited—to go to war: France could not, said Louis Marin of the Fédération républicaine, afford the luxury of a battle of the Marne every twenty years. As for ideology, peace was viewed as a victory over the Communists who sought to drag France into an ideological war for the Soviet Union: Munich was the price to pay for avoiding a Commune. Those, like Maurras, whose anti-communism had not entirely buried their traditional Germanophobia, did not pretend that Munich was a victory, but saw it as a 'necessary defeat', and a triumph over 'Israel'. Others were so obsessed by domestic hatreds as not to see a defeat at all.

Finally, Munich was supported by the pacifist left which was represented by Paul Faure's wing of the Socialist Party, by Belin's supporters in the CGT gathered around the newspaper *Syndicats*, by certain public-sector unions including postal workers and primary school teachers, and by left-wing dissidents like Gaston Bergery and Marcel Déat. A prominent role was also played by pacifist intellectuals like Alain, Giono, and Victor Margueritte whose detestation of the memory of Poincaré was so intense that they failed to see that Hitler was worse: 'rather Daladier than Poincaré' might have been their slogan. They were among the signatories of a telegram to Daladier on 11 September urging peace and the neutralization of Czechoslovakia. André Delmas, leader of the primary school teachers' union, organized a petition on 25 September proclaiming 'We do not want war'. In three days he allegedly collected 150,000 signatures.

Most of these left-wing pacifists had been strong supporters of the Popular Front when they had seen fascism as the greatest danger facing France. Now they were more worried by the threat of war and by what they saw as the warmongering of the Communists. This was the most significant realignment brought about by Munich. If the anti-communism of many conservatives had led them to pacifism, the pacifism of many Popular Front leftists had led them to anti-communism.[32]

After Munich: A New Sweden?

The British journalist Alexander Werth, an acute observer of France, noted that the French press had displayed an almost indecent glee in portraying Munich as a victory, while in Britain there had been a greater sense of guilt.[33] Werth's comment was accurate, but the French mood was uneasier than he

[32] Lacaze, *L'Opinion française et Munich*, 75–99, 441–58.
[33] A. Werth, *France and Munich: Before and After the Surrender* (1939), 343–7.

allowed. Behind the euphoria and relief that war had been avoided lay nagging questions about France's future status as a great power. The regularity with which in contemporary France the term 'Munich' still functions as a shorthand for abdication and surrender suggests the depth of the trauma which Munich represented.

Once Munich had been approved, however, the debate about its significance began. Was it the end of the road or a new beginning? A final retreat, grudgingly conceded before France returned to a continental role, or the dawn of a new era of Franco-German reconciliation? The boundaries between the four strands of opinion were very fluid. Many Socialists were in the pro-Munich camp only with reluctance—'cowardly relief' as Blum described it—and the same was true of many conservatives. Reynaud and Mandel had come close to resigning from the government. An opinion poll showed a less massive approval than might have been expected—57 per cent in favour, 37 per cent opposed—and also a striking majority (70 per cent) in favour of resisting further German demands.[34] At the Socialist congress of Montrouge in December 1938 delegates were presented with two entirely contradictory motions on foreign policy. Blum proposed a motion accepting the necessity of war in certain circumstances, Faure proposed a pacifist one. This rift between Faure and Blum finally shattered the axis which had held the party together since 1920. The CGT's Congress of November 1938 revealed similarly strong disagreements, with the pacifists around Belin and Delmas, pitted against the Communists and some non-Communists like Jouhaux.

On the right, there was a similar sorting out of positions—between those who had long anticipated an abandonment of the Czechs, and those who had accepted this outcome only with reluctance. The two groups have been described respectively as 'resigned nationalists' and 'conditional nationalists' (conditional on France being able to act). Reynaud resigned from the Alliance démocratique after Flandin sent a telegram of congratulations to all the signatories of Munich, including Hitler. The Congress of the Fédération républicaine in November 1938 rejected any disengagement from Eastern Europe, as did La Rocque's PSF. For the 'conditional nationalists', Munich was a defeat—or a tactical withdrawal—not the prelude to a strategic retreat.[35] Quite different was the position of Fabre-Luce who wrote that even if France did again win another war against Germany 'we would nonetheless continue to slide further down the scale. A military victory that is not prolonged by a permanent effort, by a startling increase in the birth rate, is only an episode.'[36]

Many pro-Munich conservatives argued that if France could no longer aspire to a major continental role, she must build on her influence in the

[34] C. Peyrefitte, 'Les Premiers Sondages d'opinion', in R. Rémond and J. Bourdin (eds.), *Édouard Daladier: Chef de gouvernement avril 1938–septembre 1939* (1977), 264–74.

[35] Micaud, *The French Right*, 190–205; Lacaze, *L'Opinion publique*, 293–307.

[36] Micaud, *The French Right*, 176.

Mediterranean and develop closer ties with Italy. This idea was often accompanied by another idea which became very popular after Munich: the 'fall back on the Empire [*repli impérial*]'. It was argued that France, free of East European commitments, should concentrate upon her imperial role. Flandin had launched the idea in the summer of 1938; Doriot visited North Africa in May, La Rocque in June. After Munich this imperial theme became even more popular. *Le Matin* declared in October 1938 that French security was not on the Danube or the Vistula but on the Vosges, Alps, Pyrenees, and Atlas Mountains: 'France has two capitals: Paris and Algiers.' This became an important theme of Doriot's PPF, but it was not confined to the extreme right. It was supported by the Alliance démocratique, and by some sections of the Radical Party. As one speaker put it at the Party's 1938 Congress:

> We are accused of being resigned to the abdication of France? . . . No, as a Western, maritime, African, and colonial nation, the development of our magnificent Empire is of much greater importance to our destiny than the unappealing role of gendarme or banker [of Europe] which in the flush of victory we felt ourselves called upon to play.[37]

The sudden popularity of the Empire in 1938 was clearly an emotional compensation for the dramatic loss of French influence in Europe which Munich seemed to presage. Few people were able to adopt the cool realism of the industrialist Auguste Detœuf, who wrote in April 1937 that he celebrated France's 'happy mediocrity' and saw Belgium and Sweden as better role models than Germany and America.[38] Thus the debate about Munich was not only about the relationship between France and Germany, but about the kind of society that France should aspire to be. In the case of Detœuf, formerly a leading light of Redressement français, the vision of a diminished international role for France was implicitly predicated on the idea that prosperity and modernization were more likely to be achieved through the renunciation of unrealistic diplomatic ambitions. This vision, which had inspired the industrialists who supported Briandism, was also to to be shared by many technocrats at Vichy: for them 'collaboration' was the route to modernization.

Quite different were those resigned nationalists who had no time for dreams of international co-operation. Their renunciation of French ambitions was based on pessimism about the realities of French power. Their answer was to turn inward and fall back on the superior qualities of French civilization. Ruralist and anti-modern representations of French identity were accompanied by a downgrading of French ambitions. This was the image of France presented at the International Trade Fairs at New York and San Francisco in 1939. The most popular attraction was the General Motors 'Futurama' exhibition and the AT&T

[37] Lacaze, *L'Opinion publique*, 571–84.
[38] Vinen, *The Politics of French Business* (Cambridge, 1991), 108.

Building where people could place long-distance telephone calls. The French Pavilion, which concentrated on French 'quality', presented a France attached to rural and provincial tradition.[39] In the French section of the catalogue, Raoul Dautry wrote: 'In France it is the peasant who holds the secret of the race. In the harmonious construction called France, the land and its cultivation provide the fundamental economic, social and cultural foundation.'[40] The novelist Jean Giraudoux, writing in 1939, took a similar line: 'France may be superior or inferior to other as regards economic power, wealth, the spread of her language, the size of her Empire. But what distinguishes her is, if I may put it like this, the moral nature of her form of life.'[41]

This traditionalist vision dovetailed remarkably with the picture of France painted in 1929 by the German journalist Friedrich Sieburg in his essay on France, *Gott in Frankreich? Ein Versuch*. It appeared in French translation in 1930, and aroused much discussion. Sieburg depicted France as a civilization of moderation and restraint, of quality not quantity, of individualism and the cultivation of private pleasures, and of literature and the celebration of the intellect. He also saw it as frustratingly inefficient and backward: defective telephones, unhygienic toilets, two-hour lunch breaks, a reluctance to take risks. Sieburg was frustrated by France's lack of European spirit, by her irremediable suspicion of outsiders upon whom she cast the same baleful stare as the concierges from their lodges.

The German essay reflecting on French culture was a fairly well-established genre, and there was nothing particularly original about Sieburg's contrast between French conservatism and German dynamism, but his book was also entirely in the spirit of the late 1920s. It is a call for the French to 'collaborate' in building Europe. He expresses frustration at the way the French are isolated from the world 'as if in a glass bubble', but he also celebrates France precisely for these qualities: 'With her charming disorder, her taste for leisure and distractions . . . France is today the last solid rampart of Europe against what it is convenient to call Americanism, that is to say the mechanization of life.' In the end Sieburg admits that 'I have the weakness to prefer staying in a neglected paradise than in a model universe, shiny, but full of despair.' In other words, although France should be ready to embrace Germany, she should also remain 'France'.[42] This vision of the Franco-German relationship fitted the resigned nationalism of Munich, and it is not surprising that Sieburg was to be

[39] P. Ory, 'L'Opinion publique et la "puissance" française vers 1938', in R. Frank and R. Girault (eds.), *La Puissance en Europe* (1984), 341–8; id., 'Plus dure sera la chute: Les Pavillons français aux Expositions internationales de 1939', *Relations internationales*, 33 (1983), 81–99.

[40] Peer, *France on Display*, 168.

[41] *Pleins pouvoirs* (1939), 22.

[42] *Dieu est-il français?* (1930); on Sieburg see W. Geiger, *L'Image de la France dans l'Allemagne nazie 1933–1945* (Rennes, 1999), 17–28; M. Gangl, 'Un Sieburg peut cacher un autre', *Allemagnes d'aujourd'hui*, 105, 7/9 (1988), 100–2.

found back in occupied Paris as one of that group of self-proclaimed Francophiles in the German Embassy whose role it was to seduce the French into accepting the place in the New Order which their conquerors had prepared for them.

5

The Daladier Moment: Prelude to Vichy or Republican Revival?

A month after Munich, Julien Benda wrote in the *NRF*: 'Will the French bourgeoisie push its submission to the Reich so far as to adopt a fascist regime, notably the suppression of freedom of expression, the destruction of the representative system, racism?' A few weeks later Emmanuel Berl replied in his paper, *Pavés de Paris*: 'If M. Benda thinks that latent fascism seems likely, it is because a Popular Front government has in some way prepared the way for fascism in reducing to nothing those liberties to which the petite bourgeoisie and middle classes have been, and remain, so attached.'[1]

This dialogue between Benda and Berl over Munich shows how deeply Munich had divided the French intelligentsia. In this case the division was especially poignant because both protagonists, although from different generations, shared similar backgrounds as members of the French Jewish bourgeoisie. Both were brilliant polemicists connected to the Gallimard publishing house. Benda (b. 1867) is most famous for his book *Treason of the Clerks* (1927) often taken to be an assault on intellectuals for becoming involved in politics. In fact Benda did not criticize intellectuals who defended 'universal' values—for example, Zola during the Dreyfus Affair—but only those—for example, Barrès, Kipling, Maurras—who became spokesmen of a 'particular' cause like nationalism.

During the war Benda had in fact written numerous patriotic articles, but his book was no *mea culpa*. On the contrary, he criticized the writer Romain Rolland for his wartime pacifism and his stand 'above the fray'. For Benda, Rolland was as wrong to criticize France in the name of pacifism as Maurras to defend her in the name of nationalism. The only correct position was to have defended France in the war because she incarnated rationalism and universal values. For Benda, the First World War had been a replay of the Dreyfus Affair with France in the victimized role of Dreyfus.

---

[1] M. Cornick, *Intellectuals in History: The Nouvelle Revue française under Jean Paulhan 1925–1940* (Amsterdam, 1995), 187–8, 191–2.

Nothing that happened during the war shook Benda's conviction about the perfect congruence between France and universalism, between the Republic and Reason.[2] This makes *Treason of the Clerks* a book which could as easily have been written before 1914 as after. For Emmanuel Berl (b. 1892), however, born twenty-five years after Benda, the war was the central experience of his life. He said in 1976: 'I remain a man of 1914 for whom war is something repugnant which consists in living in a trench while rats run over you.'[3] Already before 1914 Berl had admired Caillaux, but he succumbed temporarily to war fever and went to the front in September 1914. He emerged from this experience as a lifelong pacifist, abhorring the memory of Poincaré. Berl made his reputation with *Mort de la pensée bourgeoise* (1930) which argued that contemporary literature was redundant because it had nothing to say about the world as it had been changed by the war. Although ostensibly about literature, the book's origins lay in Berl's rage at Poincaré's return to power in 1926. Unlike *Treason of the Clerks*, which strives for Olympian timelessness, Berl's book was the *cri de cœur* of a generation. Between 1932 and 1937, Berl ran the politico-literary review *Marianne* whose political *raison d'être* was the defence of the Briandist heritage.

At this stage both Berl and Benda could have been described as figures of the left, but the threat of war pushed them in radically different directions, Benda denouncing appeasement in the *NRF*, Berl remaining committed to pacifism. Benda was eventually to become a Communist fellow-traveller, while Berl in 1940 helped write some early speeches of Pétain. His trajectory demonstrates the extent to which a certain style of pre-1914 Republican patriotism had been corroded by pacifism—although he quickly realized that Vichy's National Revolution had no room for people like him. Both he and Benda ended the Occupation hiding out in the countryside.

After Munich: Anti-Communism and Imperialism

Where Benda and Berl agreed in 1938 was in seeing Munich as a crucial moment not only for French foreign policy, but also for French domestic politics. It represented not only the avoidance of war, but also an internal victory over the 'warmongers', notably the Communist Party. Doriot saw the chance to eliminate the 'foreign army' of Communists encamped on French soil; *Action française* called for bullets for Blum, Reynaud, and Mandel.

Munich finished off the Popular Front. When Daladier came to power in April 1938, the Popular Front was on its last legs: Daladier's was the first government since 1936 to contain members of the Right. But the Communists held back from opposing him as long as there was still a possibility he would repu-

---

[2] J. Benda, *La Jeunesse d'un clerc suivi d'un régulier dans le siècle et d'exercice d'un enterré vif* (1968), 114–20, 218–19; id., *La Trahison des clercs* (1927).
[3] *Interrogatoire par Patrick Modiano* (1976), 42.

diate appeasement. This meant that, while his government was not a Popular Front one, it was not an anti-Popular Front one either. After Munich, there was no more ambiguity. By voting against the agreement, the Communists released the Radicals from any lingering attachment to the Popular Front alliance. The Radical Congress of October 1938 buried the Popular Front; those who tried to defend it were shouted down with cries of 'To Moscow'.

This new political configuration allowed Daladier to take on the powerful labour movement which remained the most significant legacy of 1936. He accomplished this by announcing the necessity to end the forty-hour week on the grounds that it was hindering rearmament. There was some truth in this, but Daladier's main objective was to pick a fight with the unions and win. The CGT fell into the trap by calling a general strike on 30 November 1938. This was a failure: strikers were sacked and occupied factories were evacuated by force. The trade-union movement was broken: the CGT had 4 million members in 1937; it had about 2.5 million at the start of 1939 with numbers falling fast.

The man who had pushed most vigorously for the end of the forty-hour week was the new conservative Finance Minister, Paul Reynaud, the dominant figure in the government after Daladier. The breaking of the labour movement restored financial confidence in the government, and led to a reversal of the capital flight which had plagued France since 1936, allowing Reynaud to fund rearmament without too much difficulty. There was even a recovery in economic activity. Reynaud surrounded himself with a dynamic team of young advisers, including the demographer and statistician Alfred Sauvy, a former member of X-Crise, and the *conseiller d'État* Michel Debré. This was part of a general trend in the Daladier government to recruit supposedly apolitical experts or technocrats to remedy the alleged failings of professional politicians. There was the engineer Jean Berthelot, brought in to the Ministry of Public Works, and most strikingly of all, there was Raoul Dautry, the technocrat par excellence, appointed to the new post of Armaments Minister. Dautry himself gave posts to such figures as Jean Jardin, a member of Ordre nouveau; Jean Bichelonne, a brilliant graduate of the École polytechnique; and François Lehideux, a manager in the Renault firm. What is interesting about these names is that many of them were to play a prominent role in the Vichy regime.[4]

In April 1940, Dautry was responsible for the so-called Majestic Accords— named after the building where his ministry was located—in which some trade-unionist and employers' leaders signed a general declaration of goodwill. This document was in no way binding, but it was presented by Dautry as an important moment of class reconciliation, and showed that there were industrialists ready, now that the labour movement had been emasculated, to consider a policy of class collaboration. In the aftermath of the general strike, Belin's anti-Communist wing of the CGT also started to rethink its vision of the role of

---

[4] L. Yagil, *'L'Homme nouveau' et la Révolution nationale de Vichy (1940–1944)* (1997), 30–4.

trade-unionism. Belin began to argue for a 'constructive syndicalism' replacing class conflict with class co-operation.

Belin became involved in the journal *Nouveaux cahiers* set up by a group of modernizing industrialists, many from X-Crise. Its leading lights were Auguste Detœuf and the banker Jacques Barnaud. Their premiss was that liberal capitalism had failed, and that the future lay in planning, class reconciliation, or some variety of corporatism or even the Social-Democratic Swedish model.[5] Whether industrialists or trade unionists, they believed that parliamentary democracy was redundant. Belin wrote in April 1938: 'what one cannot defend is the regime itself. Good citizens ask themselves . . . if the parliamentary regime, which one frequently confuses with democracy, is really worth fighting for.'[6] Although French syndicalists had traditionally no predilection for parliamentary democracy, such words, from a former participant in the Popular Front, reveal the ideological shift which had occurred within some sections of the left under the impact of anti-communism.

In theory, anti-communism also implied rapprochement with Germany. Bonnet signed a Franco-German declaration of friendship on 6 December 1938, but this agreement avoided hard questions about the future concessions France might be willing to offer in the pursuit of German goodwill. Many diplomatic and military figures were now ready for France to water down her Polish alliance, the last remaining commitment in Eastern Europe.[7] As for the Soviet pact, it had been effectively moribund since 1937, and there was no eagerness for reviving it.[8] Bonnet himself wanted a total disengagement from Eastern Europe, including a break with the Soviets.

The Franco-German declaration produced no concrete results despite some desultory negotiations on economic co-operation. Hopes of a durable rapprochement with Germany were dashed when Hitler breached the Munich agreement by occupying Prague on 15 March 1939. Although Bonnet remained Foreign Minister, the appeasers in the French government were now sidelined. On 31 March, the French and British offered Poland a security guarantee.

The loss of influence by the appeasers also affected policy towards Italy. After Munich, France had tried to court Mussolini, but this policy was torpedoed on 30 November when deputies in the Italian parliament rose to their feet clamouring 'Tunisia, Corsica, Nice'. This was the signal for an orchestrated campaign against France. Although it is unlikely that Mussolini harboured serious designs on Nice or Corsica, he did covet parts of the French Empire in Africa. This was embarrassing to those in France, like Flandin and Bonnet, whose advocacy of a

    [5] Le Crom, *Syndicats nous voilà!*, 91–103; Kuisel, *Capitalism*, 105–8.

    [6] Le Crom, *Syndicats nous voilà!*, 99.

    [7] R. Young, 'The Aftermath of Munich: The Course of French Diplomacy October 1938–March 1939', *FHS* 8/1 (1974), 309.

    [8] E. de Réau, *Édouard Daladier 1884–1970* (1973), 300; A. Adamthwaite, *France and the Coming of the Second World War* (1977), 67; R. Young, *In Command of France: French Politics and Military Planning* (1978), 217.

repli impérial had gone hand in hand with a pro-Italian policy. Daladier was undecided about Italian policy. He was under pressure from the British to be conciliatory in the hope of detaching Mussolini from Hitler. But by the spring, Daladier had set his mind firmly against concessions to Mussolini, and the British had to acquiesce. This readiness to stand up to Britain was a sign of new French confidence: Lord Halifax worried that Daladier was becoming another Poincaré.[9]

The government's firmness towards the fascist powers was mirrored by a change in French public opinion. Asked in July 1939 if a German operation against Danzig should be resisted by force if necessary, 76 per cent replied affirmatively, 17 per cent negatively; 45 per cent thought that war would occur before the end of the year. By June 1939 even *Action française* could write: 'If in the discussion of the Moscow-Berlin alternatives we lose sight of the fact that Berlin is the more menacing, then it must be said everyone is lost.' Such sentiments were a response to Hitler's occupation of Prague, but also to the defeat of the Popular Front: the Communist Party seemed less frightening.[10] On the left also, pacifism was thrown on to the defensive. At a Socialist congress in December 1938, Blum's line narrowly prevailed over Faure's. It was symptomatic of the new mood that when in May 1939 Déat wrote an article entitled 'Die for Danzig?' (expecting the answer no), he was an isolated voice.

Ironically enough, given that the advocates of the *repli impérial* had envisaged their policy as the pendant to a policy of rapprochement with Germany, the main cause of the new aggressiveness towards Germany was the outrage caused by Mussolini's sabre-rattling about the Empire. A visit by Daladier to North Africa in January 1939 was extensively covered in cinema newsreels. The Empire was suddenly a burning issue of national prestige. References to 'la Grande France' abounded in the press; *Paris-Soir* ran a series on 'The Epic of the Builders of the French Empire'; even the Communist leader Thorez visited Algeria. The evolution of opinion was also visible in opinion polls. When the post-Munich poll had asked whether colonies should be given to Germany, 59 per cent replied affirmatively; two months later (December 1938) 70 per cent replied no to the same question (although they were probably thinking of Italy).[11]

There was a flurry of films about the Empire, several of them featuring the film star Charles Vanel. In *Les Pirates du Rail*, he brought railways to Indochina; in *SOS Sahara* and *Légions d'honneur*, he imposed order on Saharan tribes. Most popular of all was *Trois de Saint-Cyr* (1939) which received a gala première in the presence of Daladier. The film celebrated a group of officers defending a colonial outpost against Arab attack until the cavalry arrive to relieve them—but not

---

[9] F. Bédarida, 'La Gouvernante anglaise', in Rémond and Bourdin (eds.), *Édouard Daladier*, 228–40; Duroselle, *La Décadence*, 412–16; Adamthwaite, *France and the Coming*, 313–14.

[10] Micaud, *The French Right*, 206–21.

[11] Peyrefitte, 'Les Premiers Sondages d'opinion', 265–75. A poll in Feb. 1939 was less conclusive.

in time to save the heroic leader who dies enfolded in a tricolour. This was the time that Édith Piaf turned the song 'Mon légionnaire' into a popular hit. Such films and songs rehabilitated military values after the popularity of pacifist films such as *La Grande Illusion* (1937). These imperial films depicted a world of simple patriotism and honest masculinity. As Vanel says in *Légions d'honneur*: 'the outback unites, women divide'.[12]

Daladier: The Authoritarian Republic

The main beneficiary of this new mood was Daladier. Being a man of few words, he had long projected an image of quiet strength which was belied by congenital indecisiveness. Now, for the first time, Daladier started to believe in his own image, and a strain of authoritarianism in his personality came to the fore. His confidence surged as a result of the extraordinary popularity he enjoyed after Munich. His reputation crystallized around two images: the saviour of peace in September 1938 and the defender of Empire in November. He was popular precisely because he reflected the ambivalence of the population: he was neither a convinced pacifist like Bonnet, nor a committed anti-appeaser like Reynaud. Daladier was also a consummate radio performer addressing his audience without any assumption of superiority, like Baldwin in Great Britain. All this combined to make him the most popular politician since Clemenceau; and like Clemenceau in wartime he governed increasingly like a dictator.

Daladier was helped by a widespread feeling that the Republic was in need of a dose of authority. For the pro-Munich conservatives this meant attacking the Communists, but similar themes were even taken up by anti-Munich conservatives like Pertinax who called for an 'authoritarian republic' or de Kérillis who wanted a government of national safety presided over by a general.[13] Capitalizing upon such sentiments, Daladier bypassed parliament. For much of the time he governed by decree powers. These became almost a permanent system of government which Daladier used with little respect for legal niceties. On 27 July 1939, he issued a decree proroguing parliament and suspending by-elections until June 1942, a measure unprecedented in peacetime.

There was remarkably little opposition to the authoritarianism of Daladier's government which was so at odds with the traditions of the Republic. The Radical Party was largely quiescent. Its executive committee, supposed to meet every month, only met once between January and September 1939. The Socialists were reduced to impotence as the Faure and Blum factions fought over their attitude to the possibility of war. Nor did Daladier face much of a threat from the extreme right. Election results after Munich suggested that the PSF, which had looked so threatening in 1937, was not heading for the electoral break-

---

[12] R. Pithon, 'Opinions publiques et représentations culturelles face aux problèmes de la puissance: Le Témoignage du cinéma Français 1938–1939', *Relations internationales*, 33 (1983), 91–102.

[13] Werth, *France and Munich*, 350; Lacaze, *L'Opinion publique*, 293–5.

through that once seemed possible. As for the PPF, it entered a major crisis after Munich. Some members were unhappy about Doriot's support for Munich; others felt that the party no longer had a *raison d'être* after the defeat of the left; others had lost confidence in Doriot's capacity to become the French Führer. The prominent figures that left the PPF at this time included Pierre Pucheu, who had been a major source of funding, and intellectuals like Drieu La Rochelle and Fabre-Luce.

One reason for the weakness of the right was the new resoluteness of the Daladier government. Another was that the Radical Party had sharply shifted to the right, disputing the same ideological terrain as the PSF. This was not the first time that a left-wing parliament had swung to the right, but never before had the shift been presided over by a Radical not a conservative: this time the Radicals were leaders, not prisoners, of a conservative government. The Radicals of 1939 were so different from what they had been three years earlier that historians talk of the emergence of neo-Radicalism at this time. In 1939, some Radicals in parliament signed a motion calling for the revision of the Secular Laws whose existence had once been the *raison d'être* of the party. Even Radicals were now ready to view the Church as a bulwark of social order.[14]

Daladier projected his government as carrying out a national and moral regeneration. In March 1939, Cardinal Verdier of Paris publicly assured Daladier of the Church's support for his 'work of national renewal'. The Church was also encouraged by the government's family policy. Concern about *dénatalité* had intensified during the so-called 'hollow years' of the 1930s when the number of eligible conscripts dipped because of the gap in births which had occurred during the war. Even the Communists, who had once opposed anti-contraception and anti-abortion laws, abandoned this position in 1936. Thorez called for the 'protection of the family and childhood'.[15] In February 1939, the government set up a population committee (Haut Comité de la Population) to examine the demographic problem. Its members included Boverat whose indefatigable pronatalist propaganda had continued throughout the inter-war years. In 1939 he published his book *Le Massacre des innocents*, an attack on abortion. Another member of the Population Committee was Georges Pernot, a Catholic senator and president of the Federation of Associations of Large Families. In February 1938, Pernot had intervened in parliament to modify a bill ending the civil incapacity of women. After much debate the bill was passed, but Pernot succeeded in getting two amendments voted, one specifying that the husband remained the head of the family, and the other allowing a husband to veto the exercise of a profession by his wife.

In July 1939, the recommendations of the Population Committee were implemented in a series of decrees known collectively as the Family Code. These

---

[14] Berstein, *Histoire du Parti radical*, ii. 565–86.

[15] Schneider, *Quality and Quantity*, 204–9. F. Delpha, 'Les Communistes français et la sexualité 1932–1938', *MS* 91 (1975), 121–52.

measures included financial incentives for large families—family allowances had been introduced in 1932, but now they were generous enough to double the income of a family with six children—a tightening up of the campaign against abortion, loans for young couples in the countryside, the teaching of demography in schools, and the repression of pornography. No government had ever come nearer to implementing the full programme of the natalist lobby.

Foreigners and Jews

The Daladier government is open to contradictory interpretations. On one hand, it seemed to portend a reassertion of national self-confidence and a rehabilitation of political institutions: the Republic seemed to be working again. In other respects—the Daladier personality cult, political authoritarianism, the influence of technocrats, anti-communism and the crushing of labour, celebration of Empire, family policy, the rhetoric of national renewal, the rapprochement between Church and State—it seems to prefigure Vichy. Nothing more strikingly anticipated Vichy, however, than the intensity of French xenophobia and anti-Semitism in 1938–9.

The roots of this xenophobia went back to the 1920s when a combination of the demographic deficit and economic growth had given France one of the largest rates of immigration in the world. By 1931, France's immigrant population was 3 million: 7 per cent of the total population as opposed to 2.8 per cent in 1911. On the whole, this influx had caused little controversy, despite sporadic outbreaks of xenophobia. Naturalization procedures were relaxed in 1927 and many immigrants became French citizens: 112,337 between 1923 and 1926, 269,872 between 1927 and 1930.[16]

The Depression transformed this tolerant atmosphere overnight—foreigners were accused of taking French jobs—just at the moment France was also admitting Jewish refugees from Nazi Germany. By the end of 1933, 25,000 German refugees had arrived, 85 per cent of them Jews. The backlash against foreigners started in August 1932 with a law, passed by a left-wing parliament, limiting the number of foreigners allowed in certain professions. From July 1934, recently naturalized French citizens had to wait ten years before being entitled to practise at the bar or hold public office. This was the first time in the history of the French Republic that a two-tier system of citizenship had been imposed for the acquisition of professional status. Similar restrictions were applied to medicine in 1935, after a strike of medical students protesting against competition from foreigners.[17]

This discriminatory legislation was tightened significantly by the Daladier government. In April 1938 Albert Sarraut, the Interior Minister, ordered 'method-

---

[16] R. Schor, *L'Opinion française et les étrangers* (1985).
[17] Ibid. 602–10; V. Caron, 'The Anti-Semitic Revival in France in the 1930s: The Socio-Economic Dimension Reconsidered', *JMH* 70/1 (1998), 24–73.

ical, energetic and prompt action to rid our country of the too numerous undesirable elements'. A decree in November made it easier to denaturalize naturalized citizens who were deemed to have proved themselves unworthy
of French nationality, and made it possible to refuse nationality to children
born in France of foreign parents if those parents were in trouble with the law.
This was another blow to the principle of equal citizenship;[18] a decree of 12
November 1938 authorized the internment of 'undesirables' when public security required it. An internment centre was set up at Rieucros in the Lozère in
February 1939. It was to be the first of many. Anti-immigrant feeling intensified
at the start of 1939 when the end of the Spanish civil war sparked off a new influx
of refugees. Between February and May 1939, about half a million Spanish
refugees, depicted in the conservative press as criminals and reds, streamed across
the Pyrenees. As an emergency measure, the government opened more internment camps in the south-west at Argelès, Saint-Cyprien, Gurs, and Le Vernet.
Vichy was to find its concentration camps already in existence. Through the
1930s, more and more police time was devoted to the surveillance of foreigners.
The Paris Prefecture of Police set up a special section for this purpose in 1933.
André Tulard who masterminded the creation under Vichy of a detailed register
of Jews—French and foreign—had honed his methods categorizing and monitoring foreigners for the prefecture in the inter-war years. There was nothing the
Germans could teach him in this respect.[19]

The xenophobia of the 1930s rekindled a tradition of anti-Semitism that had
been semi-dormant in the 1920s.[20] The fact that many Jews died defending their
country in the First World War made it less plausible to accuse Jews of a lack of
patriotism after 1918. The famous anti-Semitic newspaper *La Libre Parole* collapsed in 1924, having once sold 300,000 copies. Maurras never changed his
views on the Jews, but, as a result of the war, another former anti-Dreyfusard
nationalist, Maurice Barrès, included the Jews in his celebration of the 'spiritual
families' of France.

This tolerance disappeared in the 1930s. The fact that the Popular Front was
headed by a Jew provided an easy target for right-wing anti-Semites. 'One thing
that is dead', wrote Maurras in March 1936, 'is the spirit of semi-tolerance
accorded to the Jewish State since the war . . . A formidable "down with the Jews"
smoulders in every breast and will pour forth from every heart.'[21] Allegations
that the government was stuffed with Jews—in fact, apart from Blum, there were
only two—led to an outpouring of anti-Semitic venom against Blum himself.
When he appeared before parliament for the first time after the 1936 election

---

[18] Noiriel, *Les Origines républicaines de Vichy*, 146–9.
[19] Ibid. 176–204.
[20] R. Schor, *L'Antisémitisme en France pendant les années trente* (Brussels, 1992); P. Birnbaum, *Anti-
Semitism in France: A Political History from Léon Blum to the Present* (Oxford, 1992); id., *La France aux
Français: Histoire des haines nationales* (1993).
[21] Birnbaum, *Anti-Semitism in France*, 46.

victory, the conservative deputy Xavier Vallat caused a scandal by lamenting that 'this old Gallo-Roman country will be governed by a Jew'. Another parliamentary incident occurred in 1938 when, replying to taunts against Blum, the Socialist minister Marx Dormoy riposted that a Jew could be as French as a Breton. Since Bretons were seen by many as the epitome of the rooted French peasantry, this remark led to outrage on the right. There was a rash of caricatures of Blum in Breton costume. *Action française* commented: 'In France a Breton is in his own country. The Jew is only a leech from the Dead Sea.'[22]

In 1934, Paul Morand published his book *France la Doulce*, a tirade against the alleged Jewish domination of the French film industry. *Je suis partout* produced two special issues on the Jews in April 1938 and February 1939. On several occasions Maurras called for the murder of Blum—'in the back' as he said in 1935—but he was far from the most violent anti-Semitic propagandist. That privilege was reserved for Céline who published two anti-Semitic pamphlets: *Bagatelles pour un massacre* (1937) and *École des cadavres* (1938). Their flavour can only be conveyed by direct quotation:

> Racism above all! Ten times! a hundred times racism! Supreme racism! Disinfection! Cleansing! Only one race in France: the Aryan . . . The Jews, Afro-Asiatic hybrids have no place in this country. They should get out.

> I feel myself very friendly to Hitler, and to all Germans, whom I feel to be my brothers . . . Our real enemies are Jews and Masons.

> Yids are like bedbugs. Finding one of them in your sack means that there are ten thousand on the floor! . . . O filthy rabble! I hear you . . . rooting about in your trash bins.[23]

These pamphlets were so delirious that many critics did not know how to respond. Gide suggested that *Bagatelles* was a sort of Swiftian satire not intended to be taken literally, and certainly Céline's list of 'Jews' is so eccentric—Stendhal, Racine, Picasso, Roosevelt, the Pope, Neville Chamberlain—that the designation seems to have become a free floating term attached to everything Céline hated. One critic wondered if Céline had been paid by the Jews to discredit anti-Semitism.

Céline's violence puts him in a category of his own, but one can find the Maurrassian Pierre Gaxotte writing in *Candide* in 1938:

> How Blum hates us! he bears a grudge against our peasants for walking in clogs on French soil and for not having had ancestors who were camel drivers wandering in the Syrian desert . . . A choice has to be made between France and this accursed man. He embodies everything that revolts our blood and flesh. He is evil, he is death.[24]

[22] Schor, *L'Antisémitisme en France*, 74; Birnbaum, *Anti-Semitism in France*, 114.
[23] Birnbaum, *La France aux Français*, 213; Soucy, *French Fascism*, 302.
[24] Birnbaum, *Anti-Semitism in France*, 102.

Or there is the case of the novelist Marcel Jouhandeau who announced his personal conversion to anti-Semitism in October 1936, and in the following year produced a book entitled *The Jewish Peril*. He wrote:

> Although I feel no personal sympathy for M. Hitler, M. Blum fills me with a deeper and quite different repugnance . . . The Führer is in his own country and master of his own country . . . M. Blum is master of my country and no European can ever know what an Asiatic is thinking.[25]

These were not the views of marginal cranks. Jouhandeau was a respected author published by the *NRF*; *Candide* sold 650,000 copies weekly. Even more mainstream was the journalist Raymond Millet who wrote a series of articles on immigration in 1938 for the respected *Le Temps*. While claiming to oppose anti-Semitism, he worried about the Jewish 'invasion' of Paris, and ended by saying that 'measures must be taken against this disorder'.[26]

By 1937 anti-Semitism had also become intertwined with pacifism—the fear that the Jews, like the Communists, were driving France into an anti-Nazi crusade to defend their interests. This meant that on the right the list of Jewish enemies increased to include 'bellicist' conservatives like Mandel who had hitherto been immune from anti-Semitic propaganda. In September 1938, there were demonstrations against Jews in Paris and other cities. This association of Jews with war meant that anti-Semitism cut across traditional ideological boundaries to embrace elements of the left. There was nothing anti-Semitic about Paul Faure's statement in April 1938 that fighting for Czechoslovakia was not worth the life of a single wine-grower from Mâcon, but another line had been crossed when the Socialist Ludovic Zoretti wrote that France did not want to 'kill millions of people, and destroy a civilisation to make life a bit easier for 100,000 Sudeten Jews'.[27] Even more explicit was the Socialist deputy Armand Chouffet in 1938: 'I've had enough of the Jewish dictatorship over the Party . . . I won't march for a Jewish war.'[28] Such sentiments could also be found in the Radical Party. Paul Elbel railed against 'undesirable' Jews in *L'Œuvre*; the newspaper *L'Ère nouvelle*, which defended refugees in the early 1930s, was by 1938 mooting a possible *numerus clausus* for Jews and proposing that Jewish refugees should be sent to special training camps to turn them into farmers.[29]

Race and the Republican Tradition

The fact that such sentiments could be expressed on the left invites reflection on the relationship between the virulent xenophobia of the 1930s and the universalist traditions of French Republicanism. It was after all the Revolution

[25] Ibid. 101.   [26] Marrus and Paxton, *Vichy France and the Jews*, 44.
[27] Laborie, *L'Opinion publique*, 135.   [28] Schor, *L'Antisémitisme en France*, 48.
[29] Berstein, *Histoire du Parti radical*, ii. 586–8.

which emancipated the Jews in 1791. Supposedly race did not enter into French conceptions of nationality. In the mid-nineteenth century, the Republican historian Jules Michelet had declared that the genius of France was her 'universal receptivity' and 'intimate fusion of races'. The classic French formulation of nationhood was provided in Ernest Renan's 1882 lecture, *What is a nation?* Renan rejected any racial definition of the nation, seeing it as an artificial, historically determined construct. It was voluntaristic and subjective not ethnic and objective. He defined a nation as 'a soul . . . the culmination of a long past'; it was a 'daily plebiscite'. The immediate purpose of Renan's argument was to justify French claims to Alsace-Lorraine, recently lost to Germany, by pitting a distinctively French nationalism against a German racial one.[30]

French legislation relating to nationality was fixed in the 1889 nationality code.[31] It was a mixture of *ius sanguinis* and *ius soli*. Children of French parents were French, but so, at birth, were children born of a non-French parent who had been born in France, and so, from the age of 18, were children born in France of foreign parents providing the child had resided in France for the previous five years. This 1889 legislation was less restrictive than German legislation (of 1913), which based citizenship on race, but more restrictive than American legislation which conferred automatic citizenship on anyone born in the United States. French law required an exposure to French culture, requiring the future citizen to become French culturally before becoming so juridically. In America, censuses asked questions about ethnic origin; in France this was unthinkable, and there was no equivalent to the American notion of second-generation Italian-American or Irish-Americans. In French Republican tradition, beliefs and customs were private and did not concern the State. When the Jews were emancipated, this idea was summed up in the phrase: 'One must refuse everything to the Jews as a nation and grant everything to the Jews as individuals . . . They must be citizens as individuals.'

The 1889 law was less liberal than it seemed, however. It was inspired partly by concern at the presence of generations of foreigners without any stake in defending the country, and partly by the need, given France's sluggish birth rate, to increase the numbers liable for conscription. Its purpose was less to allow second-generation immigrants to be French than to remove their right not to be. A similar spirit lay behind the relaxation of naturalization procedures in 1927.[32] Assimilation was never quite as painless a process as abstract commentary suggested. From the Italians, who were the victims of race riots in the 1890s, to the Poles in the 1920s, each wave of immigration excited social tensions.

While disparaging German racism and congratulating itself on its universalism, France did have its own racial theorists. The most famous of these was

[30] Birnbaum, *La France aux Français*, 117–44.
[31] G. Noiriel, *Le Creuset français: Histoire de l'immigration* (1988); R. Brubaker, *Citizenship and Nationhood in France and Germany* (1992).
[32] Noiriel, *Le Creuset français*, 71–124.

Georges Vacher de Lapouge (1854–1936). Although admired by Kaiser Wilhelm and enjoying quite a following in America, Lapouge was ostracized by the French scientific community, but in the 1930s the obsession with immigration provided racial theorists with a new audience. The most influential was René Martial (1873–1955), author in 1934 of *La Race française*. Having started out as a public health administrator, Martial acquired a reputation as an expert on immigration on which he lectured at the Paris Faculty of Medicine. Although believing that all races were a mixture, Martial argued that the role of public policy was to find the appropriate racial 'graft' through selective immigration. The basis of this selection was to be blood group. His maxim was that blood group B—Jews—should be kept out.[33]

Until the arrival of the Germans in 1940, this French racial tradition remained marginal. But at the end of the nineteenth century, there was another challenge to the prevailing universalistic tradition in the emergence of what has been described as a 'closed' nationalism in contrast to the 'open' Republican tradition. This closed tradition was obsessed with French decadence. Its slogan, revived by the leagues in the 1930s, was 'France for the French'.[34] This was the tradition associated with Action française, and, in a different version, with Maurice Barrès. Supposedly repudiating racial definitions of French nationhood—Maurras defined the Jews as a people not a race, while Barrès wrote in 1921 'we are not a race but a nation'—they redefined French nationhood in terms of the Catholic tradition, or, in Barrès's case, in terms of the cult of 'the land and the dead'. Thus for the allegedly non-racist Barrès, Dreyfus's physiognomy was sufficient to explain why he was a traitor; Zola's name revealed that he would necessarily act as a 'deracinated Venetian'. The war gave new force to Barrès's idea of the soil and the dead. He suggested allowing the mothers or widows of fallen soldiers to vote on their behalf, binding the dead and the living into a common spiritual community. By definition, some were not included in this community. Charles Trochu of the National Association of Officer Veterans talked of 'the scum from the Orient recently encamped on our land, soaked with the blood of those who achieved that magnificent moral victory which is the homeland'.[35]

The closed tradition was not as far from the open one as might seem the case.[36] Renan's daily plebiscite was balanced by the weight of history and inheritance. When he wrote that 'the nation . . . is the culmination of a long past of effort, of sacrifice, of devotion . . . the cult of ancestors is absolutely legitimate since our ancestors have made us what we are', he was not so far from Barrès's cult of the soil and the dead. Barrès claimed to be a disciple of Renan, and one could say that he merely emphasized the objective over the subjective side of the

[33] P.-A. Taguieff, 'La "Science" du docteur Martial ou l'anti-sémitisme saisi par "l'anthropo-biologie des races"', in id. et al. (eds.), *L'Anti-Sémitisme de plume 1940–1944: Études et documents* (1999), 295–332.
[34] M. Winock, *Nationalisme, antisémitisme et fascisme en France* (1990), 11–40.
[35] Birnbaum, *Anti-Semitism in France*, 112.
[36] T. Todorov, *On Human Diversity: Nationalism, Racism and Exoticism in French Thought* (1993), 207–63.

equation: French identity as a sort of cultural alchemy after centuries of long assimilation. In the Republican tradition too, the key to nationhood is cultural assimilation: all 'particularisms' are confined to the sphere of the private. But by setting the bar of what constitutes assimilation sufficiently high, it was possible for Republican universalism to end up hardly less exclusive than the closed tradition of Barrès and Maurras, or even the racism of Martial.

In short, French notions of nationhood and race were confused. The word 'race' was frequently employed, but more in the sense of population stock than ethnic group. Few people openly subscribed to the idea that nationhood was related to race, but the boundaries between these concepts were blurred. Even defenders of the 1927 nationality law, which made naturalization easier to obtain, displayed barely disguised racial assumptions. It was only passed thanks to the inclusion of a clause making it possible to remove citizenship from naturalized citizens who had proved unworthy of it.[37] In the parliamentary debate on the law, one speaker wanted to 'operate a selection among foreigners living in France'; it would be undesirable to try and 'assimilate people who often fail to bring us the necessary moral and physical elements which we need'. Another speaker offered a hierarchy of assimilability at the bottom of which stood Orientals and Levantines 'whose mentality will never be ours'.[38] These were the views expressed at a moment of exceptional tolerance towards foreigners by supporters of a liberal policy.

Ten years later, such sentiments were more widespread, more violently expressed, and closer to becoming policy. Nothing better illustrates the extent to which racial assumptions had infiltrated mainstream opinion than the case of Jean Giraudoux, the man whom Daladier appointed to take charge of French government propaganda in July 1939. France had not previously had a state propaganda organization, and Giraudoux's Information Commissariat was a tiny operation compared to Goebbels's in Germany, but it was a recognition that there was a propaganda battle to be won. Giraudoux was a celebrated novelist and playwright noted for his delicacy of feeling, refinement of sentiment, and exquisiteness of style. Like Morand he had combined a literary career with a diplomatic one. In the 1920s, he was one of those writers hostile to the nationalism of Poincaré, and his play *The Trojan war will not take place* (1935) is the epitome of 1930s pacifism. None of this meant that Giraudoux was in any way a politically committed figure. He is often seen as celebrating the classical France of refinement, quality, and proportion, but he was also interested in urbanism, planning, and modernization.

In the year of his appointment to the Commissariat, Giraudoux published *Pleins pouvoirs*, outlining his diagnosis of France's malaise. For Giraudoux, one of the main problems facing France was the physical health of her population.

[37] Noiriel, *Les Origines républicaines de Vichy*, 134–5.
[38] M.-C. Laval-Reviglio, 'Parlementaires et xénophobes anti-sémites sous la IIIème République', *Le Genre humain*, 30/1 (1996), 89–91 (Special issue on 'Le Droit antisémite de Vichy').

He deplored the absence of any State policy towards sport, any co-ordinated action against TB, any policy of urban planning, but the gravest problem of all was immigration. France had become 'an invaded country' facing a 'continuous infiltration of barbarians'. It was necessary to accompany immigration by a policy of 'methodical choice' and 'pitiless surveillance' in order 'to send back those elements which could corrupt a race which owes its value to the selection and refining process of twenty centuries'. France had too many foreigners: 'We find them swarming in our arts and in our old and new industries, in a kind of spontaneous generation reminiscent of fleas on a newly born puppy.' Giraudoux painted an apocalyptic picture: 'Arabs pullulating at Grenelle or Pantin . . . an infiltration . . . by hundreds of thousands. of Ashkenazis, escaped from Polish or Romanian ghettoes . . . who eliminate our compatriots . . . from their traditions . . . and from their artisan trades . . . A horde . . . which encumbers our hospitals.'

Giraudoux's answer was the creation of a Minister of Race. He claimed that this was not a repudiation of France's traditions since the objective was to search for a 'moral and cultural type', not, as in Germany, a physical type. Whatever this meant, it did not prevent Giraudoux observing that the immigrants 'rarely beautify by their personal appearance', nor from asserting: 'we are in full agreement with Hitler in proclaiming that a policy only achieves its highest plane once it is racial'.[39] These, it must be remembered, were the words of the delicately refined writer whose task it was to defend the values of liberal and Republican France against Nazi Germany when war was declared on 3 September 1939.

[39] *Pleins pouvoirs*, 58–76.

6

The Debacle

Causes and Consequences

At the end of 1940, the popular historian Sir Arthur Bryant published his *English Saga* which depicted England as 'an island fortress . . . fighting a war of redemption, not only for Europe but for her own soul'. This was the first of several patriotic works in which Bryant celebrated the epic of English history culminating in the glorious leadership of Winston Churchill. What made these effusions particularly remarkable was the fact that, until the end of the 1930s, Bryant had been an ardent appeaser, anti-Semite, and admirer of Nazi Germany (he chose *Mein Kampf* as his book of the month in January 1939). Had British history taken a different turn in 1940, it is all too easy to imagine Bryant playing the same hagiographical role towards whoever might have become the British Pétain as he did towards Churchill. In different circumstances he would probably have become a British equivalent of René Benjamin, the writer notorious for his works of obsequious flattery of Pétain after 1940.[1]

The case of Bryant is a salutary reminder of the importance of contingency in history. As Pierre Vidal-Naquet remarks: 'History is not Tragedy. To understand historical reality, it is sometimes necessary *not to know the outcome*.'[2] One must resist the temptation to read the history of inter-war France merely as a prehistory to Vichy. Daladier's government may have represented a marked shift to the right by the Radicals, but within the Party there was still a vocal minority, led by Édouard Herriot, which still defended the Party's traditional values. Despite the obsessive natalism, women's rights did advance in the inter-war years: 1939 was the year of the Family Code, but in the previous year a law was passed bestowing civil equality on women.[3] France did have an anti-Semitic tradition, but it was the country in which Dreyfus was eventually vindicated: such a case could never have arisen in Germany since at that time no Jew would have attained comparable rank in the army. Despite the xenophobia of the late 1930s, France in that decade took a higher proportion of refugees than any other

---

[1] A. Roberts, *Eminent Churchillians* (1995), 287–322.
[2] *Les Juifs, la mémoire et le présent* (1991), 87.
[3] C. Bard, *Les Filles de Marianne: Histoire des féminismes 1914–1940* (1995).

country in the world.[4] The Daladier government may have interned foreigners, but in April 1939 it promulgated the Marchandeau decree forbidding press attacks on people of particular racial or religious groups. Daladier's decrees on foreigners were different from Vichy's laws discriminating against French Jews. In short, if there were continuities between Vichy and the Republic, there was also a radical discontinuity.

It is possible to restore continuity by arguing that the forces which came to the fore after defeat were among its causes: defeat was a consequence of what went before as much as a cause of what came after. This is the view that the defeat was partly attributable to the alienation of conservatives from a republic which they felt no longer protected their social interests. This argument should be treated sceptically. The battle against the Popular Front had been won by 1938: conservatives did not need Hitler because they already had Daladier. There was a reassertion of national self-confidence under Daladier, and the period between Munich and the Armistice was not a continuous slide from resignation to defeat.

Although it is true that after the defeat, most of the early resisters were people who had opposed Munich, and that most supporters of Vichy had supported Munich,[5] this example of continuity does not prove cause and effect. If Britain had been defeated, we would hear more about the defeatists in Churchill's War Cabinet or about the considerable pacifist lobby in parliament. The 'resolution' of the British people and the myth of Churchill were as much a consequence as a cause of victory. Or, to take another comparison, without the 'miracle of the Marne' in 1914, more would be heard about the weaknesses of the French Republic before 1914. If, then, the history of Vichy has to be understood in the light of long-term trends in French politics and society, there was nothing predetermined about that history: it could not have occurred if France had not suffered the trauma of the catastrophic defeat of 1940.

Drôle de guerre and Anti-Communism

The French government declared war on Germany at 5 p.m. on 3 September 1939, six hours later than Britain: to the end Bonnet had manoeuvred to avoid war. He was now removed from the Foreign Office. Until 10 May 1940, France lived the curious Phoney War (drôle de guerre) when the Allies, planning for a long war, avoided direct confrontation with Germany, and tried to consolidate their economic and military strength. The drôle de guerre was not just a parenthesis between peace and war. It exacerbated political and social tensions,

---

[4] V. Caron, Uneasy Asylum: France and the Jewish Refugee Crisis 1933–1942 (Stanford, Calif., 1999), 2, 14–15.
[5] There were exceptions: Henri de Montherlant, Drieu la Rochelle, and Hubert Beuve-Méry all opposed Munich but accommodated themselves in different ways to defeat; Christian Pineau had supported Munich, but became an early resister.

and revealed the fragility of the consensus which had been reached under Daladier. In more than simply chronological terms, it was the bridge between the Third Republic and Vichy.

Ostensibly the anti-war movement had collapsed. Twenty-eight anti-war *députés*, including Déat and Bergery, tried unsuccessfully to have parliament called into secret session so they could argue the case against war.[6] A manifesto calling for 'immediate peace' was published by the anarchist Louis Lecoin ten days after the declaration of war. Although signed by thirty-one prominent pacifists—including Alain, Déat, and Zoretti—the petition had no impact. Giono was briefly imprisoned for tearing down mobilization posters, but, as in 1914, only an infinitesimal number of soldiers refused the call-up.[7]

This apparent unanimity was misleading. Until censorship intervened, the extreme-right press had opposed the war. *Je suis partout*'s headline on 1 September was: 'Down with the War.' Nor had the left-wing pacifists changed their views. Paul Faure stopped contributing to *Le Populaire*, and his supporters went into a kind of internal exile in the Party. Zoretti ran a semi-clandestine paper, *Redressement*, which articulated the unreconstructed pacifism of many Socialists.[8] In parliament the mood was no more determined. The corridors were thick with intrigue against the government. Pacifists still hoped Italy might broker a peace.

Daladier appeared before the Parliamentary Foreign Affairs Commission at the start of October 1939. His performance was sufficiently robust to silence his critics.[9] He achieved this partly by deflecting opposition towards the Communist Party: anti-communism intensified dramatically during the Phoney War, forming a link between the final months of the Republic and Vichy.[10]

The pretext for anti-communism was the Non-Aggression Pact signed between Moscow and Berlin on 23 August. In fact no one had been more surprised by this than the French Communist leaders. Lacking guidance from Moscow, their first reaction was to argue that it did not alter their commitment to national defence. *L'Humanité*'s headline on 26 August ran: 'Union of the French Nation against the Hitlerian aggression.' This did not stop the government seizing the paper, and banning publications that defended the Pact. The Communist press was forced underground.

There was a second wave of anti-Communist repression at the end of September. On 26 September 1939, a decree dissolved the PCF and empowered the government to suspend Communist municipalities. No public statement from

---

[6] G. Rossi-Landi, *La Drôle de guerre* (1971), 15–23; J.-L. Crémieux-Brilhac, *Les Français de l'an 40*, i. *La Guerre oui ou non?* (1990), 48–52.

[7] Crémieux-Brilhac, *Les Français de l'an 40*, i. 55–62; Rossi-Landi, *Drôle de Guerre*, 116–17.

[8] Crémieux-Brilhac, *Les Français de l'an 40*, i. 96–8; Rossi-Landi, *Drôle de Guerre*, 120–4.

[9] Crémieux-Brilhac, *Les Français de l'an 40*, i. 135–64.

[10] On the Communists in the Phoney War, see A. Rossi, *Les Communistes français pendant la drôle de guerre* (1972); S. Courtois, *Le PCF dans la guerre* (1980), 83–122; Crémieux-Brilhac, *Les Français de l'an 40*, i. 165–201; Rossi-Landi, *Drôle de guerre*, 133–64.

the Party justified this action on grounds of national security. The Communists had unanimously voted war credits on 2 September; on 19 September they declared their 'unshakeable will' to defend France. In fact a new Comintern line was emerging in Moscow. On 27 September, this was formally communicated to the Party: the war was now condemned as an imperialist conflict in which the French Communists should not choose sides. On 1 October, the Communists called on the government to give a favourable hearing to Hitler's forthcoming peace proposals. On 4 October, Thorez deserted from the army and escaped to Moscow via Belgium. Within the next few days, thirty-five Communist *députés* had been arrested.

This sequence of events shows that the government's new anti-Communist measures preceded the Party's adoption of an anti-war line. If Daladier's priority had been to keep the Communists within the national community, he could have waited until they had formally adopted an anti-war line. This would have allowed him to play on the unease many Communists felt about the policy. The Communist Renaud Jean wrote to Daladier from gaol that if he had not been imprisoned, he would have opposed the Party's policy, but the government had rendered it impossible for him to disavow his Party in the face of unprovoked repression against it.[11] About thirty Communist *députés* (out of seventy-three) did renounce their party, but the government's primary objective was to win over the right not rally Communists who could be 'saved'. Conservative neo-pacifists could hardly advocate a positive attitude to German peace proposals when the Communists were being persecuted for doing the same.

In return for accepting a war it did not want, the right was rewarded with a campaign against Communist 'traitors'. This diversion was temporarily successful. The press succumbed to an orgy of anti-Communist hysteria, denouncing 'Hitlero-Stalinists' and reporting that Thorez had been recruited as an agent of the German high command. About Hitler there was almost nothing. When de Kérillis summoned the government to act with equal vigour against German sympathisers, he was denounced as a Soviet agent.[12]

The anti-Communist campaign intensified throughout the Phoney War. From November, citizens could be interned on suspicion alone; in February 1940, Thorez was stripped of his citizenship; in March, forty-four Communist *députés* were put on trial, most receiving sentences of upwards of five years. By March 1940 some 300 Communist municipalities had been suspended and 3,400 Communist activists arrested. Anti-fascist refugees, many of them communists, were interned in camps originally inhabited by Spanish refugees. Among these was Arthur Koestler whose book *Scum of the Earth* gives a gruesome account of the conditions in the camp of Le Vernet which was filled with anti-fascists from all over Europe. According to Koestler, veterans of Dachau judged the

---

[11] Rossi, *Les Communistes*, 49–50.
[12] Crémieux-Brilhac, *Les Français de l'an 40*, i. 346–60.

conditions to be worse in the French camp even if the cause was neglect rather than active sadism: 'In Vernet beating-up was a daily occurrence; in Dachau it was prolonged until death ensued. . . . In Vernet half of the prisoners had to sleep without blankets in 20 degrees of frost; in Dachau they were put in irons and exposed to the frost.'[13]

Domestic anti-Communism also affected French military planning and relations with Britain.[14] On 30 November, the Soviet Union invaded Finland. There was a wave of public sympathy for the Finns, and people who had once been so reluctant to die for Danzig (or Prague) were suddenly ready to do so for Helsinki. Flandin argued that a defeat of Russia in Scandinavia would be a blow struck against Germany; Émile Mireaux, director of Le Temps, claimed that driving Russia into the arms of Germany would serve France's interests by lumbering the Germans with a weak ally. Most far-fetched of all were the proposals for a pincer movement against the Soviet Union combining a force from Scandinavia with another coming through the Caucasus from the Near East.

The British government, not subject to the same anti-Communist pressures, was unwilling to provoke the Soviet Union unnecessarily. The idea of helping Finland would therefore have gone no further had it not offered the prospect of undermining Germany's war economy by acquiring control of Sweden's iron ore fields which provided much of Germany's iron. For this reason, at the end of February 1940, the British reluctantly agreed to despatch a force to Scandinavia on the pretext of helping Finland. Delays occurred, and it became clear that Finnish resistance would soon be over. Daladier, convinced that the British intended to renege on the agreement, became increasingly incensed. Anglo-French relations reached their lowest point since the start of the war. Vichy's Anglophobia went back to the misunderstandings of the Phoney War.[15]

Daladier's fury was largely caused by the fact that he needed a military success to bolster his increasingly beleaguered political position. As the Phoney War dragged on, there was a slump in morale not helped by the fact that 1939–40 was the coldest winter since 1893. Peasants resented the fact that young workers were being drafted from the front to the factories. Once again it seemed that the peasants were to be cannon fodder. Floods of letters denounced individuals who had obtained transfers from the front on fraudulent grounds—a precursor of the denunciatory frenzy which exploded after the defeat.[16] In the army, initial reports of 'magnificent' morale gave way to accounts of 'demoralization'. Morale was corroded by poor organization—the soldiers were short of socks and blankets—and by lassitude after months of forced inactivity. The mood is conveyed in the

[13] Scum of the Earth (1941), 89, 92.

[14] F. Bédarida, La Stratégie secrète de la drôle de guerre: le Conseil suprême interallié (1979).

[15] R. Parker, 'Grande Bretagne, France et Scandinavie en 1939–40: La Politique, les hommes et la stratégie', in Comité international de la deuxième guerre mondiale, Français et Britanniques dans la drôle de guerre (1979), 561–82; Crémieux-Brilhac, Les Français de l'an 40, i. 216–26, 361–72.

[16] Crémieux-Brilhac, Les Français de l'an 40, i. 412–73.

diary of Jean Paul Sartre. In November he notes: 'All the men who left with me were raring to go at the outset' but now 'they are dying of boredom.' In December: 'The soldiers returning from leave in Paris are full of complaints against the young fellows shirking in the factories.'[17]

The government failed to provide clear explanations why the war was being fought. This was partly the fault of the Propaganda Commissariat. Giraudoux's operation was underfunded and his own radio broadcasts were too fastidiously literary, but his main handicap was the lack of guidance about war objectives. Anti-German chauvinism in the style of 1914 was inappropriate for a population raised on memories of apocryphal atrocity stories. The alternative of presenting the war as an anti-fascist crusade was ruled out by the desire not to provoke Italy or alienate the French right. The censors weeded out slighting references to Mussolini. The void was filled by anti-communism, but this hardly explained a war against Germany.[18]

The failures of propaganda lay behind the impact of the Radio Stuttgart broadcasts by the French journalist Paul Ferdonnet. Hitherto an insignificant figure on the fringes of the extreme right, Ferdonnet acquired notoriety when the French government revealed his existence in October. Ferdonnet's theme was that Britain would fight to the last Frenchman: 'Britain provides the machines, France provides the bodies.' Few people heard the broadcasts, but news of them spread by rumour, and Ferdonnet acquired a fearsome reputation. He would broadcast information about France, and when this was proved correct, people believed he was being fed information by a network of spies, although he knew nothing that could not be gleaned from newspapers. The potency of rumour was another bridge between the Phoney War and French society under Vichy.[19]

All this made Daladier increasingly vulnerable. Opposition in parliament came from both the peace faction and those who felt Daladier was not prosecuting the war effectively. The convergence of these two groups signalled Daladier's demise. The *coup de grâce* was the capitulation of Finland. On 19 March, 300 *députés* abstained in a vote of confidence, and Daladier resigned. Daladier's successor, Paul Reynaud, had long believed himself to be destined to save France. During the 1930s, he was one of the few conservatives to oppose appeasement and favour a Soviet alliance. This cut him off from the right, and one of his problems in 1940 was the lack of a political base: his government had a parliamentary majority of only one. Reynaud's main support came from the anti-fascist left, but he could not fully capitalize on this for fear of alienating the right: he did not dare bring Blum into the government. Unable to form the compact war cabinet he dreamed of, Reynaud had to give posts to many people whose commitment to the war was lukewarm. Reynaud certainly made some

[17] J. P. Sartre, *War Diaries: Notebooks from a Phoney War (September 1939–May 1940)* (1984), 46–7, 163. On public opinion, see Crémieux-Brilhac, *Les Français de l'an 40*, i. 404–73, and ii. 215–370, 425–537.

[18] Crémieux-Brilhac, *Les Français de l'an 40*, i. 273–331.

[19] Ibid. 373–94.

very ill-judged appointments, among them the banker Paul Baudouin, who would eventually use his position in the government to sue for peace.

It was a striking illustration of the prevalence of anti-communism that even Reynaud was not immune from it. He promoted a plan to deprive Germany of oil imports by bombing Russian oilfields in the Caucasus. The British rejected this as a dangerous provocation of the Soviet Union.[20] They did, however, accept a scheme to mine Norway's waters in order to stop Swedish iron ore reaching Germany, but this operation was pre-empted by a German invasion of Norway on 9 April. Over the next three weeks, the Allies struggled unsuccessfully to recover their position in Norway. Anglo-French relations deteriorated further despite Reynaud's reputation for Anglophilia. So too did relations between Reynaud and the Commander-in-Chief, Maurice Gamelin, whom Reynaud accused of being responsible for the Norwegian fiasco. On 9 May, Reynaud sacked Gamelin, but he had to rescind the decision immediately because on the next morning the Germans launched their long-awaited offensive.

Defeat and Exodus

There was nothing inevitable about what followed. Although French politics were riddled with defeatism, it is not clear how this could have caused a military defeat. As for morale, censors' reports showed that it had recovered in the spring. This had less to do with Reynaud than with an improvement in the weather. The morale of the French soldiers when fighting began was no worse than in 1914. They were to fight as bravely as those of 1914 when they were properly led and equipped. The failure of 1940 was above all the failure of military planning.[21]

Anticipating the main offensive through Belgium, this was where the high command had sent the best French troops. In fact the brunt of the German attack came further south through the Ardennes. The French, believing that this sector of the frontier was protected by the natural barriers of the Meuse river and the Ardennes forest, had guarded it only by ill-equipped reservists, unprepared for the massive assault of German panzers. Within three days, the French line had been breached; on 15 May, Rommel was advancing so fast that he was overtaking the French in retreat; on 16 May, nothing lay between the Germans and Paris. Officials in the Quai d'Orsay began to burn their archives in preparation for an evacuation of the capital.[22]

Probably the battle of France was already lost, but the denouement took another three weeks. Reynaud sacked Gamelin and replaced him with General Weygand. In retrospect this was a terrible mistake. Weygand was an arch-conservative with no love for the Republic; Gamelin, whatever his faults, was a

---

[20] C. Richardson, 'French Plans for Allied attacks on the Caucusus Oilfields' *FHS* 7/1 (1973), 130–56.

[21] Crémieux-Brilhac, *Les Français de l'an 40*, ii. 518–48.

[22] R. Peyrefitte, *La fin des ambassades* (1953), 69–74.

good Republican. Weygand might originally have been the best man to produce a victory, but if the battle were lost, Gamelin would have better served Reynaud's purpose when it came to dealing with the political consequences of that fact. On 18 May Reynaud also took the fateful decision to reshuffle his cabinet and bring in the aged hero Marshal Pétain.

Weygand's plan was that the British and French troops in Belgium, who now risked being encircled by the Germans, should attack southwards while French troops further south attacked northwards. If successful, this operation would have breached the German corridor and re-established a continuous front. But poor co-ordination between the British and French commanders meant that when the British attacked southwards on 21 May, the French attack northwards did not materialize. General Gort, the British commander, fearing he would be cut off from the Channel, retreated towards Dunkirk on the coast. Between 27 May and 4 June, some 320,000 men were evacuated from Dunkirk. Since twice as many British troops were rescued as French ones, the Dunkirk operation only exacerbated the Anglophobia of Weygand who already blamed the British for sabotaging his plan in the first place.

After Dunkirk, Weygand formed a new defensive line on the rivers Aisne and Somme. But this was no more than a last-ditch battle to save the honour of the army. The unfolding of the remaining military events is easily told: the Somme front was breached on 7 June and the Aisne on 9 June; on 10 June, Mussolini declared war on France; on the same day the government left Paris and declared it an open city; the Germans entered Paris on 14 June. The fact that the battle was lost did not stop Reynaud and Weygand 'howling', in the words of a British diplomat, for more fighter planes. When these were not forthcoming, Weygand became apoplectic.

The British were not ready to commit planes essential for the defence of the British Isles to what was obviously a lost cause. The French view was that once France was beaten, Britain would have to surrender, and therefore the British had nothing to lose by pouring all their resources into France. The French calls for British aid began the process of shifting the blame for defeat and psychologically paved the way for France to abandon the British alliance with a clear conscience: at the end of this road lay the Armistice.[23]

As French military resistance disintegrated, panic-stricken refugees fled from the advancing Germans.[24] Starting from Belgium on 10 May, this panic spread to the north-east of France: on 16 May people were fleeing Reims; on 6 June they started to leave Paris. Since the government had not envisaged the possibility of such a rapid military collapse, its contingency planning for civilian evacuations was totally inadequate or non-existent. In most localities, the

---

[23] J. Cairns, 'Great Britain and the Fall of France: A Study in Allied Disunity', *JMH* 27 (1955), 365–409.

[24] In general, see J. Vidalenc, *L'Exode de mai–juin 1940* (1957); N. Dombrowski, 'Beyond the Battlefield: The French Civilian Exodus of 1940' (unpublished Ph.D. thesis, New York, 1995).

population started to leave while the authorities were still proclaiming that there was no need to panic and ordering people to stay put. By the time General Huntziger issued the order to evacuate the Marne *département* on 2 June, only livestock were left there.[25] In some localities, especially in the Nord, the municipal authorities were the first to flee.[26] Forced back on their own resources, people felt betrayed by their political leaders. This was to have important consequences in the future.

The roads became clogged by interminable columns of slow moving cars, vans, lorries, hearses, and horse-drawn carts piled up with furniture, mattresses, agricultural tools, pets, birdcages. People on foot pushed wheelbarrows or prams into which they had loaded a few possessions. From time to time, German planes attacked the refugees, adding to the atmosphere of panic. The roadsides were strewn with the corpses of horses or with cars abandoned for lack of petrol. As the refugees poured southwards, localities which they had expected to be havens of safety turned out already to have been deserted by their populations, in some case so precipitately that half-eaten meals remained on dining-room tables. People headed for the Loire, and their terror was increased when they found that the French, in the hope of impeding the Germans' advance, had destroyed most of the bridges. Even once the Loire had been crossed, it turned out that the Germans could easily cross themselves in inflatable boats. The refugees plunged ever deeper into rural France.[27]

The scale of this extraordinary population movement, christened the Exodus, astonished contemporary observers. One described it as resembling a geological cataclysm. The writer-pilot Antoine Saint-Exupéry wrote that from the air it looked as if some giant had kicked a massive anthill. It has been estimated that between 6 and 10 million people fled their homes. The population of Chartres dropped from 23,000 to 800, Lille from 200,000 to 20,000. In the village of Bosselange in the Côte d'Or all the inhabitants left except one family which committed suicide. Cities in the south had to cope with a massive influx of population: the population of Pau swelled from 38,000 to 150,000, of Brive from 30,000 to 100,000, of Bordeaux from 300,000 to 600,000.

Living through the Exodus was to experience a total disintegration of social structures. Thousands of children became separated from their families, and for months afterwards local papers contained poignant advertisements from parents trying to contact them. One refugee remembered: 'we had lost all points of reference, all our habits and all the rules of life were floating.'[28] When Marshal Pétain, on 17 June, expressed his 'compassion and solicitude' for the 'unhappy refugees', his words touched millions of people who were plunged in hopeless-

---

[25] Dombrowski, 'Beyond the Battlefield', 156–7.
[26] Y. le Namer, 'Les Municipalités du Nord/Pas-de-Calais, *Revue du Nord*, 2 hors-série (1987/8), 219–68: 224–6.
[27] Dombrowski, 'Beyond the Battlefield', 166–261.
[28] Ibid. 200.

ness and despair. Against this background, it is easy to understand why many people would greet the news of an armistice with such relief.

Armistice or Capitulation?

The possibility of an armistice had been raised as early as 25 May, but the debate in the government began in earnest after the departure from Paris.[29] It unfolded against a background of indescribable confusion as ministers were swallowed up in the Exodus and found themselves scattered around chateaux in the Loire region. The first cabinet meeting since the departure from Paris took place on 12 June, at the Château de Cangé, where for the first time Weygand formally demanded an armistice. There was such chaos that some ministers were not present because they had wrongly turned up at the Château de Candé instead. There was a second meeting at Cangé on 13 June. On the next day the government was on the move to Bordeaux where a cabinet meeting took place on 15 June. The final act was played out in two meetings at Bordeaux on 16 June. Reynaud opposed an armistice, but from meeting to meeting his resilience was whittled down as the peace faction swelled in size.

Reynaud had reshuffled his government for the last time on 5 June, bringing in General de Gaulle as Under-Secretary of State for War, but still he did not eliminate defeatists like Paul Baudouin. Once the government arrived in Bordeaux, the defeatists were assisted by the city's mayor, Adrien Marquet, a former neo-Socialist and pacifist. Marquet put every facility at their disposal while making things as difficult as possible for those who wanted to fight on. Bordeaux was thick with intrigue, and although it was impossible for parliament to meet, the defeatist *députés* operated on the sidelines with Marquet's help.

In the debate within the government, three issues were at stake.[30] The first was military: was it possible to go on fighting? The opponents of the armistice argued that resistance could continue from North Africa. The problem was that France lacked economic or logistical bases there. In the inter-war years North Africa had been seen only as a reservoir of men. In July 1939, 400,000 soldiers were stationed there, but by June 1940 only four full units were left. All the rest had been sent to the mainland.

It was on 3 June, as the last units were arriving in France from North Africa, that Reynaud first asked the military to study the possibility of transporting troops back there. De Gaulle was designated to liaise with the British, but time was short. Reynaud envisaged sending 454,000 men, but was informed that 60,000 per month was the best that could be achieved. On 15 June, Reynaud told Admiral Darlan that only ten days were left. The Admiral replied that the operation would require 200 ships, most of which were dispersed. He claimed

---

[29] P. Dhers, 'Le Comité de guerre du mai 1940', *RHDGM* 3/10–11 (1953), 165–83.
[30] There is a massive literature on this. E. Gates, *End of the Affair: The Collapse of the Anglo-French Alliance, 1939–1940* (1980) is a good narrative.

to have ten ships at Bordeaux, ready to carry 3,000 men each, but no one knew the whereabouts of the men to be transported. Troops had not yet been selected for transportation so as not to demoralize the fighting armies.[31]

These facts are worth recalling because it remains a matter of controversy whether military resistance from North Africa would have been feasible. The evidence suggests not, but because no preparations had been made, the argument within the government hardly examined the technical issues. The second debate was political: should the government go to North Africa or remain in France and sign an armistice? This argument, which was about attributing the responsibility for defeat, sparked off a serious crisis of civil–military relations. An armistice was a political act engaging the government to end hostilities in all French territories. Alternatively, by leaving France, the government would have signalled its political conviction that the war was not over. In this case, it would take as much of the army as could be salvaged, leaving the bulk of the army to surrender in the field and sign a ceasefire. Such a solution had occurred in Holland, where the government escaped to London after the capitulation of the army. Weygand refused this outcome for France, claiming it would dishonour the army. He swore that he would remain in France even if he was put in chains. Like Ludendorff in 1918, he wanted to shift the blame for defeat on to the politicians. Reynaud insisted that the military must obey the government's orders, but he lacked the confidence to impose his will by sacking Weygand.

When Reynaud cited the Dutch example, Weygand replied that a monarch who departed abroad could not be compared to 'one of these ephemeral governments of which the Third Republic has already had over a hundred in 70 years of existence'. The obvious political assumptions of this statement signalled a third issue at stake in the debate: the political future of France. On 13 June Weygand claimed that revolution had broken out in Paris, with the Communists installed in the Élysée. A telephone call from Mandel to the Prefect of Police demonstrated this rumour to be false, but the incident revealed Weygand's fear that defeat would be followed by anarchy: the precedent of the Commune was in many minds. Thus one of Weygand's motives in proposing an armistice was to safeguard the army's reputation so that it could preserve order in France.

It was a simple step to move from the argument that the army was necessary to prevent defeat from degenerating into anarchy to the argument, which was soon to be the *raison d'être* of Vichy, that defeat could be the springboard of national regeneration. This step was taken by Pétain at the second Cangé meeting, on the evening of 13 June, when he read out a statement of support for Weygand:

---

[31]   C. Levisse-Touzé, 'L'Afrique du Nord: Recours ou secours, septembre 1939 à juin 1943' (Doctorate Paris-I, 1991), 170–219; L.-C. Michelet, 'Pouvait-on réellement en juin 1940 continuer la guerre en Afrique du Nord?', *GMCC* 174 (1994), 144–60.

The duty of the government is, whatever happens, to stay in the country or lose its right to be recognised as a government. To deprive France of her natural defenders in a period of general disarray is to deliver her to the enemy. The renewal of France will come from staying in France rather than waiting for the conquest of our territory by allied forces in conditions and in a timescale impossible to predict. I am therefore of the opinion that I will not abandon the soil of France and will accept the suffering which will be imposed on the fatherland and its children. The French renaissance will be the fruit of this suffering . . . I declare that, as far as I am concerned, and outside the government if necessary, I will refuse to leave metropolitan soil and will remain among the French people to share its suffering and misery. The armistice is in my eyes the necessary condition of the durability of eternal France.[32]

Enter Pétain

Pétain's intervention decisively shifted the balance of the argument in favour of the armistice camp. It also contained a barely disguised threat: that he would stay in France whatever the government decided. Weygand's outbursts had already undermined Reynaud's position, but their impact was weakened by his reputation as a Catholic and monarchist. Pétain, on the other hand, was universally revered, and had never been associated with disloyalty to Republican governments. Weygand's unfavourable comparison between an 'ephemeral' Third Republic government and a monarchy contained an assumption unacceptable to any Republican politician, but even the most ardently Republican politician would have realized that he weighed little in the balance against Pétain.

Pétain's reputation had been built on two achievements: the defence of Verdun in 1916 and the ending of the army mutinies in 1917. His solution to the mutinies had been to shoot a few ringleaders, introduce improvements in the conditions of the ordinary soldier, and postpone further offensives until the Allies had acquired superiority with the arrival of American soldiers. Pétain's genuine concern for the lives of his soldiers distinguished him from other First World War commanders. At times, however, his caution verged on defeatism. In 1918, when the final German offensive threatened to drive a wedge between the British and French armies, Pétain was accused by the British commander Haig of being ready to desert the British. Pétain's pessimism alarmed Clemenceau himself, and it was for this reason that Foch, not Pétain, was appointed overall commander of the Allied armies.

In the 1920s, Pétain was in charge of defence policy until being replaced by Weygand in 1931; in 1934 he served as Minister of War in the Doumergue government. Gradually he turned into a living legend. After the deaths of Foch in

---

[32] Aron, *Histoire de Vichy*, 21.

1929 and Joffre in 1931, Pétain was *the* Marshal. The two other surviving Marshals, Lyautey who died in 1934 and Franchet who died in 1942, were not serious competitors. In 1929, Pétain was unanimously elected to Foch's seat in the Académie française, and the traditional eulogy of welcome pronounced by Paul Valéry gave elegant expression to the Pétain myth. Pétain's physical appearance fitted the role he was required to play. As Blum wrote after the war: 'I was struck, and I can say seduced, as were most people who met him, by his nobility of bearing, by the simple and honest gaze of his blue eyes, by the air of gravity and nobility expressed by his handsome face.'[33] Those blue eyes were integral to the Pétain myth.

The reverence for Pétain was not confined to the right. He was universally seen as the most humane commander of the war—'the most human of our military commanders', to quote Blum again. Unlike Foch, Castelnau, Lyautey, or Franchet, he was not ostentatiously Catholic or monarchist. In such company, it was not hard to acquire the reputation of being a good Republican. Pétain was also careful to keep his distance from politics. As Minister of War in Doumergue's government, he did not stray from military policy. When, during the Popular Front, his aide Loustaunau-Lacau created the Corvignolles, a secret anti-Communist network in the army, Pétain was informed but did not get involved. He was as prudent in politics as in war.

Pétain's prudence did not stop elements of the right casting him in the 1930s in the role of national saviour. He topped a poll in the conservative *Le Petit Journal* in 1935 to discover who would make the most popular dictator for France. The journalist Gustave Hervé produced a pamphlet entitled *C'est Pétain qu'il nous faut* (1935) arguing that Pétain was the providential leader who would save France from chaos. If Pétain did nothing to encourage such suggestions, he did not disavow them either. He cultivated his myth with care, ensuring that he was not forgotten. His public utterances were all the more effective for being comparatively rare. In a speech in 1934 he blamed teachers for 'destroying State and society' by bringing up children to despise patriotism. This became an obsession of Pétain's and he would like to have been Minister of Education in Doumergue's government. In 1935, inaugurating a war memorial in the Pyrenees, he pronounced a eulogy of the virtues of the peasant. Between the two rounds of the 1936 elections, he declared that France's crisis was spiritual not material, and that a new *mystique* was necessary.

These sentiments were general enough not to tarnish Pétain's reputation on the left. Although he did participate in some meetings of the Maurrassian brains trust, the Cercle Fustel de Coulanges, Pétain had little time for ideology or abstract political ideas: he viewed politics as a military man. Pétain's tragedy was to be an unremarkable person who had come to believe his own myth. In fact there was a considerable gap between the private man and the virtues he

---

[33] Servent, *Le Mythe Pétain*, 202.

preached. Although he celebrated the peasantry and his own rural roots, Pétain had long put this world behind him. He adored being a celebrity in the politico-journalistic world of Paris, basking in the flattery of the titled and famous. Although preaching family virtues, Pétain himself was a childless womanizer who finally married a divorcée in 1920 when he was 64. The marriage did not stop him continuing his philandering: the looks which seduced crowds also exercised their magic on many women.

It was wrong to believe that the myth was the man, but it was also wrong to believe that there was nothing behind the myth. This was the mistake made by Laval. Speaking during the Phoney War to a journalist who claimed that Pétain was too old to play a role, Laval replied: 'That is without importance. What would we ask of him? To be a mantlepiece, a statue on a pedestal. His name! Nothing more!'[34] In fact at the age of 83, Pétain was still in excellent physical and mental shape, apart from slight deafness. He looked twenty years younger than he was, and age had only burnished his aura of nobility, bestowing an aspect of grandfatherly benevolence. In fact Pétain was everything but benevolent. Weygand remarked 'he is very secretive. He does not like to reveal his thoughts or open them to discussion . . . His heart is very open to collective affection especially to the humble and those who have suffered—he really loves the peasants and soldiers . . .—but it is more inaccessible to individuals whatever their relations with him.'[35] It was not easy to know what Pétain was thinking, but too easy to assume he was thinking nothing. Behind the clear gaze of the blue eyes lay suspicion, self-regard, and cunning.

In March 1939, Pétain agreed to become France's first ambassador to the new Spanish regime of General Franco. The left protested that Franco did not deserve such an honour. On the outbreak of war, Daladier offered Pétain a place in his government, but Pétain declined, possibly hoping to keep himself in reserve if things went wrong. Although in Spain, he kept in touch with events in Paris. There were persistent rumours of a Pétain government. But just as on the eve of the First World War Pétain's military career had seemed at its end, so in 1940 he must have come to doubt if he would ever play the political role which had once seemed possible. In a letter of January 1940 he expressed his desire to 'steer clear' of politics: 'my physical strength would no longer permit me to bear the burden of office and I am abandoning the idea'.[36] As in 1916, impending catastrophe came to his rescue.

On 18 May, Pétain joined Reynaud's government. He kept his peace while the catastrophe unfolded. The British officer General Spears, who had known Pétain in the previous war, found him bitter about the failings of politicians and schoolteachers. Instead of discussing the conflict with Spears, Pétain read him an interminable speech he had once delivered on Joan of Arc. Spears managed

---

[34] H. Lottman, *Pétain: Hero or Traitor?* (1985), 185.
[35] *Recalled to Service* (1952), 202–3.   [36] Warner, *Pierre Laval*, 154.

to stop Pétain reading out another one about the peasantry, and instead was shown a model of a statue of the Marshal on horseback.[37]

In the armistice debate, Pétain initially allowed Weygand to make the running. There was no affinity between the two men: Weygand had been a protégé of Pétain's rival Marshal Foch. They were brought together by the conviction that the politicians were guilty of taking France into a war they had not prepared for; that France had been let down by Britain; and that to leave France at such a moment would be desertion, condemning the country to anarchy.

The Armistice

Once Pétain had come out firmly in favour of an armistice, the writing was on the wall for Reynaud. How could the politicians be more right than France's two most senior military figures? On 16 June, Reynaud resigned, and Pétain was asked to form the next government. He had a list of ministers ready in his pocket. It contained most of those ministers from the Reynaud government who favoured an armistice.

Reynaud's resignation was an act of fatal significance because it established the formal legality of Pétain's government. Had Reynaud continued in office and left French soil for Algeria or London, any government formed by Pétain would have been technically illegal. Having said that, even if Reynaud had taken the government (or those members of it willing to follow him) abroad, in the short term the outcome would not have been so different. Reynaud in London would initially have counted for less than Pétain in France. But this was also true of de Gaulle who nonetheless managed to build up his authority despite not enjoying the formal legality of a government in exile. Thus having failed to be Clemenceau in May, Reynaud missed his chance to be de Gaulle in June.

Reynaud later argued that his resignation was not itself equivalent to accepting an armistice. He claimed that he had expected the German armistice terms to prove unacceptable and allow him to re-emerge as head of a government of resistance. Reynaud may have deluded himself that this was possible, but once the mechanism for the armistice was in motion, there was little chance of stopping it. On 17 June, Pétain delivered his first broadcast to the French people: 'It is with a heavy heart that I tell you today that we must cease hostilities.' This unfortunate phrase made many people believe that a ceasefire had already been agreed rather than that the government was seeking an armistice. The broadcast was repeated with the phrase amended to: 'We must try to cease hostilities.' But the damage had already been done, and of the 1.5 million prisoners of war taken in the battle of France most were captured in the week between Pétain's speech and the signing of the Armistice. This final collapse of French resistance

[37] E. L. Spears, *Assignment to Catastrophe*, ii (1954), 87–90.

weakened the likelihood of the government rejecting whatever armistice terms the Germans chose to present.

One chance for the anti-armistice camp lay in a proposal to divide Pétain's government into two parts, one staying in France, the other heading to North Africa with some leading members of parliament. This would in theory have allowed the government to discuss the eventual armistice terms free from the threat of German troops on the doorstep. Pétain accepted the scheme although he was not himself prepared to leave. But those, like Marquet, who interpreted this plan as a final manoeuvre by the anti-armistice faction, lobbied hard to delay or reverse it. Under this pressure, Pétain started to change his mind. A decisive role was played by the junior minister Raphaël Alibert who announced on 20 June that there was less urgency for the government to leave France since the Germans had not yet crossed the Loire. On the strength of this information, which Alibert knew to be false, government ministers were instructed not to leave Bordeaux. When twenty-seven parliamentarians left Bordeaux on board the ship *Massilia* on 21 June, there were no ministers among them.

The absence of those who had departed on the *Massilia* was entirely welcome to the government since they were the people most opposed to the armistice. The *Massilia* turned out to be a trap. Having left in the belief that they were helping to prevent the signature of an armistice, those on board found, on arrival in Casablanca on 24 June, that an armistice had already been signed, and they were portrayed in the French press as deserters.

On 21 June, the German armistice terms were presented to the French representative General Huntziger in the railway carriage at Rethondes, near Compiègne, at exactly the same spot where, twenty-two years earlier, Foch had presented armistice terms to the defeated Germans. 'My poor friend', was Weygand's response when Huntziger phoned to say where he was. The German demands were few in number: France would be divided into an Occupied Zone in the North and an Unoccupied Zone in the South; the army would be demobilized apart from a force of 100,000 necessary to ensure internal order; the fleet would be disarmed and the ships would be docked in their home ports, but the Germans promised they would not touch them; the cost of maintaining German troops on French soil would be paid for by the French government; French prisoners of war would remain in captivity until the war was over.[38]

These terms were harsh, but not unreasonable enough to give ammunition to those who hoped that a majority of the government could be persuaded to reject them. They included none of the three conditions that Pétain had stipulated to Huntziger would be unacceptable: occupation of the whole of France; occupation of any part of the Empire; a handing over of any part of the fleet. Hitler's relative moderation was a calculated tactic. On 18 June he told Mussolini, who had hoped for rich pickings, that it was preferable not to provoke

[38] Duroselle, *L'Abîme*, 183–202.

a possible French refusal. It was in the Axis interest that the French fleet did not fall into British hands 'quite apart from the unpleasant administrative responsibility which the occupying powers would have to assume' if the French rejected an armistice.[39]

The Armistice was signed on 22 June. Before it could come into effect, an armistice also had to be signed with Italy. Mussolini had to listen to Hitler, and provisionally abandon any designs on the French Empire. As a consequence, the Italian terms were much more lenient than the French had feared (or hoped—if they were opponents of the armistice). The Italians received a tiny zone of Occupation stretching from Menton to the frontier. This agreement was signed on 24 June, and the two armistices came into effect on the next day. After the signature of the Armistice, the government had to move since Bordeaux was in the zone of German occupation. On 1 July, it set up its base in Vichy.

The last possible obstacle to the implementation of the Armistice might have come from the Empire. Telegrams urging the government to allow the Empire to fight on arrived in Bordeaux from the colonial administrators in the Levant, from General Boisson in French West Africa, and from General Noguès in North Africa. The strategic importance of North Africa made Noguès a key figure. On 24 June, General Mittelhauser in the Levant urged him to form an Imperial Government in North Africa and continue fighting in alliance with the British. But the imperial proconsuls, schooled in obedience, could not ultimately bring themselves to rebel, and with reluctance they rallied to the government. They were also reassured that neither armistice contained any threat to the Empire.[40] When two British envoys, Lord Gort and Duff Cooper, arrived in Rabat on 26 June to try and make contact with the passengers of the *Massilia*, they were prevented from doing so by Noguès, and sent packing on the next day. This British interference probably helped consolidate Noguès's loyalty to the government.

Subsequent British actions only reinforced that loyalty. Despite containing no German claim to the fleet, the Armistice did not entirely allay British fears that it might fall into German hands: of the five home ports to which the fleet was to be sent, all but one (Toulon) were in the Occupied Zone. On 3 July, therefore, the British government sent a naval force to Mers el Kébir on the Algerian coast where some of the French fleet was docked. The French commander was presented with an ultimatum summoning the French fleet to scuttle itself, join the British, or go to distant French colonial ports. The third of these conditions, which was the least unacceptable from the French point of view, seems not to have been transmitted to Vichy in time. But even if it had been, one cannot see how the French government could have complied, since this would have represented a breach of the Armistice, which it had only just signed.[41] The

---

[39] Jäckel, *La France dans l'Europe*, 54–8.
[40] Levisse-Touzé, 'L'Afrique du Nord', 170–219.   [41] Duroselle, *L'Abîme*, 229–34.

French Admiral, Gensoul, rejected the ultimatum, and the British opened fire, killing almost 1,300 French sailors. There was a furiously anti-British reaction in France. Noguès commented that 'the Boches would not have acted more perfidiously', and this dispelled his lingering doubts about the Armistice.[42]

The argument over the Armistice has raged ever since. Opponents of the Armistice claimed that continued military resistance from the Empire would have been possible. Although, as we have seen, it is unlikely that the French could have resisted effectively from North Africa, it would not have been easy for the Germans to transport an army to North Africa against the combined operations of the British and French fleets. Hitler's desire to avoid such an eventuality by offering comparatively lenient armistice terms lends support to the view that he still took the prospect of French resistance seriously. After the war, defenders of the Armistice argued that, by keeping the Germans out of North Africa, the Armistice had enabled the Allies to land there in November 1942 and prepare the reconquest of southern Europe. They seized upon Churchill's remark to General Georges in January 1944 that ultimately the Armistice had served the interest of the Allies by keeping French North Africa free of Germans.[43] Even if Churchill's comment is correct, however, it has no bearing on the reasons why France signed an armistice in 1940. At that time the intention was certainly not one of keeping North Africa free for the French to re-enter the war against Germany. On the contrary, it was believed that the war was over, and the Armistice was viewed as a preliminary to a fully-fledged peace.

Enter Laval: The End of the Republic

Announcing the Armistice terms to the French people on 25 June, Pétain told them that the defeat had occurred because the 'spirit of enjoyment' had prevailed over the 'spirit of sacrifice'; France needed 'a new order . . . an intellectual and moral renewal'.[44] The link between suffering and redemption, contrition and renewal, already visible in the armistice debate, now became explicit.

Before Pétain could embark on creating this new order, he had first to consolidate his power. There was still in theory a parliament and a president, and Pétain was technically only premier of a Third Republic government. Although Weygand would probably not have worried about constitutional niceties, Pétain, who always preferred to advance cautiously, was not a man to stage a coup. It was in offering another solution to the problem of what to do next that Pierre Laval saw his opening. It was a strange irony that Laval, the man who was to effect on Pétain's behalf the destruction of the Third Republic, was himself a

---

[42] Levisse-Touzé, 'L'Afrique du Nord', 371.

[43] Weygand, *Recalled to Service*, 220–1.

[44] *Discours aux Français 17 juin 1940–20 août 1944* (1989), 66. The theme of sacrifice had already been raised in his speech of 20 June, ibid. 60.

pure product of that Republic, and the incarnation of what its critics considered to be its worst vices.[45]

For Laval the presence of the government in Vichy was extremely convenient because he had a property quite close in the village of Châteldon where he had been born. Laval's father had been the village innkeeper and also had a butcher's shop. The family had been well off, but of modest social status—somewhere between the peasantry and the petite bourgeoisie. It was a classic pattern of French social history that ambitious Auvergnats went to Paris to make their fortune, usually as traders or café proprietors. In Laval's case success came at the bar. Having trained as a lawyer, he started his career defending trade unionists in the courts. It was thus entirely natural that Laval should begin his political career on the left. He was elected to parliament as a Socialist in 1914, and made his first parliamentary speech in 1917 defending French Socialists who wished to go to Stockholm to discuss peace terms with Socialists of other belligerent powers.

At the elections of 1919, Laval lost his seat. Three years later, he was elected mayor of the Parisian working-class suburb of Aubervilliers, and in 1924 he returned to parliament for the same constituency. Aubervilliers became his electoral fief. Ostensibly Laval was still on the left, and his first cabinet posts were in short-lived centre-left governments in 1925–6, but gradually he was moving to the right. His first important portfolio was as Tardieu's Minister of Labour in 1930, and when he became premier for the first time in 1931 it was as the head of a right-wing government.

To some extent, Laval's move from left to right reflected growing prosperity and social success. During the 1920s his law practice had made him into an extremely wealthy man. In 1923 he bought a property in Normandy, then a newspaper and a radio station. Laval set the seal on his social standing in 1931 when he bought the château in the village of his birth. In 1935 his daughter married the Comte de Chambrun. Laval's social ascension was not the only reason, or even the primary one, for his drift to the right. Such a trajectory was not unprecedented in the Third Republic. Aristide Briand, who became something of a role model for Laval, had also started on the extreme left before becoming a pillar of centrist politics. Laval's socialism had never been doctrinaire. It was more an instinctive sympathy with those from modest backgrounds. He always put personal contacts above ideologies.

As mayor of Aubervilliers, Laval learnt the arts of patronage and clientelism which he practised for the rest of his career. In government he operated not according to any fixed ideas, but by improvisation and persuasion. Like Briand he wrote nothing down, and spent little time studying official papers. He preferred conversation which allowed him to envelop his interlocutors in a haze of charm and cigarette smoke (like Briand he was a chain-smoker). Laval was

[45] Warner, *Pierre Laval*; F. Kupferman, *Laval 1883–1945* (1987); J.-P. Cointet, *Pierre Laval* (1993).

capable of inspiring deep personal loyalty, and returning it. Pierre Cathala, whom he first met when they were adolescents preparing their baccalaureate in the same *lycée*, was one of several followers who accompanied Laval throughout his political career, ending up as his Minister of Finance in 1942. Such enduring relationships allowed Laval to believe that in essentials he had not betrayed his origins or beliefs.

Having few settled political ideas himself, Laval did not understand politicians who could not be persuaded or flattered, bullied or bought. His enemies claimed he practised politics like a horse-trader. Laval would not necessarily have considered this an insult. He was proud of his peasant background. Nothing gave him more pleasure than inspecting livestock on his estate.

It was not true that Laval believed in nothing. Once he observed that it was wrong to describe him as a cynic since his entire career had been devoted to the cause of peace. This does not mean that he was in any ideological sense a pacifist, but he could see no sense in war, lacking the imagination to conceive a cause which might make war worth fighting. This explains Laval's affinity for Briand who initiated him into international affairs, although Laval never shared Briand's idealism about the League of Nations. When Laval returned to government after February 1934, he was convinced that he could save peace by building good relations with Mussolini's Italy.

Laval's desire for rapprochement with Italy was not inspired by any particular ideological sympathy for Mussolini's regime. But the opposition which this policy aroused on the left did start to push Laval further towards the right. He was furious when, in the name of ideology, the left jeopardized his pro-Italian policy by insisting on sanctions against Mussolini after Italy's invasion of Abyssinia in 1935. Laval's resentment against the left increased after the Popular Front drove him from power in 1936. His politics of backslapping and camaraderie worked less effectively in the more ideological climate of the late 1930s. In 1940 Laval commented: 'That Chamber spewed me up [in 1936], now I'm going to spew it up.' Laval moved from being a genial cynic to being an embittered one.

By 1939, Laval was frustrated that France was being dragged into a war from which he genuinely believed he could save her. Although lacking personal vanity, Laval, like many self-made men, had developed a strong sense of his own abilities, and was impatient that lesser men were messing things up. When told by Pétain in July 1940 that the Germans distrusted him, Laval replied that this was because they were worried he might outwit them.[46] During the Phoney War Laval was one of the most active parliamentary plotters in the peace lobby. Already in mid-September there were rumours of a Laval-Pétain government.[47] There was little temperamental affinity between the two

[46] Burrin, *La France à l'heure*, 82.
[47] P. de Villelume, *Journal d'une défaite (23 août 1939–16 juin 1940)* (1976), 41–2; Rossi-Landi, *Drôle de guerre*, 109.

men, but they respected what they had to offer each other: Pétain needed Laval's political skills; Laval needed Pétain's prestige. A personal link was provided by Laval's son-in-law, the Comte de Chambrun, who had been on Pétain's staff in 1917.

When he formed his government, Pétain had intended to make Laval Foreign Minister. This move was blocked by Weygand, for whom Laval represented everything he loathed about the Republic, and by those who wanted to avoid sending out excessively pro-German signals when bridges with England had not yet been burnt. Laval finally entered the government as deputy premier on 23 June, after the signature of the Armistice. He quickly consolidated his influence with Pétain by devising a solution to the problem of France's political future. His idea was that parliament should be persuaded to commit suicide by granting Pétain full powers to revise the constitution.

The cabinet approved Laval's scheme on 4 July, but other plans were still in the air, and Pétain seemed not to have rejected any of them. One idea, proposed by Flandin, was that President Lebrun should resign and parliament elect Pétain in his place. Pétain would thus combine the positions of president and premier within the framework of the existing constitution. Flandin's plan foundered when Lebrun made it clear he would refuse to resign: the only notable act he had performed in eight years as president. Another idea, proposed by a group of Senators, was that the constitution should be suspended until the end of the war and Pétain granted full legislative powers in the interim. In the end, Laval successfully saw off these counter-proposals which were less radical than his own. He conceded two points: that the new constitution would be submitted to popular ratification; and that Pétain would not have the power to declare war without the approval of parliament.

Laval's next step was to secure parliamentary approval. As the deputies arrived at Vichy, Laval subjected them to a mixture of charm and bullying. He reassured them that Pétain could be trusted not to abuse his power; he warned them that if they did not act first, Weygand or the Germans would do so for them. On 9 July, in the Vichy Casino, parliament met to consider the proposal that the constitution should be revised. Laval, making it clear that he spoke with Pétain's full authority, outlined the argument for constitutional revision: 'a great disaster like this cannot leave intact the institutions which brought it about'. The bill was almost unanimously approved by 624 votes to 4.

Having secured approval for the principle of revision, Laval's real success occurred on the next day when the proposal to give Pétain authority to revise the constitution was passed by 569 votes to 80 (with 17 abstentions). This massive majority was partly explained by the absence of *députés* who would have voted against: the Communists were ineligible, the parliamentarians on board the *Massilia* were still trapped in North Africa. Léon Blum, who voted against, claimed that people had voted out of fear of Weygand or the Germans. Fear was a factor, but not a decisive one. Essentially, the vote was born out of despair at the defeat. It revealed an erosion of faith in the institutions of the Republic across the entire political spectrum. On 10 July, only five *députés* of the right (two of them from the Christian Democrat PDP), voted against, but even if most of the eighty who voted 'no' came from the left, they were in a minority within their own parties (except for the five members of the left Catholic Jeune République group, all of whom voted 'no'): 57 per cent of Socialist *députés* and 58 per cent of Radicals voted full powers to Pétain.[48]

Such people were not voting for what we have come to know as 'the Vichy regime'. The size of the majority was essentially a vote of confidence in Pétain, and it is entirely explicable without invoking the black arts of Laval. If anything, Laval's involvement increased suspicion. Laval's achievement was not so much to have buried the Republic as to have convinced Pétain of his indispensability for the operation. His reward was the prospect of playing a key role in the new regime.[49] Laval was also important to Pétain because he was thought to enjoy good relations with Germany. But Laval probably overestimated the extent to which Pétain believed himself to be in his debt. When Laval brought Pétain the good news that the vote had gone smoothly, he suggested that the Marshal show himself on the balcony to receive the applause of the crowd, Pétain refused, telling one of his aides: 'He [Laval] wants to gets himself applauded behind me, but I won't play his game.'[50]

Was Vichy 'Legal'?

On 11 July, Pétain issued the first constitutional acts under his new powers. The First Act effectively terminated the Republic by abrogating the famous Wallon amendment of 1875 which had created the office of President of the Republic (and thereby the Republic): Pétain was declared to be Head of the French State. The Second Act gave Pétain full powers to appoint and dismiss ministers, and pass laws through the Council of Ministers. The Third Act adjourned parliament until further notice. The Fourth Act entitled Pétain to designate his successor: he chose Laval for this position. After the Seventh Act in January 1941, which authorized Pétain to investigate and sanction all civil servants whose performance of their duties was deemed unsatisfactory, Pétain had accumulated almost all legislative, executive, and judicial powers. One of his advisers commented that Pétain now had more power than any French leader since Louis XIV; Laval was his dauphin.

[48] J. Sagnes, 'Le Refus républicaine: Les Quatres-Vingts Parlementaires qui dirent "non" à Vichy le 10 juillet 1940', *RHMC* 38 (1991), 555–89. Burrin, *La Dérive fasciste*, 332–8; M. Sadoun, *Les Socialistes sous l'Occupation: Résistance et collaboration* (1982), 34–53.
[49] E. Berl, *La Fin de la Troisième République* (1968), 204–32.
[50] M. Ferro, *Pétain* (1987), 132.

Many of those who voted for Pétain on 10 July had not expected any of this. A lot of ink was subsequently spilled arguing whether these measures represented a kind of *coup d'état*. De Gaulle's Free French tried hard to demonstrate that the Vichy regime was illegal. In December 1940, the jurist René Cassin, who had joined de Gaulle in London, published his proof of Vichy's illegality. He argued that, quite apart from the irregular circumstances surrounding the vote of 10 July—the climate of intimidation and the absence of many deputies—parliament was not entitled to delegate its right to amend the constitution. Furthermore, by not submitting his constitutional acts for popular ratification as was stipulated by the 10 July vote, Pétain had infringed the authority he had been granted.[51]

The juridical validity of Cassin's arguments is questionable. Even if they are accepted, the illegality of Pétain's government would date from 10 July or after. Yet on other occasions the Free French offered different arguments for the illegality of Pétain's government. On 27 October 1940, de Gaulle issued a manifesto declaring the Vichy government to be unconstitutional and announcing the establishment of a council with responsibility for those parts of the Empire free from enemy control on the basis of French legislation prior to 23 June 1940. The choice of the date 23 June implied that the government's illegality dated from the signing of the Armistice because it had forfeited French sovereignty to Germany. But a later Gaullist Ordinance of 9 August 1944, which became the legal basis of the post-Liberation regime, claimed that any laws passed since 16 June 1940 were null and void. This date implied that the illegality of Pétain's regime preceded the Armistice.

This hesitation over dates—16 June? 23 June? 10 July?—underlines the weakness of the case for the illegality of Pétain's government. That is why de Gaulle also invoked the less precise notion of legitimacy. For de Gaulle, the government of a partially occupied country could not be legitimate. But legitimacy is a slippery concept. If it is conferred when a country's population supports the regime, Pétain's overwhelming popularity until 1942 certainly conferred legitimacy on him. If it is conferred by international recognition, Vichy also passed the test. Although French diplomatic relations with Britain ceased in July, Vichy in 1940–1 had diplomatic relations with forty countries including the United States, Canada, China, and Japan.[52]

There seems little doubt, therefore, that at the beginning Vichy was both legal and legitimate. This is not just a matter of academic interest. It meant that de Gaulle was technically a dissident and rebel, and made his position more precarious than that of the formally constituted governments in exile. Vichy's legality also affected the responses of the French administration: in the early days at least, disobeying the regime caused a greater crisis of conscience than

---

[51] P. Novick, *The Resistance versus Vichy: The Purge of Collaborators in Liberated France* (1968), 191–7.
[52] Duroselle, *L'Abîme*, 447–8.

obeying it. Quite apart from the glorious reputation of Pétain, the regime had law on its side.

This made the Vichy regime almost unique in occupied Western Europe. In Belgium, King Leopold II signed the capitulation of the armies on 28 May and constituted himself a prisoner of the Germans. The government fled to London, and was recognized by the Allies as the official government. Leopold, however, no longer recognized it. He met Hitler in November 1940 and would have liked to set up a rival government in Belgium, but the Germans did not want this. Instead Belgium was directly run by the German military in the person of General von Falkenhausen governing through the Belgian secretary-generals who were the top civil servants in each ministry. Before the war the government had authorized the secretary-generals to stay in place in case of defeat and guarantee that the country continued to be administered. They had to exercise their judgement about whether they could accept all the demands the Germans made of them. On occasion they were helped by the courts which remained in operation and intervened sometimes to contest the constitutionality of the acts which the secretary-generals were required to execute. In December this flared up into open conflict and the courts went on strike. But they capitulated a few days later, and from this point the secretary-generals had to fall back on their own judgement and sense of duty.

In Holland, the monarch Queen Wilhelmina fled to London with the government. There was not, as in Belgium, a conflict of legitimacy between the king and his government. The Germans installed a civil administrator, Arthur Seyss-Inquart. The administration was, as in Belgium, in the hands of secretary-generals. In Norway, King Haakon VII and his government left for London after the German occupation. The German representative in Norway, Josef Terboven, tried to get those Norwegian MPs who were still in the country to form a government and declare the deposition of the king. This was unsuccessful and the Germans were reduced to setting up a council composed of a few Norwegian fascists who represented no one but themselves. The established Norwegian politicians would not associate themselves with the occupying power. Because no instructions had been provided for the country's civil servants, they were thrown entirely on to their own devices. Some resigned and others tried to continue the task of daily administration.

The only case comparable to France was Denmark which was occupied by Germany on 9 April 1940. The monarch and Danish government decided to stay, and they were permitted to remain in power. This arrangement survived until August 1943 when the Germans, in the face of growing resistance activity, insisted that the government declare martial law. This request was refused and the Germans took full control. Up to this point, however, the Germans interfered little in Denmark's internal affairs. Democratic institutions were left intact to the extent that free elections were held in 1943. In France, however, although the government retained a similar degree of independence, it decided to embark on a fundamental transformation of French society which it christened the National Revolution. When French administrators found themselves asked to carry out anti-democratic or anti-Semitic measures, it was often French laws, not German ones, they were being asked to apply.

Part II

The Regime: National Revolution and Collaboration

Introduction to Part II

The armistice of 23 June 1940 and the vote of full powers to Pétain on 10 July 1940 defined the formal framework of Franco-German relations and internal French politics for the next four years. But many questions remained unanswered. In foreign affairs the new regime might have confined itself to the Armistice and waited on events; domestically it might have confined itself to the basic tasks of administration until the future was clearer. It did neither. For Vichy the Armistice was the prelude to a durable redefinition of Franco-German relations—what came to be called 'collaboration'—and Pétain's full powers the prelude to a fundamental transformation of politics and society—what came to be called the 'National Revolution'. The Armistice and the vote of full powers were the necessary condition of these policies, but did not make them inevitable: they were a deliberate choice.

Nor did the one policy necessarily follow from the other. In Denmark the government of Eric Scavenius aligned its foreign policy on Germany's—even joining the Anti-Comintern Pact in 1941, something that Vichy never did—but this did not substantially affect its domestic political agenda. Notwithstanding the Danish example, it was not unreasonable for Vichy leaders to assume that Germany would look more favourably on a regime that had adopted a more authoritarian political system, and this was one of Laval's arguments for a change of regime. But if it was unlikely that democratic politics could have continued entirely unchanged with half France occupied, the Germans in fact showed little interest in France's internal political arrangements for the first two years, providing public order was maintained. Indeed, to the extent that the National Revolution encouraged the traditional values of French patriotism, the Germans were suspicious of it. Such pillars of the National Revolution as the Legion of Veterans and the youth movements were prohibited in the Occupied Zone.

Not only were the National Revolution and collaboration distinct, but at Vichy not everyone supported both positions with equal enthusiasm. Weygand opposed collaboration while ardently supporting the National Revolution. He hoped that France's internal reforms would one day allow her to avenge her defeat like Prussia after Jena. This analogy was frequently repeated. Laval, on the other hand, was cynical about the National Revolution, but committed to

139

collaboration. Weygand and Laval were at the two extremes, loathing each other as a result. In general, the differing attitudes to collaboration and the National Revolution were questions of priorities and emphasis—separating those with a primarily Francocentric outlook from those with a primarily European outlook. Pétain fitted into the former category. His main requirement of collaboration was that it encourage the Germans to alleviate conditions in France in order to facilitate his government's reforms. Laval fitted into the latter category. His only requirement of domestic policy was to preserve public order so as not to upset the Germans. For Pétain collaboration was the instrument of the National Revolution; and for Laval the National Revolution the instrument of collaboration.

Without the German victory, however, those who wanted to carry out a National Revolution would not have achieved power. This meant that the distinction between collaboration and National Revolution was muddied from the beginning even for those who conceived them as separate. They were insidiously and subtly linked. In 1940 it was a logical step, easy to make, to move from saying that France's defeat, although deplorable, made reforms inevitable to saying that France's defeat was less deplorable because it made reforms possible. This was the force of the comment by the Archbishop of Lyons, Cardinal Gerlier: 'victorious we would probably have remained prisoner of our errors'.[1] On 28 May 1941, the economist Charles Rist reported hearing a more extreme version of this sentiment: 'Mme Aubouin tells me that after the Armistice she received a letter from a reactionary friend of hers containing these words: "At last we have victory!" She tells me that it took her a moment to understand.'[2] For no one was this link between National Revolution and French defeat more paradoxical than for the Germanophobe Charles Maurras. He became famous for his remark that 1940 had been a 'divine surprise'. Maurras did not mean that he welcomed the defeat, but that it had had unexpected benefits in Pétain's arrival in power. Pétain not Germany was the divine surprise. Even so Maurras found the question of collaboration embarrassing. The phrase 'divine surprise' occurred in his book *La Seule France*, published in April 1941. He summed up his position as: 'Only France [*France seule*] or, if one prefers, France alone [*La Seule France.*]' For Maurras this meant unconditional loyalty to Pétain without needing to take up a position on collaboration: he wanted to pretend that Germany was not there.

One group who had no difficulty in reconciling the internal reform of France with collaboration were those who came to be described as 'collaborationists'. For them collaboration was the condition of internal renewal, and internal renewal the guarantee of commitment to collaboration. The ideal of the most extreme collaborationists, who were based mainly in Paris, was a National Socialist France. They attacked Vichy for not going far enough, and mocked Maurras's

---

[1] Halls, *Youth and Vichy France*, 63.   [2] *Une saison gâtée*, 165.

affectation of agnosticism about Germany: one might as well, one of them claimed, argue for a policy of 'la Provence seule'.[3]

The first three chapters of Part II will treat successively the three positions which have been outlined above—National Revolution, collaboration, and collaborationism—from 1940 to 1942. Chapter 10, which takes the history of the regime from 1942 to 1944, will no longer separate out the three strands because the boundaries between the National Revolution, collaboration, and collaborationism, never entirely distinct, became in practice totally blurred. From 1942 the Germans began to interfere increasingly in French internal affairs. They started to implement a fully-fledged war economy which required France to deliver more and more to them. At the same time they began to implement the policy of exterminating the Jews, and insisted that the French government help them round up Jews. In this context the idea of pursuing an autonomous policy of internal French reform became increasingly unrealistic. Internal French policy could no longer be separated from collaboration with Germany. Those who remained loyal to Vichy had to confront the fact that their survival was dependent on a German victory in Europe, and for that reason the collaborationists became more influential at Vichy itself.

[3] J. Verdès-Leroux, *Refus et violences: Politique et littérature à l'extrême droite des années trente aux retombées de la Libération* (1996), 318.

7

The National Revolution

Vichy, a sleepy spa town, was as improbable a capital for France as Harrogate or Cheltenham for England.[1] After leaving Bordeaux, the government had initially moved to Clermont-Ferrand, in the heart of the Auvergne. It stayed only one day because the city lacked sufficient accommodation. Lyons, France's second city, would have been an obvious choice of capital, but it had a large working-class population, and its Radical mayor, Édouard Herriot, was closely identified with the Third Republic. Marseilles's unsavoury reputation as 'the French Chicago' rendered it an unsuitable location from which to launch a moral renewal of France. Toulouse was geographically too remote and had a left-wing tradition. Vichy had none of these disadvantages: it was centrally located, decorous, and with no working-class population liable to cause trouble. Most importantly, its large hotels, designed for visitors to the spa, were ideal to house the itinerant ministries. As it turned out, this Ruritanian setting was a singularly appropriate location for the chimerical project of regenerating France while half the country was occupied by Germans and war was raging in Europe: from Vichy the real world seemed far away.

Pétain installed himself on the third floor of the Hôtel du Parc, Laval on the floor below. The Ministry of the Interior took over the Casino, the Colonial Ministry, to some amusement, the Hôtel de l'Angleterre. Lesser ministries inhabited lesser hotels. Conditions were indescribably cramped: bedrooms doubled up by day as offices; bathtubs had to be used as filing cabinets. Vichy's discomforts increased in the first winter because the town was geared only for the summer tourist trade, and no provision had been made for heating arrangements. One provident minister who asked for coal was told that the government would have left Vichy by Christmas.[2] The intention was to return to Paris, as was permitted by the Armistice. But the Germans cooled towards this idea, and the negotiations about a transfer dragged on through the summer. There was also talk of a move to Versailles. In the end, however, no move occurred: the provisional capital became permanent.[3]

---

[1] On life in Vichy, M. Cointet, *Vichy Capitale 1940–1944* (1993).
[2] Ibid. 20.   [3] Jäckel, *La France dans l'Europe*, 125–30.

The smallness of the town encouraged a febrile atmosphere of gossip and intrigue. Vichy was a dull place, with few distractions; there was little to do except plot and hate. Never were the corridors of Vichy's hotels more buzzing with conspiracies, speculation, and fantasy than in the first weeks. Pundits, prophets, and politicians descended on the town, offering their services and peddling their solutions to France's problems. There was everything to play for while the regime's political orientation remained uncertain. Unlike Italy in 1922 or Germany in 1933, the regime emerged not from an internal crisis but from an external defeat. There was an internal political crisis during the 1930s in France, but a provisional resolution to it had been provided by Daladier in 1938. The Fall of France reopened that crisis without preconditioning its outcome. This meant that the situation in 1940 was relatively open-ended. There was a void—and many candidates to fill it.

The lobbying began even before parliament voted Pétain full powers. On 28 June, Weygand presented Pétain with a memorandum calling for policies inspired by 'God, *patrie*, Family, Work'.[4] Different from Weygand's traditionalist conservatism was the Declaration published on 7 July by the former Radical Gaston Bergery whose disillusion with parliamentary democracy had attracted him increasingly to fascism. His Declaration called for collaboration with Germany, and the organization of an authoritarian new order in France. Ninety-seven *députés* supported this declaration, twenty-nine of them Socialists.[5] The signatories included Marcel Déat, who was also moving towards fascism. On 8 July, he wrote in the newspaper *L'Œuvre*: 'We need, like other peoples who have carried out their revolution, whether Italy, Germany or Russia, a party, a single party, which establishes and orients the shared aspirations of the people.'[6]

The government which Pétain formed on 12 July, consisting largely of representatives of the traditional right, was a disappointment to Bergery, Déat, and other advocates of fascist policies. Déat described it as a 'consortium of old men . . . A team of reactionaries offering the prospect of a sub-Doumergue'.[7] But Déat did not despair. While lobbying Pétain and Laval for the establishment of a single party, Déat set up a committee to work out the details.[8] The committee's report, ready on 27 July, argued that a single party, acting as sole mediator between state and society, would forge a genuine national community.

Although Déat wanted all existing parties and interest groups to be absorbed into this new organization, the members of his committee could not even agree amongst themselves. Bergery wanted to go and study the single parties of Italy,

[4] Weygand, *Recalled to Service*, 229–30.   [5] Burrin, *La Dérive fasciste*, 333–6.
[6] Cointet, *Vichy et le fascisme*, 97.   [7] Burrin, *La Dérive fasciste*, 343.
[8] A. Prost, 'Le Rapport de Déat en faveur d'un parti nationale unique, essai d'analyse lexicale', *Revue française de science politique*, 23/5 (1973), 933–72; J.-P. Cointet, 'Marcel Déat et le parti unique (été 1940)', *RHDGM* 91 (1973), 1–22; Burrin, *La Dérive fasciste*, 346–59; M. Cointet-Labrousse, *Vichy et le fascisme: Les Hommes, les structures et les pouvoirs* (1987).

Germany, and Portugal; Doriot, who sent a representative to the committee, was angling to ensure a predominant role for the PPF; La Rocque put it about that Doriot was in receipt of German funds, and withdrew his support from the committee on 11 August. Even if the organizers had agreed among themselves, the scheme would never had got off the ground because Pétain was not keen on parties of any kind. Weygand and Maurras also intervened to oppose this 'totalitarian' solution. As for Laval, he was suspicious of anything which he did not control.

Pétain suggested that the supporters of a single party go on an exploratory mission around France to prepare the ground. The credulous Déat, not realizing that this was a manoeuvre to get them out of the way, was pleasantly surprised. The committee's discussions continued during August in an increasingly unrealistic atmosphere—one session even considered the party's uniforms—but even Déat knew the game was lost when it was announced on 29 August that Vichy was uniting all war veterans' associations into a single Legion of Veterans. This was not a single party, but Vichy's alternative to it.

Disgusted by the atmosphere of Vichy, and vowing never to set foot there again, on 12 September Déat left for Paris, which was to become the refuge of many disappointed fascist sympathizers.[9] Among these was Lucien Rebatet, one of the most violent journalists on *Je suis partout*, who had also arrived in Vichy during the summer. He and various associates tried to secure key posts in the regime's propaganda services, but they were seen off by Pétain's more traditionalist advisers.[10] As Rebatet later put it: 'after the great upheavals, people resumed their positions . . . Everyone with any fascist or anti-Jewish convictions left for Paris'.[11]

Vichy Governments

The departure of the 'fascists' did not end the power struggles at Vichy. Although claiming to bring efficiency and stability, Vichy's governments were no more stable than those of the Third Republic. In the four years of the regime, there were five education ministers[12] and five interior ministers.[13] Traditional ministerial responsibility did not exist at Vichy. Each minister was directly responsible to Pétain and could be sacked at will. The Council of Ministers met once a week. It was too unwieldy to take decisions, and Pétain did not like large meetings because of his deafness. He preferred to deal with small groups or individuals. Real decisions were taken by a *conseil restreint* of a few key ministers who

---

[9] J.-P. Cointet, *Marcel Déat: Du socialisme au national-socialisme* (1998), 192–3.

[10] Du Moulin, *Le Temps des illusions*, 29–30; Rebatet, *Les Décombres* (1946), 513–36.

[11] *Les Décombres*, 535.

[12] Mireaux (11 July 1940), Ripert (6 Sept.), Chevalier (13 Dec.), Carcopino (24 Feb. 1941), Bonnard (Apr. 1942). Six counting Rivaud from 16 June to 11 July 1940.

[13] Marquet (11 July 1940), Peyrouton (6 Sept.), Darlan (24 Feb. 1941), Pucheu (19 July), Laval (Apr. 1942). Six counting Pomaret from 16 June to 11 July 1940.

met daily in Pétain's office. Influence was also exercised by Pétain's own advisers, concentrated in his civil and military *cabinets* and his Personal Secretariat.

Vichy functioned like a court, albeit a shabby and impoverished one. At the centre of the court was Pétain. To be regularly admitted to dine at his table was a signal honour; Laval was rarely invited. The regime was much exercised by questions of protocol which would have delighted Saint-Simon: was it permissible, for example, for the Secretary-General of the Présidence du Conseil to accompany Pétain in his car or eat at his table?[14] Although Pétain was in remarkable condition for his age, his short-term memory was unreliable, and he tired easily. Visitors took away different impressions depending on the time of day they saw him. Politics was new to Pétain, and he was often unsure what policy to pursue. He frequently took a decision and was then persuaded to reverse it a few hours later, as over the *Massilia*. Pétain tended to listen to the last person he spoke to.

Pétain's doctor, Bernard Ménétrel, whose father had been a close friend of Pétain, exercised considerable influence over him. Ménétrel was like a son to Pétain—there were rumours he was Pétain's natural son—and Pétain loved to play with his children. Given Pétain's robust health, Ménétrel had much time to spare for politics, and he headed Pétain's Personal Secretariat. His office adjoined Pétain's, and he screened Pétain's visitors. 'I had predicted everything', remarked Laval in 1944, 'except that France would be governed by a doctor.'[15] Another influential figure in Pétain's entourage was the Finance Inspector Henri du Moulin de Labarthète, director of Pétain's civil *cabinet*, and author after the war of a cynical account of life at Vichy.

Laval was the dominant figure of the government during the first five months of the regime. Pétain was head of State and prime minister (*président du Conseil*); Laval was deputy prime minister (*vice-président du Conseil*). A ministerial reshuffle on 5 September 1940 removed the five parliamentarians still in the government, leaving Laval as the only one. But the relationship between Laval and Pétain quickly deteriorated. Laval was often in Paris negotiating with the Germans and neglected to keep Pétain informed. Pétain had never found Laval congenial despite all he owed him: Laval's scruffiness offended his sense of order, and he complained that Laval blew cigarette smoke in his face. These resentments were stoked up by Pétain's entourage, and by the many ministers who were jealous of Laval's German contacts, or despised him as the last survivor of the Third Republic. It did not help Laval's reputation at Vichy that he was praised in the Paris press, especially by Déat.

From the autumn of 1940, Pétain's advisers were plotting Laval's removal. They sounded out Flandin as a possible successor. Events were precipitated when Laval arrived at Vichy from Paris on the morning of 13 December with news of

---

[14] M.-O. Baruch, *Servir l'État français: L'Administration en France de 1940 à 1944* (1997), 177.
[15] H. Rousso, *Pétain et la fin de la collaboration: Sigmaringen 1944–1945* (Brussels, 1984), 23.

a theatrical German gesture of goodwill to France. Hitler was offering the return to France of the ashes of Napoleon's son, the Duc de Reichstadt, who had died in Austria. Pétain was invited to Paris for the reception ceremony, and Laval persuaded him that the trip could be followed by a triumphal tour of the Occupied Zone. This idea tickled Pétain's considerable vanity and he called for maps to trace the route.[16]

The anti-Laval conspirators were appalled that their efforts were about to founder. During the afternoon, they worked on Pétain, insinuating that it was Laval's intention to kidnap Pétain and take over the government. Reverting to his original anti-Laval view, Pétain called a special cabinet meeting in the evening where he summoned his ministers to write him resignation letters. The procedure had already been used for cabinet reshuffles, and the unsuspecting Laval assumed that the victim was to be the Minister of Labour, René Belin. Instead, once the letters had been signed, it was Laval who was astonished to find himself dismissed, and put under house arrest. On the next day, Déat was arrested by Vichy's representative in Paris, General de Laurencie. The 13 December crisis, a vivid illustration of Pétain's vanity, suggestibility, and duplicity, was managed in an amateurish cloak-and-dagger style characteristic of Vichy. De Laurencie had previously been informed that the code for Déat's arrest was to be 'The Marshal's wife will cross the demarcation line at 5 o'clock'. But when he received the message, he had forgotten it was a code, and complained at not having more time to make arrangements to receive her.[17]

Laval was succeeded by a triumvirate whose leading figure was Flandin. This government only lasted two months because the Germans, annoyed at Laval's dismissal, refused to do business with it. The deadlock was resolved on 10 February when Admiral Darlan was appointed deputy premier and nominated as dauphin. Darlan had been the driving force behind the expansion of the French navy in the 1930s and admiral of the fleet during the war. A blunt and gruff individual with no time for parliamentary veterans like Laval and Flandin, he preferred the company of technicians and experts. To avoid Laval's mistake of allowing his enemies to become too powerful, Darlan took on several portfolios: the Navy, the Ministry of the Interior, and the Ministry of Foreign Affairs. This did not make for increased efficiency: Darlan held so many offices that in one impersonation he sometimes wrote to himself in another (via subordinates) to refuse a request he had made to himself.[18]

Darlan remained in power from February 1941 until Laval's return to power on 18 April 1942. But even these fourteen months of relative stability were punctuated by plotting and uncertainty. In March 1941 two of Pétain's advisers even warned his wife to watch out in case his coffee had been poisoned.[19] Darlan

---

[16] Cointet, *Pierre Laval*, 322.
[17] Du Moulin, *Le Temps des illusions*, 59–87; Cointet, *Pierre Laval*, 294–326.
[18] Baruch, *Servir l'État*, 186, 455.
[19] *Carnets du Pasteur Boegner 1940–1945*, ed. P. Boegner (1992), 84.

regularly drew up lists of enemies whom he believed to be conspiring to have him removed. In July 1941, he came up with the following: the Germans in co-operation with Laval; Déat and the Paris collaborationists; Pétain's entourage; General Weygand; the British and Americans; various parliamentarians.[20] Darlan's worries about his own situation were part of a general sense in the summer of 1941 that the regime was in crisis because it was failing to carry the French population with it. To improve the government's effectiveness, Darlan gave up the Ministry of the Interior in July, and appointed the industrialist Pierre Pucheu to take it over. On 13 August, Pétain broadcast to the nation that an 'evil wind' of discontent was blowing through the country, and announced tough measures of repression. This did not end Darlan's problems. Pucheu rapidly emerged as the second most powerful man in the government, and his undisguised ambition began to worry Darlan.[21]

Despite the political instability of the Vichy regime, continuities existed between its governments. Members of the armed forces were omnipresent throughout—although the regime had been born out of military disaster. The government formed by Pétain on 12 July contained more military men than any other since Marshal Soult's administration of 1832. In the void which opened up in French society in the summer of 1940, the army was one of the only institutions (along with the Church) to remain intact. Apart from Pétain and Weygand themselves, military figures at Vichy included General Colson, Minister of War (replaced by General Huntziger on 6 September), General Pujo, Air Minister (replaced by General Bergeret on 6 September) and Admiral Platon, Colonial Minister. Darlan gave positions to so many admirals that Cardinal Linéart of Lille remarked that he would probably soon be replaced by an admiral. Military men were not only to be found as ministers. The governorships of France's five most important overseas possessions all went to members of the armed forces; Admiral Bard was Paris Prefect of Police from May 1941 to May 1942; and eight other career officers were appointed as prefects elsewhere.[22]

The regime was partly the revenge of the armed forces over the Republic; it was also, as Yves Bouthillier remarked, the 'triumph of administration over politics'. Under Vichy the line between government and administration was blurred. At the head of each ministry the regime created a new administrative post of Secretary-General on the model of British Permanent Secretaries. They were often as powerful as their ministers. Sometimes when a minister was sacked, his Secretary General replaced him. This happened when Jacques Chevalier became Minister of Education in December 1940, and Marcel Peyrouton Minister of the Interior in September 1940.[23] Members of the administrative corps who had often exercised power behind the scenes now emerged into the limelight. The

---

[20] *Lettres et notes de l'Amiral Darlan*, ed. H. Coutau-Bégarie and C. Huan (1992), 385.
[21] Ibid. 439–508.
[22] Paxton, *Parades and Politics at Vichy*, 140–52; Du Moulin, *Le Temps des illusions*, 139–42.
[23] Baruch, *Servir l'État*, 176–81.

Inspectors of Finance Yves Bouthillier and Paul Baudouin became respectively Minister of Finance (from July 1940 until April 1942) and Minister of Foreign Affairs (from July 1940 until October 1940). The experts who served Vichy were not only from the administration. The engineer Jean Berthelot was Minister of Communications from September 1940 to April 1942, and the agricultural economist Pierre Caziot Minister of Agriculture from July 1940 to April 1942.

Under Darlan the number of experts increased even further. The distinguished classicist Jerôme Carcopino became Minister of Education, and the jurist Joseph Barthélemy Minister of Justice. But a new type of expert, what today would be called technocrats, also came to prominence under Darlan. Mostly in their early forties, they stood out as young in this gerontocratic regime. They were committed not just to efficiency, as was true of administrators like Bouthillier, but also to economic modernization within a German-dominated Europe—a gleaming Europe of autobahns and autoroutes. These technocrats had backgrounds in banking or industry, and had often participated in those reforming groups, like X-Crise or *Nouveaux cahiers*, which proliferated in the 1930s. They included figures like Pierre Pucheu, formerly an international sales director for the French steel industry, who was first Minister of Industrial Production (February 1941–July 1941) and then Minister of the Interior (July 1941–April 1942); Jacques Barnaud, who was in charge of economic relations with the Germans from February 1941 to November 1942; and François Lehideux, Minister of Industrial Production from July 1941 to April 1942. Barnaud had previously worked for the Worms Bank and Lehideux had been a manager at Renault.

These Young Turks aroused much suspicion, and for people whose minds were attuned to conspiracy theories, it was easy to assume that the influence they achieved under Darlan had a sinister explanation. They were rumoured to be members of a secret organization known as the Synarchy, which was allegedly linked to the Worms Bank. The Synarchy had no basis in fact, but Jacques Benoist-Méchin, who was close to this group, writes in his memoirs that they did see themselves as a team, sharing a similar outlook and dining regularly together.[24]

The National Revolution: Doctrine

The Synarchy rumour was partly invented by conservatives around Pétain who felt that Darlan's team did not share their vision of the National Revolution. The truth was that they needed someone to blame when it appeared that the National Revolution was not working. One problem was that people had very different ideas about it. Inasmuch as there was an official version of the

[24] J. Benoist-Méchin, *A l'épreuve du temps: Souvenirs II: 1940–1947* (1989), 51–63; R. Kuisel, 'The Legend of the Vichy Synarchy', *FHS* 6/3 (1970), 365–98; O. Dard, *La Synarchie: Le Mythe du complot permanent* (1998).

National Revolution it was contained in Pétain's speeches—although Pétain himself disliked the term Revolution and only used it four times, preferring to talk of *redressement* or *rénovation.*

The National Revolution defined itself first and foremost in opposition to liberal individualism which uprooted people from the 'natural' communities of family, workplace, and region. Such communities supposedly offered 'real' freedoms unlike the abstract and hollow rights vaunted by liberals. Once society was reorganized hierarchically into organic communities, the class struggle would become redundant: the liberal obsession with rights would be replaced by a stress on duties. These duties were adumbrated in 1941 in fifteen 'Principles of the Community' which were offered as Vichy's answer to the Declaration of Rights of 1789.[25]

The most important community was the family, which Pétain declared in September 1940 to be the 'essential cell' of the social order: 'the rights of the family precede those of the State and the individual'. A law of 11 October 1940 forbade the employment of married women in the public sector; in April 1941 a law made divorce much more difficult to obtain; the regime missed no opportunity to extol the virtues of motherhood. Strengthening the family was also seen as a first step towards regenerating French youth. A Youth Secretariat (SGJ), run by the Catholic engineer Georges Lamirand, was set up to coordinate youth policies. All 22 year olds had to carry out six months' civic training in Chantiers de la jeunesse (Youth Work Sites). Partly functioning as a replacement for military service, these were intended to instil moral values in the young. There was also a new youth movement called the Compagnons de France. It was a voluntary organization, but the regime strongly encouraged people to join.

When Pétain celebrated the community of the workplace, he was thinking above all of artisans whom he addressed in a message in May 1941: 'there is no chance of the class struggle in the artisan's workshop'. He was also thinking of peasants who were portrayed as exemplifying hard work, discipline, and tradition: 'the land does not lie' was one of Pétain's most famous phrases (coined for him by the urban Jew Emmanuel Berl). Propaganda depicted Pétain as the Marshal-Peasant. In April 1941, he declared: 'France will become again what she should never have ceased to be: an essentially agricultural nation.' Subsidies were introduced to encourage a return to the land (May 1941). A law was passed in March 1941 making it easier to regroup parcels of land into single units. *Instituteurs* were required to teach basic agricultural skills. The most important measure relating to the countryside was the Peasant Charter of 2 December 1940 that instituted a corporatist framework for agriculture. Each locality was to organize a single peasant syndicate. Ascending from village to region, these would

---

[25] P. Pétain, *Discours aux Français*; H. Rousso, 'Qu'est ce que la Révolution nationale', *Histoire*, 129 (1990), 96–102; J.-M. Guillon, 'La Philosophie politique de la Révolution nationale', in *VEF*, 167–83; L. Gervereau, 'Y-a-t-il un "style Vichy"', in id. and Peschanski, *La Propagande sous Vichy*, 110–47.

form a national Peasant Corporation running agriculture in the interests of the peasantry without government interference.[26]

The celebration of the peasantry went hand in hand with the promotion of regional culture and folklore. In September 1940, Pétain sent a message of encouragement to the organizers of the 110th anniversary of the birth of Frédéric Mistral, founder of the Provençal regionalist movement. Regional costumes appeared on stamps, and architects were exhorted to build in regional styles. From December 1941 teachers were allowed to teach optional classes in dialect. The Legion of Veterans in the Landes celebrated the Marshal (Lou Manescou) in patois. Henri Pourrat, who won the 1941 Prix Goncourt for *Vent de Mars*, the latest of his regionalist works on the Auvergne, acquired almost the status of an official author. Marc Bloch wrote that Vichy was turning France into a 'vast antiquarian museum'.[27]

Some people had no place in Vichy's France of rootedness and regions. Pourrat wrote in 1940: 'the Jew, the epitome of the intellectual, is by his race fundamentally opposed to the peasant in all his being'.[28] At the apex of the communities of family, workplace, and region stood the community of the nation which had to be purged of undesirable elements: foreigners, Jews, Freemasons, and Communists. As Pétain said in September 1940: 'There is no possible neutrality between good and evil, order and disorder, France and anti-France.'

Exclusionary laws were among the first measures enacted by the regime. From 12 July, only a child of a French father could be member of a ministerial *cabinet*. Five days later, this exclusion was extended to public servants (including teachers), then to doctors, dentists, and pharmacists (16 August), and finally lawyers (10 September). In effect, these measures created a second class of French citizens whose families were deemed not to have been French sufficiently long. In addition, on 22 July, a commission was instituted to revise naturalizations that had occurred since 1927. Between 1940 and 1944, this body stripped 15,000 people of their citizenship (6,000 of them Jews).[29] Foreign refugees living in France were forced into 'foreign work units' (GTEs). The spirit behind these measures was revealed by the repeal, on 27 August 1940, of the 1939 Marchandeau decree prohibiting the publication of material inciting racial hatred. Nonetheless the precedents for Vichy's first measures against foreigners dated back to the 1930s. Vichy was only extending legislation which had been started under the Republic, and this eased the transition to laws specifically directed against Jews even if they were not foreign. The first of these laws was the Jewish Statute of 3 October which excluded *French* Jews from public service employment and from 'professions that influence people' (teaching, the cinema, press).

---

[26] G. Wright, *The Rural Revolution in France: The Peasantry in Twentieth Century France* (Stanford, Calif., 1964), 75–94.

[27] Faure, *Le Projet culturel de Vichy*, 65–88, 126–34, 200–12.   [28] Ibid. 119.

[29] B. Laguerre, 'Les Dénaturalisés de Vichy', *VSRH* 20 (1988), 3–15.

A second Statute, in July 1941, extended the list of exclusions, and was followed by quotas on Jewish employment in a whole series of professions. These two Statutes affected Jews whose families might have been French for generations. As for foreign Jews, from 4 October 1940 prefects were given the power to intern them.

The new regime also acted against political 'undesirables'. From 17 July 1940 public servants could be sacked without any formalities. The Fifth Constitutional Act set up a Supreme Court to try those 'responsible for the defeat': Blum, Reynaud, and others were interned while awaiting trial. On 13 August, 'secret societies'—which meant Freemasons—were outlawed, and civil servants had to swear that they had never belonged to a secret society and would never do so. On 3 September prefects were authorized to intern anyone judged dangerous for national security. This was primarily aimed at Communists who started to be rounded up in the autumn of 1940. By June 1941—before Germany's invasion of the Soviet Union and the Communist entry into armed resistance—between 4,000 and 5,000 Communists had been arrested. At the end of 1940 the internment camp population stood at about 55,000–60,000, consisting largely of foreign Jewish refugees, former members of the International Brigades, and French Communists. They were interned in about thirty camps scattered mainly throughout the Southern Zone, and in Algeria. These were French camps which had nothing to do with the Germans, many of them indeed dating from the late 1930s.[30]

From the beginning, then, Vichy was a regime of persecution and repression. It was also authoritarian and anti-democratic. The regime believed in hierarchy and elites. Local democracy was eliminated when elected departmental councils (*conseils généraux*) were replaced by appointed *commissions administratives* (12 October 1940). In localities with a population over 2,000, elected mayors were replaced (16 November) by appointed ones, and the municipal councils were named from a list provided by them; in localities with a population under 2,000, municipal councils could be dissolved at the discretion of the prefect.

The National Revolution: Sources

What was the inspiration behind the National Revolution? The main contemporary model was the Portuguese *Estado novo* of Salazar whose volume of collected speeches was on Pétain's table. The four parts into which this volume was divided—National Revolution, Principles of a New Order, New State, Corporative Economy—coincided perfectly with Vichy's project. The French 1942 edition of the speeches noted the similarities explicitly:

---

[30] D. Peschanski, 'Exclusion, persécution et répression', in *VEF*, 209–34; id., *Vichy 1940–1944: Contrôle et exclusion*, 87–100 (there were another 25,000 internees in North Africa). See below, Appendix, for a map and list of the camps.

Like Salazar, the declared enemy of destructive Communism, [Pétain] distances himself from Nazism and Communism, rightly believing that a totalitarian system does not correspond to the French temperament . . . Like Salazar, Marshal Pétain does not want a Single Party which under the pretext of supporting the State in fact dominates it.[31]

Salazar himself had been influenced by France's leading theorist of counter-revolution Charles Maurras, and the National Revolution owed much to the tradition of counter-revolutionary thought in France from de Maistre to Maurras via Le Play and La Tour du Pin.[32] But although *Action française* supported Pétain until the end, its direct influence on the regime should not be exaggerated. Maurras edited the newpapaper from Lyons, was rarely at Vichy, and had few meetings with Pétain.[33] The most high-profile Action française sympathizer in the government was Raphaël Alibert, Minister of Justice until January 1941. In the early days of the regime, Alibert was a powerful figure, helping to draft the first constitutional acts, and the first anti-Semitic measures. Some histories of Vichy make Alibert the evil genius of the first months of the regime, describing him as fanatical to the point of mental instability: he is described, after his sacking, as wandering around shaking his fist at Vichy's Hôtel du Parc. But the temptation to turn him into a scapegoat for the early policies of repression should be resisted. There was no significant opposition to the measures he proposed. Alibert was influential partly because, as a jurist, he was skilled at drafting laws.[34]

Other people who could broadly be categorized as 'Maurrassian' were Weygand, Vichy's proconsul in North Africa from September 1940, and Xavier Vallat, Vichy's Commissioner for Jewish Affairs from March 1941 to March 1942. Maurrassians were to be found not so much in the government as in Pétain's own entourage. The list includes aides like Generals Émile Laure and Charles Brécard; the Secretary-General of the Presidency of the Council, Admiral Fernet; and also such figures as Dumoulin de Labarthète, Ménétrel, René Gillouin, and Henri Massis. But although many of these people defined the tone of the National Revolution—Massis, Gillouin, and Dumoulin helped write several of Pétain's speeches—their real power should not be exaggerated.

Another distinctive milieu at Vichy was the group in charge of youth policy which had close links with conservative social Catholicism and with the Catholic scouting movement. Georges Lamirand, head of the SGJ, had been a vice-president of Robert Garric's Équipes sociales; Henri Dhavernas, founder of the Compagnons, and General de la Porte de Theil, founder of the Chantiers de la jeunesse, were both involved in the scouting movement; and Marcel-Denys Forestier, one of the leaders of the Catholic Rover Scouts, was appointed chap-

---

[31] Ferro, *Pétain*, 216.

[32] O. Wormser, *Les Origines doctrinales de la 'Révolution nationale'* (1971).

[33] E. Weber, *Action française* (Stanford, Calif., 1962), 446, says there were three public and six private meetings.

[34] Barthélemy, *Mémoires*, 44–5; M. Martin du Gard, *Chronique de Vichy 1940–1944* (1975), 123.

lain general of the Chantiers. Many members of this group drew inspiration from Lyautey: Lamirand's book *Le Rôle social de l'ingénieur* (1937) (with a preface by Lyautey) had tried to apply Lyautey's ideas about leadership to the factory.[35] The influence which this group acquired at Vichy from the summer of 1940 owed much to the patronage of Paul Baudouin who shared many of their views, and had in 1939 written an article in the *Revue des jeunes* calling on Catholic youth to form a new chivalry to defend the values of European civilization.

Action française traditionalists gave the regime its tone; social Catholics colonized one specific area of policy. Neither of them had as much influence at Vichy as the liberal conservatives. Apart from the already-mentioned cases of Flandin and Joseph Barthélemy, these included Lucien Romier, who was a Minister of State from August 1941, and Henri Moysset, an academic who had advised many inter-war politicians including Tardieu. Moysset became Secretary-General to the President of the Council in February 1941 and entered the government as Minister of State from August 1941 to April 1942. Such people had not been bitter enemies of the Republic or excluded from influence under it, but they had been influenced by the Maurrassian critique of democracy, and their presence at Vichy is testimony to the long-term corrosive effect of Action française on French liberalism. They did not subscribe to all aspects of Maurras's counter-revolutionary programme: their ideal was the Orleanist notion of government by the *compétences*. The presence in government of figures like Carcopino, Barthélemy, Bouthillier, or Berthelot seemed to embody that ideal perfectly.

One Vichy institution very much in the spirit of Orleanist liberalism was the Conseil national. Created in February 1941 by Flandin, the Conseil was a non-elective consultative assembly of worthies designed to give the regime a more liberal façade by building bridges to moderate conservative opinion. Seventy-eight of its 188 members were former parliamentarians. It also included non-political celebrities like the pianist Alfred Cortot, the physicist Louis de Broglie, two members of the Académie française, and some clerics. Flandin himself had left power once the Conseil had been formed, and because Pétain was irritated by the presence of so many parliamentarians, it was forbidden to sit in full session, and only permitted to convene its specialized commissions.[36]

One of the Conseil's commissions was instructed to draft the new constitution. It was chaired by Barthélemy who was certainly the most important influence on the new constitution. A version was ready by the end of 1941, although it was never promulgated. It lay somewhere between the authoritarianism of the Second Empire and the Orleanist ideal of a republic of notables. The first article read: 'the French State is national and authoritarian'. Article 8 read: 'the authority of the State is incarnated in its head. He alone decides after listening to his councillors and gathering the wishes of the nation.' There was to be a Grand

---

[35] B. Comte, *Une utopie combattante: L'École des cadres d'Uriage* (1991), 27–49.
[36] M. Cointet, *Le Conseil national de Vichy 1940–1944* (1989); G. Rossi-Landi, 'Le Conseil national', in FNSP, *Le Gouvernement de Vichy*, 47–54.

Council of 220 members representing the elites and appointed by the head of State, and a National Council of 300 members selected by provincial assemblies, professional groups, war veterans, and heads of families.[37]

The presence of liberal conservatives at Vichy is a reminder that it would be wrong to limit the inspiration, and appeal, of the National Revolution to the traditionalist right. The themes of family, authority, regionalism, communitarianism, and anti-Semitism had a much wider constituency. Not all those who believed in strengthening the family would have accepted the conservative organicist social theory which underpinned Maurrassian views of the family; not all those who wanted a stronger executive welcomed the abandonment of democracy. But there were enough overlaps to create a tentative consensus and sustain a certain ambiguity. To Maurras's chagrin, Vichy never formally renounced the Republic; 14 July remained, in theory, a national holiday. Pétain's head appeared on several series of 'État français' stamps—the first time this had happened to any living head of State since Napoleon III—but the pre-war stamps of the République française continued to appear.[38] Busts of Pétain were supposed to replace Marianne in the town halls, but the tricolour flag was retained, as was the Marseillaise. Rarely had the Marseillaise been more sung as the regime desperately attempted to cling on to the symbols of French patriotism. Pétain said that he preferred the verse beginning 'Sacred love of the Fatherland', but on his regional tours he was often greeted with the Republican refrain 'Aux armes citoyens'.[39]

It is clear from this brief survey that all strands of French conservatism were present at Vichy, but there were also representatives of the left, although they were never more than a small minority. The only one in the government was the trade unionist René Belin, Minister of Labour from July 1940 until April 1942.[40] Many of the former *Syndicats* group in the CGT joined Belin in his support of Vichy. Given Belin's pacifism and anti-communism, his presence at Vichy is not so surprising. Belin, however, was never at ease in the government, and there were constant rumours that he was to be dismissed.[41]

Conflicts I: Education

Maurrassians, social Catholics, conservative liberals, syndicalists: this is not an exhaustive list of the political sensibilities represented at Vichy but it is enough to demonstrate the regime's considerable diversity. According to Charles Rist, if Vichy had an ideology, it was not so much 'integral nationalism' as 'integral con-

---

[37] Cointet, *Le Conseil national*, 123–79.

[38] Bertrand-Dorléac, *L'Art de la défaite*, 129–30.

[39] N. Dompnier, *Vichy à travers les chants* (1996), 55–68.

[40] Until Feb. 1941 he was also Minister of Industrial Production.

[41] D. Bidussa and D. Peschanski (eds.), *La France de Vichy: Archives inédites d'Angelo Tasca* (Milan, 1996), 169–74.

fusionism'.[42] Hoffmann describes the regime as a 'pluralist dictatorship'. Whatever their differences, however, those who participated in the regime were bound
together by the conviction that Germany had won the war. They all had scores
to settle—whether with the Communists (as in the case of Belin), with the
Popular Front (the case of Laval), or with the Third Republic as a whole (the
case of Alibert). They all agreed that the new regime would be authoritarian,
anti-individualist, and anti-Semitic. But this left many questions unanswered.
How much influence should be given to the Church in education? What was
the most desirable relationship between state and society? How should labour
relations be regulated? On these matters, there were differences of outlook
between corporatists and syndicalists; clericals and anticlericals; centralizers and
regionalists; fascists and conservatives.

These conflicts were complex and cannot be reduced to any simple pattern.
The most extreme polarity was between those favouring an organicist, Catholic
society and a decentralized, minimalist State and those who favoured an interventionist State, mobilizing activist popular support and working for economic
rationalization and efficiency. Broadly speaking, this could be described as a distinction between 'traditionalists' and 'modernizers'. Of course, some people do
not fit either term neatly. Alibert, supposedly a Maurassian (hence a traditionalist), had also been in Redressement français (hence a modernizer). Darlan may
have been a modernizer when it came to the economy, but he was a traditionalist when it came to the family. Many social Catholics were traditionalists regarding morality and social policy but modernizers in respect of the economy. Many
liberal conservatives were mildly anticlerical and anti-corporatist, which separated
them from the traditionalists; but they were laissez-faire about economic policy
which distinguished them from the more interventionist modernizers. Certain
conflicts, for example between corporatists and syndicalists, do not fit the
dichotomy between traditionalists and modernizers. Nonetheless, providing these
two labels are used loosely, they provide a rough guide to the power struggles,
and factional infighting, at Vichy. Three issues were particularly contested: education; the relationship between state and society; economic and social policy.

In education, the conflict revolved around the degree of influence to be
granted to the Church. All conservatives agreed that France had been undermined by pacifist and godless *instituteurs*, and there was general approval when,
in September 1940, Vichy abolished the special colleges (Écoles normales) in
which these teachers were trained. But did the National Revolution also imply
a reversal of the secular laws which were the cornerstone of Republican education? A series of measures promulgated in the autumn of 1940 seemed to imply
that it did. Religious orders were given back their right to teach (September
1940); the Caisse d'écoles, a charitable fund for needy parents, was for the first
time made available to Catholic pupils (October 1940); 'duties to God' were

---

[42] Kuisel, *Capitalism and the State*, 131.

reinserted into the primary school syllabus (November 1940); local authorities were authorized to subsidize Catholic schools (January 1940). Most controversially of all, religious instruction was introduced as an optional subject in State schools (January 1941). Parents wishing their children to undergo religious instruction had previously had to arrange this themselves. Now it could occur in school time and on school premises: priests could enter State schools for the first time since the 1880s.

The last two measures were the work of the philosopher Jacques Chevalier who became Education Minister in December 1940. Chevalier was a devout Catholic who had been invited by Franco to prepare a plan for the reform of Spanish education. His seventy-two days as minister were the high point of Catholic influence over education, but his measures aroused considerable alarm, and he was moved to another portfolio in Darlan's ministry. Darlan, who described himself in January 1941 as 'ferociously anticlerical', had no intention of bowing to the Church lobby.[43] His Minister of Education, the classical scholar Jerôme Carcopino, reversed almost all the measures described above, apart from the abolition of Écoles normales and the decree authorizing religious orders to teach.

This did not mean that the Church gained nothing. Carcopino's defence of the religious neutrality of State schools was less rigid than the Republic's. Religious instruction was now allowed a place in the timetable and could be taught in school time (but not on school premises) for those who wished it. Following a personal intervention by Pétain, in November 1941 Carcopino offered State subsidies to Catholic schools in need. Although he presented this as a provisional emergency measure, it was a significant breach with republican practice. Overall the relationship between State education and religion remained delicate. When Darlan heard in April that many schools were taking advantage of the new climate to flout the 1880s secular laws and put up crucifixes in schools, he ordered prefects to forbid this; two months later he was forced to back down and accept the practice where it conformed to local tradition.[44]

Carcopino's reversal of Chevalier's reforms was a defeat for the most extreme Catholic traditionalist position. But Carcopino himself represented a different version of traditionalism inspired by the Cercle Fustel de Coulanges, an educational lobbying organization close to Action française, and opposed to the democratization of education promoted by the Cartel des Gauches in 1924 and the Popular Front in 1936. Léon Bérard, a leading member of the Cercle, had been one of Carcopino's main academic patrons. Carcopino was also inspired by the example of the École des roches, founded by Édmond Demolins, a disciple of the conservative thinker le Play, and modelled on the British public school. In the inter-war years it became the favoured school of the French bourgeoisie.

---

[43] *Lettres et notes*, 456.
[44] W. Halls, *Youth of Vichy France*, 62–82; Giolitto, *Histoire de la jeunesse sous Vichy*, 159–79; N. Atkin, *Church and Schools in Vichy France* (1991), 18–28, 48–51.

Carcopino's father had been its doctor and his son-in-law was its director; Jean Borotra, who was in charge of Vichy's sporting programme, sent his children there. There was a small, but influential, École des roches lobby at Vichy.[45]

A major feature of Carcopino's important education reforms, promulgated in August 1941, was the re-establishment of fees in the higher classes of the secondary education system, which had been gradually abolished by the left in the inter-war years. Carcopino also upgraded the status of technical and higher elementary schools by according them the rank of full secondary schools. Access to secondary education was acquired by the new Diploma of Primary Preparatory Studies to be taken at 11. Although this had been intended to discourage pupils from trying to enter secondary education, it had the opposite effect. On the vexed question of the role of classics in education, Carcopino, despite being himself a classicist, did not accept the full demands of the conservative Latin lobby. Latin was made compulsory for all *lycée* pupils, but other secondary schools were permitted to teach a modern language curriculum. Carcopino's reforms were therefore more complex than a simple implementation of the most conservative educational agenda.[46]

Conflicts II: State and Society: The Fascist Temptation

No theme was dearer to the traditionalists than regionalism. For Maurrassians, the celebration of regions was inspired by an idealized vision of the provinces of the *ancien régime*. In July 1940, Pétain announced that 'governors will be placed at the head of the great French provinces', and the Conseil national was instructed to draft a regional constitution. By August 1941, it had produced a division of France into twenty regions (the term sounded less *ancien régime* than provinces) each with an appointive regional assembly and a governor. This regional map took no account of the actual divisions into which the Occupation had divided the country, a characteristic piece of wish fulfilment. This did not matter because nothing came of these schemes. The governors' names remained in the yellow file where Pétain kept them. Meanwhile, in April 1941, Darlan had created the new post of regional prefect to strengthen the government's powers in its difficult task of organizing scarce food supplies. Thus Vichy got its regions, but in a spirit entirely at odds with the original intention: as a reinforcement of state control not a return to 'natural communities'.[47]

The creation of regional prefects was the prelude to the increasingly repressive policies of the regime during the summer of 1941. These were announced in Pétain's speech about the 'evil wind'. This was an admission that the National Revolution was not proving popular; it was also possibly an oblique reference to

[45] S. Corcy-Debray, 'Jérôme Carcopino: Du triomphe à la roche tarpéienne', *VSRH* 58 (1998), 70–82.

[46] Halls, *Youth of Vichy France*, 22–32; Giolitto, *Histoire de la jeunesse sous Vichy*, 213–48.

[47] P. Barral, 'Idéologie et pratique du régionalisme dans le régime de Vichy', *Revue française de science politique*, 24 (1974), 911–39; Faure, *Le Projet culturel*, 93–104; M. Cointet, *Le Conseil national*, 183–216.

the first stirrings of the Resistance. But almost immediately after that speech, the Resistance entered a new stage when the Communist Party embarked on a policy of terrorism. The first terrorist attack occurred on 21 August with the shooting of a German naval cadet in a Paris metro station. The government responded by announcing that suspected Communists would be tried by 'special sections' of courts martial, ready to act expeditiously, vigorously, and retrospectively.

This was only the most radical of a range of measures designed to counter the 'evil wind'. Political parties were suspended (a symbolic measure since parliament had not met since July 1940), a new anti-Masonic law was passed (20 August) and lists of Freemasons were published. In Paris, the Prefecture of Police resuscitated the 'Special Brigades' (BS) which had originally been created during the Phoney War to crack down on the Communists. Finally, on 7 September 1941, a State Tribunal was set up to judge 'terrorists' and pronounce the death sentence without the possibility of appeal.

Pucheu not only aimed to suppress dissent; he also wanted to mobilize popular support more systematically. In this he was supported by members of Darlan's government who were interested in experimenting with fascist-style methods of propaganda and political organization. This was particularly true of Jacques Benoist-Méchin and Paul Marion who exercised considerable influence despite only having junior posts. Marion was in effect minister of propaganda, and Benoist-Méchin had responsibility for relations with Germany. Their presence in the government reopened the issue of Vichy's relationship to fascism.[48]

Jacques Benoist-Méchin had been a journalist in the 1930s and a member of the Comité France-Allemagne. The passion of his life was the search for Franco-German reconciliation—he had written a history of the German army and translated a book on France by the well-known German writer Curtius—and it was this which drove him to fascism. He wrote in his memoirs that France should have joined the war against Britain and 'aligned her institutions on those of the totalitarian power'.[49] Paul Marion was a quintessential representative of that generation whose political anchors had been destroyed by the Great War. He had been a Communist until 1929, studying at the Leninist School in Moscow. After this he passed through a number of stages—Luchaire's *Notre Temps*, the Socialists, the neo-Socialists—before ending up in the PPF which he left after Munich. The only consistency in Marion's career was a rejection of liberalism, and a restless search for an energetic politics. He was fascinated by totalitarian methods of propaganda on which he wrote a book entitled *Leur combat: Lénine, Mussolini, Hitler, Franco* (1939). Drieu la Rochelle said of Marion: 'he was a true fascist . . . he had that mixture of love and irreducible hatred which character-

---

[48] On Vichy and fascism see R. Bourderon, 'Le Régime de Vichy était-il fasciste? Essai d'approche de la question', *RHDGM* (1973), 22–45; A. Slama, 'Vichy était-il fasciste?', *VSRH* II (1986), 41–54; Cointet-Labrousse, *Vichy et le fascisme*, 241–8.

[49] *De la défaite au désastre*, i. *Les Occasions manquées* (1984), 37.

izes real revolutionaries'.[50] Like Marion, Pucheu had also been in the PPF. This was also true of many of the advisers who staffed the *cabinets* of the technocrats: Robert Loustau and Yves Paringaux who were in Pucheu's *cabinet*, Claude Popelin in Lehideux's *cabinet*, and Maurice Touzé who was an aide to Marion. If there was a mafia at Vichy in 1941, it was not the imaginary synarchy, but the fascist network of former members of the PPF. Drieu, another ex-PPF member, was friendly with both Benoist-Méchin and Marion, and regularly met them during this period.[51]

After rejecting a single party in August 1940, the regime still had to devise a means of articulating the relationship between State and society. In theory, this role fell to the Legion of Veterans which was called upon to be the 'ears and eyes' of the Marshal. By February 1941, the Legion had 590,000 members, as well as a newspaper and a daily radio slot. But there were two problems with the Legion. First, being limited to a single—and ageing—category of the population, it was too exclusive. Secondly, its leaders saw themselves as personally loyal to Pétain, but not necessarily to his government as a whole. It was difficult to define their relationship to the administration, and conflicts frequently occurred between local Legion leaders and prefects. In April 1941 Darlan issued guidelines to clarify the situation. While the Legion was allowed the 'right and even the duty' to inform the authorities about breaches of the National Revolution, *légionnaires* were reminded that they were supposed to assist the prefects, not supplant them. Unfortunately this instruction was too ambiguous to resolve the situation.[52]

Given the Legion's shortcomings, Vichy looked for other ways to build links between State and society. The Conseil national was one such attempt, but it had no power. Another initiative was the Amicale de France, founded in November 1940 by Ménétrel and other Pétain aides, as a pawn in their battle with Laval. The Amicale had a network of Équipes du Maréchal which were supposed to spread the gospel of the National Revolution. In January 1941, Dumoulin de Labarthète, another Pétain aide, sponsored yet another idea: the Comité du rassemblement pour la Révolution nationale. Vichy intrigues were so complicated that it is impossible to be sure what Dumoulin's motives were in this case. Perhaps he wanted a possible foil to Flandin's Conseil national. The Comité contained members of the Legion, the PPF, and the PSF, but it never got off the ground because these groups could not agree amongst themselves. By the spring, Dumoulin's Comité had ceased to exist.[53]

This was the situation when Marion took over propaganda in January 1941. Immediately he set about organizing a network of propaganda delegates in each

---

[50] *Fragment de mémoires* (1982), 85–6.   [51] Ibid. 62–108.

[52] Cointet, *La Légion française*, 113–27.

[53] Ibid. 102–11; P. Nicolle, *Cinquante mois d'armistice 2 juillet–26 août: Journal d'un témoin*, 2 vols. (1947), i. 168–201; P. Amaury, *De l'information et de la propagande d'État: Les Deux Premières Expériences d'un 'ministère de l'Information' en France* (1969).

département and created a training school for them at Mayet de la Montagne. Marion intended these propaganda cadres to provide the embryo of a future single party. As a step in this direction, he took over the previously independent Amicale de France. In terms reminiscent of Goebbels, Marion declared that he wished to create a new type of Frenchman like a sculptor moulding his clay.[54] In the summer of 1941, he found an ally in Pucheu who was coming to believe that the regime needed a single party or some similar organization.[55] Pucheu hoped to get the co-operation of La Rocque whose PSF cadres still represented a considerable force. But La Rocque was unco-operative, so Pucheu and Marion turned their attention to the Legion, bringing it under closer government control in order to make it more like a single party. From November 1941, it was opened to non-veterans and its name changed to the 'French Legion of Combatants and Volunteers for the National Revolution'. But none of this made much difference. The Legion's leader, François Valentin, hung on to his independence, and just as the Legion was being given a more important role, its membership was starting to decline.[56]

The 'fascists' also had designs on youth policy. In the summer of 1940, at the same time as rejecting a single party, Vichy had also rejected the idea of a single youth movement on the model of the fascist regimes. Lamirand, head of the SGJ, had wanted to promulgate a youth charter requiring every young person to join a youth movement, only to abandon this idea in the face of Church hostility. But Lamirand never intended to create a single youth movement. This idea was explicitly ruled out by Pétain on 13 August 1940: 'all existing movements will be maintained and their specificity will be recognized'. Youth movements were required to apply for official accreditation (*agrément*), but this was granted liberally. In June 1941, it was accorded to all six scouting movements—including even the Jewish scouts (ÉIF). The regime's youth policy thus conformed to the definition offered by the Church in July 1941: 'A united youth? Yes . . . A single youth? No.' The only obligation imposed on the young was the Chantiers de la jeunesse.[57]

Marion found the SGJ too tolerant and insufficiently directive. In May 1941, he tried to secure control of the Compagnons de France and impose his protégé, Armand Petitjean, as its head. This was unsuccessful, and instead Marion tried to build up another youth movement, the Youth of France and Overseas (JFOM), which was more overtly political than the Compagnons. Despite Marion's incursions into his territory, Lamirand succeeded in keeping youth policy under the control of the SGJ. But the SGJ itself was not homogeneous.

[54] D. Peschanski, 'Vichy au singulier, Vichy au pluriel: Une tentative avortée de l'encadrement de société 1941–1942', *Annales ESC,* 43 (1988), 639–61; Peschanski, *Vichy 1940–1944,* 39–57; Amaury, *De l'information et de la propagande d'État,* 176–202.

[55] Nicolle, *Cinquante mois d'armistice,* i. 318, 331.

[56] Cointet, *La Légion française,* 132–73; Coutau-Bégarie and Huan, *Darlan,* 499–501.

[57] Halls, *Youth of Vichy France,* 132–57; Comte, *Une utopie combattante,* 155–62, 311–69.

Lamirand's immediate subordinate, Louis Garrone, a high-minded Catholic, who had taught at the École des roches, shared the same outlook as Lamirand, while the head of the SGJ's propaganda in the Occupied Zone, Georges Pelorson, had more affinity with Marion.

In March 1942, youth policy was debated by a commission of the Conseil national. Pétain opened the proceedings by reaffirming his opposition to a single youth movement. Representatives of the Churches, both Catholic and Protestant, defended pluralism. On the other side, Pucheu attacked the 'boy scout' and 'churchy' (*calotin*) spirit of the SGJ's policies, and claimed that the churches were too marked by the past to be able to train the cadres which the new France required. Pelorson argued the same, and so did Gaston Bergery who claimed that a single youth movement could create the classless society he believed to exist in Germany. The spokesmen of Pétain's *cabinet*—Massis and Dumoulin—agreed that the SGJ was too tolerant, but rejected moves towards 'totalitarianism'. In the end it was agreed to create a new non-confessional movement which would absorb the Compagnons and JFOM. This seemed like a concession to Pucheu, but before the decision became effective, Laval had returned to power, and Pucheu left the government.[58]

Conflicts III: The Economy

Social and economic policy was the area in which the rhetoric of the National Revolution was hardest to implement. In theory, the guiding principle was corporatism on which Pétain delivered two speeches in 1941. The problem was that the term was open to various interpretations. Was it about overcoming class conflict and institutionalizing conciliation between capital and labour? Was it about forcing industries into compulsory organizations whose decisions were binding on their members? The former view was inspired by the traditionalist ideal of the organic society; the latter view saw industrial organization as the key to modernization. The two shared only a common rejection of liberalism.[59]

After months of wrangling, Vichy's corporatist aspirations were enshrined in the Labour Charter published in October 1941.[60] The delay arose from differences between, on one hand, the traditionalist corporatists in Pétain's *cabinet*, who wanted workers and employers in each industry to be represented in single bodies, and, on the other, the syndicalists, around Belin at the Ministry of Labour, who wished to preserve separate representation for trades unions, although 'disciplined' within an overall corporate structure. The negotiations were so acrimonious that even after a final draft had been agreed, Belin had to literally occupy the building where the government printing presses were located

---

[58] Comte, *Une utopie combattante*, 400–19; Halls, *Youth of Vichy*, 143–57; Cointet, *Le Conseil national*, 272–91; Giolitto, *Histoire de la jeunesse sous Vichy*, 466–8.

[59] Le Crom, *Syndicats nous voilà*, 21–103.

[60] Ibid. 121–44; J. Julliard, 'La Charte du travail', in FNSP, *Le Gouvernement de Vichy*, 157–94.

so that the opposing faction, led by members of Pétain's military cabinet, would not try and alter the text at the last moment. The result was a muddled document closer to the corporatists than the syndicalists. It prescribed exclusive and obligatory syndicates for five categories of occupation—employers, cadres, foremen, white-collar employees, workers—grouped into twenty-nine 'professional families'. Strikes were outlawed. Social committees, intended to resolve welfare problems in the workplace, would be set up in every factory. Since the committees were organized on a tripartite basis, representing employers, workers, and cadres (engineers, middle managers), the workers were likely to be outvoted. Implementing this system was slow and cumbersome, and it was greeted with indifference by workers and employers.

Indifference was an appropriate response since the key decisions about running the economy had already been taken. These were determined more by immediate practical problems than by the finer points of corporatist theory. In the summer of 1940 three serious economic dangers loomed: the prospect of a systematic pillage of French industry by Germany; the inevitability of raw materials shortages resulting from the British blockade; and the spectre of unemployment once arms production had ceased. To confront this situation, the government rapidly improvised a battery of controls. There was a new Ministry of Supply, an entirely remodelled Ministry of Industrial Production, which was employing 16,000 civil servants by 1944, and a Commissariat responsible for implementing infrastructure projects (DGEN). The keystone of the system was the hastily drafted law of 16 August 1940 authorizing each branch of industry to create 'organization committees' (COs).[61]

The idea behind the COs was defensive: to oblige the Germans to negotiate with industries by sector instead of picking off firms one by one.[62] Each CO was run by a chairman and small management committee. They were empowered to carry out a census of the available stocks in their sector, allocate scarce resources, fix prices, and recommend plant closures. In reality, the power of COs was limited by the government's control over raw materials through the Central Bureau for the Distribution of Industrial Materials (OCPRI). This organism was set up in September 1940 at the behest of the Germans, who monopolized access to most raw materials, and intended French industry to work for them. OCPRI allocated raw materials to the COs which redistributed them among the industries in their sector. This gave enormous power to the Secretary-General of the Ministry of Industrial Production, Jean Bichelonne, who was in charge of OCPRI.

[61] H. Rousso, 'Les Paradoxes de Vichy et de l'Occupation', in P. Fridenson and A. Straus (eds.), *Le Capitalisme français: Blocages et dynamisme d'une croissance* (1987), 67–82; id., 'L'Organisation industrielle de Vichy', *RHDGM* 116 (1979), 27–44; A. Jones, 'Illusions of Sovereignty: Business and the Organisation Committees of Vichy France', *Social History*, 11/1 (1986), 1–31; C. Andrieu, *La Banque sous l'Occupation: Paradoxes de l'histoire d'une profession* (1990), 122–40; H. Rousso and M. Margairaz, 'Vichy, la guerre et les entreprises', *Histoire, économie et société*, 11/3 (1992), 337–67.

[62] Andrieu, *La Banque*, 131.

Bichelonne epitomized the caste of technocrats who rose to prominence at Vichy. Having graduated at the École polytechnique with the highest marks in the school's history, he was an intellectual prodigy even by the exacting standards of the French education system. He claimed not to need an address book because he could keep over 2,500 telephone numbers in his head. In the 1930s Bichelonne was involved in X-Crise and worked for the railways. In 1939 he was brought in by Dautry to organize rearmament. Worshipping the gods of efficiency, rationalization, and modernization, Bichelonne was completely naive about politics. Du Moulin de Labarthète described him as being like a brilliant child. Vichy represented the opportunity to reorganize the world without having to worry about the human beings that inhabited it.[63]

Bichelonne hoped that the economic controls introduced by Vichy would lay the foundations for the long-term modernization of the French economy. In January 1942 he announced that the COs and OCPRI would be the basis of a 'durable controlled economy': 'a modern State should not be allowed to run according to the blind and simplistic rules of the liberal economy'.[64] Bichelonne created a Commercial and Industrial Economic Council (CSEIC), chaired by Gerard Bardet, a former member of X-Crise, and made up of CO directors, civil servants, and experts. It produced a report favourable to the idea of economic planning. Similarly, the DGEN, under François Lehideux, produced two draft economic plans: a ten-year one in 1942 and another one in 1944 to prepare the transition to the post-war economy. These initiatives can be seen up to a point as precursors of French post-war planning.[65]

How did they fit into the world-view of the National Revolution? The second DGEN Plan adopted a more modernizing tone than the first, but both empha-sized the need for substantial investment in capital equipment, condemning pre-war entrepreneurs for their 'Malthusianism'. The 1942 plan described the 'return to the land' policy as 'probably utopian'; the 1944 one condemned it as liable to reduce France to the status of a second-rank power. But both accepted the assumption that social stability required the preservation of a substantial agri-cultural sector. The 1942 plan accepted the necessity to 'reinforce peasant values'; it was the countryside's 'harsh and noble discipline which has formed our race'. The word 'modernization' was not often used; the key words were 'balance' and 'stability'. This is another case where it would be wrong to exaggerate the dichotomy between modernizers and traditionalists.[66]

Neither plan was implemented or had much influence on policy.[67] In prac-

---

[63] G. Sabin, *Jean Bichelonne 1940–1944* (1991) is not very illuminating.

[64] Margairaz, *L'État, les finances et l'économie*, 538.

[65] R. Kuisel, 'Vichy et les origines de la planification économique, 1940–1946', *MS* 98 (1977), 77–101; P. Mioche, 'Aux origines du Plan Monnet: Les Discours et les contenus dans les premiers plans français (1941–1947)', *Revue historique*, 265/2 (1981), 405–38.

[66] A. Shennan, *Rethinking France: Plans for Renewal 1940–1946* (Oxford, 1989), 229–33; Kuisel, *Capitalism and the State*, 145–56; Mioche, 'Aux origines', 420–1.

[67] Margairaz, *L'État, les finances et l'économie*, 586–7.

tice, what happened to the economy under Vichy was not so much planning as a proliferation of bureaucratic controls, bestowing huge power upon an administration unchecked by democratic control. Where the system did prefigure the future was in creating a close community of interest between the State and the CO leaders, anticipating the interpenetration of administrative and business elites so characteristic of post-war France.

The chairmen and management committees of the COs were appointed by the government. The nominees tended to be representatives of big business, sometimes the bosses themselves, sometimes younger professional business administrators. Where a powerful business association had existed before the war, it often dominated the relevant CO. In theory, the State had a regulatory role since each CO was supervised by a government-appointed commissioner. In practice, these commissioners went along with the decisions taken. Although Bichelonne's role in charge of the OCPRI gave him ultimate power over the COs, he exercised it in co-operation with the main business leaders. OCPRI was itself divided into thirteen subsections which were run by the leading members of the CO in the relevant area. Thus the people who benefited from the allocation of raw materials played a key role in determining it. This created a sort of symbiosis between State officials and businessmen, most striking in the cases of CO chairmen who went on to become ministers: Lehideux had headed the automobile CO, as well as sitting on two OCPRI committees, before becoming Minister of Industrial Production, and Pucheu had been head of the mechanical industry CO, and on two OCPRI committees. In short, about 150–200 men ran the French economy under Vichy.

Representatives of small business complained that this system discriminated against them. The synarchy rumour was a symptom of this discontent. Even Pétain made a speech in 1941 denouncing the power of 'trusts' over the economy. In February 1944 a small business leader, Léon Gingembre, was taken into the *cabinet* of the Minister of Industrial Production, but this was only a sop to small business interests. The gap between word and deed in Vichy's economic policy is demonstrated by the fate of the artisans. Supposedly the regime was devoted to the interests of the artisan. An Artisans' Bureau was set up in November 1940 to protect artisanal production. But when the CO system was set up, artisans found themselves apportioned to the COs by sector—plumbers with the construction industry, tailors in the textile industry—where they sat alongside other larger employers. This made it impossible for them to protect their specific interests. When the Artisans' Bureau wrote to CO chairmen to complain that artisans were not receiving their share of State commissions, the textile CO replied that this was because of their 'feeble productive capacity'.

The Artisans' Bureau was drafting measures of support for artisans until the end, but these had few practical consequences. Artisans became increasingly critical of the regime. One of their spokesman complained in August 1942 that the COs were organized to the 'advantage of the trusts and big business and the . . . progressive suffocation of the artisan and medium-sized production'.[68] In August 1943 artisans were provided with their own corporatist organization called the Artisans' Statute. The details of the Statute were complicated, but its main effect was to integrate the many independent professional groups previously representing artisans into the State bureaucracy—not surprisingly since Bichelonne was the inspiration behind it. In short, despite the rhetoric, artisans were protected much less effectively under Vichy than they had been under the Republic where they had had an important parliamentary lobby.

If 'modernizers' had usurped 'traditionalists' in the control of Vichy's economic policy, this was largely due to the force of circumstances. The dire economic situation required interventionism and this gave the modernizers their opportunity: they saw themselves as realists. But the gap between rhetoric and reality was as great for the modernizers as for the traditionalists. It was an illusion to believe it would be possible to organize a massive overhaul of the French economy when it was hard to fulfil the most basic tasks—feeding the population, providing industry with the raw materials to keep going.

Bichelonne hoped that the COs would facilitate the modernization of the economy by closing outdated factories, but when in December 1941 Lehideux passed a law on these lines, it was because the cold winter and lack of fuel made it impossible to keep all factories running. Bichelonne admitted that the closures had nothing to do with modernizing the economy.[69] The leaders of some COs shared the modernizing perspectives of the technocrats. The automobile industry embarked upon research into the construction of an aluminium car—but there was no bauxite—and the COs of the electricity and steel industries drew up ambitious production and investment plans for the post-war period.[70] All this was for the future. In the short term, the ambitions of the modernizers were as much of a fantasy as the National Revolution of the traditionalists. But while the traditionalists, inspired by an inward-looking vision of 'la France seule', acted almost as if there were no Germans in France, the technocrats believed that the transition between the short-term penury and long-term modernization would come not by ignoring the Germans, but by negotiating with them. This was the sense in which they saw themselves as realists. To see how misguided they were, it is necessary to turn to the realities of collaboration.

[68] S. Zdatny, 'The Corporatist Word and the Modernist Deed: Artisans and Political Economy in Vichy France', *EHQ* 16 (1986), 155–79: 165.
[69] Rousso and Margairaz, 'Vichy, la guerre et les entreprises', 350–4; Margairaz, *L'État, les finances et l'économie*, 584–5.
[70] Vinen, *Politics of French Business*, 142; Margairaz, *L'État, les finances et l'économie*, 583–90.

8

Collaboration

Jean Moulin: Collaborator

On 25 June 1940, Jean Moulin, prefect of the Eure-et-Loir, had his first formal meeting with the occupying authorities. Moulin was no ordinary prefect. Unlike some who had joined the Exodus, leaving the population to fend for itself, Moulin was at his post when the Germans arrived in Chartres on 17 June. On the next day, a German officer instructed him to sign a declaration condemning alleged massacres of civilians by French Senegalese troops. Moulin refused to comply since he knew the deaths had been caused by German bombing. The Germans, surprised at such scruples when it came to protecting the reputation of black soldiers, beat Moulin up and incarcerated him for the night. Unsure if he could withstand more of this treatment without caving in, Moulin found some broken glass in his improvised cell, and cut his throat. Bleeding, but still alive when the Germans arrived the next morning, he was taken to a German doctor. The affair was embarrassing to the Germans who wished to portray a benevolent image—hence the attempt to shift responsibility for civilian deaths on to the Senegalese—and they let Moulin free.[1]

Once Moulin had recovered and resumed his duties, it fell to him, as to every prefect in the Occupied Zone, to mediate between the French population and the Germans. He was inundated with appeals from the 426 mayors of the *département*. The mayor of Gué-de-Longroi reported the arrival of 400 Germans who were commandeering lodgings without permission: were they entitled to do this? The mayor of Farvil wrote that the Germans were requisitioning local produce: how should he respond? The mayor of Jouy asked how to react to a German demand that he pay 52 marks (1,040 francs) for two photographs of Hitler and Goering.

Moulin responded as best he could, intervening with the Germans to resolve these situations amicably. On 12 September 1940 he instructed the sub-prefects and mayors of the *département* how to behave towards the Germans: 'In your relations with the occupying authorities you will display a courteous and loyal collaboration, which should not exclude dignity and firmness when the circum-

[1] Cordier, *Jean Moulin*, ii. 316–29.

stances require it.'[2] Over the next five months, until being dismissed by Vichy, Moulin tried to show by example how his instruction should be interpreted. Although he took the 'dignity and firmness' seriously, the Germans had no complaints and appreciated his efficiency. When the Feldkommandant, Colonel von Gutlingen, was replaced at the end of September 1940, he wrote a farewell letter to Moulin hoping that 'your collaboration with my successor will follow the same paths you and I have followed'. His successor described Moulin as a remarkable administrator: 'working with him has been satisfactory'.[3]

Involuntary Collaboration/Voluntary Collaboration

The case of Moulin shows that the word 'collaboration' must be used carefully. Quite apart from his later Resistance career, Moulin's behaviour on 18 June shows him to have been someone of exceptional moral courage. But his official position required him to 'collaborate' with the German authorities. This was collaboration as specified by article 3 of the Armistice, requiring the French authorities in the Occupied Zone 'to conform to the regulations of the German authorities and collaborate [*zusammenarbeiten*] with them in a correct manner'.

Collaboration in this spirit was quite different from collaboration as pursued by the Vichy regime. Stanley Hoffmann has distinguished between 'involuntary' and 'voluntary' State collaboration, the former involving a punctilious conformity to the letter of the Armistice but no more, the latter representing an attempt to go beyond the Armistice and offer more than it required.[4] After the war, Pétain's defenders claimed that he had favoured a minimalist policy of involuntary collaboration, while Laval had pursued voluntary collaboration. They presented Laval's dismissal on 13 December 1940 as a repudiation of collaboration, one even alleging that this was an event as grave for Hitler as the loss of a battle.[5] One of the many achievements of Robert Paxton is to have established that this was completely untrue: the regime was united behind the need for some degree of voluntary collaboration. But two qualifications can be made. In the first place, because Paxton made extensive use of German sources his picture may be slightly skewed. What the French felt that they had to say to the Germans was not necessarily always what they believed. In fact the subsequent opening of French archives vindicated Paxton's interpretation in most respects, but—and this is the second qualification—he did perhaps underestimate the existence of elements within the regime who were unhappy about collaboration. As we shall see, some of the first resisters in France emerged from within the orbit of the regime. Although the contradiction between a subjective disposition towards resistance within a regime that was objectively collaborating (or trying to) could not be

---

[2] Ibid. 407.   [3] Ibid. 343–416, 472–6.
[4] 'Self-Ensnared: Collaboration with Nazi Germany', 28–31.
[5] Bouthillier, *Le Drame de Vichy*, i. 283–4.

sustained indefinitely, there was a period of uncertainty about what the ultimate orientation of the regime would be.

Different responses towards Germany emerged as early as 15 July 1940 when the Germans requested the use of French bases in North Africa. This was a clear breach of the Armistice. François Charles-Roux, Secretary-General at the Quai d'Orsay, drafted a reply which politely but firmly refused, but the government opted for a refusal which tested the water for the future: 'only a new negotiation can solve these problems'.[6] In the end Hitler did not pursue the matter. The most vociferous opponent of any overtures to Germany was Weygand. In the summer of 1940, cabinet meetings frequently degenerated into slanging matches between Weygand and Laval. Although Weygand was sent away to be Delegate General in North Africa on 6 September, this was an important power base and he continued to make his views known. In November 1940 he reminded Pétain that 'Germany and Italy remain the enemies'.

The line between voluntary and involuntary State collaboration did not run between Pétain and Laval: they both believed that Germany had won the war and Britain would soon surrender. This did not mean that they, and other proponents of voluntary collaboration, shared identical views of its purpose. There were at least three different motives behind voluntary collaboration. First, there was what might be called the politico-administrative motive which aimed to protect French sovereignty. Although in theory sovereign over all French territory, Vichy's control over the Occupied Zone was at the mercy of German interference. French laws had to be submitted to the Germans before they could be published, and the Germans could veto administrative appointments. In June 1941 prefects were instructed to report German acts that they considered 'unacceptable for the maintenance of French sovereignty'. Where such acts could not be prevented, the government preferred the French to carry them out. Pucheu told the prefects in January 1942: 'the role you have to play is the maintenance of public order . . . It must be assured by French hands, French arms, French heads.'[7] Although this administrative collaboration started out as defensive and prophylactic, it became an ever more dangerous spiral of complicity: a River Kwai syndrome as one writer described it.[8]

The second motive behind collaboration might be described as politico-diplomatic: to prepare a favourable outcome for France in the peace treaty which was believed to be imminent. On 7 July, General Huntziger, the French representative on the Armistice Commission, proposed that the Commission's discussions should be supplemented by additional contacts, in view of the fact that France was 'almost at war' with her former ally. Two days later the Foreign Minister, Paul Baudouin, was trying to make contact with Ribbentrop, telling him

---

[6] Duroselle, *L'Abîme*, 236–8; Paxton, *Vichy France*, 61. For a contrary interpretation see Coutau-Bégarie and Huan, *Darlan*, 317–18.

[7] Baruch, *Servir l'État*, 78.

[8] A. Sauvy, *De Paul Reynaud à Charles de Gaulle* (1972), 134.

that France wanted to become an 'associated power'.[9] Such sentiments were partly explicable in the wake of Mers el Kebir. But French feelers towards collaboration represented not only short-term pique against the British. They were the beginning of a policy that was to be pursued in various guises for the next four years.

The first indications of German plans for a future peace treaty were worrying. On 15 July, the Germans set up customs controls on the 1871 frontiers between Alsace-Lorraine and Germany. Two Gauleiter were appointed to administer the region, suggesting that Germany intended to annex it after the war. Although technically a breach of the Armistice, this development did not entirely suprise the French. They were more alarmed by the other divisions which the Germans created within the Occupied Zone. The two *départements* of the Nord and Pas-de-Calais were attached to the German military command in Brussels. This was supposedly done to prepare the invasion of Britain, but even after the invasion was called off in September, the measure was not reversed. There was no military pretext for the creation, within the Occupied Zone, of the so-called Reserved or Forbidden Zone. Refugees who had left this area during the Exodus were not allowed to return. Even more sinister was the fact that their properties were handed over to the Ostland Company which started to settle German colonists on them. Nor did it escape notice that the boundaries of the Reserved Zone coincided more or less with the frontiers of the German Reich after the death of Charlemagne. If this was a portent of Germany's long-term plans for France, it was vital to win German goodwill before it was too late.[10]

The disruptions caused by the creation of these extra zones explain the third motive behind collaboration: the need to alleviate the impact of the Armistice on daily life in France. Originally, it had been assumed that the Armistice would only be a provisional arrangement before a speedy end to the war. As the war dragged on, the Armistice proved increasingly burdensome. One French priority was to obtain the release of the 1.5 million prisoners who were due to remain in captivity until the end of the war. Trying to relax the terms of the Armistice was all the more urgent because Germany started to apply them as rigorously as possible, treating the demarcation line as a sealed frontier which was virtually impossible to cross, and imposing huge financial burdens on the French.

The Armistice had made France responsible for paying the upkeep of the German army. In August 1940 the Germans estimated these costs at 20 million Reichsmark a day, and then fixed the franc/mark exchange rate at 20 francs to 1 mark, which represented a 50–60 per cent overvaluation of the mark. The French found themselves having to pay 400 million francs a day, enough to keep an army of 18 million men. As a result the Germans had massive spending power in France. One German official noted: 'with this money the Germans will be

---

[9] Paxton, *Vichy France*, 60–1.   [10] Ibid. 52–6; Michel, *Vichy année 40*, 164–7.

able to buy the whole of France'. On the cheap, he might have added.[11] As a final screw on the French economy, the Germans forced the French government to sign a clearing treaty. This mean that each country would pay its own exporters and then clear the trade debts nationally. French importers would pay francs into a clearing account and German importers would pay in marks. From this account the respective government would pay their exporters. But since France would be exporting much more than she imported, the account would be massively out of balance. To pay French exporters, the account would have to borrow francs from the Bank of France. Thus the French government was effectively financing Germany's imports from France.[12]

German Polyocracy: 'What a lot of authorities'

Vichy's problem in establishing contact with the occupiers was to identify who had the ear of Hitler. The Germans transplanted to France that multiplicity of competing agencies which have led historians to call the Nazi regime a 'polyocracy'. The Nazi power-brokers—Goebbels, Goering, Himmler, Ribbentrop—all had representatives in France. When told that Germany was an authoritarian state, Laval remarked this might be so, 'but what a lot of authorities'.[13]

The supreme authority in the Occupied Zone was the German military administration (MBF) based at the Hôtel Majestic in Paris under General Otto von Stülpnagel. The MBF was divided into military and civilian branches. The latter was itself subdivided into an administrative wing under the jurist Werner Best and an economic one under Elmar Michel. Best was a committed Nazi who had been in the Party since 1930; he later became Reichskommissar in Denmark. Michel was a technocratic civil servant who joined the Party only in 1939. Both were formidably able administrators. Matters arising from the Armistice were discussed at the Armistice Commission in Wiesbaden, chaired by General Karl von Stülpnagel (Otto's cousin). The Commission had its own economic commission chaired by the diplomat Richard Hemmen. Policing was the responsibility of the MBF, but Himmler managed to secure the presence of a few representatives of his security services (SD) under the SS officer Helmut Knochen. Censorship, propaganda, and cultural policy were the responsibility of the Propaganda-Abteilung (with four outposts in the provinces and one in Paris). Although incorporated into the MBF administration, the Propaganda-Abteilung was answerable to Goebbels's Propaganda Ministry in Berlin. There was also a German Embassy at the Rue de Lille in Paris. The ambassador was Ribbentrop's protégé, Otto Abetz.[14]

[11] A. Milward, *The New Order and the French Economy* (Oxford, 1970), 61.
[12] Ibid. 58–63; Hytier, *Two Years of French Foreign Policy*, 128–9.
[13] Jäckel, *La France dans l'Europe*, 110.
[14] R. Thalmann, *La Mise au pas: Idéologie et stratégie sécuritaire dans la France occupée* (1991), 23–54, 135–8; Burrin, *La France à l'heure*, 92–104; Jäckel, *La France dans l'Europe*, 104 ff.

These authorities had different priorities. The career officers at the MBF were essentially pragmatic, and ready to use the carrot as well as the stick. 'If one wants the cow to give milk, it must be fed', said Otto von Stülpnagel in September 1940.[15] They were irritated by the zealousness of hard-core Nazi ideologues like Knochen. When the SS, in co-operation with French fascists, bombed several Paris synagogues in October 1941, Stülpnagel was furious, and tried to have Knochen removed. Knochen himself resented the fact that the military controlled policing. But the line between professionals and ideologues did not necessarily separate those prepared to be gentler on the French from those prepared to be more harsh. Hemmen was distrusted by the Nazi Party, but as a negotiator he was devastatingly effective, ready to concede the French no favours.

Most German authorities in France were suspicious of the Embassy, which had the reputation of being too Francophile. Abetz's knowledge of France went back to the Sohlberg circle at the end of the 1920s. He was Francophile in that he admired French culture, food, and wine (and had a French wife), but he also believed that the French needed to know their place. The plan Abetz presented to Hitler in July 1940, before his appointment to the Embassy, was to reduce France to a 'satellite State' forced to accept 'permanent weakness'. He proposed to play on French rivalries and excite French hopes of an entente with Germany: 'a uniform attitude of rejection would provoke a single and indivisible front of all the French'. His instructions from Hitler ratified this strategy: 'everything must be done to encourage the internal divisions and thus the weakness of France'.[16] Abetz's subordinates were, like him, young and knowledgeable about France. They included Friedrich Sieburg, whose 'Francophilia' was of the same variety as Abetz's, and Karl Epting who had in the 1930s organized Franco-German student exchanges. Epting ran the German Institute which was the cultural arm of the Embassy. The Propaganda-Abteilung, whose brief was to destroy French cultural influence, did not approve Abetz's policy of cultural seduction. It was run by Major Heinz Schmidtke, a narrow Prussian officer type impervious to any attractions France might have to offer.

The relative power of these authorities oscillated. In the clash over control of cultural policy the Propaganda-Abteilung lost ground to the Embassy in the summer of 1942, but Abetz himself fell out of favour later that year. Between December 1942 and December 1943, he was replaced by his deputy Rudolf Schleier. Control over economic policy shifted from Wiesbaden to Paris when Hemmen moved there in the spring of 1941. The army lost control of policing and security to the SS from 1942. But the infighting never ceased, and there were other players to complicate the game further: the army's intelligence service, the Abwehr, and the Einsatz Rosenberg, which was in charge of pillaging of works of art, and acted as a law unto itself.

---

[15] Jäckel, *La France dans l'Europe*, 139.   [16] Burrin, *La Dérive fasciste*, 353–4.

Initiating Collaboration: Montoire

The German authorities gave out different signals, and various French politicians tried in the summer of 1940 to make contact with them. Flandin saw Friederich Grimm, of the Embassy staff, on 16 July, and told him that France must collaborate with Germany; Bonnet met Schleier on 31 July; Adrien Marquet contacted representatives of the SD and talked himself up at the expense of Laval; Pétain himself tried in the autumn to make contact with the Germans via René Fonck, a First World War air ace friendly with Goering.[17] But it was Laval who succeeded in establishing a relationship with the Germans, and it was his success in doing so, not his attempt to do so, which set him apart.

Laval's German contact was Abetz whom he met for the first time on 19 July. They discovered an affinity based on shared left-wing origins and a commitment to Franco-German reconciliation. Once Abetz was appointed ambassador on 3 August, this contact became important. As time went on, Laval and Abetz came to need each other: Laval to prove to Vichy that he had the ear of an important German, Abetz to prove to Hitler that he had found a Frenchman he could do business with.[18] Laval, who even obtained a semi-permanent *Ausweis* enabling him to travel freely between the two zones, became a frequent visitor to Paris. But it took two to collaborate, and Hitler, after his abortive attempt to get a foothold in North Africa, showed no interest. Not until the end of September did his attention turn to France again.

Hitler's attitude changed as a result of events in France's African Empire. Although most French colonies had stayed loyal to Vichy, French Equatorial Africa (Chad, the Cameroons) had rallied to de Gaulle in August. Worried that this rebellion might spread to West Africa, Vichy urgently sought German permission to reinforce French forces there. In September a joint Anglo-Gaullist force set sail for Dakar, the main port of French West Africa. But the Vichy defenders remained loyal and the Gaullists were repulsed. In retaliation the French bombarded Gibraltar. For Hitler this evidence of Vichy's determination to defend her Empire opened up the possibility of a Mediterranean and colonial strategy against Britain now that the invasion had been shelved. On 24 September Vichy was authorized to rearm the air force in North Africa. Encouraged by this, Pétain announced on 10 October that France wished to free herself of 'traditional friendships' and forge 'a new peace of collaboration'.

Hitler was now ready to launch the 'new policy'. The problem with a Mediterranean strategy was to reconcile the competing interests of Italy, Spain, and France in North Africa. One idea, never in fact presented to Vichy, was that France would be given Nigeria to compensate for the cession of Morocco to Spain and Tunisia and Corsica to Mussolini.[19] On 23 October, Hitler met Franco at Hendaye on the Franco-Spanish border to persuade him to enter the war. On

---

[17] Duroselle, *L'Abîme*, 262; Jäckel, *La France dans l'Europe*, 151.
[18] Kupferman, *Pierre Laval*, 255.   [19] Jäckel, *La France dans l'Europe*, 166–7.

his way, he stopped at Montoire, near Tours, where a surprised Laval was summoned to meet him on 22 October. A similar meeting was proposed for Pétain on the return journey two days later. Pétain's advisers were suspicious, but Pétain agreed to go, recalling the precedent of Tilsit when the defeated Alexander I of Russia had met Napoleon in 1807.

The discussions at Montoire remained general. The French had had no time to prepare their position, and Hitler made no concrete demands, partly because he had failed to win over Franco. No details were discussed and nothing was signed. At Montoire Pétain was more cautious than Laval. He called the declaration of war a blunder; Laval said it was a crime. Laval proposed collaboration; Pétain accepted it in principle, but said that he could not discuss details before talking to his government. Nonetheless, the symbolic impact of Montoire can hardly be exaggerated. Pétain was photographed shaking Hitler's hand, and in a speech on 30 October he announced that France was 'entering the path of collaboration'. He promised that in 'the near future' there would be an improvement in the situation of the prisoners of war, a reduction in occupation costs, and a relaxation of the demarcation line.[20] Montoire's importance was also shown by the fact that it led to the resignations of Charles-Roux and Baudouin; Laval now became Foreign Minister.

After Montoire, discussions started in Paris between German military representatives and envoys from Vichy (Laval, Darlan, Huntziger). The negotiations concerned a French expedition to reconquer French Equatorial Africa even at the risk of opening hostilities with the British. At the first meeting, on 31 October, General Huntziger, French Minister of Defence, told the Germans: 'The British must be chased out.' But at the second meeting, on 29 November, he disappointed the Germans by claiming that no operation against the British would be possible until the end of 1941. At the next meeting, on 10 December, he had revised his position again, and suggested that an operation might be feasible by February 1941.

These fluctuations in the French line are entirely comprehensible. At the very least, Vichy had to seem serious about defending her Empire from Britain so that the Germans were not tempted to step in themselves; on the other hand, Vichy did not want to provoke the British and Free French into launching further attacks on the Empire. In addition, French negotiators hoped to use the prospect of military operations against Britain as a way of securing German agreement for an increase in the size of French naval and military strength in the Empire. It is not clear how serious the French were about military action against Britain in Africa. Laval seems to have been the most enthusiastic—he informed Abetz that he was disappointed by Huntziger's position on 29 November—while Darlan and Huntziger seemed more cautious. On the other hand, on 12 December Pétain told the American diplomat Robert Murphy that France

[20] Ibid. 169–76; Ferro, *Pétain*, 184–92.

was organizing an expedition to recapture Chad. French policy was not fixed at the end of 1941, but it would be wrong to suppose that the idea of military action in Africa was Laval's alone.[21]

13 December: The Fall of Laval

Despite these negotiations, Montoire brought no tangible benefits to the French population apart from an agreement on 16 November to release POWs with more than four children.[22] The German representatives on the Armistice Commission remained as unco-operative as ever: Hemmen told the French that Montoire was a 'political event which has nothing to do with what we are doing here'.[23] Indeed things got even worse for the French. At the end of October the Germans expelled some 7,700 Jews from the Palatinate and Baden-Württemberg and dumped them in France. From 11 November, the Germans started to expel citizens of Lorraine who were judged to be unassimilable into Germany. Trainloads of refugees arrived daily in France. When the operation ended in mid-December, some 100,000 Lorrainers (and 4,000 Alsatians) had been unceremoniously dumped into France. This was a major blow to the German image in France, and annoyed Abetz whose seduction of the French required them to be offered some concessions. On the economic front, German demands escalated daily.

Montoire's failure to produce results poisoned relations between Pétain and Laval. It revealed a significant difference between them—not about the desirability of collaboration, but about its nature.[24] For Pétain, collaboration was a way of securing improvements in the conditions of daily life in France. The prefects reported that Montoire had shocked public opinion, and Pétain felt aggrieved at having staked his prestige on a policy which had not delivered results. For Laval, indifferent to the National Revolution, collaboration was a longer term strategy. Although disappointed that Montoire had not achieved more, his objective was a durable Franco-German reconciliation. For this he was ready to make sacrifices. On 26 November, he accepted a German request that the French surrender their capital holdings in the Bor copper mines in Yugoslavia. Three days later, he handed over, without compensation, the gold stocks that had been entrusted to France by the Bank of Belgium. In both these cases Laval, arguing that France must give 'testimony of our good faith', over-ruled the protests of the Minister of Finance, Bouthillier.[25] For all his reputation

---

[21] Paxton, *Vichy France*, 83–7; Paxton, *Parades and Politics*, 82–93; Warner, *Pierre Laval*, 242–3, 250–2; Duroselle, *L'Abîme*, 273–4.

[22] Michel, *Vichy année 40*, 335–6.

[23] Baruch, *Servir l'État*, 107; Duroselle, *L'Abîme*, 270.

[24] See R. Frank, 'Pétain, Laval, Darlan', in J.-P. Azéma and F. Bédarida (eds.), *La France des années noires*, i. *De la défaite à Vichy* (1993), 297–332.

[25] Duroselle, *L'Abîme*, 273; Margairaz, *L'État, les finances et l'économie*, 632–4.

as a cynic, Laval was extraordinarily naive. His mistake was to overestimate the importance of Abetz whose influence over German policy was less than he believed (and Abetz hoped).

Laval also became too confident of his own indispensability. He was therefore completely taken by surprise when Pétain sacked him on 13 December. Subsequent claims that he was dismissed because of his closeness to the Germans are quite wrong: only the hope that his German contacts would bear fruit had saved him from being dismissed sooner. The objection to Laval was not that he sought collaboration, but that he had achieved nothing from it.[26] On the other hand, many of Laval's enemies within the government did believe that he had executed the policy imprudently, and to that extent it is true that collaboration played some part in Laval's downfall.

Laval was replaced by a triumvirate of Flandin, Darlan, and Huntziger. Pétain assured Hitler in a letter that French policy had not altered, but Abetz was furious. Storming down to Vichy on 16 December, accompanied by some armed SS men, he had Laval released, and returned to Paris with him. Although Darlan met Hitler on 25 December, listened to a tirade, and assured him that France remained committed to collaboration, the Germans would not be appeased: they punished Vichy by closing the demarcation line even to civil servants. By January the government in desperation started to consider taking Laval back, but Laval now refused anything less than full power. In the end, however, Laval's return to government foundered not on his intransigence, but on a change of attitude by Ribbentrop who decided to keep him in reserve in case Vichy misbehaved again in future.[27] For the moment the Germans had decided that Darlan could be trusted after all. They spun the crisis out only to squeeze some extra concessions from Vichy. On 9 February, Flandin resigned and Darlan took over. The Germans received satisfaction with the dismissal of some of the 13 December conspirators (including Alibert and Peyrouton) and the entry into government of some ardent proponents of collaboration (Marion, Benoist-Méchin).[28]

Throughout the crisis the French had done all they could to assure Germany that Laval's dismissal was not a repudiation of collaboration. They would have done this whether it was true or not, but there is no reason to assume it was not. After the war, Flandin claimed that he had broken with collaboration. There was indeed almost no contact with the Germans in his short period of power, but this was not his choice.[29] Flandin, the man who sent Hitler a telegram of congratulation after Munich, did not have an anti-collaboration reputation. He had made a speech favourable to collaboration on 18 November, and he had been appointed partly to allay suspicions of anti-German motives in

[26] Kupferman, *Pierre Laval*, 268–70; Warner, *Pierre Laval*, 222.
[27] Cointet, *Pierre Laval*, 338; Warner, *Pierre Laval*, 272.
[28] Coutau-Bégarie and Huan, *Darlan*, 360–86.   [29] Paxton, *Vichy France*, 101–8.

the elimination of Laval.[30] The scheme had foundered, but through no fault of Flandin's.

The British Connection

Apart from the dismissal of Laval, those arguing that Pétain was ambivalent about collaboration point to the existence of secret contacts between Vichy France and the British. These are taken as signs of Pétain's 'double game'. Contacts with Britain certainly existed, but their importance was exaggerated after the war, and Laval's dismissal was unrelated to them.[31]

The contacts started in September 1940 via the two countries' embassies in Madrid. The French hoped to alleviate the effects of the British blockade which was starving metropolitan France of French colonial produce and the British hoped to avert any attack on their colonies or the dissident Gaullist ones. When the French refused to commit themselves on this point, the contacts were broken off. Another contact was made by Louis Rougier, a professor at Besançon, who obtained Pétain's agreement to visit London where he met Churchill on 25 October. After the war Rougier claimed, with the aid of doctored documents, that he had signed a secret protocol with Churchill. No such document existed, but Rougier's presence in London at the moment of Montoire did at least reassure the British that France had not entirely turned her back on them. It encouraged them to resuscitate the Madrid contacts. When Laval became Foreign Minister, he immediately informed the Germans and terminated these contacts again. He wanted 'loyalty' to Germany 'exclusive of any equivocal diplomacy'.[32]

Clearly there was a difference on this matter between Pétain and Laval, but events after Laval's fall showed that the difference was minimal. A third set of Franco-British contacts occurred through the Canadian diplomat Pierre Dupuy, who had contacted Jacques Chevalier just before Laval's fall. The significance of this connection was that Chevalier had once known the British Foreign Secretary Lord Halifax. Dupuy brought a message from Halifax that if France promised to keep the Empire out of German hands and leave the Gaullist colonies alone, the British would consider relaxing the blockade. On 6 December, Dupuy saw Pétain, Darlan, and Huntziger. He was assured that no action would be considered against the Gaullist territories before the spring at the earliest, and that the Germans would not be allowed in the Empire. Pétain also made the sibylline comment: 'you know where my sympathies lie'. Dupuy took this news to London. This was the extent of what Chevalier after the war

---

[30] Bidussa and Peschanski (eds.), *La France de Vichy*, 181.
[31] On Vichy–British relations see: R. T. Thomas, *Britain and Vichy: The Dilemma of Anglo-British Relations 1940–1942* (1979), 38–109; R. Frank, 'Vichy et les Britanniques 1940–1941: Double Jeu ou double langage?', in *VEF* 144–61; Duroselle, *L'Abîme*, 274–81.
[32] Duroselle, *L'Abîme*, 276.

christened the Chevalier–Halifax Agreement. In fact, nothing was signed. It is not even clear whether Dupuy had been authorized by Halifax to pass on any message; and if he had been, it only represented the private view of Halifax who was better disposed to Vichy than Churchill was.

Nonetheless on the strength of Dupuy's more extravagant assertions about Vichy's real attitude, and encouraged by Laval's dismissal, Churchill sent Pétain a secret message at the end of December suggesting possible British military assistance to North Africa if the French would contemplate an eventual entry into the war. Pétain did not reply. Another consequence of the hopes aroused by Dupuy was the resumption of the talks in Madrid (for the third time) in January, but British suspicion was aroused when Flandin informed the Germans about these. At Madrid the French presented the British with unrealistic demands for the importation of massive quantities of supplies. The negotiations petered out in February 1941, and the Franco-British contacts were now over. Dupuy went on proffering his services, but no one took any notice.

There was no French double game either before or after Laval's dismissal. The French hoped for an alleviation of the blockade, but they offered no concessions in return: nothing that Dupuy was told on 6 December was not already French policy. If the French subsequently sabotaged the Madrid negotiations, it was because they realized that the British lacked the resources to enforce a blockade: in the first three months of 1941, only eight out of 108 French ships passing through the Straits of Gibraltar were intercepted.[33]

France's plight was also eased after the American government started sending supplies to French North Africa, subject to certain conditions. This was the result of an agreement negotiated in February between General Weygand and President Roosevelt's representative in North Africa, James Murphy. The Murphy–Weygand agreement was motivated by Roosevelt's belief that if the Allies showed goodwill towards Vichy, it would be possible to bring France back into the war on the Allied side. Roosevelt's ambassador at Vichy, Admiral William Leahy, built up excellent relations with Pétain. But the Americans had even greater hopes of Weygand, seeing him, in the words of the Secretary of State, Cordell Hull, as 'a cornerstone around which to build a policy of resistance towards Germany'. The British were not convinced about this strategy, but they could not stop it.[34]

After the end of 1940, there was no more talk of retaking Chad, but this was not because Laval had gone. The policy had never been Laval's alone: when Darlan and Pétain saw Dupuy on 6 December they had refused to rule out a Chad expedition. If the project was abandoned, it was partly because Hitler had lost interest in the Mediterranean–African arena and was already planning the invasion of Russia. This meant that he was unlikely to allow the French to equip

[33] Thomas, *Britain and Vichy*, 101; Coutau-Bégarie and Huan, *Darlan*, 325, argue the blockade was relaxed as a result of the negotiations, but the British records show this to be wrong.

[34] Thomas, *Britain and Vichy*, 88–106.

the necessary forces.[35] It was also clear that the British, scarred by the failure of the Dakar expedition, were not going to sponsor such operations in future. Thus it made sense for Vichy tacitly to accept the colonial status quo rather than risk provoking the British unnecessarily.

Relaunching Collaboration: The Protocols of Paris

Nothing more conclusively contradicts the view that Laval's dismissal was a repudiation of collaboration than the fact that the apogee of the policy occurred under Admiral Darlan, his successor. Darlan was a devious figure in whose career it is hard to find any consistency. In the Third Republic, he had never displayed anti-Republican sentiments, and his sympathies were considered to lie on the left, yet in 1941 he claimed to believe that France's problems had been caused by the weaknesses of the Republic, its schoolteachers, and its 'Judaeo-Masonic political habits'. Unlike Weygand, he had not been an early advocate of the Armistice, yet he had changed his mind at the last moment. He was not involved in the plot against Laval, yet he became its main beneficiary. Apart from a tenacious Anglophobia tradition in the navy—in May 1942 he remarked: 'I worked with the British for 15 years and they always lied to me; I have worked with the Germans for 3 months, and they have never deceived me'[36]—Darlan's only principle was opportunism. He also enjoyed the trappings of office, and had a taste for the high life which contrasted with the austere tone of Vichy. Apart from two residences in Vichy itself, he had a sumptuous official villa in Toulon. He entertained lavishly, and liked to be accompanied wherever he went by a large military band.[37]

Darlan's views in 1941 can be easily reconstructed because he had a predilection for composing long memoranda which decked out his opportunism in grand geopolitical speculations. He believed that whether the war resulted in a stalemate or a German victory, its consequence would be a world divided into two blocs—a European one dominated by Germany and an Anglo-Saxon one dominated by America—and the end of the British Empire. Although one day France might become a bridge between these two blocs, her immediate destiny was to be part of German Europe.[38] Not only did Darlan think a German Europe was the likeliest outcome; he also thought it the desirable one. A British victory would lead to France being treated as a third-class dominion; a negotiated peace between Germany and Britain would allow them to carve up France's Empire to their mutual advantage; a German victory would offer France some sort of continental role and posed the least threat to her Empire.[39] Some of Darlan's pre-

[35] Paxton, *Vichy France*, 94–7.   [36] Boegner, *Carnets du Pasteur Boegner*, 112.
[37] H. Michel, *François Darlan* (1993), 143–7.
[38] Notes of 8 Nov. 1940, 17 Nov. 1940, 14 May 1940, in Darlan, *Lettres et notes*, 245–52, 325–8.
[39] Note of Dec. 1940, ibid. 264–5.

dictions have been borne out by history, but for an opportunist it is fruitless to be right fifty years early.

After Laval's insouciance and secrecy, Pétain appreciated Darlan's orderly reports. His view on collaboration did not differ substantially from Darlan's, although he noted in the margin of one of Darlan's memoranda that collaboration must not be military or involve the cession of bases.[40] If Pétain was not as sure as Darlan that Germany would win, he was no less convinced she would not lose: 'if Germany wins the war, we must have settled our account with her while she still has need of us'.[41] Darlan's main difference from Pétain was on domestic policy. His priority, and that of the technocrats in his government, was to enable France to hold her own economically in the new Europe. With Darlan therefore the congruence between domestic and foreign policy was greatest: where Laval was cynical about domestic reform and primarily interested in collaboration and Pétain primarily interested in collaboration to facilitate domestic reform, for Darlan the two were inseparable.[42]

To relaunch collaboration it was necessary to interest Hitler in France again. This became possible after February 1941 when Hitler sent Rommel to North Africa to assist the Italians. France's opportunity to capitalize on this occurred in April when Hitler decided to support an anti-British coup that had broken out in Iraq. Abetz asked for Germany to be allowed to use airbases in French Syria. On 5 May Darlan agreed and the first German planes arrived four days later. Darlan's understanding was that in return the French would win some of the concessions they so desperately wanted: a reduction in occupation costs and the release of more POWs. But Abetz had promised more than he could deliver, and no concessions were forthcoming.

On 11 May, Darlan met Hitler at Berchtesgaden. Hitler told him that although Germany would win the war anyway, France could speed up victory. For every large concession France made to Germany, the Germans would make a large one in return; for every small one, the Germans would make a small one. Back in France Darlan reported:

> This is the last chance for us of a rapprochement with Germany . . . If we collaborate with Germany . . . that is to say, if we work for her in our factories, if we give her certain facilities, we can save the French nation; reduce to a minimum our territorial losses in the colonies and on the mainland; play an honourable— if not important—role in the future Europe.
>
> My choice is made: it is collaboration . . . France's interest is to live and to remain a great power . . . In the present state of the world, and taking account of our terrible defeat, I see no other solution to protect our interests.[43]

[40] Note of 21 July, ibid. 383.   [41] Burrin, *La France à l'heure*, 125–6.
[42] Frank, 'Pétain, Laval, Darlan', in Azéma and Bédarida (eds.), *La France des Années noires* i. 297–332.
[43] Communication of 14 May 1941, in *Lettres et notes*, 325–7.

The cabinet approved these conclusions. The ensuing negotiations with Germany resulted in the signature on 27 May 1941 of the Protocols of Paris. These contained three major French concessions: German use of Syrian airfields (formal confirmation of the 5 May agreement); German use of the Tunisian port of Bizerta to supply Rommel in North Africa; submarine facilities for the Germans at Dakar. Annexed was a fourth protocol mentioning political concessions to give the French government the 'means to justify to public opinion the eventuality of an armed conflict with Britain or the United States'. The first three protocols were signed by Darlan, Abetz, and the German military negotiators; the fourth was signed by Abetz and Darlan alone. While France remained officially neutral, in practice that neutrality was increasingly asymmetrical.

When the Protocols came up for approval on 3 June, Weygand, who had hurried over from North Africa, threatened to resign. Darlan conceded that before proceeding further, the government would itemize the political concessions it required. A list of these was handed to Germany on 6 June. The German reaction was unforthcoming and the negotiations stalled. Weygand was back in Vichy on 11 July, and on 14 July the government presented Germany with another note. Again the German response was negative, and the application of the Protocols was suspended. Nonetheless the affair had had grave consequences for France. The Iraqi revolt had been crushed by the end of May which allowed Darlan to obtain the removal of German planes from Syria. But this was too late to prevent the Anglo-Gaullists launching an attack on Syria on 8 June. After a month of fighting, the Vichy forces surrendered. Vichy had lost another piece of her Empire; Vichy forces had fought the Anglo-Gaullists; no German concessions had been obtained.

These events have been interpreted in various ways. Weygand believed that his intervention was decisive in forcing Darlan to abandon the military collaboration he was contemplating. The French diplomatic historian Jean-Baptiste Duroselle accepts this claim. According to this interpretation, the French notes of 6 June and 14 July were drafted to invite a German refusal and sabotage the protocols.[44] Jäckel and Paxton, on the other hand, utilizing German sources, downplay Weygand's role. Noting that Darlan continued to negotiate with the Germans after Weygand's intervention, they see the note of 14 July as a bid to put Franco-German relations on a new footing going beyond the Armistice, and taking Hitler's words at Berchtesgaden at face value. Benoist-Méchin, who helped to draft the note, certainly claims in his memoirs that this was its purpose.[45] According to Paxton, if Germany did not take the bait, it was because the invasion of the Soviet Union again redirected Hitler's priorities away from the Mediterranean: Abetz informed the French on 13 August that Germany could not consider their proposals because she was now tied up in the East.

[44] Duroselle, *L'Abîme*, 285–90; Weygand, *Recalled to Service*, 326–37.

[45] Paxton, *Vichy France*, 116–27; Jäckel, *La France dans l'Europe*, 251–8. Benoist-Méchin, *A l'épreuve du temps*, 212–17; id. *De la défaite au désastre*, i. 237–53.

Pétain's biographer, Marc Ferro, offers a different interpretation. He believes that Darlan quickly became suspicious about Germany's willingness to offer concessions. Weygand therefore pushed Darlan in a direction he wished to go, providing an alibi for retreat.[46] Thus Weygand wrote to Noguès on 15 July: 'I must say that I had to fight less hard than I had expected.'[47] Darlan's biographers, in their heroic attempt to salvage the Admiral's reputation, have pushed this line even further. They argue that even when he signed the Protocols, Darlan, who felt the Germans had cheated him on 5 May, was already wary of their intentions: he had inserted the fourth protocol as an escape route.[48]

The only certainty is that Darlan had taken France to the brink of military collaboration and that he drew back for want of German political concessions. The view that the Protocols foundered because Germany lost interest does not square entirely with Germany's irritation at the new French position. Even if the view is correct, it is not incompatible with the idea that the 14 July note was intended to elicit a negative response. Probably the various protagonists had different expectations of the note, Benoist-Méchin hoping it would relaunch collaboration as a genuine partnership, Weygand believing it met his requirement of 'keeping our political demands very high',[49] Darlan probably expecting a German refusal, but unsure if he wanted one.

After the Protocols: Collaboration goes on

The Protocols, however, were only part of a longer process of Franco-German co-operation in North Africa which had started before the Syrian affair and went on after it. French North Africa had become important as a base of supply for Rommel's armies. On 25 April 1941, the Germans asked to purchase French military vehicles. Vichy agreed and a contract was signed in May for the provision of 1,100 lorries and 300 liaison vehicles.[50] Negotiations on this subject reopened in September. In general Darlan's behaviour in the second half of 1941 suggests, even to his own apologetic biographers, that 'he persisted in the idea that France could obtain from Germany more favourable conditions and even a modification of her political statute'.[51] He did everything possible to win German approval, starting in July with the removal of General Doyen from the Armistice Commission for being too anti-German.

Vichy's adoption of more repressive internal policies in August was partly a response to the deteriorating internal situation, but it was also linked to collaboration. Policing was at the intersection of politico-administrative and politico-

[46] Ferro, *Pétain*, 316–24.   [47] Levisse-Touzé, 'L'Afrique du Nord', 465.
[48] Coutau-Bégarie and Huan, *Darlan*, 395–438.
[49] Levisse-Touzé, 'L'Afrique du Nord', 465.
[50] Ibid. 314–16; Jäckel, *La France dans l'Europe*, 233–4.
[51] Coutau-Bégarie and Huan, *Darlan*, 442.

diplomatic collaboration: it was a way of preserving sovereignty by preventing the Germans from interfering in French internal security; and a way of winning German approval for the wider project of relaunching political collaboration. It was also a means of pre-empting more ruthless German measures likely to render both the regime and collaboration more unpopular. The Germans had responded to the first Communist terrorist attacks in August by executing five French hostages, and Hitler ordered that future attacks should be punished by the execution of 50–100 hostages per victim. To keep some control over the situation, the French themselves executed three Communists on 28 August after a trial in a 'Special Section' and another three on 24 September after a trial by the Special Tribunal. These six victims, guilty of no more than being Communist, were in no way implicated in the terrorist attacks.

If these measures proved insufficient to stop the German policy of shooting hostages, Vichy at least wanted to limit the unpopularity of that policy. On 23 October, the government proposed co-operation between the French and German police to avoid the Germans shooting the wrong people: 'it is eminently desirable in the future that the Communist hostages are selected by the German authorities but after consultation with the relevant French authorities'.[52] Prefects were instructed to hand the Germans lists of those arrested as Communists. This was only a step away from the French government selecting French citizens to be shot by the Germans. Anti-communism blunted Vichy's recognition of the invidious territory into which it was straying.

The resistance attacks continued, and the Germans went on exacting their revenge. After a German soldier was shot in Bordeaux on 20 October and another at Nantes the next day, ninety-eight French hostages were executed. These executions became particularly controversial because Pucheu, having managed to get the number of victims reduced, was later accused of having selected the names of Communists from among the hostages. He had apparently asked the Germans to spare the names of some people with heroic war records, and then presented with another list containing the names mainly of Communists, he kept silent. The executions caused a wave of national outrage, and Pétain decided to present himself as a hostage at the demarcation line. He was talked out of the idea, but news of it spread sufficiently for Pétain to secure credit for it without having had to carry it out. In fact the German reprisals did not let up. Ninety-five more hostages were shot after another resistance attack on 28 November. In total, 471 hostages were executed by the Germans between September 1941 and May 1942.

To win German approval, Darlan was also ready to sack Weygand who had done his best during September to slow down deliveries for Rommel.[53] On 8 November 1941, Darlan delivered Pétain an ultimatum: 'France, having been

---

[52] Quoted by D. Peschanski, 'Le Régime de Vichy a existé', in D. Peschanski (ed.), *Vichy 1940–1944: Archives de guerre d'Angelo Tasca* (1986), 3–49: 30.
[53] Levisse-Touzé, 'L'Afrique du Nord', 336–9.

beaten by Germany, cannot hope to survive unless she draw closer to her conqueror who desires this not out of sentiment but self-interest . . . I have chosen
the path of integrating France into the European bloc.' If Pétain would not sack
Weygand, Darlan would resign.[54] Weygand was finally dismissed on 18 November and replaced by General Juin who was given military command over North
Africa, but not the political powers which Weygand had also exercised.
Weygand's dismissal did more to alienate American opinion than to win concessions from Germany.

As Rommel's position in North Africa deteriorated at the end of 1941, Vichy
came under more pressure to provide him with help. Juin was sent to negotiate
in Berlin. Asked whether France would defend Tunisia even if this meant French
troops alongside Rommel, he was evasive, saying that it was necessary to create
the 'necessary climate for the French troops to accept the idea of fighting side
by side with the Germans'. As usual Germany would not offer the concessions
which this statement implied. Nonetheless at the end of December Darlan was
forced to provide more supplies and promise that the French would resist any
British incursion into Tunisia if Rommel were forced to retreat there. In effect,
then, the Germans had secured the second of the Protocols without giving anything in return. Luckily for French neutrality, it never became necessary to offer
a refuge to Rommel because the British offensive faltered. But France delivered
supplies to Rommel until the Americans threatened to stop their deliveries under
the Murphy accords. Between June 1941 and May 1942, France had provided
Rommel with about 1,700 vehicles, a small quantity of arms, and about 3,600
tons of fuel.[55]

None of this brought a political settlement any closer. In return for sacking
Weygand, Pétain was granted an interview with Goering at Saint-Florentin on
1 December. But when he presented the usual French demands and complained
at Germany's lack of co-operation, he was told: 'Who won this war, you or us?'[56]
This was what 'collaboration' had come to. A glimmer of hope that the Germans
might consider a general settlement was offered by Abetz after a rare meeting
with Hitler on 5 January. He told Benoist-Méchin that Hitler really seemed interested in offering a peace treaty 'which will astonish the French' if they would
declare war on the Allies. Benoist-Méchin enthusiastically reported this to
Darlan. The information was discussed by a small group of ministers in Pétain's
presence on 10 January. Despite Pétain's reluctance, they decided not to reject
the overture flatly, but explore what was on offer. Benoist-Méchin reported back
positively to Abetz who immediately informed Ribbentrop that the French were
ready to declare war.

In the end, nothing came of this. If Hitler had fleetingly nursed the idea of

[54] Darlan, *Lettres et notes*, 414–22.
[55] Coutau-Bégarie and Huan, *Darlan*, 469–71; Paxton, *Vichy France*, 127–8; Levisse-Touzé, 'L'Afrique
du Nord', 318–28, 487–501.
[56] Coutau-Bégarie and Huan, *Darlan*, 457–70; Ferro, *Pétain*, 355–65.

offering France something, he did not do so for long. He told Goebbels on 22 January that 'France renders us certain services in Africa but not of sufficient importance for us to offer concessions.' On the French side, this curious incident is difficult to interpret. What seems to have happened was that at every stage Abetz and Benoist-Méchin inflated the significance of what they had been told: Abetz exaggerated to Benoist-Méchin a few reveries by Hitler; Benoist-Méchin exaggerated to Darlan what Abetz had told him, and then exaggerated to Abetz the way Darlan had responded; and finally Abetz exaggerated to Ribbentrop what Benoist-Méchin had told him. This makes it difficult to reconstruct exactly how the French government did respond, but it seems certain that the response was to keep the door open. Darlan rushed to Paris in the hope of meeting Ribbentrop. He returned empty-handed. The whole affair was a tragicomic condensation of the entire history of collaboration.[57]

Darlan still hoped for a general settlement, but it is unclear how far he was now prepared to go to obtain it. In February 1942, he sent notes to Abetz and Stülpnagel expressing his continued interest in a rapprochement 'indispensable to the establishment of a new stable order in Europe', but he added that 'rapprochement does not mean participation in the war, at least as long as the country is neither materially nor morally ready'. Privately, however, Darlan had begun to lose hope. He wrote to Admiral Duplat who was negotiating with the Italians:

> While for a year I have deliberately oriented French policy towards a rapprochement, I have only met mistrust from both the Germans and the Italians. The proof of this is given by the constant refusal to give us the military means to respond to the Anglo-Saxon reprisals which are risked by our transports for the Axis . . . So it is not surprising if I respond to mistrust with prudence.[58]

The American entry into the war in December 1941 was a further blow to Vichy's policy of asymmetrical neutrality. Worried that the Germans might use French bases in the Caribbean, Washington insisted in February 1942 that Darlan refuse Germany any facilities in France's Caribbean possessions. The Germans pressurized him to resist American pressure. Darlan's freedom of manoeuvre was rapidly shrinking.[59]

By the end of 1941, Darlan's policy was as discredited as Laval's had been a year earlier, and he was losing favour with Pétain. He resented Darlan's failure to produce results, and had been deeply disappointed by the interview with Goering. Pétain's frustration emerged in his New Year message where he spoke of his 'partial exile' and 'semi-liberty'. Darlan tried to stop Pétain delivering this speech, and the Germans would not allow it to be reproduced in the North.

[57] Paxton, *Vichy France*, 387–90; Jäckel, *La France dans l'Europe*, 302–10; Benoist-Méchin, *De la défaite au désastre*, 351–69; Burrin, *La France à l'heure*, 132–4; Coutau-Bégarie and Huan, *Darlan*, 512–15.
[58] Note of 9 Sept. 1942, in *Lettres et notes*, 473.
[59] Paxton, *Vichy France*, 130–1.

Darlan's position was not helped by the opening on 19 February 1942 of the long-delayed trial, at Riom, of those judged responsible for the defeat. The two most prominent defendants, Daladier and Blum, had little difficulty in showing the flimsiness of the charges against them, and turned the occasion into a public relations disaster for the regime. The Germans, on the other hand, were furious that the accused were being tried not for causing the war, but for losing it. Under German pressure the trial was suspended in April. Darlan had few friends left.

The weeks of scheming preceding Darlan's dismissal were Byzantine even by Vichy standards. On 26 March 1942, Pétain had a secret meeting with Laval. In fact he remained as hostile to Laval as he had ever been, but Darlan took fright and showed the German consul at Vichy a note from the American ambassador, Leahy, informing Pétain of America's opposition to Laval's return. This was a tactical error on Darlan's part. Apart from Abetz, whose star was waning, the Germans had not been pushing for Laval's return, but once Darlan turned his own survival into a trial of strength between Germany and America, he obliged Berlin to swing behind Laval. On 17 April Darlan resigned, and Laval returned to power.[60] Collaboration was now to enter a new stage.

Economic Collaboration

Leaving aside any moral objections to the policy as pursued up to April 1942, collaboration followed logically from the premiss that Germany had won the war, just as de Gaulle's resistance followed logically from the opposite premiss. Although Vichy's premiss turned out to be wrong, it was not an absurd one between 1940 and 1942. In that sense, as Henri Michel observed, the policy of Darlan and Laval made more sense than Weygand's position of noble obstinacy, which drew the opposite conclusion from the same premiss.[61]

Even allowing for the flawed premiss, however, collaboration turned out to be a chimera because Vichy grossly overestimated the degree to which France mattered to Hitler. Vichy Realpolitik was wishful thinking based on a complete misreading of Germany. Although Hitler had not made up his mind about France's long-term fate, in conversation he mused about annexing Burgundy and Flanders to the greater Reich, and returning France to her borders of 1500. Of course, Vichy leaders were not privy to these thoughts, but available indications of German intentions towards France were hardly promising. The German Propaganda Ministry had announced on 9 July 1940 that France's future would be to become 'a greater Switzerland, a country of tourism . . . and fashion'.[62]

---

[60] Coutau-Bégarie and Huan, *Darlan*, 509–44 gives most detailed account.

[61] *Vichy année 40*, 274. But even Weygand did not oppose any possible deviation from the Armistice. When arguing against the Protocols, Weygand said that 'there is no question of breaking with Germany . . . The continuation of the negotiation which has started is indispensable for our military reinforcement.' Levisse-Touzé, 'L'Afrique du Nord', 274.

[62] Milward, *New Order*, 40.

As far as the future peace treaty was concerned, Hitler had debts to pay to Italy, and these were likely to be at France's expense. Laval made the mistake of misreading Abetz's intentions and overestimating his influence. As Philippe Burrin observes, collaboration was based on a double manipulation: that perpetrated on the French by Abetz who was really seeking 'France as a satellite not a partner'; that perpetrated on Abetz by Hitler who allowed Abetz to believe he wanted France as a satellite whereas in reality he intended to crush her.[63]

How could Vichy have been so credulous about Germany? A partial explanation can be found if one moves from the high politics of collaboration, which was a dialogue of the deaf, to collaboration as a daily process of negotiation. State collaboration was the story of a French government desperately seeking a response from a German government which was usually not interested. But it is not true that there was nothing the Germans wanted from the French. On the contrary, they embarked on a systematic milking of the French economy. Having abandoned a policy of outright requisition in the autumn of 1940, the Germans engaged the French in complex economic negotiations. These had the consequence of accustoming high-level French officials to the idea of doing business with the Germans. Administrative, economic, and political collaboration followed different rhythms. Montoire did not help the French negotiators on the Armistice Commission, but Abetz's hostile reaction to the sacking of Laval did not disrupt Franco-German negotiations which were taking place in Paris to work out how much influence Germany should be allowed over civil service appointments in the Occupied Zone.[64]

Vichy tried to monitor, and control, economic negotiations between industrialists and the Germans. For this reason it set up, in February 1941, the General Delegation for Franco-German Economic Affairs (DGREFA), under Jacques Barnaud, to co-ordinate all Franco-German economic negotiations. The French aimed to link economic negotiations, where the Germans wanted something, to political negotiations, where the French wanted something. The highly sensitive case of the aircraft industry showed, however, that the Germans refused to connect politics and economics in this way. Here the initiative for collaboration came from the Germans who wanted French factories (in both zones) to produce planes for them. In September 1940 Vichy agreed to allow French factories to produce military aircraft for Germany, except fighter planes which might be used offensively against Britain. The Germans asked the French to produce German models as well. In return Vichy asked for concessions on the demarcation line and the release of prisoners, but with no success. It was Flandin who in January 1941 abandoned this bargaining position and let the negotiations proceed nonetheless. An agreement was finally signed in July 1941. In return for producing planes for Germany, the French were also authorized to produce aircraft

[63] Burrin, *La France à l'heure*, 104.   [64] Baruch, *Servir l'État*, 80–1.

for themselves (something previously forbidden by the Armistice). The proportion of German to French planes would be approximately 2:1. The French were to produce 2,275 for Germany (including 1,480 German models) and 1,101 for France.

By November 1942, when the Germans occupied the whole country, they had still received only about half of the planes due. The shortfall, which also affected the planes for France, was due not to any French resistance, but to shortages of raw materials and to the difficulty of adjusting to German models. Nonetheless, the total contribution of the French aircraft industry to Germany was not insignificant: 27 per cent of Germany's transport planes in 1942, 42 per cent in 1943, and 49 per cent in 1944 had come from France. Planes produced in France supplied Rommel's African army in 1942 and German troops at Stalingrad in 1943.

If Vichy had not collaborated in this matter, the Germans would probably have dismantled French aviation factories and reassembled them in Germany. But there were more positive motives for co-operation. German orders kept the French aircraft industry going, allowed France to envisage building up an air force again, and provided employment to the aircraft workers who had been laid off after the Armistice. Their number had dropped from 250,000 in May 1940 to 40,000 in June; by 1942 it was back to 80,000; by 1944, 100,000.[65] The aircraft industry embodied a paradox which applied to French industry as a whole: the Germans posed a threat to the French economy, but they also provided the only prospect of its recovery. Negotiations were therefore unavoidable. Even if political concessions were not forthcoming, the French were also interested in other concessions—for example, the provision of raw materials lacking in France or guarantees that some production would be reserved for the French market. If the Germans wanted the French to supply them with manufactures, they had to allow them raw materials in return.

During all economic negotiations Vichy was vigilant about a possible penetration of German capital into France. At the Ministry of Finance, Maurice Couve de Murville was put in charge of monitoring this issue. In fact, this was one area where the Germans proved less predatory than expected. The one exception was the dye industry where the German chemical giant, IG Farben, backed by the German authorities, intended to restore the dominant position in the French market which it had lost after the First World War. An agreement signed in March 1941 compelled French manufacturers to join a new Franco-German mixed company, Francolor, where IG Farben held 51 per cent of the capital. The French government in return obtained some concessions: the president of the company would be French, and the agreement would not be taken as a proto-

[65] P. Klemm, 'La Production aéronautique française de 1940 à 1942', RHDGM 107 (1977), 53–74; 'Aperçus sur la collaboration aéronautique franco-allemande 1940–1943', RHDGM 108 (1977), 85–102; H. Chapman, State Capitalism and Working Class Radicalism in the French Aircraft Industry (Berkeley, 1991), 238–42.

type for other industries, as the Germans had originally wanted.[66] Other examples of financial penetration occurred not as part of a general strategy, but in piecemeal fashion, and for specific reasons. In the cases of the Denoël and Sorlot publishing houses, and the Havas press agency, the motive was one of ideological control. In the case of the Galeries Lafayette department store and Calmann-Lévy publishing house, the Germans seized an opportunity presented by 'Aryanization'. In the case of the Mumm champagne firm, the Germans recovered control of a firm which had been German-owned before 1914 and been taken over by France on the outbreak of war.

The absence of a concerted German plan for financial penetration of the economy indicated how unimportant a place was ascribed to the French economy in the post-war New Order. In the immediate term, they could obtain all they wanted from France thanks to their massive purchasing power and to the mechanisms of economic control they forced the French to set up. The most important of these was OCPRI on which an MBF report in September 1940 commented: 'a foundation has been laid on which French industrial production and distribution can be directed in a unified way under German control throughout the whole of France'.[67]

A whole series of contracts were signed with French industry: the Kehrl Agreement in February 1941 for the purchase of French textiles, various contracts for the purchase of bauxite, the Grunberg Plan for the delivery of shoes.[68] Invariably the terms were unfavourable to the French, but there was little choice. As Bouthillier told the government when recommending acceptance of the Kehrl Agreement: 'If this operation is not accepted in an agreement, it will be imposed upon us.'[69] In the case of some lost causes, Vichy did not exert itself to protect French industrial interests. This was true of the steel industry where the likelihood of losing Alsace-Lorraine permanently did not make it worth arguing too hard about a sector where German pre-eminence seemed assured.[70] By the end of 1941 the Germans were taking 40 per cent of French bauxite, 55 per cent of aluminium, 90 per cent of cement, 50 per cent of wool, 60 per cent of champagne, and 45 per cent of shoes and leather products.[71]

Even if economic negotiations were often disappointing to the French, the officials with whom they negotiated were more flexible than the higher political authorities. These were at least negotiations. Although unhappy about the terms of the textile agreement, the French negotiators found their opposite number, Hans Kehrl, encouraging in his views about the future of France's textile industry in the new Europe. He was said to have shown 'a spirit of comprehension . . . and a genuine desire for collaboration'.[72] Summarizing economic collaboration at the end of 1941, one high-ranking official noted that, however tough

---

[66] Margairaz, *L'État, les finances et l'économie*, 637–51.
[67] Milward, *New Order*, 69.
[68] Margairaz, *L'État, les finances et l'économie*, 591–668.
[69] Ibid. 610.
[70] Mioche 'Les Entreprises sidérurgiques sous l'occupation', 397–414.
[71] Margairaz, *L'État, les finances et l'économie*, 599–600.
[72] Ibid. 609–13.

Germany had been, she had been less 'eager than the Anglo-Saxon powers would have been in a similar situation to take commercial stakes'.[73]

Overall, then, these contacts helped to fuel the expectations of technocrats in the Darlan administration that ultimately collaboration could be conducted on a rational basis: economic logic would prevail over political prejudice. They viewed economic collaboration as a step towards the construction of a new Europe in which France would play a major role. Lehideux nursed the idea of three great road systems linking Bordeaux and Berlin, Cherbourg and Basel, Marseilles and Hamburg. In France itself sixteen roads would converge on Paris through sixteen monumental 'gates of the Marshal'.[74] The irony was that this vision of France as a modern industrial nation corresponded less to German plans for France as a weak agricultural economy than did the vision of the more anti-German traditionalists around Pétain. In that sense at least, the traditionalists were more realistic than the technocrats. But when it came to fantasy politics neither could compete with the Paris collaborationists.

[73] Ibid. 592–4; Rousso and Margairaz, 'Vichy la guerre et les entreprises', 358.
[74] Benoist-Méchin, *De la défaite au désastre*, ii. 71.

9

Collaborationism

Fanatics, Criminals, and Adventurers

Parisian collaborationism has fascinated film-makers and novelists. It is depicted as a world of louche marginality and decadence: fraternization with Germans over champagne in Maxims or the Tour d'Argent; glamorous first nights at the Opéra and galas at the German Embassy; job openings for informers, sadists, and black marketeers; opportunities for fanatics to indulge their hatred of Jews, Communists, Freemasons, or the British; the chance for failures to settle scores with rivals; or, finally, for those bored with existence, the excitement of transgressing conventional moral codes. In this light collaborationism becomes a series of individual stories of fanaticism, naivety, opportunism, and adventure.

Naivety and adventure were certainly present in the case of Marc Augier, a former pacifist who ended up fighting for Germany on the eastern front. In the 1930s Augier had been a leader of the non-Catholic youth hostel movement, with links to the Popular Front, but like many pacifists he became increasingly anti-Communist. By defending 'Europe' in the French (Charlemagne) division of the Waffen-SS, he rediscovered the outdoor life and youthful camaraderie which he had celebrated while supporting the Popular Front: this was 'collaborationism' as youth-hostelling and male fraternity.[1]

Fanaticism was present in the case of the historian Bernard Fäy, a professor at the Collège de France, who was made director of the Bibliothèque nationale, in place of Julien Cain, sacked because he was a Jew. Fäy, who ran a supposedly scholarly publication called *Documents Maçonniques,* was obsessed by Freemasonry; he even suspected Freemasons among the episcopate.[2] Among those with scores to settle was the journalist Alain Laubreaux, a leading light of *Je suis partout.* During the Occupation he became the most powerful Parisian theatre critic, on one occasion lavishing praise on a play he had himself written under a pseudonym. But how does one characterize the strange journey of Maurice Sachs? Before the war he had been a minor literary figure, friendly

---

[1] Gordon, *Collaborationism in France,* 254–6.   [2] Rist, *Un saison gâtée,* 433–4.

with Gide, Cocteau, and others. After the defeat, he lived for a while with a German officer. He started playing the black market and also spent some time in a homosexual brothel. In the autumn of 1942 he went to Germany, ending up in Hamburg where he worked as a crane operator, before becoming a Gestapo informer.[3]

The Occupation provided rich pickings for racketeers. The exorbitant occupation costs meant that there were German buyers disposing of sums too huge to spend legally. Equally there was no shortage of French sellers looking to sell above the official fixed price. These were perfect conditions for the emergence of a black market. Most German authorities in France set up purchasing services which operated on the black market, buying in France and reselling in Germany. The most important of these was the 'Otto Bureau', started by the Abwehr. By the spring of 1941 it employed 400 people, and had taken over rail-yards in the north of Paris from which it despatched its merchandise to Germany.

This system required a swarm of French middlemen. The most flamboyantly successful were two Jewish immigrants, Joseph Joinovici and Mandel Szkolnikov. Joinovici, of Romanian origin, had arrived in France in 1921 and made a fortune in scrap metal before the war; Szkolnikov, of Russian origin, had arrived in 1933 and worked in the garment trade. On the eve of the war, he was under threat of expulsion for issuing false cheques. After the Germans' arrival Szkolnikov's rise was meteoric. He supplied the Kriegsmarine, the SS, and the Otto bureau, building up a fortune which allowed him to accumulate huge amounts of property. Joinovici's success was on a less grand scale, but he built a large circle of contacts, among them the sinister Bonny-Lafont gang.

Lafont, whose real name was Henri Chamberlin, had a long criminal record for robbery. In 1940 he offered his services to the Abwehr. His speciality was finding premises vacated by Jews who had fled south. Their contents would end up with the Otto Bureau. Lafont was also called upon to do police work for the Germans, and he recruited accomplices from acquaintances he had encountered in gaol. He became a captain in the SS in 1941, and in the next year he teamed up with Pierre Bonny, a former police inspector sacked for corruption in 1934. The success of their activities allowed Lafont to buy an hôtel particulier in the rue Lauriston. Here they hosted lavish receptions at which German officers could meet collaborationist press barons and French actresses procure German patrons. In 1943, the Germans clamped down on the black market because it was drying up materials necessary for the German war effort. But if there were fewer opportunities for profits, there were more for torture as the Bonny-Lafont gang helped the Germans to track down resisters. The rue Lauriston torture chambers became infamous.[4]

---

[3] J.-M. Belle, *Les Folles Années de Maurice Sachs* (1979).

[4] Rochebrune and Hazera, *Les Patrons sous l'Occupation*, 182–246; J. Delarue, *Trafics et crimes sous l'Occupation* (1988), 17–142.

Frères-Ennemis: Doriot and Déat

Collaborationism was not only an accumulation of individual stories. It was also a political world setting itself up against Vichy, and offering a more radical vision of France's future. One should not, however, exaggerate the dichotomy between Vichy and Paris. Vichy often practised discreetly what the collaborationists preached vociferously. Vichy ministers like Marion and Benoist-Méchin were totally committed to a collaborationist position; various collaborationist groups received intermittent Vichy subsidies. Nonetheless the language employed by the Paris collaborationists was different from that of Vichy.[5] They talked more of Europe than France, viewing Hitler as a new Charlemagne reuniting Europe, or, after June 1941, as a holy crusader against Bolshevism. Where Vichy talked of national reconciliation, collaborationists preferred the language of denunciation. There was a newspaper, *Au pilori*, which existed just to denounce enemies of France—Communists, Freemasons, and above all, Jews.

The collaborationist world was not homogeneous—it contained pacifists and fascists, Socialists and Catholics—and the choice of collaborationism was not predetermined. Some former members of the clandestine right-wing organization, the Cagoule, became collaborationists, some ended up at Vichy, others in London.[6] Collaborationist politics was a vipers' nest of hatreds, all the more intense because power was so remote. There was a constellation of tiny organizations, all aspiring to become France's single fascist party. There were more candidates for this role in occupied Paris than there had been parties in the Third Republic. Some collaborationist groups, like Marcel Bucard's Francistes, had existed before the war; others, like Robert Hersant's Jeune Front, were new. Many groups had only the most notional existence. The Jeune Front's only sign of activity was to break the windows of Jewish shops on the Champs-Élysées.

Tiny organizations gave themselves grandiose names like the Ligue française d'épuration, d'entr' aide sociale et de collaboration européenne founded by Pierre Costantini and four friends in September 1940. Costantini was violently anti-British—he put up posters announcing that he had declared war on Britain—and anti-Semitic. His newspaper *L'Appel* ran a series of articles in 1941 on the theme 'Should the Jews be Exterminated?' He ended his life in a mental asylum.[7] More significant was Eugène Deloncle's Revolutionary Social Movement (MSR) which possibly had as many as 20,000 members in 1941. These included Eugène Schueller, founder of the cosmetics firm L'Oréal. Deloncle had been a leading member of the Cagoule, and was unable to throw off his habits of terrorism and conspiracy. On the night of 2 Ocotober 1941, he was responsible for the bombing of several Paris synagogues; he was also strongly suspected of involvement in the assassination in July 1941 of Marx Dormoy, the Socialist who had helped to break

---

[5] Ory, *Les Collaborateurs*, 146–67.   [6] Gordon, *Collaborationism in France*, 60.
[7] Ory, *Les Collaborateurs*, 91–8.

the Cagoule during the Popular Front government. These activities alienated some of Deloncle's followers and led to an internal coup against him from within the MSR in May 1942. By July 1942 he was plotting with the Abwehr, and possibly also with the Allies, against Hitler; in January 1944 he was shot by the Gestapo.[8]

Among this plethora of groups, two stand out: Marcel Déat's Rassemblement national populaire (RNP) and Jacques Doriot's PPF. In September 1940 Déat took over the pre-war Radical newspaper, *L'Œuvre*, using it to attack Vichy's half-hearted attitude to collaboration. In January 1941, he founded his own party, the RNP, which was an alliance between former neo-Socialists and Deloncle's MSR. This curious cohabitation between the earnest, former Socialist intellectual and the inveterate right-wing conspirator was Déat's attempt to build a movement transcending left and right, the embryo of a fascist single party. The RNP's immediate objective was to bring Laval back to power, and Déat with him. Characteristically Deloncle wanted to achieve this by a march on Vichy (*à la* Mussolini).

The RNP was founded with Abetz's approval, but once Germany no longer insisted on Laval's return to power, it lost its *raison d'être* and was reduced to railing harmlessly against Vichy 'reactionaries'. The RNP was also weakened by incompatibility between its two leaders. While Déat aspired to build a mass party, Deloncle was more interested in an elite force of shock troops; Déat's supporters wore suits, Deloncle's uniforms. When Déat was the victim of an assassination attempt in August 1941, he assumed Deloncle was the culprit. Whether or not this was true, the fact Déat suspected it showed the state their relations had reached. The break with Deloncle occurred in September 1941, and although this brought into the RNP some neo-Socialists who had been suspicious of Deloncle, it lost most of its MSR members and ended Déat's dream of a movement transcending previous divisions. By the end of the year, the coming man was Doriot.[9]

While Déat made the initial running, Doriot was reduced to reacting to him. Since Déat attacked Vichy, Doriot tried to ingratiate himself with it by publishing a collection of speeches under the title 'The Marshal's Man'. Since Déat was unreserved about collaboration, Doriot was cautious (possibly because of the Nazi–Soviet Pact). Since Déat had Abetz's support, Doriot cultivated the SS and the Abwehr. Gradually his rhetoric became more violent. 'It is intolerable', he declared in May 1941, 'that Mandel's blood has not served to mark a red line between the Third Republic and the National Revolution.'[10] It was Hitler's invasion of the Soviet Union which released Doriot's energies and gave him a cause.

---

[8] B. Gordon, 'The Condottieri of the Collaboration: Le Mouvement social révolutionnaire', *JCH* 10/2 (1975) 261–82; id., *Collaborationism in France*, 196–213.

[9] Id., *Collaborationism in France*, 90–129; Burrin, *La Dérive fasciste*, 385–419; M. Déat, *Mémoires politiques* (1989), 587–634.

[10] Burrin, *La Dérive fasciste*, 428.

He immediately advocated the creation of a volunteer force to join the German fight against Bolshevism. Déat, Deloncle, and the collaborationist leaders had no choice but to agree, and an anti-Bolshevik Legion (LVF) was formed.[11]

Vichy discouraged the recruitment of LVF volunteers in the South, although in November 1941 Pétain sent a message of support to the men who were defending 'part of our military honour'. The ambiguity was characteristic of Vichy's ambiguous stance towards collaborationism. The main problem for the LVF was that the Germans neither felt they needed help against the Soviet Union, nor wished to encourage French activism even in a good cause. For this reason, they imposed a ceiling of 10,000 men on the LVF. It took two years to reach 10,000 volunteers, and half of these were turned down by the Germans as unfit. The first three LVF battalions arrived on the eastern front in October 1941. Among them was Doriot, setting off to fight Bolshevism almost twenty years after he had arrived in Moscow as an idealistic young Communist disgusted by war. The LVF troops were unequipped for the Russian winter, and unhappy at having to fight in German uniform (with only a tricolour badge on the sleeve to signify their French affiliation). Their effectiveness was further undermined by squabbles between followers of Doriot and Deloncle. Two weeks later, after 250 casualties, they were removed from the front line and subsequently used only for police duties and action against partisans.[12]

Despite the LVF's unheroic record, Doriot acquired the prestige of being the only collaborationist leader to fight on the eastern front, apart from Deloncle who, after an endless series of 'farewell dinners', also went east, but only in a propaganda capacity.[13] The LVF kept Doriot away from France intermittently, but the meetings held on his return were triumphalist, and boosted the PPF's influence.

The Rank and File

Membership of the collaborationist movements is difficult to estimate. At its peak in 1942, the PPF had around 40,000–50,000 members (including North Africa), the RNP between 20,000 and 30,000.[14] Collaborationism was never a mass movement. If one adds up the membership of all the various movements between 1940 and 1944 (including some like Collaboration and the Milice to be discussed later) the total would not exceed 220,000, with the peak being reached at the end of 1942 when German success seemed at its height. But this cumula-

---

[11] Gordon, *Collaborationism in France*, 130–65; Burrin, *La Dérive fasciste*, 420–46; D. Wolf, *Doriot: Du communisme à la collaboration* (1969), 317–49; J.-P. Brunet, *Jacques Doriot* (1986), 309–64.

[12] Gordon, *Collaborationism in France*, 244–64; Wolf, *Doriot*, 350–7; Ory, *Les Collaborateurs*, 240–7; O. Davey, 'The Origins of the Légion des Volontaires contre le Bolchévisme', *JCH* 6/4 (1971), 29–45.

[13] Brunet, *Jacques Doriot*, 367.

[14] Gordon, *Collaborationism in France*, 119, 145, estimates 20,000–30,000 for the RNP, and 20,000 for the PPF; Burrin, *La France à l'heure*, 398, 422, estimates 20,000 for the RNP and 40,000–50,000 for the PPF.

tive figure overestimates the total numbers since some people joined more than one movement, or moved from one to another.[15]

Figures available for thirty-eight *départements* reveal no significant difference between the social bases of the movements. Their members were largely urban and lower middle class, with an under-representation of workers and peasants, and an over-representation of office workers, small businessmen, artisans, and shopkeepers. The PPF members were slightly younger than the RNP; the RNP had more functionaries and more women. Although both were strongest in the Paris region, the PPF also had provincial bases—especially in the south-east and North Africa—which it owed to its pre-war existence. In Marseilles, one of its regional strongholds before 1940, the PPF had around 1,500 members in 1942, while the RNP never had more than 60.[16]

What made people join these movements? Sometimes the motive may have been opportunism—a way of winning German favour. In Louis Malle's film *Lacombe Lucien*, the young peasant who joins the German police acquires a sense of power he has never enjoyed before. But joining the German police was an extreme step that few people took, and most members of French collaborationist movements acquired little social validation. Collaborationist activists were not popular, and in small communities they met with suspicion. The case of the small town in the Eure where the fifty RNP members kept their membership a secret was probably not untypical.[17] From the beginning, the windows of collaborationist offices were regularly smashed; by 1943, collaborationists were at risk of their lives from the Resistance. People ready to run such risks obviously had a high level of political commitment. About a third of those who joined collaborationist movements before the end of 1942 had some political past. Of these, about two-thirds came from the extreme right, about a quarter from the left, and less than 10 per cent from the moderate right. Members of collaborationist groups spent much time brawling with each other. The rest of the time they distributed tracts and papers, destroyed busts of Marianne, defaced Republican street names, denounced people to the authorities, or smashed up Jewish shops. In short, they remained outsiders, even after 1940.[18]

Leftist Collaborationism

If it is hardly surprising that the collaborationist rank and file mostly came from the extreme right, it is also important to note several former leftists among the collaborationist cadres. These were not, like Doriot or Déat, renegades from

---

[15] Burrin, *La France à l'heure*, 438 suggests a total of 250,000.

[16] Gordon, *Collaborationism in France*, 120–3; Ory, *Les Collaborateurs*, 110–15; Burrin, *La France à l'heure*, 431–8; P. Jankowski, *Communism and Collaboration: Simon Sabiani and Politics in Marseilles 1919–1944* (1985), 80–5.

[17] Burrin, *La France à l'heure*, 432.

[18] M. Sueur, 'La Collaboration politique dans le département du Nord (1940–1944)', *RHDGM* 135 (1984), 3–45.

the left since the mid-1930s, but people who had participated in the Popular Front: for example, the syndicalist Ludovic Zoretti, who had organized workers' educational projects during the Popular Front, or the Socialist Charles Spinasse, who had been in Blum's government.[19]

Usually pacifism and anti-communism both figured in their journey towards collaborationism. For trade unionists, the journey was eased by a lack of commitment to parliamentary liberalism. Some leftist collaborationists were former *planistes*—de Man followed the same route in Belgium—who had moved from non-Marxist socialism to anti-Marxist socialism. Some were seduced by the 'socialism' of the 'National Socialists': a delegation of trade unionists who visited Germany in March 1941 returned impressed by the conditions in German factories.[20] Some sought to recover a non-Marxist and French socialist tradition inspired by Proudhon, Saint-Simon, and Fourier. Spinasse denied that his commitment to a German Europe contradicted this return to French roots: 'I do not accept that by aligning [with Germany], we will have to accept a terrifying unity of thought . . . and action . . . It is what she offers that is original and unique that makes France useful to the European community.'[21]

In the end, the belief that collaborationism was compatible with any meaningful left-wing politics was based on an entire misreading of Nazism. Those who did not eventually jump off the collaborationist bandwagon ended up breaking with their left-wing origins. This was discovered by Spinasse who had in November 1941 founded a weekly paper, *Le Rouge et le bleu*, which defended collaboration while remaining sufficiently faithful to the values of the Popular Front to criticize the Riom trial and attack Déat's advocacy of a single party. The paper was banned in August 1942, showing that there was diminishing space for a collaborationism which was not fascist.[22]

No trajectory was more tortured than that of the Socialist Georges Soulès who had in the 1930s been on the left of the Party. As a former *polytechnicien*, Soulès was attracted by economic planning and had acted as an adviser to Blum's aide Jules Moch during the Popular Front. Soulès's support of collaborationism after 1940 is partially explicable by pacifism. More surprising was that he joined the MSR. He seems to have believed that, unlike the eternal talker Déat, Deloncle was a genuine man of action in search of an ideology. This offered the opportunity for an intellectual like Soulès to make his mark. At the end of 1941, however, Soulès started to lose faith in Deloncle, and together with the former Communist André Mahé, he formed a dissident faction within the MSR. They carried out a palace revolution, drove Deloncle out of the movement, and by the end of 1942 had taken control of it. They published a book calling for the rejuvenation of France by a new elite, inspired by a racist mystique. The book's heady

---

[19] In general see Ory, *Les Collaborateurs*, 128–45; M. Sadoun, *Les Socialistes sous l'Occupation résistance et collaboration* (1982), 77–108; Burrin, *La France à l'heure*, 391–402.

[20] Burrin, *La France à l'heure*, 394.

[21] Sadoun, *Les Socialistes sous l'Occupation*, 89.   [22] Ibid. 85–96.

mixture of Sorel, Rosenberg, and Nietzsche had little practical relevance since the MSR had few members left. At the end of 1943, Soulès founded a new movement called the Mouvement révolutionnaire français. Although despising Déat's intellectualism, Soulès suffered from the same defect. He also had Déat's infinite capacity for self-delusion, allied to a marked predilection for plotting. Soulès's was a mystical temperament in search of certainties, and from 1944 he turned to esotericism and the Cabbala.[23]

Unlike Soulès, most leftist collaborationists gravitated towards the RNP, especially after Déat's break with Deloncle. Five of the thirteen members of the RNP's governing committee were former Socialist activists. The RNP showed a lot of interest in social problems, especially workers' education which was looked after by Zoretti. In the orbit of the RNP were the collaborationist syndicalists who set up a paper, L'Atelier, a Syndicalist Centre for Propaganda (CSP), and a Social Labour Front (FST), whose name was inspired by the Nazi Arbeitsfront. The syndicalists who ran these organizations included important former CGT leaders like Georges Dumoulin, former head of the Nord Federation, and Marcel Roy who had run the Metallurgical Federation. Although such men had been central figures in pre-war trade unionism, the popular appeal of this leftist current of collaboration was minuscule. Dumoulin commented in June 1941: 'the base is hostile, indifferent or refractory'.[24] L'Atelier sold about 2,000 copies. The so-called Congress of the FST managed to attract 600 people thanks to an allowance of 150 francs per day paid to each delegate by the Germans. In twelve départements for which detailed figures are available, out of 32,400 pre-war Socialists, only thirty can be found among members of collaborationist groups.[25] Left-wing collaborationism had cadres without followers.

Nonetheless the presence of former left-wing leaders in the RNP gave it a distinctive sensibility in the politics of collaborationism. It represented a left wing and the PPF a right wing, although the distinction blurred with time.[26] Déat himself was reluctant to jettison all republican values. He condemned the removal of Marianne from schools and denounced Vichy's clericalism. He confided in the autumn of 1942 that his French philosophical training made it hard for him to swallow German racist thought.[27] Déat saw the Nazis as a twentieth-century incarnation of the soldiers of Year Two who had taken revolution to Europe on their bayonets. Doriot, on the other hand, was unbridled in his denunciations of traitors, Freemasons (suggesting that Déat was one), and Jews. The differences between Doriot and Déat were partly opportunistic: they both

---

[23] R. Abellio, Ma dernière mémoire, iii. Sol Invictus 1939–1947 (1980), 188–340; Gordon, Collaborationism in France, 204–11.

[24] Burrin, La France à l'heure, 394.

[25] Le Crom, Syndicats, nous voilà!, 210; Sadoun, 'Les Contraintes de la position', in Peschanski (ed.), Vichy 1940–1944, 51–67: 63.

[26] Burrin, 'Le Collaborationisme', in Azéma and Bédarida (eds.), La France des années noires, i. 364–83: 367–74.

[27] Tasca, in Peschanski (ed.), Vichy 1940–1944, 418.

wanted power and were trying to outflank each other in winning German favour. There were also temperamental antipathies deriving from their past careers. Doriot retained the ruthlessness of a former Bolshevik; Déat the earnestness of a former Socialist. In character they were the Danton and Robespierre of the National Revolution: Doriot the working-class rebel, Déat the lower middle-class scholarship boy; Doriot the earthy street fighter, Déat the ascetic intellectual (he did not smoke or drink); Doriot driven by passion, Déat by logic. The source of Doriot's passion was his hatred of communism. Déat was immured in the dialectical inevitability of his arguments: he allegedly wrote his six daily editorials for *L'Œuvre* at the start of the week. Each week he proved irrefutably, as he had done for ten years, that his political moment was about to dawn.[28]

Despite their differences, Doriot and Déat shared the same dilemma. They depended entirely on German patronage, but the Germans had no intention of bringing them to power. The French fascists could not win. To the extent that they had no popular base, they were of dubious value to Hitler; to the extent that they might acquire popularity, they were a possible threat to him: National Socialism was not for export. If Abetz encouraged Déat over Doriot, it was partly because Doriot seemed more liable to succeed.[29] Abetz wanted not to promote a French fascist movement which might one day take power, but to fragment French politics further. The collaborationists were to be a sword of Damocles suspended over the Vichy government—threatening enough to keep it in line, never strong enough to unseat it (unless the Germans wished).[30]

Circles of Influence

The audience for collaborationist ideas was larger than the membership of the collaborationist parties. Political activism was the most intense form of commitment, but not the only one. There were those who attended collaborationist meetings; those who read their newspapers; those who visited the exhibitions organized by the Germans to promote collaboration.

The first of these exhibitions, at the Petit Palais in October 1940, was on Freemasonry. Visitors could see objects seized from the lodges and read information about Freemasonry's links to the British and the Jews. In five weeks over 900,000 people visited this free exhibition, and then another 113,930 when it toured the provinces. An exhibition on 'European France' at the Grand Palais, between June and October 1941, attracted 635,000 visitors. It was followed between September 1941 and January 1942 by an exhibition on the 'Jew and France' at the Palais Berlitz. This attracted 255,600 visitors in Paris, and another 95,000 in the provinces. Finally, in March 1942, an exhibition on 'Bolshevism

---

[28] Ory, *Les Collaborateurs*, 90–115.   [29] Wolf, *Doriot*, 333.
[30] Burrin, *La Dérive fasciste*, 355; Gordon, *Collaborationism in France*, 66–7.

against Europe', at the Salle Wagram, attracted 370,000 visitors, and another 300,000 in the provinces.[31] These figures are not insignificant but hard to interpret. Presumably many visitors went out of simple curiosity; the numbers visiting the exhibition on 'the Jew and France' were inflated by school visits. The Masonic and Jewish exhibitions may have attracted people who were sympathetic with the objectives of the organizers without necessarily being pro-German: although the Germans subsidized these exhibitions, they were ostensibly organized by French frontmen.[32]

The Germans put considerable effort into propaganda with the Embassy and the Propaganda-Abteilung both vying for control.[33] The Propaganda-Abteilung had a staff of over 1,200 and six sections dealing with the press, radio, literature, propaganda, cinema, and culture (including theatre, art, and music). Its objective was to promote German influence, and annihilate French cultural dominance in Europe. But Abetz, who was conducting a more subtle game of seduction, wanted to restrict the Propaganda-Abteilung to press censorship and run cultural affairs himself. In July 1942, he won this battle. The German Institute became a centre of cultural collaboration, organizing exhibitions, lectures, language classes, and concerts. It revived the pre-war *Cahiers franco-allemands*.

German Institutes were also set up in the main provincial towns. There were fifteen of them in existence by 1944. In the first two years of the Occupation their language courses were so successful that people had to be turned away. Over 12,000 people enrolled in the autumn of 1941, but in the next year the numbers started to decline.[34] Efforts were also made to promote German literature. This was one of the jobs of Epting's deputy Karl-Heinz Bremer, who had been a lecturer at the École normale before the war. In January 1941 Bremer drew up a list of 500 works to be translated into French. In the end 331 of these did actually appear, but most of them were classics—twenty-one by Goethe, eleven by the Grimm brothers, seven by Schiller—rather than specifically Nazi products.[35]

Reading Goethe did not make one a collborator; nor indeed did learning German—even if there was something in Fabre-Luce's observation that 'the French bourgeois fulminates against collaboration, but learns German: that means that he thinks it is durable'.[36] But the Germans also found French people willing to work for them in the areas of more overtly ideological propaganda. These were often professional anti-Semites and anti-Freemasons who now had access to funds for the first time in their lives. Henry Coston, one of the most indefatigable anti-Masonic polemicists of the 1930s, set up an anti-Masonic

[31] Burrin, *La France à l'heure*, 297–301.

[32] A. Kaspi, *Les Juifs pendant l'Occupation* (1991), 105–110.

[33] J. Nobécourt, 'L'Occupant allemand', in Gervereau and Peschanski (eds.), *La Propagande sous Vichy*, 82–91; Burrin, *La France à l'heure*, 92–104; Bertrand Dorléac, *L'Art de la défaite*, 45–50; C. Lévy, 'L'Organisation de la propagande', *RHDGM* 64 (1966), 7–28.

[34] Burrin, *La France à l'heure*, 303–10; Geiger, *L'Image de la France*, 245–7.

[35] Geiger, *L'Image de la France*, 250–1.   [36] Burrin, *La France à l'heure*, 305.

Action and Documentation Centre (CAD) in the premises of the Grand Lodge; the former naval officer Paul Chack created a Centre of Anti-Bolshevik Studies and a Committee of Anti-Bolshevik Action; Paul Sézille, a retired army officer, created the Institute for the Study of Jewish Questions (IEQJ).[37]

These pseudo-scientific bodies reached an infinitesimal audience. More important was the collaborationist press. Even a vicious rag like *Au pilori* sold about 50,000 copies; Déat reached more people as editorialist of *L'Œuvre* (with sales of around 130,000) than as leader of the RNP. After the arrival of the Germans, most of the pre-war Paris press had moved to the Free Zone. Of the forty-odd daily and weekly papers published in occupied Paris, only six were survivors from before 1940, but these included three very famous titles: *Le Matin*, which resumed publication on 17 June, three days after the arrival of the Germans, *L'Illustration*, which resumed on 10 August, and *Le Petit Parisien* which resumed on 8 October.

The presence of these familiar titles was important to the Germans because it nurtured the illusion that life was continuing as normal. To fill the void left by the absence of *Le Temps*, France's most respected newspaper, Abetz sponsored a replacement, *Les Nouveaux Temps*, which appeared from November 1940. The editor was Abetz's old friend Jean Luchaire, a lifelong Briandist. As a journalist in the 1930s, Luchaire had been supplied with funds by the Quai d'Orsay; after 1940, he was equally happy to take them from the Germans. One observer commented that he would have taken money from the Mongols if they had arrived in Paris. Luchaire was not alone in this. The collaborationist press was heavily subsidized and firmly controlled by the Germans. Increasingly also, they sought a financial stake in it. With the backing of the German Embassy, the German businessman Gerhard Hibbelen built up a press empire in France. By 1944, he controlled almost half of the Parisian press.[38]

The total readership of the Parisian daily press was considerable—about 3 million in October 1940, about 1.7 million by 1944—but this cannot be assumed to reflect the real audience of collaborationism. There are many practical reasons why people read daily newspapers. The case of political weeklies, however, is different: they imply some level of interest in, or support for, the principles they represent. The total circulation of political weeklies in the Occupied Zone was about 300,000. If this figure is supplemented by the circulation of weeklies in the Unoccupied Zone defending a similar line, one reaches a total readership of about one million. This implies a considerable audience for, or at least curiosity about, collaborationist ideas.[39]

The first new collaborationist weekly founded in the Occupied Zone was Alphonse de Chateaubriant's *La Gerbe*, founded in July 1940. De Chateaubriant

[37] Taguieff et al., *L'Antisémitisme de plume*, 351–7, 370–84, 442–6.

[38] P.-M. Dioudonnat, *L'Argent Nazi à la conquête de la presse française 1940–1944* (1981); C. Lévy, 'Les Nouveaux Temps' et l'idéologie de la collaboration (1974); Thalmann, *La Mise au pas*, 158–61.

[39] Burrin, *La France à l'heure*, suggests between one and two million readers.

was a self-important minor novelist who had won the Prix Goncourt in 1911. He was a conservative Catholic whose epiphany had been a meeting with Hitler in 1936. On his return he wrote that if Hitler's one hand was stretched out in Nazi salute, the other invisibly clasped the hand of God.[40] At the time even French fascists had ridiculed such pronouncements, but Chateaubriant increasingly saw himself as a sage and prophet. *La Gerbe* became the vehicle of his conviction that Nazism was the only spiritual force capable of withstanding communism. The paper paid its contributors well and attracted significant names like Henri de Montherlant, Colette, and Jean Giono. Chateaubriant was too distracted to interfere much with what they wrote. It sold as many as 100,000 copies, and its readers received a somewhat partial view of the realities of Germany. One article in 1943 was devoted to Goering, the huntsman and lover of forests.[41]

Chateaubriant's other venture was the group Collaboration founded at the end of 1940. Its governing committee included worthies like the rector of the Catholic Institute of Paris, the director of the Opéra-Comique, and the curator of the Musée Rodin. The movement sold the message of collaboration through lectures, cultural events, and in the columns of its journal, *Collaboration*. Although the group claimed 100,000 members, the real number was nearer 40,000. Nonetheless, its events attracted good audiences: a lecture tour of the Unoccupied Zone by Professor Friedrich Grimm was greeted by full houses everywhere. The Embassy estimated in September 1943 that some 200,000 people had attended events organized by Collaboration. The movement was authorized in the Vichy Zone, demonstrating again the porousness of the frontier between Vichy and Paris. It was the respectable face of collaborationism, and the elite of local society, including usually a representative of the prefect, attended its events. This was collaboration as provincial self-improvement, a world away from the street brawlers of the PPF.[42]

Collaboration as Hatred and Fraternity: *Je suis partout*

More strident was the tone of the weekly *Je suis partout*, which resumed publication in February 1941 and became the most successful politico-literary collaborationist weekly, selling up to 250,000 copies in 1942, 300,000 by 1944.[43] Like *La Gerbe*, it attracted some distinguished writers who were not politically committed (Marcel Aymé, Jean Anouilh), but its regular contributors were unconditional supporters of collaboration. The editor, Robert Brasillach (1909-45), was one of those young Maurrassians increasingly attracted to fascism during

[40] P. Ory, *La France allemande: Paroles du collaborationisme français (1933–1945)* (1977), 36–9.
[41] Verdès-Leroux, *Refus et Violences*, 192–8.
[42] Ory, *Les Collaborateurs*, 62–4; Gordon, *Collaborationism in France*, 230–43; Burrin, *La France à l'heure*, 411–16; C. Brice, 'Le Groupe "Collaboration" 1940–1944' (unpublished *mémoire de maîtrise*, Paris-I, 1978).
[43] Dioudonnat, *Je suis partout*, 346.

the 1930s. Sharing his generation's disgust with parliamentary politics, Brasillach's original interests had been more literary than political. He became literary editor of *Action française* at the age of 22, and by 1937 he had published four novels. It was after 6 February 1934 that politics started impinging on him. Writing for *Je suis partout* in the late 1930s, he developed a strong sense of camaraderie with the other young contributors. Ever since his student days at the École normale supérieure, Brasillach idealized what he described, using the English word, as the life of the 'gang', the group of convivial comrades, linked by a common vision of the world. He had never entirely got over the memory of student life or developed emotionally beyond it. One theme running through his novels is that life is not worth living after 30. The same cult of camaraderie and youth informed his vision of fascism.[44]

Brasillach's fascination with fascism was sparked by a meeting with the Belgian fascist leader Léon Degrelle in 1936. The small, chubby, and bespectacled Brasillach was seduced by Degrelle's youthful good looks, describing him as a 'poet of action'. Brasillach's views were reinforced by a visit to Nuremberg in 1937 where he was enraptured by this politics of 'poetry', 'youth', and 'joy' (all key words for Brasillach). Fascism offered an aesthetic politics to rescue the world from decadence. But Brasillach's residual Maurrassianism prevented him from succumbing totally to Nazism at this stage. He had not been impressed by Hitler—'a sad vegetarian functionary'. Brasillach felt more drawn to the Falange, and he wrote a pamphlet in homage to the Cadets of the Alcazar of Toledo (another group of young men) holding out against the Republicans. His cult of youth and the outdoor life led him also to admire the young hitchhikers of the Popular Front. There is an undeniable homoeroticism in Brasillach's writing.

After 1940, Brasillach's reticence towards Nazism disappeared. Victory had shown that fascism was the poetry of the century, the 'highest artistic creation' of the time.[45] With six other French writers, Brasillach attended a 'European' Congress of Writers organized at Weimar in October 1941. There he discovered Germany's 'eternal spirit of creative youth', so different from the 'wrinkled and decrepit' French Republic, 'a syphilitic strumpet, smelling of cheap perfume and vaginal discharge'.[46] He became friendly with Karl-Heinz Bremer, this 'big blond boy', a 'young Siegfried', as he put it. Bremer's death on the eastern front in 1942 affected Brasillach greatly.[47]

Those who celebrate Brasillach's lyrical, almost innocent, fascism, overlook the other side of his wartime journalism: the incitements to murder, the implacable calls to violence, and the frenzied anti-Semitism. On one occasion he wrote: 'What are we waiting for to assassinate the Communist leaders already

[44] R. Tucker, *The Fascist Ego: A Political Biography of Robert Brasillach* (1975) is the best study.
[45] Carroll, *French Literary Fascism*, 118.
[46] Tucker, *Fascist Ego*, 231.   [47] Ibid. 228.

imprisoned . . . Against those who want the death of the country, EVERYTHING is legitimate.' In the Occupation such articles were not the kind of adolescent provocation they might once have been. The same is true of Brasillach's notorious comment about the Jews in September 1942: 'We must remove the Jews in a block, and not keep the young ones.' In 1943, when it became clear that the war was lost, Brasillach felt *Je suis partout* should reduce its political content and concentrate more on literature. This issue split the editorial team, and Brasillach stopped writing for the journal from August. But he never disavowed collaboration, and continued to write for other collaborationist papers.[48]

In this editorial dispute, Lucien Rebatet (1903-72) was on the other side. Rebatet started his career in 1929 writing music and film criticism for *Action française*. He was one of a younger group of contributors (like Brasillach) who joined the paper at this time, and introduced a breath of artistic modernism. Although this had no effect on Maurras whose cultural tastes had not moved beyond 1890, the fact that people like Rebatet nonetheless felt at home in *Action française* is further proof of Maurras's immense power of attraction in the inter-war years. During the Occupation Rebatet wrote for *Je suis partout* on both political and artistic subjects—he was the regular film critic—but what made him famous was the publication, in July 1942, of his book *Les Décombres*.

Despite its length, *Les Décombres*, a memoir mixed with long reflections on the current state of France, became the publishing sensation of the Occupation: 65,000 copies were sold in the first month, and Denoël, its publisher, claimed that only paper shortage prevented him selling another 200,000. In *Les Décombres*, Rebatet proclaimed his total commitment to Germany: 'I wish the victory of Germany because her war is my war.' One of Rebatet's main targets was his former mentor Maurras. The book's tone is best rendered by direct quotation. One passage nurses fantasies of murder: 'Oh, my machine gun, so often caressed in my dreams, facing the despised gangs of the Popular Front . . . the gilded ghettos of Sodom . . . A hundred well-aimed machine gunners . . . I shoot like a god, greedily, passionately, in small steady bursts.' Of François Mauriac, he writes: 'a rich bourgeois with the shifty face of a false El Greco . . . oscillating in his prose between the eucharist and the pederastic brothel . . . is one of the most obscene rascals to have sprouted from the Christian dung-heap of our era'.

The book is riddled with an almost delirious anti-Semitism. One of Rebatet's criticisms of Maurras was his lack of racism. Rebatet's comment on the film *Jew Süss* was that it was agreeable to watch, even if only fictionalized, the hanging of a Jew; he expressed his joy at seeing Jews forced to wear a yellow star; he poured out his bile on Jewish art, Jewish writers, the Jewish 'bacillus', the Jewish 'microbe'. Rebatet admitted that some Jews had talent, but this concession only

---

[48] Verdès-Leroux, *Refus et violences*, 99–124, 151–63; Tucker, *Fascist Ego*, 253–60.

allowed him to demonstrate the disinterested purity of his anti-Semitism: he declared himself ready to smash the 'marvellous' recordings by Menuhin and Horowitz, and to incinerate the paintings of Pisarro, 'the only great painter of Israel'.[49]

The only writer whose rage matched Rebatet's was Céline. But Céline was not a member of the *Je suis partout* group, which he described as a 'feverish club of ambitious little pederasts'.[50] In fact Céline was too anarchistic to belong to any coterie. For this reason, his defenders exculpate him from any accusation of collaboration. At a dinner at the German Embassy in February 1944, he brooded in surly silence before launching into an impassioned tirade whose theme was that the Germans had lost the war, and that Hitler was dead and had been secretly replaced by a Jew. The rant went on until Abetz had him taken home by the embassy chauffeur.[51] But although the Germans found Céline difficult, they certainly considered him an ally, and the picture of Céline as an irascible and eccentric misanthrope, disconnected from politics, is too convenient.

In 1941, Céline published a third anti-Semitic pamphlet, *Les Beaux Draps*, and reissued the previous two. In his new preface to the *École des cadavres* he proudly affirmed that it had been the only work of its date to be anti-Semitic, racist, and collaborationist. He visited the anti-Semitic exhibition and wrote to complain about the absence of his books, and he was present for the opening of the IEQJ. In March 1942 he was at a dinner organized by the Association of Anti-Jewish Journalists, attended by the cream of the collaborationist press, as well as by Abetz's deputy Schleier. He was also on good terms with several figures in the SS.

Although it is true that Céline contributed no article to the collaborationist press, he wrote numerous letters to it (five to *Au pilori*, six to *Je suis partout*), usually to denounce the inadequacy of anti-Semitic measures and the prevalence of philo-Semitism. The extremism of some of Céline's statments made people wonder sometimes if he meant to be taken seriously—the German officer Ernst Jünger reports him as saying in December 1941 that he was 'amazed that we don't shoot, hang, exterminate the Jews . . . Amazed that someone possessing a bayonet doesn't make use of it'[52]—but his letters to the collaborationist press in fact represented greater political involvement than he had ever shown before the war.[53]

[49] Rebatet, *Les Décombres*; R. Belot, *Lucien Rebatet: Un itinéraire fasciste* (1994); R. Belot, 'Lucien Rebatet, ou l'antisémitisme comme événement littéraire', in Taguieff et al. (eds.), *L'Antisémitisme de plume*, 205–30; Ory, *Les Collaborateurs*, 116–27; Verdès-Leroux, *Refus et violences*, 163–73.

[50] Belot, *Lucien Rebatet*, 315.

[51] Benoist-Méchin, *À l'épreuve*, 345–58.

[52] Verdès-Leroux, *Refus et violences*, 232.

[53] In general see P. Alméras, *Les Idées de Céline* (1992); F. Gibault, *Céline 1932–1944: Délires et pérsécutions* (1985); A. Duraffour, 'Céline, un antijuif fanatique', in Taguieff et al. (eds.), *L'Antisémitisme de plume*, 147–97.

Drieu's NRF: Literary Collaborationism

The ravings of Céline or the fury of Rebatet were less valuable to the Germans than the support of writers not previously known for pro-German sentiments. For this reason they attached great importance to the editorship of the *NRF* by the fascist writer Drieu la Rochelle, hoping that the journal's prestige would encourage distinguished writers to contribute to it. Abetz allegedly remarked: 'there are three great powers in France: communism, the big banks, and the *NRF*'.[54] Drieu had originally gone to see Abetz about setting up a single party, but there were quite enough of these on the horizon already, and he was instead charged with taking over the *NRF*. He secured the agreement of its publisher Gaston Gallimard who hoped this would safeguard his publishing house. For the same reason, the *NRF*'s former editor Jean Paulhan also gave his benediction, but refused any further association with the *NRF* for himself.[55]

Writing for Drieu's *NRF* did not make one a collaborator, even less a collaborationist. This was certainly not the case of Paul Valéry (despite his ardent support of Pétain),[56] who contributed a poem to the second issue in January 1941, nor André Gide who contributed pieces to the first and third issues. But many who agreed to write, particularly if they continued after the initial few issues, were aware of the implications of their decision, and the roster of contributors provides a gallery of the more celebrated writers willing to lend their name, at some level, to collaboration. Of the sixty or so writers who agreed to contribute something, slightly over half had already written for the *NRF* before the war.

A writer whose contribution to the first issue in December 1940 caused considerable shock was Jacques Chardonne. Born into a wealthy Cognac family from the south-west, Chardonne owned the Stock publishing house. He was most famous for his novel *Le Bonheur de Barbezieux* (1938) which celebrated the *douceur de vie* of the community of Barbezieux in the Charente and presented it as an epitome of the charms of provincial France. After the defeat Chardonne rushed to Paris to see if Stock was safe, and was pleasantly surprised by the welcome he received from the Germans. Out of this surprise was born the notorious article, 'L'Été à La Maurie', in which Chardonne described a meeting between a French peasant wine-grower and the German colonel posted in his region, both of them Verdun veterans. The German behaves with 'courtesy' and 'distinction', commenting to his French host: 'It must be painful for you to see us here.' The peasant replies: 'I would have preferred to have invited you. But there is nothing I can do to change things. Enjoy my Cognac. I offer it to you gladly.' In 1941 Chardonne republished this piece in the book *Chronique privée*

[54] P. Hebey, *'La Nouvelle Revue française' des années sombres juin 1940 à juin 1941: Des intellectuels à la dérive* (1992), 123.
[55] Ibid. 115–32.
[56] Verdès-Leroux, *Refus et violences*, 283–8.

de l'an 1940 which expanded on the theme of reconciliation.[57] His next book
Voir la figure (October 1941) went further, arguing that Germany, so generous in
victory, offered France her only prospect of survival in a reorganized Europe. As
Chardonne wrote to Paulhan in November 1940: 'France was dead, Hitler is our
providence.'[58] In this second book Chardonne expressed his fear of communism,
and perhaps the best explanation of the conversion of a writer not previously
known for political statements, was his conviction that Germany was the only
protection which the cosy world of Barbizieux enjoyed against this threat.[59]

Another writer known for his descriptions of provincial society was Marcel
Jouhandeau who had created in his fiction the imaginary community of
Chaminadour in the south-west. His public conversion to anti-Semitism in 1936
went hand in hand with increasingly conservative politics. In this context his
eight contributions to Drieu's *NRF* are not surprising. He also attended the Congress of European writers at Weimar in 1941. In his diary of the trip he wrote
that his presence was meant to demonstrate that 'France is not necessarily Germanophobe even in the present circumstances' and 'to make my body a fraternal bridge between France and Germany'. Given that he was pursuing an affair
with a German officer while on the trip, this was, as Burrin remarks, more than
a figure of speech.[60]

Henry de Montherlant was also not insensible to the physical charms of
German soldiers, although he is not recorded as having any affairs with them.
Montherlant arrived in Paris in May 1941 after his compulsive pursuit of young
boys had led to two close shaves with the police in the Unoccupied Zone. His
rallying to collaboration was not to have been predicted since no one had more
violently excoriated the Munich agreement. He declared that the French had
become a nation capable only of listening to the Corsican crooner Tino Rossi
and playing *belote*. The same contempt for weakness which inspired Montherlant's condemnation of Munich now led him to admire the force which had
swept France away. For Montherlant, who liked sporting metaphors, France had
been fairly beaten, and she must be sportsmanlike in defeat. It was not for
'narrow-shouldered . . . balding' intellectuals to carp at the vitality of these young
German troops 'streaming with sweat'. In *Je suis partout* in November 1941
Montherlant wrote: 'Europe will only be saved by a virile aristocracy, a heroic
elite which has always to go against Christian morality.'

Montherlant published his reflections on the defeat in *Solstice de juin* (1941),
a collection of articles which had previously appeared in *La Gerbe* and the *NRF*.
He saw France's defeat as the victory of healthy paganism over feeble Christian-

[57] J. Chardonne, *Chronique privée de l'an 1940* (1940), 94, 115, 138–43, 214–17.
[58] Hebey, *'La Nouvelle Revue française'*, 130.
[59] G. Guitard-Auviste, *Jacques Chardonne* (1984); Hebey, *'La Nouvelle Revue française'*, 287–98; Verdès-Leroux, *Refus et violences*, 233–40.
[60] M. Jouhandeau, *Journal sous l'Occupation* (1980), 84; Verdès-Leroux, *Refus et violences*, 225–7; Burrin, *La France à l'heure*, 354; J. Grenier, *Sous l'Occupation* (1997), 293 n.; Hebey, *'La Nouvelle Revue française'*, 350–60.

ity. The swastika was the wheel of fate, and 1940 was a moment in the eternal cycle of defeat and victory. The passage that caused most shock was Montherlant's description of a moment in the summer of 1940 when he had watched the writhing of a caterpillar on which he was urinating. Having shown his power over the creature, he had then spared it. The analogy was clear enough—the French being cast in the role of the caterpillar—and so was the moral: the defeated must throw themselves on the mercy of their conquerors. For all his celebration of virility, Montherlant's was a counsel of prudence and realism. In fact he was an exceptionally timid individual always worried that his sexual escapades would come to the attention of the police. Walking around Paris one day with the writer Jean Grenier, he insisted they lower their voice when passing in front of a building occupied by the Germans in case they were overheard.[61]

Montherlant's argument for collaboration as a moment in the millennial rise and fall of civilizations was also employed by Alfred Fabre-Luce who compared France's defeat to that of Greece by Rome. Like the Romans, Fabre-Luce argued, the Germans were 'respectful, almost timid, conquerors' whose rough edges would be smoothed out by time: French intelligence would prevail over German force. A long-standing advocate of Franco-German reconciliation, in the Occupation Fabre-Luce was one of the most seductive and sophisticated proponents of collaboration. His anthology of French writers who allegedly prefigured 'the New Europe' gave Hitler a pedigree which included Renan, Paul Valéry, Péguy, Maurras, Pascal, and Gide. Nazism was almost transformed into part of the French patrimony.

Fabre-Luce was one of those *grands bourgeois*—son of the founder of the Crédit Lyonnais bank—whose Europeanism derived from a sense of belonging to a cosmopolitan civilization of taste, refinement, money, and manners, collaboration as viewed from a grand apartment on the Avenue Foch. During the Occupation, he published three successive volumes of his *Journal de la France*. These offer a well-informed portrait of the period and also function as subtle apologetics. The first volume contains a passage showing that the disadvantages of Occupation had compensations: cars might no longer be available but one could cross the road safely; there might be fewer books published but one could return to the classics. (This celebration of the more austere virtues was a stock-in-trade of collaborationist writers, especially those likely to be seen at glamorous Embassy parties.) But one hardly has to scratch the surface of Fabre-Luce's polish to find some standard themes: the decadence of the old regime, the Jewish 'problem'.[62]

Far removed from Fabre-Luce's Parisian sophistication was Jean Giono who

---

[61] Grenier, *Sous l'Occupation*, 297; Hebey, *'La Nouvelle Revue française'*, 377–90; J.-L. Garet, 'Montherlant sous l'Occupation', *VSRH* 31 (1991), 65–73; R. Golsan, 'Henry de Montherlant: Itinerary of an Ambivalent Fascist', in id. (ed.), *Fascism, Aesthetics and Culture* (1992), 143–63.

[62] G. Loiseaux, *La Littérature de la défaite et de la collaboration* (1984), 314–16, 358; A. Fabre-Luce, *Journal de la France 1939–1940* (Geneva, 1946); Hebey, *'La Nouvelle Revue française'*, 305–17.

spent most of the Occupation in Provence, dreaming of the day when the peasantry would march on Paris and sweep away the rotten civilization of the city. When indulging these fantasies, the supposedly pacific Giono happily imagined 'rivers of blood'. In this context it is not surprising to find him telling a fellow-writer in August 1940 that the defeat of France was insignificant compared to the fact that a world based on machines was coming to an end. Since German civilization was based on machines, it was doomed, and if the defeat had ruined the industry of the north-east of France, it was to be welcomed. In these circumstances, Giono's five contributions to Drieu's *NRF* and others to *La Gerbe* are not surprising, nor that he was the subject of a flattering article in the German magazine *Signal* in March 1942.[63]

Other *NRF* contributors included the philosopher Alain whose lifelong pacifism made him an easy target for Drieu's invitation, even if his entire philosophical and political writing had been about defending the freedom of the individual; the critic Ramon Fernandez, unable to survive without his name in print; and Paul Morand whose anti-Semitism and conservatism had become more pronounced in the 1930s: his *Chroniques de l'homme maigre* (1941) celebrated a Paris free of Americans and Polish Jews.[64]

These trajectories all have their own logic: pacifism in the case of Alain; a sort of peasant Messianism in the case of Giono; a cult of force in the case of Montherlant; conservative solipsism in the case of Chardonne; Europeanism in the case of Fabre-Luce. Their degree of commitment varied. How many collaborationist papers did they write for? How long did they continue doing so? How political were their contributions? Did they go on either of the two trips to Weimar organized by the Germans in October 1941 and October 1942? The answers to these questions defined each individual's level of commitment.

Chardonne was one of only three writers on both Weimar visits, but after 1942 he abstained from further public statements, and decided not to publish a third collaborationist volume, already in proof, from which his already tarnished reputation would never have recovered. Jouhandeau went on the first Weimar trip, but avoided public statements. Giono, who was well viewed by the Germans, went on neither trip. He turned down an invitation to the second on the grounds that his mother was sick, and despite the fact, as he wrote to the German consulate in Marseilles, that 'I had been waiting for it with impatience' since it 'would have allowed me to continue with yet more faith in the work of Franco-German reconciliation for which I have worked since 1931'.[65] Montherlant went on neither trip and gradually distanced himself from collaboration. He contributed to no more collaborationist publications after February 1943.

One must not exaggerate the number or importance of the writers on this

[63] Grenier, *Journal de l'Occupation*, 209; Hebey, *'La Nouvelle Revue française'*, 332–9; P. Citron, *Giono* (1995) is somewhat apologetic.

[64] Burrin, *La France à l'heure*, 351; Hebey, *Nouvelle Revue française*, 318–31, 391–7.

[65] Burrin, *La France à l'heure*, 354.

list. Intellectual collaboration was the case of a few names spread thinly, not the abdication of an entire elite. Raymond Aron in London concluded that 'none of the great names' of French literature were collaborating, the most significant ones being, in his estimation, Chardonne, Montherlant, and Fabre-Luce.[66] A year into running the *NRF*, Drieu noted that he had attracted only 'second rank' people: 'apart from a few pages of Montherlant I have published nothing worthwhile'. In January 1943 he recognized that 'almost all that is intelligent and lyrical in France is against us'.[67] In June 1943 he abandoned the editorship, aware that he had failed and Germany was going to lose.

Drieu: Collaborationism as Self-Hatred

Such weary disillusionment was a leitmotif of Drieu's entire career. This made him quite different from Brasillach who genuinely enjoyed the presence of the Germans and felt nostalgic, but never regretful, as the war drew to its conclusion. In February 1944, he wrote his famous phrase: 'All Frenchmen of intelligence have more or less slept with Germany during these last years, not without quarrels, and the memory will remain sweet.'[68] Drieu, however, moved from disappointment to disappointment, into ever deeper waters of rancour and self-pity.

Drieu was the most talented intellectual to throw himself so fully into collaborationism. In 1939 he was an established writer with eight novels and numerous short stories to his name. The Communist writer Louis Aragon had been one of his closest friends, and Malraux, who had been another, could write of him in 1959 that he was 'one of the most noble beings I have ever met' and a 'magnificent writer, a stylist of the first order'.[69] Anyone who has sampled the bile of Drieu's war diaries must take the nobility on trust, but the eclecticism of Drieu's friendships reveals his substantial reputation among his contemporaries.

Drieu was one of those intellectuals whose moorings were definitively broken by the Great War. From the war, which was the defining experience of his life, he drew contradictory conclusions. In his *Comédie de Charleroi* (1934), Drieu described war as an epiphanal experience, revealing that it was possible to become a Man. Elsewhere he wrote the opposite, asserting that modern technology had deprived war of its heroism: it had become impersonal and industrial. Such contradictions are characteristic of Drieu: there was little coherence in his restless quest for political bearings. He flirted with Dadaism and surrealism in the early 1920s; he briefly participated in Redressement français and then joined Bergery's Front commun in 1933; he announced his conversion to fascism in the book

[66] Verdès-Leroux, *Refus et violences*, 145, 234.
[67] P. Drieu la Rochelle, *Journal 1939–1945* (1992), 273; Loiseaux, *La Littérature de la défaite*, 504.
[68] Verdès-Leroux, *Refus et violences*, 155–62, 191.
[69] R. Soucy, *Fascist Intellectual: Drieu la Rochelle* (1979), 7.

Socialisme fasciste in 1934; he joined Doriot's PPF in 1936, and resigned from it in October 1938; he opposed the Munich agreement and considered going to Britain after the Fall of France, but instead stayed, and rallied to collaboration.[70]

The only consistent thread to Drieu's politics lay in his belief in France's decadence. In *Mesure de France* (1922), he concluded that France's victory had set the seal on this decadence. France had only won thanks to her allies, and the French soldier had not shown the fighting qualities of the British or Germans. Drieu felt increasing disgust for his compatriots: 'it is horrible to go for a walk and encounter so much decadence and ugliness . . . the bent backs, the slumped shoulders, the swollen stomachs, the small thighs, the flabby faces'.[71] He particularly despised the 'small, brown Frenchmen of the South and the Centre'. The French, he said, were only interested in fishing, aperitifs, and *belote*.

During his PPF period Drieu wrote a hagiographical biography of Doriot. Unlike the average 'pot-bellied intellectual' politician, Drieu's Doriot was a real man, 'an athlete who embraces the debilitated body of France . . . and breathes into it his own bursting health'.[72] But France's decadence was moral as well as physical. The hero of Drieu's autobiographical novel, *Gilles*, returns from the front to find Paris rotted by drugs, sodomy, modern art, and dancing. The symbol of this decomposing modernity was the Jew: 'I cannot stand the Jews because they are par excellence the modern world', says one of his characters.[73] 'I hate the Jews. I have always hated the Jews', he wrote in 1942.[74] In fact, he was not even consistent in this. In the 1920s, he claimed not to be a racist. His first wife, Colette Jeramec, whom he married in 1917 and divorced three years later, was Jewish. If the depiction of the marriage in *Gilles* is to be believed, Drieu could not forgive her for the fact that he had married her for her money.

Against the modern world, Drieu idealized the golden age of medieval Europe as an ascetic epoch of warriors and master builders. His book *Geneva or Moscow* (1928) argued that the only cure for French decadence was a European federation. After 6 February 1934, Drieu decided that only fascism could regenerate France. The dilettante hero of *Gilles* redeems himself fighting for Franco. By the outbreak of war, disappointed by Doriot, Drieu had become detached from politics. He was now obsessed by the idea that he was insufficiently appreciated by the *NRF* literary establishment, and one consolation he took from France's defeat was a chance for revenge over the 'gang of Jews, pederasts and timid surrealists' who ran the *NRF*.[75] Drieu had not otherwise welcomed defeat. Before 1940, he was not particularly Germanophile despite being enthralled by a visit to Nuremberg in 1935. He had left the PPF because of Doriot's support for Munich. After France's defeat, however, Drieu came to see Hitler as the incarnation of fascist force and the instrument of European unity. The continuity

---

[70] In general see: Soucy, *Fascist Intellectual.*   [71] Ibid. 205.   [72] Ibid.

[73] M. Winock, 'Une parabole fasciste: *Gilles* de Drieu La Rochelle', in id., *Nationalisme, antisémitisme et fascisme*, 346–73.

[74] *Journal*, 308.   [75] Ibid. 246.

between Drieu's collaborationism and his previous beliefs lay in his conviction that France's salvation would be found in a unified Europe: Drieu's fascism was genuinely European.

In arguing that the French should succumb to the virile embrace of their conquerors, Drieu displayed in almost pathological form the prostration before strength—even self-annihilation—so characteristic of many intellectual collaborationists: 'I have loved force . . . Since my childhood I have known what force is, but the French no longer like it.'[76] The case of Drieu was one of the inspirations for Jean-Paul Sartre's famous 1945 essay 'What is a Collaborator?' which diagnosed a 'mixture of masochism and homosexuality' in collaborationism. Sartre noted the recurrence in collaborationist writing of metaphors 'presenting France's relationship as a sexual union, in which France plays the woman's role'.[77] Sartre was not alone in noting that collaborationism was supported by a surprising number of homosexual intellectuals. Apart from Jouhandeau, Montherlant, Bernard Fäy, and possibly also Brasillach (although his sexuality remains unclear), one could mention Roger Peyrefitte who wrote to his friend Montherlant that the 'Germanic ideal is closer to that of antiquity, and thus our own' than France's 'civilization of shopgirls'.[78] Although he was no collaborator, homosexual fascination with the German occupier is a theme of Jean Genet's *Funeral Rites*,[79] although he was no homosexual, the idea that the French had become 'devirilized' is a key theme in the writing of Rebatet.

Drieu was not homosexual—although his obsession with 'pederasts' (the second favourite insult in his *Journal*, after 'Jew') and his combination of profound misogyny with a Don Juanesque pursuit of women has led to suggestions of repressed homosexuality—but otherwise he fits Sartre's analysis well. Ashamed of his petit-bourgeois background and of his periodic bouts of indolence; wanting to be a warrior, but feeling himself to be only a narcissistic dilettante; haunted by fear of sexual impotence, despite being one of the sexual athletes of his era, Drieu, in his own words, 'transposed on to France the weakness of my being [*la défaillance de l'être en moi*]'.[80] Later, his foreboding of German defeat turned his thoughts to suicide: 'Always masochistic for France as for myself.'[81]

Even while hoping in June 1940 that Nazism might be the 'aristocratic and warlike socialism', the 'virile force', which Europe required, Drieu was wondering if Germany would be infected by France's decadence like the 'soldier by the syphilitic girl'. By 1942 he concluded that collaboration had not worked, and he reverted to the morbid pessimism with which he was most at ease. His final definition of collaboration was: 'Germans who did not believe in Hitler enough supposedly indoctrinating French who believed in him too much.'[82] Once he

---

[76] Verdès-Leroux, *Refus et violences*, 222–3.

[77] 'Qu'est-ce qu'un collaborateur', in *Situations*, iii (1949), 43–61: 58–9.

[78] Burrin, *La France à l'heure*, 349.

[79] *Henry de Montherlant/Roger Peyrefitte: Correspondance* (1983), 285.

[80] *Journal*, 136–7, 143, 153, 171.   [81] Ibid. 396.   [82] Ibid. 308, 191, 254, 407.

realized that Germany had lost, Drieu's consolation was that Stalin would succeed where Hitler had failed: in destroying the rotten French bourgeoisie. With 'savage joy', he contemplated a Europe dominated by Stalin whose men were 'aristocrats such as have not been seen for centuries'. They would represent the triumph of 'totalitarian man', of strength over weakness.[83] But Drieu knew there was no place for him in that new world. As he dreamt of the immolation of bourgeois Europe, he pondered Hinduism and the peace of non-being. He refused all opportunities to escape, and after two failed suicide attempts in the summer of 1944, he finally succeeded in poisoning himself, on 15 March 1945, in an apartment belonging to his first wife.

[83] *Journal,* 320, 386–7.

10

Laval in Power: 1942–1943

The Authoritarian Republic

On Laval's return to power in April 1942, the Parisian ultras believed their moment had arrived. But Laval had no intention of bringing such voraciously ambitious figures as Doriot or Déat into his government. Having regained power, he was determined to exercise it alone. He received the new title of 'head of Government', leaving Pétain only as titular head of State. Pétain mattered less and less. Du Moulin de Labarthète resigned after Laval's return to power, leaving Pétain increasingly isolated. His mind wandered more, but he was without illusions. In a speech on 17 June, he admitted that the National Revolution had been a series of 'setbacks, uncertainties and disappointments'.[1]

Laval took over the key portfolios—Foreign Affairs, the Interior, and Information—and confided the Finance Ministry to his trusted crony, Pierre Cathala. Only five members remained from the previous government. Those who departed included Bouthillier and Caziot, whom Laval had not forgiven for their involvement in the 13 December plot, and Pierre Pucheu, who was too ambitious to be trusted. Barthélemy and Lucien Romier remained as sops to Pétain, but they had little influence. Despite the absence of Doriot and Déat, Laval's government was markedly more collaborationist than its predecessors. Benoist-Méchin and Marion remained; the extremely pro-German Fernand de Brinon, Vichy's Delegate in the Occupied Zone, entered the government as Secretary of State without Portfolio; and the Education Minister, Abel Bonnard, was an ardent collaborationist whose appointment had previously been blocked by Pétain. Bonnard was a littérateur and member of the Academie française who had become fascinated by Nazi Germany in the 1930s. After 1940 he wrote for *La Gerbe* and *Je suis partout*, and joined the committee of Chateaubriant's Collaboration group. Laval once described Bonnard as more German than the Germans. As Minister of Education, he surrounded himself with ultra-collaborationists: his first *chef de cabinet*, Jacques Bousquet, shocked Ministry officials by giving the Hitler salute.[2]

---

[1] *Discours aux Francais*, 262.
[2] J. Mièvre, 'L'Évolution politique d'Abel Bonnard', *RHDGM* 108 (1977), 1–26; Giolitto, *Histoire de la jeunesse*, 114–23; Halls, *Youth of Vichy France*, 34–41.

Despite this collaborationist presence, Laval's return did not pull Vichy in a more 'fascist' direction. Laval used the collaborationists because they improved his standing with Germany. He was as indifferent to fascist politics in 1942 as to the National Revolution in 1940. New reviews and and journals devoted to the National Revolution continued to appear: *Idées* in November 1941, *France, revue de l'État nouveau* in May 1942. Although the contributors to these journals had links to the regime—the editors of *Idées* were close to Marion—the fact is that they were reduced to writing about their ideas because they had diminishing hopes of actually seeing them implemented.[3] Marion remained formally in charge of propaganda, but he lost influence to the former Radical politician, Paul Creyssel, a Laval loyalist since 1930. Creyssel announced to the Propaganda delegates in May 1943: 'the single party solution, for various reasons, has been abandoned . . . French society, more and more, can only be guided by its natural leaders, by the intermediary of the political notables'.[4] This signalled a return to the clientelist practices of the Third Republic with which Laval felt most at home.

The *commissions administratives* set up in 1940 were replaced with *conseils départementaux* which were closer in style to the *conseils généraux* of the Third Republic. Their members were chosen by the prefects, but Laval specified that preference be given to figures with local reputations, especially if they had held office under the Republic. The persecution of Freemasons was relaxed. Laval also carried out a reshuffle of prefects (twenty prefects and nine regional prefects were changed), reinstating some who had been sacked in 1940. Laval was not well disposed to those reactionary prefects who had been too enthusiastic about the National Revolution in 1940. Even Jean Moulin, who had been sacked by Vichy in 1940, was offered reinstatement although, unknown to the authorities, he was now de Gaulle's main emissary in France.[5]

This did not mean Laval planned a return to democracy. His ideal was an authoritarian republic reminiscent of Daladier's style of government in 1939. Although Laval required loyalty, he also respected efficiency and technical competence. For this reason he promoted Bichelonne to be Minister of Industrial Production. Considerable power was also bestowed upon two prefects, Georges Hilaire and René Bousquet, who became Secretary-Generals at the Ministry of the Interior. Laval's government was thus one of administrators as much as cronies.[6] All Laval required from domestic politics was that nothing interfere with collaboration. Remaining convinced that Germany had won the war, he intended to resume the policy which he believed would have worked in 1940 if he had not been dismissed. In the summer of 1942, Germany seemed at the peak of success: Rommel had launched an offensive in North Africa, and the Germans

---

[3] M.-O. Baruch, 'Les Revues de l'État français', *La Revue des revues*, 24 (1997), 35–43.

[4] Peschanski (ed.), *Vichy 1940–1944*, 23.

[5] Baruch, *Servir l'État*, 333–50; Cordier, *Jean Moulin: La République des catacombes*, 43.

[6] Baruch, *Servir l'État*, 323–63.

were advancing into the Caucausus. Laval told a meeting of CO Presidents on 30 May:

> France's salvation, at a moment when Germany is preparing the final offensive against Russia, is in total obedience, without mental reservations. France can seize, in playing an economic role in the victory, a historic chance to modify her destiny. From being a defeated country she can become a nation integrated in the new European ensemble.[7]

The pragmatic case for collaboration was now reinforced by an ideological one. In a speech on 22 June 1942 Laval made the remark for which he was never to be forgiven: 'I desire the victory of Germany, for without it, Bolshevism would tomorrow install itself everywhere.'

Tightening the Screw: Oberg, Sauckel, Dannecker, Röthke

Conditions had changed since Laval's first period in power. In 1940, his policy of collaboration had had little chance of success because the Germans hardly wanted anything France had to offer; in 1942 it had no chance of success because the Germans wanted so much that nothing the French offered would be enough. As Goering put it in August: 'If the French hand over until they can't hand over any more, and if they do it of their own free will, then I'll say I'm collaborating.'[8]

There were three ways in which German policy towards France was about to become harsher. First, at the beginning of 1942, Germany abandoned Blitzkrieg and started to convert to a full-scale war economy. This meant that all the occupied territories had to supply workers for German factories. In March 1942 the Gauleiter Fritz Sauckel was appointed Commissar-General for Labour to oversee this policy. Sauckel was a blusterer and a bully, later to be the bane of Albert Speer's efforts to introduce rationality into the German war economy. Secondly, in January 1942, the Germans had decided upon the extermination of all the Jews of Europe. Responsibility for organizing the deportation of Jews from France fell initially to the young and energetic SS officer Theodor Dannecker who had represented Eichmann in Paris since 1940 as head of the Judenamt (Jewish Office). After July 1942, when Dannecker was transferred to Bulgaria, he was replaced by Heinz Röthke who was no less zealous. Thirdly, the growth of resistance made the Germans increasingly concerned about security. In May, control of German policing in France was removed from the army and handed to the SS officer Carl Oberg, who had previously served as a Nazi police official in Poland. Oberg's two chief assistants, Herbert Hagen and Helmut Knochen, were, like him, fanatical Nazis entirely devoted to Himmler's deputy, Heydrich. To demonstrate the significance of Oberg's appointment, Heydrich accompanied him personally to Paris when he took up his post.

---

[7] Rousso, *Pétain et la fin de la collaboration*, 33.   [8] Warner, *Pierre Laval*, 297.

Since all the new German policies required co-operation from the French police, a key role on the French side was played by René Bousquet, Secretary-General in charge of the police. Today Bousquet is largely remembered for his role in deporting Jews from France. In the Third Republic, however, he had been the rising star of the prefectoral corps, and a protégé of the Radical politician Albert Sarraut. He became a national celebrity in 1930 when, at the age of 21, he saved many people from drowning during floods in the Tarn *département* where he was working in the prefecture. One observer of the Vichy scene noted of Bousquet: 'he had the misfortune to become a hero at the age of 20, and that sent him off the rails'.[9] In 1931 Bousquet served in the *cabinet* of Pierre Cathala, in Laval's first government. Although it was Vichy which, in September 1940, named Bousquet as the youngest prefect in France, he showed no signs of repudiating his previous affinities. A bust of Marianne remained in his office, and he tried to protect Freemasons from persecution. Bousquet's willingness to serve the new regime was helped by its commitment to order and anti-communism, but otherwise he was not ideological. Committing his crimes as a zealous administrator not a fanatic, he was the perfect servant of Laval's authoritarian Republic.[10]

Policing was now at the heart of collaboration. Any German interference in French internal policing would further erode that sovereignty which Vichy was so committed to preserving. This could only be avoided by reassuring Germany that the French would carry out the necessary measures. Bousquet had his first meeting with Oberg on 6 May. Negotiations proceeded for three months until, on 8 August, Oberg and Bousquet signed an agreement recognizing the independence of the French police. It stipulated that the Germans would no longer issue direct orders to the French police; the Germans would abandon collective executions of hostages; and French courts would judge all crimes except those committed specifically against the Germans. In return, the French promised to struggle against 'terrorism, anarchism, and communism'. The bargain was simple: Vichy promised to keep order on the Germans' behalf; the Germans promised to respect Vichy's sovereignty over policing.

Bousquet considered this agreement as a victory, but Oberg was no less happy. The repression against the Resistance intensified. Between May 1942 and May 1943 roughly 16,000 Communists or Gaullists were arrested by French police working closely with the Germans. The head of the Paris Special Brigades (BS) met the Paris Gestapo chief every Wednesday; the French police used torture systematically. In cases directly involving the Germans, suspects were handed to the Gestapo. Despite the Bousquet–Oberg agreement, the Germans did not immediately abandon the execution of hostages. On 11 August 1942, 88 Frenchmen were executed to avenge the death of two Germans after a bomb was thrown

[9] Limagne quoted in Baruch, *Servir l'État*, 388.
[10] P. Froment, *René Bousquet* (1994); J.-P. Husson, 'Itinéraire d'un haut fonctionnaire: René Bousquet', in *VEF*, 287–301.

into a sports stadium in Paris, and on 17 September another 116 were executed after an attack on a cinema patronized by Germans. But after September, this policy was largely abandoned, and 'only' 254 hostages were shot between May 1942 and December 1943 (as opposed to 471 between September 1941 and May 1942).[11] After the war, Knochen was clear about the advantages of the deal with Bousquet: 'If we were able to have smaller police forces in France [than in Belgium or Holland] it was because there existed an established government and an official police.'[12]

The Vel d'Hiv: 16 July 1942

French police co-operation also proved indispensable to the Germans in the deportation of the Jews. Already on three occasions in 1941, the Germans had, with French police co-operation, rounded up Jews in Paris as a reprisal against Resistance attacks. These Jews were sent to internment camps, and filled the first deportation convoys that left for Auschwitz on 27 March, 5 June, and 22 June 1942, including over 1,000 French Jews. But this piecemeal policy was now to be replaced by the 'Final Solution'.

At his meeting with Oberg on 6 May, Bousquet was informed by Heydrich that the Germans were intending to deport foreign Jews from the Occupied Zone to camps in the East. Bousquet asked if foreign Jews in the Unoccupied Zone, who were in internment camps, could be included. No decisions were taken on this occasion because the Germans had not decided their strategy. In mid-June, Dannecker demanded the initial deportation of 40,000 Jews between the ages of 16 and 40: 10,000 were to come from the Unoccupied Zone, the rest from the Occupied Zone; 40 per cent of them were to be French. Negotiations on this issue proceeded throughout the rest of the month, Eichmann himself paying a fleeting visit to Paris on 1 July.

The key meeting took place on 2 July between Bousquet and Oberg. Bousquet raised no objections to the arrests. For him the only 'embarrassing [*gênante*]' fact was that they were to be carried out by the French police; for the Germans this was a prerequisite of the operation's success. A compromise was reached: the French police would round up the Jews but the operation would be restricted to foreign Jews from both zones. The government ratified the agreement on the next day. The Germans had intended only to arrest Jews between the ages of 16 and 40 in order to preserve the fiction that they were being deported to work camps. But Laval proposed that the deportations also include children under 16. After some hesitation, Eichmann gave his approval. Laval claimed to be inspired

---

[11] D. Peschanski, 'Exclusion, persécution, répression', in *VEF*, 224–5; J. Delarue, 'La Police', in *VEF*, 303–11; Klarsfeld, *Vichy-Auschwitz*, i. 52–3; Courtois et al., *Le Sang de l'étranger*, 221–34; Baruch, *Servir l'État*, 382–403; H. Luther, *Der französische Widerstand gegen die deutsche Besatzungsmacht und seine Bekämpfung* (Tübingen, 1957), 183–90.

[12] Froment, *René Bousquet*, 221.

by a 'humanitarian' desire to keep families together. He may indeed have feared the effect on public opinion of scenes of screaming children being forcibly separated from their parents, but his main motive was practical: Vichy did not want to be saddled with organizing care for the children once their parents had gone.[13]

The operation began in Paris on 16 and 17 July; it was planned with military precision and involved 9,000 French police. In two days, 12,884 Jews were arrested; 7,000 of the victims (including 4,000 children) were parked for five days in the Vel d'Hiver sports stadium where they languished in indescribable squalor with little food or water. They were then taken to special camps before being deported to Auschwitz. The Rafle du Vel d'Hiver (Vel d'Hiver Round-Up) was the largest single operation, but it was accompanied by other arrests in the Occupied Zone. These were followed on 26–8 August by more round-ups in the Unoccupied Zone which netted over 6,500 more Jews.

The government modified its position in September in the face of public outrage and Church protests. Seeing Oberg on 2 September, Laval asked not to be required to find more Jews. Handing over Jews was not, he said (whether regretfully or not is unclear), like buying items in a discount store. Although the deportations proceeded through September, they then ceased for the rest of the year, except for four convoys in November. Röthke, the ideologue, had hoped to sustain the rhythm of a convoy per day until the end of October, but Knochen and Oberg were willing to take account of Laval's difficulties, and preferred not to compromise Franco-German police co-operation.[14]

In total, 36,802 Jews (6,053 of them children under 16) were deported from France between July and the end of the year (41,951 in the year as a whole including the earlier convoys). Almost all of them were foreign. Laval's post-war defenders argued that French police co-operation was the price he paid to save the French Jews. Quite apart from the morally dubious notion that some Jews were more precious than others, or the fact that the government made no protest about the deportations in March and June, which had included French Jews, the idea that foreign Jews were sacrificed to save French ones founders on the fact that, without French co-operation, the Germans lacked the manpower or information to round up significant numbers of either foreign or French Jews. Dannecker could not even find enough German troops available to escort the first convoy on 27 March until French police stepped into the breach.[15] Throughout the negotiations, the Jews were viewed as expendable in the wider scheme of collaboration: Bousquet's priority was to regain control over French policing. The only fact that conflicts with this interpretation was Bousquet's initial objection on 2 July to French police involvement, but since he dropped the objection

---

[13] Klarsfeld, *Vichy-Auschwitz*, i. 55–87; Marrus and Paxton, *Vichy France and the Jews*, 217–78.

[14] This explanation why the deportations ceased in Oct. is that of Klarsfeld, *Vichy-Auschwitz*, i. 168–78. Marrus and Paxton, *Vichy France and the Jews*, 260, have no explanation of why the convoys stopped in Oct. other than a possible 'unexpected interruption of railway timetables'.

[15] Cohen, *Persécutions et sauvetages*, 258.

almost at once, it seems that his purpose was to underline to the Germans their need for French police co-operation.[16]

The truth was that Vichy shed no tears over the fate of foreign Jews in France who were seen as a nuisance, 'dregs [*déchets*]' in Laval's words.[17] He told an American diplomat that he was 'happy' to have a chance to get rid of them.[18] It was after all Bousquet who had initially suggested including foreign Jews from the Unoccupied Zone, to the surprise of the Germans. When the arrests started there, he instructed the prefects to 'break all resistance' and 'free your area of all foreign Jews'. He asked for the names of officials whose zeal was suspect.[19]

Would Vichy have acted differently if the fate of the Jews had been known? Laval told the cabinet that the Jews were apparently being sent to a Jewish state in Eastern Europe, but neither he nor Bousquet enquired whether this was true. On 2 September Laval informed Oberg that he was telling foreign diplomats that the Jews were being sent to Poland. He asked whether this was the right answer, explaining that his concern was to avoid discrepancies between what the Germans and French were saying, but showed no sign of being interested in what was really happening. When the Protestant leader Pastor Boegner saw Laval on 9 September, he was fed the official line that the Jews were building an agricultural colony in the East. Boegner remarked after the war: 'I talked to him about murder, he answered me with gardening.'[20]

The regime's callousness emerged again in its treatment of Jewish children. In October, the American government offered to take 1,000 Jewish children whose parents had been deported. Laval and Bousquet insisted that only certified orphans be granted visas. Since nothing was known of the fate of the deported parents, such proof was impossible to obtain, and the children were never allowed to leave. The reason for this obstructiveness was a German warning that the departure of children for the United States must not become an occasion for anti-German propaganda. For Vichy, the lives of 1,000 Jewish children were a reasonable price to pay for retaining German favour.[21]

The Collaborationists Attack

Laval bargained harder when it came to sending French workers to Germany. In May 1942, Sauckel demanded the recruitment of 350,000 French workers. It was almost impossible to have a civil dialogue with Sauckel, who was impervious to French protestations of faith in the new Europe. But Laval finally obtained two concessions: the figure was reduced to 250,000 (of whom 150,000

---

[16] Ibid. 266.   [17] Klarsfeld, *Vichy-Auschwitz*, i. 101.
[18] Kupferman, *Pierre Laval*, 350.
[19] Klarsfeld, *Vichy-Auschwitz*, i. 150; Marrus and Paxton, *Vichy France and the Jews*, 257–8.
[20] Marrus and Paxton, *Vichy France and the Jews*, 355.
[21] Ibid. 263–9; Klarsfeld, *Vichy-Auchwitz*, i. 189–92.

were to be skilled workers) and for every three skilled workers who departed one prisoner of war would be released. This *relève* (relief) scheme was announced in a fanfare of publicity in June. Although Laval in person welcomed the first trainload of returning prisoners on 11 August, the results of the *relève* were disappointing. By mid-August only 40,000 workers had volunteered. Sauckel threatened that if necessary he would requisition the workers himself. To prevent this, Laval promulgated a law on 4 September, making all Frenchmen between 18 and 50, and all unmarried Frenchwomen between 21 and 35, liable to carry out whatever work the government deemed necessary. Employers were required to draw up lists of those who fell under the terms of this law. By the end of the year Sauckel's figures had been reached.[22]

Laval's attempt to bargain with the Germans, rather than accept their demands unconditionally, made him vulnerable to attack from the Paris collaborationists. They had turned against him once his return to power brought them nothing. During the summer, Doriot stepped up his attacks on Vichy. Announcing that the PPF was preparing for power, he started describing Laval as Kerensky to his Lenin. Not to be outdone, Déat also radicalized his rhetoric: he talked of 'blood and soil', and began appearing in uniform. In September, with Abetz's approval, Déat organized the National Revolutionary Front (FRN) to group together all collaborationist parties. The RNP, the MSR (now in the hands of Soulès), and the Francistes all agreed to join, but Doriot's refusal doomed the enterprise to failure. Doriot was meanwhile being encouraged by the SS and the SD to believe that he was Germany's candidate to replace Laval. But his hopes were dashed in September when Ribbentrop reassured Abetz that Hitler still backed Laval. Doriot was to be a sword of Damocles over Laval, as Laval had been over Darlan, but Laval would stay as long as he was useful.[23]

The collaborationists became increasingly interested in North Africa as an arena where the French could be more useful to the Germans than on the eastern front: while Germany defended Europe from Bolshevism in the East, France would defend her from the Anglo-Saxon allies of the Bolsheviks in the South. Doriot set up an Empire youth movement in May 1942; barely a day went by without an article by Déat on the Empire.[24] Laval tried to neutralize the collaborationists by authorizing Benoist-Méchin to turn the LVF into a new organization called the Légion tricolore. Where the LVF had been an independent organization, enjoying Vichy's unofficial blessing, its volunteers were now treated as full members of the army who could fight on the eastern front, but also in the colonies. Laval hoped this would both tame the LVF and win collaborationist approval. Benoist-Méchin, however, saw it as the embryo of full-scale military collaboration between France and Germany. But Laval soon became worried that

---

[22] Warner, *Pierre Laval*, 299–300, 307–11.
[23] Abellio, *Ma dernière mémoire*, 333–5; Burrin, *La Dérive fasciste*, 403–6, 430–9; Wolf, *Doriot*, 367; M. Cotta, *La Collaboration 1940–1944* (1964), 260–9.
[24] Tasca, *La France de Vichy*, 417.

Benoist-Méchin might use the Légion tricolore as an independent power base, and sacked him in September 1942. The LVF reverted to its former name.[25]

Although Laval remained convinced that Germany had won the war, he had lost any appetite for military collaboration. Unlike the collaborationists, he wished to preserve French neutrality, but this became increasingly difficult as the war beat at France's door both inside and outside Europe. In the Caribbean, the Americans, still concerned that French possessions might be used by the Germans, asked Laval to agree that all French ships in the area be totally immobilized. The Germans, fearing that America wanted to take control of France's Caribbean possessions, tried to get Laval to stand firm.[26] The war came even closer in August 1942 when the Allies launched a raid on Dieppe to test German coastal defences. The Germans easily destroyed the Allied force, and Vichy propaganda praised the local population for refusing to aid the Allied aggressors. Pétain wrote to Hitler on 21 August proposing joint military action to repulse further attacks, but received no reply. Pétain's motive was possibly to win the French army a toehold in the Occupied Zone and get the Germans to allow a reinforcement of the Armistice Army. But he clearly considered the British attack an aggression to be resisted at the risk of jeopardizing neutrality.[27]

It was increasingly feared the Allies intended to attack next in Africa. For this reason, on August 27, Vichy was permitted to organize an armed unit in West Africa to resist a possible Allied invasion in return for allowing the Germans to charter neutral ships docked in French ports since 1940.[28] For Vichy, the prospect of an Allied attack offered an opportunity to squeeze concessions from Germany, but if an attack actually came, it risked jeopardizing French neutrality. Thus when the Americans finally landed in North Africa on 8 November 1942, the conditions which permitted Laval's delicate balancing act of satisfying Germany while preserving French neutrality were finally shattered.

The North African Imbroglio

The Americans had been preparing the ground in North Africa for several months.[29] In line with Roosevelt's policy of trying to win Pétainists over to the Allies, Roosevelt's representative in North Africa, Robert Murphy, had approached local figures of influence. From his soundings emerged the so-called

---

[25] Paxton, *Parades and Politics*, 273–6; Benoist-Méchin, *À l'épreuve*, 134–205; Tasca, *La France de Vichy*, 411–12; Abellio, *Ma dernière mémoire*, 299–300.

[26] Paxton, *Vichy France*, 312–13.

[27] Ferro, *Pétain*, 404–6; Burrin, *La France à l'heure*, 154–5.

[28] Paxton, *Vichy France*, 303–5.

[29] A. Funk, *The Politics of Torch: The Allied Landings and the Algiers Putsch* (1974). On the subsequent North African events, see Levisse-Touzé, 'L'Afrique du Nord', 632–719; Duroselle, *L'Abîme*, 364–401; Paxton, *Parades and Politics*, 344–90; Jäckel, *La France dans l'Europe*, 334–60; Warner, *Pierre Laval*, 318–57; for Darlan's position see Coutau-Bégarie and Huan, *Darlan*, 573–650, which needs to be read in conjunction with the corrective by R. Paxton, 'Un amiral entre deux blocs', *VSRH* 36 (1992), 3–19.

Group of Five who prepared a plan to neutralize French resistance to the landings. It remained to find a figurehead to rally support to the Allies. This had to be someone who could win over the army. Weygand, the obvious choice, refused. The decision fell upon General Henri Giraud who had become nationally famous after escaping from a German prisoner of war camp in April 1942. Giraud's arrival at Vichy had not helped Laval in his task of winning German goodwill, but the General had refused to give himself up to the Germans. The most he agreed to do was sign an undertaking of loyalty to Pétain. As an anti-German Pétainist, he was the perfect symbol for America's strategy in North Africa. Approached by the conspirators, Giraud agreed to help. But when the landings occurred, he was still in Gibraltar negotiating with Eisenhower. Owing to further delays caused by difficulties in transporting him to North Africa, Giraud did not arrive in Algiers for another twenty-four hours. Giraud's absence was one hitch in the plan. More serious was the fact that the Americans were so keen to achieve surprise that they gave insufficient advance warning of the landings to their North African contacts. The Group of Five were therefore unable to assist them by seizing strategic points, and the Americans were met by armed resistance.

The news of the invasion reached Vichy at 3 a.m. on 8 November. Woken at 7 a.m., Pétain signed a message, drafted by Laval, calling for armed resistance. Laval stalled on German demands for a declaration of war on the United States, but had to accept an ultimatum that airbases in Tunisia be made available to the Germans so that they could transport men and material to North Africa. By midday on 9 November, the German planes had started to arrive.

Laval's problem was that if France could not repulse the attackers alone, the Germans would intervene, threatening France's sovereignty over her Empire. Laval, therefore, had to reassure Hitler that France could be trusted to defend North Africa or ensure that German assistance to France in North Africa was accompanied by guarantees about the future of the Empire. This was the last chance to win German concessions while Vichy still had something to bargain with. Laval may have been encouraged by a German message of 8 November calling on France to declare war on America and promising to stand by her 'through thick and thin'. In fact, these final words were personally added by Abetz and meant nothing. Abetz again muddied the waters and raised Laval's hopes. In December 1942, he was summoned back to Berlin, and remained there in semi-disgrace for a year.

Summoned to Hitler's presence, Laval set off by car for Munich on the morning of 9 November, but bad weather delayed his arrival until the early hours of the next morning. Hitler kept him waiting several hours longer, and finally received him on the afternoon of 10 November. Laval's hopes of winning Hitler's confidence were compromised by Vichy's lack of control over events in North Africa. Quite fortuitously, Darlan was in Algiers visiting his sick son when the invasion occurred. When it became clear on the evening of 8 November that further resistance in Algiers was impossible, Darlan authorized General Juin to sign a ceasefire for Algiers, although fighting continued elsewhere. Thus Darlan unexpectedly emerged as a key player with more influence than Giraud, who finally arrived on the afternoon of 9 November. During that day, the Americans pressurized Darlan to sign a total ceasefire in Algeria. He temporized, claiming that he could not act without orders from Vichy. On the morning of 10 November, however, he gave way since military resistance was no longer viable.

This news reached Laval shortly before he was due to see Hitler, and he urgently telephoned Vichy that, if his negotiations were to enjoy any chance of success, resistance to the Americans must continue. Darlan was instructed to rescind his ceasefire order. He obeyed, declaring himself impotent to act, and constituted himself technically a prisoner of the Americans. This was too late to help Laval. He found Hitler in glacial mood, offering nothing and interested only in securing access to Tunisian bases. Laval had barely left the meeting and lit his first cigarette when Hitler ordered the occupation of the Free Zone without even telling him. Laval's exhausting journey through the fog and snow, only to be snubbed by Hitler yet again, had proved futile. Even before meeting Laval, Hitler told Ciano that he intended to occupy the Free Zone. Laval's problem was that France had nothing to offer which Hitler could not as easily take himself. Even if Hitler had believed in Laval's good faith, he could see that Vichy had lost control in North Africa. At 7 a.m., on the symbolic date of 11 November, German troops crossed the demarcation line. All France was now occupied. The Vichy government instructed its armed forces to remain in their barracks and avoid provoking the Germans. Two weeks later, Hitler ordered France's Armistice Army to be disbanded. Again there was no opposition.[30]

On the pretext that after the occupation of the south Pétain was no longer a free agent, Darlan could have now rallied to the Americans. But he waited two days longer to do this. For an opportunist, he was remarkably slow to seize his opportunities. This was all the more surprising because, during 1942, Darlan, losing confidence in German victory, had begun to put out feelers to America. His son Alain had contacted Murphy in March 1942. Nonetheless Darlan's view remained what it had been in August 1941, when he told Leahy that only if the Americans were ready to arrive on the south coast of France in force—6,000 planes and half a million men—would he welcome them.[31] Because he had not expected this before 1943, the events of November 1942 took him by surprise, and struck him as premature. His vacillation was, for once, a result of confusion more than duplicity.

When Darlan declared himself a prisoner of the Americans, Pétain had appointed the military commander in Morocco, General Noguès, to replace him as Vichy's representative. Darlan, clinging to the fiction of obedience to the

[30] Paxton, *Parades and Politics*, 371–89.   [31] Ibid. 339.

Marshal, refused to commit himself to the Americans before consulting Noguès. In Morocco, Noguès refused to treat locally with the Americans until he had met Darlan in Algiers, where he did not arrive until 12 November. The dithering of these French commanders irritated the Americans. Their forces had prevailed in Morocco as well as Algeria, and what they now required was that the French forces in Tunisia be instructed to resist the Germans.

The situation in Tunisia was confused. Vichy had ordered the local commanders in Tunisia to facilitate the arrival of the German forces. On 11 November General Juin told them to do the opposite, only to reverse this order a few hours later until he had heard what Noguès was going to decide. Noguès and Juin were petrified at the idea of being disloyal to Pétain. As Juin said on 12 June: 'since the Americans are here, it is necessary to choose. I incline towards the struggle against Germany, but I will obey orders'.[32] Desperate to prevent the Germans installing themselves in Tunisia, the Americans were ready to treat with any French commander who could help. The problem with their original protégé, Giraud, was that, despite his impeccable anti-German credentials, his early involvement in the conspiracy alienated loyal Pétainists and made them reluctant to obey his orders. With Darlan the terms of the equation were reversed: his anti-German credentials were suspect, but he was more likely to be obeyed by Pétain loyalists. On balance this made Darlan more useful to the Americans. As Darlan said on 11 November: 'the Americans must understand that they can either have Giraud without the army or the army without Giraud'.[33]

Darlan wanted to sideline Giraud because he regarded him as a traitor to Pétain and because of his enthusiasm to re-enter the war. Darlan's objective was not to re-enter the war on America's side, but to preserve French sovereignty over North Africa and hang on to neutrality. His position in the face of the Americans in November 1942 was thus a mirror image of Laval's in the face of the Germans: a desperate struggle to hang on to the shreds of French neutrality and sovereignty. Once Darlan had ascertained that Noguès was prepared to follow his lead on the grounds that Pétain was no longer a free agent—there was no longer an independent Vichy government to be loyal to—a deal was struck with the American commander, General Mark Clark. On 12 November the Darlan–Clark agreement recognized Darlan as the head of the government of French North Africa. Giraud, with whom Noguès and Darlan would not shake hands, was authorized to raise a volunteer army to fight the Germans. But when the original conspirators—the Group of Five—saw that Giraud had been excluded, they despatched him to protest to the Americans. As a result Giraud's status was upgraded, making him army commander under Darlan's authority. The agreement was finally signed on 13 November, six days after the American

[32] Levisse-Touzé, 'L'Afrique du Nord', 701, 735–40.   [33] Ibid. 690.

landings. The whole affair had cost 479 American deaths and 720 wounded, and 1,346 French dead and 997 wounded.[34]

Even after the signing of the Darlan–Clark agreement, the hapless commanders in Tunisia, who had received such bewilderingly contradictory orders, were given no clear instruction to resist the Germans. Even Darlan probably no longer expected to be able to preserve French neutrality, and the further delay occurred because the Germans had now arrived in such force that French resistance would have been futile until the Americans were ready to move east and help. Darlan may also have felt the need to proceed cautiously because the Governor-General of Tunisia, Admiral Estéva, and the commander of the naval base at Bizerta, Admiral Derrien, remained faithful to Vichy. Had they been followed, there was the risk of a dangerous division within the French army. The army commander, General Georges Barré, however, decided to rally to Darlan, and the first French fired their first shots against the Germans in Tunisia on 19 November. But by then the Germans were firmly installed, and it would take six months to dislodge them.

Darlan's switch of sides had not even succeeded in bringing over the French fleet. After the Germans occupied the South, Darlan ordered Admiral de Laborde, commander of the fleet in Toulon, to transfer his ships to French West Africa rather than risk them falling into German hands. Laborde refused unless given the order by Pétain himself. When on 27 November, German troops moved into Toulon to take control of the fleet, it was too late to leave, and the fleet scuttled itself. Darlan's most useful service to the Americans was to ensure the rallying of Equatorial Africa, whose Governor, General Pierre Boisson, had fired on the Gaullists and British in September 1940. With its key strategic base of Dakar, and an army of 75,000, Equatorial Africa was a major prize.

Darlan's proclamation announcing his agreement with Clark ended with the words 'Long live the Marshal', but this did not stop Pétain on the next day condemning Darlan's violation of his orders. Subsequently, Pétain's defenders claimed that he had sent secret telegrams privately approving Darlan's actions. The most important telegram, on 13 November, allegedly conveyed Pétain's 'intimate accord' when hearing of the Darlan–Clark agreement. For years the existence of this telegram was contested, but it has now been discovered by Darlan's most recent biographers. The telegram, however, does not mean what Pétain's defenders claimed when it was only known about by hearsay. It was an answer to a telegram from Noguès explaining how the agreement with the Americans had successfully sidelined Giraud who wanted to 'chase Germany out of Tunisia'. In other words, Pétain was giving his 'intimate accord' for a continuation of neutrality not a rallying to the Allies.[35]

Although Pétain did protest against the occupation of the south, he did not

---

[34] Ibid. 700–1.   [35] The telegram is reprod. in Coutau-Bégarie and Huan, *Darlan*, 618.

order the fleet to leave France or the Armistice Army to resist the Germans. Despite the urging of several advisers, he also refused to leave France for Algeria. During most of the crisis Pétain played an entirely passive role. For the first time since 1940, his age became a significant factor in a situation which changed every minute and demanded rapid reactions. His advisers had only woken him four hours after the news of the American landings in North Africa reached Vichy; nor did they wake him when Hitler's message announcing the occupation of the South arrived at Vichy at 5.30 a.m. By the end of the eventful week, Pétain was overcome by mental exhaustion. But his decision to stay in France was in line with his belief since 1940 that he could best serve French interests by remaining on metropolitan soil. Up to November 1942, this was at least an arguable case, and had Pétain left then, he could have survived the war with his reputation intact, possibly even as a hero. If there was a moment when Pétain—however misguidedly—sacrificed himself for his country, it was not June 1940, when the 'sacrifice' was amply compensated by adulation and the likelihood of being on the winning side, but November 1942, when all that beckoned was obloquy and defeat, and everything Vichy had salvaged from the catastrophe of 1940 was irremediably lost: the fleet, the Armistice Army, the Free Zone, and the Empire.

Vichy 1943: Shrinking Power

Vichy was now living on borrowed time. The existence in North Africa of an alternative French administration offered an escape route to those who no longer believed that Vichy had any *raison d'être*, but were unwilling to join de Gaulle, or too compromised to consider doing so. Those who defected to Algeria in May included such high-ranking figures as Pierre Pucheu and the civil servant Maurice Couve de Murville. By the autumn, only sixteen countries continued to have diplomatic relations with Vichy.[36] The town itself was no longer the hive of activity it had been two years earlier. It was gloomy and semi-deserted— ministers found it hard to find chauffeurs—although there were now many Germans.[37]

A big conference to discuss the National Revolution was organized at Mont-Dore, not far from Vichy, in April 1943. Several of Pétain's advisers were involved in these four days of fantasy.[38] But André Lavagne, deputy director of Pétain's civil *cabinet*, had no illusions. In a note drafted in March 1943, he admitted that the National Revolution was not for this world:

Still reeling from the blow she suffered in 1940, France immediately tried to set about renewing herself. She still had enough strength, enough freedom, to

---

[36] Duroselle, *L'Abîme*, 448.   [37] Baruch, *Servir l'État*, 446.
[38] *Vers la Révolution communautaire: Les Journées de Mont-Dore* (1943); Abellio, *Ma dernière mémoire*, 337–9.

attempt this recovery . . . Two years passed in this way. France had believed in her resurrection, but resurrection is only possible after Golgotha . . . Contrary to what she believed, France had in 1940 scarcely begun her road of the cross . . . Now the end approaches. Everything has been used up. The last arms, the last resources, the last able-bodied men, the last colonies, the last possibilities of freedom, have one by one disappeared. Everything has fallen from her hands. Abandoned and immobile, France today does not participate any longer in the life of peoples. Her kingdom is no longer of this world . . . All alone, without fearing the incomprehension and insults of the watching crowds, an old soldier, covered in glories and victories, accompanies France step by step to support her cross.[39]

After the crisis of November 1942 Pétain become entirely a figurehead. Constitutional Act Twelve granted Laval the full authority to promulgate laws under his own signature. Pétain, whose powers had been compared to those of Louis XIV two years earlier, was now more like a Third Republic president. In March 1943, Laval reshuffled his cabinet, sacking Joseph Barthélemy, who was almost the last Pétain loyalist left in the government. The other one, Lucien Romier, remained, but he was too ill to offer Pétain much support.

To what purpose did Laval exercise the power he now possessed? In public, he still proclaimed that Germany was the only bulwark against Bolshevism. As late as December 1943 he announced: 'the victory of Germany will prevent our civilisation collapsing into communism. The victory of the Americans would be the triumph of the Jew and of communism.' But in private he was now less sure. In November 1943, he remarked:

Will the Germans win the war? I haven't a clue, I am not clairvoyant! The more time goes on the less I think so . . . If the Germans are beaten, General de Gaulle will return. He is supported—and I have no illusions about this—by 80 or 90 per cent of the French people. And I shall be hung . . . There are two men who can save France now; and if I was not Laval I would like to be de Gaulle.[40]

Laval took sombre comfort in his unpopularity, as if it conferred the nobility of sacrifice upon him. It confirmed a tendency to self-pity, and a conviction that he had always been misunderstood.

Although Laval no longer believed in German victory, he clung to the hope of a compromise peace. He continued to work for an agreement with Germany, managing to obtain two meetings with Hitler—on 19 December 1942 and 29 April 1943—but they were as fruitless as the previous ones. On 19 December, having made the two-day journey to Hitler's headquarters in East Prussia, Laval was barely allowed to open his mouth. On the second occasion, his last meeting with Hitler, Laval tried telling him that war must give rise to a United States of Europe. At these two meetings, Laval obtained a few concessions. In place of the defunct Armistice Army, the French were authorized to raise a volunteer force—the Phalange africaine—to defend what remained of the Empire. Crossing the

[39] Baruch, *Servir l'État*, 331–2.   [40] Warner, *Pierre Laval*, 352.

Demarcation Line became a formality after March 1943, but because the whole country was now occupied, this mattered less than it would have two years earlier.[41]

These tiny concessions were nothing compared to the new burdens which France had to bear. The occupation costs were raised to 25 million Reichsmark. Sauckel pressed relentlessly for more French workers to be sent to Germany. In January 1943, no sooner had the first quota been fulfilled than he demanded another 250,000 by March. To meet these demands, Laval was forced on 16 February to introduce Compulsory Labour Service (STO) conscripting all young men born between 1920 and 1922 to work in Germany (apart from some exempted categories like miners, peasants, and police).

Thanks to STO, Sauckel's new target was achieved by the end of March. He thereupon demanded another 220,000 workers by the end of June, and Laval had to agree, extending the categories of those liable for STO. But when on 6 August Sauckel demanded another 500,000 workers (including for the first time women) before the end of the year, Laval dug his heels in. Their meeting lasted six hours, and Sauckel was so truculent that Laval suffered a fainting fit, but he did not give in. Sauckel reported to Berlin that he had now lost all faith in Laval. Laval held firm because he knew that there was increasing criticism of Sauckel's methods within Germany. After initially boosting the numbers of labour recruits, STO had quickly proved counter-productive. Thousands of those liable to be sent to Germany fled to the countryside, often swelling the ranks of the Resistance. In the first three months of 1943, 251,000 workers had left for Germany; in the next two, only 37,000. The German Armaments Minister, Albert Speer, was ready to rethink Sauckel's crude policy.

Between 16 and 18 September 1943, Speer had a number of meetings in Berlin with Jean Bichelonne, French Minister of Industrial Production. They agreed that factories working in France for German war production (designated *Sperrbetriebe*) would be given special protection, sparing them from the labour draft. Instead of being forced to work in Germany, French workers could now work for Germany in France. For Laval, this was an important respite; for Bichelonne, it was the foundation of a rationally conceived policy of Franco-German economic collaboration. As Speer writes in his memoirs, he and Bichelonne had immediately taken to each other. The minds of these two young, brilliant, politically autistic, technocrats soared above the contingencies of war to envisage a future Europe of planning and harmony, steel and concrete.[42]

Bichelonne allowed nothing to sully the purity of his vision of collaboration. The evolution of René Bousquet, that other brilliant, apolitical technician, was different. In April 1943 Bousquet succeeded in getting his police agreement with Oberg extended to the South (where the Germans were now present). Present-

---

[41] Jäckel, *La France dans l'Europe*, 373–80; Cointet, *Pierre Laval*, 422–5, 437–9.
[42] Milward, *The New Order*, 149–73; A. Speer, *Inside the Third Reich* (1970), 310–11.

ing the agreement to the regional prefects, he stressed that Germany and France shared the same enemies: 'terrorists, Communists, Jews, Gaullists and foreign agents'. But in truth the French police were becoming less reliable, and the Germans increasingly had to interfere in policing. In August 1943, the SS authorities summoned the regional prefects and issued them directly with orders to repress disorder. From this point Bousquet began to distance himself from collaboration. In October, he refused to give the Germans lists of Jews in the Southern Zone; in November, he told Knochen that being a Jew was not in itself a presumption of guilt—a belated discovery. Perhaps it was harder to shut out reality when running the police than when dreaming about the economic reconstruction of Europe. Whatever the reason, Bichelonne was to follow collaboration to its end; Bousquet was to extricate himself just in time.[43]

Laval too became less accommodating to the Germans from the middle of 1943. Standing up to Sauckel in August was one example of this; another, in the same month, was his attitude towards the Jews. Although in September 1942 Laval had marked his reluctance to be involved in further deportations, this had not signalled the end of French involvement in the policy. In February 1943, when the Germans indicated that deportations must resume, the French police again helped arrest foreign Jews. The round-ups that occurred in the South in February 1943 were the most extensive since August 1942. Vichy's continuing indifference to the fate of the Jews was clear in its response to events in the Italian Zone where the authorities frequently interceded to protect Jews from the French police. Annoyed by this infringement of France's sovereignty, Laval protested to the Germans. But German pressure on Italy had no effect, and the Italian Zone became a haven for Jews fleeing the Germans—and the French.[44]

As it became harder to find enough foreign Jews, the Germans demanded the denaturalization of all Jews naturalized since 1927. Bousquet and Laval at first held out for a later date of 1932–3, and then in August Laval refused point blank. In the words of Marrus and Paxton: 'For the first time in the history of the Final Solution in France, Laval had said "No".'[45] In July, Röthke had to abandon another major round-up in Paris because the government refused the necessary police co-operation.[46] In August, he reported: 'it is no longer possible to count on the assistance of the French police on a significant scale for the arrests of Jews'.[47]

All this made Laval increasingly vulnerable to being outflanked by the Paris collaborationists, eager to prove that they could best serve Germany's interests. When the Americans landed in North Africa, the PPF was holding its congress. There were calls for a declaration of war on Britain and America, and cries of

[43] Baruch, *Servir l'État*, 403–6.
[44] Marrus and Paxton, V*ichy France and the Jews*, 315–21; Klarsfeld, *Vichy-Auschwitz*, ii. 11–18, 37.
[45] *Vichy France and the Jews*, 325.
[46] G. Wellers, A. Kaspi, and S. Klarsfeld (eds.), *La France et la question juive 1940/1944* (1981), 72.
[47] S. Zuccotti, *The Holocaust, the French and the Jews* (New York, 1993), 178.

'Laval to the scaffold'.[48] Doriot was ready to march on Vichy. Again he had over-played his hand. In December 1942, Hitler wrote to Abetz's successor, Rudolf Schleier, reiterating his support for Laval. A disappointed Doriot left again for the eastern front where he spent most of the next year.

Although PPF activists played a part helping the Germans against the Allies in Tunisia, the PPF's stock was falling.[49] Laval hoped to seize the opportunity to do away with his enemies once and for all. At his meeting with Hitler on 19 December, he tried to secure German agreement to dissolve all the collabora-tionist movements and merge them into a single movement loyal to Vichy. Hitler refused this request, but he did authorize Laval to set up a force of his own. This was the origin of the founding of the infamous Milice française (French Militia) in January 1943. Its nominal president was Laval, but the driving force was its Secretary General, Joseph Darnand.

Towards Terror: The Milice

Darnand was one of those war veterans who never entirely readapted to civilian life after 1919. He had been a celebrated war hero and was bitter that the army would not keep him on as an officer. His resentment turned him against the Republic. In the inter-war years he ran a garage business in Nice while par-ticipating in extreme right-wing politics. Here he rediscovered the mixture of adventure and fraternity which he missed from the war. In 1940 he again fought heroically, and after the defeat became leader of the Legion of Veterans in Nice.

Darnand quickly found the Legion too staid to quench his thirst for action, and he created within it an activist elite called the Service d'ordre légionnaire (SOL) which spread outside the region. The SOL received official government recognition in January 1942, and Darnand left for Vichy to head it. The SOL had its own uiform—khaki shirt, blue trousers, black tie, black beret—and came to see itself as independent of the Legion from which it had emanated. Darnand was now the coming man on the extreme right, and in January 1943 the SOL became the Milice.[50]

Laval, always confident of his ability to manipulate others, viewed Darnand as a simple-minded, honest soldier without the political ambitions of Doriot or Déat. He wanted the Milice both as a sort of praetorian guard and a force to counter the Paris collaborationists. Darnand, however, envisaged a more exten-sive role for the Milice than this, hoping to create a political movement on the model of a fascist party. With this aim in mind, he divided the Milice into several sections. Most members continued a normal professional life, devoting a few hours a week to Milice activities, but there was also the Avant-Garde section, for

---

[48] Peschanski (ed.), *Vichy 1940–1944*, 433.
[49] Wolf, *Doriot*, 371–3; Gordon, *Collaborationism in France*, 155–62.
[50] J.-P. Azéma, 'La Milice', *VSRH* 28 (1990), 83–105; B. Gordon, 'Un soldat du fascisme: L'Évolution de Joseph Darnand', *RHDGM* 108 (1977), 43–70.

boys and girls, and the Franc-Garde, a fully militarized section which would be permanently mobilized and live in barracks. In addition, there was a propaganda service, and a weekly newspaper, *Combats*. The *miliciens* cultivated the image of a chivalric elite like the Romanian fascist movement the Legion of the Archangel Michael. Swearing a twenty-one-point oath condemning democracy, individualism, international capitalism, bolshevism, Freemasonry, and 'Jewish leprosy', they vowed to defend Christian civilization.

Membership of the Milice, between 25,000 and 30,000, was far below Darnand's expectations. The recruits included virulent anti-Communists, fanatical Catholics, former legionnaires who still believed they were being faithful to the Marshal, and young men, of no fixed political opinion, who saw an opportunity to escape from STO. If the Milice never became the mass movement Darnand had hoped, it did become increasingly important later in 1943 as the Resistance expanded and Vichy was less able to rely on the police. The Milice stepped into the breach.

At first, the Milice's effectiveness was hampered by German suspicion of any French paramilitary organization. Like the Legion, it was banned in the Northern Zone. It lacked arms and some *miliciens* stuffed their empty holsters with paper. Darnand became so frustrated that in June he even tried to contact the Free French. In August, however, he burnt all his bridges by swearing a personal oath of loyalty to Hitler and becoming a Sturmbannführer in the Waffen-SS. This spectacular decision—one no other collaborationist leader had taken—was all the more remarkable from a decorated hero of two anti-German wars. It won Darnand the approval of the SS, who started to supply the Milice with money and arms.

At the moment that Darnand had uncompromisingly committed himself to Germany, Laval was trying to mark his distance. The relations between the two men deteriorated, and Darnand decided to throw in his lot with the Paris collaborationists. On 17 September 1943, he signed a joint manifesto with Déat, Luchaire, and others. They called for all collaborationist groups to merge into one party committed to total collaboration with Germany and the imposition in France of a fully-fledged National Socialist regime. Although the five signatories claimed they wanted Laval to head the new government, Darnand's intention was that the Germans should install him instead.

Endgame

This assault on Laval from the collaborationists coincided with a conspiracy against Laval at Vichy by the Pétain loyalists. In April 1943 Pétain had sounded out his closest advisers about forming a government without Laval.[51]

---

[51] Duroselle, *L'Abîme*, 453–4.

Any such temptation was scotched by a letter from Hitler warning Pétain against a repetition of 13 December. But the idea resurfaced in the autumn when some Vichy leaders started to nurse the idea that if they detached themselves from Germany in time, it might still be possible to do a deal with the Allies. They were encouraged by the example of Italy where in July the king had dismissed Mussolini, and on 8 September the Americans had signed an armistice with his successor Marshal Badoglio.

For such a manoeuvre to work in France, it was necessary to form a government with which the Allies would negotiate. Both Laval and some Pétain aides began to explore this possibility. Laval tried contacting parliamentarians and members of the left in the hope of broadening the base of his government. But no one was willing to join him at this late stage.[52] Meanwhile a group of Pétain loyalists set about trying to give the regime a democratic facelift. Bouthillier, Moysset, and Romier started to prepare another draft constitution. By September they had produced something considerably less authoritarian than the 1941 version, a constitution somewhat like the way the Third Republic had been expected to work in 1875: this was the last fling of Orleanism in France. Pétain, despite finding the document too democratic, agreed to play his part.[53]

The next stage in the plot was to get rid of Laval. On 12 November, Pétain told Laval he intended to broadcast the next day. He would announce that a constitution was ready, and that if he died before it could be ratified, his constituent powers would pass to the National Assembly. The Germans refused to allow the broadcast to go ahead. In its place listeners heard music from a light operetta. Pétain retaliated by going on strike, refusing to carry out his duties. This stand-off lasted for the rest of November, until the Germans decided to raise the stakes. Abetz, back in favour, arrived in Vichy on 4 December with a letter from von Ribbentrop ordering Pétain to form a government fully committed to Germany. Hitler was now ready to ditch Pétain in case of a refusal, but after a day's reflection Pétain capitulated. The Germans sent an envoy, Cecil von Renthe-Fink, to act as Pétain's watchdog. The old man was now effectively a prisoner. As for Laval, the price he had to pay for being saved again by the Germans was to bring into his government those collaborationists from whom he had been trying to distance himself. Bousquet was replaced at the head of the police by Darnand who became Secretary-General for the Maintenance of Order; and another ultra-collaborationist, Philippe Henriot, was put in charge of propaganda. The Milice was now authorized to operate in the North. Thus the paradoxical result of Laval and Pétain's separate machinations to republicanize the regime was to bring it closer to fascism than it had ever been.[54] The collaborationists now had power—but in a State which barely existed.

[52] Warner, *Pierre Laval*, 382–3.   [53] Cointet, *Le Conseil national*, 316–27.
[54] Burrin, *La France à l'heure*, 177.

Collaboration: The Balance Sheet

What had collaboration achieved? It is hard to dissent from the view that it failed by any standard against which it is judged. Certainly it failed to win the French a privileged place in the German Europe. At no point did the Germans even hint at any kind of partnership. Laval never obtained any guarantees about the future peace treaty, and even in November 1942 when it would have cost Hitler nothing to offer the French some promises about the future of an Empire they were about to lose, he would not do so. The few examples of the Germans failing to get what they wanted—the demand for bases in North Africa on 15 July 1940 and again in July 1941—occurred only because the Germans decided not to press the matter further. Vichy believed that it had trump cards—the fleet, the Empire, the Free Zone—but paradoxically the very existence of these prevented a more robust policy. Precisely because it did have something to lose, the Vichy government was always terrified to push its case too far for fear of provoking the Germans.

Vichy only won paltry concessions: a reduction in Occupation costs between May 1941 and November 1942; the suppression of the Demarcation Line in March 1943 (but by this stage the whole country had been occupied); the right to equip France's armed forces beyond the levels prescribed in the Armistice (but it was in Germany's interest that France should be able to defend her Empire). Vichy did enjoy some limited success in getting Germany to release French prisoners of war, but this cost Germany nothing, and kept the French dangling in the hope that good behaviour would obtain yet more releases. In any case, the prisoners were more useful to the Germans working for Germany in France than languishing in camps. Some prisoners were let out after Montoire, another 6,800 after the signing of the Protocols of Paris in June 1941, 1,075 after the sacking of Weygand, 90,747 under the terms of the *relève*. In total 600,000 prisoners came back during the war, about 220,800 thanks to Vichy's efforts (the others escaped or owed their release to illness).

After the war, defenders of Vichy conveniently forgot the more ambitious expectations they had harboured for collaboration, and constructed the theory that Pétain had acted as a 'shield', protecting France from suffering the fate of Poland. How does this claim stand up? It is true that France did not suffer like Poland, but it had never been Germany's intention that she should. The Nazis did not class the French in the same ethnic category as Slavs. France was to be exploited, but not destroyed. The only valid comparison would be with the rest of Western Europe, and it does not suggest that France received favourable treatment. Comparisons of caloric intakes are difficult because regional variations were so considerable. But France's figures seem to have been the lowest in Western Europe.[55] Germany siphoned off so much of the French economy that

[55] Paxton, *Vichy France*, 359–60.

it would have become counter-productive to take any more. In 1943, Germany was taking 50 per cent of French iron ore, 99 per cent of French cement, 92 per cent of French lorries, and 76 per cent of French locomotives. The Economic Section of the MBF estimated that by the end of 1943 as much as 50 per cent of all French non-agricultural production was for German purposes. Massive quantities of agricultural produce also went to Germany. Hemen's prediction in 1940 that the Germans would be able to buy up the French economy had been largely fulfilled.[56] The shield was more like a sieve.

In the end, the 'shield' defence revolved around two claims: that thanks to Vichy's efforts a smaller proportion of workers had been sent from France to Germany than from Holland and Belgium; and that a larger proportion of Jews survived in France than in other occupied countries. The first of these claims was simply untrue. By the end of 1943, there were 646,421 French workers in Germany. This represented 10.8 per cent of the total number of foreign workers, making the French the third largest foreign contingent after the Soviets (36.4 per cent) and the Poles (18.5 per cent). The big difference was that women accounted for only 6.6 per cent of the French workers, as opposed to 51 per cent of the Soviets and 34 per cent of the Poles.

In total, Paxton estimates that total numbers of French working in Germany amounted to 3.3 per cent of the French population, as opposed to 3.4 per cent in Belgium and 3 per cent in Holland. Thus although Laval was able to claim that, thanks to the *relève*, labour conscription arrived later in France than Belgium and Holland, this did not in the end make much difference. It was true that the numbers conscripted to work in Germany fell far below Sauckel's demands, but this was due partly to the Bichelonne–Speer agreement, and partly to the fact that increasing numbers of Frenchmen refused to obey the law. A huge amount of Vichy propaganda was devoted in 1942 to encouraging people to work in Germany; and a huge amount of police time was devoted in 1943 to forcing them to do so. If the Germans did not obtain all the workers they desired, this was largely in spite of Vichy.[57]

The same observation can be made about Vichy's claim to have protected the Jews. It is true that a larger proportion of Jews survived the Holocaust than in almost any other European country, but the real issue is whether, without Vichy's co-operation, even fewer Jews would have perished. The comparison ought not to be with Holland and Belgium, which did not have supposedly independent governments, but with those countries which did, like Denmark and (up to September 1943) Italy. If this comparison is made, Vichy emerges very unfavourably. The massive deportations of the summer of 1942 had been made possible by the Vichy government and its police. To the extent that the regime did, after September 1942, display a slightly less co-operative spirit—though French police in

---

[56] Milward, *French Economy*, 131–4, 256–9.
[57] Y. Durand, 'STO: Vichy au service de l'Allemagne', *L'Histoire*, 167 (1993), 14–23.

Bordeaux were still arresting Jews in January 1944—this was due to Laval's awareness of the adverse popular reaction to the round-ups of the summer.

In short, if there was a shield in France between 1940 and 1944 it was less Vichy's shield against Germany than the shield which the reactions of French civil society created between the French people and the regime supposedly protecting them against the Germans. It is to society that we must now turn.

Part III

Vichy, the Germans, and
the French People

Part III

Vichy, the Germans, and the French People

Introduction to Part III

As we have seen in Part II, only a tiny minority of people were actively involved in political collaboration, and as we shall see in Part IV, only a small minority were actively engaged in the organized Resistance. But what of the large majority who were actively engaged in neither, and often described as *attentiste*? One approach might be to argue, like the historian Richard Cobb, that for most people the daily rhythms of private life are more important than the public sphere. In the preface to his evocative book on the Occupation, Cobb proposes for his own autobiography a chronology marked by a private calendar of ferocious toothaches. The novelist Jacques Laurent agrees:

> One must remember that the Occupation did not entirely occupy the thoughts of my contemporaries, whether it be my parents, whose only concern was to resolve the indirect consequences of the Occupation, notably the lack of coal which obliged them to move into the smallest room of the apartment, the bathroom, or my parents' concierge, whose concern was that her husband's bronchitis would become chronic despite the lack of tobacco, and who was sad at the death of her cat.[1]

But was it possible to live outside politics in the peculiar conditions of the Occupation when 'ordinariness' has implications it would not have in other circumstances? One aim of German propaganda was to encourage a return to 'normal'. Did the attempt to continue an ordinary life not render one complicit in that enterprise? Is indifference not a form of complicity? As Pascal Ory has written: 'At the most extreme, everyone who remained on territory occupied by the German army or that was under its control had to some degree collaborated.' This is what Robert Paxton means by describing even those who 'did' nothing as 'functional collaborators'. But everything depends on context. Another historian, John Sweets, has convincingly suggested that many of the silent majority could just as accurately be described as 'functional resisters'. If a concierge who did nothing while witnessing a Jew being escorted out of her building by the police was a functional collaborator, was not a concierge who did nothing when

---

[1] R. Cobb, *French and Germans, Germans and French: A Personal Interpretation of France under Two Occupations* (1983), pp. xi–xiii; Laurent, *Histoire egoïste*, 360–1.

239

seeing someone stuffing Resistance tracts in the letter boxes of her building a functional resister?[2]

In other words, silence during the Occupation had multiple meanings. A writer who did not actively participate in resistance, although refusing to publish while the Germans were in France, may not have been 'doing' anything, but this silence could carry the weight of an accusation. As Jacques Debû-Bridel put it: 'Only silence has grandeur, all the rest is weakness . . . I sincerely pity those who mistake this necessary silence for resignation and refuse to understand the full force of its eloquence.'[3] Or in the words of the writer and editor Max-Pol Fouchet: 'Silence, far from being an absence, is a presence which is waiting.'[4] On the other hand, another observer, the Jewish lawyer Lucien Vidal-Naquet, wrote in his journal in September 1942 to stigmatize what he called the 'silence of abjectness'.[5] Yet the most famous Resistance novel, *Le Silence de la mer* (The Silence of the Sea), published clandestinely in 1942, celebrates silence: the silent resistance of a girl and her uncle who refuse to address a word to the German officer who has been billeted upon them.

Although we must try to penetrate the various meanings of silence, it would be wrong to go to the other extreme of trying to fit all conduct on to the spectrum of resistance and collaboration. These categories barely existed at the start of the Occupation. Until at least the end of 1942, the Resistance was too small to be a presence in the experience, even consciousness, of most people: choices did not seem to exist in 1940. One could say that the avoidance of choice is in itself a kind of choice in the way that Alain once claimed that someone who denied the existence of left and right was by definition of the right. Individuals were confronted with moral choices every time they came into contact with a German and they had to fashion individual codes of conduct compatible with dignity, self-respect, conscience, and survival. Such dilemmas are the inevitable consequence of any foreign occupation. They are present in Maupassant's stories about the occupation of 1870–1. The writer Léon Werth, who kept a journal during the Occupation, remembered the case of his aunt who regretted for the next thirty years that she had in 1870 shaken the hand of a German officer because he had allowed her to visit her prisoner-of-war husband.[6] The Occupation presented innumerable such dilemmas. Did one accept a seat proffered by a German soldier in the metro? Did one give directions to a German soldier if asked?

How do we assess the case of Edmond Dumérial, a teacher of German, who kept a diary during the Occupation, subsequently published under the title *Journal d'un honnête homme pendant l'Occupation* (Journal of an Honest Man

---

[2] Ory, *Les Collaborateurs*, 10; Paxton, *Vichy France*, 235, 240–1; J. Sweets, 'Hold that Pendulum! Redefining Fascism, Collaborationism and Resistance in France', *FHS* 15/4 (1988), 730–58.

[3] *La Résistance intellectuelle: Textes et témoignages* (1970), 40–1.

[4] Quoted in M. Trebitsch, 'Nécrologie: Les Revues qui s'arrêtent en 1939–1940', *La Revue des revues*, 24 (1997), 19–33: 33.

[5] L. Vidal-Naquet, 'Journal (15 septembre 1942–29 février 1944)', *Annales ESC* 48/3 (1993), 513–43: 515.

[6] Burrin, *La France à l'heure*, 199.

during the Occupation). After the start of the Occupation, Dumérial offered his linguistic services to the prefect of the Loire-Inférieur. He was given considerable responsibility in the official contacts between the German and French authorities. A man of patriotic sentiments, conservative but not anti-republican, Dumérial deplored Vichy's anti-republican and anti-Semitic legislation, and the policy of collaboration: after Montoire, he put flowers on English graves in the local cemetery. But Dumérial also saw it as his duty to smooth over problems between the Germans and the French. His view was that 'the only policy is to accept the situation and adapt oneself diplomatically as best one can'. He formed a good relationship with the local German commander, who was assassinated in October 1941, and he regretted Resistance attacks on Germans as 'regrettable for the harmony of Franco-German relations'.[7] The Manichaean vocabulary of 'resistance' and 'collaboration' hardly seems appropriate to Dumérial. If he used his linguistic skills to mediate between the population and the Germans, it was because he wanted to protect his compatriots from the worst effects of the Occupation.

How do we assess the case of Frédéric Joliot, one of France's most distinguished scientists? Winner of the Nobel prize for chemistry in 1935, Joliot held the chair of nuclear chemistry at the Collège de France. Having acquired the funding to build a particle accelerator (cyclotron)—the only one in Europe—he was in the forefront of research into the study of nuclear chain reactions and the potential development of nuclear energy. Immediately after the defeat Joliot had taken the precaution of sending abroad France's stock of heavy water—used as a moderator in nuclear reactors—but he decided himself to stay on despite pressing invitations to go to Britain or America. Returning to Paris after the Exodus, Joliot found his laboratory had been taken over by the Germans, and he immediately embarked on negotiations to recover possession of it. It was clearly to Germany's advantage that he should return to the laboratory, but before doing so he wanted assurances that any Germans working in the laboratory would not carry out research which could be detrimental to the military interests of France. He wrote to one colleague that these negotiations certainly pained him but the alternative might be 'to exclude us from our place of work and dispossess us of our material'. Up to a point he was reassured by the fact that the German negotiators included the scientist Wolfgang Gentner who had worked in Joliot's laboratory in the 1930s and was known to him as a former anti-Nazi. Joliot wrote to his wife that in the negotiations the Germans had shown themselves to be 'correct, even respectful'. In the end Joliot never obtained all the guarantees he would have liked, but a modus vivendi was reached. Joliot continued to run the laboratory and the German scientists had two rooms of their own. The French and Germans did work together in the basement where the cyclotron was situated, but apart from this they met only in the lifts.

---

[7] *Journal d'un honnête homme pendant l'Occupation (juin 1940–août 1944)*, ed. J. Bourgeon (Thonon-les-Bains, 1990), 72–83, 233.

Despite this semi-amicable accommodation Joliot was not favourably viewed by the occupying authorities, not least because in the 1930s he had been closely involved with the Popular Front and the anti-fascist left. In early November 1940 he was involved in one of the first public manifestations of opposition to the occupiers after the Germans arrested the distinguished physicist Jean Langevin on suspicion of being involved in early resistance efforts. This arrest outraged Parisian academic circles. At what would have been Langevin's first lecture Joliot took the podium and made a public protest. On 11 November he was involved in a demonstration at the War Memorial of the Sorbonne. On two occasions in 1941 Joliot was arrested, but on both occasions almost immediately released thanks to the intervention of Gentner. Some time in 1942 he joined the clandestine Communist Party and was on the executive committttee of the Communist Resistance organization, the Front national.

How, then, does one characterize Joliot's conduct? To work in a laboratory which was technically under the protection of the German army was clearly in some sense collaboration. Justifying his decision to stay in France, Joliot wrote to a colleague that it was 'of primordial importance to maintain scientific activity intact' in France: he was staying to protect his laboratory and France's scientific future. Could this be described as 'prophylactic collaboration', even 'patriotic collaboration'? But was not Joliot in quite a literal sense playing with fire given that the development of nuclear weapons in America was only two years away? Even if, as seems the case, Joliot did not realize that this development was so close—the cyclotron in Chicago which produced the first quantities of plutonium in 1942 was much more powerful than the French one—was he not too confident of his own ability to keep several balls in the air at once? Was he too reassured by the presence of Gentner? Did his resistance activities outweigh the degree of pragmatic collaboration which he felt to be necessary? How are such comparisons and measurements to be carried out?[8]

The near impossibility of answering such questions satisfactorily suggests that it might be more useful to jettison these categories of resistance and collaboration for all but the small activist minorities. Perhaps for the mass of the population it would be preferable to use the less morally charged term 'accommodation' proposed by Philippe Burrin. He has distinguished between 'structural' or forced accommodation imposed by the need to keep services running; 'voluntary accommodation' in which the French took initiatives of their own for a variety of motives ranging from the defence of professional or corporate interests to simple self-interest; and political accommodation inspired by some degree of ideological sympathy with the occupier.[9]

---

[8] M. Pinault, 'Frédéric Joliot, la science et la société, un itinéraire de la physique nucléaire à la politique nucléaire 1900–1958' (unpublished thesis, University of Paris-I, 1999), 220–421; 'Frédéric Joliot, les Allemands et l'université aux premier mois de l'occupation', *VSRH* 50 (1996), 67–88; Burrin, *La France à l'heure*, 315–22.

[9] *La France à l'heure*, 468–70.

Burrin's conceptualization, which owes something to Hoffmann's distinctions between different kinds of collaboration, is extremely useful, but there are problems with entirely abandoning the category of collaboration, or at least restricting its application to a small minority. Given that the tendency of recent historiography is to extend resistance from the activist minority and site it within a broad social context, it would surely be illogical simultaneously to narrow the category of collaboration. It is also the case that the concept of collaboration did eventually come to structure the way people perceived their own conduct and the conduct of others. In that sense collaboration 'existed'. It existed, however, as a historically contingent category. During the Great War, in the part of north-eastern France which was occupied, the French lived in proximity to the Germans as they did between 1940 and 1944. But after 1918 only 123 people were tried for 'intelligence with the enemy', and they were people who had carried out flagrant acts of assistance to the Germans (such as denouncing people who were hiding French citizens on the run from the Germans).[10] After 1945 the notion of what was considered reprehensible conduct was extended much more widely.

Even if collaboration exists, defining it remains very difficult. One celebrated contemporary definition was provided by Sartre in his essay 'What is a Collaborator?' Sartre defines the collaborator as a 'feminine' psychological type with certain predispositions which are latent and emerge in certain circumstances. For Sartre collaboration was a vocation to be explained by certain certain 'psychological and social laws'.[11] In fact Sartre was talking more about the extreme and committed cases like Drieu la Rochelle, who was probably his model. Another solution would be to take the definitions used by the post-Liberation courts and purge commissions. But even here there was much ambiguity. For example, there was uncertainty as to how to deal with 'sexual collaboration' between French women and German men. Some courts judged it as a crime of 'intelligence with the enemy'; others saw it only as a misdemeanour punishable by the loss of civic rights.[12] Social representations of collaboration were constantly shifting: its history is to some extent the history of the construction of the concept. The term must therefore be used in a fluid way, and we must be aware of the importance also of what Italian historians, following Primo Levi, call the 'grey zone'. Conduct which might be described as collaboration could incorporate a myriad of motives including self-protection, the protection of others, even patriotism.

These problems were complicated by the existence of the Vichy regime. How do we judge those people who applied Vichy's Jewish Statute, excluding Jews from various categories of employment? The term 'collaborator' is technically

[10] R. Martinage, 'Les Collaborateurs devant les Cours d'Assises du Nord après la très grande guerre', *Revue du Nord,* 309 (1995), 95–115.

[11] 'Qu'est-ce qu'un collaborateur?', 43–5.

[12] H. Diamond, *Women and the Second World War in France 1939–1948* (1999), 145–6.

inappropriate since the law in question was a French law not a German one. The case is different from that of French policemen who rounded up Jews in July 1942: this was a German policy not a French one, and so the term 'collaborator' might be appropriate (although the orders had been given by the French government). Vichy further complicated matters because some who ardently opposed Germany were ready to serve the regime either out of personal loyalty to Pétain, believing he was playing a double game, or because they believed in the National Revolution. It has to be remembered that Vichy started with a radical project to change France. Like the so-called totalitarian regimes, Vichy up to a point aspired to create a New Man (and Woman). Examining the experience of life under the regime therefore also requires examining how people responded to this project. How much 'resistance' was there to it?

The more that is known about the social history of 'totalitarian' societies, the more it is clear how unsuccessful they were in transforming civil society, even when people did not resist in any organized or political way. The German term for political resistance is *Widerstand*, but Martin Broszat has suggested that the term *Resistenz*, the medical term describing the body's resistance to infection, could also be given a social meaning to describe the multifarious ways in which the social organism resists attempts to transform it. Society develops its own anti-bodies: the Russian peasants whom Stalin collectivized could be physically moved, but they could not so easily be remade, and their values reacted back on the state which tried to transform them.[13] At one level, therefore, totalitarian regimes are hard to resist because their control of society is so all-encompassing. But by trying to influence behaviour that more liberal states ignore, or leave in the domain of private life, they politicize what had previously been unpolitical and private, and thereby increase the surface of possible opposition. If, say, listening to jazz is prohibited, a previously innocent activity becomes a sort of resistance, or at least pushes civil society into an opposition that is the precondition of organized resistance. This makes it necessary to extend the notion of resistance beyond politics. The extent to which individuals retain autonomy defines the limits of a totalitarian regime's success in transforming civil society.

Up to a point, this model applies to Vichy—but only up to a point. Despite its ambitious reform projects, the regime explicitly eschewed 'totalitarianism', and allowed a considerable measure of pluralism. This created another level of ambiguities. Having rejected the single party, Vichy was forced to rely upon the co-operation of pre-existing organizations and institutions to carry out its transformation of society. Since the regime supposedly believed in handing power back to the 'real' communities, this was entirely in line with its ideological preconceptions: there was to be no *Gleichschaltung*. Vichy did not invent all that many new institutions so much as encourage initiatives that were believed to be

---

[13] S. Fitzpatrick, *Stalin's Peasants: Resistance and Survival in the Russian Village after Collectivization* (Oxford, 1994).

in the right spirit. This created, between the regime and civil society, what Henri Rousso has called 'spaces of liberty'.[14] As a result, between the policies of the regime and their implementation, there were contradictions and misunderstandings which derived from the large margin of manoeuvre that Vichy left to many executants of those policies.

This meant that initially Vichy had something to offer not only traditional conservatives and diehard anti-Republicans. Some of those who had supported the Popular Front not out of passionate republicanism but because they believed it was an opportunity to remedy some of the defects of the liberal state were also ready to give Vichy the benefit of the doubt, or at least see how much of its project was compatible with theirs. This was not opportunism or betrayal but a sign that there were many for whom the divisions between Republicans and anti-Republicans were no longer the ones that counted most.

These are the questions which will be discussed in the following chapters. Chapter 11 examines propaganda, policing, and administration, and the ways in which the Vichy regime tried to mobilize support. Chapter 12 looks at the responses of the population towards both Vichy and the German occupier. Here we will be primarily concerned with the period up to the end of 1942 but not beyond. This is because once the organized Resistance became a more important presence in 1943, people found themselves reacting not simply to the Germans and to Vichy but also to the Resistance. We shall, therefore, return to this question when discussing the organized Resistance in Part IV. Chapter 13 is concerned with the responses of artists and intellectuals, not those, already examined, who were politically committed to collaboration, or those, to be examined later, who were politically committed to resistance, but rather the majority who were testing what could be achieved with the new constraints, and probing the limits of acceptable compromise.

Chapter 14 examines the regime's policy towards women and the young. The intention here is not only to evaluate the impact of those policies but also to analyse an area in which the 'spaces of liberty' were particularly important, and the ambiguities also. Finally, Chapter 15 looks at the experience of the Jews, examining how their fate was bound up in the interaction between the policies of the Germans, the policies of the Vichy regime, and the responses of French civil society.

[14] 'L'Impact du régime sur la société', in *VEF*, 573–600: 588–9.

11

Propaganda, Policing, and Administration

Balkanization

Assessing the impact of the Occupation on the French population is difficult because a unified France no longer existed: there were at least six Frances. First, the Unoccupied Zone covering 45 per cent of French territory and about a third of the population. Secondly, the tiny Italian Zone (extended after November 1942). Thirdly, Alsace-Lorraine which had been effectively annexed by Germany and was run by two Gauleiter: the two *départements* of Alsace were attached to the Gau of Baden, and Moselle in Lorraine was attached to the Gau of Saar-Palatinate. Fourthly, the two *départements* of the Nord and Pas-de-Calais (*zone rattachée*) were attached to the German military command in Brussels. Fifthly, there was the Forbidden Zone (*Zone interdite*) or Reserved Zone (*Zone réservée*), comprising a total of six *départements* and part of four others, running from the mouth of the Somme in the north down to the Swiss frontier in the Jura. This area was separated from the rest of the Occupied Zone by another demarcation line, and refugees who had fled from it during the Exodus were not allowed back. Finally, there was the rest of the Occupied Zone.[1]

To these six Frances, one could add three more. From April 1941, another 'forbidden zone' about 20 kilometres deep ran along the coast from Dunkirk

[1] There was some terminological variation in the designation of these zones. The terms Reserved and Forbidden Zone were often used interchangeably, and the line separating this area from the rest of France was variously called 'Green Line', 'Führer Line', or *Nordostlinie*. Confusion has persisted ever since. Some books distinguish a smaller Forbidden Zone, comprising part of the Somme, Aisne, and Ardennes *départements*, from a larger Reserved Zone, stretching from the Ardennes to the Jura. Even if contemporary usage sometimes gives credence to this view, in reality this extra line never seems to have existed on the ground. The local historian of the Ardennes, e.g., while insisting on the importance of the line dividing the Reserved/Forbidden Zone from the rest of the Occupied Zone, which ran through the *département*, has nothing to say about any division between the Reserved and Forbidden Zones although, if such a division had existed, the line would also have run through the *département*. See J. Vadon, *Les Ardennes dans la guerre 1939–1945* (Le Coteau, 1985), 63. What does seem to be true, however, is that in the north of the Forbidden Zone, near to the Nord/Pas-de-Calais, German control was more oppressive than further south.

to Hendaye. There was Algeria which remained free of German troops through-out the Occupation. Finally, there was the diaspora of 1.5 million prisoners of war in Germany who were assiduously courted by the Vichy regime.

The divisions between these zones respected no previous administrative boundaries. The demarcation line between the Unoccupied and the Occupied Zones ran through the middle of thirteen *départements*; in the Occupied Zone only twelve *départements* were not crossed by at least one line. The Jura *département* lay in three different zones. These lines were genuine internal frontiers. Obtaining a pass (*Ausweis*) could be difficult. Even communicating across the demarcation line was problematic. People could only write to family members, and had to do so using a card thirteen lines long where they ticked the appropriate words: 'in good health', 'tired', 'slightly/seriously ill', 'wounded', 'prisoner', 'dead', 'no news of'.

Conditions in the two main zones were very different. The North was on German time, one hour ahead of the South. This meant that during midwinter in the North it was not light before 9 a.m. In the North, there was a curfew from 10 p.m. to 5 a.m.; in the South there was none. In the North, American films were forbidden; in the South, they were available until November 1942. In much of the North, it was difficult to hear Vichy radio, and easier to hear Radio Paris, or the BBC. In the South there were French flags; in the North swastikas. In the South, the Marseillaise was sung; in the North it was prohibited. Because the Germans feared any possible revival of French militarism, several distinctive features of the Vichy regime, like the Chantiers de la jeunesse and the Veterans' Legion, were banned in the North.

The division between Free Zone and Occupied Zone was not the only one that mattered. The population of the Nord/Pas-de-Calais felt entirely cut off from the rest of France. The German presence was oppressive from the start; workers were being drafted to Germany from the summer of 1940. The history of the Nord/Pas-de-Calais under occupation belongs as much to the history of Belgium as France. Visiting the area in May 1941, a Vichy representative reported: 'there is as much difference between this Zone and the Occupied Zone as between the Occupied Zone and the Free Zone'.[2]

Alsace-Lorraine underwent total Germanization. School lessons were conducted in German; citizens not considered to be assimilable were deported to France; Nazi organizations like the Hitler Youth were introduced; statues of Joan of Arc were pulled down; and berets forbidden. The 410,000 refugees who had fled south were ordered to return; about two-thirds of them did so. From August 1942, men of eligible age had to join the Wehrmacht. If they tried to escape, they were warned that reprisals would be exacted on their families. There were about 130,000 of these 'malgré nous' (Against Our Will), as they were called. Dispersed

---

[2] E. Dejonghe, 'Le Nord et le Pas-de-Calais pendant la première année d'occupation: Un régime d'exception', *Revue du nord*, 76/306 (1994), 487–99: 487.

in different army units, most were sent to the eastern front, from where 40,000 never returned.[3]

The disruptions caused by France's geographical fragmentation were exacerbated by constant changes in the rules. After May 1941, all zones were on German time. The system of correspondence across the Line was progressively relaxed: from June 1941, there was a blank card of seven lines; from September 1941, ordinary cards could be sent; from March 1943, all restrictions were lifted. The German troops policing the *Nordostlinie* were removed in December 1941. The separation of the Nord/Pas-de-Calais remained in force, but from the spring of 1941 Vichy representatives were allowed in, and people permitted to display photographs of Pétain.

Given the Nazis' predilection for ethnic theorizing, it is perhaps surprising that the 'six Frances' were not joined by others: a Flemish one and a Breton one. In the north-east, where only about 170,000 French people spoke Flemish and, unlike in Belgium, there were no community tensions, the Germans allowed the separatist leader the Abbé Gantois to organize regionalist cultural events, but not to promote separatism. In Brittany there were a million Breton speakers, and a tiny Breton nationalist party (PNB) had existed since 1931. After the defeat, its leaders, who escaped to Germany on the outbreak of war, believed their moment had arrived. In July 1940, they proclaimed the Breton National Council, and set up a paper, *L'Heure bretonne*, which had about 8,000 readers. But after momentary hesitation, the Germans decided that the advantages of supporting a movement which enjoyed such minuscule support were outweighed by the disadvantages of causing friction with Vichy. The PNB was taken over by a moderate leader who approved Vichy's regionalist policies. At the end of 1943, however, the more radical wing seceded, and in May 1944 founded a pro-German PNB and a Breton *milice* (the Perrot group) whose fifty members ended up fighting for Breton independence wearing German uniform with a Breton badge.[4]

Other Maps

The occupation map of France must also be fitted over an older map of French memories and traditions. These two maps did not necessarily match. Much of the Unoccupied Zone included the traditional Republican heartlands of the south which might have been expected to be more resistant to Vichy's message than the traditionally conservative west which was in the Occupied Zone. In some Protestant areas of the south, 'resistance' had a history going back

---

[3] P. Barral, 'L'Alsace-Lorraine: Trois départements sous la botte', in Azéma and Bédarida (eds.), *Les Années noires*, i. 233–49; Ory, *Les Collaborateurs*, 183–90.

[4] Burrin, *La France à l'heure*, 54–8, 371–7; Ory, *Les Collaborateurs*, 168–200; M. H. Butler, 'La Collaboration dans la préfecture régionale de Rennes', *RHDGM* 117 (1980), 3–23; H. Fréville, *Archives secrètes de Bretagne 1940–1944* (Rennes, 1985).

to the seventeenth century. During the Occupation, the Catholic north of the Lozère *département* proved less favourable to the Resistance than the Protestant south.[5]

One intense regional memory survived in those north-eastern *départements* which had been occupied during the First World War. This was the only part of France where people started out with concrete images of what occupation meant.[6] An ingrained suspicion of southerners made people ready to believe that the Armistice had been signed because the timorous meridionals wanted to keep the war off their territory. The region was traditionally Anglophile—Roubaix was the second town in France to form a football club—and the Germans remained 'Boches' throughout the years of Briandism. Lille has five monuments commemorating the city's suffering between 1914 and 1918, and several streets celebrating local resistance heroes of the First World War. Jean Lebas, Socialist Mayor of Roubaix, had been deported to Germany in the First World War and suffered the same fate in the Second—but this time he did not return. Many restrictions imposed in the second occupation were familiar from the first: the curfews, the obligation to step off the pavement if German soldiers were passing, the taking of hostages, and the confiscation of carrier pigeons in an area where pigeon fancying was a popular pastime. Lille had erected a statue to the sixteen 'colombophiles morts pour la France' in the First World War. Although such memories helped to forge a unified regional identity, one must not underestimate the countervailing effects of the Popular Front which had exacerbated class tensions in this highly industrialized region with its deeply conservative and Catholic bourgeoisie.

To these maps—the conjunctural map imposed by the Occupation and the deeper structural map of memory—should be added a third one: that of food shortages. By September 1940 most essential goods were rationed. The struggle for survival forms the background to every memoir of the period. The most literary of diarists spent time obsessively compiling lists of prices and noting the time spent in queues. Thus the journalist Galtier-Boissière on 12 January 1941: 'Atmosphere reminiscent of the Siege of Paris; interminable queues.' Or the writer Jean Guéhenno on 3 January 1941: 'We have coupons but cannot buy anything with them; the shops are empty.' Or the journalist Jacques Biélinky on 29 December 1940: 'Rue Mouffetard there is no food. In the queues the subject is discussed energetically.' On 10 February 1941, Biélinky noted that he had queued one and a half hours for an egg.[7]

The level of rations for the largest category of the population was 1,327

[5] J.-M. Guillon and C. Bougeard, 'La Résistance et l'histoire, passé/présent', *La Résistance et les Français: Nouvelles approches, Cahiers de l'IHTP*, 37 (1997), 29–45: 29–33.

[6] Cobb, *French and Germans*, 3–56; A. Becker, 'Memoire et commémoration: Les "Atrocités" allemandes de la Première Guerre mondiale dans le Nord de la France', *Revue du Nord*, 295 (1992), 339–54.

[7] J. Galtier-Boissière, *Mon journal pendant l'Occupation* (1944), 32; J. Guéhenno, *Journal des années noires* (1947), 101; J. Biélinky, *Journal, 1940–1942: Un journaliste juif sous l'occupation* (1992), 85, 98.

calories per day as opposed to an average of 3,000 per day before the war.[8] This barely adequate ration was steadily reduced, but even then it was difficult to find. There were many reasons for the shortages: the British blockade, German requisitioning of French produce, and falling agricultural production caused by lack of labour, livestock, and fertilizer. To make matters worse, the Occupation divided the France of grain-producers from the France of wine-growers. Before the war the Occupied Zone had produced all the sugar grown in France, three-quarters of all wheat, 87 per cent of all butter.

The market became so fragmented that it is impossible to draw a comprehensive map of shortages. People in the South believed that food problems did not exist in the North. In fact the most fundamental division was between town and country. In thirty-nine mainly rural *départements*, mortality rates in 1941–3 were lower than in 1936–8; in cities they were higher.[9] City dwellers with country relatives, or country property, were privileged. Others would embark on scavenging expeditions into the countryside. In Dijon, hundreds of people regularly headed to the countryside on bicycles with trailers attached in order to stock up on provisions.[10] The rural commune of Arnecke in the Nord was frequently invaded by townspeople. Up to 200 people at a time would descend from the train from Lille to find provisions for their families, or buy for resale on the black market. The local populace viewed these expeditions with apprehension.[11]

Some country areas of monocultural production, like the wine-producing Var and Hérault, suffered as badly as towns. Regions of mixed production, like the Seine-et-Marne or Loiret, suffered least.[12] Nowhere suffered more than cities like Marseilles and Montpellier, which were surrounded by monocultural production. Montpellier in 1944 was said to be the town with the least meat, least bread, least eggs, least milk, and most wine in France. In the Hérault, in November 1942, all outside supplies of vegetables had dried up, and people lived on a diet of chestnuts and potatoes.[13] Everywhere meat became a luxury; swedes and Jerusalem artichokes made their appearance in the winter of 1940. Recalling the Occupation fifty years later, the Resistance leader Jean-Pierre Lévy remembered above all hunger.[14]

When prefects listened to popular opinion, the loudest sounds they heard were not political slogans but rumbling stomachs. This had profound political

---

[8] D. Veillon, *Vivre et survivre en France, 1939–1947* (1995), 116.

[9] P. Abrahams, 'Haute-Savoie at War: 1939–1945' (Ph.D. thesis, Cambridge University, 1992), 76.

[10] H. Drouot, *Notes d'un Dijonnais pendant l'occupation allemande 1940–1944* (Dijon, 1998), 261, 284.

[11] L. Taylor, 'The Black Market in Occupied Northern France, 1940–1944', *Contemporary European History*, 6/2 (1997), 153–76: 163.

[12] D. Veillon and J.-M. Flonneau (eds.), *Les Temps des restrictions 1939–1947* (IHTP, 1996).

[13] R. Austin, 'The Education and Youth Policies of the Vichy Government in the Department of the Hérault, 1940–1944' (unpublished Ph.D. thesis, Manchester University, 1981), 292.

[14] *Mémoires d'un franc-tireur: Itinéraire d'un résistant* (1998), 44.

consequences. It undermined Pétain's claim that by signing the Armistice he had saved France from the deprivations of war; and it subverted Vichy's rhetoric of moral unity. The struggle to survive created a general *sauve-qui-peut* which was far from the propaganda image of the nation gathering around the Father-Protector. The mothers of large families were fêted by the regime, but in reality people resented them for enjoying the privilege of being allowed to join the front of food queues.[15] Despite propaganda extolling the virtues of the peasantry, town-dwellers blamed peasant cupidity for the shortages, and believed that the countryside was groaning with unsold produce. Urban resentment reached such proportions that in some areas the authorities worried that people from towns would invade the countryside and violently seize the food they lacked; occasionally this did happen.[16]

Trying to control prices forced the regime into ever more bureaucratic intervention which alienated the peasants it courted so assiduously: there was more State, not less. Farmers held back or hid their produce, and black market prices soared. In the Haute-Savoie these were sometimes 1,000 per cent above official prices.[17] In March 1942, the regime acknowledged its inability to eradicate the black market by accepting that those who infringed the regulations would not be prosecuted if they had acted to satisfy family needs.[18] Tacit tolerance of the black market nonetheless created grey areas which caused friction between the population and the authorities. On two days in April 1942, the police searched every passenger descending from the train at Lille station. In the course of this operation they seized 9,550 kilos of potatoes, 170 kilos of beans, 120 kilos of peas, 430 kilos of wheat, 70 kilos of meat, 230 eggs, and 16 chickens. But most individuals were only carrying small quantities of goods (between 10 and 30 kilos) for their own use. They felt that they were entitled to keep their merchandise, and the atmosphere in the station turned ugly. In such situations, serious incidents often flared up.[19]

Shortages did not affect food alone. Obtaining fuel was also a major problem. The winter of 1940 was exceptionally cold—in Paris there were seventy days of frost—and coal was scarce. Lack of petrol led to the appearance of cars powered by gas or woodburning (*gazogènes*); in Paris people turned to bicycle-rickshaws (*vélo-taxis*). Since the Germans issued permits for only 7,000 private cars in Paris, the streets of the city were eerily empty. This was the heyday of the bicycle. But even these were not so easy to acquire: they were subject to German requisitioning and the scarcity of rubber made tyres difficult to replace. The price

[15] M. Pollard, 'Vichy and the Politics of Gender, 1940–1944' (Ph.D. thesis, Trinity College, Dublin, 1990), 357.
[16] F. Marcot, 'Étude régionale: Le Franche-Comté', in *VEF*, 644; M. Luirard, *La Région stéphanoise dans la guerre et dans la paix* (Saint-Étienne, 1980), 629; Abrahams, 'Haute-Savoie', 130–3.
[17] Abrahams, 'Haute-Savoie', 74–94.
[18] Veillon, *Vivre et survivre*, 180.   [19] Taylor, 'Black Market', 163–4.

of bicycles rocketed, and there was a black market in stolen ones.[20] In general, the Occupation was the time of the ersatz economy: wooden soles instead of leather, grilled acorns instead of coffee, sunflower leaves instead of tobacco.

Selling the National Revolution: Propaganda

It was against this background of penury and fragmentation that Vichy set about implementing its National Revolution. The division of France into zones complicated the most basic tasks of government. Ministers were located in Vichy, but their civil servants were mostly in Paris. Keeping contact depended on German co-operation. When the Germans were displeased with the French they would refuse to issue an *Ausweis*. Yves Bouthillier and René Belin, the Ministers of Finance and Labour, were not allowed to go to Paris between December 1940 and April 1941. Such restrictions became less severe during the course of 1941, but Berthelot, the Minister of Transport, who went to Bordeaux in October 1941 without permission was unceremoniously ordered to leave. The first minister authorized to visit the *Zone rattachée* was Pucheu in September 1941. Only some civil servants were permitted to carry files across the Line. The Germans could also suspend authorization to telephone across it, and they listened in to conversations. This made civil servants more liable to write things down, adding to the flood of paper produced. Like everything, paper was scarce, and officials were instructed to write on both sides of it; and also to dust their lampshades regularly to save electricity.[21]

To govern at all in such conditions was an achievement, but the regime claimed to be inaugurating a new era of administrative efficiency. Pétain announced on 11 July 1940: 'The impotence of the State must no longer paralyse the Nation ... Civil servants will no longer be hindered by narrow regulations and excessive controls. ... They will act faster ... We will create an organized France.'[22] The reality was quite different as was noted by an internal report of 1941: 'The Vice-President of the Council is not informed about the internal situation of the country ... The ministers do not control their administrations which usually betray them ... The result is that the country is neither administered nor governed.' One of the government's main preoccupations was drumming up enthusiasm for the Marshal, but it could not even provide sufficient portraits of him. The Ministry of the Interior had instructed all public buildings to display Pétain's portrait, but in February 1941 the prefect of Belfort complained that of the 392 portraits he had ordered four months earlier, only twenty had arrived![23]

---

[20] H. Diamond, 'Women's Experience during and after World War Two in the Toulouse Area 1939–1948: Choices and Constraints' (D.Phil. thesis, Sussex, 1992), 24.

[21] Baruch, *Servir l'État*, 84–91, 216–17.

[22] Pétain, *Discours*, 69.   [23] Baruch, *Servir l'État*, 187, 98.

Nonetheless, the regime's propaganda was on a scale unprecedented in France.[24] It was reported in January 1942 that there were so many posters on city walls that no one read them any more.[25] Saturation had been reached. The effectiveness of propaganda was also undermined by factional infighting. Until 13 December 1940, Laval tried to keep control over propaganda, and stuffed his cronies into key positions. To counter Laval's influence, Ménétrel set up the Amicale de France. Once Marion took over propaganda, he imposed a degree of consolidation, but although he took over the Amicale, its teams of propagandists—the Amis du Maréchal—continued to compete with Marion's Propaganda Delegates. On Laval's return, Marion was sidelined, though not sacked, and Laval again put in his own team. Laval did not suspect Marion of being lukewarm about collaboration, but he always preferred having personal control over everything and was happier using traditional propaganda methods than experimenting with new techniques. Laval believed essentially in newspapers.

Apart from problems caused by these internecine conflicts, Vichy propaganda was also competing with the Germans. In two years, the German Embassy, less active in this area than the Propaganda-Abteilung, distributed 17 million brochures, 10 million tracts, and 400,000 copies of 23 posters.[26] The Germans created a Press Agency, and the Propaganda-Abteilung gave detailed guidelines to the 350 papers or periodicals of the Occupied Zone. To counter this, in November 1940, Vichy took over France's main independent press organization, the Havas agency, which was renamed the French Information Office (OFI). Vichy censorship was supplemented by a stream of instructions and 'guidance notes [notes d'orientation]' sent out by OFI.[27] These ranged from matters of high policy—an instruction to play up a meeting between Laval and Goering and downplay the celebration of the Armistice (11 November 1940)—to minute points of detail—an instruction prohibiting reference to the menus offered to the Marshal on his provincial visits (presumably in deference to food shortages) or mention of his birthday in 1941 (presumably in order not to remind people of his age).[28]

In December 1940, the censors instructed papers to hammer their messages home: 'it is through obstinate repetition that propaganda for the New Order will bear fruit'.[29] In fact, obstinate repetition led to boredom. By the start of 1941, the press of the Southern Zone was losing readers, especially to Swiss newspapers. If people read the press at all, it was to discover precious information about

[24] In general see Amaury, De l'information et de la propagande d'État; C. Lévy and D. Veillon, 'Propagande et modélage des esprits', in VEF, 184–202; D. Rossignol, Histoire de la propagande en France de 1940 à 1944 (1991); Peschanski (ed.), Vichy 1940–1944, 39–58.

[25] Pollard, 'Politics of Gender', 129–30.

[26] Burrin, La France à l'heure, 187.

[27] M. Palmer, 'L'Office français d'information (1940–1944)', RHDGM 101 (1976), 19–40.

[28] P. Limagne, Éphémerides de quatre années tragiques 1940–1944 (Lavilledieu, 1987), 46, 141, 191.

[29] Ibid. 60.

rationing. When Marion took over, he tried to operate a more flexible system, encouraging newspapers to present the news in the way best suited to their readers. After Pétain's 'evil wind' speech, some papers were encouraged to stress the speech's authoritarian aspects, others its social content (the attack on the trusts).[30] But Marion's attempt to allow more leeway foundered since he could not stop ministers intervening on their own account to censor material: censorship created its own momentum.[31]

How did the press of the Free Zone respond to these conditions? There were 330 titles, including nine dailies and thirty weeklies which had left Paris, and an extensive regional press. Some publications like *Gringoire* or *Action française* identified entirely with Vichy's core philosophy, and if they criticized the regime, it was for not going far enough.[32] Maurras, however, had to go through contortions to reconcile his support for Vichy with his antipathy for Germany. He avoided saying anything positive about the Germans, and evaded the issue of collaboration, as emerges from the following dialogue from his book, *La France seule*:

> 'Are you a partisan of what the Marshal calls "collaboration"?'
> 'I don't have to be a partisan of it.'
> 'So you are against?'
> 'Not against it either.'
> 'Neutral?'
> 'Not neutral either.'
> 'You accept it then?'
> 'I have neither to accept it nor to oppose it'.

The moral was to have complete confidence in Pétain.[33]

For those papers out of sympathy with the regime, like the Catholic *La Croix* and the liberal conservative *Le Figaro*, or leftish regional papers, like the *Depêche de Toulouse* or *Le Progrès de Lyon*, editorial compromises were unavoidable. Dissent could only be expressed in oblique ways. *Le Figaro* published the Jewish Statute without commentary, which was as close as one could come to disapproval; *Le Croix* indicated when editorials had been imposed upon it by signing them 'NC' ('Note Communiqué'). But newspapers always ran the risk of suspension. This happened to *Le Figaro*, between 6 January and 14 January 1942, for being too favourable to the Red Army, and to *Le Progrès de Lyon* in June 1942 because it refused to accompany a report of the British bombing raid on Boulogne-Billancourt with headlines proclaiming 'The English and the Communists agree to assassinate France'.

After the Germans occupied the South in November 1942 some papers suspended publication: *Le Figaro* and *Le Progrès de Lyon* on 12 November, and *Le*

[30] Limagne, *Éphémerides*, 224.
[31] C. Lévy, 'L'Organisation de la propagande', *RHDGM* 64 (Oct. 1966), 7–28: 20.
[32] Verdès-Leroux, *Refus et violences*, 300–11.
[33] C. Maurras, *La Seule France: Chronique des jours d'épreuve* (Lyons, 1941), 286–7.

Temps on 29 November (too late to prevent its prohibition at the Liberation).[34] But Pierre Limagne of *La Croix* justified the continued appearance of his paper on the grounds that 'the press has had to stoop so low under Pétain that Hitler can hardly be worse'; in these circumstances it was better to 'hold the fort'.[35] *Paris-Soir*, which tried to suspend publication on 11 November, was forced to continue printing, or see its staff deported to Germany. It fought back by giving headline billing to minor events and consigning pro-German news to the inside pages. Eventually it ceased publication in May 1943. The more flexible policy which Marion had favoured was implemented in January 1943 when the remaining papers signed an agreement with Vichy allowing them to present news as they wished providing they respected the general government line. This system of self-censorship did nothing to staunch the haemorrhaging readership.[36]

Newsreel propaganda in the two main zones was so different that it might have been describing two separate countries.[37] In the Occupied Zone, cinemas had to show German newsreels. At first these were very crude: the speaker denouncing Mers el Kébir had a German accent. So the Germans set up an agency producing French versions of their newsreels, under the name Actualités mondiales. In the Unoccupied Zone, Vichy forced the three existing newsreel companies into a single organization, France-Actualités. The German Actualités mondiales devoted much time to anti-British propaganda and news about the war. In the Vichy newsreels, however, the outside world was largely absent: the only other countries which seemed to exist were Spain and Switzerland. Seeing these newsreels today, one might not realize a European war was taking place. They depicted a peaceful and rural France, offering extensive coverage of Pétain's provincial visits, and reports on French traditions and French craftsmen; there was also a lot about the Empire. The newsreels of the two zones overlapped only in ignoring the presence of the Germans—apart from items in Actualités mondiales about German soldiers helping French women and children.

Vichy was not happy that its newsreels were seen by only half the country. After prolonged negotiations, a single company was set up in August 1942 with exclusive rights to edit and distribute all newsreels in France. The board of the company was composed of two Germans and three Frenchmen, with a 60 per cent French stake, but since its French president, Henri Clerc, was committed to collaboration, the newsreels conformed more to Germany's vision than Vichy's.

---

[34] For *Le Temps* under Vichy see A. Slama, 'Un quotidien républicain sous Vichy: "Le Temps" (juin 1940–novembre 1942)', *Revue française des sciences politiques* 22/4 (1972), 719–49.

[35] Limagne, *Éphémerides*, ii. 898.

[36] C. Lévy and D. Veillon, 'La Presse', in Peschanski and Gervereau (eds.), *La Propagande*, 164–71.

[37] P. Sorlin, 'The Struggle for Control of French Minds 1940–1944', in K. Short (ed.), *Film and Radio Propaganda in World War Two* (1983), 245–70: at 258–9; F. Garçon, 'Nazi Film Propaganda in Occupied France', in D. Welch (ed.), *Nazi Propaganda: The Power and the Limitations* (1983), 161–79. Newsreels form the basis of Claude Chabrol's film *L'Œil de Vichy* (1993) but he fails to distinguish between Vichy and German propaganda.

In radio propaganda, no such amalgamation occurred. The Germans set up their own radio station in Paris, entirely staffed and run by the French. Its transmitters covered most of the country. Vichy had no control over the content, although the Germans did allow two daily broadcasts of Vichy news bulletins. Vichy National Radio, with transmitters in some southern cities, had a much less extensive reach. The style of the two radios could not have been more different. Radio Paris, run by a younger team, had the pick of French singers and musicians, and developed innovative styles of broadcasting. One of its innovations was the Compass card, inviting listeners to write in with their views which were then read out over the air. This programme proved so popular that it was broadcast twice weekly at peak time. In comparison, Vichy radio was stuffy and unimaginative, and listeners found it boring.[38]

The political tone of the radios was also different. Radio Paris contained subtle propaganda for the new Europe, virulent anti-Semitism, irreverent mockery of Vichy conservatism, and, after June 1941, anti-Bolshevism. On the day the Germans invaded Russia, Radio Paris applauded this 'liberating' conflict to rid Europe of 'the Bolshevik nightmare which has haunted it for twenty years'. Radio Vichy merely announced an event 'of great importance' whose outcome was 'unpredictable'. Vichy reported the course of the war on the eastern front in a detached way, as if describing an event of distant history. Apart from this characteristic evasion of reality, Vichy radio lacked a clear propaganda line. A plethora of Vichy organizations were allotted their own radio time—the Legion, with five minutes daily, the Youth Commissariat with a slot called Radio jeunesse, the Family Secretariat—and this led Darlan to complain in March 1942 that this cacophony was putting listeners off.[39]

Intermediaries

Despite these internal contradictions, Vichy did create a distinctive political style. When Jean Guéhenno arrived from Paris for his first visit to the Unoccupied Zone in June 1942, he encountered 'a strange country, a sort of principality where everyone seems to be in uniform: from children of six regimented into "Youth Groups" up to war veterans wearing *francisques* or the insignia of the Legion. Where is France in all this?'[40] Vichy's obsession with choreographed public festivals, ritual, and pageantry was about trying to develop a new political culture. History teaching in schools was reformed in order to play down the significance of the Revolution.[41] Although 14 July remained an official public holiday, its significance was reinterpreted. It was no longer a day of cele-

[38] Sorlin, 'The Struggle for Control', 254–5; H. Eck and J.-L. Crémieux-Brilhac, *La Guerre des ondes: Histoire des radios de langue française pendant la Deuxième Guerre mondiale* (1985), 39–49.

[39] Eck and Crémieux-Brilhac, *La Guerre des ondes*, 50–7.

[40] *Journal des années noires*, 313.

[41] M. Cointet-Labrousse, 'Le Gouvernement de Vichy et les réformes de l'enseignement de l'histoire (1940–1944)', *RHMC*, hors-séries (1984), 41–8.

bration, commemorating the Fall of the Bastille, but, as Pétain said in 1941, a day of 'meditation' on France's misfortunes—the war dead, the prisoners in Germany, the ruined cities—and on her hopes for recovery. There was to be no 'street agitation'. Even this was too much for Maurras or the fascists of *Je suis partout* who wanted 14 July erased from the official calendar.

Having downplayed 14 July, Vichy developed its own calendar of commemoration. The three most important events took place in May. Since this was also traditionally the season of rural rituals of rebirth and fertility, it fitted well with Vichy's folkloric and regionalist rhetoric. The first of May, which before 1940 had been a working-class holiday, now became the festival of work—no longer, in Pétain's words, a 'symbol of division and hatred' but one of 'union and friendship'. The festival of Joan of Arc, on the first Sunday after 8 May, had been celebrated since Joan's canonization in 1920, but its importance was upgraded by Vichy: it was a chance to recall that France's hereditary enemy had not changed over six hundred years. Finally, Mother's Day, the last Sunday in May, became the occasion of a massive propaganda campaign. These fêtes celebrated the guiding principles of the regime: Work, Family, *Patrie*.[42]

A central role in Vichy's public ceremonial was played by the Legion. The legionnaires, attired in their berets, are one of the most familiar sights in photographs of the period. The anniversary celebrations of the Legion's foundation on 28–31 August, when the legionnaires solemnly renewed their oath, was another key date in Vichy's calendar. The legionnaires were supposed to sell the message of the National Revolution, but their missionary zeal was counterproductive. Local Legion leaders caused irritation by acting as petty vigilantes: rebuking prefects because portraits of the Marshal were not prominently displayed or denouncing schoolteachers considered to be lukewarm about the National Revolution. Some prefects submitted lists of proposed local appointments to the Legion in order to avoid problems later.[43] The Legion's officiousness was particularly oppressive in small communities. In Jean Guéhenno's village, the Legion president was the pharmacist 'avenging over the last two years the fact that for the rest of his life he has exercised no influence at all'. The vice-president was the local hairdresser who contrived to be busy whenever Guéhenno presented himself for a haircut: 'At last I understood. He wants to cut off my head, but not to cut my hair. He is counting on all the credit he will derive from this when he retails it to the new notabilities of the region.'[44]

---

[42] A. Ben Amos, 'La Commémoration sous le régime de Vichy: Les Limites de la maîtrise du passé', in C. Charle et al. (eds.), *La France démocratique: Mélanges offertes à Maurice Agulhon* (1998), 397–408. See also M. Agulhon, 'Combat d'images: La République au temps de Vichy', *Ethnologie française*, 24/2 (1994), 209–15.

[43] R. Zaretsky, *Nîmes at War: Religion, Politics and Public Opinion in the Gard, 1938–1944* (University Park, Pa., 1995), 127–31; J.-L. Panicacci, *Les Alpes-Maritimes pendant la Seconde Guerre mondiale* (Nice, 1984), 18; R. Austin, 'Political Surveillance and Ideological Control in Vichy France', in R. Kedward and R. Austin (eds.), *Vichy France and the Resistance: Culture and Ideology* (1985), 13–35: 22–3; Guillon, 'La Resistance dans le Var', 32–3.

[44] *Journal des années noires*, 326–8.

Whatever its shortcomings, the Legion was effective enough to sabotage other organizations created to propagate the gospel of the National Revolution. The Comité du rassemblement national was stillborn because the Legion would not co-operate with it.[45] The Amicale de France had more success, at least on paper. Its 'Amis du Maréchal' claimed to have bases in forty-five cities of the Free Zone, and 600,000 subscribers to its *Bulletin*. Unlike the Legion, it was allowed in the Occupied Zone. In the two Norman departments of the Eure and Seine-Inférieure, there were allegedly between 11,000 and 15,000 members at the end of 1942. But these claims seem optimistic, and the paucity of references to the Amicale in local studies suggests that it had a negligible impact.[46] The most sustained attempt to create an effective propaganda organization was Marion's network of regional propaganda delegates. In the department of the Bouches du Rhône alone (excluding Marseilles), ninety people worked for Marion's propaganda services. In the summer of 1941, they circulated 60,000 tracts, and 7,000 posters reproducing Pétain's speech of 12 August; between June 1941 and February 1942, they organized 350 speeches or lectures.[47] But this intense activity encountered local hostility from the Legion, and most of it fell on deaf ears.[48]

Aware that its message was not getting through, in the autumn of 1941 the regime created the *commissaires du pouvoir*. These were a corps of officials, to be recruited outside the administration, who would travel the country inspecting abuses of state power, and offering redress against them. In the end, however, the *commissaires* all came from the administration, except for one trade unionist, whose appointment shocked the Legion because he had been a Freemason. The *commissaires* turned out to be so ineffectual that it was not even worth abolishing them.[49] These endless propaganda initiatives meant that even in many towns the regime could be represented by numerous different spokesmen: the local Legion leader, a propaganda delegate, a delegate of the Youth Secretariat, and so on.[50] This did not make for coherence.

One organization which the regime might have used to harness support was La Rocque's PSF which was the only party to survive the disintegration of 1940 with its structure more or less intact. In August 1940, La Rocque had changed the name of the party to the Progrès social français to signify that it was now confining itself to charitable and social activities. Given that Vichy's rhetoric was similar to that of the PSF in the 1930s—the motto 'Work, Family, *Patrie*' had

[45] Amaury, *De l'information*, 176–80.

[46] e.g. Luirard, *La Région stéphanoise*, 336–7; J. Papp, *La Collaboration dans l'Eure 1940–1944* (1993), 107–29.

[47] R. Mencherini, 'La Propagande dans les Bouches-du-Rhône', in *VEF*, 203–8; see also Papp, *La Collaboration dans l'Eure*, 91–106.

[48] Martin du Gard, *Chronique de Vichy*, 146, on the monthly meeting of the propaganda delegates at Vichy.

[49] Baruch, *Servir l'État*, 315–21.

[50] Austin, 'Education and Youth Policies', 267.

originally been La Rocque's—it would have been natural to try and make use of La Rocque's cadres. La Rocque tried on various occasions to offer his services, but he was not even able to secure an interview with Pétain who did not want to share his glory with anyone else. There was much suspicion of La Rocque who had always clung to his independence. La Rocque viewed the Legion as partly directed against him, but he did not stop PSF members joining it. Six departmental heads of the Legion were from the PSF.

La Rocque finally got an interview with Pétain in September 1941 at the time when Pucheu was nursing the idea of building a single party. He wanted to per-suade La Rocque to merge the PSF with the Legion. Although La Rocque would not agree to this, he did agree to co-operate with the Legion, probably as a way of fending off the dissolution of the PSF. He was also given an advisory position in Pétain's *cabinet*. But La Rocque's tactical rapprochement with Vichy soon ended since it became clear that he had no intention of allowing the PSF to be absorbed by the regime.[51]

In addition to the Legion, Vichy also relied upon a number of parapolitical organizations to sell its message. The most important of these was the Secours national, a charitable organization founded in 1914 to aid victims of the war, and headed throughout the Occupation by Robert Garric. Partially funded by the State, the Secours national also raised money by selling portraits of Pétain. It called itself the Entre-Aide d'Hiver du Maréchal (The Marshal's Winter Relief). This was Vichy's attempt to exploit the mood of charity and solidarity which had been aroused by the plight of the refugees in 1940. The same function was performed by the ubiquitous Prisoner of War Aid Committees which existed in every *département*.

This propaganda was particularly directed at children who were urged to 'adopt' a prisoner of war. They were also exhorted to alleviate the food crisis by foraging for acorns and chestnuts; or to join in rooting out the Colorado beetles (*doryphores*) which had recently arrived from America. (This turned against its instigators when the term *doryphore* became one of the slang terms for German.) In the autumn of 1940 teachers were told to organize their pupils to collect wild fruit. This was done, but the food was allowed to rot instead of being distributed. In the next year, enthusiasm for the campaign had diminished. As so often, Vichy squandered its initial capital of goodwill—in this case through bureaucratic inefficiency.[52]

Repression and Administration

Propaganda was accompanied by repression. Vichy France was a highly policed society: one of its legacies to contemporary France was the introduction of identity cards. On average about 350,000 letters were opened each week. In

[51] Cointet, *La Légion*, 196–9; J. Nobécourt, *Le Colonel de la Rocque (1885–1946)* (1996), 685–760.
[52] Baruch, *Servir l'État*, 216–17.

December 1943 alone about 2.5 million letters, 1.8 million telegrams, and 21,000 telephone conversations were intercepted.[53] This is why we are so well informed about public opinion under the Occupation.

Before Pétain's two-day visit to Marseilles in December 1940, the police carried out 20,000 preventive arrests of possible troublemakers, who were parked in prisons or in boats, barracks, and cinemas which had been commissioned for the purpose. Before Pétain arrived in Toulouse, in June 1942, prostitutes were rounded up and sent to the camp of Récébedou. This is the side of Pétain's visits not revealed by the newsreels of cheering crowds.[54] In January 1943, Marseilles was the site of another major police operation when the Germans insisted on clearing—and then destroying—the Old Port. Some 9,000 police were brought in to supplement the local forces, and in one week 400,000 identities were checked, and almost 6,000 individuals apprehended. This was the largest police operation in French history.[55]

Between April and July 1941, there were eleven major laws or decrees reorganizing the police. The result was to create a national police in France for the first time: in towns with a population above 10,000, the policing was taken out of municipal control and put under the control of the State (prefects).[56] Another law created the GMR (Groupes mobiles de réserve), a new force specializing in crowd control (the ancestor of today's CRS). The Brigades spéciales (BS) which had been reactivated in August 1941 to track Communists were supplemented in 1942 by the creation of a second division (BS2) which specialized in hunting down immigrant resisters.[57]

In addition to this reinforcement of the traditional police, a number of parallel police forces were established. The first of these were Colonel Georges Groussard's Groupes de protection designed as a sort of praetorian guard for Pétain. But at the end of 1940 they were disbanded on the instructions of the Germans because of their involvement in the plot against Laval. After the regime's repressive turn in the summer of 1941, Pucheu created three new police services in October: the Anti-Communist Police (SPAC), the Jewish Police (PQJ), and the Secret Societies (i.e. Freemasons) Police (SSS). These were staffed by professional anti-Semites or collaborationist activists who made up in zeal what they lacked in professionalism—another indication of the porousness of the frontier between Vichy and collaborationism.

When Bousquet took over the police in 1942 he tried to emasculate these new police forces. In July 1942 the PQJ was renamed the Investigation and Inspection Division (SEC) and had its powers reduced. The SPAC was harder to crack

[53] Laborie, L'Opinion publique, 35.
[54] Kitson, 'The Marseilles Police in their Context: From the Popular Front to the Liberation' (D.Phil. thesis, University of Sussex, 1995), 69; V. Fry, Surrender on Demand (New York, 1965), 130–48; Diamond, 'Women's Experience', 108.
[55] Kitson, 'Marseilles Police', 132–4.   [56] Baruch, Servir l'État, 377–88.
[57] Courtois et al., Le Sang de l'étranger, 193–6.

since its PPF director, Charles Detmar, was much appreciated by the German SD. But in August it was absorbed into the regular police and became the Service of Repression of Anti-National Activity (SRMAN). Bousquet's motive in bringing these organizations under State control was administrative tidiness, not any ideological or sentimental objection to their activities. He was irritated that the PQJ had carried out arrests of Jews which it was not authorized to do. His method of neutralizing these rivals was to show that the official police could do the job better. Thus Vichy's designated enemies—Jews or Communists—found themselves not only the victims of competitive zeal between the French and Germans, but of institutional rivalries within the Vichy regime.[58]

Bousquet's reassertion of the authority of the traditional administration after Pucheu's attempt to politicize the State apparatus shows how wrong it would be to characterize Vichy as moving closer to fascism in 1942. The regime certainly became more repressive in 1942, but fascism is about more than repression. The spirit of Pucheu and Marion's policies in 1941 was more fascist than that of Laval and Bousquet in 1942. Even under Pucheu, however, the backbone of Vichy remained the French State bureaucracy. Despite promises of a leaner administration, the number of state employees swelled from 650,000 in 1939 to 900,000 in 1944.[59]

At least until the end of 1942, the regime was served loyally by the police.[60] Vichy's anti-communism and hostility to foreigners struck a chord with the police. They had already been arresting Communists in the last stages of the Third Republic, and in this respect Vichy at first represented no major change. If the police were discontented under Vichy, it was for practical rather than political reasons. Even before the imposition of STO and the growth of resistance in 1943, workloads had significantly increased. Policing the black market was a full-time job in itself. Wading through sacks of letters of denunciation was as dispiriting as it was time-consuming. These letters had to be followed up, but the accusations mostly turned out to be groundless. The police liked this job all the less because the letters often denounced them as Freemasons or Communists.

To cope with their new burdens, the police benefited from no increase in resources. A police chief in Clermont complained that his men lacked whistles, truncheons, handcuffs, new uniforms, and even proper shoes. The police were also short-staffed. Many policemen were in prisoner of war camps, and it was difficult to attract replacements. A recruitment campaign with the slogan 'Police nationale, Révolution nationale' was such a failure that in November 1941 Darlan ordered that the words 'National Revolution' be erased from the posters. The

[58] J.-M. Berlière, *Le Monde des polices en France xixe–xxe siècles* (Brussels, 1996) 163–202; Froment, *René Bousquet*, 190–7.

[59] Baruch, *Le Régime de Vichy* (1996), 71.

[60] For this and the following paragraph, see Kitson, 'Marseilles Police'; J. Sweets, 'La Police et la population dans la France de Vichy: Une étude de cas conforme et fidèle', *GMCC* 155 (1989), 63–73.

idea that the police was being offered a more political role than under the Republic clearly discouraged potential recruits.

Nor did the police appreciate the creation of the new supplementary police forces. They resented the GMR because it was better paid, and they considered the anti-Jewish police to be a nuisance. Because these anti-Jewish police were only authorized to gather information on infractions of the law and recommend action to the police, they were constantly sending them on what turned out to be wild goose chases. In 1942, the police started to become demoralized, and became nostalgic for the Republic when working conditions had been better. At a demonstration organized by the Resistance in Marseilles on 14 July 1942, police tolerance of the demonstrators was flagrant enough to arouse the fury of collaborationists, and win praise on the BBC. This was a warning to the regime that the police might not be counted on indefinitely. Nonetheless before 1943 the degree of police disaffection must not be exaggerated.

Vichy could also count on the loyalty of judges and magistrates. This could not necessarily have been taken for granted given how little concern was shown for legal niceties, especially once Pucheu became Interior Minister: in August 1942, one German observer noted approvingly that, in the pursuit of Communists, Vichy seemed ready to 'abandon the sacrosanct conceptions of traditional French law'.[61] The most striking example of this was the Special Sections set up on 23 August to act expeditiously against 'Communists and anarchists'. This law was backdated to 14 August so that it could be applied retroactively. Two weeks later a special court—the State Tribunal—was set up to judge acts endangering 'the unity and security' of the State: it could order the immediate application of the death penalty with no possibility of appeal. Barthélemy, the Justice Minister, who had reservations about these measures, worried that it would be impossible to find judges to serve in these courts. His concern was unwarranted.

To ensure obedience Vichy did not even need to carry out a significant purge of judicial personnel.[62] No existing careers were broken, but accelerated promotion was available for those known, in Barthélemy's words, for their 'firmness of character and devotion to the State'. No judges or magistrates protested publicly about the new duties they were required to perform. Only one, Paul Didier, refused to swear the oath to Pétain, and he was immediately sacked; another one who tried to restrict the oath to the person of the Marshal alone was suspended.[63] No sanctions, however, were taken against the judge who refused to preside over

---

[61] H. Villéré, L'Affaire de la section spéciale (1973), 146.

[62] For this and the next paragraph, see A. Bancaud, 'La Haute Magistrature sous Vichy', VSRH 49 (1996), 45–62; id., 'La Magistrature et la répression politique de Vichy ou l'histoire d'un demi-échec', Droit et société, 34 (1996), 557–74; id., 'Les Magistrats face à la lutte armée', in Marcot (ed.), Lutte armée et maquis, 183–92; Y. Lecouturier, 'Section spéciale', VSRH 28 (1990), 107–13.

[63] Baruch, Servir l'État, 312–13.

the Paris Special Section in August 1941, and he subsequently received the promotion he was due. It was therefore possible to distance oneself from the regime,
but few judges did so, at least before 1943. The habit of obedience was deeply
ingrained, and most judges shared the prevailing anti-Communist prejudices.
Exceptional measures against the Communists had after all started under the
Third Republic. Judges were also susceptible to the argument that they were
preserving French justice from German interference.

It is hard to generalize much beyond this point. The severity of the Special
Sections varied considerably. The Special Section of Douai considered 550 cases,
and pronounced five death sentences; that of Bourges considered twenty-eight
cases and pronounced no death penalties. In total thirty-three death penalties
were pronounced, and one carried out; 129 people were condemned to forced
labour for life, and 1,130 for fixed periods. It would be wrong, however, to think
that the activity of these courts mostly concerned the repression of communism.
Of the eighty-two cases judged by the Special Section of Caen, only seven related
to offences committed by Communists; three-quarters concerned the theft of
animals or the theft of the contents of parcels being sent to prisoners of war.

The loyalty displayed by the police and the judiciary was representative of the
administration as a whole. The bureaucracy worked smoothly and toed the line.
For the first time since the Second Empire, high-ranking public servants had to
swear an oath of loyalty to the head of State. The most important ceremony
occurred on 19 February 1942 when all prefects gathered at Vichy to swear the
oath. The regime discouraged zealous prefects from getting all their subordinates
to swear as well: it was feared that this would devalue the oath or that the number
of refusals would swell embarrassingly.[64]

It is difficult for administrators in any system to break with habits of
obedience. As Peyrouton, an administrator turned minister, said at his post-war
trial: 'I did not pose questions. I repeat: I am not Republican, I am not anti-
Republican, I am an agent, a functionary. If I had to pose such questions to
myself in thirty-five years of service, I would have had to pose them thirty-five
times.'[65] Top civil servants were attracted by the regime's supposed commitment
to administrative efficiency. Many Vichy reforms, including the creation of a
national police force, were measures that politicians had been trying to achieve
for years.[66] Some branches of the administration were more exposed to morally
invidious situations than others. It was easier for a young official in the Finance
Ministry, like Maurice Couve de Murville, to keep his hands clean, than for a
young official in the prefectoral administration, like Maurice Papon. But officials did not only have the choice between obedience or dismissal. The top civil
servants at the Ministry of Education found it easy to sabotage most of Bonnard's
ideas—especially since Bonnard was not interested in the details of administra-

---

[64] Ibid. 309–14.   [65] Ibid. 353.   [66] Berlière, *Le Mondes des polices*, 164–5.

tion and would sometimes deal with documents by waving a pendulum over them. The surest way of getting him to approve a policy was to say that it was modelled on Germany.[67]

Bonnard was not hard to outwit. In other cases, officials went into a kind of internal exile. This was the tactic adopted by François Bloch-Lainé, a Finance Ministry official whom Bichelonne asked to prepare a statistical inventory of French industry. Excited by this chance to remedy France's glaring deficiencies in statistical information, Bloch-Lainé enquired how these statistics would be kept from the Germans. On being told that the information was to be provided to both the French and the Germans, he had himself posted to a less interesting, but less exposed, assignment.[68] Very occasionally officials refused point blank to carry out orders. In January 1943, Joseph Rivalland, regional prefect in Marseilles, refused to provide the Germans with a list of hostages. Instead he offered only his own name. He was immediately sacked, and moved to the Cour des Comptes.[69]

The Prefects: 'Propagandists of Truth'

Rivalland's case is celebrated because of its rarity. In general, French administrators executed their orders with efficiency. Of no group was this truer than the prefects, who had personified State authority in the *départements* since their creation by Napoleon. The prefects were infinitely more important to Vichy than any of its own innovations. In this respect, the regime resembled the Second Empire more than Nazi Germany. A circular of October 1940 informed the prefects that they were to be 'the propagandists of truth, of hope and of liberating action, the defenders of a France bruised by twenty years of errors and follies'.

In the summer and autumn of 1940, thirty-five prefects were sacked (among them Jean Moulin). Prefects who remained in office were moved to new *départements* in case they had become too dependent on local influences: by the end of August 1940, only twenty-seven prefects (out of eighty-seven) remained in the *département* to which they had been appointed under the Republic; by July 1941, only five. There was a half-hearted attempt to bring new blood into the corps: 18 per cent of new prefects were recruited from outside the prefectoral corps, including seven from the armed forces. Pucheu also wanted prefects to undergo a political re-education to 'rid them of everything in their intellectual formation which could impede their support of the movement of national renovation'.[70]

The prefects' powers were extended and they were given a new uniform with

---

[67] Baruch, *Servir l'État*, 420.   [68] Ibid. 373.
[69] Ibid. 374; Kitson, 'Marseilles Police', 132–3.
[70] Baruch, *Servir l'État*, 233–5. On the prefects in general, see S. Mazey and V. Wright, 'Les Prefets', in *VEF*, 267–86.

gold braid (another imperial touch) to enhance their prestige. Nonetheless their role under Vichy was unenviable. Besides warding off interference from the Legion or from the propaganda delegates, they were also undermined by the creation of regional prefects in April 1941. The regional prefects were supposed to remedy supply problems by breaking down departmental autonomy. But there were unresolved issues of jurisdiction between them and the ordinary prefects. The prefects found themselves increasingly tied up in red tape: the minutiae of daily administration left little time to be 'propagandists of truth'. It was all the harder to work effectively because they were continuously being moved around. Although most transfers and sackings occurred in 1940, there were six more occasions when these took place on a large scale. An average *département* had three or four prefects in just four years.

Prefects in the Occupied Zone also found their power whittled away by the German occupiers. Each prefect faced in microcosm the problem of the regime as a whole: whether to co-operate with the Germans in order to preserve French sovereignty or whether to be obstructive at the risk of provoking German intervention.[71] When it came to anti-communism, however, many prefects shared a sense of purpose with the Germans. The first arrests of Communists in the autumn of 1940 did not occur under German pressure. Sometimes indeed the French authorities felt they did not enjoy full German support because of the Nazi–Soviet Pact. Up to June 1941, anti-Communist repression was toughest in the South, where Vichy was most in control, and least severe in the *Zone rattachée*, where Vichy had least influence: the German authorities in the Nord refused to allow the prefect to open an internment camp for Communists.[72] Once anti-communism became a German priority as well, French and German police co-operated on anti-Communist repression at local level even before the formalization of arrangements between Bousquet and Oberg in August 1942. The prefect of the Nord got his internment camp in September 1941. Camps were set up in the Loiret in April 1941, in the Saône-et-Loire in March 1942.[73]

The *relève* and STO pushed the French authorities into even closer administrative collaboration at local level. In a perfect illustration of the 'River Kwai' syndrome, the prefect of Loiret reported in the autumn of 1942 that 'we have tried to protect the workers against arbitrariness and show the local occupation authorities a demonstration of the efficiency of the French administration'. The local Feldkommandant reported on his 'exemplary' attitude. The Germans played on the French obsession with sovereignty by holding out rewards for good

[71] Y. Durand, 'L'Administration de Vichy en zone occupée: Loiret et région d'Orléans', *Revue du Nord*, 2, hors-séries (1987/8), 103–17: 104.

[72] Peschanski, 'Exclusion, persécution et répression', 213–14; J.-P. Azéma et al., 'Certitudes et hésitations des préfets de Vichy', in id., *Le Parti communiste français des années sombres*, 150–72: 164–5.

[73] Durand, 'L'Administration', 105; J. Gillot-Voisin, 'La Répression allemande dans le département de Saône-et-Loire' (unpublished thesis, University of Bourgogne, 1992), 146–7.

behaviour. In May 1943, Sauckel's representative reassured this prefect that the Germans would leave the implementation of STO to the French, and offered a bait to encourage them to co-operate: 'The success of the operation could [cause] . . . a marked attenuation of the interference of the German military administration in French internal matters . . . The result of this operation will represent a touchstone of the capacity of the French administration to carry out its tasks independently.'[74]

For at least two years, the Germans had few complaints about the prefects. It was even reported at the end of 1942 that the 'spirit of collaboration' of the top French officials was improving. During his lecture tour of the South in 1942, Professor Grimm was impressed by the courtesy and friendliness of the prefects who received him.[75]

Only a tiny number of prefects, driven by ideological hostility to Communists, Jews, and Masons, could be said to have collaborated enthusiastically (Chiappe in the Gard). More of them were enthusiastic about the National Revolution (Morane in the Loiret, Carles in the Nord), but unsympathetic to the Germans. The majority, however, merely carried out their duties in a spirit of professionalism rather than political zeal. What made the prefects' task difficult was that the destruction of local democracy had left them operating in a vacuum. In the Republic, local government operated through a delicate balance of power between the prefect, representing the State, and the locally elected representatives (mayors, conseillers généraux) who mediated between them and the population. The destruction of the conseils généraux was judged by Dumoulin de Labarthète to be Vichy's biggest mistake because it created a void which the replacement commissions administratives were inadequate to fill.[76]

The prefects found themselves bearing the brunt of the regime's unpopularity. Vichy considered creating a new administrative rank of 'cantonal agents' to explain policy and build contacts with the local population. But Laval wound up this experiment after it had been tried in a few localities.[77] Laval's replacement of the commissions administratives with conseils départementaux in August 1942 was a recognition that it had been misguided to abolish those bodies which genuinely represented local opinion. But this step towards the Republic was too half-hearted—there were still no elections—and too belated to win back support for Vichy.

To compensate for the destruction of local democracy prefects had to try and cultivate local figures of influence, even those with strong Republican affiliations. Certainly such people were hardly in favour with the new regime. Of 311 former conseillers généraux who were selected to sit on the new commissions administratives, only 10 per cent were from the left, mainly the moderate left. Of 355 Socialist conseillers généraux before the Armistice—11 per cent of the total—only

[74] Durand, 'L'Administration', 114–16.   [75] Thalmann, La Mise au pas, 60–1.
[76] Du Moulin, Le Temps des illusions, 261–2.   [77] Baruch, Servir l'État, 358–9.

two were retained in the *commissions administratives*.[78] But the way that the new law on municipalities was applied suggests that the extent of the local purge should not be exaggerated. In towns with a population over 10,000, over one-third of mayors remained in place. Forty-seven Socialist mayors of towns with a population of over 2,000 were sacked, and twenty-three retained.[79] In the mining areas of the Nord, the sub-prefect wanted to avoid 'too great a gap between the appointed mayor and the population by the designation of personalities too markedly of the right'; in the left-wing Pas-de-Calais, 73 per cent of mayors were retained. In Lille, the Socialist mayor, Saint-Venant, was replaced by another Socialist, Paul Dehove; in Lens the Socialist Alfred Maes, a great local figure, was kept on despite his opposition to Marshal Putain (the French for 'tart'), as he was wont to call the Marshal.[80]

The Nord/Pas de Calais was perhaps unusual because Vichy's lack of influence in the area meant that the priority was less to implement the National Revolution than preserve some contact with the local population. But even in a *département* like the Loiret, the prefect avoided a sectarian approach, despite being personally committed to the principles of the regime. Of the twenty-six councils in the Loiret affected by the law on municipalities (those with a population above 2,000), twelve kept the same mayor, of whom half were Radical, and one was even a Freemason. This was recognition of the local importance of the Radical Party. As for the new appointees, they were chosen with an eye to local opinion. The new mayor of Orleans, Dr Simonin, a member of the moderate centre PDP, replaced a Radical. This represented a move from left to right, but within the boundaries of moderate Third Republic politics.[81] In the Saint-Étienne region, the prefect, Georges Potut, himself formerly a centre-right politician, kept contacts with local left-wing politicians.[82]

Vichy approved such contacts. In the first flush of enthusiasm of 1940, Vichy had encouraged a purge of political undesirables, exhorting prefects not to be satisfied with 'demonstrations of loyalty' and to undertake 'the minutest enquiries' about the beliefs of local figures in influential positions.[83] By January 1941, however, this zeal had passed. Prefects were told that it was not their job to try and establish a 'new moral order' or exact 'revenge for the events of 1936'. The aim was now stabilization.[84] In the summer of 1940, *instituteurs* had been viewed with suspicion by the regime; by the beginning of 1942 they were being

---

[78] J. Steel, W. Kidd, D. Weiss, 'Les Commissions administratives départementales', in *VEF*, 55–64.

[79] Sadoun, *Les Socialistes sous l'Occupation*, 65–70; M. Luirard, 'L'Administration de la Zone Sud', *Revue du Nord*, 2, hors-séries (1987/8), 119–36: 121.

[80] Y. Le Maner, 'Les Municipalités du Nord sous "Occupation"', *Revue du Nord* 2, hors-séries, 219–68: 241–5.

[81] Y. Durand, 'La Politique de Vichy mise en œuvre au niveau d'un département: Le Loiret', *VEF*, 37–45: 41.

[82] Luirard, *La Région stéphanoise*, 296–7.

[83] Baruch, *Servir l'État*, 124, 515.

[84] Luirard, *La Région stéphanoise*, 308–9.

courted for the local support they could mobilize.[85] The regime was now reluctant to antagonize opinion gratuitously since food shortages already caused enough problems. A bust of Pétain by the sculptor François Congé was supposed to replace busts of Marianne in town halls, but this was not strictly enforced: in the Paris Hôtel de Ville the two busts coexisted.[86] Similarly prefects ordered unsuitable street names—Jaurès, Barbusse, Guesde, Proudhon—to be replaced, but they did not insist too officiously, and frequently the old signs were not removed.[87]

The Church: 'Loyalty without Enthralment'

One institution on which prefects could count for support was the Church, which remained a pillar of the regime until the end.[88] Pétain himself had never been devout. He had married a divorcee in a civil ceremony in 1920, which caused Catholics some embarrassment, until the marriage was solemnized by the Church at a secret ceremony in 1941. But Pétain was happy to embrace the Church as a bastion of social order whose objectives dovetailed with the National Revolution. Church leaders initially confined themselves to guarded support for the new regime on the principle of respect for established authority. But in the autumn of 1940, when the government's political orientation became clearer, the Church succumbed totally to the cult of the providential leader. The tone was set by Cardinal Gerlier, Archbishop of Lyons, welcoming Pétain to the]city in November 1940 with the words: 'Pétain is France, and France, today, is Pétain.'

Prelates were present on most official occasions and bishops were frequent guests at Pétain's table. Cardinal Suhard of Paris was named a member of the Conseil national. Clerics were to be found in ten departmental committees of the Legion; and 200 others were in leadership positions at the level of commune and canton (forty-five of these in the very Catholic Lozère).[89] In July 1941 the Assembly of Cardinals and Archbishops (ACA) of the Free Zone (followed in the North in September) declared officially that 'we venerate the Head of State' and called for 'complete and sincere loyalty, without enthralment, to the established order'. In practice the qualification 'without enthralment' did not prevent delirious effusions of devotion to Pétain from individual prelates. Many went beyond the formula 'established order' and described the government as 'legitimate'.[90]

---

[85] Halls, *Youth of Vichy France*, 121–30.   [86] Dorléac, *L'Art de la défaite*, 114–18.
[87] Sweets, *Choices in Vichy France*, 80–1.
[88] On this subjet in general see J. Duquesne, *Les Catholiques français sous l'Occupation* (1996 edn.); E. Fouilloux, *Les Chrétiens français entre crise et libération 1937–1947* (1997); W. Halls, *Politics, Society and Christianity in Vichy France* (Oxford, 1995); X. de Montclos (ed.), *Églises et Chrétiens dans la Deuxième Guerre mondiale: La Région Rhône-Alpes* (Lyons, 1978).
[89] J.-P. Cointet, *Histoire de Vichy* (1996), 140.   [90] Duquesne, *Les Catholiques*, 112–16.

The reasons for the Church's enthusiasm are obvious. Vichy's themes of contrition, sacrifice, and suffering resonated with Catholics. 'Work, family, fatherland: these words are ours', declared Gerlier. Not since the 1870s had the Church seen a greater opportunity to advance its interests. Few clerics might have gone as far as the Bishop of Dax who declared that the 'cursed year for us was not 1940, that of our external defeat, but 1936, that of our internal defeat',[91] but most were ready to welcome Pétain as a saviour. Despite the condemnation of Action française in 1926, and the fact that 70 per cent of French bishops had been appointed since that date, it became clear how skin-deep the Church's acceptance of Republicanism had been in many cases. Mgr. Araquy, archdeacon of Cahors, declared in the cathedral on 14 July 1941 that 'many intelligent Frenchmen have never celebrated 14 July with much enthusiasm'.[92]

Some Church leaders showed more caution, and in general their adulation became less effusive after 1941. The more reserved prelates included Archbishops Gerlier of Lyons (despite his notorious remark about Pétain being France) and Saliège of Toulouse. Saliège's views were so notorious that de Gaulle addressed a personal message to him in May 1942. Among the more loyalist leaders was Cardinal Suhard of Paris who wrote to Pétain in June 1943: 'More than ever France has need of you . . . of a voice which gives leadership to follow.'[93] Despite these nuances, the hierarchy as a whole remained loyal until the end although tensions arose sporadically on specific issues. The Church was vigilant about defending the independence of its youth movements. There was conflict in the summer of 1942 when five leading prelates, including Gerlier and Saliège, publicly criticized the deportation of the Jews. But they had made their peace with Vichy by the start of 1943.

Support for Vichy did not mean that the Church lent its support to collaboration, apart from a few striking exceptions. The Bishop of Arras, Dutoit, publicly supported Montoire. The German war against the Soviet Union was enthusiastically supported by Cardinal Baudrillart, rector of the Catholic Institute of Paris, who was on the governing committee of Chateaubriant's Collaboration group. Probably senile (he died in 1942 aged 83), Baudrillart had become unhinged by anti-communism. He described the LVF as the 'crusaders of the twentieth century. May their arms be blessed! The tomb of Christ shall be delivered.' No collaborationist cleric was more colourful that Mgr. Mayol de Lupé—another collaborator inspired by the sight of blond youths in uniform—who had himself appointed chaplain to the LVF. His bravery in the field, at the age of 69, won him the Iron Cross. He would end Sunday Mass with the cry 'Heil Hitler!'[94]

These were extreme and unusual cases. On the other hand it could not be said that the Church offered an anti-German lead. Cardinal Suhard was obsequious to Abetz, who felt he could be counted on; he had himself

[91] F. Muel-Dreyfus, *Vichy et l'éternel féminin* (1996), 66–7.
[92] Laborie, *Résistants, Vichyssois*, 205.   [93] Burrin, *La France à l'heure*, 229.
[94] Halls, *Politics, Society and Christianity*, 349–50.

represented at a reception at the German Institute in honour of Goering;[95] and he gave absolution at a Mass in August 1942 for LVF volunteers who had fallen in battle. There was certainly no such treatment for the Communist hostages shot by the Germans. In general the Church's reluctance to break with Vichy prevented it from distancing itself firmly from the occupier.

The Church, of course, consisted of more than its bishops, but before 1943 most priests do not seem to have dissented from the official line. The Catholic Action Organization (ACJF) took the toughest stance on protecting the independence of the youth movements. The Catholic trade unionists (CFTC) were unhappy about the Labour Charter whose abolition of trade-union pluralism included them, and they were divided about whether they should participate in the institutions set up by the Charter.[96] But the greatest source of Catholic dissent towards Vichy came from intellectuals in the religious orders like the Dominican Father Jean Maydieu and the Jesuits Gaston Fessard, Father Pierre Chaillet, and Stanislas Fumet: it was from these circles that Catholic resistance was to develop.

To what extent did the Church's support for the regime reflect the opinion of ordinary Catholics? The Occupation came when the Church was becoming deeply concerned by the dechristianization of French society, but in fact in the short term its influence was increasing. Everywhere the number of children in Catholic primary and secondary education increased, in some *départements* by more than 10 per cent.[97] This may have had practical as much as religious causes, but there are other signs during the Occupation of an increase in popular religiosity. Many Catholics retreated from the difficulties of daily existence into a more intense spiritual life. A recent study of religious practice in Occupied Paris reveals a world of active Catholic citizenship in which the calendar of feast days, pilgrimages, holy days of obligation, and parish works looms more largely than the more well-known chronology of national events. The author argues that ordinary Catholics 'by remaining loyal to the structures of parish life, succeeded in protecting themselves and their families . . . from the violent ideological onslaught of Nazi and collaborationist propaganda'.[98] But, even if this is true, it begs the question how Catholics responded to Vichy: did the regime's quasi-religious rhetoric of repentance, contrition, and resurrection win it the political support of ordinary Catholics?

One particularly intense moment of religious fervour, which the regime tried to harness to political ends, was the pilgrimage organized by the Catholic Rover Scouts to the basilica of Le Puy-en-Velay, famous for its Black Virgin. Thousands of Catholic members of the Catholic Action youth groups descended on Le Puy from all over France on 15 August 1942, Assumption Day. Twenty-five statues of the Virgin from different French churches were ceremoniously trans-

[95] Burrin, *La France à l'heure*, 187.   [96] Halls, *Politics, Society and Christianity*, 247–55.
[97] Id., *Youth of Vichy France*, 95–6.
[98] V. Drapac, *War and Religion: Catholics in the Churches of Occupied Paris* (Washington, 1998), 113.

ported to Puy. Among them was the much-venerated Virgin from Boulogne cathedral which was smuggled across the demarcation line in a vegetable truck. Cardinal Gerlier and the Papal Nuncio presided over the Puy ceremonies in the presence of nine bishops. Pétain sent a message, and the occasion was attended by representatives of the Legion, the local prefect, and the head of Vichy's Youth Secretariat, Georges Lamirand. This was the apotheosis of the relationship between Vichy and the Catholic Church.[99]

In the wake of the Puy celebrations came the movement known as the Grand Retour (The Great Return), an upsurge of Catholic fervour whose significance is harder to fathom. After the Puy pilgrimage, the statue of Notre-Dame de Boulogne was taken to Lourdes where it arrived in September, having attracted huge crowds on its journey. This success led to the idea of allowing more people to see the statue before its return to Boulogne. Three replicas of the statue were constructed, and the four statues then embarked on a progress across the country, each taking a different route. The return of the statues to Boulogne was also to be a return of the people of France to God.

Originally the four statues were intended to reach Boulogne by the end of 1944, but the Liberation slowed their progress. The Grand Retour was not over until August 1948. The statues passed through some 16,000 parishes, exciting scenes of enthusiasm which amazed many priests who had often been sceptical about the project. The largest gathering occurred at the Colombes Stadium in Paris in October 1945 where some 100,000 people went to see the statue. This was one of the climaxes of popular Catholicism in twentieth-century France. It led the Bishop of Arras—before the Liberation—to see another sign of the miraculous powers of Pétain. After the Liberation, some Communist municipalities tried to block the progress of the Grand Retour through their localities. But the phenomenon, which straddled the period from the Occupation to the Liberation, defies simple political categorization. The prayers which people deposited by the statues reflected the preoccupations of the moment. At first, they prayed for prisoner of war relatives to return safely; later they prayed that their villages be spared from destruction at the Liberation. In one locality, 122 Resistance fighters called upon the Virgin to protect their region. The Grand Retour was too vast to be contained by the mobilization of religion for political ends which had occurred at Puy in 1942. The Catholic Church supported Vichy until the end; the same was not true of most Catholics.[100]

---

[99] Faure, *Le Projet culturel*, 187–90; C. Guérin, *L'Utopie Scouts de France: Histoire d'une identité collective catholique et sociale 1920–1995* (1997), 266–70.

[100] There is no full study of the Grand Retour, but see S. Laury, 'Le Culte marial dans le Pas-de-Calais (1938–1948)', *RHDGM* 128 (1982), 25–47; L. Pérouas, 'Le Grand Retour de Notre-Dame de Boulogne à travers la France (1943–1948), essai de reconstitution', *Annales de Bretagne et des Pays de l'Ouest*, 90/2 (1983), 171–83; L. Pérouas, 'Le Grand Retour de Notre-Dame de Boulogne à travers la France (1943–1948), essai d'interprétation', *Archives des sciences sociales des religions*, 56/1 (1983), 37–57.

12

Public Opinion, Vichy, and the Germans

In the first weeks after the defeat, people responded to the Germans with relief, surprise, and curiosity: relief that the fighting was over; surprise at the restrained behaviour of the Germans; curiosity to see these godlike creatures who had triumphed so decisively. On the heels of the German troops soup kitchens arrived to provide relief to the population. Posters underscored the message: 'Abandoned populations—put your trust in the German soldier.' The word of the moment to describe the conduct of the Germans was 'correct'.[1] In the first weeks in Paris, they carried cameras as often as guns.[2] They all seemed young, bronzed, and handsome. One observer wondered if they were a 'beauty chorus reserved for triumphal entries'.[3]

The terror that the Germans had aroused in anticipation rendered the first encounters strangely reassuring. Women refugees caught up in the Exodus, who had smeared themselves with mustard to burn German soldiers who might rape them, were pleasantly surprised to meet disciplined German soldiers more helpful to them than the haggard French soldiers they had come across as they fled south. Viewed at close quarters the Germans turned out to be human. One witness remembered her amusement, as a little girl, at seeing these odd creatures clumsily trying to eat seafood for the first time. Such incidents made the Germans seem almost vulnerable.[4] Léon Werth remarked in his memoir of the Exodus: 'It was the time when they were "correct" which preceded the time when they gave us lessons in manners.'[5] This period of correctness was only a moment in the history of the Occupation, but it left traces even after the 'lessons in manners' had begun.

It was part of a conscious German strategy to erase the memory of alleged German atrocities in 1914 which lived on in folk memory. Simone de Beauvoir

---

[1] Burrin, *La France à l'heure*, 24–38.
[2] P. Audiat, *Paris pendant la guerre, juin 1940–août 1944* (1946), 27.
[3] N. Jucker, *Curfew in Paris* (1960), 98.
[4] Dombrowski, 'Beyond the Battlefield', 204, 247–9.   [5] *33 Jours: Récit* (1992), 9.

in 1940 encountered people in the west with stories of children who had had their hands cut off. In 1940 the Germans seized any Allied military documents relating to atrocities in 1914, and destroyed any monuments which commemorated them.[6]

From the beginning, however, German 'correctness' was ambiguous. As Werth wrote: 'We are "kept". The German soldiers distribute tins of bully beef and sardines . . . chocolate and sweets. But it is all made in France. It all comes from Rouen or Orléans, it has all been looted.'[7] The German Ernst Jünger's diary of the invasion reads at times like a gastronomic tour washed down by good Champagne and Burgundy, but these delicacies did not come from nowhere. At Sedan in May 1940 Jünger watched German soldiers lowering bottles of Burgundy down from the upper windows of houses: 'I snatched one in mid-air like a fish snapping at bait: a Châteauneuf-du-Pape 1937' (revealingly, this passage was cut from the diary when it was published in 1942 and only appeared in print for the first time after the war).[8] But since most of the French population of the north-east had fled before the Germans arrived, they were not present to witness scenes of looting. Even Werth noted that the Germans in his area were only pillaging abandoned property,[9] and whatever the superficiality of German correctness, the invaders' behaviour in France was very different from what it had been in Poland or was later to be in the Soviet Union. In comparative terms, at least, correctness was not entirely a myth. In the north-east, however, this cut no ice, not only because of the memories of 1914–18, but also because of atrocities carried out by the Germans during the 1940 invasion: 98 civilians had been massacred at Aubigny-en-Artois (22 May), 124 at Oignies and Courrières (28 May).[10]

Elsewhere, in the summer of 1940, most people were too traumatized to think beyond the problem of getting home, tracing relatives who had disappeared in the Exodus, worrying about sons or husbands who had fallen into German hands. Society was in a state of total fragmentation, people experiencing, in one prefect's words, 'intellectual and moral anaesthesia'.[11] What mattered was that the fighting was over. People knew what the Armistice had ended; they did not yet know what it had begun. In areas evacuated by the Germans because they lay outside the Occupied Zone, the Armistice almost seemed like a victory. When the Germans left Saint-Étienne on 6 July, the tricolour was raised and people gathered to sing the Marseillaise.[12]

---

[6] J. Horne, 'L'Invasion dans la mémoire (France, Grande-Bretagne, Belgique, Allemagne)', in S. Caucanas and R. Cazals (eds.), *Traces de 14–18: Actes du colloque de Carcassonne* (Carcassonne, 1996), 115–26: 124–5.

[7] Werth, *33 Jours*, 124. [8] Geiger, *L'Image de la France*, 206.

[9] Werth, *33 Jours*, 90.

[10] K. Deberles, 'Les Atrocités commises par la division SS Totenkopf dans le Pas-de-Calais', *Revue du nord*, 76/306 (1994), 519–22.

[11] Marrus and Paxton, *Vichy France and the Jews*, 16.

[12] Kedward, *Resistance in Vichy*, 14.

Even François Mauriac, a writer later unambiguously associated with resistance, was initially unsure how to react. On 3 July 1940, he wrote an enthusiastic article in *Le Figaro* about Pétain's broadcast of 25 June; and on 15 July, another one venting his fury at Mers el Kébir. But a few days later he wrote to a friend: 'we are so tossed about that our feelings change from day to day. Undoubtedly the wise course would be to remain silent until our destiny takes shape.' In September, Guéhenno found him 'in despair', repeating 'what to do, what to do?' To another correspondent he wrote: 'I think that despite everything it is necessary to support Pétain in spite of what he is *obliged* to do.'[13]

Gide's 1940 *Journal* reveals similar fluctuations of mood:

[14 June] Pétain's speech [on the 'esprit de jouissance'] is simply admirable.

[24 June] Yesterday we heard with stupor Pétain's new speech . . . Was it really Pétain who pronounced it? Freely? . . . How can one talk of France as 'intact' after handing over half the country to the enemy . . . How can one not give wholehearted support for the speech of General de Gaulle?

[5 September] To treat with yesterday's enemy is not cowardice, it is wisdom; the acceptance of the inevitable . . . What is the point in battering oneself against the bars of one's cage? To suffer less from the smallness of the gaol, one should stay in the centre of it. I feel myself to have unlimited possibilities of acceptance.

By the start of 1941, Gide was so confused that he felt that the 'swings of my thoughts' could only be adequately expressed by a dialogue presenting two sets of opposing views.[14] As for Gide's friend Roger Martin du Gard, in July 1940 he felt like a cork floating on the filthiest water.[15]

Public Opinion: From Disenchantment to Opposition

After the initial shock of defeat, however, and despite the propaganda surrounding Mers el Kébir, opinion had by the autumn become anti-German and pro-British. It remained so throughout the Occupation. This is confirmed by every source which monitored public opinion, whether in the Lot (south-west) or the Var (south-east), whether in Clermont-Ferrand (Auvergne) or in the north-east.[16] Anti-German feeling was initially most intense in the Forbidden Zone, but the rest of the Occupied Zone soon followed suit. In the Unoccupied Zone, the expulsion of the Lorrainers in November caused a shock to public opinion, leading the prefect of Hérault to comment: 'the principle of collabora-

---

[13] Hebey, *La Nouvelle Revue française*, 185–90; Verdès-Leroux, *Refus et violences*, 267; Guéhenno, *Journal des années noires*, 49.

[14] *Journal 1939–1949* (1954), 29, 53, 65.

[15] Martin du Gard, *Journal*, iii. *1937–1949* (1993), 347.

[16] Laborie, *Résistants, Vichyssois*; Guillon, 'La Résistance dans le Var'; Sweets, *Choices in Vichy France*; E. Dejonghe, 'Le Nord isolé: Occupation et résistance (mai 1940–mars 1942), *RHMC* 26 (1979), 48–97.

tion has regressed with a large part of opinion. The feeling of revolt against the aggressors only continues to grow.' 'Almost unanimously favourable to Great Britain' was how the pro-Vichy prefect of Ariège described his *département* in February 1941.[17]

One sign of this was the popularity of the BBC. In October 1940, Vichy forbade people to listen to British radio in public places. Offenders were liable to a 100 franc fine or six days in prison. A year later the ban was extended to listening in private as well, with the penalty raised to a 10,000 franc fine or two years in prison. General Stülpnagel, usually seen as a moderate, wanted the maximum penalty to be death, but Darlan resisted on the grounds this would only further antagonize the population. He preferred to reinforce the jamming of BBC broadcasts. The Germans got their way at the end of 1942, but the escalation of penalties only demonstrated the extent of the problem.[18]

Although people were almost unanimous in their attitude towards the Germans, initially it remained possible for people of opposing views to maintain cordial relations. In May 1941, Drieu sent his latest book to Guéhenno whose opposition to collaboration was unambiguous from the start. The dedication read: 'as a token of complete disagreement'; Guéhenno found this 'rather touching [*plutôt gentil*]'. Similarly Mauriac wrote to Drieu in December 1940 that, while not agreeing with him, he found his views 'defensible'. By the end of 1941, contact between them was broken off. But when in November 1941 the writer Jean Grenier consulted Mauriac about the propriety of contributing to the *NRF*, Mauriac's reply was: 'No need to tell you that I in no way go along with Drieu; but I am not indignant at his attitude. Such is the position of France today that no one has the right to cast a stone at anybody.' By 1942 such tolerance was a thing of the past. The Occupation was said to divide families like the Dreyfus Affair. By the end of 1942, Mauriac and his brother were 'separated by such an abyss that they only dare speak to each other with the most extreme caution'. These were no longer differences of opinion but matters of treason.[19]

This heightened intensity of feeling was a response to the increasing violence of the Occupation. Well before the hostage shootings, which started in 1941, the image of correctness had become tarnished. The first victim of the Germans in Paris was Jacques Bonsergent, a 28-year-old engineer, who was in a group which jostled some German soldiers. In the ensuing argument, Bonsergent raised his fist against a German. He was arrested and shot on 23 December 1940. German posters announcing this event were posted throughout the city, and they became little shrines at which people laid flowers.[20]

[17] Cordier, *Jean Moulin*, iii. 83; Laborie, *L'Opinion publique*, 240.

[18] Lévy, 'L'Organisation de la propagande', 25.

[19] Burrin, *La France à l'heure*, 196–7; Hebey, *La Nouvelle Revue française*, 192–3; Grenier, *Sous l'Occupation*, 264.

[20] H. Michel, *Paris résistant* (1982), 44, 164.

From the summer of 1941 such sinister posters became a familiar sight, over-laying any lingering memory of images of Germans protecting civilians. One prefect reported that the hostage shootings had created 'an abyss between the French and Germans which it will be difficult to overcome'. By 1942 words like 'hate' and 'rage' frequently occur in prefects' accounts of attitudes towards the occupier.[21] Jean Paulhan described seeing in his local café an old bookbinder, usually calm, trembling with joy at the news of an assassination attempt on Laval.[22] Such attitudes were hardly affected by the Allied air raids on France which started in 1942. When Boulogne-Billancourt in the Paris suburbs was bombed in March 1942, killing 623 people, public opinion was favourable to the British despite official propaganda.

The unpopularity of the Germans did not, however, translate directly into disaffection from the Vichy regime. Except in the Forbidden Zone, most people in 1940 believed that the regime was doing its best to resist Germany and protect the French. Montoire, almost universally unpopular, shook this conviction, but the sacking of Laval helped to restore it. This early indulgence towards the regime does not mean that people subscribed to the National Revolution. The regular report on telephone conversations concluded in March 1941 that the National Revolution met with 'almost total indifference'.[23] Probably it would be truer to say that attitudes varied according to political belief and local tradition. In conservative, Catholic, and rural Haute Savoie, up to 42 per cent of the male population was in the Legion, more than in any other *département* of France.[24]

During the winter of 1940–1, food shortages undermined the regime's popu-larity. In the Hérault, the prefect feared as early as December 1940 that these might lead to a 'breakdown of public order'; housewives demonstrated against shortages in Carcassonne, Béziers, and Marseilles.[25] In the winter of 1940–1, forty-six such demonstrations occurred in the Occupied Zone—especially the Paris region—and the Nord/Pas-de-Calais.[26] In the Var, the first food demonstrations occurred in August 1941.[27] When the regime celebrated pre-Revolutionary France, bread riots had certainly not been in its mind. This back-ground made it harder to sell the National Revolution: Pétain's 'evil wind' speech was an admission that the regime's message was not getting through. By June 1941, in one Normandy *département*—an area not known for political radical-

[21] Laborie, *Résistants, Vichyssois*, 188; id., *L'Opinion publique*, 267.

[22] Paulhan, *Choix de lettres*, ii. *1937–1945: Traité des jours sombres* (1992), 232.

[23] Burrin, *La France à l'heure*, 188.

[24] Cointet, *Le Légion française*, 300–1; Abrahams, 'Haute-Savoie at War', 37.

[25] R. Austin, 'Propaganda and Public Opinion in Vichy France: The Department of Hérault, 1940–1944', *European Studies Review*, 13 (1983), 455–82: 466.

[26] D. Tartakowsky, 'Manifester pour le pain', in D. Veillon and J.-M. Flonneau (eds.), *Les Temps des restrictions 1939–1947* (1996), 465–79; Y. Avakoumovitch, 'Les Manifestations de femmes 1940–1944', *Cahiers de l'Institut Maurice Thorez*, 45 (1991), 5–53.

[27] Guillon, 'La Résistance dans le Var', 63.

ism and less affected by food shortages than others—the regime was judged to have only 'an infinitesimal handful' of supporters. In the summer of 1942, in the Var, which did have a left-wing tradition, it was reported: 'the population has not varied in its convictions and is quietly favourable to a new democratic and Republican regime purged of the evils of the previous one'.[28]

During 1942, the breach between the people and the regime deepened. More food demonstrations occurred in the winter of 1941–2, affecting twenty-six *départements*: there were nineteen in the Bouches du Rhône in January and February; forty-two in the Var between January and May.[29] In total, there were 149 such demonstrations between November 1940 and April 1942. Usually these demonstrations were small, occurring on market day, and often accompanied by pillaging. They were generally ended by an emergency distribution of food—which sometimes caused counter-demonstrations in villages protesting against the preferential treatment accorded to the towns.[30] A few demonstrations were quite large: one at Sète, on 20 January 1942, involved 2,000 people. In general they were not explicitly political, but in Montpellier on 15 January and Sète on 20 January 1942 there were cries of 'Down with Pétain', 'Pétain the Starver', and even some singing of the Internationale.

Although the food situation was better by the spring, Laval's return was unpopular. His speech of 22 June 1942 caused a terrible shock throughout the country. The word 'collaboration' ceased to be abstract after Laval had clearly said that he wanted a German victory.[31] The round-ups of Jews in the summer also caused outrage. From the middle of 1942, mayors started to resign, and it became increasingly difficult to replace them. Vichy's decreasing popularity was reflected by the difficulties of the Legion. A rally to commemorate the first anniversary of the Legion attracted 10,000 people in Toulon in August 1941; a year later the event pulled in only 1,800.[32] Even in the Haute-Savoie where the Legion had been so successful, its popularity was declining from the spring of 1942.[33]

The Legion was increasingly discredited by the aggressive tactics of the SOL. A notorious example occurred in April 1942 when, to retaliate against the cutting down of a tree planted to commemorate Pétain's visit to Annecy, some SOL activists assaulted the respected local figure François de Menthon, whose hostility to Vichy was notorious, and threw him into a fountain. Although local Legion leaders condemned this action, the Legion was tainted by it.[34] If many people had long been irritated by the Legion's officiousness, it had at least seemed to represent order; now it seemed to be moving towards rowdiness. In May 1942

---

[28] Ibid. 120.			[29] Ibid. 121–4.

[30] Austin, 'Propaganda and Public Opinion', 468.

[31] L. Werth, *Déposition: Journal 1940–1944* (1992), 314–15.

[32] Guillon, 'La Résistance dans le Var', 38, 113.

[33] Abrahams, 'Haute-Savoie at War', 60–5.

[34] Kedward, *Resistance in Vichy*, 87–8; Abrahams, 'Haute-Savoie at War', 67–9.

the SOL held an anti-British demonstration in Toulon: there were scuffles with the police and twenty-two people arrested.[35] By the end of 1942 the Legion had entered a state of chronic crisis. This was a good barometer of Vichy's decreasing popularity.

The Pétain Cult

The French population, immediately hostile to Germany, and progressively disillusioned with Vichy, was much slower to lose confidence in Marshal Pétain. Reports in 1941 about growing opposition to the regime often referred simultaneously to Pétain's growing popularity. The censors observed in October 1941: 'only the popularity of the Head of State is holding together an artificial unity'.[36] For a long time, people distinguished between Pétain and his government. In the countryside it was commonly said, 'Ah, if only the Marshal knew'.[37] Even when Pétain's actions excited disapproval, he was able recover support. The sacking of Laval in December 1940 appeased the disaffection caused by Montoire. A year later, newsreels of Pétain meeting Goering at Saint-Florentin caused such an uproar in the cinemas of the Unoccupied Zone that the authorities considered issuing an appeal for calm,[38] but Pétain's speech on New Year's Day 1942 complaining at his situation of 'semi-liberty' won back waverers.

Pétain was the subject of an extraordinary personality cult.[39] Vichy set up a special department to create an 'Art Maréchal'. Images of Pétain were produced on an industrial scale. One could buy Pétain posters, postcards, calendars, plates, cups, chairs, handkerchiefs, stamps, colouring books, matchboxes, tapestries, paperweights, medals, vases, board games, ashtrays, penknives, barometers. One could have him in Aubusson tapestry, Baccarat glass, Sèvres porcelain, or plastic.[40] Pétain's portrait was omnipresent. So was the song 'Maréchal, nous voilà' with its refrain 'Before you, the saviour of France, We, your lads, we swear to follow in your steps' and its final line 'For Pétain is France, France is Pétain'. The song, which achieved the status of a semi-official anthem, was written in 1941 by André Montagnard, previously known for lyrics written with the financial support of the pastis producer Paul Ricard.[41] The Pétain cult was assiduously propagated in the schools. For the 1941 New Year, teachers exhorted their pupils to write to the Marshal: one and a half million letters, and thousands of presents, were sent.

The cult was sustained by Pétain's provincial visits throughout the Free Zone, starting with Toulouse on 5 November, and followed by Clermont, Lyons,

---

[35] Guillon, 'La Résistance dans le Var', 112.
[37] Austin, 'Education and Youth Policies', 330.
[38] Lévy, 'L'Organisation de la propagande', 27.
[39] G. Miller, *Les Pousse-au-jouir du Maréchal Pétain* (1975).
[40] Bertrand-Dorléac, *L'Art de la défaite*, 107–28.
[41] Dompnier, *Vichy à travers les chants*, 41–53, 108–10.

[36] Laborie, *L'Opinion publique*, 256.

Marseilles, Toulon. Pétain visited almost fifty cities between 1940 and 1942. Those unable to witness his presence in person could see it on newsreels. The visits were meticulously orchestrated. Pétain's two-day visit to Marseilles on 3 December 1940 took in the prefecture, the cathedral, the war memorial, and the hospital—symbols of authority, repentance, mourning, and suffering—and then he attended a meeting at which the assembled members of the Legion, arms outstretched, swore their oath of loyalty. On the next day, he went to Toulon to see the fleet, symbol of France's imperial power.[42] On all such visits, newspapers were given strict guidelines as to how the Marshal should be described:

> in referring to the Head of State the expression 'old gentleman' must be avoided, even when preceded by a well-disposed adjective like 'illustrious' or 'valiant'. Terms evoking his military past should be used as little as possible, though in certain circumstances it is permitted to employ the term 'victor of Verdun'. On the other hand frequent mention should be made of the Marshal's moral and physical vigour, his generous disposition, his lucidity, and the interest he takes in every problem. Such qualities do not have to be directly described, but should be shown in action, as if incidentally. For example:
>
> 'The Marshal came forward with a quick and decisive step'. 'He takes the liveliest interest in explanations which are given to him'.[43]

The Pétain cult had its high priests in the hagiographical effusions of authors like Pourrat, Thibon, Romier, Henry Bordeaux.[44] But no one surpassed René Benjamin whose three books on Pétain defy parody.[45] Benjamin's rhapsodic description of coming upon Pétain's overcoat is characteristic of his prose:

> After several moving and happy meetings [with Pétain] I had one which I believe was more extraordinary than all the others. I found myself one day alone with his overcoat. Yes, his overcoat, which was lying just like that on the armchair in his study. It was a magnificent moment. I was overcome. Then all of a sudden I became as motionless as the coat when I noticed that the seven stars were gleaming like the seven stars of wisdom of which the ancients tell us.

The seven stars worn by Marshals of France were a favourite theme of hagiographers. So were Pétain's blue eyes and his moustache 'white with the impeccable white of virtue'. Benjamin recounted a conversation between a priest and parishioner: ' "My friend, do you know that God created man in his image, and do you know what that means?" . . . "I do understand . . . I have seen the Marshal".'[46]

A hymn celebrating the Marshal as 'an envoy from God | To save beloved France | O you whose age | Matches in its nobility | The youthfulness of Joan

---

[42] See the documentary film *Les Voyages du Maréchal* (1990) directed by C. Delage.
[43] Kedward, *Resistance in Vichy*, 188.
[44] H. Pourrat, *Le Chef français* (1942); H. Bordeaux, *Images du Maréchal Pétain* (1941).
[45] *Le Maréchal et son peuple* (1941); *Les Sept Étoiles de France* (1942); *Le Grand Homme seul* (1943).
[46] Benjamin, *Les Sept Étoiles*, 138.

of Arc' was not liked by the authorities because of its reference to the Marshal's age.[47] They were less worried by blasphemy. One newspaper published a 'Credo de la France' which paraphrased the Lord's Prayer, ending with the words, 'deliver us from Evil, O Marshal'. Pierre Taittinger dedicated his book *Les Leçons d'une défaite* to 'Marshal Pétain, a new Christ, who has sacrificed himself, to allow the regeneration of defeated France'. Pétain himself had announced on 17 June that he was making the 'gift of my person' to France. This rhetoric of sacrifice and redemption was central to Vichy: the Pétain cult tapped into the mood of popular religiosity.

It is tempting to mock the excesses of the cult, but it would be wrong to see it as constructed entirely from above. On the contrary, Pétainism—or 'Maréchalism' as it has been described to distinguish it from support for the regime—represented a genuinely popular political culture born out of the Exodus, those six weeks sandwiched between the German invasion and the Armistice.[48] In the Exodus, individuals experienced in person the disintegration of the French State: in many cases, the authorities were among the first to flee. Faced with this void, people retreated from politics into self-reliance. Pétain's apolitical language of good sense and honest talk ('I hate the lies which have done you so much harm') touched a chord. His first speech expressed his 'compassion and solicitude' for the 'unhappy refugees'. His fourth one offered this advice: 'Do not hope for too much from the State which cannot give back more than it receives. Count for the present on yourselves and on those you have brought up in the sentiment of duty.' For the first time since the declaration of war, when the gap between official propaganda and reality had grown by the day, the French were being addressed in words that genuinely reflected their own experiences. Pétain acquired a debt of gratitude which outlasted the popularity of his regime. As Fabre-Luce observed: 'the terrible Exodus created the moral foundations of the Armistice'.[49]

If people risked forgetting what Pétain had saved them from, he was quick to remind them. In June 1941, he chided dissenters: 'You have really short memories. Remember the columns of refugees.' The refugees' experience of disintegration, dislocation, and upheaval explains the appeal of Pétain's language of rootedness: home and hearth, family and security. To a suffering nation, Pétain was not only the redemptive saviour but also the Father-Protector, sometimes severe ('today, it is from yourselves that I want to protect you': 12 August 1941), sometimes comforting ('my children . . . Gather this evening around me': 25 December 1940), but always solid as the oak tree in the Forest of Tronçonnais which was formally christened with his name in November 1940.[50] In Vichy pro-

[47] Halls, *Youth of Vichy*, 295.
[48] H. R. Kedward, 'Patriots and Patriotism in Vichy France', *Transactions of the Royal Historical Society*, 32 (1982), 175–92.
[49] *Journal de la France*, 220.   [50] Pétain, *Discours*, 103, 172.

paganda, Pétain's life was given the simplicity of a fairy story: Pétain offered himself as a father; the French were ready to be his children.

From the spring of 1942, this situation began to change. Anti-Pétain graffiti appeared more frequently, and Pétain's appearances in newsreels were no longer greeted with applause.[51] But even if reverence for Pétain as political leader had diminished, many people retained a residual respect. One prefect observed in September 1942: 'The majority of the population continues to venerate the Marshal, but it follows him less as a leader than as a personality of legend, a magnificent old man of astonishing virtues.'[52]

Private Lives

Disaffection from Vichy did not necessarily lead to active opposition or support for the emerging Resistance: caution and fatalism prevailed. People were suspicious of official propaganda and did not know what to believe. They lived on rumours, myths, and prophecies. One prophecy which circulated widely was that made by St Odile, patron saint of Alsace, in 890. She had predicted that terrible violence would be unleashed on the world by 'Germania', but also that the conqueror would reach the pinnacle of success in the sixth month of the second year of the war, and then the tide would turn.[53] As prophecies go, this was more accurate than many of Darlan's predictions in 1941.

People listened to the BBC because they trusted it more than Vichy propaganda. This eventually created a kind of clandestine community, but initially the Occupation generated an accumulation of individual discontents rather than any collective movement of dissent. One sign of this was the notorious epidemic of denunciations.[54] *Gringoire* had a special rubric encouraging delation called 'Répétez-le'. Already in December 1940, prefects reported a 'veritable deluge of anonymous letters'.[55] Curés denounced *instituteurs*, doctors their patients, patients their doctors; women denounced the immorality of POW wives in the absence of their husbands, shopkeepers denounced rivals for trading on the black market, non-Jews denounced Jews, French denounced foreigners, husbands denounced wives.[56] This came to be seen a major problem by the authorities, and prefects were told in February 1942 to discourage delation, and pursue those supplying false information.[57]

The daily preoccupation with survival encouraged a *sauve-qui-peut* mentality.

[51] Burrin, *La France à l'heure*, 190.   [52] Laborie, *L'Opinion publique*, 257.
[53] Ibid. 245–6; Drouot, *Notes d'un Dijonnais*, 98; Marcot, 'La Résistance', 57.
[54] A. Halimi, *La Délation sous l'Occupation* (1983), provides extracts from letters but fails to distinguish between letters opened by the censors and letters of delation.
[55] Cordier, *Jean Moulin*, iii. 281.   [56] Laborie, *Résistants, Vichyssois*, 197–9.
[57] Cordier, *Jean Moulin*, iii. 239; Baruch, *Servir l'État*, 513.

Prefects frequently commented on people's passivity and apathy. At the beginning of the school year in October 1940, Guéhenno observed the amorphous attitude of his pupils, worried only about their own problems and exams. The postal control report noted in October 1941: 'One of the present characteristics of the French population is that individuals are turning in on themselves. For some months the French have become alienated from their government, but without significantly swelling the ranks of the opponents: they are retreating into their shells.'[58] Fifteen months later, the synthesis of prefects' reports observed a similar phenomenon: 'a sort of indifference . . . towards collective issues. Each person limits themselves to their individual life and the egotistical pursuit of their immediate material interests.'[59]

In one of Maupassant's stories about the occupation of 1871 two friends try to recreate a semblance of normality by going on a fishing expedition which ends badly because the Germans take them to be spies. In the Occupation of 1940–4, fishing again allowed men to retreat from the public sphere into private leisure. Hunting was banned in the Occupied Zone, and the confiscation of carrier pigeons put an end to a traditionally popular pastime in the north-east. Fishing, however, was still possible. Never had the Bazar de l'Hôtel de Ville, one of Paris's biggest stores, sold more fishing tackle. One morning in August 1941, Jean Guéhenno, taking the first metro at 5.30 a.m., in order to secure a good place in the queue for an *Ausweis* (he was unsuccessful since there were already 300 people when he arrived), watched as the carriages filled up with fishermen who descended at Châtelet station to take up their places on the banks of the Seine.[60]

Fishing rods sometimes assumed political significance since carrying two rods ('deux gaules') could be a coded reference to de Gaulle. Such gestures could hardly be characterized as resistance, but they were part of a developing culture of opposition and irreverence. There was a rich seam of Occupation jokes. Three early jokes are among the best-known:

The definition of collaboration: 'Give me your watch and I'll tell you the time.'[61]

Hitler, desperate to get across the Channel, promises the Grand Rabbi of Berlin he will abandon anti-Semitic measures if he is told how Moses succeeded in crossing the Red Sea. The reply comes that Moses's magic wand could be found in . . . the British Museum.[62]

On the return of Napoleon II's remains in December 1940: the Parisians say they prefer coal to ashes.[63]

---

[58] Peschanski, 'Vichy au singulier', 656.   [59] Baruch, *Servir l'État*, 443.

[60] Cobb, *French and Germans*, 93–4.

[61] Galtier-Boissière, *Mon journal*, 27; M. Bood, *Les Années doubles: Journal d'une lycéenne sous l'Occupation* (1974), 87 (8 Mar. 1941).

[62] Grenier, *Sous l'Occupation*, 156; Galtier-Boissière, *Mon journal*, 18 (18 Oct. 1940); Bood, *Les Années doubles*, 72 (22 Jan. 1941).

[63] Galtier-Boissière, *Mon journal*, 25 (15 Dec. 1940); Paulhan, *Choix de lettres*, 210 (16 Dec. 1940).

A 1941 joke:

> Hitler telephones Mussolini after the failure of Italy's attack on Greece:
> 'Benito, aren't you in Athens yet?'
> 'I can't hear you, Adolf.'
> 'I said, aren't you in Athens yet?'
> 'I can't hear you. You must be ringing from a long way—presumably London.'

A later joke:

> Did you know the Marshal was dead?
> No. Since when?
> Three months ago, but his entourage have hidden it from him.[64]

Many Occupation jokes were collected in 1945 in a book with the title 'Resistance through Humour'.[65] Although the term 'resistance' seems excessive, jokes were certainly seen as subversive by the authorities: two peasants from a village near Draguignan were prosecuted for naming their horse 'Darlan'.[66] Before Pétain's visit to Marseilles in December 1940 the police arrested a bookseller whose window contained portraits of Pétain and Darlan surrounded by piles of Hugo's *Les Misérables*.[67] Displaying portraits of Darlan and Laval with the word 'vendu' ('sold out') underneath was a common form of not so innocent humour. One can track the progress of jokes in the journals of the period, an ever-thickening thread of dissent, creating complicity where there had previously been only suspicion.

Responding to the Germans

Whatever their private views of the Germans, inhabitants of the Occupied Zone had to construct codes of conduct towards them. On his first visit to the German Institute in Paris, Chardonne spotted Giraudoux in a corridor: 'each of us averted his eyes like two men meeting in a brothel'.[68] But familiarity blunted embarrassment. As Fabre-Luce described these Institute occasions, 'when the French and Germans meet on an equal footing, they start by displaying coldness and end in cordiality'.[69] These were at least encounters by choice, but François Mauriac's son, Claude, described the difficulties of having a German officer billeted in the family house:

> Yesterday the Captain came into the salon to present himself to my parents. Young, with a fairly sympathetic manner, distinguished, with a great desire to be correct. But he does not speak our language and we do not speak his. There is

[64] I. Naour and M. Rajfus, *L'Humour des Français sous l'Occupation* (1995) contains many more examples.

[65] R. Régis, *La Résistance par l'humour: Histoires recueillies* (1945).

[66] Guillon, 'La Résistance dans le Var', 46.   [67] Kitson, 'Marseilles Police', 70.

[68] Guitard-Auviste, *Jacques Chardonne*, 207.   [69] Burrin, *La France à l'heure*, 210.

such an abyss between us . . . Catherine (who is Alsatian) serves as interpreter. The conversation languishes. Everyone makes an effort and tries to bring out the few words they know. He is certainly no less embarrassed than us, clicking his heels and bowing at everything . . . He dares not take his leave. We don't like to give him the leave to do so. The minutes drag . . . We meet again after dinner. One cannot tell him to go. One has at least to make the gesture of inviting him to sit down. But he takes the gesture at face value. Does he feel obliged to stay or does he prefer this embarrassed *tête-à-tête* to the solitude of his frozen room? He sits down and stays . . . To try and look at ease I turn on the radio: never have the English stations been more arrogant. With strained smiles on both sides, we finish by finding a neutral station and stay with it.[70]

This nervous testing of the waters was characteristic of the early days of Occupation. People who did not have such proximity forced upon them could try to ignore the Germans, who were kept separate from the French as much as possible. Certain restaurants, brothels, and cinemas (*Soldatenkino*) were reserved for exclusive German use. But the Germans also brought a mass of vexatious regulations which they enforced with efficiency, not to say officiousness: people were fined for not crossing the road at proper crossings, cyclists were stopped for riding three abreast, pedestrians had to step off the pavements to let Germans pass. The Germans were suspicious of French hygiene, and tried to impose their own standards where their soldiers were affected.[71] In the larger cities, they found French women to be excessively made-up and were shocked by the sight of so many blacks.[72]

As well as an irritation, the German presence also became a habit, as Sartre observed of Paris:

> Clearly the immense majority of the population abstained from any contact with the German army. But one must not forget that the occupation was part of *daily* life . . . We pressed against the Germans in the metro, we bumped into them in the dark evening . . . In the long run a sort of shameful and indefinable solidarity developed between the Parisians and these soldiers who were so similar, in the end, to French soldiers. A solidarity which was not accompanied by sympathy . . . At the start, the sight of the Germans was offensive to us, and then, little by little, we learnt not to notice them, they took on an institutional appearance. What completed the process of making them inoffensive was their ignorance of our language . . . They were more like the furniture than they were like men.

On one occasion, Sartre saw a car knock over a German colonel, and ten French bystanders ran to help:

> They hated the occupier, I am sure; and among them, there were undoubtedly some future resistance fighters who fired on the Germans on that same street two

---

[70] *La Terrasse de Malagar* (1977), 144–5.
[71] Amouroux, *La Grande Histoire des Français sous l'Occupation*, ii. 115–16.
[72] Geiger, *L'Image de la France*, 361.

years later . . . But was the man lying under the car an occupier? What should one have done? The concept of an enemy is only clear and fixed if the enemy is separated from us by the barrier of gunfire.[73]

In smaller communities, the Germans inevitably became part of the rhythms of local life. As Richard Cobb observes, in the notebooks of the Breton novelist Louis Guilloux, describing life in Saint-Brieuc, the Germans become 'so familiar as to be taken as a matter of course, unaccompanied by expressions of anger, indignation or surprise': the French policeman raises his hat in greeting to the German policeman standing on the step; a friend whom Guilloux visits is giving a young German officer a French lesson which is interrupted for a friendly argument about the outcome of the war; a beach in July is so crowded with swimmers that it is impossible to distinguish French swimmers from German ones; French children know which Germans are likely to be a soft touch for sweets.[74] In such communities, 'the Germans' inevitably became individuals. People quickly learnt to distinguish the differences between army officers, the *Feldgendarmerie* (nicknamed 'bulldogs' because of their chains worn around the neck), the female auxiliaries (nicknamed 'grey mice' because of the colour of their uniforms).

Familiarity might salve the wound of occupation, but the Germans knew they were not popular. As early as August 1940 a German army report on public opinion in thirteen *départements* noted that the 'exemplary, amiable and helpful behaviour of the German soldiers towards the population has aroused little sympathy'.[75] The tone of these army reports remained consistently pessimistic. In early June 1941 it was noted that 'even Britain's hostile acts against France do not change the population's attitude'; a month later, that the German invasion of the Soviet Union had not made the French more favourably disposed towards Germany. Even Professor Grimm whose pro-collaboration lecture tour was such a success, observed in June 1941: 'My friends tell me that the climate has never been so bad . . . The French rejoice at the fact that British planes are attacking their cities . . . The French who are well-disposed to us despair of their compatriots.'[76]

How did people manifest their hostility to the Germans? Charles Rist observed of Paris in November 1940: 'People pass by the Germans without seeing them. They are surrounded by silence. Silence in the trains, in the metro, in the street. Each keeps his thoughts to himself. And yet one *senses* the hostility.' Paris was christened by the Germans 'Stadt ohne Blick'.[77] People tried to express disapproval and retain dignity while avoiding overt provocation. The Paris Métro was one site of enforced proximity where people improvised their responses.

[73] J.-P. Sartre, 'Paris sous l'Occupation', in *Situations*, iii (1949), 18–21.
[74] *French and Germans*, 108–10.
[75] Cordier, *Jean Moulin*, iii. 179–80, 207, 215–16, 1362.
[76] Geiger, *L'Image de la France*, 217–36.
[77] *Une saison gâtée*, 107. See the similar description in Grenier, *Sous l'Occupation*, 21.

Jacques Biélinky, ultimately to perish in Sobibor, noted one day that a German soldier had politely offered his seat in the metro: 'I accepted with thanks'. Two weeks later he saw a 'pleasant-looking' German smile at a child sitting opposite on his mother's knee. The woman looked away brusquely. Galtier-Boissière reported: 'In the metro a very young German with a gentle face gets up to offer his seat to Charlotte. She refuses. The soldier, disconcerted, offers it to me. I refuse. The poor man does not know how to get out of this ridiculous situation and he remains standing, all embarrassed, next to this empty seat which no one wants.' Guéhenno summed up the situation in February 1943: 'when you get on the metro we squeeze closer to each other to make you a place. You are untouchable. I lower my head so that you don't see my eyes, to deny you the joy of an exchanged glance. You are in the middle of us, like an object, in a circle of silence and ice.' The German writer Felix Hartlaub, on the receiving end of this silence, noted the 'arctic' climate in June 1941.[78]

From the beginning of the Occupation, however, the Germans also faced more active opposition than this. The first months of Occupation in Bordeaux—not a city with a heroic reputation—witnessed many anti-German incidents:

9 August 1940: a Gendarme was arrested for saying that it was 'painful to have to salute these Germans pigs'. He had been denounced to the authorities by a Swiss man who overheard the remark.

14 August: in the early hours of the morning a German marine was shot dead in Royan. The culprit was never identified, and Royan had to pay a fine of 3 million francs.

23 August: in the Olympia cinema, German newsreels of Hitler caused hilarity among the audience. The Germans ordered future newsreels to be shown with the lights on.

27 August: a Polish Jew, Israel Leizer Karp, was executed for shouting insults at a passing German column.

28 August: in the early hours, shots were fired at a German patrol. The culprits were not found, but the local police were informed that in future such incidents would cause severe reprisals.

28 August: an 18-year-old sailor was found slashing German posters in the Place des Quinconces. He was sentenced to three months in prison for sabotage.

2 September: the German telephone cable linking La Rochelle to Royan was cut. The culprit, 19-year-old Pierre Roche, was shot by the Germans on 7 September.[79]

Similar incidents occurred throughout the Occupied Zone in the first months after the Armistice.[80] But they petered out at the end of the year because, without

[78] Biélinky, *Journal*, 110, 114; Galtier-Boissière, *Mon journal*, 42; Guéhenno, *Journal des années noires*, 369–70; Burrin, *La France à l'heure*, 204.

[79] R. Terrisse, *Bordeaux 1940–1944* (1993), 170–7.

[80] e.g. Cordier, *Jean Moulin*, iii. 215–16, 240; Dumérial, *Journal d'un honnête homme*, 41, 51.

any organized Resistance movement to give them a purpose, they were futile, dangerous, and led nowhere. The booing of German newsreels, however, remained a major irritation for the Occupation authorities. Turning up the lights only caused people to arrive at the cinema after the newsreels were over. In the first months of the Occupation, there was also a lot of anti-German graffiti. In one week of January 1941, the Paris police counted 400 handwritten anti-German stickers on walls.[81]

There were some early instances of collective opposition to the Germans. The funerals of Allied pilots who had been shot down gave people an opportunity to manifest their feelings. In Lanester in Britanny some 2,000 people gathered in December 1941, apparently spontaneously, for the funeral of three British pilots; 5,000 gathered in Rennes in April 1941. Twenty-one demonstrations of this kind have been recorded between August 1940 and November 1942.[82] Usually they passed off without incident—unlike the famous demonstration that occurred in Paris on 11 November 1940. On that day several thousand students assembled at the place de l'Étoile in Paris, singing the Marseillaise and shouting 'Long live de Gaulle'. News of this event spread throughout France, but the severity of the German reaction surprised the participants, and discouraged any repetition. On 14 July 1941, 488 people in the Paris suburbs were stopped by police for gathering illegally or wearing patriotic colours.[83] On 11 November 1941, however, the whole country was quiet.

Not all anti-German gestures were spontaneous and uncoordinated. When de Gaulle from London called on the population to show hostility to the Germans by staying at home between 2 p.m. and 3 p.m. (3 p.m. and 4 p.m. in the Occupied Zone) on 1 January 1941, the appeal was quite well observed in the North, less so in the South.[84] One observer wrote: 'for a week everyone I meet has only spoken about this hour of protest against the invader'.[85] In Quimper the street was crowded at 2.55 p.m. and deserted five minutes later.[86] On Joan of Arc day, 11 May 1941, de Gaulle asked people to be silently present in the streets between 3 p.m. and 4 p.m., again with some success.[87] In March 1941, the BBC called on people to draw Vs for victory on walls. This idea caught on and the prefecture of Paris counted 1,000 Vs on 7 April 1941. In Montpellier the prefect complained that the extent of such defacement had become 'disagreeable to the eye'. To undermine this campaign, the Germans started putting up their own V

[81] D. Veillon, 'La Ville comme creuset de Résistance', in Douzou et al. (eds.), La Résistance: Villes, 136–48: 144.

[82] C. Bougeard, 'La Résistance bretonne et les Anglais', in Frank and Gotovitch (eds.), La Résistance et les Européens du Nord, 21–9: 23; Tartakowsky, Les Manifestations de rue en France 1918–1968 (1997), 456.

[83] Veillon, 'La Ville comme creuset de Résistance', 146.

[84] Cordier, Jean Moulin, iii. 306.

[85] J.-L. Crémieux-Brilhac, La France libre: De l'appel du 18 juin à la Libération (1996), 219.

[86] I. Ousby, Occupation, the Ordeal of France, 1940–1944 (1997), 208; the same was true in Dijon: Drouot, Notes d'un Dijonnais, 65.

[87] Cordier, Jean Moulin, iii. 379–80.

posters in Paris. This 'battle of the Vs' was significant enough to be noted by several diarists of the period.[88]

One should not exaggerate the importance of these gestures. Only after the Resistance imposed itself as a realistic alternative to Vichy did people start to believe they could change their situation. Before this, they followed events in the outside world, and desired a British victory, but without seeing how they could contribute to it. One observer wrote: 'France is like a not very well off tourist who visits a casino and watches the roulette being played without playing himself. Now he watches the English game, now the Russian.'[89]

In the first eighteen months of Occupation the Germans were more concerned about maintaining the discipline of their own troops than responding to opposition from the French population. A German report in October 1940 observed that the amount of sabotage was 'neither particularly high, nor particularly preoccupying for the troops'.[90] Especially in the early days of the Occupation, Goebbels's main concern was that the German public might have too favourable a view of France. He ordered that 'papers must not paint Paris in too attractive a way'.[91] France remained a privileged posting for most German soldiers throughout the Occupation. As one of them wrote: 'the charm of Paris is difficult to deny. It bewitches even those least sensitive to it.' Even the military authorities, although aware of the unpopularity of the Germans in France, accepted that this caused them few problems. An army report in August 1941 noted: 'the French adapt themselves to the requirements of the occupying powers and behave in a correct manner'.[92]

The Sociology of Opinion: *Notables* and Peasants

Were there significant differences in the attitudes of different social groups towards Vichy and the Germans? Prefects' reports provide only the most general answers to this question. Early in 1941, the prefect of the Lot noted that collaboration was supported by the bourgeoisie; the peasants showed no open hostility; and the workers were against it. In December of the same year, the prefect of the Limoges region reported: 'Very striking hostility to the government from most workers, small farmers, small shopkeepers and artisans; unreserved support from big business and big shopkeepers, magistrates and *notables*.'[93]

The French term *notable*, which has no sociological precision, describes figures of local influence such as landowners, doctors, vets, lawyers, and pharmacists.

---

[88] Veillon, 'La Ville comme creuset de Résistance', 144–5; Galtier-Boissière, *Mon journal*, 62; Guéhenno, *Journal des années noires*, 193; Drouot, *Notes d'un Dijonnais*, 152–3.

[89] Werth, *Déposition*, 232 (1 Aug. 1941).

[90] Cordier, *Jean Moulin: La République des catacombes*, 108.

[91] Geiger, *L'Image de la France*, 134–5.   [92] Ibid. 358–61, 235–6.

[93] Laborie, *Résistants, Vichyssois*, 182; G. Madjarian, *Conflits, pouvoirs et société à la Libération* (1980), 440.

Some were figures of social importance who felt that republican democracy had displaced them from rightful positions of leadership. But in other cases the social status of *notable* was conferred by election: in the Nord, with its strong tradition of municipal pride, many Socialist mayors had been in office for so long that they had become the *notables* of the region.

For at least two years, Vichy enjoyed considerable support from *notables*. They staffed its institutions as they had those of the Republic, acting as mayors, sitting on *commissions administratives*, providing the local cadres of the Peasant Corporation or the Secours national. They were not all from the right. In the Loiret the different kinds of *notables* who served Vichy included a royalist aristocrat who saw an opportunity to eliminate the influence of an anticlerical *institutrice*; a Socialist *instituteur* who in 1941 agreed to become mayor of one of the four largest towns in the *département*; and the moderate conservative doctor who served as mayor of Orleans from 1940 to 1944.[94] In the Nord, as we have seen, most Socialist mayors remained in office, although they had to bring some conservatives into their municipal councils. In some *départements*, the cadres of the Legion came from the Radical Party. This improved the local image of an organization that was frequently viewed as sectarian and intolerantly right-wing.[95]

Why did such former stalwarts of the Republic agree to serve Vichy? Often they acted from social duty, trying to protect the population from the consequences of the Occupation. This was especially true in the Nord/Pas-de-Calais where the German presence was so oppressive. The pre-war mayor of Roubaix, Jean Lebas, who was involved in the Resistance from the beginning, had no qualms about encouraging his Socialist colleague Victor Provo to accept the post of mayor in 1942 on the grounds that the alternatives might be worse. For the same reason, he persuaded the Vichyite prefect Carles not to resign in 1941.[96]

Some of those who felt it their duty to protect their fellow citizens devised ways of distancing themselves from the regime. In the Eure, most Socialist mayors avoided putting up photographs of Pétain; the Socialist mayor of Moulins refused to remove the bust of Marianne; the mayor of Argenton put Pétain's photograph next to one of Jaurès.[97] But many mayors, even Socialist ones, initially felt no need to apologize for their willingness to serve the regime. At the Liberation, those who had refused to do so were viewed as patriotic. But patriotism was viewed differently in 1940 when mayors who had abandoned their posts during the exodus were resented: the stigma of 'desertion' preceded the stigma of collaboration. In the context of 1940—of social collapse and national disintegration—Vichy's rhetoric of unity made sense, and the

[94] Y. Durand, 'Les Notables', in *VEF*, 372–81.   [95] J.-P. Cointet, *Histoire de Vichy*, 148.
[96] J.-P. Florin, 'Pouvoir municipal et occupation à Roubaix', *Revue du Nord*, 2, hors-séries (1987), 269–312.
[97] Sadoun, *Les Socialistes sous l'Occupation*, 70–1.

ideological project behind it was not immediately obvious. The Republic's reputation was tarnished, and the seemingly apolitical moralism of Pétain's speeches had great appeal. It was not so removed from the kind of austere republican values held by many *instituteurs*. In the traditionally left-wing Var, several Socialist mayors expressed allegiance to Pétain: the Socialist mayor of Bandol joined the Legion, as did many *instituteurs* who had once been seen as bastions of Republicanism. Such conversions may have been motivated by opportunism or prudence, but also, in many cases, by conviction.[98]

No group was more assiduously courted by the regime than the peasantry. How successful was this? The outside world seemed remote in the countryside, and the rhythms of rural life proceeded as before. Many villages never saw a German soldier in four years of Occupation. Léon Werth who spent the war in a village in the Jura was surprised by his first visit to Lyons in December 1940:

> In the countryside the image of the Marshal is not so all-obsessing. We only see his picture in the papers. The postcard-sellers have not reached isolated farmers. But in Lyons the Marshal is everywhere. His portraits, his messages, his radio speeches are stuck in the windows of shops.[99]

Werth throus interesting light on the local peasantry. He observed their complacency that 'whatever occurs they at least will never go hungry'. Mostly the peasants were 'absolutely indifferent to everything that the government says and does . . . All the acts and projects of Vichy go largely unnoticed.' One day in August 1941, after a copious meal of two rabbits and two chickens washed down with *marc*, the conversation turned to the outside world:

> They are suspicious of everything, of Germany and England, of Communism and the government. But they have one common hatred, the hatred of the workers: 'they envy us, but they do not envy our work. If there was a revolution they would come and take their revenge on us . . . they would pillage us.'

The peasants felt satisfaction that the workers, envied for their short working days and high wages, should now also suffer: 'there are those who say that five years like this would do the workers no harm'. This also provided a reason to support Vichy: if a revolution came, the workers might be tempted to take their revenge on the peasants![100]

In theory, the main impact of the National Revolution on the countryside was the Peasant Corporation. Each village was supposed to create a single corporative syndicate. These would combine to form an ascending hierarchy of regional syndicates at the apex of which was a national corporative council. Previously there had been two agricultural syndicates in France, the conservative National Union of Agricultural Syndicates (UNSA), and another one linked to

---

[98] Guillon, 'La Résistance dans le Var', 32, 35–8.
[99] *Déposition*, 139.   [100] Ibid. 116, 238, 262, 301, 254.

the Radical Party. The Corporation represented a victory for the ideas of UNSA, and its members staffed the regional syndicates.[101] Corporatism was supposed to give the peasantry a collective identity and allow them to organize their affairs independently. But as the government was faced with organizing an economy of scarcity and fulfilling German demands for food deliveries, it used the Corporation as an instrument of economic regulation. The corporatist theorists became disillusioned, and the peasants, far from seeing the Corporation as defending their interests, came to see it as an intrusion on their freedom.[102]

The peasants were, as Werth noted, practised in the skills of evasion. They would appear at the town hall to declare their produce to officials 'who don't know if a cow gives two or twenty litres of milk a day'. One Sunday the authorities imposed price ceilings at the local market; on the following market days no produce appeared at the market.[103] But peasants became increasingly unhappy at having to wage constant guerilla war against a regime that claimed to protect them. Werth heard people in the village café saying in February 1942 that 'we'd rather see the Soviets than see what we see at the moment'.[104] Prefects became frustrated by the peasantry's evasion of economic controls.[105] One of them observed that he needed 'a gendarme on every farm'. The servitors of a regime which so adulated the peasantry referred increasingly to peasant 'selfishness', even peasant 'resistance'.[106] In the Hérault, in February 1942, it was reported that the 'peasants feel for the Marshal the hatred they feel for his government', and a year later that 'the peasantry has lost all confidence in the government and in some cases people go as far as to accuse the Marshal of duping the agricultural population'. By 1943, peasant disaffection was almost universal, even in conservative *départements* like the Haute-Savoie.[107]

The Sociology of Opinion: Business

At the Liberation, it was believed that business had acquitted itself badly under the Occupation. De Gaulle allegedly told a business delegation in 1944: 'I did not see many of you in London.' Undoubtedly the Vichy regime enabled employers to complete their revenge over 1936. Even if, as Richard Vinen suggests, they had already done this by 1938,[108] the memory of 1936 remained raw: in a class war there are always new battles to win.

The employers were not a single block. One division was between the elite

---

[101] J. Sainclivier, 'La France de l'Ouest', in Azéma and Bédarida (eds.), *La France des Années noires*, 335–53: 339; Luirard, *La Région stéphanoise*, 364–72.

[102] Wright, *Rural Revolution*, 77–92; I. Boussard, *Vichy et la corporation paysanne* (1980).

[103] Werth, *Déposition*, 116, 65.   [104] Ibid. 263.

[105] R. Kedward, 'Le Monde rural face au maquis', in Marcot (ed.), *La Résistance: Lutte armée et maquis*, 339–50: 342; Laborie, *Résistants, Vichyssois*, 184.

[106] Abrahams, 'Haute-Savoie at War', 91, 104.

[107] Austin, 'Education and Youth Policies', 292, 332; Abrahams, 'Haute-Savoie at War', 113.

[108] *Politics of French Business*, 134–7.

who dominated the COs, and the mass of small employers who felt Vichy was not serving their interests. Pierre Nicolle, one of the small employers' leaders, aired his resentments in his diary of the period. Nonetheless Nicolle was a Vichy insider—his diary is a precious source of Vichy gossip—and one should not exaggerate the discontents of small employers: even if they did not get all they wanted from Vichy, they sympathized with its social values.

What about attitudes to Germany? By the end of 1941, 7,000 businesses were producing directly for German orders; this figure had doubled by 1944.[109] This underestimates the real level of economic collaboration since many firms not directly exporting to Germany supplied firms who were. Between 70 and 90 per cent of metallurgical goods produced in the Nord ended up in Germany although only about 50 per cent of this showed up in the official figures.[110] German pressure on French business was not confined to heavy industry: the Germans were as interested in clothing and champagne as in aluminium and lorries. Some French industrialists were better placed than others to respond to German pressure. The iron producers of the annexed Lorraine, under direct German control, were in a weaker position than the bauxite producers, who were all situated in the Unoccupied Zone. Marius Berliet, the lorry manufacturer based in Lyons, had more leeway than other vehicle manufacturers, who were all in the Occupied Zone. But he was not free of German pressure since he had a factory outside Paris producing parts for his lorries, and only the Germans could authorize these to be sent South.[111]

Industrialists were subject to the regulations imposed by their CO. Despite being located in the Unoccupied Zone, Berliet was instructed by the automobile CO to sell a percentage of his output to the Germans since it would be unfair on his competitors if their dependence on German orders allowed him to supplant them in the French market.[112] Berliet needed little prompting to sell to Germany. The same was true of most other industrialists. German representatives of the Armistice Commission, travelling in the Southern Zone in the autumn of 1940, reported that industrialists were keen to procure German orders. In his memoirs, Pucheu recalled that his efforts as Industry Minister to monitor the signing of contracts with the Germans were 'forestalled by the industrialists themselves, which placed me in an impossible position with regard to the occupier'.[113] Pucheu knew only too well what he was talking about. Before becoming a minister, he had complained, as an industrialist, that businessmen who wanted to make contact with the Germans were being hampered by the government.[114]

---

[109] Burrin, *La France à l'heure*, 250.   [110] Beltram et al., *La Vie des entreprises*, 22.
[111] Rochebrune and Hazera, *Les Patrons sous l'Occupation*, 42–52.
[112] Ibid. 53–4.   [113] Ibid. 313.
[114] A. Lacroix-Riz, *Industriels et banquiers sous l'Occupation: La Collaboration économique avec le Reich et Vichy* (1999), 116–17.

In July 1940, when General Huntziger, French representative on the Armistice Commission, told the German negotiator Hemmen that French industrialists would be likely to experience 'moral and almost sentimental difficulties' about the idea that their manufactures might end up being used in the battle against Britain, he met with a sceptical response. Hemmen's cynicism was vindicated, and in the first weeks after occupation industrialists displayed almost indecent haste in making contact with the Germans. The directors of the Kuhlmann chemical company were trying to contact representatives of the German dye industry as early as 26 July despite receiving counsels of caution from Vichy. But the German representative of IG Farben in Paris was slow to respond, preferring, as he put it later, to 'let the French stew in their juice'. Another Farben representative reported that Kuhlmann had been looking for an 'intimate collaboration' allowing 'the integration of French industry into a new Europe under German leadership'.[115] If Vichy tried to restrain this enthusiasm it was in order to impose some control over the negotiations and obtain German concessions in return. But in the late summer and autumn a whole series of industries—bauxite, aluminium, chemicals, building—signed contracts with the Germans with little heed for Vichy. Barnaud who was supposedly monitoring the process of negotiations complained in May 1941 that he had lost track of them.[116]

In February 1941, the Germans organized an industrial fair at the Petit Palais, exhibiting items they required. The operation was a success: 10,000 French companies put in bids. French industrialists frequently visited German factories to view industrial techniques: in the single month of November 1941, six such delegations visited Germany.[117] A congress of French and German chambers of Commerce took place in September 1941. This occasion was so successful that it was followed by others.[118] Social encounters between top businessmen and Germans were frequent. At one such occasion, a reception at the German Embassy to meet a German trade minister, the banker Henri Ardant, head of the Société Générale, spoke of his hopes that the Germans would set up a single customs zone in Europe and create a single European currency.[119] The highest and most visible level of Franco-German economic and commercial contacts was the so-called Table ronde lunches held at the Ritz between February and October 1942 where top French businessmen met their German counterparts.

Flagrant examples of political commitment to collaboration, like Eugène Schueller's backing of the MSR, were exceptional. One extreme case was the eccentric Georges Claude, inventor of liquid air and founder of the Air liquide company. Obsessed by Bolshevism, Claude became a passionate advocate of

[115] Ibid. 68, 88.   [116] Ibid. 88–106, 125.
[117] Burrin, *La France à l'heure*, 240, 256–7.   [118] Lacroix-Riz, *Industriels et banquiers*, 430–5.
[119] Andrieu, *La Banque sous l'occupation*, 265.

Franco-German reconciliation, and a leading member of the Collaboration group. After the Allies landed in North Africa, he gave spectacular proof of his devotion to Hitler, announcing, at the end of a lecture delivered in Bordeaux, that he was swallowing a fatal dose of strychnine in the hope that his sacrifice would touch Hitler and persuade him to offer France a privileged place in the new Europe. In fact Claude's strychnine did not kill him, allowing him to be arrested in August 1944.[120]

There were industrialists who merely tried to profit opportunistically from the Occupation and others who enthusiastically embraced the idea of a durable economic reorganization of Europe around Franco-German co-operation. In the former category was the Photomaton company which suggested in May 1941 that, since interned Jews needed to be photographed for administrative purposes, the Germans might like to invest in the company's high-quality photo machine.[121] Long-term co-operation with Germany was attractive to the automobile industry where the main pre-war competitor had been America. In March 1941 French automobile industrialists set up a committee with the Germans to prepare the 'collaboration of the European automobile industry'. One Vichy official commented on the 'bad impression' created by the sight of Germans in Paris riding around in Renault, Citroën, and Peugeot cars, and wondered if the Germans could not be persuaded to do this more discreetly, preferably early in the morning.[122] But where the main pre-war competitor had been Germany, as was true of the coal and steel industry, the attractions of long-term collaboration were less obvious—although during the Occupation the coal industry found itself working flat out for Germany. After the Liberation, coal owners defended themselves by claiming that only 4 per cent of their output had been exported to Germany, but this neglected the fact that most coal was distributed to industries like steel which were working directly for the Germans. Demand was so great that the coal owners used the opportunity to exploit less profitable seams of lower quality coal, keeping the better coal for after the war.[123]

STO was a major cause of tension between industrialists and the Germans. In the coal mines, employers protected their employees from being drafted to Germany, and subsequently claimed credit for this 'resistance'. But just as the motives for co-operation with the Germans were usually more commercial than political, the same applies in the opposite case. Employers who shielded workers from STO did so because they were desperately short of labour. Since workers were probably more productive in France than Germany, saving them from being drafted abroad could be said to have objectively helped the German war economy.[124] The same coal owners who protected their workers in 1943 did not

---

[120] Rochebrune and Hazera , *Les Patrons sous l'Occupation,* 249–54.
[121] Ibid. 313–14.
[122] Lacroix-Riz, *Industriels et banquiers,* 142.
[123] Burrin, *La France à l'heure,* 233–66; Vinen, *Politics of French Business,* 152–5.
[124] R. Vinen, 'The French Coal Industry during the Occupation', *HJ* 33/1 (1990), 105–30.

hesitate to use German help to quash labour unrest in May 1941; and this was also true in the aircraft industries.[125]

For these reasons, the terms 'collaboration' and 'resistance' do not apply neatly to the world of business. Not everything was what it seemed. The directors of the AFC aluminium company—the future Péchiney—were unhappy about contracts which had been negotiated with Germany by the French government, and after the war they cited their objections as an example of resistance. But their arguments against the contracts had been commercial not patriotic: fearing that the Germans would steal their export markets, they wanted assurances that the aluminium would only be used for German war industry and not re-exported to former French customers. These same industrialists spent months discussing a German proposal to build jointly a new aluminium factory in France.[126] They were worried that otherwise the Germans would go ahead instead with a plan to build their own factory in Yugoslavia and weaken France's share of the market after the return of peace. Although the discussions broke down in May 1942, the rhetoric of resistance with which they were invested after the war bears no relation to how they were perceived at the time. The assumption was that the Germans had won the war, and the issue was seen only in terms of future commercial strategy. The same was true of Michelin, another industrialist with a resistance reputation. Michelin's supplies of rubber from Indochina had been disrupted, but he refused to concede German participation in his French firm or cede control of his Dutch and Belgian branches in return for a German offer to supply him with synthetic rubber. Despite pressure from the French government, Michelin said: 'I have made my choice: sacrifice the present for the future.'[127] His calculation was vindicated.

In the end, Berliet's remark at his trial that he 'viewed the matter only as a head of industry' applied to most industrialists. When patriotism did not coincide with commercial interest, the latter was rarely sacrificed to the former. There clearly was a difference between Berliet, who sent two of his sons to Germany as voluntary workers to set a good example, and the Peugeot family who helped STO evaders and developed contacts with the Resistance, but neither Peugeot nor Berliet could have survived without German orders.[128] Even the aircraft industry, tightly integrated into economic collaboration, contained Resistance heroes, like Jacques Kellner and Marcel Robert Bloch, while others, like Félix Amiot and Louis Renault, were happy to provide all the Germans wanted. Most aircraft makers fitted into neither category and tried only to keep their factories running, while implicating themselves as little as they could: Louis Verdier, head

---

[125] Chapman, *State Capitalism and Working Class Radicalism*, 251.

[126] Rochebrune and Hazera, *Les Patrons sous l'Occupation*, 129–30; Margairaz, *L'État, l'économie et les finances*, 614–28.

[127] Rochebrune and Hazera, *Les Patrons sous l'Occupation*, 123; Margairaz, *L'État, l'économie et les finances*, 662–4; Lacroix-Riz, *Industriels et banquiers*, 312–20.

[128] Rochebrune and Hazera, *Les Patrons sous l'Occupation*, 74–5, 388–90.

of the Gnôme-et-Rhône company, greeted an Anglo-American Inspection team in August 1944 with champagne, as he had the Germans in 1941.[129]

The Sociology of Opinion: The Workers

At the Liberation, it was the received wisdom that the working classes had been the heart of the Resistance. Mauriac wrote: 'the working class alone are faithful to the profaned *patrie*'. By 1944, workers were certainly over-represented in the active Resistance,[130] but this did not apply to the period 1940–2, to the extent that Resistance existed at this stage. In the first two years of Occupation, the workers were often described as the most apathetic and passive section of the population. 'We're going to work for the Boches. So what, one has to live', was a comment overheard by one observer in 1940.[131] All reports suggested that workers had no sympathy for Vichy, but they remained quiescent. It was noted in February 1942 that the 'workers suffer the most and protest the least'.[132]

This fatalism is easy to understand. The political demobilization of the working class went back to the defeat of the trade-union movement in 1938. Immediately after the Armistice, the main preoccupation was unemployment. Once unemployment fell in 1941, there was the problem of survival. As prices rose and wages were blocked, real incomes fell: in Paris at the end of 1943 they were about half the level of 1939.[133] Quite apart from wage levels, it was difficult to find food to buy, and many workers started to grow their own. Workers' gardens in the Loire increased tenfold in the period.[134] If workers shunned politics, it was often literally to cultivate their gardens.[135]

The working class received no clear guidance from its former leaders. After the defeat, the pre-war tension between the Belin and Jouhaux factions of the CGT became an open breach. Belin's supporters organized themselves into a new Trade Union Co-ordination Committee (CSC) and created a newspaper, *Au travail*, which defended Belin's policies.[136] There were also trade unionists who opposed the new regime. On 15 November 1940, twelve union leaders, including nine members of the CGT (among them Jouhaux) and three Catholic trade unionists, signed a manifesto reaffirming their commitment to free trade unions and denouncing racist legislation (which few other people did at this stage).

---

[129] Chapman, *State Capitalism and Working Class Radicalism*, 244–5.
[130] P. Fridenson and J.-L. Robert, 'Les Ouvriers dans la France de la Seconde Guerre mondiale', *MS* 158 (1992), 117–147: 145.
[131] Burrin, *La France à l'heure*, 34.
[132] Marcot, 'Résistance et population', 64.
[133] Fridenson and Robert, 'Les Ouvriers dans la France', 130–1.
[134] Le Crom, *Syndicats nous voilà*, 328.
[135] J.-M. Guillon, 'Y-a-t-il un comportement ouvrier spécifique? Les Ouvriers varois', in Peschanski and Robert (eds.), *Les Ouvriers*, 469–76: 469–70.
[136] Le Crom, *Syndicats nous voilà*, 211–12.

They constituted themselves as the Committee of Social and Economic Studies (CEES). Their manifesto was a marker for the future, and most of its signatories ended up in the Resistance.

Although national trade-union confederations had been outlawed in November 1940, trade unions were allowed to continue a regional and departmental existence. Many trade unionists participated in Vichyite bodies like the Workers' Committee of Emergency Aid (COSI), which was set up to assist the victims of Allied bombing (with funds taken from Jews), the Secours national, the Committee for the Reinsertion of POWS, and various boards administering the *relève*. Of the thirty-five former *confédérés* elected to the Executive Committee of the CGT in 1938, fourteen are known to have played a role in the institutions of the regime, as did at least sixteen leaders of the thirty-one union federations. Their motives were varied. Union leaders from the former pacifist and anti-Communist wing of the CGT may genuinely have supported the regime, whose Labour Minister up to April 1942 had after all been deputy leader of the CGT in the 1930s. Syndicalists had never considered the political form of the State to be important: their duty was to defend workers within existing political structures. Some may even have seen the Charter as a step towards the depoliticized producers' society of which they dreamed. Even the CEES, which opposed the Labour Charter, did not propose a total boycott of its institutions.[137]

The technicalities of implementing the Charter were so complex that by 1944 the creation of the single syndicates had made only limited progress. As for the factory social committees prescribed by the Charter, 372 of these had been formed by January 1942, 4,644 a year later, 7,807 in January 1944. These committees were useful in organizing food supplies, creating workers' gardens, and organizing leisure activities, but most workers showed no interest in them. Even where the committees were elected, which was not obligatorily the case, few workers participated. Those trade-union leaders who rallied actively to the regime found little response from their members. Even *L'Atelier* noted in 1942 the 'scepticism, indifference or hostility' of most workers to the Charter.[138]

What about the working class and the Germans? By 1944 there were about 660,000 workers in Germany. Most of them were not there voluntarily but as a result of STO. Before the introduction of STO, about 150,000 workers had volunteered to work in Germany (many of them on short contracts so that the number in Germany at any one moment never exceeded 75,000). Another 35,000 had volunteered under the *relève* scheme. This gives a total of about 185,000 volunteers (less, as a proportion of the workforce, than the number of volunteers

[137] Ibid. 185–256; J. Rancière, 'De Pelloutier à Hitler: Syndicalisme et collaboration', *Les Révoltes logiques*, 4 (1971), 23–61.

[138] Le Crom, *Syndicats nous voilà*, 308–36; J.-M. Guillon, 'Le Syndicalisme ouvrier varois de l'effondrement à l'apogée (1939–1944)', *MS* 158 (1992), 50–1; Chapman, *State Capitalism and Working Class Radicalism*, 249; Luirard, *La Région stéphanoise*, 372–84; Rancière, 'De Pelloutier à Hitler', 42.

from Belgium, Holland, or Denmark).[139] These volunteers were motivated less by politics than the prospect of higher wages and reports of good working conditions. Nor was it necessarily politics which prevented others going: workers were not so much put off by working for Germany as by doing so if this involved travelling abroad. In the Breton *département* of Morbihan, there were 370 volunteers to work in Germany, but 3,000 others worked for the Todt Company in France (on constructing the Atlantic wall).[140] Todt, which paid up to three times higher than French firms, had no problem in recruiting labour.

Given that most of French industry was producing for Germany, it was impossible for workers not to find themselves producing for the German war economy. Sometimes workers tried to slow down production, and there were even cases of sabotage. In the spring of 1942, productivity at Renault was 40 per cent lower than in September 1939; the same was true in the coal mines. Since both these industries worked extensively for the Germans, this could have been a kind of resistance, but it could also have been a result of undernourishment and fatigue.[141] In the mines, factory inspectors reported that the workers seemed worn out; cases of fainting were more numerous than before the war.[142] Absenteeism was also higher because workers spent time on their gardens.

When industrial action did occur in the first two years of occupation, it did not necessarily have a patriotic motivation. The most important strike of the Occupation, involving up to 80 per cent of the labour force, took place in the mines of the Nord/Pas-de-Calais between 27 May and 9 June 1941. The Communists later celebrated this strike as one of the bravest examples of working-class resistance. There is no doubt that this was an exceptionally anti-German region. On 11 November 1940, about a third of the Pas-de-Calais miners demonstrated their patriotism by not turning up to work, and were punished by a fine from the Germans. But apart from this incident, the social tension that had been simmering in the coalfields since the autumn of 1940 had little to do with the Germans. The miners were angry about falling real wages and by the fact that the coal-owners, exacting their final revenge on the Popular Front, had reimposed the hated Bedaux system which had been abolished in 1936.

Working-class militancy was directed against employers, not against the Germans, who tried to keep out of the conflict. The Communists, whose role in fomenting the strikes was important, were not yet pursuing an anti-German line. Indeed workers' representatives tried appealing to the Germans to intervene on their behalf. The Germans relished the opportunity to play employer off

[139] Burrin, *La France à l'heure*, 289. R. Handourtzel, 'Pourquoi ont-ils choisi la Relève?', in Peschanski and Robert (eds.), *Les Ouvriers*, 477–82, gives a figure of 185,000 volunteers between the start of 1941 and Sept. 1942 of whom 30,00 under the auspices of the *relève*.
[140] Ory, *Les Collaborateurs*, 44.
[141] Fridenson and Robert, 'Les Ouvriers dans la France', 142.
[142] Peschanski and Robert (eds.), *Les Ouvriers*, 124.

against worker. On one occasion, the local German commander ordered an increase in the number of workers' delegates in the mines although the prefect warned him this would let in 'extremists' eliminated in 1938. But German tolerance of working-class activism soon started to wear thin because it disrupted production. During the strike itself, the Germans worked closely with the employers and local French authorities: about 325 miners were arrested, and cafés and cinemas were closed. In this way, the Germans helped turn what had started out as a social conflict into a patriotic one.[143]

In the end, it was impossible for most employers or workers to avoid some degree of implication in the German war economy unless they wished to go out of business or find themselves unemployed. It is necessary now, however, to turn to one professional group that did enjoy a greater freedom of manoeuvre: artists, entertainers, and intellectuals. No one forced writers to publish or intellectuals to take up public positions: when they did so the impact was all the greater.

[143] E. Dejonghe and Y. Le Maner, 'Un bastion au Nord', in Rioux, Prost, Azéma (eds.), *Les Communistes français de Munich à Chateaubriant*, 249–65; L. Taylor, *Between Resistance and Collaboration: Popular Protest in Northern France, 1940–1945* (New York, 2000), 72–80.

13

Intellectuals, Artists, and Entertainers

'When M. Montherlant went to receptions at the German Institute, he consented to Auschwitz', wrote the Communist writer Claude Morgan in 1945.[1] Although this remark was an extreme assertion of the responsibility of intellectuals, the prestige attaching to intellectuals in France did invest their actions with huge significance. The trials of intellectuals at the Liberation attracted as much publicity as those of Pétain and Laval: they were punished more for who they were than what they had done.

The surest way to avoid compromising oneself was to go abroad. This was a real possibility for artists and intellectuals, many of whom had foreign contacts. American institutions like the Rockefeller Foundation provided grants and organized visas. From New York, the biologist Louis Rapkine organized the departure of French scientists who wished to leave. The most important initiative of this kind was the Emergency Rescue Committee (ERC), a privately funded American organization set up immediately after France's defeat, and run from Marseilles by a young Harvard classicist called Varian Fry.

Despite limited funds, and harassment by the French authorities, the ERC helped some 1,500 people to escape, including Hannah Arendt, André Masson, André Breton, Max Ernst, and Heinrich Mann. Some sailed from Marseilles after visas, legal or forged, had been obtained for them; others were smuggled across the Spanish border. Some had to be persuaded to leave. Marc Chagall was slow to accept that his French citizenship would not protect him from anti-Semitism. He left in March 1941, having been reassured by Fry that there were cows in the United States. Fry was eventually expelled from France in August 1941, but his assistant, David Bénédite, continued the rescue work for a few more months. The ERC's last 'client' was Marcel Duchamp who sailed from Marseilles in May 1942.[2]

---

[1] Verdès-Leroux, *Refus et violences*, 399.

[2] V. Fry, *Surrender on Demand* (New York, 1945); I. Guenther, 'Emergency Rescue Committee', in B. Gordon (ed.), *Historical Dictionary of World War Two France: The Occupation, Vichy and the Resistance, 1938–1946* (Westport, Conn., 1998), 119–20; D. Bénédite, *La Filière marseillaise* (1984).

A considerable number of French artists and intellectuals did choose exile. They included the film directors Jean Renoir, René Clair, Julien Duvivier, and Max Ophuls; the actors and actresses Michèle Morgan, Jean Gabin, Louis Jouvet, Françoise Rosay, and Jean-Pierre Aumont; the aritsts Marc Chagall, Tanguy, Man Ray, Amédée Ozenfant, Jacques Lipchitz, and Fernand Léger; the writers André Breton, Saint-John Perse, Georges Bernanos, Julien Green, Jules Romains, André Maurois, Antoine de Saint-Exupéry, and Jacques Maritain; the journalists Geneviève Tabouis, André Géraud (Pertinax), and Emile Buré; and academics like the biologist Louis Rapkine, the physicist Francis Perrin, the physiologist Henri Laugier, the historian Gustave Cohen, the anthropologist Claude Lévi-Strauss, and the philosopher Raymond Aron. Most of them ended up in America: Greenwich Village became a sort of Manhattan Montparnasse.[3] But there were entirely respectable reasons not to go abroad. Was this not a 'desertion' of France in her greatest hour of need? *L'Université libre*, an underground Resistance paper run by Communist academics in Paris, argued against leaving the cultural field open to the Germans.[4] André Breton's decision to leave for South America in March 1941 was condemned by other surrealists who chose to remain in France. After the war, Tristan Tzara argued that the surrealists who abandoned France had for ever discredited the movement.[5]

Reputations

The post-war reputations of those who stayed in France have often been based more on rumour and innuendo than a balanced assessment of their conduct during the Occupation. Certain reputations never fully recovered from a few endlessly recycled half-truths. Take for example the Catholic poet and play-wright Paul Claudel, whose activity in the Occupation is frequently reduced to two 'facts': that he wrote an 'Ode' to Pétain in 1940 and another one to de Gaulle in 1944. Claudel's diary, however, reveals a more complex story. Certainly he was one of those conservatives without nostalgia for the defunct Republic. He exulted in July 1940: 'France is delivered after sixty years from the yoke of the Radical and anti-Catholic party (teachers, lawyers, Jews and Freemasons).' But the same diary entry showed no indulgence towards the Armistice: 'we have lost all the conditions which constitute independence . . . we have alienated England which represents our only eventual hope'. In November 1940, he was shocked by Cardinal Baudrillart's 'monstrous' article calling for collaboration. Claudel judged Catholics who adopted this position to be 'nauseating in their stupidity and cowardice'. In December, he wrote a long poem entitled *Paroles au Maréchal*

---

[3] Lindenberg, *Les Années souterraines*, 153. On exiles in America see C. Nettlebeck, *Forever French: Exile in the United States 1939–1945* (Oxford, 1991).
[4] Pinault, 'Frédéric Joliot, la science et la société', 292.
[5] R. Belot, *Aux frontières de la liberté* (1998), 22.

(not an ode) which was a patriotic call for France's resurrection under the guidance of Pétain.

On this evidence, Claudel was a Pétainist who opposed collaboration. But he was not a Pétainist like any other. On 24 December 1941, he wrote a letter to the Grand Rabbi, which soon became public, expressing 'the disgust, horror and indignation which all good Frenchmen and especially Catholics feel about the iniquities . . . and ill treatment inflicted on our Israelite compatriots'. No other writer had at this stage so forcibly condemned anti-Semitic persecution; most never did so. During 1941 Claudel became increasingly hostile to Pétain, and his diary contained mocking references to 'our venerated Leader'. He noted how Péguy has been so 'lamentably distorted and deformed' by the National Revolution. It is true that in November 1943 Claudel allowed his play *Le Soulier de satin* to be staged in Paris, but Camus and Sartre also had plays performed in occupied Paris. In August 1942 Claudel refused to allow a production of his play *Protée* without the music of the Jewish Darius Milhaud. On hearing of the American landing in North Africa, he wrote: 'My God I thank you for allowing me to see this hour.'[6]

If Claudel in the Occupation has often been reduced to his 'Ode', Picasso has been reduced to his alleged riposte to Abetz when asked if he was the creator of *Guernica*: 'No, you were'. The story was apocryphal, but Picasso himself later said: 'I used to distribute reproductions of *Guernica* to visiting Germans and say to them "take it, souvenir, souvenir".' Another anecdote claims that Picasso refused a German offer of heating fuel with the words 'a Spaniard is never cold'. On such fragile foundations, after the Liberation, Picasso acquired the reputation of a minor Resistance hero. Was this justified?

After fleeing to the south-west during the Exodus, Picasso had chosen to return to Paris, although he could have escaped to America. He moved his studio to the Left Bank, worked with frenzy, and socialized intensely with a small group of friends, many of whom were involved in the Resistance. No 'messages' can be convincingly read into his work at this time although the shortages of the period are reflected in the materials used for some of his sculptures: cardboard, cigarette boxes, matchboxes, a piece of bread. Speaking later of his decision to remain in France, Picasso told his mistress Françoise Gilot; 'staying on isn't a manifestation of courage; it's just a form of inertia'. But his pro-Republican sympathies during the Spanish civil war, and the fact that Hitler had personally singled him out as a degenerate artist, meant that this 'inertia' was itself quite courageous. As he also remarked to Gilot: 'in a passive sort of way I don't care to yield either to force or terror'. He was not permitted to exhibit, and he was sometimes visited by the German police looking for incriminating evidence. On one occasion, some canvases were slashed. But Picasso also received politely German visitors who wished to see his studio. Among these were Gerhard Heller, who worked

---

[6] See P. Claudel, *Journal*, ii. *1933–1955* (1969), 298–470; Verdès-Leroux, *Refus et violences*, 273–83; G. Antoine, *Paul Claudel ou l'enfer du génie* (1988).

for the literature section of the Propaganda-Abteilung, and the writer Ernest Jünger, who was stationed in Paris. They were not offered postcards of *Guernica*, and Jünger noted in his diary that Picasso told him: 'the two of us sitting here together could work out a peace treaty this very afternoon'.

The photographer Brassaï, who may or may not have known about such visits, was not alone in seeing Picasso's very presence in Paris as an act of courage, a 'comfort and a stimulant'. After the Liberation, Picasso was severe about painters who had compromised themselves, telling one interviewer he hoped Derain would be shot. But although preventing others making claims for him, Picasso was modest. He told one friend: 'There was nothing to do but work and struggle for food, see one's friends quietly, and look forward to the day of freedom.' Calling Picasso a resister is no more helpful than describing Claudel as a collaborator.[7]

Looking back on the Occupation, writers often indulged in minor distortions of the truth to place their conduct in a favourable light. Simone de Beauvoir later said that the first rule of Resistance intellectuals was 'no writing for the Occupied Zone papers',[8] but Sartre published an article in the Paris review *Comoedia*. The novelist Edith Thomas claimed that she had refused to publish during the Occupation, but this 'choice' was helped by Gallimard's rejection of her manuscript in 1942.[9] Distinctions also have to be drawn between the reception of a work and its author's intention. Claude Vermorel's play about Joan of Arc, *Jeanne avec nous*, staged in August 1942, was viewed after the war as a Resistance piece. In fact the play had been written in 1938, and shortly before its staging, Vermorel had been trying to get German approval for a youth theatre project to establish links between German and French theatre. In 1941, he wrote in *Le Gerbe* that the theatre should turn its back on the 'taste for rottenness'. Vermorel's play was approved by collaborationist critics: Rebatet saw his Joan as a possible 'patroness of French fascism.'[10]

It is also necessary, as in the case of Claudel, to distinguish between attitudes towards Vichy and towards the Germans. When Abel Bonnard proposed to his fellow members of the Académie française that they send Pétain a letter of support after Montoire, the idea was blocked by Georges Duhamel and Paul Valéry. What made Bonnard's idea so inopportune was that its timing implied approval of collaboration. Only four academicians were openly pro-German, but most others were ardent Pétainists apart from a small minority of whom Duhamel was the leading light.[11] For these conservative intellectuals, Vichy

---

[7] M. Cone, *Artists under Vichy: A Case of Prejudice and Persecution* (1992), 131–53; Bertrand Dorléac, *L'Art de la défaite*, 190–202.

[8] *Dans le force de l'âge* (1960), 528.

[9] See Dorothy Kaufmann's introd. to E. Thomas, *Le Témoin compromis* (1995), 10.

[10] S. Added, 'Peut-on parler de "théâtre résistant?"', *RHMC* 37 (1990), 128–47; id., *Le Théâtre dans les années Vichy*. See also the case of Anouilh's *Antigone*, M. Witt, 'Fascist Ideology and Theatre under the Occupation: The Case of Anouilh', *Journal of European Studies*, 23 (1993), 47–69.

[11] Hebey, *La Nouvelle Revue française*, 222–3; Sapiro, *La Guerre des écrivains*, 249–315.

represented the chance for revenge on the literary avant-garde represented by the *NRF*. *Le Figaro* launched a debate in August 1940 on the responsibilities of literature for the defeat. One target was Gide, the supposed corrupter of youth, who was attacked by the academician Henry Bordeaux in a book at the end of 1940.[12] In May 1941, members of the Legion in Nice prevented the 'immoral' Gide from delivering a lecture on the poet Henri Michaux. The cartoonist Sennep satirized such attitudes in a caricature of two bemused peasants being told: 'How can you be surprised [about the defeat]; you gorged yourself on Proust, Gide and Cocteau.'[13] Many of the writers interrogated by *Le Figaro* refused to participate in this witch-hunt. No such reticence was displayed by the collaborationist press in Paris. Its favourite target was Mauriac who was vilified in language of extraordinary violence. One paper wrote: 'Mauriac is not Jewish but he deserves to be . . . Everything about him is muddy, false, satanic, degenerate, stinking . . . scrofulous, with the appearance of an over-brimming chamber pot.'[14]

Writers who were the victims of such abuse found it easier to choose their camp. Mauriac wrote of his own case:

> The glorious name of Marshal Pétain resonated for me as for all the French . . . But at the same time I reacted instinctively, without calculating, in the direction of the Resistance—or rather I found myself on that side without even having to choose it: my enemies, much more numerous and virulent than I had imagined, designated my true place for me by their calumnies, from the first day.[15]

Gide was also saved from compromising himself by the attacks to which he was subjected. In Gide's case it had been a close thing, and for a long time he had to struggle against what he called his 'demon of curiosity'. When Gallimard laid siege to him, trying to persuade him to contribute to Drieu's *NRF*, Gide's attitude changed almost daily. Although he contributed to the first and third issues, in April 1940 he attacked Chardonne's notorious article 'Été à Maurie', and announced that he would cease writing for the *NRF*.[16]

Culture under Vichy

The dilemmas facing intellectuals were different in each zone. In February 1941, a group of Communist intellectuals in Paris started a clandestine journal entitled *La Pensée libre*. Its first issue declared: 'Today in France legal literature

---

[12] H. Bordeaux, *Les Murs sont bons: Nos erreurs et nos éspérances* (1940). See also Henri Massis, *Les Idées restent* (1940).

[13] Reprod. in *Le Nouvel Observateur*, 14 June 1980.

[14] W. Babilas, 'La Querelle des mauvais maîtres', in *La Littérature française sous l'Occupation* (1989), 197–226.

[15] G. Sapiro, 'La Raison littéraire: Le Champ littéraire français sous l'Occupation', *Actes de la recherche en sciences sociales*, III/112 (1996), 3–35: 11.

[16] Hebey, *La Nouvelle Revue française*, 48, 153–80.

means: literature of treason.' If this was appropriate for Paris, did it also apply to the South? Not in the opinion of another Communist, Louis Aragon, living near Carcassonne. In September 1940, Aragon published a poem, 'Les Lilas et les roses', in *Le Figaro*. It was reprinted in the collection *Le Crève-Cœur*, published by Gallimard in April 1941. These associations might seem suspect, but Aragon conceived his poem, and others which followed, as a coded form of resistance. He developed the notion of 'contraband' literature which he had formulated during the Phoney War in response to anti-Communist repression. In his poem 'Art poétique', published in August 1942, the lines

> Pour nos amis morts en mai
> Et pour eux seulement désormais
> Que mes rimes aient le charme
> Qu'ont les larmes sur les armes

passed the censor because the 'amis morts en mai' ('the friends who died in May') could be taken to refer to those who had died in the battle of France. But it was the execution of a group of Communist intellectuals in May 1942 which had inspired Aragon's poem. In the essay 'La Leçon de Riberac' (June 1941) Aragon, discussing his experiments with the styles of medieval poetry, invoked the *clus trouver* (the closed art), of the Troubadours which allowed them 'to sing to their ladies in the presence of their Lords'. He argued that contemporary poetry could exploit similar stratagems. Aragon's poems had a great impact, and *Le Crève-Cœur* was reprinted in London in 1942.[17]

Aragon was not the only poet to exploit the possibilities of sending coded messages through legal publication. Openings were available in several avant-garde literary reviews published in the South. Among these were the Marseilles-based periodical *Les Cahiers du Sud*; Max-Pol Fouchet's review *Fontaine*, founded in Algiers in 1939; René Tavernier's *Confluences*, published in Lyons from July 1941; Albert Béguin's *Les Cahiers du Rhône*, published at Neuchâtel in Switzerland but read in France; Pierre Seghers's *Poésie*, started in 1939 under the name *Poètes casquées 39* (Poets under Arms 1939) to publish poets mobilized into the army (the first issue was dedicated to Péguy), and then continued as *Poésie 40*, *Poésie 41*, and so on. Poetry became important in literary resistance because it lent itself to ambiguity. Perhaps also, once open publication became too risky, the move underground was easier for poets accustomed to small readerships of initiates than for novelists accustomed to large audiences and public acclaim.[18]

These avant-garde reviews were not all unambiguously opposed to Vichy. Each had its own individual voice. The July 1940 issue of *Fontaine* declared defiantly 'We are not defeated', while *Confluences* was initially pro-Vichy. In

---

[17] P. Daix, *Aragon: Une vie à changer* (1994), 378–86; P. Seghers, *La Résistance et ses poètes* (1974), 118–20; Aragon's article is repr. in Georges Sadoul, *Aragon* (1967), 72–6.
[18] Sapiro, 'La Raison littéraire', 8.

December 1941, its editor, Tavernier, enthusiastically reviewed an edition of Pétain's speeches. But whatever their stance towards Vichy, these publications all provided a tolerant forum for both established and new poets—Aragon published in *Les Cahiers du Rhône, Confluences, Poésie, Fontaine*—and increasingly they sailed close to the wind of Vichy disapproval. *Confluences* was banned for two months in August 1941 after publishing a poem by Aragon whose message was too transparent.[19] The last poem Aragon published under his own name was 'La Rose et le Réséda' in March 1943. His subsequent writing appeared in clandestine publications.

For two years, however, the free Zone did offer some freedom of manoeuvre. Despite the cultural somnolence of the town of Vichy itself, a surprisingly rich cultural life existed in many cities of the South. The Occupation witnessed an unprecedented cultural decentralization because many Parisian intellectuals who had joined the Exodus decided to stay in the South after the Armistice. One intellectual magnet was Lyons, where many Parisian newspapers—*Le Temps, Le Figaro, Action française*—were now published. Lyons also had a reputation as a centre of Catholic thought, and for that reason several Catholic intellectuals (Mounier, Gabriel Marcel) took refuge there. Marseilles was also culturally vibrant thanks to the presence of so many French and European intellectuals, waiting to escape. Cultural life in Clermont-Ferrand was stimulated by the University of Strasbourg which had moved there after the Armistice. Nice benefited from the proximity of Gide, Malraux, and sometimes Aragon.[20]

Although some degree of cultural diversity was possible in the shadow of Vichy, the official tone of the regime was moralizing, *bien-pensant*, and culturally stifling. Unlike Nazi Germany or Fascist Italy, however, Vichy did not have a prescriptive cultural agenda. There was a project to create an Order of Artists, bestowing professional status and regulating artistic standards. Louis Hautcœur, Secretary General of the Fine Arts Ministry, believed that the decadence of Western art derived from the collapse of the studio system in which artists had been trained up as apprentices. The Order of Artists, by developing a corporatist structure for artists, was conceived as a step towards restoring such a system. But it never advanced beyond the planning stage.[21]

Vichy ultimately lacked the means, the coherence, or the time to develop an artistic policy. Some collaborationists in Paris called for 'art in the service of the National Revolution',[22] and Rebatet denounced the decadence and Jewishness of modern French art (he liked Corot, Renoir, Degas, Rousseau, Utrillo), but the

---

[19] Kedward, *Resistance in Vichy France*, 189–95; Debû-Bridel, *La Résistance intellectuelle*, 80–94.

[20] J.-M. Guiraud, *La Vie intellectuelle et artistique à Marseille à l'époque de Vichy et sous l'Occupation* (Marseilles, 1987); Lindenberg, *Les Années souterraines*, 127–52; G. and J.-R. Ragache, *La Vie quotidiennne des écrivains et des artistes sous l'Occupation* (1989), 93–118.

[21] L. Bertrand Dorléac, 'L'Ordre des artistes et l'utopie corporatiste: Les Tentatives de régir la scène artistique française', *RHMC* 37 (1990), 64–87.

[22] S. Wilson, 'La Vie artistique à Paris sous l'Occupation', in Centre Georges Pompidou, *Paris-Paris 1937–1957* (1992), 163–70.

nearest Vichy got to a 'cultural project' was the promotion of folklore.[23] Pétain's only interest in art was to ensure that portraits sufficiently emphasized the blue of his eyes; Laval's only interest was to use works of art coveted by the Germans as possible bargaining counters in collaboration.

There was no 'Vichy art' except in the sheer proliferation of representations of Pétain. There was a department (Imagerie du Maréchal) to orchestrate images of the Marshal; and another one, the Service artistique du Maréchal, to create an 'art Maréchal'. The Service artistique was run by the ceramicist Robert Lallemant whose own work was influenced by cubism. He recruited his artists eclectically, and his own contributions—a plastic paperweight and a Sèvres vase—were of modernist inspiration. If there was a Vichy style, it was embodied in Gérard Ambroselli's album on the life of Pétain, produced for the Imagerie du Maréchal. Using the folkloric style of the Image d'Épinal woodcuts, Ambroselli transformed Pétain's life into the simplicity of a fairy story: content and style fused perfectly.[24]

German Ambiguities

What was life like for intellectuals in the Occupied Zone? In two respects, the Germans' attitude to French cultural production was uncompromisingly repressive: they banned any manifestation of anti-German sentiment and eliminated any Jewish presence. Plays written or even translated by Jews were banned from the stage. From September 1940, publishers had to respect the so-called Otto List containing 1,060 works by Jewish and allegedly anti-German authors including Thomas Mann, Sigmund Freud, Julien Benda, Claudel, de Gaulle, and Malraux. All books on this list had to be destroyed. More extensive lists followed in March 1942 and May 1943. In return for complying with these lists (which only applied in the Occupied Zone), publishers were theoretically free to publish what new works they pleased providing these were not injurious to the Germans. Doubtful cases had to be referred to the German censors. In effect therefore the Germans put the responsibility of censorship upon the French themselves although the freedom of publishers was further constrained from the start of 1942 when the Germans started to use the distribution of paper, which was tightly rationed, as a form of control.

French publishers accepted this dispensation without protest. In most cases they did so without enthusiasm, apart from a few who rallied entirely to the New Order like Robert Denoël who published Céline and a collection of Hitler's speeches. Another enthusiast was Bernard Grasset who returned promptly to Paris after the Exodus. He started a collection called *In Search of France* in which he published such collaborationist luminaries as Abel Bonnard,

[23] Dorléac, *L'Art de la défaite*, 54–8; Cone, *Artists under Vichy*, 20–34.
[24] Dorleac, *L'Art de la défaite*, 112–29; Faure, *Le Projet culturel*, 156–76, reproduces many of the images; Cone, *Artists under Vichy*, 72–81.

Chardonne, Drieu, and Déat. In November 1940 Grasset declared publicly that the Occupation would be 'an opportunity to rediscover the real Frenchness of our being'.[25]

In the visual arts, the Germans banned Jews from exhibiting; Jewish galleries were 'Aryanized' and Jewish collections seized. Many of these works were stored at the Jeu de Paume Museum. Large quantities of booty were taken to Germany, but the effectiveness of the pillage was hampered by rivalries between different German departments. No one was more avaricious than Goering, who pillaged on a Napoleonic scale. In the course of his twenty visits to the Jeu de Paume, he seized ten Renoirs, ten Monets, and even works by artists who breached Nazi canons of correctness, such as the Jewish Pisarro. Those works left over once the Nazi barons had had their pick of the best flooded on to the Parisian art market which was more active during the Occupation than it had been for many years. Some works, however, were considered beyond the pale, and on 27 May 1943 the Germans organized a secret auto-da-fé at the Jeu de Paume, burning paintings by Picasso, Miró, and Ernst.[26]

In other respects, however, German cultural policy in occupied Paris was comparatively relaxed. The Germans pursued the bread and circuses principle that cultural distractions would keep the population happy.[27] Behind this pragmatism, their real attitude to French culture was a schizophrenic mixture of jealousy and contempt: jealousy of France's cultural predominance; contempt at French artistic decadence. Hitler who visited Paris only once, on 23 June 1940, was so in awe of the city, especially the Opéra, that he sometimes mused about razing it to the ground. In the end, he decided that the new Berlin would dwarf Paris in magnificence: Paris could be spared because Germany would do better. The Propaganda-Abteilung's long-term objective was to break French cultural hegemony, but this did not mean imposing Nazi cultural norms in France or revealing to France 'the secrets of Germany's cultural renaissance': Nazi values were not for export.[28] In Nazi eyes, there was no contradiction between permitting France some cultural freedom and wanting to destroy French cultural hegemony. 'What does the spiritual health of the French people matter to us?', Hitler told Speer; 'Let them degenerate!'

Allowing the French to choke on their culture suited those Germans in Paris who admired French culture and were keen for the opportunity to choke on it themselves. These cultural Francophiles were mostly employed at the Embassy, but there were also some, like Heller, working for the Propaganda-Abteilung. In

[25] P. Fouché, L'Édition française sous l'Occupation 1940–1945, i (1987), 19–56, 304–47.

[26] L. Nicholas, The Rape of Europa: The Fate of Europe's Treasures in the Third Reich and the Second World War (1994); H. Feliciano, Le Musée disparu (1995); R. Valland, Le Front de l'art: Défense des collections françaises 1939–1945 (1961).

[27] Added, Le Théâtre dans les années Vichy, 99, 101; Dorléac, L'Art de la défaite, 44, 49.

[28] G. Eismann, 'La Politique culturelle du "Militärbefehlshaber in Frankreich" pendant l'Occupation' (unpublished DEA thesis, Paris-IEP, 1993), 104–5.

1981 Heller published a memoir describing his wartime experiences in Paris: his disillusionment with Nazism, his assistance to French writers in trouble with the authorities, his visits to Picasso's studio. Presenting his book on French television, Heller seduced the public as effectively as he did French writers during the war, but his artfully selective account must be taken with a pinch of salt. Most Germans who displayed a marked affinity for the French were usually noticed and suffered for it by being sent to the eastern front (as happened to Bremer in 1942), or at least recalled to Berlin (as happened to Epting from June 1942 to January 1943). Heller's feat of lasting the entire war in Paris suggests he had not taken that many risks. Certainly he was zealous in applying the anti-Semitic instructions to literature.[29]

Germans like Heller or the writer Ernst Jünger did certainly see themselves as Francophile, but as we have already observed in the cases of Abetz and Siegburg, German 'Francophilia' was often double-edged. It could coexist with an attitude of superiority bordering on contempt: precisely those aspects of France which made her so attractive—her refinement and *douceur de vie*—also condemned her to the second rank.[30] But many French intellectuals were so relieved by the urbanity and admiration displayed by their conquerors (or some of them) that they failed to detect what lay beneath it. German Francophilia salved uneasy French consciences and lulled the unwary. Joliot felt reassured by the presence of his colleague Gentner. Jean Cocteau had a clearer conscience for being able to write in his diary that the Germans he met were people with a 'profound French culture.'[31] Even Claude Mauriac, who felt only antipathy to the Germans and avoided their company, was witness on one occasion to the spell cast by Heller. In February 1943 he found himself unexpectedly at a social gathering where the other guests included two Germans: Heller and a German playright. Although 'stupefied to be shaking hands with one of those officers whose contact I find so repugnant on the metro', he could not deny the 'irresistible charm' of Heller, 'laughing and smiling, witty and friendly'. Heller told him such encounters showed that this 'horrible war hasn't stifled every trace of civilization and humanism'. On the next morning Mauriac noted his sense of shame: 'The champagne and the atmosphere of sympathy and youth made everything too easy. I should not have been there.' He reassured himself with the thought that since the Germans were obviously going to lose the war, his presence could not be interpreted as toadying to them whereas a year earlier he would have left such a gathering as soon as he had seen who was present. Nonetheless, despite his guilt, Mauriac still felt that those present had represented a 'small island of honest men'.[32]

---

[29] G. Heller, *Un allemand à Paris* (1981); G. Loiseaux, *La Littérature de la défaite et de la collaboration* (1984), 470–83, provides a ferocious demolition; Burrin, *La France à l'heure*, 332.

[30] Geiger, *L'Image de la France*, 207–8.   [31] *Journal 1942–1945* (1989), 31, 85.

[32] C. Mauriac, *Bergère ô tour Eiffel* (1985), 222–5.

Glittering Paris: Temptations and Sophistries

For such reasons, the Occupation was a glittering period of Parisian cultural life. The collaborationists compared the cultural openness of Paris favourably with the puritan stuffiness of Vichy. The Vichy authorities believed that German tolerance of pornography in the Occupied Zone jeopardized the task of remoralizing France.[33] So tolerant could the Germans be, that in April 1941 the Propaganda-Abteilung intervened, in the name of 'artistic freedom', to allow the performance in Paris of Cocteau's play *Machine à écrire* which the Vichy government had wanted to ban given the dubious morality of its author.[34] One or two adventurous Paris galleries even showed works by Kandinsky, Léger, Ernst, Klee, Miró, none of whom could be exhibited in Germany.[35]

Over four hundred plays were performed in Paris during the Occupation. Among them were the first plays of Sartre, Camus, and Montherlant, and the first performances of plays by Anouilh, Cocteau, Guitry, Claudel, and Giraudoux. No less striking was the increasing number of theatregoers: rarely had theatre been more brilliant or more popular. The same was true of other arts as well. The number of visitors to galleries was greater than at any time since 1937; 1942 saw the opening of the Museum of Modern Art at the Palais de Tokyo. Culture perhaps offered a refuge from the difficulties of daily life; cinemas and theatres were also a way of keeping warm when fuel was scarce. After the introduction of STO, however, they could be dangerous once the police started carrying out raids to track down *réfractaires*.

If the atmosphere of occupied Paris was surprisingly liberal, this also made it dangerous for the unwary. In this period, enemies could be more useful than friends, as Mauriac and Gide discovered. For those who were not the target of collaborationist attacks, the temptations were legion. First, there was the social temptation: the receptions at the German Institute, the Gallery openings at which one mingled with the Germans, the first nights at the Opéra. The Parisian salons of Florence Gould (where Claude Mauriac had met Heller) and Marie-Louise Bousquet continued through the war, as they did after it: Bousquet's salon was attended by Evelyn Waugh and Nancy Mitford in 1946, as it had been by Ernst Jünger in 1943.[36] The butler at the residence of Baron Robert de Rothschild, now occupied by the German General Hanesse, told Cocteau: 'I am not unhappy working for the Baron, I mean the General, since he receives the same people as the Baron used to.'[37] The 1942–4 social diary of the German *chargé de presse* Schwendemann contained sixty-four French names, ten of them with particles.[38]

---

[33] Baruch, *Servir l'État*, 92.
[34] Added, *Le Théâtre dans les années Vichy*, 43.
[35] Dorléac, *L'Art de la défaite*, 268–9.
[36] R. Griffiths, 'A Certain Idea of France: Ernst Jünger's Paris Diaries', *Journal of European Studies*, 23 (1993), 101–20: 109–10.
[37] Cocteau, *Journal*, 125.   [38] Burrin, *La France à l'heure*, 210.

Jünger's Parisian journal offers a catalogue of the cultural *tout Paris* during the war. We find him meeting the decorator Christian Bérard and the actress Arletty, as well as Gaston Gallimard, Cocteau, Giraudoux, Morand, Jean Marais, Mme Boudot-Lamotte, Florence Gould, the Marquise de Polignac, and, of course, Drieu la Rochelle, Jouhandeau, Fabre-Luce, and Bonnard. He drinks the best Burgundies and champagnes at Pruniers, the Tour d'Argent, Maxims, La Pérouse, and the Ritz. He visits the studios of Picasso and Braque. A fairly typical occasion would be 8 October 1941 when he was invited to lunch by de Brinon. His host, whose wife was Jewish, made remarks about 'Yids' (youpins); the playwright and actor Sacha Guitry made a bad joke about collaboration; Arletty laughed uproariously throughout.[39]

Sacha Guitry, a sort of French (heterosexual) Noel Coward, was a frequent star of such occasions. He made no political statements during the Occupation, and afterwards felt aggrieved to find himself pilloried for doing what he had always done: seeking to be the centre of attention in all circumstances. The same was true of Jean Cocteau. His wartime diary displays staggering political naivety allied to an irresistible compulsion to dazzle, regardless of the context. The naivety was particularly evident in his remarks about Hitler. In July 1942 he wrote that the chance offered by Montoire had been missed because Pétain lacked a sense of imagination worthy of Hitler: 'One does not respond to grand theatre with the reactions of an usherette.' Hearing that after Munich Hitler had proposed that French and German soldiers throw their arms into the Rhine to repudiate war, he regretted that this poetic gesture had been spurned by narrow-minded politicians like Daladier. Cocteau was much taken by the remark made to him by the German sculptor Arno Breker about Hitler's deep artistic sensitivity. Idealizing the artist as a free spirit, Cocteau was conveniently able to pass off his accommodation to circumstances as a grand assertion of artistic integrity: 'one must not let oneself be distracted at any price from serious matters by the dramatic frivolity of the war'.[40] Hearing himself denounced as a collaborator on the BBC, Cocteau was aggrieved at the injustice of the world.

Cocteau cannot be classed as a collaborator in the manner of a Brasillach, a Chardonne, or even a Montherlant. The nearest he came to burning his wings irremediably was his involvement in one of the high spots of cultural collaboration: the exhibition, at the Orangerie, of works by Breker who was Hitler's favourite sculptor. Breker's monumental male nudes conformed perfectly to the Nazi Aryan ideal: Sacha Guitry commented to Cocteau that if the statues had been in a state of erection, it would have been impossible to circulate around the room.[41] What gave the exhibition such significance was the official character conferred on it: Laval invited Breker to lunch; Bonnard made a speech at the opening; the most famous living French sculptor, Aristide Maillol, came specially to Paris for it and declared his admiration for Breker's art. Cocteau's

---

[39] E. Jünger, *Premier journal parisien: Journal II 1941–1943* (1980), 48–9.
[40] *Journal*, 173, 188.   [41] Ibid. 125.

contribution was an article in May 1942 entitled 'Salute to Breker'. Breker was an astute choice to symbolize Franco-German cultural collaboration. Having worked in Paris in the 1920s, he retained many French friends to whom he was now ready to lend assistance. Maillol was grateful to him for intervening to save his young Jewish model Dina Vierny. As Laurence Bertrand Dorléac has noted, France's homage to Breker's studies in virility, and Breker's admiration for the curvaceous female forms of Maillol's sculpture, could be read as a metaphor for collaboration as a whole, an artistic replication, or anticipation, of the respective roles of the two countries in the New Europe.[42]

Playing on the idea of the 'good' Germany of Beethoven, the Germans used music even more systematically than art as an instrument of cultural seduction. The cream of German musicians—von Karajan, Jochum, Kempff, Schwarzkopf—gave concerts in France. The Berlin Staatsoper performed *Tristan und Isolde* in May 1941 (with a French singer as Isolde). The German Institute organized seventy-one concerts between May 1942 and July 1943.[43] There were also visits by German theatrical groups—starting with the Schiller theatre of Berlin in 1941—but the language barrier made these less successful.

Cultural exchanges operated in both directions. Invitations to visit Germany represented a temptation that many found irresistible. If the writers who attended the two literary conferences at Weimar in 1941 and 1942 were already so notorious for their pro-German views that their participation was of limited propaganda value to the Germans, the same was not true of the eight leading film stars who accepted an invitation to Germany in March 1942. They met Goebbels, visited Sans Souci, and attended the Vienna Opera. For German propaganda, this was worth a thousand editorials by Déat. The trip was so successful that another one was planned for the summer. Twenty-one directors or actors were sounded out, and all but four (Jean-Louis Barrault, Madeleine Renaud, Yvonne Printemps, Pierre Fresnay) accepted. The trip never took place because the Germans were furious to discover that the French actor Harry Baur, who had made a film in Germany and met Hitler, was of Jewish origin.[44]

There were other celebrated visitors to Germany. The pianist Alfred Cortot— an ardent Pétainist and member of the Conseil National—gave concerts there. French musicians—including Jacques Rouché, director of the Opéra, and the composer Arthur Honegger—attended a Mozart festival in Vienna in December 1941. The dancer Serge Lifar paid frequent visits to Berlin.[45] But the most notorious cultural tour to Germany was made in October 1941 by thirteen leading French sculptors and artists, including Derain, Maurice de Vlaminck, Cornelis van Dongen, and André Dunoyer de Segonzac. Their motivations were mixed: the promise of getting some POWs released, the desire to keep the banner

[42] *L'Art de la défaite*, 104–6.   [43] Burrin, *La France à l'heure*, 302.

[44] Thalmann, *La Mise au pas*, 212.

[45] Ragache, *La Vie quotidiennne des artistes*, 156–61; Burrin, *La France à l'heure*, 35–6, 346.

of French art flying, even simple curiosity. Most of them had hoped the visit would be a discreet affair, but the Germans made sure of the opposite. Setting off from the Gare de l'Est, the painters were greeted by a barrage of cameras. Some were chastened by the affair; the more credulous, like Dunoyer, declared themselves impressed at the interest shown in art by the Nazis. For Vlaminck, the visit had more conscious political overtones. As a repentant Fauve, he had written an article in 1942 attacking Picasso as a painter of 'impotence and death'.[46]

Several popular French singers—Maurice Chevalier, Edith Piaf, Charles Trenet—went to Germany not at the invitation of the Germans, but to sing for French prisoners of war or volunteer workers in Germany. Piaf subsequently said that she had smuggled in some false identity cards; Chevalier said that he had sung on condition that his visit would be given no publicity and that ten prisoners would be released. Even if such claims were true—which they often were—the Germans could not be prevented from exploiting such trips for their propaganda purposes. As a result, Chevalier was listed in *Life* magazine in August 1942 as a collaborator. Although he had made ardently pro-Pétainist remarks, Chevalier was understandably upset that what he genuinely perceived as a humanitarian visit to Germany should cause him to be singled out in this way. The moral was that the only way to avoid compromising oneself was to abstain from any public gestures.[47]

For writers this meant refusing to publish. The few writers who followed this policy were Guéhenno, Tristan Tzara, Malraux, Roger Martin du Gard, André Chamson, and the poet René Char. Their silence was a positive choice. Char, who fought in the armed Resistance, refused to publish until the Liberation. He later wrote that during the Occupation the poet could only 'complete the sense of his message by the refusal of himself'. Similarly, when Seghers invited the poet René Lacôte to contribute to *Poésie*, the reply was: 'I've read your letter and honestly I couldn't be less sympathetic. My literary attitude under current circumstances can only be expressed by silence.'[48] The Breton writer Louis Guilloux was more cynical: 'the big question is to work out what least serves the interests of the occupier: to speak or remain silent. In reality, the occupier couldn't care less.'[49]

Silence was perhaps easier for an obscure poet like Lacôte than for writers in great demand. As Guéhenno noted: 'the man of letters is not one of the most impressive species on earth . . . He would sell his soul so that he can *appear*.' In his opinion, Montherlant's 'worst fault is undoubtedly never to be able to keep quiet'.[50] Montherlant's own view was that 'I preferred to risk writing stupidities

---

[46] Dorléac, *L'Art de la défaite*, 74–83, 187–190, 211–16; Cone, *Artists under Vichy*, 65–72.
[47] E. Behr, *Thank Heaven for Little Girls: The True Story of Maurice Chevalier* (1993).
[48] R. Scharfman, 'The Honour of Poets', in D. Hollier (ed.), *A New History of French Literature* (1994), 948–53: 951.
[49] Hebey, *La Nouvelle Revue française*, 67.   [50] *Journal des années noires*, 80.

than risk an abstention which could have been interpreted as indifference'. The risk was easier to take when Montherlant could command 2,000 francs for a newspaper article and over 3,000 francs for a radio talk. His journalistic earnings in the Occupation were over 140,000 francs.[51] On the other hand, it was easier for Guéhenno to take a moral stand because, as a teacher, he did not need to write to earn his living.

Even Mauriac, who in October 1942 summoned writers to accept 'the trial of silence', had not always observed this rule himself. Mauriac was the only member of the Académie to participate in the literary resistance, but he took time to find his way. The one article he contributed to the press of the Occupied Zone—to a local newspaper in December 1940—was trivial. More compromising was the visit Mauriac paid to Epting in February 1941 to secure German authorization for the publication of his novel *La Pharisienne*. He told his wife: 'They made me a little speech on tomorrow's Europe which I listened to almost in silence. I understood that they would not cause me problems.' He saw the visit as 'a simple *démarche* which commits me to nothing, although clearly it does have significance'. Even after Mauriac had obtained German authorization, his collaborationist enemies had the print run limited to 5,000 copies. Mauriac therefore went to see Heller on 13 May 1941 and got the restriction lifted. In four months, 35,000 copies of the novel were sold. Mauriac sent personally dedicated copies to Heller and Epting as a token of gratitude. After the war Mauriac's enemies periodically resuscitated this affair to discredit him. Mauriac recognized that he had made an error of judgement although he had refused Heller's request to declare his support for collaboration. He never set foot in the Institute again. In June 1941, he refused a dinner invitation from Morand because 'the gentlemen of the Institute will be there'.[52]

The problem with publishing anything was that compromises were almost inevitable. To secure publication of his *Myth of Sysiphus* in 1943, the rising literary star Albert Camus had to remove references to Kafka whose Jewishness made him an unacceptable authority to quote. Before publishing Aragon's novel *Les Voyageurs de l'impériale*, Gallimard insisted on cuts to satisfy the censor. Aragon accepted this, but when the novel appeared in December 1942, it had been so disfigured that there was even a passage which made it appear that Dreyfus had been guilty. In fact, Aragon had not seen the corrections which were made by Gallimard himself. The book was soon withdrawn from circulation, but the affair demonstrated the need for vigilance.[53]

Some writers in Paris claimed, like those in the South, that their work contained coded resistance messages. It was later useful to Montherlant that the line

[51] Sapiro, 'La Raison littéraire', 29.

[52] Hebey, *La Nouvelle Revue française*, 199–203; Touzot, *Mauriac sous l'Occupation*, 29–35, 105–20.

[53] M. Apel-Muller, 'L'Édition de 1942 des *Voyageurs de l'impériale*: Une entreprise "diabolique"', *Recherches croisées Aragon/Elsa Triolet* (1988), 167–208.

'En prison se trouve la fine fleur du royaume' in his play *La Reine morte*, performed at the Comédie-Française in 1942, should be interpreted as a criticism
of the Germans. Given Montherlant's political statements at this time, the interpretation was patently absurd. But what about Sartre's play *Les Mouches*, his
version of the Orestes/Agamemnon legend, which was first staged in 1943? The
play might deserve the resistance interpretation Sartre later claimed for it—'why
write about the Greeks', he said, 'unless to disguise one's thoughts under a fascist
regime?'—but if one was not attuned to his philosophical language, the message
was thickly disguised. It was not picked up by the collaborationist Paris critics
who were always on the lookout for political dissidence. Indeed they even offered
a Nazi reading of the play, interpreting Orestes as a sort of Nietzschean super-
man pitted against Jupiter as tyrannical rabbi. What, then, was the value of a
resistance message that was so oblique as to be invisible to all but a few initiates? Did it not matter more that the theatre in which the play was performed,
originally the Théâtre Sarah Bernhardt, had been renamed 'Théâtre de la Cité',
owing to anti-Semitism, or that Charles Dullin, the director, was viewed
favourably by the Propaganda-Abteilung? Can the message be so easily separated
from this context?[54]

Context could transform the implications of the most anodyne literary efforts.
Joliot gave an interview to the collaborationist *Notre temps* about the need to
reform the teaching of French science. This may have been innocent or naive;
it was certainly unwise. Was it ever innocent to write purely literary and unpolitical texts if they appeared in collaborationist journals like *La Gerbe*? Cocteau
wrote in *La Gerbe*, Anouilh in both *La Gerbe* and *Je suis partout*. When Drieu
became disillusioned with running the *NRF*, he took solace in the fact that he
had at least caused some writers to compromise themselves.[55] The risk of guilt
by association was particularly insidious in the case of the cultural magazine
Comoedia, launched in 1941. *Comoedia* was soon attracting the cream of literary
Paris much more successfully than the *NRF*. Contributors included Cocteau,
Colette, Paul Valéry, Claudel, and Jean-Louis Barrault. It was here that Cocteau
published his homage to Breker.

Comoedia contained nothing directly political, but every issue carried a page
on 'European' culture. This was not an innocent Europe: it meant primarily
Germany (Bayreuth, Mozart, 'contemporary German poetry') but also Italy,
Hungary, Romania, Slovakia, and Croatia. The European page was under the
control of the German Institute (although it was not always viewed favourably
by the Propaganda-Abteilung).[56] Mauriac, who was invited to contribute,
wrote to Duhamel in June 1941: 'it is quite tempting and all the names are

[54] I. Galster, *Le Théâtre de Jean-Paul Sartre devant ses premiers critiques* (1986), 501–92; Added, *Le Théâtre dans les années Vichy*, 257–73.

[55] Hebey, *La Nouvelle Revue française*, 69.

[56] Verdès-Leroux, *Refus et violences*, 218; Eismann, 'La Politique culturelle', 29.

acceptable . . . it would be good to be able to express oneself sometimes on the literary front . . . What do you think?' In the end he decided against.[57] But not everyone was so cautious. The first issue contained Jean-Louis Barrault, Arthur Honegger, Jean-Paul Sartre (on *Moby Dick*)—and also Henry de Montherlant. Was the proximity of Montherlant sufficient to compromise those who appeared besides him? Was the European cultural orientation of the magazine not a form of 'soft' collaboration? Whether it was acceptable to contribute to *Comoedia* continued to exercise many writers who had no doubts that it would not be acceptable to write for the *NRF*.[58] The answer was not obvious. It was after all the Jewish journalist Joseph Biélinky who noted in his diary in December 1941: 'we regularly read *Comoedia*, the only paper in Paris which does not insult the Jews'.[59]

How far could one push the argument of contamination by context? Was it wrong for Aragon to publish with Gallimard, who also published the *NRF*, or for his wife Elsa to publish a novel with Denoël, who also published Céline and Rebatet? One writer whose rejection of the argument of guilt by association has to be taken seriously was Jean Paulhan, because in his case there is no suspicion of special pleading. Editor of the *NRF* before 1940, he had been involved since August 1940 in the first resistance group to emerge in Paris. The group was broken by the Germans and Paulhan arrested in March 1941. In the nick of time, he threw into the Seine the stencil machine on which the group produced its newspaper. He spent a week in prison, but was released thanks to the intervention of Drieu. Paulhan went on to play a pivotal role in organizing resistance among writers, but none of this stopped him encouraging writers to contribute to the *NRF*, or even himself contributing to *Comoedia* in 1943. Paulhan's processes of thought were famously subtle, but his position seems to have been that everybody was 'terribly responsible' for what they wrote—he judged Chardonne to be 'abject'—but not for what others wrote alongside them.[60] For this reason, after the war he denounced the excesses in the purge of intellectuals.

Continuing France

Those who wished to continue publishing frequently employed the defence that any assertion of the vitality of French culture was a sort of resistance. This was the sense of Matisse's comment in September 1940: 'If everyone of any value leaves France, what remains of France?'[61] An eloquent statement of this case appeared in Sacha Guitry's film *Donne-moi tes yeux* (1943). The film

---

[57] Touzot, *Mauriac sous l'Occupation*, 77.   [58] Grenier, *Sous l'Occupation*, 284, 286.
[59] *Journal 1940–1942*, 174, 230.
[60] Hebey, *La Nouvelle Revue française*, 73–9, 139–40; F. Badré, *Paulhan le juste* (1996), 182–95; Paulhan, *Choix de lettres*, 209.
[61] Cone, *Artists under Vichy*, 51.

opens with two friends visiting a gallery. One of them points out some works painted in 1871 (Monet, Renoir) and then some contemporary French paintings (Utrillo, Derain). He comments:

> And so in 1943 it goes on. France continues . . . This is what men of genius could do at a moment when France had just lost the war . . . Before these marvels one has the impression that what was lost on one side has been regained on the other . . . One has the right to consider these works as substitutes for victories.

This position was somewhat undermined by the relative cultural open-mindedness of the Germans in Paris. In May 1941, there was an exhibition of the rising generation of young painters—'Young Painters in the French Tradition'—presented by its organizer Jean Bazaine as an assertion of the French spirit in the face of adversity. He proclaimed the need to display a 'certain taste for risk' since 'our military defeat should not by extension be seen as the general rout of all the best that our civilization has given'. But the German authorities, having visiting the exhibition, found no quarrel with it; and the only satisfaction came from the attacks of the collaborationist press.[62]

Whether compromise was legitimate as a means of preserving a 'French' voice was the burden of the discussion between the historians Marc Bloch and Lucien Febvre over the future of *Annales*, the journal they had founded in 1929. From the autumn of 1940, Febvre was in Paris; Bloch, one of the few Jews exempted from Vichy's law banning Jews from education, was teaching in Montpellier. Febvre wished to continue producing *Annales* from Paris, but this meant that Bloch's name would have to disappear. Since they were co-proprietors, Bloch's approval was necessary. Bloch preferred to suspend publication or to move *Annales* to the Unoccupied Zone. He wrote to Febvre: 'If our work has had any meaning at all, it has been in its independence, its refusal to accept the pressure of what Péguy . . . called the "temporal" . . . The suppression of my name would be an abdication.'

To Bloch's arguments of principle, Febvre opposed arguments of expediency: the death of *Annales* would be another victory for those who wished to crush the spirit of France, 'another death for my [*sic*] country'. To publish in the South would cut the journal off from most of its readers. To publish in the North required some compromises to be made: '[we must] roll up our sleeves, take heart, and shout: "save what can be saved". One name on the cover? So what? It's the enterprise that counts . . . Maintain it. Let's swim till the water's in our mouth. And fight.' After two months, Bloch finally conceded.

Febvre's position has recently been criticized by Philippe Burrin. Certainly Febvre displayed tactless insensitivity in presenting his arguments, seeming more irritated at the problems Bloch's Jewishness was causing than outraged at the legislation which made it a problem. But, as Peter Schöttler points out, one can

---

[62] Dorléac, *L'Art de la défaite*, 217–23; Cone, *Artists under Vichy*, 40–5.

be too alert to potential slights: Burrin's criticism of Febvre's reference to 'my' country is misplaced since Febvre used the same formulation to his own children. This was less a conflict between an opportunistic Febvre and a noble Bloch than a painful dialogue between two intellectuals sharing similar values, but divided about how to remain faithful to them. Bloch continued contributing to the journal under a pseudonym until resistance activities consumed all his time. In March 1944, he was arrested, tortured, and shot. His continued participation in *Annales* suggests that he did not feel that an unacceptable moral line had been crossed by Febvre. And Febvre's argument that the continuation of *Annales* was a way of 'continuing France' was not merely a rationalization of self-interest. The philosopher Georges Friedmann who, as a Jew, Marxist, and resister, had no reason to display indulgence, wrote to Febvre in 1942 to congratulate him on the recent issue of *Annales*: 'One can already see that you have, in the present conditions, resolved a difficult problem. As far as I am concerned, I disapprove of the publication of certain journals whose editors have paid too dearly . . . But *Annales* serves only the best causes, and its courageous continuity is a comfort to me.' It was, he wrote on another occasion, 'a thread which links me to what we called and continue to call science and culture . . . the continuity of all that is best in France'. The contemporary historian surely has no right to a greater severity of judgement than Friedmann's.[63]

The Cinema: Ambiguities and Paradoxes

'The continuity of all that is best in France': at the Liberation, nowhere was this ideal thought to have been more perfectly exemplified than in the cinema.[64] As the film-maker Abel Gance put it, cinema had carried 'abroad the message of France, the message of a spirit that cannot be vanquished'.[65] Inevitably the truth was more complicated.

Cinema audiences had never been larger: 220 million in 1938, 225 million in 1941, over 300 million in 1943. The film industry, like all others, was forced to establish its own Organization Committee, the COIC. Formed in November 1940, the COIC imposed a long overdue rationalization on an industry close to financial disaster. Many of its reforms, such as the prohibition of double features, were retained at the Liberation, and continue to regulate the French film industry today.[66] It also imposed the elimination of all Jews from the industry.

[63] Burrin, *La France à l'heure*, 322–8; id., 'Fausse querelle autour de Lucien Febvre', *Histoire*, 189 (1995); P. Schöttler, 'Marc Bloch et Lucien Febvre face à l'Allemagne nazie', *Genèses*, 21 (1995), 75–95; N. Z. Davis, 'Rabelais among the Censors 1940s, 1540s', *Representations*, 32 (1990), 1–32; ead., 'Censorship, Silence and Resistance: The *Annales* during the German Occupation of France', *Historical Reflections*, 24/2 (1998), 351–74.

[64] See R. Régent, *Cinéma de France sous l'Occupation* (1948); F. Garçon, 'Ce curieux âge d'or des cinéastes français', in Rioux (ed.), *La Vie culturelle*, 293–313: 297.

[65] E. Ehrlich, *Cinema of Paradox: French Filmmaking under the German Occupation* (New York, 1985), 23.

[66] Jeancolas, *Quinze ans*, 301–3.

Any Jews who worked on films had to do so secretly, like the composer Joseph Kosma and the designer Alexandre Trauner who collaborated on Marcel Carné's film *Les Enfants du Paradis*. In most respects, however, films provided audiences with a reassuring sense of continuity and familiarity. Of the eighty-one film-makers of the Occupation, only nineteen were making their first film, and many of the actors were familiar names from the 1930s, despite some gaps left by those who had escaped abroad, including the two biggest stars of the day, Jean Gabin and Michèle Morgan.

Approximately 220 feature films were made during the Occupation, includ-ing some of the most celebrated French films ever made. This output represented a decline over the pre-war period—120 films had been produced annually in the 1930s—but profits soared. The industry was helped by the virtual elimination of American competition. The gap was partially filled by German films, but, after an initial flurry of curiosity, these never won over French audiences: German films accounted for 5 per cent of those distributed in France in the 1930s, 56 per cent in 1941, 22 per cent in 1943. The commercial success of the French film industry was all the more striking since film-makers had to contend with short-ages of all kinds. While filming the banquet scene of *Les Visiteurs du soir* (1942), Marcel Carné injected the fruit with carbolic acid to prevent the hungry film crews from stealing it.[67]

At first, the Germans did not allow French films to cross the demarcation line. But after February 1941, this restriction was lifted, subject to German approval. This was not a reciprocal arrangement since all films approved by the German censors could be shown in the South. Partly for this reason, film-making came to be concentrated in the North. Although Vichy had hopes of creating big studios in the South, even turning Nice into a French Hollywood, in the end most films were made in the Occupied Zone—thirty-five were made in the South—where the production facilities were better, and the cultural climate less stuffy.

What kinds of films were made? It has often been noted that the films of the Occupation seem to exist in a time capsule. With one or two exceptions—a fleet-ing shot of the car-free streets of occupied Paris (*Falbalas*, 1944), a German soldier in an art gallery (*Donne-moi tes yeux*, 1943)—one could view most of these films without realizing that they were made while France was occupied. On the other hand, the themes of the National Revolution were omnipresent in films. The greatest commercial success of the period was *La Voile bleue* (1942), a tear-jerking melodrama which tells the story of a young woman who loses her husband and only child in the First World War. Refusing to remarry, she spends the rest of her life as a governess bringing up other people's children, moving on to a new family when they grow up. At the end, when she is an old lady, all her former 'children' reunite around her at Christmas. The Vichyite resonance of this

---

[67] E. Turk, *Child of Paradise: Marcel Carné and the Golden Age of French Cinema* (1989), 189.

celebration of motherhood—in this case surrogate motherhood—is obvious. So is that of *Monsieur de Lourdines* (1943) whose main protagonist is a young man, bored with country life, who goes to Paris, abandoning his landowning parents. In the frivolity of Paris, he squanders their fortune, obliging his father to sell his property. Out of grief, his mother falls ill and only when her son returns to her deathbed does he understand the folly of his ways. He stays in the country to rebuild his family estates, ready to respect his father's judgement: 'your role is to replace me here among our peasants'. The film was based on a novel by Alphonse de Chateaubriant.

When a novel did not contain the right message, it could be doctored for the purpose. In the courtroom drama *Les Inconnus dans la maison* (1941), based on a Simenon novel, there is a scene with a lawyer defending a young man who is innocent of the murder for which he is being tried. One of the set pieces of the film is the lawyer's speech, not to be found in the novel, attacking the society which has not been able to provide its young people with healthy distractions:

> Members of the Jury, can you show me the way to the stadium or the swimming pool? . . . No, there is no stadium or swimming pool. There are 132 cafes and bistrots, I have counted them; and four brothels, I have not counted them since all my fellow citizens are only too well aware of them.

There are numerous other examples of films reflecting Vichy values. But the problem with this line of argument is that such themes were also prevalent in the cinema of the 1930s. Paradoxically, many themes that one might expect to have figured more prominently after 1940, almost disappeared from the screen. Before 1940, many French films contained critical portrayals of British characters; after 1940 the British are absent. Before 1940, films had frequently depicted Germans sympathetically; after 1940, despite collaboration, Germans almost disappear from the screen. In the 1930s, antagonism to foreigners had been a frequent theme; after 1940 it was less present. In Vichy cinema there are few depictions of happy families and many of family disintegration. It is hard to imagine a representation of peasants more cynical, selfish, and vicious than *Goupi mains rouges* (1942).[68]

Most surprisingly of all, whereas hostile depictions of Jews had proliferated in the 1930s, they are almost absent after 1940. Thus Pierre Billon's 1943 Balzac adaptation, *Vautrin*, underplayed the Jewishness of the villainous Baron de Nucingen, although the same film-maker had emphasized the Jewishness of the sinister banker Gudermann in his 1936 version of Zola's *L'Argent*.[69] The one Occupation film in which many critics have detected anti-Semitism was *Les*

[68] For this general interpretation, F. Garçon, *De Blum à Pétain: Cinéma et société française 1936–1944* (1984); J.-P. Bertin-Maghit, *Le Cinéma français sous Vichy* (1980) argues, however, for the specificity of Vichy cinema.
[69] Garçon, *De Blum à Pétain*, 172, 183.

Inconnus dans la maison where the murderer is revealed to be a Jew called Luska. But in the film his Jewishness is much less obvious, if at all, than in the novel, where we are told that his first name is Ephraim. Seeing the film today, one is hardly aware of anti-Semitic undercurrents; certainly the collaborationist press did not notice any. Even if the film does deserve its reputation, this would still make it an exception in the cinema of the Occupation.[70]

Perhaps the film acquired its reputation because it was distributed with a short anti-Semitic propaganda film, *Les Corrupteurs*. This coupling was not innocent, and these short documentaries accompanying the main feature should not be overlooked when discussing the Occupation cinema. The banning of double features caused a massive output of documentary shorts. Some 400 documentaries were made, but because most of them have not survived, they remain the hidden face of the Occupation cinema. The available evidence suggests they were fairly anodyne, but not without ideological significance. There were many celebrations of artisanal labour and evocations of medieval Paris. There were also overt propaganda productions ranging from celebration of the Empire to diatribes like *Les Corrupteurs* or the anti-Masonic *Les Forces occultes*. These last two were produced by Nova Films, a German-backed production company. Such films were widely distributed, but it is difficult to know how they were received. It is well recorded that the German propaganda newsreels were unpopular, and the film historian Jacques Siclier, whose memories of the period are vivid, says that the shorts were viewed as the necessary pill which had to be swallowed before the feature.[71]

As far as feature films are concerned, if they reflect anything different from the films of the 1930s, it is Vichy's desperate wish to believe the outside world did not exist. There were many costume dramas (six adaptations of Balzac) and historical reconstructions. Sometimes these historical films lent themselves to contemporary interpretations. The film *Pontcarral, colonel d'Empire* (1942), the story of a Napoleonic army officer who refused to accept the Restoration, was seen as containing a resistance message: it ends with the hero setting out to conquer Algeria and redeem French glory. The film was frequently applauded; 'Pontcarral is Giraud' could be read on walls.[72] But the film's patriotism and celebration of Empire were also in the spirit of Vichy and not liked by the Germans who imposed cuts.

There was also a vogue in the Occupation for fantastical films, with magical or legendary subjects. Celebrated examples of this genre were Marcel Carné's *Les*

[70] This interpretation is followed by Ehrlich, *Cinema of Paradox*, 181–2; Garçon, *De Blum à Pétain*, 50–2; E. Strebel, 'Vichy Cinema and Propaganda', in K. Short (ed.), *Film and Radio Propaganda in World War Two* (1983), 271–89: 283–4 takes a different view, but having recently seen the film, I find her interpretation unconvincing.

[71] J. Siclier, *La France de Pétain et son cinéma* (1981), 35–9; Jeancolas, *Quinze ans*, 342–61; Strebel, 'Vichy Cinema', 275–9; J.-P. Bertin-Maghit, 'Le Documentaire de propagande sons l'Occupation', *VSRH* 63 (1999), 23–50.

[72] Jeancolas, *Quinze ans*, 333.

Visiteurs du soir, the story of the devil's visit to a medieval court, or *L'Éternel retour* (1943), Jean Cocteau's reworking of the Tristan and Isolde legend with Jean Marais in the role of Tristan. These films were characterized by an extreme formality of composition, an icy classicism, which was hailed by many critics as the emergence of a new aesthetic. If the lived-in face of Jean Gabin against an urban background was the icon of 1930s cinema, the equivalent in the 1940s might be the pure features of Jean Marais—'a Breker type' as Cocteau himself admitted—against a timeless mythological setting.[73]

The film critic André Bazin dubbed this the 'cinema of evasion', but other critics have tried to offer allegorical readings. In *Les Visiteurs du soir*, the devil's machinations are thwarted when one of his envoys falls in love with his victim. The devil turns the two lovers to stone, but their hearts go on beating: was this France's heart beating despite the Occupation?[74] Such interpretations need to be treated with a lot of scepticism. Jacques Prévert, who wrote the scenario of *Les Visiteurs du soir*, subsequently disclaimed any allegorical intentions. Jean Delannoy, the director of *L'Éternel retour*, wrote: 'The essential feature of this period was that one tried in the public interest to make people forget about what was dreadful and demeaning about the present . . . why did we make *L'Éternel retour*? Why was *Les Visiteurs du soir* made? Always for the same reason: to try and help people escape from daily life.'[75]

Even if Delannoy's statement is accepted at face value, this does not necessarily render the cinema of evasion entirely apolitical. The aesthetic of such films was strongly approved by collaborationist critics like Rebatet who applauded a return to a pure French style of cinema free of foreign influences. Rebatet described *Les Visiteurs du soir* as a 'delicately chiselled piece of jewellery', although he saw Carné's 1930s films as the epitome of 'Judaized' cinema. When Marcel L'Herbier declared that his fantastical film *La Nuit fantastique* (1941) (also admired by Rebatet) was inspired by Meliès and the origins of French cinema, the comment needs to put in the context of his observation that in the Occupation French film-makers were liberated from the 'climate of cinematic slavery' (i.e. Hollywood and Jews) of the 1930s. Or as another director, Claude Autant-Lara, put it: 'freed from a certain number of parasites . . . French film-makers were able to work for the French people'. In the light of such comments, the new aesthetic represented a kind of stylistic 'retour à l'ordre' which was not politically innocent.[76]

It was later argued that the continued production of high-quality French films was itself an assertion of the vitality of French culture. But was this necessarily

[73] Ehrlich, *Cinema of Paradox*, 93–102; Cocteau, *Journal*, 130.

[74] Turk, *Child of Paradise*, 187–218, offers a long, but unconvincing, allegorical reading.

[75] G. Sims, '*Tristan en chandail* Poetry as Politics in Jean Cocteau's *L'Éternel Retour*', *French Cultural Studies*, 9/25 (1998), 19–50: 31.

[76] The interpretation in this paragraph closely follows Sims, '*Tristan en chandail*'. See Régent, *Cinéma de France*, 70–3, 90–4, for a contemporary view of the new aesthetic. L'Herbier's comment is in M. L'Herbier, *La Tête qui me tourne* (1979), 283.

contrary to German objectives? As usual, the Germans did not speak with one voice. One priority was to keep the French public docile. In May 1942, Goebbels wrote in his diary that the French should only be allowed to make 'light and corny' films which would not 'cultivate their nationalism'; such 'cheap trash' would allow German cinema to dominate. But these remarks were not official policy. The Propaganda-Abteilung also nursed the idea of using French cinema to create a continental film industry which could mount a challenge to the Americans. Conscious of the greater popularity of French over German films, in 1941 the Propaganda Ministry authorized the export of French films to other Axis-controlled countries: France would play the role of entertainer in a Europe where power lay with the Germans.[77]

The instrument of this strategy was the Continental film company. Set up in October 1940, the Continental was a German-owned company making French films. Its director, Alfred Greven, was directly answerable to Goebbels, and his brief was to make commercially successful films, not propaganda.[78] Greven had resources surpassing any French company and this permitted him to sign up leading French actors and directors: Barrault, Pierre Fresnay, Danielle Darrieux, Tino Rossi, Fernandel. Many of those agreeing to work for the Continental may have viewed this as a continuation of their previous 'collaboration' with UFA in the 1930s: in 1939 Fernandel was filming a French-speaking, German-financed film in Berlin; in 1941 he was doing the same for the Continental, this time in France.[79] Nor had the content of the films changed much either. The thirty films made by the Continental covered most genres—American-style comedies, French period reconstructions, police dramas (including *Les Inconnus de la maison*), French comedies (three with Fernandel)—and most spectators had no idea that the company was German.

Another attraction of working for Greven was the fact that his company's German ownership offered greater freedom from censorship than was available to French companies. The only film of the period containing female nakedness was the Continental's *Le Dernier des six*. In the Catholic Church's rating of Occupation films, the two which scored the top disapproval rating ('essentially pernicious') were Continental films; and of the seven which scored the next highest rating ('to be proscribed absolutely'), three were made by the Continental.[80] This was not a machiavellian German plot to lower the moral standards of the French, but a case of film-makers exploiting the artistic freedom which the Continental allowed them. This freedom offered more than the possibility to broach 'immoral' subjects. At least three Continental films had patriotic overtones, even covert resistance messages. This was most explicit in *La Symphonie fantastique*

---

[77] Ehrlich, *Cinema of Paradox*, 148–56.
[78] On Greven, see the different assessments of C. Crisp, *The Classic French Cinema* (1993), 49–50, and Siclier, *La France de Pétain*, 41–8.
[79] Jeancolas, *Quinze ans*, 17.
[80] The list is in Siclier, *La France de Pétain*, 445–57.

(1942), a film about the life of Berlioz (played by Jean-Louis Barrault) in which the nationalism of French romanticism is fully brought out. Goebbels was most displeased by this film which he described as a 'national fanfare.'[81]

If, then, the most French of films were made by a German production company, who was using whom? To work for the Continental was clearly to 'collaborate' in some sense. But what if the outcome was to keep French cinema alive, and even allow a patriotic voice to be heard? On the other hand, if the German aim was to allow high-quality films to be made in France as part of a European strategy, was the production of 'good' French films less a subversion of German aims than a fulfilment of them?

Nowhere are the ambiguities of Occupation cinema more evident than in the critical reception of two films of the period: Jean Grémillon's *Le Ciel est à vous* (1944) and Henri-Georges Clouzot's *Le Corbeau* (1943). *Le Ciel est à vous* is the story of a modest provincial couple, Thérèse and Pierre Gauthier (Madeleine Renaud and Charles Vanel), who sacrifice everything so that Thérèse can break a flying record. How the spectator is supposed to judge their obsession is not always clear. In some scenes the couple display quite extraordinary selfishness towards their two children. When they set off to the flying contest, the children are left alone with no one to look after them. One does not need to be a Pétainist to wonder if family responsibility is not being unduly neglected. Yet when the Gauthiers solicit funds from a board of middle-aged bourgeois worthies—classic Vichy *notables*—and are refused partly on the ground that the woman's place is in the home, it is clear that we being asked to sympathize with them in their struggle against mediocrity.

The contradiction between family and ambition is resolved when Thérèse arrives in the desert at the end of her flight. Her first thoughts are for her family, and she follows this by complaining, as a good housewife, that the soldiers welcoming her are unable to make a proper cup of tea: adventure is reconciled with domesticity. But it has been a close thing, and the film ends, as it had opened, with children from the local orphanage being led obediently through the streets by a priest. Are they an accusatory reminder of the risk to which Thérèse has subjected her children or an image of the stifling provincial life against which she has valiantly reacted?

Grémillon was someone of left-wing sympathies, a member of a clandestine Resistance organization of film-makers, whose previous film, *Lumière d'été* (1942), offers a heroic vision of the working class which would not have seemed out of place in 1936, and was almost banned by Vichy. The title *Le Ciel est à vous* had surprising resonances for an Occupation film: the film which Renoir had made for the Communist election campaign in 1936 was called *La Vie est à nous*, and the promotion of aviation as a popular sport had been one of the ambitions of the Popular Front. But *Le Ciel est à vous* was received ecstatically by both the

---

[81] Ehrlich, *Cinema of Paradox*, 53–4.

Vichyite and collaborationist press; there was a special showing for Pétain. It was described as the best film since the Armistice, exuding 'moral health', a film about what ordinary French people could achieve, an 'exalting and moving work . . . showing the role of the wife in the home and the beauty of the family'. The film, however, was no less applauded by the underground Resistance press. The Resistance reading of the film was helped by the final scene showing Thérèse arriving home to be greeted by a crowd waving French flags. In *Confluences*, the Communist critic Georges Sadoul described Gauthier as a modern d'Artagnan. In general, the terms in which the Resistance described the film were remarkably similar to those of the Vichy press: it 'salvaged the honour of the French cinema'; its characters were brimming with 'French sap' and moral health; Thérèse was a 'young French mother, modest and strong, who carries out without grandiloquence all her duties and whose heart is also vast enough to conceive a heroic dream'.[82]

The only similarity between *Le Ciel est à vous* and *Le Corbeau* was the unanimity of response they elicited—in the case of *Le Corbeau*, a unanimity of rejection. Produced by the Continental, *Le Corbeau* tells the story of a small provincial town afflicted by an outbreak of anonymous letters of denunciation signed 'The Crow'. One letter accuses the doctor (Pierre Fresnay) of being an abortionist; another tells a hospital patient that he is dying of cancer: in despair he cuts his throat with a razor. Other characters include a nurse who steals morphine for her former fiancé; and her sexually frustrated sister who tries to blame the letters on an innocent woman of whom she is jealous. These are hardly Vichy's images of ideal womanhood. Even the children in the film seem malevolent. If there is a hero, it is the abortionist doctor; if there is a heroine, it is a sexually lubricious cripple who is first seen in bed, smoking, and painting her toenails. She alone refuses to participate in the lynch mob (including the priest) which drives an innocent woman out of the town believing her to be the Crow.

The film was based on an incident which had occurred at Tulle in 1922, but the stifling atmosphere of the rotten little community could stand as a metaphor for occupied France: the theme of delation could hardly have been more contemporary. This was not a picture of healthy provincial life as Vichy conceived it, and it is not surprising that the film was criticized by the Vichy press for traducing all the icons of the National Revolution. Nor was the film ever released in Germany: it was judged it to be morbid, and the authorities could not approve a film that implicitly criticized delation. But criticisms in the Resistance press were no less strident: it vilified the film for portraying such a debased image of France. At the Liberation, anyone involved in the film was under suspicion. The Resistance press explicitly contrasted *Le Corbeau* with *Le Ciel est à vous* whose

[82] J. Semple, 'Ambiguities in the Film *Le Ciel est à vous*', in Kedward and Austin (eds.), *Vichy France*, 123–32; Jeancolas, *Quinze ans*, 331–2; O. Barrot, *L'Écran français 1943–1953: Histoire d'un journal et d'une époque* (1979), 13–15; Siclier, *La France de Pétain*, 202–7.

morally exalting characters were so removed from the 'club-footed tart' and the 'hypocritical and criminal doctor'.[83]

While *Le Ciel est à vous* showed the Resistance and Vichy to be competing up to a point for shared ground, *Le Corbeau*, simultaneously disapproved of by the Resistance, Vichy, and the Germans, was disconcerting because it offered no simple answers. It contains one scene that could serve as a commentary on the entire experience of occupied France. A seemingly respectable psychiatrist, who in the end turns out to be the Crow, gives a lesson on morality to the doctor:

The psychiatrist: 'You think that all people are good or evil [he grasps a hanging light which casts a pool of light in the otherwise dark room]. But where is darkness [he pushes the lamp and it begins to swing], where is light? Where is the border of evil? [The lamp illuminates different parts of the room as it swings]. Do you know which side you are on? Think about it and examine your conscience. You will perhaps be surprised'.

The doctor: 'I know myself'.

The psychiatrist: 'Since a whirlwind of hate and denunciation has blown through this town all moral values are more or less corrupted. You have been afflicted like the others. One only has choices you know'.[84]

---

[83] Barrot, *L'Écran français*, 13–15; Ehrlich, *Cinema of Paradox*, 177–87; Siclier, *La France de Pétain*, 62–3, 236–9.

[84] The trans. is from A. Williams, *Republic of Images: A History of French Filmmaking* (1992), 271.

14

Reconstructing Mankind

'The sexes have again to be clearly defined. Each individual must be either male or female, and never manifest the sexual tendencies, mental characteristics, and ambitions of the opposite sex.' Thus wrote Alexis Carrel in his international best-seller *Man the Unknown* (1935).[1] Carrel was a Nobel prizewinning scientist, but in this book he assumed the role of sage and prophet. Arguing that science had disrupted the natural relationship between man and his environment, Carrel proposed to remedy this by a synthesis of sciences and social sciences. Such grandiose syncretic intellectual constructions were in the spirit of the technocratic reforming groups of the 1930s and Carrel had some contact with that other aspiring sage, Jean Coutrot.

In November 1941, Carrel was appointed to head the Foundation for the Study of Human Problems (Fondation pour l'étude des problèmes humains).[2] The Fondation was set up to 'study the most appropriate measures to safeguard, improve and develop the French population'. Its staff consisted mostly of medical specialists, like Carrel himself, but there were also engineers and economists. Research groups were organized on public health, urbanism, nutrition, immigration, criminality, and childhood development. Carrel wrote that the Fondation aimed at the 'systematic construction of civilized man in the totality of his corporal, social, and racial activities'. It was necessary to 'reconstruct mankind according to natural laws'.[3] The Fondation Carrel's importance in the overall history of Vichy should not be exaggerated, but its objective of 'reconstructing mankind' was central to Vichy's project of national renewal.

Moral Hygiene/Social Hygiene

The 'reconstruction of mankind' began with women and the young. In the language of Vichy, the 'young' meant boys and young men; 'women' meant mothers. Boys were to be brought up to become the virile elite of the new France;

---

[1] pp. 314–15.
[2] See A. Drouard, *Une inconnue des sciences sociales: La Fondation Alexis Carrel, 1941–1945* (1992).
[3] A. Carrel, 'La Science de l'homme', in H. Massis (ed.), *La France de l'esprit 1940–1943: Enquête sur les nouveaux destins de l'intelligence française* (1943), 106–12.

women to become their mothers, wives, and helpmates. As one writer put it: 'we must never tire of repeating this: woman, wife and mother, is made for man, for the home, for the child. As long as the young wives of France do not understand this, do not live out this truth of nature, nothing can be achieved.'[4] Remedying France's decadence required a restoration of the 'natural' sexual order.

The defeat of 1940 was often described in gendered imagery: France was 'devirilized' and her defeat was a 'rape'.[5] Many observers compared the unhealthy and unmanly appearance of the French troops with the youth and vigour of the conquering Germans—'young war gods', 'angels of death'.[6] One of Marion's aides described the National Revolution as 'a virile and human reaction to a feminized Republic, a Republic of women and inverts'.[7] The collaborationist Costantini wrote: 'What France, a female nation, lacks is a male . . . The purge will allow her to be soldered to Germany.' For Vichy conservatives, however, France's problem was not so much that she was feminine as that she had repudiated the 'feminine' virtues of fidelity and sacrifice, which had brought victory in 1918, in favour of the 'feminine' vices of frivolity and weakness, which had brought defeat in 1940. The 'morality of the shopgirl' was Montherlant's verdict on Munich. National Revolution propagandists criticized 'modern' women who read women's magazines and modelled themselves on Hollywood stars. As Thibon wrote, women should be 'rooted in nature without horizon beyond their hearth and without any aspiration beyond the joys of motherhood'.[8]

The decadence of French womanhood was viewed as the symptom of a general moral breakdown. In Pétain's words: 'the spirit of enjoyment has prevailed over the spirit of sacrifice'. Gide was frequently accused of having corrupted the young, but even his diary for 28 July 1940, lamenting the 'sorry reign of indulgence', sounded a similar note: 'Softness, surrender, relaxation in grace and ease, so many charming qualities that were to lead us, blindfolded, to defeat.' One Vichy documentary diagnosed the problem of France as 'the English weekend, American bars, Russian choirs, and Argentinian tangos'.[9] Pierre Dunoyer de Segonzac, an army officer who later founded a school to educate France's elite, had his own insight into France's collapse when, during the Phoney War, he witnessed his men listening to France's most popular singer, Tino Rossi:

> This international Corsican singer . . . whose warbling voice transforms consonants into vowels, had taken on the proportions of a myth—a eunuch who made

---

[4] Muel-Dreyfus, *Vichy et l'éternel*, 184.
[5] M. Weitz, *Sisters in the Resistance: How Women fought to free France* (New York, 1995), 2.
[6] Ibid. 272; Luirard, *La Région stéphanoise*, 286–7.
[7] M. Bordeaux, 'Femmes hors d'État français, 1940–1944', in R.Thalmann (ed.), *Femmes et fascismes* (1986), 135–55: 138.
[8] Muel-Dreyfus, *Vichy et l'éternel*, 35, 208.
[9] Bertin-Maghit, 'Le Documentaire de propagande', 32.

French women dream, and in whom their husbands revered their own mediocrity. Tino Rossi in the trenches: this scandal required a redemption—a virile song of men working on the fields.[10]

In Vichy's discourse, France's moral disorder was related to her physical decline—the 'collective suicide of the nation' represented by *dénatalité*. A survey organized by the regime in 1941 asked people to choose among the following causes of *dénatalité*: young couples who preferred cinema-going or car ownership to bringing up children; the decline of religion; the expense of raising a family; women's worries about their figure; the ready availability of divorce; the rural exodus; housing difficulties; unemployment. The decline of religion came top, but the answers, which have no statistical validity, are less interesting than the assumptions revealed by the question.[11] The inter-war obsession with *dénatalité* reached its climax in a law of February 1942 (commonly known as the Three Hundred Law since it was the 300th to be passed under Vichy) transforming abortion from a crime against the individual into a crime against society, the State, and the 'race'. Offenders would be tried by the special State Tribunal set up in 1941 to judge Communists; abortion was now punishable by death.

The population debate concerned quality as much as quantity: moral hygiene was inseparable from social hygiene. In August 1940, measures were taken against alcoholism (including the banning of pastis); anti-venereal decrees were passed in 1941; a premarital examination law of 1942 required both partners to undergo medical examination before marriage. The French Eugenics Society had long advocated such a measure, but in the inter-war years it had been considered too controversial. The 1942 law did not prohibit couples from marrying even if the results of the examination did reveal congenital defects, but the intention was to confront people with their responsibilities.[12]

This was the only eugenicist measure promulgated by Vichy. Nonetheless eugenics under Vichy has recently attracted attention because the Fondation Carrel had a research group studying it. The last chapter of *Man the Unknown* was devoted to eugenics—or the 'remaking of man' as Carrel called it. The Fondation was committed to the notion of biological regeneration and it studied ways of determining the most biologically appropriate immigrants. But quite apart from the fact that support for eugenics did not make one fascist—the intellectual inspiration for Carrel's eugenicism was America where he had spent most of his career—eugenics was not central to the work of the Fondation whose agenda was a broader social hygienist one. The real significance of the Fondation Carrel was to provide a quasi-scientific legitimization of the traditionalist agenda of the National Revolution.[13] Carrel argued that women 'attained their

---

[10] Fabre-Luce, *Journal de France*, 378.
[11] M. Pollard, *Reign of Virtue: Mobilising Gender in Vichy France* (Chicago, 1998), 36–40.
[12] Schneider, *Quantity and Quality*, 268–72.
[13] Muel-Dreyfus, *Vichy et l'éternel*, 332–3.

full development after one or two pregnancies' and that it was 'absurd to divert women from maternity'. The vice-regent of the Fondation, Félix-André Missenard, proposed that women be debarred from too much education or from entering unsuitable professions like the law.[14]

Family Values

At the centre of Vichy's policy towards women was the family. Family policy was the responsibility of the Secretary of State for Family and Health, and, after September 1941, of the new Family Commissariat which was directly responsible to the head of government. The lobbyists of the natalist organizations enjoyed greater influence than ever before: Pernot sat on the Conseil national; the works of the indefatigable Boverat became recommended texts for demographic instruction (he was also involved in the Fondation Carrel); Paul Haury, former vice-president of the ANAPF, headed the *cabinet* of the Secretary of State for the Family.[15]

Although familialism and natalism had now entirely converged, even at Vichy the imperatives of repopulation could override those of family morality. A law of September 1941 allowed children born out of wedlock to become legitimate providing their parents married subsequently. Known as the Loi du Jardinier because Pétain had supposedly insisted upon it to regularize the situation of his gardener, the law is sometimes presented as Pétain's whim. The law did shock many Vichy familialists, including André Lavagne of Pétain's civil *cabinet*, but it is explicable in terms of the natalist agenda.[16] There was a surprisingly tolerant attitude towards illegitimacy in the cinema of the occupation, as there had been in the pre-war films of Pagnol.[17]

In other respects, Vichy fully accepted the familialist agenda. Articles 53 to 59 of the 1941 draft constitution proclaimed the family to be the 'basic social group assuring the physical continuity of the nation'. It went on: 'the family has a head; the husband is the head of the household, the father is the head of the family'. The Gounot Law of December 1942 provided for the creation, in every locality, of a family association. Attributed a semi-official role advising the government and local authorities on family affairs, these associations were to be linked into a national federation. Existing family associations remained free to continue their activities in a private capacity—Vichy always shied away from 'totalitarianism'— but they were encouraged to affiliate to the new federation. The Gounot Law was presented as a sort of Family Charter to accompany the Peasant Charter and

---

[14] Drouard's somewhat apologetic *Une inconnue des sciences sociales* is the only study of the Fondation; see also Muel-Dreyfus, *Vichy et l'éternel*, 339–56; Schneider, *Quantity and Quality*, 272–80; Lindenberg, *Les Années souterraines*, 177–94.

[15] Pollard, 'Vichy and the Politics of Gender', 99–113.

[16] Id., *Reign of Virtue*, 64–6.

[17] Garçon, *De Blum à Pétain*, 85–95.

the Labour Charter, building a structural relationship between family and State as the first step towards integrating the family into the future corporatist constitution.[18]

Vichy orchestrated massive propaganda celebrating motherhood and the family. Mother's Day became a major date in the calendar. Festivities were organized in schools and local communities; medals were awarded to deserving mothers; on Mother's Day in 1941, Pétain broadcast to the mothers of France.[19] Since the regime also celebrated Joan of Arc, school manuals were rewritten to show that, apart from her martial virtues, she had also practised the domestic arts of cooking and sewing (and also came from a *famille nombreuse!*).[20] From March 1942 girls were required to study domestic science (*enseignement ménager*) at school for at least one hour a week.[21] Positive propaganda about motherhood was accompanied by more coercive measures. The divorce laws, untouched since 1884, were modified by the law of 2 April 1941 which forbade divorce within three years of marriage. After that, severe mistreatment was considered grounds for divorce, but the process could take up to seven years. The Justice Minister Barthélemy instructed the courts to apply the divorce law retroactively to cases already under way.[22]

A law of 11 October 1940 banned the recruitment of married women into public service except when their husbands could not support them. Unmarried women working in public service were offered incentives to leave and get married. As for married women already employed in public service, where their husbands' means were adequate to support them, they could be put on unpaid leave. This legislation was presented as a provisional measure to tackle unemployment, but it was announced that similar legislation for the private sector would follow. By the spring of 1941, however, unemployment was falling, and the Minister of Labour, Belin, considered modifying the legislation restricting female employment. This was opposed by the Family Secretariat and also by Darlan who argued that it was essential to 'ensure the return of the mother to the household'.[23]

Women, Vichy, and the Germans

In fact the employment laws became increasingly anomalous as labour shortages developed. It became impossible to fill public-sector posts, and in September 1942 the law on women's employment was suspended. By 1943 prefects

---

[18] Muel-Dreyfus, *Vichy et l'éternel*, 217–23; Pollard, 'Vichy and the Politics of Gender', 134–9.

[19] Pollard, *Reign of Virtue*, 45–56; Muel-Dreyfus, *Vichy et l'éternel*, 135–48.

[20] E. Jennings, 'Reinventing Jeanne: The Iconology of Joan of Arc in Vichy Schools', *JCH* 29 (1994), 711–34.

[21] Pollard, *Reign of Virtue*, 80–4.

[22] Paxton, *Vichy France*, 167; Muel-Dreyfus, *Vichy et l'éternel*, 198–9.

[23] Pollard, *Reign of Virtue*, 145–64; id., 'La Politique du travail féminin', in Azéma and Bédarida (eds.), *Vichy et les Français*, 242–5.

were being urged to employ women in preference to men in the administration and to encourage them into industry by raising wages.[24] In the aircraft industry, where 8 per cent of workers were women in 1941, the proportion had risen to a quarter in 1944, higher than it had been in May 1940.[25] In February 1944, married women became liable for labour service in Germany, a policy denounced by the Church as the final nail in the coffin of a family policy.

This triumph of economic reality over social policy was one instance among many of the abyss between image and reality in Vichy's policy towards women. The law prescribing domestic science was rarely applied because there were too few trained teachers available.[26] The Gounot Law remained symbolic: by the Liberation only three departmental associations had been set up. The regime did seemingly enjoy more success in its efforts to combat *dénatalité*. In 1942 the birth rate started to rise, and by the end of the war it was higher than it had been for a century. The causes of demographic trends are notoriously difficult to establish. The rise in the birth rate may have been encouraged by the generous family allowance system established in the 1930s; it may have been one of those impalpable shifts in national mood which defy analysis; it probably had little to do with Vichy policy.

Certainly the Vichy regime failed in its effort to stamp out abortion despite promulgating of one of the most repressive abortion laws in Europe. Forty-two abortion cases were considered by the State Tribunal under the terms of the Three Hundred Law: fourteen people were sentenced to life imprisonment and twenty-six others to prison terms of up to twenty years. Two death sentences were carried out: Marie-Louise Girard, a laundress who had performed twenty-six abortions, was guillotined on 30 July 1942 (the last woman to be guillotined in France); Désiré P—— (the only man to be convicted under this law) was guillotined on 22 October 1943. Giraud was singled out for her flagrantly 'immoral' lifestyle and disregard for public opinion. She rented out rooms to prostitutes and carried on open affairs in full view of her family until denounced to the authorities, apparently by her husband. As for Desiré P—— he had taken no precautions to hide what he was doing, and even performed an abortion in public.[27]

Most abortion cases continued to be dealt with by the normal courts. In the Seine *département*, 1,300 police inquiries into abortion cases were made in 1943. More than three times the number of cases came before the courts in 1942 than in 1940. In the circumstances of the Occupation—the presence of strangers in local communities (whether Germans or refugees), the absence of husbands, and the burden represented by unwanted babies in a period of shortages—it is hardly surprising that the number of abortions increased. The real figures can only be guessed, but the evidence of post-abortion cases arriving in hospitals suggests

[24] Kedward, *In Search of the Maquis*, 54.
[25] Fridenson and Robert, 'Les Ouvriers dans la France', 126.
[26] Pollard, *Reign of Virtue*, 82.   [27] Ibid. 174–94.

a sharp rise in 1941–2, possibly between 400,000 and one million per annum. They were usually married women of modest means, often with a small family. Mostly the abortions were carried out by family friends not professional abortionists.[28]

Whether in trying to keep women out of the workplace or in repressing abortion, Vichy found that it was not so easy to 'remake' women. But did women view the regime differently from men? The Exodus had been primarily an experience of women and children, and it possibly made women initially receptive to Pétain's rhetoric of hearth and home.[29] But they were also among the first to see how little it corresponded to the realities of life under the Occupation. Women were the people most directly affected by food shortages since it usually fell to them to find the food. Food queues brought women together in large numbers, and frequently witnessed violent criticism of the authorities.[30] Food demonstrations, mainly involving women, were the first major challenge to public order facing Vichy.

While Vichy exhorted women to return to traditional roles, many women were being forced, by the absence of their husbands in prisoner-of-war camps, to undertake new responsibilities to keep their families alive. The most gener-ous social benefits were allocated to large families where mothers stayed at home and were supported by a working husband, but this was a mockery of the situation facing many women. In fact Vichy did concede one modification of existing legislation to take account of reality. From March 1941 the Republic's *allocation de la mère au foyer* (benefit for mothers at home), which had provided women with a benefit to compensate for lost income if they stayed at home with the children, was replaced by the *allocation de salaire unique* (single wage benefit), available to any household with only one income, irrespective whether that income was earned by the man or the woman. This provided an incentive for women to seek a job.[31]

No women were more brutally confronted by the contradictions of the regime than prisoner-of-war wives. Vichy propaganda endlessly celebrated their absent husbands whose suffering was portrayed as an expiation of the nation's sin.[32] Prisoner-of-war wives were also accorded an iconic status in propaganda, but in daily life they were the object of suspicion and jealousy. If they were seen enjoy-ing themselves, they were judged to lack decorum; friendly relations with any man made them victims of gossip and letters of denunciation.[33] It was so widely

[28] C. Watson, 'Birth Control and Abortion in France since 1939', *Population Studies,* 5/3 (1952), 261–86: 286.

[29] Pollard, *Reign of Virtue,* 30.

[30] Id., 'Vichy and the Politics of Gender', 358; Biélinky, *Journal 1940–1942,* 85; P. Schwartz, 'The Politics of Food and Gender in Occupied Paris', *Modern and Contemporary France,* 7/1 (1999), 35–45.

[31] Diamond, 'Women's Experience', 45–58; Pollard, *Reign of Virtue,* 124–5.

[32] Fishman, 'Grand Delusions: The Unintended Consequences of Vichy France's Prisoner of War Propaganda', *JCH* 26/2 (1991), 229–54.

[33] Fishman, *We will wait,* 65, 74–5.

believed that many of them had turned to prostitution that the government passed a law against adultery in December 1942 with special penalties for prisoners' wives.[34] In order to overcome their isolation, and provide each other with practical assistance, prisoner-of-war wives organized themselves into groups. These eventually formed into a national federation which had 12,000 members in March 1942 and 40,000 by May 1943. They set up parcel-making centres, organized holiday camps for children, and published a bulletin. What is interesting about these groups is that they were created by women themselves. Although Vichy talked a lot to women, it did not expect them to talk back or to show that they had a separate voice: the interests of women and the family were seen as identical. But the existence of this women's activism does not necessarily imply estrangement from the regime. The publications of the prisoner-of-war wives' associations claimed to be non-political. They gave advice on how to be a good wife and mother, and exhorted their readers to consult absent husbands on family decisions. In short, their language and values mirrored Vichy's official values.[35]

It may even be that the vulnerability of prisoner-of-war wives rendered them more liable to support collaboration than other sections of the population. A report of the postal censors in the autumn of 1941 noted that in the Occupied Zone collaboration was supported only by wives of prisoners of war; and a year later a report noted that these circles were characterized by 'a generalized tendency to Anglophobia'.[36] Some women joined the RNP in the belief that this would get their husbands released.[37] In general, however, few women joined collaborationist movements. When collaboration is discussed in relation to women, two issues are usually highlighted: denunciations and sexual relationships with Germans. Of the 901 women tried for collaboration after the war in the Seine *département*, 687 (76 per cent) were accused of denunciations; of 225 cases of denunciation which came to light in the Norman *département* of the Eure at the Liberation, 65 per cent had been committed by women.[38] There is no quantitative study of delation to tell us whether women were more prone to it than men, but this is what was popularly believed. Female denunciators appear in novels about the period, like Dutourd's *Au bon beurre*, and it is no coincidence that the only woman to be interviewed in the *Sorrow and the Pity* was an unrepentant Pétainist involved in a sordid case of denunciation.[39]

The liaisons between French women and German men are the aspect of

[34] Fishman, *We will wait*, 134–42.

[35] Ibid. 99–112; Diamond, 'Women's Experience', 124–7.

[36] Burrin, *La France à l'heure*, 192–3.

[37] Diamond, 'Women's Experience', 128–9; Fishman, *We will wait*, 35–6; Gordon, *Collaborationism in France*, 123.

[38] F. Leclerc and M. Weindling, 'La Répression des femmes coupables d'avoir collaboré pendant l'Occupation', *Clio: Histoire, femmes et sociétés*, 1 (1995), 129–50: 139; Papp, *Collaboration dans l'Eure*, 180–2.

[39] Cobb, *French and Germans*, 105–6; Diamond, 'Women's Experience', 133–6. Halimi, *La Délation*, gives no gender breakdown of the authors of the letters.

female 'collaboration' which most exercised the popular imagination at the Liberation. Between 10,000 and 20,000 women accused of so-called 'horizontal collaboration' had their heads shaved and swastikas daubed on their skulls; sometimes they were also stripped naked. Prostitutes were singled out for particular opprobrium. During the Occupation many brothels were officially reserved for German military personnel, and those working in them had no choice but to comply. The most famous brothel in Paris was the One Two Two (named after its address at 122 Rue de Provence). Its manager Fabienne Jamet managed to get the German authorities to allow it to be patronized both by Germans and French—'I had won the One Two Two back for France'—and it was frequented by rich black marketeers like Joinovici, members of the Bonny-Lafont gang, celebrities like Sacha Guitry and Tino Rossi. Recollecting her war years Jamet looked back nostalgically on the handsome SS officers who frequented her establishment: 'I've never had such a good time in my life.'[40]

In the Paris region, there were thirty-two brothels operating for the Germans in 1941; there were seven in Toulouse in November 1942 with sixty-three prostitutes serving the Germans in fortnightly shifts. There were also many unregistered prostitutes—the Germans estimated 80,000–100,000 in the Paris region in 1941—most of whom were driven to prostitution by the financial necessity and the existence of a large new market. Henri Michel remarks that the 'honourable' prostitute of Maupassant's *Boule de suif* did not find many exemplars in the 1940s, but 'Boule de Suif' was quite prosperous, and probably in a better position to refuse than many women finding themselves in similar circumstances in the 1940s. There are also examples of resisters who were hidden in brothels or fed information by those working in them.[41]

It was not only prostitutes who were punished at the Liberation. Any woman seen in the company of a German risked finding herself accused of horizontal collaboration. The kinds of employment open to women—secretarial jobs or domestic service—were more likely to bring them into contact with Germans than was true of French men, and this did not imply any preference on their part. But it is true that many liaisons did occur. By mid-1943 80,000 Frenchwomen from the Occupied Zone alone had claimed benefit from the Germans for their offspring.[42] Those who had affairs with Germans included celebrities like the actress Arletty and the couturière Coco Chanel. At the Liberation, Arletty famously dismissed the idea that her sexual choices diminished her patriotism: 'my ass is international, my heart is French'. Both she and Chanel, however, certainly had right-wing sympathies. The actress Corinne Luchaire, daughter of Jean

---

[40] *Palace of Sweet Sin* (1977), 81–145.
[41] Diamond, 'Women's Experience', 141; Pollard, *Reign of Virtue*, 67–9; Cobb, *French and Germans*, 122–3.
[42] Cobb, *French and Germans*, 66–7. The Germans estimated that there were between 50,000 and 75,000 offspring of such liaisons: Burrin, *La France à l'heure*, 213.

Luchaire, wrote empty-headed reminiscences about partying with Germans in occupied Paris while protesting that she was not in any way political.[43] Luchaire moved in a tiny, self-contained, and privileged Parisian *beau monde*. But where we have information about ordinary women who became sentimentally involved with Germans, they seem to have come from the most vulnerable sections of society. They were young, single or divorced, often with one or both parents deceased, and lacking much formal education. Often their first contact with a German had been in the workplace.[44]

How were these liaisons generally viewed? Simone de Beauvoir claimed that in the early days of the Occupation, watching French women and Germans together, she often overheard people remark, with amusement rather than disapproval, 'soon there'll be lots of little Germans'.[45] Yet in many diaries of the period, the first sighting of Germans with French women is recorded with outrage, as a moment revealing the humiliation of Occupation. The first incident dealt with by the Paris police commissioner Georges Ballyot, after the arrival of the Germans, involved a German soldier who claimed to have been insulted by a French war veteran in the street. The veteran was allowed to go free after he had explained that his insults were directed at the French woman in the company of the German.[46] Women who worked for the extremely dangerous 'Travail allemand' section of the Resistance, which involved making friends with Germans in order to obtain information or encourage them to desert, found that the most difficult aspect of the work was braving the hostile stares of French onlookers.[47]

Sexual contacts between French women and German soldiers were numerous, but the post-war fixation upon them is largely revealing of male sexual anxieties and jealousies. Quite apart from the homosexual encounters between German soldiers and Frenchmen, which history has not recorded,[48] little was said after the war about the numerous liaisons between German girls and French POWs or French workers in Germany. How many of those who shaved the heads of women were assuaging their own guilt at having done so little to resist the Germans? How many of the *maquisards* who punished women were expressing their own sexual frustrations after months of enforced sexual deprivation?

Rather than viewing the relationships between French women and German men as a particularly flagrant form of collaboration, they should be seen as one of the many moral dilemmas confronted by people living under foreign occu-

---

[43] *Ma drôle de vie* (1949).

[44] Diamond, *Women and the Second World War*, 82–6; L. Capdevila, *Les Bretons au lendemain de l'Occupation: Imaginaire et comportement d'une sortie de guerre 1944–1945* (Rennes, 1999), 223–36.

[45] Burrin, *La France à l'heure*, 29.

[46] G. Ballyot, *Un flic dans la tourmente: Souvenirs (1937–1944)* (1992), 72.

[47] P. Schwartz, 'Women, Resistance and Communism in France 1939–1945' (Ph.D. thesis, New York University, 1998), 152.

[48] For an exception to this silence, see P. Sperat-Czar, 'Le Carnet noir: Journal d'un jeune homme amoureux sous l'Occupation', *Masques*, 89 (1981), 93–108.

pation. Were relationships with anti-Nazi Germans justifiable or was a Boche always a Boche? There were no clear rules of conduct. One woman in Normandy, who had had a child by a German, told a post-Liberation court that she did not consider the liaison reprehensible: 'neither he nor his relatives have ever shared the ideas of the Nazi regime. His uncle spent ten years in a concentration camp because of his anti-Nazi views.'[49]

The diary of Micheline Bood, a Parisian schoolgirl, 14 years old in 1940, shows one individual coping with the temptations of Occupation, and trying to reoncile curiosity and conscience. Bood's family was Gaullist; her brother was in England during the war, flying with the RAF. Her diary is full of pro-British and pro-Gaullist sentiments. Pétain is described as senile from the start, and she is continuously getting into trouble because of her pro-Gaullist sympathies— writing 'vive de Gaulle' on the blackboard or drawing Vs on walls. But her diary is also about the difficulties of living out these principles in the face of daily contacts with friendly Germans.

Most of her encounters took place at the swimming pool. In April 1941 she exchanged pleasantries (in English) with a blond 25-year-old German called Walter, who told her Paris was the most beautiful city in the world. He accompanied her to the metro and she felt 'ashamed at the way people were looking at me'. Out of 'propriety', she tells him they cannot walk together; she has a clear conscience because 'I told him all my views'. Two days later, they meet again at the pool and again she refuses to walk with him because 'the French don't like it'. Her mother reproaches her for talking to him, and she agrees: 'I should never have spoken to a Boche.' She goes to confession, but the priest is no help: he is only interested in whether sex has occurred. In June she adopts a new position: 'I detest and will always detest the Boches . . . but Germans taken individually are very nice, usually well-brought up and correct . . . I no longer feel it is wrong to speak to a German.'[50]

In July, at the pool, she encounters another German, the 19-year-old Peter, and they have several meetings which she hides from her mother. But in August, she decides again that she can never love a Boche: 'there will always be something in me, my education probably, and my love for England which will save me'. A few days later she notes her hatred of collaboration: 'sinking into the mire'. In December, shocked by her friend Monique, who has fallen totally in love with a German and allowed herself to be kissed by him several times, she resolves never to allow herself to be kissed by a Boche: 'One might love a Boche, but he remains a Boche.' With the arrival of summer the following year, however, swimming-pool flirtations with Germans resumed.[51]

Micheline Bood's experiences illustrate the limited usefulness of the vocabulary of resistance and collaboration. However one views her amorous encounters,

---

[49] Papp, *Collaboration dans l'Eure*, 173.
[50] *Les Années doubles*, 96–106.   [51] Ibid. 109, 115–17, 125–6.

her pro-Gaullist pranks could have got her into real trouble. Doubtless her life mirrored that of thousands of other girls of her age and situation.

Remaking the Young: Aspirations and Reality

Vichy wished to promote collaboration between France and Germany, but it would certainly not have approved of Bood's flirtations with Germans—nor with French boys either. Vichy wanted boys and girls to be kept separate; co-education was frowned upon. The regime's education policies towards the sexes overlapped on only one point: the harmfulness of too much learning. Books filled girls' minds with thoughts unsuitable for future mothers; boys needed to build up their characters more than their minds. Bonnard had once written a book 'in praise of ignorance'.[52] One Youth Ministry representative wrote in 1940: 'less literature and more nature . . . more baths, more walks, more sun'.[53]

No previous government in France, including the Popular Front, had done more to promote sport than Vichy. In July 1940, it created a Commissariat for General and Sporting Education headed by the tennis star Jean Borotra, twice a Wimbledon singles champion. Borotra viewed sport as a way of improving physical fitness, building character, and instilling moral values. He wanted to phase out professionalism and allow sport to become 'chivalrous and disinterested'. Before sports contests, participants had to swear the Athlete's Oath: 'I promise on my honour to practise sport disinterestedly, with discipline and firmness, so as to become a better person and serve my country better.' To motivate young people to practise sport, Borotra created a National Sporting Certificate. Nine hours of 'general education' (primarily sport but also artistic activities) were introduced into the school curriculum.[54]

Borotra's aims meshed perfectly with those of the Youth Secretariat (SGJ). Georges Lamirand, its head, supported the creation of Vichy's two new youth movements: the Chantiers de la jeunesse and the Compagnons de France. The Chantiers, run by General de la Porte du Theil, were compulsory for all 20-year-olds, who were sent to camps for eight months to undergo a regime of strenuous outdoor physical activity away from the corrupting influence of the city. Visits were arranged to local communities so that the recruits could learn about the realities of peasant life. Each camp leader (*chef*) was supposed to encourage comradeship, and organize games and singing around the fire in the evenings. The Chantiers were to be the embodiment of the community ideal.[55]

The Compagnons de France were a voluntary organization for teenagers, founded in July 1940 by the former civil servant Henri Dhavernas. After May

---

[52] 'Vichy, idéologue de l'école', *RHMC* 38 (1991), 560–616.
[53] Austin, 'Education and Youth Policies', 54.
[54] J.-L. Gay-Lescot, *Sport et éducation sous Vichy (1940–1944)* (Lyons, 1991); Halls, *Youth of Vichy France*, 186–92.
[55] Halls, *Youth of Vichy France*, 284–307; R. Hervet, *Les Chantiers de la jeunesse* (1962).

1941, they were run by a career officer, Guillaume de Tournemire. The aim was to inculcate community spirit and patriotism. Recruits were admitted as 'apprentices' and graduated to become 'journeymen' (compagnons); they wore scouting-style uniforms. Full-time members lived in camps according to a strict routine. They performed useful works like forestry but also cultural activities like choral singing and drama. There were never more than about 29,000 Compagnons (of whom about 3,500 were full-time), but no other voluntary youth organization was more generously subsidized.[56]

Lamirand, de la Porte du Theil, Dhavernas, Tournemire, and many others associated with the SGJ all came, as we have seen, from the milieu of conservative social Catholicism and Catholic scouting. Their aim was to regenerate France by creating a national spiritual community. They believed in honour, duty, discipline, faith, and class reconciliation; they opposed materialism and liberal individualism. They were not, however, without competitors for the control of Vichy youth policy. There was Marion's Information Secretariat whose *fascisant* views were represented within the SGJ itself by Pelorson. There were Pétain's own advisers on youth policy, like the Maurrassian Henri Massis, who shared the political conservatism of the SGJ, but not its naive social ideas. There was the Education Ministry which saw character building as a distraction from the intellectual values which had traditionally been the priority of French education. Lamirand, who was not much of an administrator or politician, had to navigate continuously between these conflicting currents.

Lamirand's real problem, however, was that his ambitions came up against the realities of life in occupied France. Schools were supposed to remove unsuitable textbooks, but paper shortages made this impracticable, and the old books continued to be used.[57] Borotra's nine hours of general education were soon reduced to three because undernourishment made excessive physical activity undesirable, and most children lacked appropriate clothes and footwear. Parents were suspicious of general education in the curriculum. This explains the increasing popularity of Catholic schools which were seen as providing a serious education, not one encouraging children to 'sing, dance, and jump'. The Church was suspicious of any cult of the body.[58]

Throughout France, there was a lack of sports facilities. Although Borotra encouraged villages to apply for government subsidies to build them, most were unwilling to sacrifice agricultural land for this purpose. When they did, the result was to unleash conflicts between Catholics and anticlericals about whether the facilities should be sited near the school or the church. Instead of promoting national reconciliation, sport reopened old quarrels. Participation in sport did

[56] Halls, *Youth of Vichy France*, 267–307.

[57] O. Dumoulin, 'L'Histoire et les historiens', in Rioux (ed.), *Vie culturelle*, 241–68: 252; C. Singer, *Vichy, l'univérsité et les juifs*, 200.

[58] Austin, 'Education and Youth Policies', 195–7; Halls, *Youth of Vichy France*, 200–1; Giolitto, *Histoire de la jeunesse*, 192–206.

increase during the Occupation. By 1943, there were 6,100 football clubs, three times more than in 1939; the athletics federation increased its membership from 90,365 to 208,425 between 1940 and 1941. But this had little to do with Borotra's Commissariat: a 1942 survey in Paris showed few people had heard of it.[59] The enthusiasm for sport was a manifestation of the turning away from politics which so many prefects noticed. In the Nord/Pas-de-Calais, the population was described as incapable of enthusiasm for anything other than the success of local football teams.[60]

There is no sign, to the extent this can be measured, that young people were being won over to the values which Vichy wished to encourage. Its puritanism succeeded in creating opposition countercultures, the most celebrated being the 'Zazous' in Paris. They were middle-class youth rebels who affected an effete style—long hair, drainpipe trousers—listened to jazz and swing, and used their own slang ('vachement bath', 'drôlement chouette'). There was nothing political about the Zazous—except the fact that they affected English expressions in their slang—but this did not stop them being chased by PPF thugs who would shave their heads.[61] The Zazous were a tiny minority whose notoriety derived from the attacks of the collaborationist press. But there are other examples of youth disaffection. Although public dances were banned because they were deemed indecent while the POWs were languishing in Germany, by 1942 this prohibition was increasingly flouted and *bals clandestins* became common. In a period when resourcefulness was essential for survival and many fathers were absent in prisoner-of-war camps, petty crime and delinquency increased. The number of minors convicted of delinquency almost trebled from 13,000 in 1938 to 35,000 in 1942.[62]

The Chantiers, which were the heart of Vichy's enterprise to re-educate the young, were particularly hated. In the first winter, the camps lacked the most elementary facilities. Conditions improved, but the idea of dividing the day between physical labour and intellectual development or technical training never materialized. Many camps were characterized by a brutal army discipline which antagonized young men already alienated by boredom and hunger. Their letters home reflected apathy and cynicism; there were floods of letters from parents protesting at the treatment of their children. As for the political opinions of the recruits, the prefect of the Lozère reported that the youths in his local camp were 'still imbued with Popular Front ideas'. An enquiry into 263 recruits in an Allier camp found that 150 believed the Republic was the ideal regime (presumably if

---

[59] Gay-Lescot, *Sport et éducation*, 132–3.

[60] E. Dejonghe, 'Les Départements du Nord et du Pas-de-Calais', in Azéma and Bédarida (eds.), *La France des années noires*, i. 505.

[61] E. Rioux, 'Les Zazous: un phénomène socio-culturel pendant l'Occupation' (Mémoire de maîtrise, Paris X, 1987); Halls, *Youth of Vichy France*, 177; Giolitto, *Histoire de la jeunesse*, 480–93.

[62] Halls, *Youth of Vichy France*, 181–2.

so many said so, even more thought it).[63] Those who ran the Chantiers, however, remained loyal to the regime almost until the end.

The situation of the Compagnons was the opposite from that of the Chantiers: they did arouse genuine enthusiasm from their members, but their leaders were less conformist than those of the Chantiers. A government inquiry in March 1941 noted that the Compagnons had 'taken on habits of independence . . . the appearance of a small state in a state'.[64] This was the origin of the crisis of May 1941 when Dhavernas was forced out. His successor, Tournemire, was a reliable Pétainist army officer, and Pétain's presence at the first anniversary of the Compagnons in July 1941 indicated that they were back in favour. Nonetheless their weekly journal *Compagnons* gave little coverage of the National Revolution, and in November 1941 it criticized attacks on Jewish synagogues in Paris. In the Catholic Lozère and Aveyron *départements*, the Compagnons were viewed with hostility, as a bunch of Communists and anarchists; the Bishop of Montepellier reminded his flock that Catholic children should join Catholic groups.[65]

Uriage: A Pétainist Deviation?

The Compagnons showed how little control Vichy might exercise even over a movement that it subsidized. This was even truer of one of the most famous initiatives supported by Vichy: the School of Uriage founded in the summer of 1940 by Pierre Dunoyer de Segonzac.[66] An admirer of Lyautey, Dunoyer believed that France had been let down by her elites. He resolved to create a school to train the nation's future leaders. With the backing of the Youth Secretariat, his school was given the official task of offering courses for Vichy youth leaders. It acquired great prestige, and was visited by Pétain in October 1940 and Darlan in June 1941. After Darlan's visit, Uriage's brief was widened to include training courses for higher civil servants. Publishing a journal and a number of pamphlets, it aspired to become a laboratory of reflection for the National Revolution.

Located at the Château d'Uriage, in the bracing air of the Alps above Grenoble, the school viewed itself as a sort of chivalric order. The standard course lasted three weeks, and consisted of lectures, study groups, and visits to local farms or factories. The atmosphere was somewhere between a religious community and a scout camp. Trainees wore a simple uniform—smock, blue shirt, and

---

[63] Austin, 'Education and Youth Policies', 116; Giolitto, *Histoire de la jeunesse*, 567–70, 586–94; S. Fishman, 'Youth in Vichy France: The Juvenile Crime Wave and its Implications', in id. et al. (eds.), *France at War*, 205–20.

[64] Austin, 'Education and Youth Policies', 403.

[65] Ibid. 390, 458–9.

[66] On Uriage, see Comte, *Une utopie combattante*, and J. Hellman, *The Knight-Monks of Vichy France* (1993).

beret—and every day there was one and a half hours' compulsory collective exercise. Meals were preceded by a song and followed by a reading. The guiding principles were team spirit, service to the community, and loyalty to Dunoyer, the 'Vieux Chef', as he was known.

Despite the emphasis on community life, the atmosphere of Uriage was tolerant, and Dunoyer attracted some serious intellectual figures to his staff. Many of them were Catholics who had been associated with *Esprit*: the Jesuit theologian Henri de Lubac, who was interested in Proudhon and Marx, the Dominican René de Naurois, a former member of Izard's Third Force, the philosopher Jean Lacroix. Emmanuel Mounier himself was not on the staff, but he lectured at Uriage where 'personalism' acquired something of the status of an unofficial ideology. But there were also people from other backgrounds: Joffre Dumazedier, a young atheist with Socialist leanings, who had been involved in the youth hostel movement during the Popular Front; Pierre Ollier de Marichard, a Protestant and Socialist in the orbit of *Esprit*, who had advised Leo Lagrange during the Popular Front; the Grenoble professor Jean-Jacques Chevalier, a former member of the PDP. Until he went to work for Borotra's Sports Commissariat, Chevalier combined Uriage's dual preoccupation with spiritual and bodily health by regularly cycling 15 miles up the mountain to lecture on the need to create an *ordre viril*.

The dominant intellectual at Uriage was Hubert Beuve-Méry, who was from June 1941 in charge of the research department. Before the war, Beuve-Méry had taught in Prague from where he also acted as the correspondent of *Le Temps*. He resigned from this post in disgust when the paper refused to publish his criticisms of Munich. After the defeat, he joined the board of *Esprit*. Beuve-Méry was a Catholic intellectual much influenced by Dominican theology. His experience of the venality of the French press in the 1930s made him congenitally suspicious of power and those who wielded it. In character he was austere to the point of asceticism, indifferent to money, and anti-materialist.[67]

No one at Uriage had any nostalgia for the Third Republic or parliamentary democracy in general. The school's doctrine has been variously described by historians as *the* ideology of Vichy, as a left-wing Pétainism, or even as semi-fascist.[68] But the school also has its ferocious defenders. Critics of Uriage focus on two issues: its attitude to Germany and its attitude to the National Revolution. Dunoyer was fiercely patriotic. In March 1941 he said publicly to the students that he wanted a British victory, and that Nazi Germany was the enemy number one.[69] Uriage had no ideological sympathy with Nazism. Naurois had spent time

---

[67] L. Greilsamer, *Hubert Beuve-Méry (1902–1989)* (1990).

[68] Hellman, *The Kinght-Monks*, pp. vii–ix; Giolitto, *Histoire de la jeunesse*, 649; Lévy, *L'Idéologie française*; P. Bitoum, *Les Hommes d'Uriage* (1988), 13–25 gives an account of the controversy aroused by Lévy's book.

[69] Comte, *Une utopie combattante*, 241, 375.

in Germany and his lectures were eloquent about the evils of Nazism. Some writers claim that in 1941 both Beuve-Méry and Mounier were ready to accept a German-occupied Europe. This is obviously true to the extent that, like anyone willing to work within the framework of the Armistice, they believed Germany's victory was a fact, at least provisionally. The Resistance was deemed heroic but unrealistic. Beuve-Méry turned down an overture to join a resistance movement, and Mounier rejected the temptation to go abroad, saying 'this is not the moment to desert'. But Uriage did not support collaboration: it wanted to test what could be achieved in France despite Germany.[70]

This leads to the second question: what was Uriage's attitude to the National Revolution? A giant portrait of Pétain hung over the entrance hall. Dunoyer was unconditionally loyal to Pétain until November 1942; Beuve-Méry was more reserved. But despite his adulation of Pétain, Dunoyer jealously guarded Uriage's independence. The school shared much with Vichy—criticism of liberalism, materialism, and individualism, contempt for the Third Republic—but it was vague about positive policies. Its discussions were largely about values, the search, as Mounier wrote, for a 'French humanism of the person and the community'. Uriage itself embodied the kind of moral community it idealized. The presiding influence was Péguy: each new course began with a reading from a passage by Péguy on 'work well done'. Uriage sought a third way between mystical fascism and materialistic liberalism.

Uriage soon fell under official suspicion because it was too distanced from the day-to-day preoccupations of the National Revolution. As early as December 1940, Chantier leaders criticized the school's religious neutrality. A visiting lecture by Massis was badly received.[71] In July 1941, *Action française* attacked Mounier's influence at Uriage while a collaborationist publication accused it of being pro-British and pro-Jewish. In the summer of 1941, Mounier and Naurois were forbidden to continue lecturing there. A government spy in the school reported in September 1941 that it 'refused to admit the fact of our defeat and was exhorting people to a utopian return to arms'; two months later, members of Pétain's *cabinet* criticized its teachers for acting as the 'champions of a spiritual cause . . . rather than as instructors in the service of the political order'.[72] At the meeting of the Conseil national to discuss youth policy in March 1942, Uriage was attacked for lacking sufficient 'ideological content' and being infected by Mounierism. Dunoyer was allowed to carry on, but under sufferance. In short, although it never condemned the National Revolution, Uriage was at the least a Pétainist deviation—or, to quote Roderick Kedward, 'a Vichy that might have been'.[73]

---

[70] Hellman, *The Knight-Monks*, 37–43; Winock, *Histoire politique de la revue Esprit*, 207–8; L. Greilsamer, *Hubert Beuve-Méry (1902–1989)* (1990), 143–52.
[71] Comte, *Une utopie combattante*, 70, 119–20.
[72] Austin, 'Education and Youth Policies', 356.
[73] *Resistance in Vichy*, 209.

'Pockets of Health' (Mounier)

Uriage tried to occupy a middle ground between unconditional support for the regime and opposition to it. No one more perfectly exemplified this ambiguity than Mounier. He had no nostalgia for the fallen regime: 'what was dead is dead; the History which awaits us has a new face, an authoritarian face; we cannot escape the massive oscillations of history, nor work against its fundamental premisses'. But this did not mean submitting totally to Vichy's values. Mounier wanted 'to profit from the verbal similarities between our values and the publicly proclaimed values in order to introduce . . . the content we desire'. The situation was 'very open', an opportunity to be seized. The alternative was to retreat into a 'fruitless solitude' and 'abandon Vichy to its internal determinism'.[74]

For these reasons, Mounier decided to resume publishing *Esprit*, despite the opposition of several contributors. *Esprit* reappeared from November 1940, offering a guardedly sympathetic critique of the early days of the National Revolution—with criticism gradually overcoming sympathy. Mounier came under pressure from his own circle to stop publishing, but he continued to believe, as he wrote in February 1941, that it was not necessary 'to choose between yes or no'. This could become 'an alibi for total inaction . . . taking refuge in the absolute and allowing history to run on without us'.[75]

At the same time as writing this, Mounier was making more vigorous criticisms, in private, of Vichy anti-Semitism than one would find from many early resisters.[76] He told his critics that *Esprit* was read by many people as a journal of resistance and independence. In the February 1941 issue he used Péguy to criticize anti-Semitism; in the June issue there was strong criticism of the film *Jew Süss* and an article pointing out that Péguy had 'remained loyal to his republicanism and even to his revolutionary faith'. Mounier wrote in June 1941: 'Each month I pull a little harder on the rope and one day it will break.' It finally did in August 1941 when Vichy banned *Esprit*. Mounier wrote to his parents: 'What a joy not to be on the side of cowardice and to be made, by an official decree, the brother of all the innocents suffering for their faith in the concentration camps.'[77] Mounier's critics are right that he was no defender of liberalism or democracy in 1940; but he was no orthodox Pétainist either.

Despite his relief at the banning of *Esprit*, Mounier's judgement on his balancing act was positive: 'because we did not withdraw into our tents, we have known real pockets of health, corners of France truly free'.[78] Among these pockets of health, he included Uriage, and also another experiment with which

---

[74] *Mounier et sa génération: Lettres, carnets et inédits* (1956), 268 (10 Nov. 1940). On Mounier in 1940 see P. Laborie, '*Esprit* en 1940: De l'usage de la défaite', *Esprit*, 254 (1999), 44–60.

[75] *Mounier et sa génération*, 285–6 (22 Feb. 1941).

[76] Ibid. 267, 279.

[77] Kedward, *Resistance in Vichy*, 199–203.

[78] *Mounier et sa génération*, 286.

he was associated: the Jeune France organization.[79] Founded in November 1940, by Pierre Schaeffer, a young broadcasting engineer, Jeune France started out as a means of assisting unemployed young artists. Subsidized by the SGJ, it soon developed the more ambitious project of reinvigorating the arts and bringing culture to the people. One of its objectives was to set up local cultural centres, *maisons Jeune France*. Although only five of these saw the light of day, no previous government had subsidized such an ambitious enterprise of cultural decentralization.

In the 1930s, Schaeffer had been associated with *Esprit*, and Mounier agreed to help Jeune France. Other participants included Jean de Fabrègues, editor of *Combat* in the 1930s, Claude Roy who had written for *Combat*, and Albert Ollivier who had been in Ordre nouveau. These people were from the generation of 1930s nonconformists, but represented different strands of it. As a result, like other institutions of Vichy youth policy, Jeune France soon became torn by conflict. Fabrègues wanted it to defend the political objectives of the National Revolution and repudiate Mounier's 'intellectual liberalism . . . and political non-conformity'. The government was informed that Fabrègues was a 'solid Catholic, a hardliner' who wanted to combat the 'danger of Mounier's "Christian Bolshevism" '.[80] Schaeffer eventually sacrificed the Mounierists in the autumn of 1941, but Fabrègues still found Jeune France too heterodox, and he eventually left it to work with prisoners of war instead.[81]

Jeune France was indeed culturally open-minded. Organizing a meeting of musicians and poets at the Château de Loumarin in September 1941, it invited contributors to magazines like *Poésie*, *Confluences*, and *Fontaine*. Aragon himself was invited, but did not go. At the end of the day some of the participants ran through the streets shouting 'vive de Gaulle'. Jeune France's main effort went into backing theatrical groups, often experimental ones: La Roulotte, Les Quatre Saisons, and the Comédiens routiers. The inspiration behind many of these groups was Jacques Copeau, whose entire career had been devoted to challenging the stuffiness of bourgeois boulevard theatre. In 1913 he had set up the Théâtre du Vieux Colombier in Paris; between 1924 and 1929 he formed a community of actors in Burgundy. His disciple Léon Chancerel had set up the Comédiens routiers, the theatrical movement of the Catholic scouts; another disciple Olivier Hussenot set up a theatrical group at Uriage. Influenced by Stanislavsky, Greek classical theatre, and the Commedia del dell' Arte, they wanted to reinvigorate theatre and bring it to the people. Many of these groups were inspired by the social Catholic ambition of respiritualizing society. But they also drew on the Popular Front's experiments in cultural democratization. They were precursors of the revival of France's theatrical life in the Fourth Republic.

[79] V. Chabrol, 'L'Ambition de "Jeune France" ', in Rioux (ed.), *Vie culturelle*, 161–78; Added, *Le Théâtre dans les années Vichy*, 203–24; Faure, *Le Projet culturel*, 57–65, 136–42, 154, 214–27; Dorléac, *L'Art de la défaite*, 223–39.
[80] M. Bergès, *Vichy contre Mounier: Les Non-Conformistes face aux années 40* (1997), 111–12.
[81] Ibid. 142–68.

Jean Vilar, a major figure in that revival, was involved with Jeune France in the Occupied Zone.

Jeune France's reputation has suffered from its association with Vichy; Schaeffer omits any mention of it from his long *Who's Who?* entry. But rather than allowing its Vichyite origins to discredit Jeune France, one could use Jeune France to rethink Vichy. It was an example of the possibilities that Vichy seemed to offer to people who did not necessarily accept its conservative agenda, as the Popular Front had done to people who did not necessarily accept its Republican agenda. Vichy's official values were susceptible to various interpretations. This was true, for example, of folklore. For Vichy, folklore was the decor of a nostalgic quest for *vieille France*. By the young innovators of Jeune France, folklore was viewed as a way of reinvigorating an atrophied local cultural life, bridging the chasm between cultural experimentation and popular culture. It was after all the Popular Front which had created France's first folklore museum, the Musée des Arts et Traditions Populaires (ATP), in 1937.

The ATP's first director was Georges-Henri Rivière who remained in place throughout the Vichy regime and continued to head it until 1967. In the 1920s Rivière who originally wanted to be a musician, was a member of the glittering Right Bank set—playing jazz at the Bœuf sur le Toit, writing songs for Josephine Baker—but he also mixed with the cultural avant-garde. It was surrealists like Michel Leiris, Robert Desnos, and Georges Bataille who had introduced him to primitive art. He organized an exhibition of pre-Colombian art which came to the attention of the ethnologist Paul Rivet, director of France's main ethnographic museum. As a committed Socialist academic, and one of the intellectuals most committed to the Popular Front, Rivet could not have been more different from the dandyish dilettante Rivière, but he appreciated Rivière's flair and enterprise. Rivet's patronage gave Rivière the directorship of the ATP. Rivière had no strong political identity, but his cultural priorities meshed with those of the Popular Front: cultural democratization and the rediscovery of authentic popular cultures.[82]

Rivière, who had owed his career to the patronage of the left, thrived equally well under Vichy. When the regime launched the idea of *chantiers intellectuels* ('intellectual worksites') to employ out-of-work intellectuals, Rivière proposed three projects: a survey of rural architecture; a survey of rural furniture; a survey of the arts and traditions of the peasantry. This was entirely in the spirit of Vichy, and Rivière received generous subsidies to employ teams of workers to catalogue the varieties of regional styles. This was among the most important research of its kind ever conducted in France. In carrying it out, Rivière co-operated with the Peasant Corporation, and published a study of peasant folklore in its journal, *Études agricoles*. At the Liberation, he was briefly under a cloud, but accusations of collaboration were not substantiated.

---

[82] H. Lebovics, *True France: The Wars over Cultural Identity 1900–1945* (1982), 162–86.

Rivière was a survivor, unencumbered by political baggage, ready to seize any opportunities to achieve his aims. This makes it difficult, in his relationship to Vichy, to draw the line between tactical accommodation and genuine commitment. In 1942 he wrote: 'The new French State, and with it all Europe, senses the importance of hereditary values under threat and wants to incorporate the most precious substance of them into the new order which is emerging.'[83] Rivet's colleagues were shocked that books by Jews had apparently disappeared from the shelves of the ATP.[84] But Rivière did not subscribe to Vichy's archaic romanticism. He criticized the obsession with tradition which kept the peasant in poverty, talking of the need to adapt to the modern, and allow 'a new beauty to come forth from the industrial revolution'.[85]

Twentieth-Century Utopia: An Architect at Vichy

Rivière's ambiguities were to some extent those of the regime itself. Borotra, although revering Pétain, was quite ready to admit what his sports policy owed to the Popular Front. In October 1941, he held a big meeting to pay tribute to the memory and work of Léo Lagrange, the Popular Front minister in charge of leisure, who had been killed in the battle of France.[86] But there is no more striking evidence of the ambiguities of Vichy than the brief Vichyite career of the architect Le Corbusier, who had also offered his services to the Popular Front. On the face of it nothing seems more improbable than the flirtation between the pope of architectural modernism and the France of folklore. But like that other social engineer, Alexis Carrel, Le Corbusier fully subscribed to Vichy's ambition to 'reconstruct mankind'. In Le Corbusier's case, this role was to be fulfilled not by science but by architecture. This was a message he had been preaching for twenty years. Now the physical destruction that had occurred during the battle of France provided an opportunity to be seized.

After 1919 the State had provided the funds for reconstruction, but did not interfere in the way it was spent. Vichy, however, intended to monitor the process closely. Urban squalor was considered to have been one of the Republic's main failures; the need for a policy of enlightened urbanism was a major theme of Giraudoux's *Pleins pouvoirs*. Vichy set up a Commissariat for the Reconstruction of Buildings (CRI) to oversee reconstruction. Its staff swelled from 894 in 1941 to 2,855 by the Liberation. Many of the experts who staffed it were running French urban policy into the 1960s. Inevitably there was an air of unreality about the CRI's plans. Allied bombing, which started in 1941, made a mockery of the hope that France would escape further physical devastation, and rebuilding was

[83] Faure, *Le Projet culturel*, 73.   [84] Lindenberg, *Les Années souterraines*, 256–7.
[85] Lebovics, *True France*, 182–3.   [86] Gay-Lescot, *Sport et éducation*, 135.

only possible to the extent that the Germans, who controlled access to France's raw materials, were willing to allow it.[87]

The CRI was not given a totally free hand. Its decisions had to be submitted to another body set up at the same time, the National Committee for Reconstruction. In June 1943, Vichy promulgated an urbanism code and put all the bodies responsible for urban planning under a National Committee of Urbanism (CNU). This was characteristic of Vichy's solution to most problems: the setting up of innumerable new commissariats, committees, commissions, and secretariats whose efforts cancelled each other out. A reconstruction plan for the city of Châteauneuf which was ready in April 1941 had still not been officially approved by 1944. The CNU was sympathetic to architectural modernism while the Architecture Committee of CRI was not. It organized competitions to guide architects towards traditional 'non-degenerate' French art, and warned against 'deracinated' architecture.

It was into this maze that Le Corbusier stumbled in January 1941. For twenty years, he had not been unduly discriminating in searching for patrons to implement his grandiose schemes. In the 1920s he was a prophet of Taylorism, seeing businessmen, not governments, as the key to reform: he was a member of the urban study group of Redressement français, and believed that the world would be remade by an alliance of architect and engineer. From 1930 Le Corbusier became involved in neo-syndicalist and technocratic reviews like *Plans*, *Prélude*, and *L'Homme réel*. He became increasingly interested in urban planning and drafted plans for Rio, Buenos Aires, Paris, and Algiers. In 1928–30 he visited Moscow three times and was invited to give his views on the redevelopment of Moscow. He now saw the Soviet Union as 'the promised land of the engineer' until the turn to Stalinism scotched any prospect of his ideas being adopted. In 1934–5 he started to cultivate fascist Italy. He sent Mussolini an inscribed copy of one of his works, and submitted an urban plan for Italy's new conquest Addis Ababa. Again this came to nothing. In 1936 Le Corbusier had hopes of the Popular Front. But although he was allowed to exhibit his ideas in the Pavillon des Temps Nouveaux at the 1937 Exhibition, he got nowhere in trying to sell the new government his proposal for the model farm—'la ferme radieuse'—which he had first devised in 1932.[88]

After the defeat Le Corbusier wrote a short book, *Destin de Paris*, which argued that better housing could lead to a regeneration of the family. He also wrote a piece dedicated to the Compagnons de France. Having demonstrated in this way that he was in tune with the prevailing rhetoric, Le Corbusier arrived

[87] D. Voldman, *La Reconstruction des villes françaises 1940–1944* (1997) 1–85.

[88] M. McCleod, 'Urbanism and Utopia: Le Corbusier from Regional Syndicalism to Vichy' (Ph.D. thesis, Princeton, 1985); R. Baudoui, *Planification territoriale et reconstruction 1940–1946* (1984); id., 'L'Architecture en France des années 1930 aux années 1940', in P. Milza and F. Roche-Pezard (eds.), *Art et fascisme* (Brussels, 1988)), 79–100; R. Fishman, *Urban Utopias in the Twentieth Century: Ebenezer Howard, Frank Lloyd Wright and Le Corbusier* (1977).

at Vichy in January 1941. He wrote: 'I enter the ranks after six months of doing nothing and twenty years of hopes.'[89] He was put in charge of a DGEN Study Commission for questions relating to housing and building. Enthusiastic about Vichy's creation of an Order of Architects, Le Corbusier compared it to the master builders of medieval Europe. He envisaged the order carrying out a massive reconstruction programme under the direction of an official (presumably himself) to be called 'the regulator (*l'ordonnateur*)'.

While awaiting the realization of this scheme, Le Corbusier lobbied for the Algiers reconstruction plan he had drafted in the 1930s. This was to no avail. The Algiers Plan infuriated the city's European population and the mayor denounced him as a Communist. Meanwhile the Study Commission ran into the opposition of the DGEN's head, Lehideux. Le Corbusier returned from Algiers to find that it had been downgraded before being finally wound up in January 1942. Le Corbusier was kept off the CNU on the pretext that he had not been a French citizen long enough, but the real reason was that he had too many enemies. In frustration, Le Corbusier lobbied to get an interview with Pétain. He wrote to one friend: 'I'm down on my hands and knees doing everything to get results.' The most he obtained was a letter from Ménétrel acknowledging the receipt of Corbusier's book *Sur les quatre routes* and transmitting the Marshal's opinion that it contained 'many suggestions for the regeneration of urban life, often happy ones'. After more fuming at the 'mediocrity, hostility, and cliques' of Vichy, Le Corbusier finally left the town in April 1942: 'Farewell dear shitty Vichy! I shake the last speck of your dust from my shoes.'[90]

Le Corbusier's eighteen months at Vichy are only a footnote in the history of the regime, and he never approached its inner circles. That he should have hoped for anything from Vichy demonstrates his opportunistic naivety, but it also shows the diversity of expectations aroused by the regime in its early days. That Vichy could ever have held out the prospect of using him is another illustration of the many currents that coexisted within the regime. That he was finally thwarted was less an example of the victory of 'traditionalists' over 'modernizers'—on the contrary one of his main enemies was Lehideux while one of his supporters was Dumoulin—than an illustration of the Byzantine workings of the regime where corridor intrigues so often ended in stalemate.

Utopian Communities: An Economist at Vichy

By the end of 1942, few ambiguities remained at Vichy: the Vichy utopians buried their illusions. *Esprit* had been silenced in the summer of 1941; Jeune France was closed down in March 1942. Dunoyer's faith in Pétain did not survive the events of November 1942, and Uriage was closed in the following month (it

[89] Macleod, 'Urbanism and Utopia', 384.
[90] Fishman, *Urban Utopias*, 243–52; R. Baudoui, 'L'Attitude de Le Corbusier pendant la guerre', in Centre Georges Pompidou (ed.), *Le Corbusier: Une encyclopédie* (1987), 455–9.

became a Milice school instead). Most of Dunoyer's team went into hiding or joined the Resistance. Vichy youth policy, long a contested arena between traditionalists and fascists, underwent a marked radicalization after Bonnard became Minister of Education in April 1942. Georges Pelorson became Lamirand's deputy, and proclaimed that he intended to provide the 'political and revolutionary formation necessary for the New French State'. This was the role he envisaged for the Équipes nationales, volunteer groups originally created in the Occupied Zone to clear bomb damage. In August 1942 Pelorson summoned the leaders of youth movements to inform them that the Équipes were to become the core of a single youth movement swearing total obedience to the Marshal. This ambition came to nothing because the leaders of the other youth movements resisted any infringement of their independence, and Pelorson was not allowed by his superiors to abandon entirely the pluralistic youth policy which remained the regime's official policy. He did, however, give official accreditation to collaborationist youth movements like the JFOM and the Jeunesse franciste which had previously been held at arm's length by the SGJ.[91]

Lamirand resigned from the SGJ in March 1943. Youth movements were now required to renegotiate the accreditation which Lamirand had granted them in 1941; the Jewish scouting organization (EIF) was banned. Borotra, who had never disguised his anti-German convictions, was ousted from the Sports Commissariat in April 1942, and subsequently arrested while trying to cross the Pyrenees. He had run the Commissariat in an ecumenical spirit. Collaborationists had disapproved of his readiness to celebrate the feats of France's swimming champion Alfred Nakache, who happened to be Jewish. In 1941, Nakache accompanied Borotra on a tour of North Africa and was asked by him on various occasions to raise the colours. In 1943, after Borotra had gone, Nakache was arrested and deported with his family to Germany.[92]

From the middle of 1942, there was less and less space within Vichy for a Mounier, Beuve-Méry, Dunoyer de Segonzac, Schaeffer, Le Corbusier, or Borotra. But the fact that the regime, or organizations which developed with its benediction, had, up to a point, enjoyed their support, is testimony to the crisis of traditional Republican values in France at the end of the 1930s. All these people had shared a certain number of preoccupations: a sense of living through a profound crisis of civilization which required a remaking of mankind; a belief that liberal individualism was incapable of embracing humanity in all its wholeness; and a conviction that the void which had opened up in France in 1940 offered vast possibilities. To the extent that they shared a positive doctrine to offer in opposition to liberalism, it was centred upon the idea of 'community'.

No one more ardently espoused this theme than another young reformer attracted to Vichy: the economist François Perroux (1903–87). Having been one

---

[91] Duquesne, *Les Catholiques français*, 233–4; Comte, *Une utopie combattante*, 501–2; Austin, 'Education and Youth Policies', 368.

[92] Gay-Lescot, *Sport et éducation*, 94, 113–15.

of the first interpreters of Schumpeterian economics in France before 1939, Perroux was a pioneer in the application of Keynesian economics in France after 1945. In 1944, he founded the Institute of Applied Economic Science; in 1947, he produced the first French study of national accounts; he later became a seminal contributor to Third World economics. These and many other original contributions to economics are mentioned in the works of homage to him. Few of these works, however, mention his activities during the Occupation, unless to mention his pre-war book *Les Mythes hitlériens* in which he supposedly warned his compatriots about the dangers of Nazism, making it possible to portray him like a sort of resister *avant la lettre*.[93]

In fact, Perroux was actively involved with Vichy at several levels. He was a member of the Conseil national, sitting on its Constitutional Reform Commission; he acted as a technical adviser to the Ministry of Finance;[94] from September 1942 he was Secretary-General of the Fondation Carrel from which he resigned in December 1943 after quarrelling with Carrel. The quarrel was not about the work the Fondation was carrying out, but about the way it was run. Perroux claimed that it was riddled with inefficiency and that funds were being wasted.[95] In September 1941 Perroux was also a founding member, along with Pétain's pet philosopher Gustave Thibon, of the group Économie et humanisme whose leading light was the Dominican Louis Joseph Lebret. Économie et humanisme aimed to create a forum for dialogue between Catholics and the social and human sciences. After the war it became involved in Third World development and was ready to engage in a dialogue with Marxism. But during the Occupation it was guardedly sympathetic towards the National Revolution. Économie et humanisme participated in the 'Journées communautaires de Mont Dore' organized in April 1943 by Pétain's *cabinet* to reflect (albeit rather hypothetically) on the future of the National Revolution. It received a subsidy from Vichy in 1943, and whatever Lebret's doubts about Vichy, in August 1944 his main worry was that the Liberation would be a pretext for 'Judaeo-Marxist revenge'.[96]

In July 1942, Perroux also set up a group called Renaître whose objective was to offer doctrinal reflection on the National Revolution and help to 'find the elite who will make it'. Renaître in fact consisted only of Perroux himself and the Africanist Yves Urvoy, director until April 1942 of an institute to provide légionnaires with a political education.[97] Renaître's output consisted of six dense brochures outlining proposals for reform. In addition to all these activities, Perroux can also be found editing a series entitled *La Bibliothèque du peuple*

[93] F. Denoël (ed.), *François Perroux* (Lausanne, 1990).
[94] Margairaz, *L'État, les finances et l'économie*, 510.
[95] Drouard, *Une inconnue des sciences sociales*, 154–65.
[96] D. Pelletier, *Économie et humanisme* (1996), 60–65.
[97] D. Urvoy, 'Témoignage: Yves Urvoy (1900–1944)', *Revue française d'histoire d'Outre-Mer*, 65 (1978), 64–98.

with the Catholic Jacques Madaule, lecturing in October 1941 to the École nationale de cadres civiques, which was the training school for Marion's propaganda delegates.[98] Although Perroux never lectured at Uriage, Beuve-Méry, to whom he remained close all his life, disseminated some of his ideas there. But Perroux felt Beuve-Méry had not properly emancipated himself from the ideology of 1789.[99]

What did Perroux mean by this, and what was it about Vichy that he supported? Throughout the 1930s, Perroux had been the indefatigable advocate of a form of corporatism which he called the 'Community of Labour'.[100] He started from the position that the liberal state had no answer to the crisis of modern man. The totalitarian states (Germany and the Soviet Union) had succeeded no better although at least they had addressed the problem of trying to integrate the proletariat into the national community. The revolution of 1848, the Commune, and the Popular Front had tried to do this, but each of them had failed. Given that modern capitalism separated the worker from the means of production, it was necessary to reorganize industry around corporatist communities of labour giving equal rights to employers and workers. These communities would be the prelude to a restructuring of society on communitarian lines. Once 'dissolving and mutilating individualism' had been overcome, it would be possible to 'reconstruct mankind' in a society of 'communitarian humanism'.[101]

This communitarian society would move beyond parliamentarianism—the 'fiction of representation'—and rediscover the notion of elites: 'it is only around the leader and through the leader that the group becomes conscious of itself'. Elites emerged from 'concrete communities, centred on definite activities' ascending like a pyramid from the smallest local communities to the apex of the national community. The country would no longer be governed by professional politicians 'separated from the deep life of the country'.

Perroux's anti-indivdualism was grounded in his strong Catholic convictions; his suspicion of democratic politics was shared by many young intellectuals of the 1930s. He wrote in 1938 that Ordre nouveau, *Esprit, Homme réel,* and *Nouveaux cahiers* had 'in a few years brought more original and realistic ideas into circulation that any French political party in the last half century'.[102] After 1945, Perroux's interest in working out an economics of Third World development that respected local cultures was consistent with his suspicion of the disintegrating force of untrammelled capitalism. So was his interest, in the late 1960s, in the ideas of Herbert Marcuse.[103]

---

[98] The lecture was published as 'Le Problème français du prolétariat', *Idées* (Nov. 1941).
[99] Comte, *Une utopie combattante,* 307.
[100] *Capitalisme et communauté de travail* (1938), 154–65.
[101] Id. and Urvoy, *Renaître,* i. *La Révolution en Marche* (1943) and iv. *Politique* (1943).
[102] *Capitalisme et communauté,* 316–17.
[103] F. Perroux, *François Perroux interroge Herbert Marcuse* (1969).

Probably no one had reflected more carefully on the doctrine of communitarianism than Perroux. Not everyone would have subscribed to his interpretation of it, but the concept was sufficiently protean and ambiguous to accommodate reactionaries like Maurras, Catholic conservatives like Thibon, authoritarian Catholics like de Fabrègues, leftist Catholics like Mounier, social Catholics like Lebret, and syndicalists like Hubert Lagardelle. Communitarianism was the nearest Vichy came to developing a single, overarching ideology.

Communities are of course defined by whom they exclude as well as whom they include. Perroux himself did not address this matter in any detail. In one of the *Renaître* brochures he wrote:

> In a nation articulated into numerous overlapping and interlocking groups, one becomes more fully a citizen as one participates in a larger number of communities . . . There are infinite degrees, all possible nuances of citizenship . . . It is possible to conceive different kinds of status which could for some people involve participation in ordinary communities, for others participation in specialized communities reserved to people of specific origins. This would no longer involve people being thrown out of the single common national community, but reflect concrete realities, so that just as certain groups are more or less purely national communities, people would be more or less 'pure' citizens. This would be the most flexible way of . . . recognizing the real diversities while also assisting unity. This would also be the best way of resolving the 'Jewish problem'.[104]

Although vague on details, this was at least framed in relatively inclusive terms. There were others, however, for whom the French national community would have no place for Jews.

[104] Id. and Urvoy, *Renaître*, iv. 36–7.

15

Vichy and the Jews

At his trial for collaboration in 1947, Xavier Vallat, Vichy's Commissioner for Jewish Affairs, defended himself by arguing that he had always been an anti-Semite. As a defence, this is not as paradoxical as it sounds. Vallat's point was that he could not be accused of having worked for Germany since his anti-Semitism was authentically French, 'inspired by my personal conception of the Jewish problem'. That Vallat could even consider offering this defence is striking evidence of the fact that, although the fate of the Jews was not entirely ignored at the Liberation,[1] anti-Semitism in itself was considered secondary to the crime of collaboration.

Today the situation is reversed. The experience of the Jews is central to contemporary perceptions of the Occupation. This can create new distortions: it would be as wrong to read the entire history of the Occupation through the prism of anti-Semitism as it would to leave it out entirely. Little of the regime's propaganda targeted the Jews. It commissioned no anti-Semitic posters; there was no anti-Semitism in any of the official film documentaries produced by the regime;[2] no speech by Pétain directly mentioned the Jews. When Vichy issued its first Jewish Statute in October 1940, it did so almost apologetically. The accompanying communiqué announced that the government 'respects Jewish persons and property . . . There is no question of easy vengeance but of indispensable security.' The Statute would be applied in a 'spirit of humanity'.[3]

The tone was different in the Occupied Zone where the collaborationist press was violently anti-Semitic. *Au pilori* declared in March 1941: 'Jews are not men. They are stinking beasts. One gets rid of fleas. One fights against epidemics.'[4] The main centre of anti-Semitic propaganda in Paris was the IEQJ, nominally run by a thuggish French officer, Paul Sézille, but financed entirely by Germany. Its most ambitious undertaking was the notorious exhibition on the Jew and France at the Palais Berlitz. As always, however, it would be wrong to exagger-

---

[1] H. Rousso, 'Une justice impossible: L'Épuration et la politique antijuive de Vichy', *Annales ESC*, 48/3 (1993), 745–70.

[2] Bertin-Maghit, 'Le Documentaire de propagande', 32.

[3] Singer, *Vichy, l'université et les juifs*, 73–4.   [4] Cotta, *La Collaboration*, 141.

ate the contrast between the two zones. Pétain's entourage contained fanatical anti-Semites like Ménétrel and Alibert. As for propaganda, much of the southern press was so anti-Semitic that the regime hardly needed to organize its own campaigns. Anti-Semitism was a dominant theme of the Legion's daily radio broadcasts. Even if Vichy's anti-Semitism was less radical than Germany's, it was an autonomous policy, with its own indigenous roots. There were two separate anti-Semitic projects in France between 1940 and 1944, and the Jews were caught between them.

Emulative Zeal: Vichy Anti-Semitism/Nazi Anti-Semitism

The Jewish 'problem' was one of Vichy's earliest preoccupations. Alibert had immediately started to prepare legislation against the Jews. In September 1940, Peyrouton was exploring the possibility of sending 2,000 Jews to Madagascar, but the Ministry of Finance was worried by the cost.[5] The first law specifically aimed at Jews (as opposed to measures against foreigners also affecting some Jews) was the Jewish Statute of 3 October 1940. The Statute was drafted by Alibert, but apparently Pétain was the 'most harsh' when the government discussed the project.[6]

Despite what Vichy apologists later claimed,[7] the Statute was not imposed by the Germans. Some Vichy leaders, however, did view anti-Semitism as a means of winning German favour: Flandin told a German interlocutor on 16 July 1940 that collaboration would require France 'completely to rid herself' of Jewish influence.[8] On 24 September, General de Laurencie reported that the Germans were enquiring whether Vichy planned any measures against the Jews, adding that there was no pressure from them for such measures.[9] Three days later, the Germans issued an ordinance requiring Jews in the Occupied Zone to register with the authorities, but a German memorandum reveals that this measure was passed in the knowledge that the French were about to act: 'it was consciously judged necessary to have it antedate the French law so that the regulation of the Jewish question appeared to emanate from the German authorities'.[10]

The Jewish Statute was the start of a thickening web of regulations directed against the Jews. Over the next twelve months, Vichy issued twenty-six laws and twenty-four decrees on the Jews. In June 1941, a second Jewish Statute widened the definition of Jewishness and introduced more occupations banned to Jews. It was followed by decrees imposing quotas on Jewish lawyers, doctors, students, architects, and pharmacists. In July 1941, Vichy ordered a census of the entire

---

[5] Baruch, *Servir l'État*, 130.
[6] P. Baudouin, *The Private Diaries (March 1940 to January 1941)* (1948), 254–5.
[7] J. Carcopino, *Souvenirs de sept ans*, 358; Barthélemy, *Mémoires*, 311; Berthelot, *Sur les rails*, 106–7; Peyrouton, *Du service public*, 155–6. Du Moulin, *Le Temps des illusions*, 280, does admit the opposite.
[8] Burrin, *La Dérive fasciste*, 352.
[9] Baruch, *Servir l'État*, 129.   [10] Peschanski, *Contrôle et exclusion*, 146.

Jewish population in the Unoccupied Zone. This was a breach with the Republican tradition confining questions of religion and ethnic origin to the private sphere; it had grave consequences when Jews started to be rounded up in 1942.[11]

Vichy's treatment of foreign Jews was even more callous. From 4 October 1940, they could be interned at the discretion of prefects. Seven main camps were used for this purpose, and by the start of 1941 about 40,000 Jews were held in them. The conditions were atrocious: in total about 3,000 Jews perished in the French camps from undernourishment and cold before the Final Solution had begun. The number of internees dropped in 1941, but this was due to the efforts of relief organizations, not to the government. Indeed Darlan ordered in June 1941 that Jews who had not been resident in France before May 1940 should not be released in case they tried to integrate into French society.[12]

Left to itself, then, Vichy's policy was to turn French Jews into second-class citizens, and treat foreign Jews as an encumbrance to whose fate it was indifferent. But Vichy was not left to itself for long. By the end of 1940 Dannecker in Paris was pushing his own anti-Semitic agenda. He was certainly emboldened by Vichy's own example. At a meeting at the German Embassy in February 1941 he declared: 'the fact that more than 40,000 Jews are interned in the Free Zone is an argument one can advance to encourage the military to give the SD immediate and full powers for the arrest of all Jews'.[13]

Once Dannecker started to press for a radicalization of anti-Semitism, Vichy had a simple choice: to let the Germans proceed in the Occupied Zone, at the cost of allowing infringements of sovereignty and jeopardizing France's unity, or to preserve nominal sovereignty at the cost of doing the Germans' dirty work for them. Usually the latter course was chosen. When on 18 October 1940, the Germans passed a second ordinance, requiring all Jewish enterprises in the Occupied Zone to be placed under trusteeship as a preliminary to 'Aryanization', Vichy, fearing that this was a German plan to penetrate the French economy, instituted an agency of 'temporary administrators' (SCAP) to ensure that the trustees were French. By the summer of 1941, half the Jews of Paris had been deprived of any means of existence. In July 1941, to preserve administrative unity, Vichy also imposed Aryanization on the Unoccupied Zone.

The Germans also pushed for the setting up of a Jewish office to co-ordinate anti-Semitic policy. Darlan was not enthusiastic, but having just come to power he was keen to win German approval. He also preferred the existence of a French organization responsible for all France to a German one operating in the North alone. The result was the creation in March 1941 of the Commissariat-General

---

[11] Marrus and Paxton, *Vichy France and the Jews*, 83–105.

[12] A. Grynberg, *Les Camps de la honte: Les Internés juifs des camps français* (1991); Marrus and Paxton, *Vichy France and the Jews*, 165–76; Kaspi, *Les Juifs pendant l'Occupation*, 131–44; Cohen, *Persécutions et sauvetages*, 92–112.

[13] Billig, *Le Commissariat général aux questions juives*, i. 44.

for Jewish Affairs (CGQJ), headed by Vallat. Although less fanatical than some of Germany's candidates for the job—who included Céline—Vallat considered himself a 'serious anti-Semite'. He once told Dannecker: 'I have been an anti-Semite for much longer than you.' The theoretical difference between Vallat's State anti-Semitism, which viewed the Jews as unassimilable to the French Catholic tradition, and German racial anti-Semitism, was that it allowed exemptions for Jews who had served France with distinction. German anti-Semitism did not embrace the concept of the good Jew. But Vallat granted exemptions so parsimoniously that the practical consequences for French Jews were negligible.

Having obtained the setting up of the CGQJ, Dannecker's next objective was to force all the Jews in France into a single organization somewhat like the Eastern European *Judenräte*—those Jewish councils obliged to administer their own misery. This was contrary to the logic of Vichy policy which preserved a distinction between French and foreign Jews. Vallat therefore procrastinated until it became clear that Germany was ready to act unilaterally. Rather than allow this, in November 1941, Vichy set up it own General Union of the Israelites of France (UGIF). This organization, which subsumed existing Jewish organizations under its authority, covered both zones, and was answerable to the French government.[14]

Vichy's desire always to keep up with the Germans meant that anti-Semitism spiralled continuously in a more radical direction. This is clearly visible in the Aryanization process. In fact the Germans had no major designs on the French economy, but they were happy for this to be believed, so that the French would act prophylactically. The aim, as Elmar Michel stated in November 1940, was 'To make the French authorities participate in the elimination of the Jews. In this way we shall make the French share the responsibility for Aryanization and we shall have at our disposal the French administrative apparatus.'[15]

This Machiavellian strategy was extremely successful. Although the initiative for Aryanization came from Germany, many French interests became implicated in it, seizing the opportunity to advance their own agendas: Vallat wanted to reduce Jewish influence; the Ministry of Industrial Production saw a chance to impose further economic 'rationalization'; the COs, administering Aryanization in their industries, hoped to eliminate Jewish competition. These sectional interests frequently clashed, but they were united in displaying little sentimentality about the fortune(s) that circumstances had presented them with. By May 1944, over 40,000 Jewish enterprises had been placed in trusteeship, and of these three-quarters had been sold to 'Aryans'.[16]

[14] Marrus and Paxton, *Vichy France and the Jews*, 108–9; Cohen, *Persécutions et sauvetages*, 165–78.
[15] H. Rousso, 'L'Aryanisation économique: Vichy, l'occupant et la spoliation des juifs', *Yod*, 15/16 (1982), 51–77: 56.
[16] Ibid; Kaspi, *Les Juifs pendant l'Occupation*, 112–28; Cohen, *Persécutions et sauvetages*, 113–24; Marrus and Paxton, *Vichy France and the Jews*, 100–3, 152–60.

Vallat's attempt to preserve French control over anti-Semitic policy eventually caused the Germans to lose patience with him. His patriotic dislike of the occupier was only too evident. In April 1942 Laval replaced him by Louis Darquier de Pellepoix, a corrupt and violently anti-Semitic journalist who had often been arrested in the 1930s for brawling with Jews. Darquier's approach was apparent in a memorandum he issued to his personnel instructing them that Jews should no longer be referred to as M. Levy or M. Dreyfus, but as 'the Jew Levy' or 'the Jew Dreyfus'.[17]

Under Darquier, the CGQJ stepped up anti-Semitic propaganda. From September 1942 it had three weekly radio slots on French national radio. The South now received the same kind of anti-Semitic propaganda as the North. Darquier sponsored a number of pseudo-scientific bodies devoted to studying race, such as the Institute of Anthropo-Sociology under Claude Vacher de la Pouge (son of the famous Georges). A Chair in the History of Judaism was created at the Sorbonne, and its first holder, Henri Labroue, author of a pamphlet entitled *Voltaire antijuif*, gave his first lecture in December 1942.[18] The IEQJ was transformed into the Insitute for the Study of Jewish and Ethno-Racial Questions (IEQJER) under the direction of Georges Montandon (with René Martial on its board of directors).

Montandon had since 1935 held the Chair of Ethnology at the conservative École d'anthropologie. During the 1930s his ideas had become increasingly racist and anti-Semitic. In 1938 he proposed a Jewish statute and suggested that Jewish men who disobeyed it should be castrated. Accused by a left-wing newspaper, during the Phoney War, of having taken up the ideas of Hitler, he claimed that on the contrary Hitler had copied his ideas. In 1941 he founded a new anthropology journal called *L'Ethnie française* and he was also author of the book *Comment reconnaitre un juif?* (How to recognise a Jew). Less harmless than these pseudo-scholarly speculations was Montandon's role as the CGQJ's ethnological expert adjudicating whether a person was Jewish or not. He spent much time examining penises, noses, and earlobes. People who hoped he might procure them a certificate of non-Jewishness had to pay for his services with no guarantee that he would decide in their favour.[19]

Darquier was an incompetent administrator and the Germans took a low view of the effectiveness of these bodies. The IEQJER was wound up in the autumn of 1943. Another problem, from the German point of view, was that these bodies genuinely believed in racial theory, but the Nazis were not happy with the French designating themselves as Aryans.[20] Darquier was despised at

---

[17] Billig, *Le Commissariat général*, i. 113.

[18] On Labroue, see C. Singer, 'Henri Labroue', in Taguieff (ed.), *L'Antisémitisme de plume*, 233–44.

[19] M. Knobel, 'L'Ethnologie à la dérive: Georges Montandon et l'ethnoracisme', *Ethnologie française*, 18/2 (1988), 107–13; Billig, *Le Commissariat général*, ii. 243–8.

[20] G. Wellers, *L'Étoile jaune à l'heure de Vichy* (1973), 86–95; Cohen, *Persécutions et sauvetages*, 344–54; Marrus and Paxton, *Vichy France and the Jews*, 294–301.

Vichy, where he rarely set foot. He wanted to exclude Jewish children from schools and force all Jews to wear a yellow star, but Vichy rejected these ideas. The Germans were also pressing for the imposition of the yellow star, and in June 1942 they acted unilaterally and imposed it in the Occupied Zone. For once, Vichy refused to follow, more out of fear of public reaction than out of concern for the Jews.[21]

The yellow star was part of a steady tightening of the screw on the lives of Jews in the Occupied Zone. From August 1941, Jews were forbidden to own radios and bicycles; from February 1942, they were subject to a special curfew; from June 1942, they were allowed only to travel in the last carriage on the metro and shop only between 3 p.m. and 4 p.m., and were banned from all public places (cinemas, restaurants, libraries, public gardens, sports fields). When the deportations began in July 1942, the Jews of Paris had been excluded from participation in normal daily life.

These were German, not French, policies. But Vichy continued to implement its own separate policy of persecution. Even after the Germans started to deport Jews from France, the Vichy authorities were, for their own reasons, expelling Jews from certain *départements*. In April 1943, the 332 Jews (French and foreign) of La Bourboule, near Vichy, were forcibly shunted to another locality because Pétain was moving into the town.[22] Even more dangerously, in December 1942 Vichy required all Jews, French and foreign, to have their identity and ration cards stamped 'juif'. This made the Jews all the more vulnerable to the German policy of arrests.[23]

The way that French and German policies interacted to the detriment of the Jews emerges clearly from the progressive amendments made to the definition of Jewishness. The first definition was provided by the Germans in the ordinance of 27 September 1940: it did not use the word 'race', and defined as Jewish anyone of the Jewish religion or having at least three Jewish grandparents. A week later, Vichy's Jewish Statute spread its net further: it used the criterion of 'race' and defined as Jewish anyone with at least three Jewish grandparents or two if the spouse was Jewish. In an ordinance of 26 April 1941, the Germans adopted Vichy's definition but extended it further: half-Jews (people with two Jewish grandparents) who were married to Jews would now be considered Jewish unless they had divorced before the publication of the ordinance. Vichy's second Jewish Statute in June 1941 widened the boundary further by backdating the point at which divorce could exempt half-Jews from being included as Jews to 25 June 1940. Once the German round-ups started in the summer of 1942, Dannecker ordered the wider French definition of Jewishness to be used in preference to the slightly more restrictive German one.[24]

[21] Marrus and Paxton, *Vichy France and the Jews*, 234–40.
[22] Poznanski, *Être juif en France*, 537–9.
[23] Ibid. 522–7.   [24] Billig, *Le Commissariat général*, i. 42–4, 56–8, 242.

When Vichy apologists later claimed that Vichy anti-Semitism was not, like the German one, driven by the ultimate aim of exterminating the Jews, they were correct. But this did not stop Vichy simultaneously continuing its own policy of depriving French Jews of their livelihoods, shunting them around, arresting them for minor infractions of the law, stamping their papers— oblivious of the fact that in the background the German convoys were rolling east. From 1942, Vichy behaved towards the Jews like a family building a bonfire in its backyard despite its knowledge that a forest fire is raging just over the fence.

The Holocaust in France

Even before the Wannsee conference in January 1942, arrests of Jews had occurred in the Occupied Zone. The first took place on 14 May 1941 when 3,710 foreign Jews were arrested. In August 1941, there was a raid on the 11th arrondissement in Paris, resulting in the arrest of 4,230 Jews, both French and foreign. Finally, in December 1941, 734 prominent French Jews (and 250 immigrant Jews), were arrested, allegedly as a reprisal for an attack on German soldiers. The victims were interned in four camps: Pithiviers and Rolande-la-Beaune in the Loiret (about 100 km from Paris), Compiègne to the north-east of Paris, and Drancy, an unfinished municipal housing estate just outside Paris. Apart from Compiègne, all these camps were run by the French. Drancy was so lacking in basic facilities that in October 1941 the Germans ordered 900 sick and dying internees to be released.[25] One observer noted in November: 'I have met several living skeletons who can hardly stand. They are the Jews freed from Drancy.'[26]

The arrests of 1941 prepared the ground for the deportations of 1942. Laval and Bousquet's complicity in this policy has been discussed earlier because it was dictated more by the logic of Vichy's collaboration policy than by its anti-Semitism: it was the most horrific example of the consequences which could flow from collaboration. Most of those arrested in the summer of 1942 were sent to Drancy. Conditions in the camp had improved, but no one stayed long enough to benefit from this: Drancy became the departure point for almost all the trains leaving for Auschwitz. After the Vel d'Hiver round-up in July 1942, many Jews fled to the South, assuming they would be safe there. In fact, in the South, between 6 August and 15 September, the French authorities slightly exceeded the 10,000 Jews they had promised to arrest. About 4,700 of these came from the internment camps. In total, 41,951 Jews were deported from France in 1942.

In 1943, 17,069 Jews were deported. Vichy's slightly less co-operative attitude may have partly accounted for this lower figure, but the extent of Vichy non-

---

[25] Marrus and Paxton, *Vichy France and the Jews*, 252–5; Kaspi, *Les Juifs pendant l'Occupation*, 264–74.
[26] Biélinky, *Journal 1940–1942*, 163.

cooperation should not be exaggerated. In early 1943, when Knochen and Röthke demanded the arrests of French Jews, Bousquet refused, but again he offered to arrest foreign Jews. There was a wave of arrests in Paris on 10 February, when 1,549 people were arrested, 500 of them in their seventies or older.[27] Another 2,000 were found in the South, again by the French police. In January 1943, the Germans destroyed the Old Port at Marseilles, and this allowed them, with French co-operation, to round up 800 Jews, of whom 211 were French. Never before had the French police in the Unoccupied Zone participated in arresting French Jews.[28] But generally from the spring of 1943, the Germans carried out arrests alone.

In June 1943, the administration of Drancy was taken over by the Germans. The camp was now run by the violently sadistic Aloïs Brunner who had organized the elimination of the Jewish community of Salonika. Now that the Germans were carrying out most arrests, the distinction between French and foreign Jews no longer counted. The arrests were more random and more brutal, but less efficient. The biggest operation occurred in the autumn in Nice to which 30,000 Jews had fled while the city was occupied by the Italians. When the Italians signed an armistice, Brunner moved in. Over the next four months, with the help of PPF activists, and white Russian 'physiognomists', the Germans hunted all the Jews they could find. Their lack of documentation only made the operation more arbitrary. One survivor remembered:

> Official black Citroëns cruised the streets of Nice, and passengers attentively scrutinised passers-by. At any moment, a pedestrian would be asked to get into a car. No useless questions or identity checks. The car went to a synagogue. There the victim was undressed. If he was circumcised, he automatically took his place in the next convoy to Drancy.[29]

Altogether 1,800 Jews were arrested, many fewer than the 25,000 the Germans had hoped for. The victims included the father of the future historian of the Holocaust in France, Serge Klarsfeld.[30]

The anti-Semitic fury of the Nazis reached a peak in the first months of 1944. Darquier had been removed because he was too ineffectual. His replacement Paty de Clam was no more effective, despite his promising name, and matters were really run by his second-in-command Joseph Antignac who took over in the spring. In the eight months of 1944 before the Liberation, 14,833 Jews were deported. This was a slightly higher monthly figure than the previous year. The French police still participated in some operations involving non-French Jews, but most work was now done by the Germans with help from the Milice. The arrests were carried out in a frenzied and indiscriminate way. No Jews were safe, whether French or foreign, young or old, sick or healthy:

---

[27] Klarsfeld, *Vichy-Auschwitz*, ii. 24–5.   [28] Poznanski, *Être juif en France*, 542–3.
[29] Léon Poliakov, quoted in Zuccotti, *Holocaust*, 181.
[30] Zuccotti, *Holocaust*, 180–7; Cohen, *Persécutions et sauvetages*, 449–62.

hospitals and orphanages were combed for Jews. One notorious episode occurred in July when the Lyons Gestapo chief Klaus Barbie seized forty-four small children from a children's refuge in Izieu near Lyons. All ended up in Auschwitz. The last convoy left Drancy on 17 August 1944, eight days before the Liberation of Paris.

A total of 75,721 Jews was deported from France if one includes those from the Nord/Pas-de-Calais, which was attached to Belgium, and those deported individually as resisters. About another 4,000 Jews died in French camps or were executed in France. This gives about 80,000 Jewish victims of the Holocaust in France—of whom about 3.5 per cent (2,500) returned alive. Approximately 24,000 (32 per cent) of those deported were French Jews and 56,500 (68 per cent) foreign. This represented approximately 12 per cent of French Jews and 41 per cent of foreign Jews in France.[31] So two-thirds of the Jews deported were foreign although they had comprised only about half the Jews in France.

As has already been noted, it would be wrong to infer from these figures that Laval sacrificed almost half the foreign Jews *to* save French ones. Without French police co-operation, it would have been difficult for the Germans to arrest the foreign Jews. About three-quarters of all Jews were arrested by the French police. There were only about 2,500–3,000 German police in France in mid-1942. After November 1942 the German police were more thinly spread than ever: in Saint-Étienne, the Gestapo arrived in February 1943, and it only had four men and one commander for a population of 200,000. When Röthke pleaded with Berlin in June 1943 for 250 extra French-speaking Gestapo men to assist in the round-ups, he was told to manage with what he had.[32]

If one compares Vichy's role in the Final Solution to that of other semi-independent governments in Nazi Europe, there are few others who offered as much help as Vichy. It was Vichy which, to German surprise, had originally volunteered to deport foreign Jews from the Free Zone over which the Germans had no jurisdiction. Pétain's Vichy was not as co-operative as Slovakia, which delivered native and foreign Jews from its own heartland, but it was more so than Horthy's Hungary which, despite having had indigenous anti-Semitic legislation since 1920, handed over no Jews until the German occupation in March 1944. But there is a paradox: France was also one of the countries with the largest surviving Jewish population. Apart from Denmark, where only 7 per cent of Jews perished and most of the tiny Jewish population was spirited across the water to Sweden, and Italy, where the non-cooperation of the authorities meant that only 16 per cent were deported, nowhere compared more favourably than France from where 'only' 24 per cent of Jews were deported, as opposed to 78 per cent from Holland, 45 per cent from Belgium, and 50 per cent from Hungary. This

[31] If one includes among foreign Jews the 8,000 children born in France of foreign parents and therefore technically French, although in effect treated as foreign, the figures are 64,000 foreign and 16,000 French Jews, 45 per cent and 9 per cent respectively.

[32] Klarsfeld, *Vichy-Auschwitz*, ii. 81–2; Marrus and Paxton, *Vichy France and the Jews*, 241, 303.

paradox can only be explained by looking at the responses of both the Jews—
who were not merely passive victims of their fate—and the non-Jewish French
population.

Jewish Responses: French and Immigrants

In 1939, there were about 300,000 Jews in France, 190,000 of them French
citizens and the rest foreign. Most of the foreign Jews had arrived as immigrants
from Eastern Europe in the 1920s or refugees from Nazism during the 1930s. The
assimilated French Jews, many of them pillars of the bourgeoisie, frequently
looked down on the recent arrivals from Eastern Europe, who were mainly artisans and petits bourgeois. In Paris, where most Jews lived, the latter lived in the
poorer quarters of the east and centre (the Marais and Belleville), and the former
in the west.[33] The numbers of foreigners had been swelled by about 20,000
in 1940 with the addition of Dutch and Belgian Jewish refugees during the
Exodus, and 6,500 Jews expelled into France from the Palatinate and Baden-
Württemberg.

Whether French or foreign, the reaction of most Jews in 1940 was to obey
the law and hope for better times. About 90 per cent of Jews in the Occupied
Zone registered under the German ordinance of 27 September 1940. Even nine
months later, when Vichy introduced a census, and there was mounting evidence
of the danger ahead, about 108,000 Jews registered within two months. In total,
287,962 Jews registered in the two zones. This was a fateful step since the
census lists provided the authorities with the names and addresses used when
carrying out arrests. Astonishingly, many French Jews who fled Paris during the
Exodus returned afterwards, either because they underestimated Nazi intentions
or because they refused to be intimidated.

The distinguished paediatrician Robert Debré, father of the future Gaullist
prime minister Michel Debré, felt it his duty to 'act like our Alsatian ancestors,
live under the yoke and work to get rid of them'.[34] The civil servant Philip
Erlanger considered joining de Gaulle but decided to remain and 'bear witness';
his friend René Blum, director of the Monte Carlo Ballet and brother of Léon,
felt the same. Such people refused to deny their origins and continued to trust
in France.[35] Raymond-Raoul Lambert, who came of an old French Jewish family,
wept when Vichy's first Jewish Statute was announced. He wrote in his diary:
'one does not judge one's mother when she is unjust. One suffers and waits. Thus
we Jews of France must bow our heads and suffer.'[36]

The response of Jewish organizations was complicated by the divisions

---

[33] Kaspi, *Les Juifs pendant l'Occupation*, 17–50; Cohen, *Persécutions et sauvetages*, 25–30.
[34] Kaspi, *Les Juifs pendant l'Occupation*, 94.
[35] Zuccotti, *Holocaust*, 44–5, 54–6; Kaspi, *Les Juifs pendant l'Occupation*, 77–98: A. Wieviorka, *Ils
étaient juifs, résistants, communistes* (1986), 72–4.
[36] R.-R. Lambert, *Carnet d'un témoin* (1985), 85.

between French and foreign Jews. For French Jews to identify with the foreign Jews involved renouncing a tradition of assimilation and French patriotism. One French Jewish inmate of the Compiègne camp wrote: 'If I should perish in this adventure, it is for France that I will have died; I do not wish to be considered a victim of Judaism'.[37] Vichy paid lip-service to the tradition of French Jewish patriotism by offering exemptions to French Jews who were judged to have rendered services to France. French Jews were initially allowed to join the Legion; the Jewish scouting movement (EIF) was one of the youth movements officially accredited by the regime, and it received government grants until 1941. Indeed some French Jewish organizations were fully in sympathy with aspects of the Vichy regime. In September 1940, the Council of French Rabbis drafted a declaration of allegiance to Pétain, and affirmed its support for the values of the National Revolution. The EIF, which was trying to set up rural communities for Jews, fully subscribed to Vichy's ruralist rhetoric.[38]

Some French Jews wished to believe Darlan's remark: 'The stateless Jews, who for the past fifteen years have invaded our country, do not interest me. But the others, the good old French Jews, are entitled to all the protection we can give them.'[39] Jacques Helbronner, President of the Central Consistory (the top administrative body of French Jewry), had known Pétain since 1917 and visited him frequently during the Occupation. In the immigrant Jewish community, he was known as 'the Marshal's Jew'.[40] Pétain mendaciously let Helbronner believe that the Statute had been the work of extremists in his government, and that he wanted it repealed.[41] In April 1941, the Consistory suggested to Vallat that immigrant Jews could be placed in work camps. Helbronner himself even proposed to Pétain a revised Jewish statute which would eliminate from public life 'elements which cannot be assimilated to the national spirit'.[42]

For French Jews, the objection to the UGIF was that it lumped Jews together, ignoring the distinction between French and non-French Jews. Most Consistory leaders, who saw themselves as the representatives of French Judaism, refused to play any role in the UGIF, but Vallat secured the co-operation of other French Jewish leaders by threatening that otherwise he would appoint outsiders of his own choosing. These French Jewish leaders offered little guidance and stuck to legality. The UGIF was informed in advance by Germans of the Vel d'Hiver operation so it could prepare food for those to be arrested. It kept the informa-

---

[37] F. and R. Bédarida, 'La Persécution des juifs', in Azéma and Bédarida (eds.), *La France des années noires*, ii. 129–58: 131.

[38] R. Cohen, *The Burden of Conscience: French Jewish Leadership during the Holocaust* (Bloomington, Ind., 1987), 20; Poznanski, *Être juif en France*, 214–16.

[39] J. Adler, *The Jews of Paris and the Final Solution* (New York, 1985), 84; see also Darlan's note to Moysset in Jan. 1941, complaining that Vallat was 'going a bit too far' in his treatment of 'old French Jews': Darlan, *Lettres et notes*, 468.

[40] Adler, *Jews of Paris*, 95.   [41] Poznanski, *Être juif en France*, 132.

[42] F. and R. Bédarida, 'La Persécution des juifs', 142.

tion to itself almost until the last minute in order not to cause panic among the Jewish population.[43] In August, it even wrote to Pétain, thanking him for the protection offered to French Jews.

French Jewish leaders clung desperately to the idea that Vichy would not betray the French Jews. It was not surprising that Helbronner should feel relatively reassured when comparing his cordial meetings with Vallat to those with Dannecker who ostentatiously called for a bowl of water to wash his hands after going to the Consistory. Far from shielding French Jews, however, Vichy helped to lull them into a false sense of security. One of the UGIF leaders was Raymond-Raoul Lambert, who had once enjoyed the confidence of many leading French politicians. His wartime diaries testify to his good faith, decency, and tragic naivety. 'One has to play on the sincerity of Vallat', he wrote. He found Vallat 'correct', 'cordial', 'open and frank'. In June 1941, he anguished whether to send his children to New York: 'I will remain a Frenchman until my death, but if the French nation legally rejects me from its midst, do I have the right to decide that my children must be pariahs?' He named his daughter, born in January 1942, Marie-France, as an act of 'affirmation and hope'.[44] In December 1943, Lambert was deported to Auschwitz along with his wife and all four children; none of them returned.

The UGIF never fully broke with legality, and some historians have accused it of culpable complicity in the Final Solution.[45] Although it cannot be compared to that of the East European *Judenräte*—it did not organize convoys—it certainly failed to provide France's Jews with inspiring leadership. Some of its leaders believed that its activities as a relief organization justified unpalatable compromises. The UGIF's complacency emerged in the way it treated the orphan children in its care. Keen to respect legality, it lodged them in residences whose names were registered with the police. This exposed them to the risk of arbitrary arrest. Even in 1944, when the danger had become all too clear, the UGIF leadership in Paris rejected a plan by a Jewish resistance group to organize the escape of children remaining in UGIF residences in the Paris area. Between 20 and 24 July 1944 the residences were raided by the Gestapo: 233 children were arrested and taken to Drancy. Over 200 of them were deported to Auschwitz on 31 July.[46]

The immigrant Jews, who often had previous experience of persecution, were psychologically better equipped to respond to it than French Jews. In Paris, their numerous relief organizations decided to co-ordinate their action in the so-called Amelot Committee (after the street in which it met). The Communists had a specific immigrant organization—the Immigrant Workers' Movement (MOI)—

---

[43] Adler, *Jews of Paris*, 121–4.   [44] *Carnet d'un témoin*, 103, 130, 146, 149–50.
[45] M. Rajsfus, *Des juifs dans la collaboration: L'Union générale des israélites de France* (1980) is critical; Cohen, *Burden of Conscience*, is more nuanced.
[46] Adler, *Jews of Paris*, 159; Cohen, *Burden of Conscience*, 97–8.

grouped into language sections. The Yiddish one was the most important, with about 250 members, although Jews were also scattered among other language groups (Poles, Hungarians, and Romanians). MOI published a clandestine yiddish paper, *Unzer Wort*, and was also linked to a Communist relief organization called Solidarité.[47]

At first, the Communist Jewish leaders were as unsure how to act as anyone. When the Germans ordered Jews to register in September 1940, neither Solidarité nor MOI called for non-compliance. Their leaders submitted to the census like most Jews. Similarly, they were totally unprepared for the first round-up of Jews in May 1941. Looking back on their attitude subsequently, one of the MOI leaders, Louis Gronowski, wrote:

> In the light of the Holocaust I have wondered if our attitude at the time was right, and if we should not have, from the start, called on the Jewish population to disobey the Vichy ordinances. But it was unimaginable, at that moment, to envisage the idea of thousands of people crossing into illegality overnight. Besides, our minds had not yet taken on board the horrors inflicted on the world by the Nazis.[48]

Who knew what is one of the most vexed questions about the Holocaust. Evidence about the extermination of the Jews was filtering out by the middle of 1942. But what does 'knowing' mean? The images of Auschwitz, which haunt our imagination, did not exist. Raymond Aron, who spent the war in London, where much information was available, wrote later: 'What did we know of the genocide? . . . I must confess that I did not imagine it, and because I could not imagine it, I did not know.'[49] Similarly Georges Wellers, a Jewish doctor in Drancy for two and a half years, until being deported in 1944, wrote that he did not 'know' even on arrival at the gates of Auschwitz: 'one had to be mad to believe it'. The children in Drancy invented the name Pitchipoi for the destination of which they knew so little, but which we know as Auschwitz.[50]

MOI and Solidarité were the first organizations to start warning the Jews. Solidarité published a tract in May 1941 denouncing the recent arrests. It organized clandestine committees in the Pithiviers and Beaune-la-Rolande camps, and demonstrations outside the camp gates by wives of the internees.[51] When, in August, Radio Moscow broadcast an appeal to world Jewry by a Soviet Yiddish poet, David Bergelson, warning that Polish Jews were facing extermination, Solidarité reproduced the text in Yiddish and French. At this stage, there was little to support such allegations, but when the first deportation convoy left Compiègne in March 1942, they seemed less far-fetched. MOI urged activists in

---

[47] Adler, *Jews of Paris*, 53–8; Courtois, et al., *Le Sang de l'étranger*, 85–116.
[48] Courtois et al., *Le Sang de l'étranger*, 108–9.
[49] Zuccotti, *Holocaust*, 152.
[50] Cohen, *Persécutions et sauvetages*, 317–27; Rayski, *Le Choix des juifs*, 154–6.
[51] Adler, *Jews of Paris*, 178.

the internment camps to inform the wives of inmates that their husbands were being sent to their deaths. Some activists, however, were reluctant to do this, fearing that it would only spread panic.[52]

Despite these doubts among immigrant Jewish leaders about how to respond, the first round-ups in May and August 1941 had already led many Jews—French and foreign—to take their destiny into their own hands. Philippe Erlanger escaped the December 1941 round-up by slipping to the South, but not his friend René Blum, who saw this as desertion: Blum was arrested in December 1941 and later died in Auschwitz.[53] For most Jews, however, the moment of truth was the Vel d'Hiver round-up in July 1942. That day has been vividly described by the historian Annie Kriegel, who was 15 years old at the time. On the morning of 16 July, she encountered the following sight on turning into the Rue de Turenne in the Jewish quarter where she lived:

> I saw a policeman in uniform who was carrying a suitcase in each hand and crying. I distinctly remember those tears running down a rugged, rather reddish face because you would agree that it is rare to see a policeman cry in public. He walked down the street, followed by a small group of children and old people carrying little bundles . . . It was the round-up . . . I continued on my way when at the crossroads . . . I heard screams rising to the heavens: not cries and squawks such as you hear in noisy and excited crowds, but the sort of screams you hear in hospital delivery rooms.

At a loss what to do, she sat down on a park bench and waited: 'It was on that bench that I left my childhood.'[54] At the same time, the Jews of France collectively lost their innocence. Thousands went into hiding; others turned to resistance.

Jewish Resistance

One can distinguish three categories of Jewish resistance: first, individual French Jews in the general Resistance; secondly, specifically Jewish organizations in the general Resistance; thirdly, Resistance organizations (not necessarily comprising Jews alone) with specifically Jewish objectives.[55]

Many individual French Jews played a significant role in Resistance movements. One of the most important movements, Franc-Tireur, was led by a Jew, Jean-Pierre Lévy; among its other members was Marc Bloch. Another prominent Jewish resister, Daniel Mayer, founded the clandestine Socialist Party. There were also many Jews in de Gaulle's Free French. But none of these individuals were

---

[52] Courtois et al., *Le Sang de l'étranger*, 158.   [53] Cohen, *Persécutions et sauvetages*, 147–8.

[54] *Ce que j'ai cru comprendre*, 153–4.

[55] On the debate over Jewish resistance, see H. Weinberg, 'The Debate over the Jewish Resistance in France', *Contemporary French Civilization*, 15/1 (1991), 1–17; C. Lévy, 'La Résistance juive en France: De l'enjeu de mémoire à l'histoire critique', *VSRH*, 22 (1989), 117–28. See also L. Lazare, *La Résistance juive en France* (1987); Kaspi, *Les Juifs pendant l'Occupation*, 299–322; Cohen, *Persécutions et sauvetages*, 359–97.

acting specifically as Jews: Mayer claimed to be a Socialist first, a Frenchman second, and a Jew third. Another French Jewish resister, Léo Hamon, said that for him joining the Resistance was the 'deliberate choice of France'.[56]

The second category—specifically Jewish Resistance organizations—included the tiny Jewish Army (Armée juive), the brainchild of two Russian-born Zionists, David Knout and Abraham Polonski. Based in Toulouse, they began in 1940 to organize young Zionists into commando groups for eventual military action against the Germans. Recruits trained under a Jewish flag, and underwent an initiation ceremony, swearing a Hebrew oath. Armed units were also organized by the EIF after it was banned in 1943. In 1944, these two organizations combined into the Jewish Combat Organization (OJC). They attracted about 400 members, and at the Liberation they fought alongside the general resistance forces, although keeping their blue and white armbands.[57]

No Jews were more active in the armed resistance than the Communists of the MOI. After the Communist Party turned to armed action in the summer of 1941, it set up a specialized military-terrorist branch, the FTP, which had a special immigrant section (FTP-MOI). The fifty to sixty members of the Jewish section of the FTP-MOI carried out most of the Communists' guerrilla operations in Paris. There has, however, been much debate among historians whether this should be characterized as Jewish resistance.[58] Were the members of the MOI resisting as Jews or Communists? Certainly they did not target specifically Jewish objectives. Their most spectacular operation was the assassination in 1943 of Julius Ritter, who, as Sauckel's representative in France, was responsible for implementing the STO—a policy not aimed at the Jews. In December 1943, one of the Jewish Communist organizers, Adam Rayski, refused to countenance any 'hierarchy of atrocities committed by the Nazis' when it came to deciding whether 'to give priority to the Jewish question or the question of the deportation of the French [STO]'.[59] This has led some Jewish historians to argue that the MOI's activities had little relevance to the specific circumstances of the Jews. Nothing, for example, was done to attack Jewish deportation trains.

An interesting argument to show how the MOI did serve the interests of the Jews is offered by Annie Kriegel who joined MOI herself, once her family had escaped South after the Vel d'Hiver round-up. Many of the Jewish fighters in the MOI were extremely young—often adolescents—and had lost their entire families. Kriegel argues that the Communist Jewish Resistance restored a sense of identity to these young Jews whose lives had been shattered by the events of 1942, and contributed to their own psychological survival. She writes:

[56] Kaspi, Les Juifs pendant l'Occupation, 300; Poznanski, 'Résistance juive, résistants juifs', in Guillon and Laborie (eds.), Mémoire et histoire, 227–45: 232.

[57] Lazare, La Résistance juive, 99–100; Zuccotti, Holocaust, 274–5.

[58] See A. Kriegel, 'De la Résistance juive', Pardès (1985), 191–209; and the debate on 'La Résistance communiste juive', Pardès (1987), 159–96.

[59] Wieviorka in Ils étaient juifs, communistes résistants, 248–9.

To understand [these young Jewish Communist resisters] it is necessary to start from one basic fact: the brutal collapse for them of all those systems of protection, even if sometimes oppressive, which an individual acquires from belonging to a regulated society. Homeland, name, family, house, school, neighbourhood, work, everything which provides a point of fixity, and definition of self, had been swallowed up in nothingness. The revolt of adolescents, we are told, usually aims to throw off the constraints imposed on them by the generation of their elders: it was on the contrary to restore these constraints, often in the name of their father who had gone, that so many adolescents feverishly demanded arms . . . Thus the resistance provided membership of a group, a narrow group, but one which was tightly structured and hierarchical, the reconstitution of a network of interpersonal relations where the survival of each depended on the solidarity of all the others. The slow, repetitive but regular round of tasks . . . the incredible intensity and variety of material and intellectual effort which the tiniest of operations required, once again peopled the days with faces and gave them back a savour and a value, an existence freighted with both fear and hope.[60]

Even if it was true that the Communist Jewish Resistance put the interests of the Communists before the fate of the Jews, it was also true that no other group did more to disseminate information about the fate of the Jews. A few days before the Vel d'Hiver arrests, Solidarité distributed a tract warning Jews to go into hiding. Two Communist Jewish leaders penetrated into the Vel d'Hiver and produced a clandestine pamphlet describing the conditions in the stadium. This was one of the few documents produced by the entire Resistance on the Vel d'Hiver round-up.[61] Jewish Communist propaganda was not restricted to the immigrant Jewish community or the Yiddish language. The autumn of 1942 saw the setting up of the National Movement against Racism (MNCR), to develop solidarity between Jews and non-Jews. This was effectively a Communist front organization, but in October 1942 its French language paper, J'Accuse, published the news that gas was being used on Jews.[62]

Informing Jews of the danger confronting them was a step to saving them from it. The next step was to organize help that went beyond the legalism of the UGIF. This brings us to the third category of Jewish resistance: saving Jews from deportation. Although this did not involve fighting the Germans, the term 'resistance' seems appropriate since the purpose was to thwart a fundamental Nazi objective. Rescuing Jews, although an underground activity, was undertaken primarily by organizations which had originally enjoyed a legal existence, and found themselves pulled into illegality. In Paris, the Amelot Committee continued to provide relief and medical care, but also started to produce false papers and smuggle children across the line. By the autumn of 1943, its leaders had been

---

[60] 'Résistants communistes et juifs persécutés', in G. Wellers et al. (eds.), *La France et la question juive* (1981), 345–70: 361–2.

[61] Adler, *Jews of Paris*, 194–5; Courtois et al., *Le Sang de l'étranger*, 159–60; but Wieviorka, *Ils étaient juifs, communistes, résistants*, 148–51, 162–4, is sceptical about the significance of this.

[62] S. Courtois and A. Rayski, *Qui savait quoi?* (1987), 115–228.

arrested, and its legal existence ceased entirely. The Communist MNCR also organized networks for Jewish children, and, unlike the Amelot Committee, it was prepared to work outside immigrant communities. But rescue was never a primary objective of the Communist Jewish resistance.[63]

In the South, a major role was played by the Children's Relief Organization (OSE), founded in 1912 after the Russian pogroms. In 1940 and 1941, it worked to improve the conditions of children in the internment camps. By the end of 1942, it was engaged in clandestine activity to save Jewish children: smuggling them across the borders, forging papers, or arranging hiding places. One escape network run from Lyons by a Jewish engineer, Georges Garel, and operating under the legal cover of the OSE, managed to hide about 1,600 children. Another network, run from Nice by a Syrian Jew, Moussa Abadi, dispersed about 500 children in orphanages, convents, and schools. The OSE also had its own legal centres for children, but, as the German arrests became more arbitrary, it started to close these and disperse the children. Tragically, at the OSE centre at Izieu, the Germans arrived just before the children were about to be moved. However, overall the OSE saved between 7,500 and 9,000 children.[64]

Rescue efforts would not have succeeded without the complicity of non-Jews: many children were looked after by non-Jewish families or hidden in religious institutions. As Garel said: 'In every department or diocese there was a religious or lay, public or private charity or institution which involved itself in the protection of our children.' In short, the fate of France's Jews cannot be understood without examining the response of the population at large.

French Society and the Jews 1940–1942: Indifference and Hostility

During the first two years of Occupation, the prevailing sentiment towards the Jews ranged from indifference to hostility. The first Jewish Statute aroused little interest. People had more pressing concerns on their minds. Only fourteen out of forty-two prefects in the Unoccupied Zone reported any reaction at all—unfavourable in four cases.[65] One exception to this general indifference was the Protestant leader Pastor Boegner who wrote a much-publicized letter to the Chief Rabbi on 26 March 1941 protesting against the Statute. But he accepted that there was a 'problem' regarding recent Jewish immigrants; Catholic leaders said nothing.[66]

Indifference to the fate of the Jews was not the same as non-involvement in

---

[63] Adler, *Jews of Paris*, 165–95.

[64] S. Zeitboum, *L'Œuvre de secours aux enfants (OSE) sous l'occupation en France* (1990); also Cohen, *Persécutions et sauvetages*, 390–7; Zuccotti, *Holocaust*, 210–26.

[65] Marrus and Paxton, *Vichy France and the Jews*, 15–16.

[66] *Carnets du Pasteur Boegner 1940–1945*, 93–4. Even before this date, Boegner was much troubled by the plight of the Jews.

it. The application of both Statutes drew people into complicity with anti-Semitism. It was the professional organizations of doctors, dentists, lawyers, and architects who administered the quotas in their professions; it was the universities who excluded Jewish teachers; it was the COs who helped to administer Aryanization; it was prefectoral officials who organized censuses. The fact that the Statutes relied upon the co-operation of people who were not necessarily virulent anti-Semites makes their participation all the more significant—just as within the government, the anti-Semitic, but ineffectual Bonnard, probably did less active harm to the Jews than his respected predecessor Carcopino who applied the Statute to the education system, and even proposed the idea (never implemented) of a quota of Jewish students.[67]

The Jewish Statutes were applied with few visible scruples. By March 1942, approximately 3,400 public servants had been dismissed in metropolitan France, and another 2,500 in Algeria. There was little opposition in the universities although twelve of the university rectors had been appointed under the Popular Front. The administrative machine operated with implacable efficiency: two jurists teaching respectively in Brazil and Indochina received notice of their dismissal on 19 December 1940, exactly the same day as their colleagues in France. The only academic who refused, in November 1940, to apply the law was Gustave Monod, a top-ranking academic in the University of Paris, and member of a distinguished Protestant dynasty. Monod was relieved of his duties and went back to teaching in a *lycée*.[68] Sometimes the 'last class' was the occasion of moving scenes. But there were no organized student protests of the kind that occurred in Holland or Belgium. The difference was that in France the exclusion measures had been imposed by the French government not the Germans. According to a survey carried out in the Southern Zone by the Jewish Commissariat in 1943, students were among the social categories most hostile to Jews.[69]

There were few problems in the application of quotas to the professions although it is difficult to generalize. In Marseilles, the Order of Doctors set about implementing the quota with zeal. By May 1943, ninety-five Jewish doctors in the *département* had lost the right to practise. But this did not stop the Order complaining to the Commissariat in July 1942 that Jews in medical schools enjoyed an unfair advantage because they did not lose study time in the Chantiers.[70] In the medical profession, fear about foreign competition had been intense in the 1930s, but Vichy quotas also concerned French Jews. In Paris, however, the Order of Doctors defied the law by allowing 203 doctors to

[67] Singer, *Vichy, l'université et les juifs*, 91–101.
[68] Ibid. 100, 191–2; Baruch, *Servir l'État*, 127–69.
[69] Singer, *Vichy, l'université et les juifs*, 170–8.
[70] D. Ryan, *The Holocaust and the Jews of Marseilles: The Enforcement of Anti-Semitic Policies in Vichy France* (Champaign, Ill., 1996), 44–5.

practise when there should only have been 108.[71] In Marseilles, only architects delayed in applying the quotas to their profession, for what reason is unclear.[72]

Lawyers, who applied the quotas as smoothly as in other professions, were drawn into even greater complicity with the anti-Semitic legislation.[73] The notion of race contained in the Jewish Statutes was unprecedented in French jurisprudence, and definitions of Jewishness were open to interpretation. Lawyers had a field day, and an entirely new branch of law developed. One problem was whether it fell to the State to prove Jewishness, or to the individual to prove the contrary. Lawyers defending Jewish clients could hardly be blamed for entering into these debates, but what about the jurists who wrote learned commentaries on the Statutes? In 1941, Maurice Duverger, later to become a celebrated political scientist of left-wing sympathies, was a young jurist making his name when he published a commentary on the legal implications of the Jewish Statutes. His phraseology certainly seems to have adopted the assumptions of the law's drafters—'If one adopts the religious criterion it is to be feared that most Jews will feign a conversion'—but even if one accepts Duverger's subsequent defence that technical commentary did not imply approbation, such professional neutrality assisted the 'normalization' of something which had no precedent in France. Detachment was more insidious than overt anti-Semitism.[74]

Duverger's case became notorious when his article was exhumed for polemical purposes in the 1960s—causing two libel cases which he won—but there was nothing extraordinary about his article in itself. No commentary on the Jewish Statutes in the specialized legal press expressed any reservations. Yet dissent was not impossible in Vichy France. Jacques Charpentier, head of the Paris Bar Council, criticized Pétain at the time of the Riom trial for abusing his power by delivering the verdict in advance. About the Jewish legislation, however, Charpentier said nothing, probably because he believed that, as he wrote quite unselfconsciously in his post-war memoirs, 'there had always been a Jewish problem' at the Paris Bar.[75] The Conseil d'État, France's ultimate court of appeal in disputes between the State and individuals, also adapted itself remarkably easily to this legislation so at odds with republican tradition. When it came to deciding on exemptions from the Statutes, the Conseil (having purged itself of its own Jewish members) tended towards severity.[76] Whether the attitude of the legal profession was an example of the pitfalls of strict legal positivism, or whether the prevailing anti-Semitic assumptions made the legal community only too receptive to the new laws, the fact is that the French legal profession applied them with no visible scruples.

---

[71] Adler, *Jews of Paris*, 25.   [72] Ryan, *The Holocaust and the Jews*, 48–50.

[73] R. Badinter, *Un antisémitisme ordinaire: Vichy et les avocats juifs 1940–1944* (1997).

[74] D. Lochak, 'La Doctrine sous Vichy où les mésaventures du postivisme', in *Les Usages sociaux du droit* (1989), 250–85; R. H. Weisberg, *Vichy Law and the Holocaust in France* (New York, 1996).

[75] Weisberg, *Vichy Law and the Holocaust*, 84–5.

[76] Baruch, *Servir l'État*, 344–5.

Was this mixture of indifference to the fate of the Jews, and complicity in their persecution, enough to characterize the attitude of the French population as one of active anti-Semitism? Not in the view of the CGQJ which monitored public opinion and frequently bemoaned the lack of anti-Semitism, although its standards in the matter were exacting.[77] Labroue's lectures at the Sorbonne were a disaster: at the first one, describing Jewish racial characteristics, he was booed; the following ones were almost unattended.[78] The exhibition on the Jew and France was visited by over 350,000 people. Was this a lot or a little? It was certainly less than other exhibitions organized by the Germans, but perhaps this was because it was held later than them.[79] The German anti-Semitic film *Jew Süss* was a major box-office success. It did cause demonstrations in Lyons and Bourg-en-Bresse in 1941, but (to show how difficult it is to generalize) it was cheered in Marseilles a year later.[80]

The reactions of the population to the Jews were less sympathetic in the Free Zone, where anti-Semitic legislation had the imprimatur of the Vichy regime, than in the Occupied Zone. In the South, the Exodus had swelled the number of Jews in some localities (especially the Côte d'Azur) or brought Jews to places where almost none had existed before (especially some rural communities in the south-west). In Nice, where the SOL and PPF were strong, anti-Semitic incidents were frequent. In the Occupied Zone, which meant essentially Paris, where all but about 20,000 Jews were concentrated, the Jewish population was if anything smaller than before, and the anti-Semitic measures were directly associated with the Germans. The Jewish journalist Jacques Biélinky, who kept a careful diary of people's reactions, encountered few signs of anti-Semitism. He observed that when Jewish-owned shops were required to put up a special sign, many of them reported an increase in non-Jewish clients offering solidarity. He noted that sellers of *Au pilori* received frequent abuse from passersby.[81] One Jewish observer commented at this time about the Free Zone: 'here we can still move around freely and don't fear arrest at any moment. But as for the attitude of the French, one feels more at home in France in the Occupied Zone.'[82]

Nor did the Resistance or Free French display much concern for the Jews at first. No speech of de Gaulle specifically mentioned the Jews although he did send messages to the World Jewish Congress (November 1940) and the American Jewish Congress (August 1941) condemning anti-Semitic measures. One of de Gaulle's followers, René Cassin, condemned the anti-Semitic legislation on the BBC on 12 April 1941, but it was specifically to the French Jews that he

[77] A. Cohen, 'Le "Peuple aryen" vu par le Commissariat général aux questions juives', *RHMC*, 35 (1988), 482–94; Poznanski, *Être juif en France*, 553–4.

[78] Singer, *Vichy, l'université et les juifs*, 204–6; Singer, 'L'Échec du cours antisémite de H. Labroue à la Sorbonne (1942–1944)', *VSRH* 39 (1993), 3–9.

[79] Kaspi, *Juifs pendant l'Occupation*, 104–9; Burrin, *La France à l'heure*, 299.

[80] Poznanski, *Être juif*, 140–1.

[81] Biélinky, *Journal 1940–1942*, 69–76.   [82] Poznanski, *Être juif en France*, 142.

addressed himself. Another Free French member, Pierre Tissier, wrote in 1942, in a book published in London: 'the Jewish problem does exist in France . . . [the Jew] instead of attaching himself to the territory in which he lives, maintains his international links'.[83] When Jean Moulin arrived in London in October 1941 his report on France said nothing about anti-Semitic persecution although it mentioned other aspects of Vichy repression. With a few exceptions this indifference reflected the attitude of the Resistance within France until at least the second half of 1941.

The discretion of the Resistance regarding anti-Semitism has to be carefully interpreted. Sometimes it did signify indifference to the Jews, even sympathy with the Vichy policy, but it must be remembered that there were many Jews in the Resistance. In their case, the silence had other causes. For French Jews to link their opposition to Vichy to their Jewishness, risked conceding Vichy's case that they were not French citizens like any other. On hearing about the Jewish Statute, Roger Stéphane felt 'humiliated' at the idea that 'from today I will be suspected of opposing Vichy only because I am a Jew'. When in 1944 Pierre Mendès France, who ran the Free French finances, was asked to provide funds for some Jewish children who had been rescued from France, he agreed. But, as a French Jew himself, he went on to specify: 'they are French children to be saved and I do not know of any special category called French Jews'.[84]

The Resistance did become more critical of Vichy's anti-Semitism in the second half of 1941, but the same was not true of public opinion. On the contrary, in some areas resentment of Jews increased in the first half of 1942. As food shortages got worse, Jews were accused of being black marketeers. These feelings were strongest in the Côte d'Azur and the rural south-west—Dordogne, Limousin—where Jewish refugees attracted the opprobrium attaching to all outsiders in times of difficulty.[85]

French Society and the Jews 1942–1944: Solidarity and Rescue

The events of the summer of 1942 transformed French responses to the plight of the Jews. Already in June 1942, the authorities noted the adverse reaction of the Parisian population to the imposition of the yellow star. Most people affected not to notice the star, a response appreciated by Jews, who feared being the object of ostentatious curiosity. Perhaps what some Jews, desperate for reassurance, interpreted as sympathy was really indifference, but there were also open manifestations of solidarity. Some people even put on stars in sympathy,

[83] Le Gouvernement de Vichy (London, 1942), 161.
[84] Poznanski, 'Résistance juive, résistants juifs', 229, 235.
[85] Cohen, Persécutions et sauvetages, 191–203, 228–40; Marrus and Paxton, Vichy France and the Jews, 179–91.

and were punished by being sent to Drancy.[86] Biélinky witnessed many more examples of active sympathy than of hostility: twice he witnessed shop-keepers singling out Jews in food queues to serve them first. On 8 June 1942 he wrote:

> First day out with my star: in the street no one pays any attention to my decor-ation, nor at the tobacconist or newsagent. A neighbour whom I meet . . . says hello to me as amiably as always . . . In the milk queue all my acquaintances greet me amiably, and we chat as usual. No hostile looks . . . A wife of a friend of mine went to the cheese shop where white cheese was being distributed person by person. To show her sympathy the shopkeeper gave her two cheeses. Lobermann's daughter was very scared she might lose her Catholic friends. In fact, they all came to her house to show their sympathy and then wanted to go out with her wearing her decoration.

Guéhenno, who had no indulgence for the behaviour of his compatriots, also noted that the star had led people to show sympathy to the Jews.[87] It should be noted, however, that similar reactions were recorded by the Jewish writer Victor Klemperer to the imposition of the star in Berlin in September 1941.[88]

The real turning point in French public opinion came with the arrests of the summer of 1942.[89] In Paris in July, and then in the South in August, people were shocked by the horrifying scenes of screaming children being arrested with their parents or being forcibly separated from them. All prefects' reports in the summer of 1942 mentioned popular reactions to the arrests of Jews; in almost all cases to report outrage. One woman from the small town of Saint-Girons in the Ariège wrote to the Marshal: 'France has dishonoured herself in inflicting such cruel treatment on people who thought they were finding an asylum in our country. We are ashamed to be French, to be Christian . . . and the veneration which sur-rounds your person had been unsettled if not indeed swept away.'[90] By no means everyone demonstrated open sympathy to the Jews—in the round-ups there were helpful and indifferent concierges, sympathetic and brutal police—but for the first time the issue was forced on everyone's attention.

On Sunday 23 August 1942, the Archbishop of Toulouse, Cardinal Saliège, at last broke the silence of the Catholic Church. In the cathedral, he read out a pastoral letter unequivocally condemning the arrests and reminding his listeners that the Jews were 'our brothers'. This message was read out in every church in the diocese, despite being forbidden by the prefect. Saliège's example was fol-lowed by four other leading prelates: Bishop Théas of Montauban, Archbishop

---

[86] Cohen, *Persécutions et sauvetages*, 254–6; Poznanski, *Être juif en France*, 352–62; Cocteau, *Journal*, 148.

[87] Biélinky, *Journal 1940–1942*, 216; Guéhenno, *Journal des années noires*, 306.

[88] V. Klemperer, *I Shall Bear Witness: The Diaries of Victor Klemperer 1933–1941* (1998), 531, 535, 543.

[89] Marrus and Paxton, *Vichy France and the Jews*, 270–9; Cohen, *Persécutions et sauvetages*, 277–82.

[90] Poznanski, *Être juif en France*, 431.

Gerlier of Lyons, Bishops Delay of Marseilles and Moussaron of Albi. The last three were more restrained in their condemnation—Gerlier admitted that there was a 'problem to resolve'—but this counted less than the cumulative impact of the messages. Five bishops and archbishops out of thirty-five (in the Southern Zone) were perhaps not many, but their messages received wide publicity. The Resistance press that had been so discreet on the Jewish issue joined the chorus of condemnation.[91]

By the end of the year, however, the outrage had died down. After Gerlier and Pétain met in October, the Church and Vichy seemed to have made it up. The public also seemed to lose interest in the Jews, perhaps because although the deportations continued throughout 1943, there were no more massive round-ups on the scale of 1942. The introduction of the STO also diverted attention away from the Jews: in 1943 the term *déporté* described labour recruits not Jews. To some people, indeed, the Jews now appeared as privileged because they were not liable for labour service.[92] But something had irrevocably changed in the summer of 1942. The open protests may not have lasted, but they gave way to active solidarity and the development of an infrastructure to aid the Jews.

The first rescue efforts were spontaneous and improvised. During the round-up in the Lyons region in August 1942, Jewish children had been parked in a disused barracks at Vénisseux outside Lyons. Exploiting the confusion whether or not the children were to be deported, the OSE representatives had managed to get about 100 of them out. Amitié chrétienne, an organization run by two Catholic priests, Pierre Chaillet and the Abbé Alexandre Glasberg, helped to place the children in safety, dispersing them in religious houses and among Catholic families. When the prefect heard what had happened, he asked for the children to be given up. Chaillet refused and was supported by his superior, Archbishop Gerlier.

This was the start of more formal links between Jewish rescue organizations and sympathetic Catholics. Amitié chrétienne, which had been founded to help foreign refugees, set up a clandestine operation to help Jews. Its activities were brought to an end in the spring of 1943 when the Gestapo raided its offices, and Chaillet went into hiding. The Jewish rescue network set up by Georges Garel, himself involved in the Vénisseux rescue, began after he visited Archbishop Saliège of Toulouse. Saliège gave Garrel entry to religious institutions in his diocese where Jewish children could be hidden. Moussa Abadi's network in Nice was assisted by Bishop Paul Rémond who offered Abadi a cover by appointing him 'inspector of independent education' and gave him a room in the bishopric from which to operate. The nuns of the order of Notre-Dame-de-Sion in Paris sheltered children and placed around 450 of them in non-Jewish families in the region. In Lyons the nuns of the same order specialized in forging identity papers.

---

[91] Halls, *Politics, Society and Christianity*, 113–24.
[92] Marrus and Paxton, *Vichy France and the Jews*, 328–30; Cohen, *Persécutions et sauvetages*, 362.

Father Pierre Marie-Benoît, a Capuchin friar based in Marseilles, intervened with the Italian authorities to transfer some 30,000 Jews to the Italian Zone of occupation after November 1942. He was also responsible for helping up to 4,000 Jews escape to Switzerland.[93]

Even more important was the help provided by the Protestants. This was initiated by CIMADE, a Protestant organization founded in 1939 to help refugees. Continuing its work among inhabitants of the camps after 1940, it contacted sympathetic pastors willing to provide refuges for children in their communities. Many of these were in the Cévennes, a mountainous area of the Languedoc with a large Protestant population. The Protestants of this area viewed the persecuted Jews in the light of their own history of resistance to persecution from the French Catholic state over the centuries. In numerous small Cévennes communities, hundreds of Jews took refuge, relying on the support and complicity of almost the entire population. In the village of Saint-Germain-de-Calberte, for example, eight Jewish families—including Greeks, Russians, Hungarians, and Poles—were hidden in the hotel; another five Jews were hidden by the local schoolteacher; and when a non-Jewish family in the hotel wrote a letter of denunciation, it was intercepted at the village post office.[94] Nowhere saved more Jews than the isolated Protestant village of Le Chambon-sur-Lignon (Haute-Loire). Under the leadership of their pastor, André Trocmé, the 3,000 villagers hid around 5,000 Jews during the Occupation, some for a few days, some for months, even years. When the police arrived, the children would be dispersed in the thick local forests. Trocmé was arrested in February 1943 and released after a month. He then went into hiding, and his wife, Magda, continued the rescue work.[95]

Large numbers of Jews, however, were saved not by organized rescue networks, but by the spontaneous actions of individuals from all walks of life: Auguste Boyer, the guard at the Les Milles camps near Marseilles, who helped several inmates escape in 1942 before being himself arrested and tortured; Jean Chaigneau, prefect of the Alpes-Maritimes, who destroyed the lists of Jews held at the prefecture; Camille Matthieu, a guard at Drancy who assisted the escape of Simon Fuks, a Paris tailor, and then hid his whole family for the rest of the Occupation at his mother's house in a village in the Aude.[96]

Many Jewish children owed their lives to the efforts of such individuals. Pavel-Saul Friedländer, today a historian at Tel Aviv, was 9 years old in 1940 when his family, who had escaped the previous year from Prague to Paris, settled in the small town of Neris-les-Bains in the Allier. He was befriended by a local

[93] Cohen, *Persécutions et sauvetages*, 428–70.

[94] P. Joutard, J. Poujol, P. Cabanel, *Cévennes terre de réfuge 1940–1944* (Montpellier, 1987), 265–75.

[95] P. Hallie, *Lest Innocent Blood be Shed: The Story of Le Chambon and How Goodness Happened There* (New York, 1979); Cohen, *Persécutions et sauvetages*, 427–32; Zuccotti, *Holocaust*, 227–31.

[96] Ryan, *The Holocaust and the Jews*, 105, 124; Rayski, *Le Choix des juifs*, 144–5; Marrus and Paxton, *Vichy France and the Jews*, 320; Cohen, *Persécutions et sauvetages*, 439–40.

librarian who placed him, with the consent of his parents, in a Catholic board-
ing school at Montluçon. Friedländer's parents were themselves deported to
Auschwitz on 4 November 1942; they were never to return.[97]

Pierre Vidal-Naquet, today a classical historian in Paris, was 10 when his
family arrived in Marseilles in 1940. The Vidal-Naquets were a distinguished
French Jewish family, Republican and fiercely patriotic. His father was a lawyer
barred from practising by Vichy's Jewish legislation. On 15 May 1944 the Gestapo
arrived to arrest him and his wife. Pierre was not at home, and one of his schoolteachers organized a group of fellow pupils to track the boy down and prevent
him returning home. Thanks to this intervention Pierre was saved, along with
his two brothers and sister. His parents perished in Auschwitz. For the rest of
the Occupation, the children were put up by an old Protestant lady in the village
of Sainte-Agrève (Ardèche), about 10 miles from Chambon, and later in the
village of Dieulefit (Drôme). These were both Cévennes villages with large
Protestant communities.[98]

Stanley Hoffmann, today a political scientist at Harvard, was 12 in 1940. Born
in Vienna, and technically an Austrian citizen, he had been bought up in France.
Although baptised Protestant, he was Jewish according to Vichy's laws. He and
his mother spent the Occupation in Nice; his uncle, who stayed in Paris, was
deported to Germany in 1943. In Nice, Hoffmann encountered some anti-
Semitism from his schoolmates, but also kindness from some of his teachers.
When the Germans arrived in Nice in September 1943, he and his mother
practised the art of escaping from the balcony of their flat to the roof in case
the knock on the door should come. After three months, the strain became too
much. The boy's history teacher forged identity papers for them, and they
spent the rest of the Occupation in the tiny spa of Lamalou-les-Bains in the
Languedoc. In the end, Hoffmann's memories of his own experience were positive: 'one should not expect a nation to be made only of heroes, but one could
ask for decency, and decency prevailed'.[99] When the film *The Sorrow and the Pity*
came out in 1971, Hoffmann felt unable to accept fully its bleak vision of the
French under Occupation. In his article on the film, he wrote:

> In my memory, the schoolteacher . . . who taught me French history, gave me
> hope in the worst days, dried my tears when my best friend was deported along
> with his mother, and gave false papers to my mother and me so that we could
> flee a Gestapo-infested city in which the complicity of friends and neighbours
> was no longer a guarantee of safety—this man wipes out all the bad moments,
> and the humiliations, and the terrors. He and his wife were not Resistance heroes,
> but if there is an average Frenchman, it was this man.[100]

---

[97] S. Friedländer, *Quand vient le souvenir* (1978).

[98] P. Vidal-Naquet, *Mémoires: La Brisure et l'attente, 1930–1955* (1995); id., 'Protestants et juifs pendant
la Seconde Guerre mondiale en France', in id., *Les Juifs, la mémoire et le présent* (1991), 359–81.

[99] 'To be or not to be French', in L. Miller and M. J. Smith (eds.), *Ideas and Ideals: Essays on
Politics in Honor of Stanley Hoffmann* (Boulder, Colo., 1993), 19–46.

[100] *Decline or Renewal? France since the 1930s* (1974), 60.

In the end, there is no single reason why a higher number of Jews from France survived the war than in much of the rest of Western Europe.[101] Throughout Nazi Europe, the fate of the Jews depended on a variety of factors: the presence of an independent government able to interpose itself between the Jews and the Germans; the willingness of such a government to do so; the numbers of German occupation troops; the timing of German anti-Jewish policies; the reactions of public opinion and the organizations which expressed it; the effectiveness of rescue networks; the geography and topography of the country; the size and distribution of the Jewish population.

None of these factors was decisive in itself, and what mattered was how they combined. Holland and Belgium are both small and highly urbanized countries, but only a quarter of Jews survived in Holland as opposed to almost two-thirds in Belgium. Holland witnessed significant public protests against anti-Semitism in the autumn of 1940 and again in February 1941, but Dutch rescue networks were less effective than those in Belgium. It may also have been significant that the Nazi Party had more influence in Holland, which was run by a Reichskommissar, than in Belgium, where the army was in charge.[102] By the time it was clear what fate awaited the Dutch Jews, most of them had been concentrated into three ghetto districts of Amsterdam. Geography—proximity to Sweden— may have saved the Jews of Denmark, but it was not enough to help those of Norway, most of whom perished. The successful rescue of the Danish Jews was due to the combination of factors: the obstructiveness of the government, the solidarity of civil society, the effectiveness of the rescue networks, and the fact that the Germans, reluctant to antagonize the Danish government, did not act against the Jews until the summer of 1943.

How many of these factors operated in France? In the first place, was the existence of the Vichy regime in any way beneficial to the Jews? Annie Kriegel, despite her wartime involvement in the Jewish Communist Resistance, later came to believe that without the existence of an independent French government, even more Jews would have perished, as in Holland and Belgium where independent governments did not exist. Even if one were to accept this argument—and it is true that on a very few occasions Vichy did say 'no' to the Germans: refusing to impose the star in the Unoccupied Zone in June 1942 or to denaturalize more Jews in August 1943—the question should be not how many Jews Vichy's existence did save, but how many more its existence could have saved if the will had been there. But in fact Kriegel's argument is unconvincing. The safest place for the Jews of France was not the so-called Free Zone; it was the Italian zone of occupation (as long as it lasted). The truth is that without Vichy's co-operation, it would have been impossible for the Germans to arrest

---

[101] R. Paxton and M. Marrus, 'The Nazis and the Jews in Occupied Europe', *JMH* 54 (1982), 687–714; Poznanski, *Être juif,* 685–710.
[102] B. Moore, *Victims and Survivors: The Nazi Persecution of the Jews in the Netherlands 1940–1945* (1997), 55, 71–2, 254.

as many Jews as they did. This is clear if one compares the results of the Vel d'Hiver operation in July 1942 with those of the Brunner operation in Nice just over a year later.

The Germans' failure to round up as many Jews as they had hoped in Nice can also be ascribed to the later date of the operation. In 1942, the Vel d'Hiver operation had been a bolt from the blue; in 1943, the Jews knew what to expect, and rescue networks had been created. Michael Marrus and Robert Paxton, however, are not convinced of the importance of such factors. They claim that, in the last analysis, the survival rate of the Jews depended on 'the degree to which the Nazis were willing and able to apply themselves to their task'.[103] But in all cases this willingness and ability were not independent variables. They were a function of other factors such as the reactions of civil society and the attitudes of the governments with which they had to deal. On the other hand, it is true that once the Nazis in France pursued their murderous task without restraint of any kind, as was the case in 1944, there was an increase in the rate of arrests—despite the fact that the French police had almost ceased to co-operate and that rescue networks were in existence.

Nonetheless the role of rescue networks was crucial in explaining the survival of many thousands of Jews, especially children. Why were these efforts so successful? Undoubtedly geography was important: France was a large and mountainous country, sharing borders with two non-belligerent countries, Spain and Switzerland. Possibly some 44,000 Jews escaped across these two frontiers, 24,000 legally and 20,000 illegally.[104] Chronology was also important: the existence of the Italian safe haven until September 1943 won the Jews valuable time. But in the end the effectiveness of the rescue organizations required the solidarity, passive or active, formal or informal, of the French population. For 150 years the Jews of France had looked to the State to protect them, if necessary, from the sudden anti-Semitic outbursts of civil society; in the Occupation, it was civil society that helped to protect the Jews from the State.

The experience of the Jews under Vichy offers more general lessons for the history of Occupied France. It reveals the extent to which Vichy, like any authoritarian state, relied for its effectiveness on consent and approval from its population. Vichy's anti-Semitism in 1940–1 was the aspect of the National Revolution which seems to have aroused the least opposition: the complicity of civil society considerably facilitated the implementation of that policy. Once the anti-Semitic consensus was shattered in 1942, the effectiveness of State anti-Semitism was undermined by the 'resistance' of civil society. The saving of Jewish lives can certainly be categorized as a form of 'resistance', although different from the more well-known forms of resistance like sabotage, the planting of bombs, or the production of propaganda. It was a resistance which relied upon the complicity of

---

[103] 'The Nazis and the Jews', 688.   [104] R. Belot, *Aux frontières de la liberté* (1998), 702 n. 22.

the population as a whole. However much Vichy tried to exclude the Jews from France, the effectiveness of Jewish resistance was intimately linked to the responses of civil society. The same, as we shall see, was to be true of the Resistance as a whole.

Part IV

The Resistance

Introduction to Part IV

When Jean Moulin arrived in London in October 1941 with his report on the situation in France, he used various terms to characterize the movements of opposition to the Occupation: 'French patriots', people 'professing Anglophilia', 'Anglophile movements', a 'surge of revolt and popular indignation', 'degaullists'. Once he also referred to the 'movements of French resistance', but never to 'resisters' nor to 'the Resistance'.[1] Moulin's uncertainty about terminology demonstrates the novelty of what came to be called 'the Resistance'. The word itself had no particular historical resonance. Creating 'resistance' involved creating the idea of the Resistance. In the nineteenth century, the 'party of the resistance' described the conservative Orleanists who opposed the July Monarchy.[2] There had been 'resisters' to the German occupation of northern France and Belgium in the First World War, but there had been no 'Resistance'. One early resistance group in 1940 alighted on the word 'Resistance' for its associations with the struggle of the Huguenots against the French monarchy.[3]

Certainly the word 'resistance' was used from the beginning of the Occupation, but the meanings attached to it were not precise. In his first speech from London on 18 June 1940, de Gaulle declared: 'the flame of French resistance must not be extinguished and will not be extinguished'. He was using the term in the military sense of armed resistance: 'every Frenchman who is still armed has the absolute duty to continue the resistance'. The word 'resistance' was used differently by another general, the air-force officer Gabriel Cochet, who had, unlike de Gaulle, chosen to remain in France. In September 1940, Cochet circulated a tract calling on people to 'resist and unite'. He conceived resistance primarily as a state of mind: 'moral force in the absence of material force, the will to resist given the absence of means to resist'. Different again was the use of the term 'resistance' by a group based in Paris's anthropological museum, the Musée de l'homme. In December 1940, they had started producing a newspaper called *Résistance*. For them resistance meant organizing groups in France to carry out

---

[1] Cordier, *Jean Moulin*, iii. 789–90 The two slightly different versions of his report are reprod. ibid. 1210–26.
[2] J. Semelin, *Sans armes face à Hitler: La Résistance civile en Europe 1939–1945* (1989), p. vii.
[3] M. Blumenson, *The Vildé Affair: Beginnings of the French Resistance* (1977), 20–1.

practical tasks: collating information about the enemy, helping Allied airmen to escape.

Even when the word 'resistance' had acquired a more fixed meaning, the history of the Resistance remained many histories. Several distinctions need to be made. The most important is between London and France, between de Gaulle's Free French and the metropolitan Resistance. De Gaulle's first speech had not been addressed to the people of France, but to Frenchmen abroad, or Frenchmen who might be able to come abroad. He was thinking of resistance outside France not within it. His argument was that the British were not beaten and that the British had at their disposal the resources of the American economy. In short, the conflict would become a world war, and the French must once again become part of it. From the end of 1941, the history of de Gaulle's Free French starts to converge with the history of the Resistance in France, but they always remained distinct. Many metropolitan resisters resented the fact that the start of resistance had come to be associated with de Gaulle. One of them, Henry Frenay, recalled: 'It was not at the call of the General that we rose up.'[4] Most early resisters had not even heard de Gaulle's speech of 18 June.

Many resisters also felt that de Gaulle did not sufficiently appreciate the risks they ran or the significance of what they were doing. One scene which recurs in similar terms in the memoirs of many Resistance leaders is the first meeting with de Gaulle in London, when the visitor first encounters the general's lofty coldness. Christian Pineau, an early arrival, described finding himself in the presence of an 'authoritarian prelate' who sat him down and commanded without any introduction: 'Now tell me about France.' Having listened impassively, de Gaulle then launched into a monologue on the perfidy of the British. He asked no personal questions, showed no curiosity about life in the Resistance.[5] Given how de Gaulle describes the Resistance in his memoirs, one can understand why its members felt aggrieved about his view of them:

> Having given the Resistance the inspiration and leadership which saved it from anarchy, I found it, at the right moment, a useful instrument in the struggle against the enemy and with regard to the Allies a useful support for my policy of independence and unity.[6]

The misunderstanding between London and France was reciprocal. Resisters in France criticized what they sometimes referred to as the émigrés of London, but those in London felt that they had no lessons to receive in heroism from those who had chosen to stay in France. Arriving in London in July 1940, a future member of the Free French, Jacques Bingen, wrote:

---

[4] Frenay, *La Nuit finira*, 16; or see Pineau, *La Simple Vérité*, 156.
[5] Pineau, *La Simple Vérité*, 158; see also Frenay, *La Nuit finira*, 232–3; d'Astier de la Vigerie, *Sept fois sept jours*, 82–3.
[6] *Mémoires* (2000), 303.

Here I am, escaped from Nazi soil and ready . . . to fight Hitler until the end . . . I have lost all I had, my money . . . my work, my family which has stayed in France, and perhaps I will never again see my country and my beloved Paris . . . But I remain a free man in a free country and that counts more than anything.[7]

The suddenness of Bingen's total rupture with the past was not experienced by most resisters in France whose move into clandestinity was usually more gradual. In that sense, his decision to go to London was as radical and courageous an act as any performed by most resisters in France in 1940. The point of the comparison is not to award marks for heroism, but to stress the psychological divide between those who left France and those who stayed. Neither was able fully to appreciate the virtues of the other.

In addition to the distinction between France and London, a distinction needs to be drawn between the minority of actively committed resisters in France and those who participated in more informal types of resistance. There are two possible pitfalls to avoid when broaching this subject. The first is the temptation to adopt an excessively narrow and military interpretation of resistance. This was the approach of British intelligence and military planners who were sceptical about the value of much of what passed for resistance in France. From the Allies' point of view, this might have been justifiable, but the historian of France is not required to confine resistance to those aspects of it which can be shown genuinely to have hastened the Liberation. In the history of France, resistance is more important as a social and political phenomenon than a military one.

It is also necessary to avoid the other extreme of adopting an excessively broad interpretation of resistance, extending the term to include any manifestation of opposition to the German presence. This was the attitude satirized by Anouilh in his play *L'Orchestre* where one character who had performed in an orchestra during the Occupation defends herself by saying that it was an orchestra of resisters: 'When there were German officers in the audience, we played wrong notes. It took a certain courage! We risked being denounced at any moment; they were all very musical.'[8] Several observers during the war were even to claim that the elegance of Parisian women was a form of resistance against the German attempt to break France's spirit.[9]

The Resistance was increasingly sustained by the hostility of the mass of the population towards the Occupation, but not all acts of individual hostility can be characterized as resistance, although they are the necessary precondition of it. A distinction needs to be drawn between dissidence and resistance. Workers who evaded STO, or Jews who escaped the round-ups, or peasants who withheld their produce from the Germans, were transgressing the law, and their actions were subversive of authority. But they were not resisters in the same way as those who

---

[7] L. Douzou , 'L'Entrée en Résistance', *MS* 180 (1997), 9–20: 11.
[8] Wieviorka, *Une certaine idée*, 137.   [9] Cocteau, *Journal*, 113–14.

organized the escape of *réfractaires* and Jews. Contesting or disobeying a law on an individual basis is not the same as challenging the authority that makes those laws.[10]

Resistance, then, requires some congruence between intentions and actions. Just as it is not enough to think anti-German thoughts to be a resister if nothing results from these thoughts, so acts which might have had unintended consequences beneficial to the Resistance cannot be qualified as resistance. On the other hand, once the organized Resistance grew in strength, and became a presence in society, there were increasing opportunities for individuals to contribute to it in informal ways. What might have once been individual acts of disobedience became part of the Resistance. In short, the Resistance must always be considered dynamically in relationship to the population at large.

Resistance, finally, must also be studied in relation to Vichy. The Resistance comprised not only those who had always opposed Vichy, but also those who had originally supported it or at least been willing to work within the legal framework of the regime. Individuals like Mounier or Segonzac, reviews like *Confluences* or *Poésie*, organizations like Jeune France or Uriage had tried to explore the leeway that Vichy offered them to express nonconformist views. As the situation revealed itself to be less open than they had believed, they found themselves pulled into dissidence and sometimes resistance. The Resistance did not suddenly emerge fully formed to challenge the Vichy regime: its contours were moulded by Vichy.

These are the issues which will be examined in Part IV of this book. Chapter 16 examines the origins and emergence of de Gaulle's Free French in London; Chapter 17 the origins and emergence of resistance in France. Chapters 18 and 19 examine how these two originally parallel and separate enterprises converged and interlinked. Chapter 20 examines the relationship between the Resistance and the mass of the French population. Finally, Chapter 21 looks at the development of Resistance ideology, viewing that ideology not only as an opposition to the values of Vichy but also as a dialogue with them.

[10] J. Semelin, 'Qu'est-ce-que "résister"'?, *Esprit* 198 (1994), 50–63: 52–3.

16

The Free French 1940–1942

Beginnings

When the 49-year-old General de Gaulle broadcast from London on 18 June 1940, he was an almost unknown figure. Alexander Cadogan, the Permanent Under-Secretary at the Foreign Office, knew only that de Gaulle had 'a head like a pineapple and hips like a woman's'; most French people, unable to see him, knew even less.[1] Few people heard his speech; fewer still acted upon it; the BBC did not even bother to record it. In political and military circles, de Gaulle was notorious in the 1930s for his advocacy of the mechanization of the army and the offensive deployment of tanks. The stridency with which he argued this case had won de Gaulle many enemies. The only leading politician to back him was Paul Reynaud. As a result, de Gaulle's military career had been respectable, but not spectacular. He was promoted to the rank of Brigadier-general on 1 June 1940, making him the most junior general in the army.

On 5 June 1940, Reynaud took de Gaulle into his government as Under-Secretary of State for War, a post that he held for twelve days until Reynaud's resignation. In Reynaud's government, de Gaulle was one of the most vigorous opponents of an armistice. When he arrived in London on the morning of 17 June, the day after Reynaud's resignation, de Gaulle had previously met Churchill on only four occasions. Churchill allowed de Gaulle to broadcast on the BBC despite the scepticism of other British ministers who wanted to avoid antagonizing the new Pétain government at such a delicate juncture. For this reason de Gaulle was not authorized to broadcast again until 22 June.[2] Once the signature of the Armistice reduced the need to treat Pétain with kid gloves, Churchill was ready to accord de Gaulle formal recognition, despite the reservations of the Foreign Secretary Lord Halifax.

Originally Churchill hoped that de Gaulle might attract more important French personalities. This did not occur. Not only did few people come from France to join de Gaulle, most leading French figures already in London decided to return to France. Even many of those who wanted to go on fighting had no

[1] *The Diaries of Sir Alexander Cadogan*, ed. D. Dilks (1971), 302.
[2] Crémieux-Brilhac, *La France libre*, 48–53.

confidence in a crusade headed by an obscure general: they preferred to go to North America. This was true of Jean Monnet, who had co-ordinated Anglo-French economic co-operation until the defeat; Alexis Léger, former head of the Quai d'Orsay; and Geneviève Tabouis and Henri de Kérillis who were celebrated anti-Munich journalists.

De Gaulle had hoped to set up a French national committee in London, but there was no one of any importance to sit on it. Churchill therefore told him: 'You are alone, I shall recognise you alone.'[3] On 28 June, the British government recognized de Gaulle officially as 'leader of all the Free French, wherever they are to be found, who rally to him in support of the Allied cause'. On 7 August, de Gaulle and Churchill signed a formal agreement stipulating that the British would supply the Free French, and in return de Gaulle would accept the general directives of the British High Command, although exercising 'supreme command' over his forces.

Among those who did rally to de Gaulle in 1940, there were no prefects or ambassadors, no academicians or professors, no top civil servants or politicians. The names of his first followers would have been unknown to most French people. What is interesting about those names is the diversity of age, social origins, and political beliefs they represented. They included Georges Boris, a left-wing journalist and economist who had been an adviser to Blum; René Cassin, a 55-year-old jurist; Captain André Dewavrin, a 22-year-old lecturer at the Saint-Cyr military college; Maurice Schumann, a left Catholic journalist; René Pleven, a businessman who had worked with Monnet in London during the Phoney War; Émile Muselier, a retired admiral. These people were allocated tasks more or less suited to their expertise: Cassin became the Free French legal expert, Schumann became a broadcaster, Muselier became head of the Free French naval forces. Dewavrin, however, was assigned a task for which he had no qualifications or experience: to organize a Free French intelligence service.

The leading personality to rally to de Gaulle was General Georges Catroux, Governor-General of Indochina until being sacked by Vichy. Catroux arrived in England in September while de Gaulle was away in Africa. Because he was a more high-profile figure than de Gaulle, Churchill hoped he might take over the leadership of the Free French. But Catroux proved ready to work under de Gaulle. His urbanity and charm proved a welcome complement to de Gaulle's intransigence and asperity. As the British discovered more about de Gaulle's personality, Catroux represented everything they would have liked de Gaulle to be.[4]

De Gaulle's prospects of recruiting from the army and naval personnel who had ended up in Britain after the evacuations from Norway and Dunkirk were not helped by the British attack at Mers el Kébir. But the greatest blow to de Gaulle's initial hopes was that most of France's Empire remained loyal to Vichy.

---

[3] F. Kersaudy, *Churchill and de Gaulle* (1990), 85.
[4] Crémieux-Brilhac, *La France libre*, 128–9.

The only significant exceptions to this were French Equatorial Africa (Chad, French Congo, Ubangi-Shari, Gabon) and the Cameroons, which rallied to de Gaulle in August 1940. Gabon, the last enclave in Equatorial Africa, was won back in October. This furnished de Gaulle with a foothold outside England, and a base from which, ultimately, Free French troops would participate in North African military operations. This success was quickly overshadowed by the catastrophic failure of the expedition to win over French West Africa. British and French intelligence had reported considerable local hostility to Vichy, but when an Anglo-French force, with de Gaulle on board, arrived off Dakar on 23 September, the defending Vichy forces, under the command of Governor-General Pierre Boisson, fired back. The operation was suspended after two days.

This fiasco was a terrible blow to de Gaulle's prestige. Dakar also had long-term repercussions on his relations with the Allies. It was widely believed that the operation had failed owing to indiscretions from Free French members in London. The British decided that the Free French could not be trusted with intelligence information. As a result, for the rest of the war, de Gaulle was kept in ignorance of every operation involving France. Dakar also reinforced the argument of those in the British government who wanted to build bridges to Vichy instead of backing a maverick general—'that ass de Gaulle' as Cadogan wrote—who seemed to have little support among the French. 'We should treat Vichy tenderly', wrote Halifax at the end of November 1940.[5] Dakar also helps explain the unrelenting hostility that Roosevelt was later to display towards de Gaulle.

De Gaulle recovered his confidence by spending six weeks visiting French Equatorial Africa. The tumultuous reception he received in Doula, capital of the Cameroons, helped erase the humiliation of Dakar. Possessing a French base, de Gaulle used it to seize back the initiative. On 27 October 1940, at Brazzaville in the Congo, he announced the creation of a committee of imperial defence to direct the French effort in the war. This was a substitute for the national committee he had failed to set up in June. De Gaulle proclaimed that he was exercising his power in the name of France and made a solemn commitment to submit his actions to the judgement of the French people as soon as they were free again.[6]

The Committee of Imperial Defence was the first step on the road towards de Gaulle's acquiring the status of the head of a provisional government. In the immediate term, it was a response to Pétain's meeting with Hitler at Montoire on 24 October, and also a way of sabotaging any possible British rapprochement with Vichy. All this confirmed Foreign Office suspicions of de Gaulle. One official commented, 'he has of late got rather out of hand'.[7] The British believed de Gaulle should confine himself to building up a military force. Even some of de

[5] P. Bell, *A Certain Eventuality: Britain and the Fall of France* (1974), 260; *Diaries of Alexander Cadogan*, 334 (8 Nov. 1940).
[6] De Gaulle, *Mémoires* 120–2.   [7] Bell, *Certain Eventuality*, 241.

Gaulle's followers took a similar view. Gaston Palewski, a former aide to Paul Reynaud, who had joined de Gaulle in the summer of 1940, told a Foreign Office official that de Gaulle should 'above all be military . . . get away from the idea of a nigger kingdom and repair his damaged military prestige, for example by a successful action against the Italians'.[8]

Conflict: De Gaulle and his Allies

De Gaulle's assertions of independence did not initially cloud his relationship with Churchill. The romantic in Churchill admired de Gaulle's epic adventure; they shared a love of drama and a deep sense of history. In the end, however, a clash was inevitable because de Gaulle conceived his role differently from the British. Possessing no military resources, he was forced into a political role. When Cassin enquired about the juridical status of the Free French, de Gaulle had replied 'We are France'. Refusing to accept the legitimacy of the Vichy government, de Gaulle saw himself as the sole repository of French sovereignty. He was prepared to defend that sovereignty from all sides—including the British. This emerged already in the negotiations over the Franco-British agreement of 7 August. Churchill had committed himself to support the 'integral restoration of the independence and grandeur of France'. In a secret letter to de Gaulle, he explained that this phrase implied no commitment to preserving France's frontiers as they had existed before the war. De Gaulle could only register his hope that 'events will one day enable the British government to consider the question with less reserve'.

The suspicion which lay behind this barbed exchange exploded into open hostility less than a year later in the Middle East, a region of long-standing Anglo-French tension. De Gaulle had long nursed the idea of an operation to reclaim Syria from Vichy. Initially the British claimed not to have sufficient forces available, until the outbreak of the anti-British revolt in Iraq raised the prospect of the Germans acquiring a toehold in the Levant. On 8 June 1941, an Anglo-French force, containing mostly Free French troops, attacked Syria. The Vichy forces fought back, and for the first time French soldiers found themselves fighting each other. At Dakar, the operation had been suspended before this could occur.

After four weeks, the Vichy commander, General Dentz, surrendered, and signed an armistice with the British General Maitland Wilson. This document contained no reference to the Free French. It offered the defeated Vichy troops a choice between repatriation to France or joining the Allied forces. Seeing this as a 'pure and simple transference of Syria and the Lebanon to the British', de Gaulle reacted furiously. He threatened to withdraw his Middle East troops from

[8] Bell, *Certain Eventuality*, 233; Crémieux-Brilhac, *La France libre*, 134–41.

British command. What de Gaulle viewed as a plot was largely the result of the incompetence of the local British representatives, but he was understandably resentful that the Armistice had provided him no opportunity to recruit from Dentz's forces.[9]

De Gaulle succeeded in having the armistice amended, but the local British authorities remained obstructive. In one place, the British commander moved into the French residency, replacing the Tricolour by a Union Jack. De Gaulle sent a force to reclaim it, even at the risk of employing force against the British. His frustration at this situation spilled out in an extraordinary interview he gave from Brazzaville to the *Chicago Daily News* on 27 July. For the first time, he publicly expressed his differences with the British, even claiming that Britain was doing a 'wartime deal with Hitler'. Churchill wondered if de Gaulle had 'gone off his head'. Anthony Eden, one of de Gaulle's staunchest defenders in the government, reminded Churchill of de Gaulle's importance as a 'rallying point against Vichy', but even he speculated that de Gaulle might be crazy.[10] Probably the same thought occurred to many Free French members in London. Churchill gave orders that on his return to London, de Gaulle was to be ostracized. After a stormy meeting between the two men on 12 September, a superficial harmony was re-established, but the relationship was never to be the same.[11]

De Gaulle's fury had not been feigned. This did not mean that he was crazy, but the vehemence of his reaction did partly have psychological causes. For someone of de Gaulle's temperament, his total dependence on the British was intolerably difficult to bear. The defeat of 1940 had been a humiliation which he felt with terrible intensity. One observer commented: 'I think he was like a man, during these days, who had been skinned alive.'[12] All that pain erupted in the summer of 1941. But de Gaulle was also testing how far he could push his allies. His conclusion after the Syrian affair was that 'With the English one must bang on the table and they will submit'.[13] De Gaulle was also acutely aware that if he were not seen to be defending French interests in the Empire, he would be vulnerable to Vichy accusations of being a British stooge. Telling Churchill 'I am too poor to be able to bow', de Gaulle bit the hand that fed him because it was his only way of showing that France still had teeth.

As de Gaulle's difficulties with Churchill developed in 1941, he tried to court America.[14] In June, he suggested that if Roosevelt entered the war, he might prefer French Equatorial Africa to Britain as base of operations. But he was unsuccessful in playing America off against Britain. On the contrary, America's entry into the war in December 1941 compounded de Gaulle's problems with the Allies. Roosevelt was dubious about de Gaulle's utility to them: Dakar and

[9] A. Gaunson, *The Anglo-French Clash in Lebanon and Syria 1940–1945* (1986).
[10] Kersaudy, *Churchill and de Gaulle*, 153–4.   [11] Ibid. 136–60.
[12] M. Borden, *Journey down a Blind Alley* (1946), 113–15.
[13] Crémieux-Brilhac, *La France libre*, 161; Gaunson, *Anglo-French Clash*, 62.
[14] De Gaulle, *Lettres, notes et carnets: juin 1940–juillet 1941* (1981), 330–1, 346, 350–2.

Syria had demonstrated that Gaullist involvement in operations against Vichy-controlled areas could be counter-productive. This confirmed Roosevelt's preference for retaining contacts with Vichy and trying to bring Pétain around to an anti-German position.

Relations between de Gaulle and Roosevelt were aggravated by de Gaulle's decision, in December 1941, to send a force to recover the two tiny French islands of Saint-Pierre-et-Miquelon, off the Newfoundland coast. Roosevelt opposed anything liable to alienate Vichy, and his Secretary of State, Cordell Hull, condemned this 'arbitrary action' by the 'so-called Free French'. Hull's comment outraged American public opinion and offered de Gaulle an insight into the possibilities of using Allied public opinion against the Allied governments. Roosevelt insisted that the Free French evacuate the islands. A compromise was reached which saved face on both sides, but left simmering grievances.

During 1942 de Gaulle's relations with the Allies deteriorated further. One French observer in London commented: 'The General must be constantly reminded that our enemy number one is Germany. If he followed his natural inclination it would rather be the British.'[15] There was another flare-up when the British launched an expedition on 5 May to the French colony of Madagascar without including (or consulting) the Free French. This crisis rumbled on for six weeks. De Gaulle was so incensed that at the start of June 1942 he asked the Russian ambassador in London whether the Soviet Union would offer a refuge if he decided to break with Britain.[16]

By the middle of June 1942, de Gaulle was persuaded that the British harboured no nefarious designs on Madagascar. His mood improved when the Free French scored their first military success at the battle of Bir Hakeim in Libya. Between 2 and 11 June, the Free French General Koenig, with about 4,000 troops under his command, repelled the forces of Rommel, which were massively superior in number. This was a battle with real strategic importance, winning a respite for British forces retreating eastward. In a month when other military news for the Allies was negative, Bir Hakeim received worldwide publicity. The Americans even accredited an official representative to the Free French in July.

The honeymoon did not last long. In the summer de Gaulle was again in the Levant where he had violent encounters with Churchill's envoy in the area, General Spears. Once back in London, de Gaulle had another epic confrontation with Churchill on 30 September. Eden commented that he had not witnessed such rudeness since Ribbentrop. The burden of the argument was contained in the following exchange:

Churchill: You say you are France! You are not France! I do not recognise you as France.
De Gaulle: Why are you discussing these questions with me if I am not France?

---

[15] Pierre Brossolette, quoted in Kersaudy, *Churchill and de Gaulle*, 186.
[16] Crémieux-Brilhac, *La France libre*, 311–12.

... I am acting in the name of France. I am fighting alongside England, I am
not fighting for England . . .
Churchill: The problem is to decide what France is . . . There are other fractions
and other elements of France who could one day play a larger role.[17]

The National Committee

Churchill was too committed to de Gaulle to be willing—yet—to explore
these 'other elements'. But from 1941 he was looking for ways to bring de Gaulle
to heel. One possibility was to exploit the distrust existing towards him among
the French in London. Like most émigré communities, the French in London
were riven by factional infighting. One persistent intriguer was Admiral Muselier who resented his subordination to de Gaulle. Muselier was encouraged by
another born mischief-maker, André Labarthe, who had been an aide to the
Popular Front Air Minister Pierre Cot. In November 1940, Labarthe founded a
review entitled *La France libre* which, despite its title, had no connection with
the Free French movement, and adopted a mildly critical stance towards it.
Thanks to the participation of the young philosopher Raymond Aron, the
journal had real intellectual weight, and enjoyed considerable influence in
London.[18]

Churchill was aware of these currents of dissent. In September 1941, he suggested that de Gaulle set up an advisory committee to make the Free French less
of a one-man show. In this way he hoped to curb the troublesome general. The
scheme backfired. Taking Churchill's idea as his cue to attempt a palace revolution, Muselier summoned de Gaulle to form a council composed of himself,
Labarthe, and others. De Gaulle counter-attacked by declaring that he would set
up a committee of his own choosing. Muselier thereupon threatened to secede
from the Free French, taking the fleet with him. After British mediation, the
contest was won by de Gaulle. On 25 September Muselier was forced to accept
the creation of a national committee with de Gaulle as president. Churchill told
Eden: 'this is very unpleasant. Our intention was to compel de Gaulle to accept
a suitable council. All we have done is to compel Muselier and Co. to submit
themselves to de Gaulle.'[19] Muselier, who was not entirely trusted by the British,
had pitched his ambitions too high. The British had wanted to reduce de Gaulle's
power, not emasculate him.

The eight-member National Committee began to give the Free French the
appearance of a provisional government. It claimed to be 'the sole representative
of France and the empire' although the British did not recognize it as such.[20]
Although de Gaulle's authority was now greater than it had ever been, criticisms

[17] Kersaudy, *Churchill and de Gaulle*, 206–7.
[18] A. Gillois, *Histoire secrète des Français à Londres* (1972).
[19] Kersaudy, *Churchill and de Gaulle*, 169.
[20] Crémieux-Brilhac, *La France libre*, 209; Cordier, *Jean Moulin*, iii. 569–646.

of him continued. Labarthe's *La France libre* kept its distance: in all the articles written by Raymond Aron, which run to 1,000 pages, the name of de Gaulle appears only eleven times. Criticism of de Gaulle was also expressed in the newspaper *France*, edited by Pierre Comert, a former press officer at the Quai d'Orsay who had been sacked for his anti-Munich opinions. Comert was assisted by two Socialists, Louis Lévy and Georges Gombault. Lévy organized the French Socialists in London into the 'Jean-Jaurès Group' which became another centre of anti-Gaullist sentiment. After the setting up of the National Committee, the Jaurès Group refused to recognize it.[21] This sniping against de Gaulle continued throughout the next year. It influenced perceptions of de Gaulle among the British left, and gave ammunition to those in America who argued de Gaulle could not be trusted.

De Gaulle's Ideology

These criticisms of de Gaulle were fuelled by suspicion of his political ambitions. There was a long-standing republican mistrust of generals becoming involved in politics which de Gaulle's aloof manner and authoritarian style did nothing to allay. Gombault remarked after his first meeting with de Gaulle in July 1940: 'I had not expected to meet General Boulanger.'[22] There was a persistent rumour, sedulously cultivated by Labarthe, that Dewavrin was a former Cagoulard, and had stuffed the Free French intelligence services with right-wing extremists. Rumours circulated about 'torture chambers' in Duke Street, where these intelligence operations were located. Although Dewavrin was certainly not a left-wing sympathizer, the only substance to these allegations was that one of his first agents had been a Cagoulard. But the mud stuck.[23]

It was true, however, that many of de Gaulle's first followers were army officers, with no love for democracy. When Pierre Cot presented himself to de Gaulle in June 1940, claiming that he was ready to serve in any way, even to sweep the stairs, his offer was rebuffed on the grounds that his reputation would frighten away air-force officers. But there were figures of the left in de Gaulle's movement from the start, among them Boris, Schumann, Cassin, and the trade unionist Henry Hauck. They were willing to give de Gaulle the benefit of the doubt or at least shelve politics until the end of the war.[24]

In fact, no one knew much about de Gaulle's political ideas. Certainly he did not have republicanism in his bones. His parents were Catholic and monarchist, although his father had been unusual in believing Dreyfus to be innocent. But well before 1940 de Gaulle had parted ways with the prejudices of his family. This is clear from his book *France and her Army* (1938), a history of France told

[21] Crémieux-Brilhac, *La France libre*, 207; Cordier, *Jean Moulin*, iii. 634–40.
[22] Gillois, *Histoire secrète*, 52.
[23] Crémieux-Brilhac, *La France libre*, 176, 726–8.
[24] Ibid. 195–8, 209–10; J. P. and M. Cointet, *La France à Londres* (1990), 166–74.

through the history of her army. Its interpretation of French history is entirely unideological. France's many regimes are judged only according to whether they had contributed to the country's military greatness: such a book could not have been written by Maurras. De Gaulle was positive about the *ancien régime* but also the revolutionary armies; scathing about the period 1815–70, viewed as a mediocre interlude between disasters; admiring of the Third Republic up to 1918 for restoring French military strength. Such views were not self-evident for someone from de Gaulle's milieu: his eulogy of the revolutionary General Hoche attracted a grieved rebuke from his father.[25]

In 1940, de Gaulle was happy to take on followers from all political backgrounds. He had no trouble accepting that one could be a Socialist, a Jew, and a patriotic Frenchman. De Gaulle was intransigent in defence of what he believed to be France's national interests, but pragmatic about everything else. In *The Edge of the Sword*, a book he published on the nature of leadership in 1932, one guiding theme is that leaders must be able to adapt to circumstances. When lobbying for his campaign for army modernization in the 1930s, de Gaulle readily approached politicians of all stripes.

None of this makes de Gaulle a Republican, but it does not make him an anti-Republican either. It is true that the first months of the Free French were striking for the absence of references to the Republic. Free French broadcasts were introduced by the motto 'Honour and *patrie*' not the Republican motto 'Liberty, Equality, Fraternity'. In November 1941 de Gaulle declared that his condemnation of the 'appalling tyranny' of Vichy did not signify any indulgence for the 'anarchic abuses' of the decadent Third Republic: both should be swept away.[26] But the idea there had been much wrong with the Third Republic in its last years was widely shared in 1940. De Gaulle's motives in avoiding any association with republicanism were also tactical. He wanted to avoid specific political labels so as to attract the widest support. When Cassin tried in July 1941 to obtain a clearer commitment to democracy, he was told that the French people currently identified democracy with the fallen Republic which had been 'condemned by the facts and by public opinion'.[27] On the other hand, at Brazzaville in October 1940, de Gaulle promised that the French people would choose their form of government after liberation.

In short, de Gaulle's political radicalization over the next two years was not a complete break with his previous beliefs. In January 1941, he invoked 'all the traditions of French freedoms'; in March, the 'two-thousand-year pact between the grandeur of France and the liberty of the world'. The real turning point came in November 1941 when de Gaulle embraced the slogan 'Liberty, Fraternity, Equality' in order to 'remain faithful to the democratic principles . . . which are

---

[25] De Gaulle, *La France et son armée* (1938); J. Lacouture, *De Gaulle*, i. *Le Rebelle* (1984), 176–7.
[26] De Gaulle, *Discours et messages: Pendant la guerre (1940–1946)* (1970 edn.), 146.
[27] Id., *Lettres, notes et carnets: juin 1940–juillet 1941*, 385; also H. Alphand, *L'Étonnement de l'être: Journal 1939–1973* (1977), 111.

at stake in this war of life and death'. In April 1942, he proclaimed that France was going through the greatest revolution in her history. He preferred to 'win a war with Marshal Hoche than lose it with [the *ancien régime* general] Marshal Soubise'.[28] One of de Gaulle's representatives in Washington, Adrien Tixier, was told in December 1941 to explain in America that de Gaulle was a 'firm partisan of the democratic principles' of the French Revolution. The word 'revolution' appears seven times in his speeches and writings in April 1942 alone.[29] In the same month, he referred for the first time to the Republic.

De Gaulle's radicalization partly reflected his resentment of what he saw as France's betrayal by her elites. He once observed that his earliest followers had all been Jews and Socialists. Visiting New York in 1944 he remarked: 'My supporters are Negroes and Puerto Ricans, cripples and cuckolds, émigrés and Jews.'[30] De Gaulle's radicalization was also a tactical response to circumstances. He was quick to grasp the ideological nature of the war, especially after the entry of the Soviet Union. In addition, it was increasingly difficult to separate opposition to Vichy's collaboration policy from opposition to Vichy's domestic agenda. If in 1940–1 de Gaulle felt that associating the Free French with republicanism might alienate French opinion, there was reason to believe in 1942 that this situation was changing. For all his quarrels with his allies, de Gaulle never lost sight of France.

De Gaulle and the French

De Gaulle's first speech had been addressed less to the people of France than to French citizens outside or prepared to leave France. From the beginning, however, he was aware of the importance of propaganda within France itself. The radio was his most powerful weapon. The Free French had five minutes on the BBC every evening. De Gaulle spoke on the big occasions—sixty-seven times in total—but the most frequent broadcaster was Maurice Schumann, who spoke over a thousand times. The British had the right to vet the speeches, and when they wished to punish de Gaulle, they stopped him broadcasting. De Gaulle could also speak from Brazzaville, where the British did not control him, but until June 1943 there was no transmitter powerful enough to be heard in France.[31]

In addition to the Free French radio slot, there were also the French broadcasts of the BBC which increased from two and a half hours daily in 1940 to five hours in 1942. One of the most successful programmes was 'Les Français parlent aux Français' run by Jacques Duchesne, a theatre director who stayed in England

---

[28] *Discours et messages*, 63, 78, 146, 188–9.
[29] C. Andrieu, 'Charles de Gaulle, héritier de la Révolution française', in Institut Charles de Gaulle (ed.), *De Gaulle en son siècle*, ii. *La République* (1992), 48–63.
[30] Birnbaum, *Anti-Semitism in France*, 124.
[31] Crémieux-Brilhac, *La France libre*, 229–31.

after Dunkirk. Duchesne's team was not under de Gaulle's control, and he did not always appreciate their broadcasts. Although 'Les Français parlent aux Français' could not match the stars of Radio Paris, it cultivated an irreverent style which was no less lively. One characteristic invention was the ditty (sung to the tune of La Cucaracha):

Radio Paris ment
Radio Paris ment
Radio Paris est allemand.[32]

(Radio Paris lies, Radio Paris lies, Radio Paris is German).

From the beginning, de Gaulle was keen to test opinion in France. In his tenth speech, on 23 July 1940, he appealed to anyone working for the Germans to 'resist passively by all the means at their disposal'. He also called on people to keep off the streets for one hour on 1 January 1941, and to go into the streets on 11 May.

In December 1940, de Gaulle created a department responsible for 'action in the occupied territories'. This portfolio was given initially to Gaston Palewski, and then in March 1941 to Maurice Dejean, a former aide to Daladier. Palewski conceived the idea of setting up a network Free French committees in France. But he lacked the resources to implement this plan, and nothing came of it. Dejean decided that rather than trying to create committees out of nowhere, he would build contacts with French trade-union circles, and win them over to the Free French. This mission was given to Léon Morandat, a trade unionist who had stayed in London after the signature of the Armistice. Morandat had been the head of the Catholic CFTC in the Savoie, and he had good trade-union contacts. But in the autumn of 1941, several months after the decision to send him to France, Morandat was still in London: it was easier to make plans than to execute them.[33]

The only contacts which had been made with France were the work of Dewavrin's intelligence service. What Dewavrin knew about intelligence work when he started came from spy thrillers. He and his first associates began by selecting their pseudonyms from the Paris metro map: Dewavrin became 'Passy'. Everything had to be created from scratch. His agents were not professionals; he took anyone willing to volunteer. The first one, Jacques Mansion, was landed in Brittany in July by two fishermen. He returned with a map of German installations in Brittany. Another agent was Gilbert Renault, a 35-year-old film producer, who was sent to organize an escape route through the Pyrenees.[34]

To transport his agents to France and provide them with radio contact and equipment, Passy needed the co-operation of the British intelligence service,

[32] Ibid. 211–18; Eck and Crémieux-Brilhac, *Guerre des ondes*, 60–70.
[33] Cordier, *Jean Moulin*, iii. 704–11, 748–9.   [34] Passy, 2ᵉ *Bureau Londres*, 52–78.

MI6. He also had to deal with the newly created Special Operations Executive (SOE) which had a special section (RF) to liaise specifically with the Free French, but also its own French section (section F) which carried out independent operations in France. Passy's relations with these British services—themselves at loggerheads with each other—were tense. Colonel Buckmaster, the head of Section F, was his particular *bête noire*. But Passy could not have functioned without the British, and they needed any intelligence information he could provide them.

By the end of 1941 Passy had sent twenty-nine agents to France. The most successful was Renault, better known to posterity under his pseudonym Colonel Rémy, who set up an intelligence network, the Confrérie Notre Dame (CND), which developed tentacles throughout France. Passy's ultimate ambition was to carry out military actions—especially sabotage—as well as gather intelligence. De Gaulle was sceptical about this but did not forbid it, and in July 1941 Passy set up a military action section to work with SOE. Passy's overall operation was now called the Central Bureau of Intelligence Information and Military Action (BCRAM). The 'M' for 'Military' was added because although de Gaulle was happy to let Passy organize military operations, he believed that these must be separated from political action and propaganda (which was Dejean's responsibility).

In the autumn of 1941, de Gaulle tried to instil a greater urgency in those responsible for political action: so far not a single envoy had been sent to France. When the National Committee was set up, responsibility for political action in France was given to a Commissariat of the Interior, under André Diethelm, a civil servant who had joined de Gaulle in 1941. On 7 November, Morandat was finally parachuted into France on his much-delayed political mission. Passy believed that the distinction between political action and military/intelligence operations was artificial, and once the Commissariat of the Interior did start sending envoys to France, there were rivalries and crossed wires between its agents and Passy's. This plagued the entire history of the Free French.

Diethelm drew up a plan to organize a propaganda network in France and recruit political personalities to it. He contacted his acquaintance Philippe Roques, a former adviser to Mandel, who visited Mandel regularly in prison. Roques was given the task of sounding out former parliamentarians about their attitude to de Gaulle.[35] The problem with this idea, as with the previous schemes of Palewski or Dejean, was that it failed to build upon the activities of Resistance organizations which were beginning to emerge in France—for the simple reason that almost nothing was known about these organizations. In August 1941, one of Passy's agents, Pierre Forman, had stumbled upon a resistance movement called Liberté. He was sent back in October to develop the contact. But Forman's relations with Liberté deteriorated when he was accused by the group of being responsible for indiscretions which had led to arrests of its members. Forman

---

[35] Cordier, *Jean Moulin*, iii. 762–4, 885–7; Crémieux-Brilhac, *La France libre*, 342–3.

became less enthusiastic about Liberté, and his final report in December 1941 accused them of being merely 'idealistic intellectuals'.[36]

De Gaulle expressed his own attitude to what little was known about the Resistance in a press conference on 2 October 1941. He announced: 'A vast resistance is gradually forming . . . To organize and direct this resistance, not only in the already liberated territories, but everywhere in France and the empire, that is the task which the French National Committee has undertaken.' Given that he knew nothing about this 'vast resistance', de Gaulle's claim to direct it was extraordinarily presumptuous. He was even more explicit in a speech on 23 October, reacting to the shooting of hostages which had occurred after the first Communist terrorist attacks. De Gaulle criticized such attacks as premature and likely to lead to demoralizing reprisals: 'The war of the French people must be conducted by those whose responsibility it is, that is to say by me and by the National Committee . . . For the present time the order I give for the occupied territory is not to kill the Germans.'[37]

De Gaulle had no means of applying this 'order'. His real problem at the end of 1941 was not so much that he knew nothing about the Resistance—in fact the Forman reports, the terrorist attacks, the arrival of some Resistance newspapers, were allowing a vague picture to emerge—but that the Resistance was not integrated into any strategy that London might have towards France. It was at this opportune moment that Jean Moulin arrived in London with his authoritative report about the Resistance—what it had so far achieved, and what uses might be made of it.

[36] Cordier, *Jean Moulin*, iii. 750–9, 900–2, 913–14.   [37] *Discours et Messages*, 127–32.

17

The Resistance 1940–1942

Where does the history of the Resistance begin? From the first weeks of the Occupation there were sporadic anti-German incidents: stray shots fired on German patrols, German posters slashed, cables cut. Clearly these brave but futile acts were gestures of 'resistance', but rather than anticipating what came to be 'the Resistance', they represented desperate final skirmishes in the battle of France.[1] They were an end, not a beginning, and their perpetrators were usually young men or boys, acting alone, and often paying with their lives. The future Resistance also started with the acts of isolated individuals, but individuals seeking to make contacts and develop new responses rather than continue a lost battle.

Personalities

In July 1940, the Socialist Jean Texcier, witnessing the first contacts between the Paris population and smiling German soldiers photographing each other in front of Parisian monuments, penned his *Conseils à l'occupé* (Advice to an Occupied Population) which comprised thirty-three 'rules of conduct for the population of an occupied country'. Texcier's *Conseils* originally circulated like a chain letter; two months later he heard them quoted on the BBC.[2] In September 1940, in the Free Zone, General Cochet started producing a series of tracts called *Tour d'horizon*, calling on the French to 'watch, resist and unite'. His readers formed groups to disseminate the tracts more widely.[3]

While Cochet was attempting to appeal to opinion, other army officers were trying to act more discreetly against the Germans. Many of these were to be found within the army intelligence services, the 2ème Bureau. There was, for example, Colonel Alfred Heurtaux, also a vice-president of the Legion of Veterans and Captain Paul Paillole, head of the counter-espionage department. Also operating within the orbit of the Vichy regime was Colonel Georges

---

[1] F. Marcot, 'Resistance et population 1940–1944', 45; id., 'Villes et pouvoir de commandement', in Douzou et al. (eds.), *La Résistance: Villes*, 215–28: 217–18.

[2] J. Texcier, *Écrits dans la nuit* (1945).

[3] Kedward, *Resistance in Vichy*, 37.

Groussard who founded the Groupes de protection, a supplemental police intended both to act as a sort of praetorian guard for Pétain and become the nucleus of a future anti-German military force. That many future resisters started out working for the Vichy regime is only surprising in the light of the later history of the Resistance, which developed its identity in opposition to Vichy. But this could not have been predicted at the beginning. In 1940–1, when there was not yet a Resistance, but there were tiny numbers of people ready to work to remove the Germans from France, many of them could be found at Vichy.[4]

These patriotic and conservative soldiers could hardly have been more different from the group of intellectuals which formed in the summer of 1940 at the Musée de l'homme. Most of them were from the left, some of them were not of French origin. Both these facts applied to the most active member of the group, Boris Vildé, a linguist of anarchist inclinations and Estonian background, who started to build a network of contacts both in Paris and outside. The group's activities included collecting information about German installations, helping British aviators or escaped prisoners of war to escape to Britain, producing and distributing tracts. At the peak there were probably up to 300 people involved. In December, they started a newspaper called *Résistance*.[5]

Although they did not know it, they were not the first to do this. The earliest newspapers to have left a trace were *Pantagruel* and *Libre France* (later called *Arc*) which both appeared in Paris in October 1940.[6] Another precocious centre of activity was Roubaix where the city's Socialist mayor, Jean Lebas, was involved in the production of a paper called *L'Homme libre* from October 1940. In the Unoccupied Zone, the earliest clandestine newspaper was *Liberté*, whose first issue appeared on 25 November 1940 with a quotation from Marshal Foch: 'a people is only conquered when it accepts defeat'.

Who were these resistance pioneers? Claude Bourdet, a leader of the Combat movement, suggested that they were people who had already 'broken with their social and professional milieu'.[7] Another resister, Jean Cassou, said that he had always been someone 'without possessions, without inheritance or title, with no fixed home, no social status, no real profession'. Emmanuel d'Astier de la Vigerie, founder of the southern resistance movement Libération-Sud, asserted that 'one could only be a resister if one was maladjusted'.[8] This may have been true of the flamboyant d'Astier, the black sheep of an aristocratic family, who before 1940 had been a journalist of no fixed opinions. He was a heavy user of opium and

[4] G. Groussard, *Service secret, 1940–1945* (1964); P. Paillole, *Services spéciaux 1935–1945* (1945).

[5] For the Musée de l'homme network, see Blumenson, *The Vildé Affair*; G. Tillion, 'Première Résistance en zone occupée (du côté du Réseau "Musée de l'homme-Hauet-Vildé"', *RHDGM* 30 (1958), 6–22; J. Blanc, 'Le Réseau de Musée de l'Homme', *Esprit* 261 (2000), 89–103.

[6] See the *Catalogue des périodiques clandestins (1939–1945)* (1954); H. Michel, 'Une feuille clandestine: "Arc"', *RHDGM* 30 (1958), 23–32 (it does not appear in the Catalogue); in general, C. Bellanger, *Presse clandestine 1940–1944* (1961).

[7] *L'Aventure incertaine*, 26–7.

[8] Kedward, *Resistance in Vichy*, 76–7.

felt obliged to undergo detoxification before embarking on resistance. Those who knew d'Astier before the war as an aimless dilettante were amazed at the determination and single-mindedness he would display during the Occupation, and he never entirely shook off his reputation as a *condottiere* and adventurer.

The cases of Bourdet, Cassou, and d'Astier should not be generalized. Most early resisters were far from being outsiders. The founder of *Liberté* was François de Menthon, a law professor who secured a post at the University of Lyons after the Armistice. In the autumn of 1940, de Menthon began to sound out the views of other academic colleagues: Pierre-Henri Teitgen and René Courtin at the University of Montpellier, Alfred Coste-Floret at Clermont-Ferrand. Like de Menthon, they had all been committed Christian Democrats before the war. Their deliberations resulted in the decision to produce the newspaper *Liberté*, whose first issue de Menthon drafted at his family chateau near Annecy.[9]

No less respectable than François de Menthon was Captain Henri Frenay, a career officer from a traditional Lyons family. All that set Frenay apart from his conservative Catholic background was his relationship with Bertie Albrecht, who was married to an Englishman. Working in the field of factory welfare provision, Albrecht had introduced Frenay into left-wing circles before the war, and he later claimed that she was responsible for his political education. After the Armistice, Frenay was posted to the Marseilles garrison where he began approaching colleagues about forming a secret military organization that he decided to call the Mouvement de libération nationale. Frenay continued his soundings after being transferred to Vichy in December 1940 to work for the 2ème Bureau.[10]

Worlds apart from Frenay, but no less rooted in a professional milieu, was the trade-union official Christian Pineau. After the Armistice Pineau got himself a job at the Ministry of Supply, and this allowed him to move between the zones without causing suspicion. With another trade unionist, Robert Lacoste, he drafted the CEES manifesto of trade unionists opposed to Vichy. In addition to this public activity, he started a clandestine newspaper called *Libération*, whose first issue appeared in Paris in December 1940.[11]

Philippe Viannay was a 23-year-old Sorbonne student from a middle-class family. Like many of his generation, he despised politics as exemplified by the Third Republic. But immediately after the defeat, Viannay felt the need to 'do' something. An industrialist friend, Marcel Lebon, suggested that he start a paper, and offered to provide funds. The first issue of the paper, *Défense de la France*, eventually appeared in August 1941.[12]

Jean-Pierre Lévy worked for a small Strasbourg-based business which moved to Lyons after the defeat. There he encountered a group called France-Liberté which had grown out of meetings of friends and acquaintances. Many of them

[9] Kedward, *Resistance in Vichy*, 29–35.   [10] Frenay, *La Nuit finira*, 15–86.
[11] Pineau, *La Simple Vérité*, 81–95.   [12] Wieviorka, *Une certaine idée*, 21–4.

were businessmen and professionals, with varying political beliefs, but all opposed to Vichy's authoritarianism. Lévy, who had contacts among the Alsatian refugee community in Lyons, provided many early recruits to the group, and soon became its dominant figure.[13]

Raymond Burgard was a teacher at the Lycée Buffon in Paris. He was an active member of the Christian democratic movement Jeune République. With four other Jeune République activists from the fifth arrondissement of Paris, he formed a group in September 1940. They began by putting anti-German stickers in the metro and on walls. Their motto was: 'Only one enemy, the invader.' In January 1941, they started a newspaper called *Valmy*, and this became the name of their group.[14]

Menthon, Frenay, and Lévy in the Unoccupied Zone; Viannay, Pineau, and Burgard in the Occupied Zone: an academic, an officer, a businessman, a student, a trade unionist, a teacher. These were not maladjusted mavericks although clearly they were individuals of exceptional strong-mindedness, ready to break with family and friends. When Frenay's mother, an ardent Pétainist, heard about his activities in 1941, she threatened to denounce him to the authorities: he did not see her again until the war was over.[15] If the first resisters were sometimes led to rebel against their backgrounds, it was as often within their own milieu, even their families, that they sought their first contacts: Frenay among army officers, Viannay among students, Menthon among Christian Democratic academics. D'Astier's earliest recruits included his own nephew and niece.

Glimmers in the Night

In Resistance memoirs, the theme of night emerges frequently. Texcier collected his Resistance writings under the title *Écrits dans la nuit*; Frenay entitled his memoirs *La Nuit finira*. The publishing house which produced clandestine resistance texts called itself the Éditions de Minuit (the Midnight Press).[16] The night is a conventional image of oppression, but in this case it also conveys the idea of isolation—literally 'living in the dark'. As Marc Bloch wrote to Lucien Febvre, the Occupation meant 'the impossibility of knowing what our closest neighbour thinks. We live surrounded by monads.'[17] The first priority was to find other glimmers in the night, to make contacts. These were usually with old friends or former colleagues,[18] not only for reasons of safety but also to build

---

[13] Veillon, *Le Franc-Tireur*, 45–59.

[14] Noguères, *Histoire de la Résistance*, ii. 130, 269, 388.

[15] Frenay, *La Nuit finira*, 117.

[16] See also A. Vistel, *La Nuit sans ombre: Histoire des mouvements unis de Résistance, leur rôle dans la libération du sud-est* (1970).

[17] C. Fink, *Marc Bloch: A Life in History* (Cambridge, 1989), 278.

[18] Tillion, 'Première résistance en zone occupée', 6; Guehénno, in Debû-Bridel, *La Résistance intellectuelle*, 29.

bridges to the world before defeat: there was reassurance in continuity.[19] One Christian Democratic resister said of his participation in the Resistance that it was not a 'passing phase in my life; it was a continuity: I carried it in me through all my past'.[20]

As contacts widened, new encounters occurred: Catholics found themselves alongside anticlericals, Socialists alongside conservatives. Chance often determined the group one joined. It was on a train that Frenay met Claude Bourdet, who became one of his closest collaborators. Had this not occurred, Bourdet says that he might have ended up in London. Two founders of Libération-Sud, Lucie Samuel (Aubrac) and Jean Cavaillès, teamed up with d'Astier after he overheard their conversation in a Clermont café. Jacques Copeau, who joined Libération-Sud later, and became d'Astier's deputy, remarked: 'I could just as easily have stumbled upon [Frenay's movement] Combat.'[21]

What did 'resistance' mean to these people? One must cast aside romantic images of groups feverishly deciphering coded messages from London, unpacking parachute drops, or sabotaging trains. In 1940–1, there were no contacts with London and no parachute drops; most early resisters had no idea how to sabotage a train or the means to do it. Equally, the hackneyed phrase 'he or she joined the Resistance', is entirely inappropriate to 1940–1. Before it could be joined, resistance had to be invented. So indeed did the very concept of resistance. It was true that the founding of *Défense de la France* had been prompted by the memory of *La Libre belgique*, a Belgian underground newspaper in the First World War, or that in Lille people laid flowers by the statue of the First World War heroine Louise de Bettignies,[22] but most resisters, in Frenay's words, 'had no precedents to guide our thoughts and acts'.[23]

Resistance was a territory without maps, and sometimes developed differently from what the first pioneers had expected. D'Astier, who christened his group 'La Dernière Colonne', wanted to organize attacks on collaborators. This proved to be beyond the capacity of his handful of recruits, and instead they tried propaganda. On the night of 27 February 1941, in several cities of the Southern Zone, they posted up stickers denouncing the newspaper *Gringoire*. This ended in disaster. Five of them, including d'Astier's niece, Bertrande, were arrested. The group was close to extinction. After other false starts, d'Astier decided to produce a newspaper, called *Libération*. The first issue appeared in July 1941, and it rapidly created its own momentum. A newspaper required money, printing facilities, paper, and ink; it had to be collected and distributed. As circulation expanded, these became full-time tasks, and false identity papers had to be forged for those

[19] Kedward, *Resistance in Vichy*, 22–64.
[20] N. Dumez, *Le Mensonge reculera* (Lille, 1946), 58.
[21] Bourdet, *L'Aventure incertaine*, 33–5; Douzou, *La Désobéissance*, 19; Noguères, *Histoire de la Résistance*, ii. 548.
[22] Wieviorka, *Une certaine idée*, 22–3; A. Becker, 'Les Britanniques dans la Grande Guerre', in Frank and Gotovitch (eds.), *La Résistance et les Européens du Nord*, 13.
[23] Frenay, *La Nuit finira*, 11; see also Lévy, *Mémoires d'un franc-tireur*, 42.

who performed them. In this way, the newspaper *Libération* changed the priorities of the group which had created it. The newspaper in a sense created the movement: La Dernière Colonne became Libération.[24]

Frenay's National Liberation Movement developed differently, but a newspaper also became central in a way that he had not expected. Frenay originally intended to create paramilitary units, organized into groups of six or thirty, which would form the embryo of a liberation army. With Bertie Albrecht, he also began producing an information bulletin which could be slipped inside magazines. This bulletin became a newspaper called successively *Les Petites Ailes* and *Vérités*. In November 1941, Frenay's group merged with the Liberté group, and they formed a single newspaper called *Combat*. Frenay did not abandon his military plans, but the newspaper's importance was revealed by the fact that the new movement, although taking the name Mouvement de libération française, became generally known as Combat.[25]

In 1941, resistance meant above all propaganda, especially in the South, and newspapers were its main vehicle. When Jean-Pierre Lévy, on a visit to Marseilles, saw a 'proper' clandestine paper, he realized his movement, which had only distributed tracts, must produce one as well. This resulted, in December 1941, in the first issue of *Franc-Tireur*, henceforth the name by which the movement was known.[26] However modest its appearance, a newspaper projected a future: numbering a sheet 'one' suggested that others would follow. Some resisters were worried about tempting fate in this way. Lévy's group decided not to number the first issue of *Franc-Tireur* in case they were unable to produce a second one. Only with the appearance of the eighth issue in June 1942 did they feel confident enough to begin numbering the paper.[27] Newspapers were also a tangible proof of existence, a way of becoming known and a means of recruitment. Distributing a paper allowed ordinary people to do something. Creating solidarity between those who produced a paper was initially as important as conveying any message to those who might stumble upon it.

The term 'newspaper' is too grandiose for the first artisanal efforts. The first 'issue' of *Liberté* was three pages long; there were only seven copies of the first number of *Libération-Nord*, produced on a typewriter; *Valmy*'s first issue was produced on a child's press. These 'newspapers' were left on trains and in post offices, or slipped into letter boxes, a primitive form of distribution which relied on shopkeepers or concierges turning a blind eye. In these early days, much time was spent scrounging money and travelling the country to extend contacts. Frenay later wrote: 'we did not have a penny . . . We ate in 15-franc restaurants, travelled third class, economized on envelopes. This was the heroic epoch during

[24] Douzou, *La Désobéissance*, 47–79.
[25] Michel and Granet, *Combat*, 34–48.
[26] L. Douzou and D. Veillon, 'Mouvements de Résistance non communiste et lutte armée', in Marcot (ed.), *La Résistance: Lutte armée et maquis*, 83–96: 87.
[27] Lévy, *Mémoires d'un franc-tireur*, 52.

which solid bonds of friendship and confidence were built up.'[28] The rules of clandestinity had to be learnt by experience. On one train journey, Frenay suddenly noticed that the initials in his hat band did not correspond to his alias, and he rushed to the lavatory to remove them.[29] The memory of these early adventures explains why Resistance leaders were later so resentful of attempts by outsiders to infringe their independence.

When their resources were so exiguous, early resisters had to bluff to win new recruits. The first issue of *Libération-Sud* was grandiloquently subtitled 'Organ of the Directory of the Forces of French Liberation'.[30] Vildé's paper *Résistance* claimed to be the 'Official Bulletin of the National Committee of Public Safety'. Pineau wrote the first issues of *Libération-Nord* on his own, attributing to himself a number of pseudonyms to convey the illusion of an editorial team: on military matters he was Captain Brécourt, on economics he was François Berteval.[31] Frenay impressed potential recruits with complicated diagrams of the structure of his organization, but this structure existed largely in his head.[32]

Consolidation I: Movements and Networks

Structures did gradually emerge, and gave rise to two distinct types of resistance organizations: networks (*réseaux*) and movements. The networks were set up with specific military objectives—the collection of information, sabotage, organizing escape routes—and were linked to the intelligence networks of the Allies (SOE, MI6, OSS) or the Free French (BCRAM). Some networks developed from spontaneous local initiatives, such as efforts to help British soldiers stranded in France after the Armistice. Others were set up from scratch by intelligence agents sent out from London. In either case, the link with the outside world was their *raison d'être*—there was no point in collecting information without somewhere to send it—and the condition of their effectiveness: they needed codes, radio transmission facilities, and money. For security reasons, networks had to be rigidly compartmentalized and hierarchically organized. They did not have newspapers because the overriding priority was secrecy. By contrast, newspapers were central to the existence of most movements. Although these also collected information and sought links outside France, their priority was to target the French population: to shake it out of its lethargy and eventually organize it for action.[33]

The differentiation between movements and networks crystallized gradually. The first resisters did whatever seemed possible. The Musée de l'homme group

---

[28] Noguères, *Histoire de la Résistance*, i. 101. See also d'Astier, *Sept fois sept jours*, 35–7.
[29] Cordier, *Jean Moulin*, iii. 1231.
[30] Douzou, *La Désobéissance*, 77.
[31] Aglan, 'Le Mouvement Libération-Nord', 91–2.
[32] Douzou, *La Désobéissance*, 77; Aglan, 'Le Mouvement Libération-Nord', 91–2; Bourdet, *L'Aventure incertaine*, 34.
[33] Bourdet, *L'Aventure incertaine*, 95–6.

started by smuggling escaped prisoners to the Free Zone; then it moved on to collecting information; then, finally, it founded a newspaper. In theory it had gone from being a network to a movement, but such distinctions did not yet exist. Once the networks became more professionalized and started receiving aid from London, the rule was that their members could not also be in a movement. But this was difficult to enforce. When Christian Pineau agreed to create an intelligence network for the Free French in 1942, he recruited from his Libéra-tion-Nord movement. Pineau himself ceased working for the movement, but at the base some agents remained involved in both movement and network.[34]

Nonetheless the distinction between movements and networks was funda-mental. The networks were specialized, secretive, and usually small: effectiveness and security might be jeopardized by size. The movements, on the other hand, sought to increase their numbers. The networks had mysterious coded names— Ali-France, Jade-Fitzroy, Caviar, Brutus, Comète—while the names of the move-ments spoke for themselves: Libération, Défense de la France, Résistance. After the war, official recognition was conferred on 266 networks, representing a total of 150,000 agents. There were huge variations: the Ossau network was restricted to the Basque region and had seventeen full-time agents and ninety-four part-time ones; Zéro-France had 1,000 agents, of whom 150 were full-time. The net-works' social composition also varied. Some specialized in infiltrating a particular institution, like the Ajax network which recruited among the police. Others, like Jade-Fitzroy, recruited eclectically: its members included railway workers, postal workers, garage owners, a prefect of police, hairdressers, restaurateurs, gen-darmes, doctors, teachers, lawyers, priests, students, engineers.[35]

The networks incarnated the cloak-and-dagger aspects of the Resistance so familiar in the popular imagination.[36] Their military contribution to the war may have been more significant than that of the movements, but they belong more to the history of military intelligence, and the Allied war effort than to the social and political history of France. The movements, however, were intimately linked to that history. Among the movements, 1941 was a year of consolidation. Some groups went under; others expanded. New recruits tapped their own circles of contacts. One local organizer of Défense de la France approached friends who had played in the same football team; another contacted pharmacists he had known while working as a medical visitor before the war; most of the move-ment's members in Brest had been at school together.[37] Once existing contacts were exhausted, it was necessary to prospect further afield. Some small groups were absorbed by, or attached themselves to, larger ones. In Britanny, the first group in the Ille-et-Vilaine Department was founded by the guardian of the

[34] D. Veillon, 'Les Réseaux de résistance', in Azéma and Bédarida (eds.), *La France des années noires*, i. 385–412.
[35] A. Aglan, *Mémoires résistantes: Histoire du réseau Jade-Fitzroy 1940–1944* (1994).
[36] Colonel Rémy, *Mémoires d'un agent secret de la France Libre*, 7 vols. (Paris and Monte Carlo, 1947–50).
[37] Wieviorka, *Une certaine idée*, 76.

Château de Fougères, with his wife and daughter. It grew in size, and then attached itself in August 1941 to a larger movement called Ceux de la Libération.[38] Défense de la France also absorbed a number of groups in Britanny: by the end of the Occupation, of its 800 members in the region, 40 per cent had started in a separate group.[39]

Frenay was much assisted by the merger with the Liberté group in November 1941. D'Astier's route to success was to build links to the Socialists and trade unions. In the spring of 1941, he secured backing from Daniel Mayer, who was reconstructing a clandestine Socialist Party, and in the autumn from the venerable trade-union leader Léon Jouhaux. The fact that d'Astier, the highly strung French aristocrat, should have won over Jouhaux, the taciturn and cautious trade unionist, was testimony to d'Astier's considerable eloquence. Jouhaux published an anonymous 'Appeal to Workers' in Libération's fourth issue in December. Socialist and trade-union representatives joined Libération's Executive Committee. The movement was powerfully reinforced by having a network of Socialist and trade-union activists at its disposal.[40] In the case of Libération-Nord, which had been founded by trade unionists and Socialists, such links already existed.

Consolidation II: North and South

Another pattern which developed within the Resistance was a differentiation between the two main zones. Initially there were contacts between resisters in both zones. Frenay sent Robert Guédon, a contemporary from the Saint-Cyr military school, to organize groups in the North during 1941; Philippe Viannay asked a relative in Lyons to contact southern groups. As for the two Libération movements, d'Astier's in the South and Pineau's in the North, they originally had no connection with each other. But a link was established when the philosopher Jean Cavaillès, one of d'Astier's first recruits, was transferred to the Sorbonne. In January 1942, the two Libération newspapers announced that the movements were uniting; in August, it was claimed that a single inter-zone coordinating committee had been set up.[41] None of these efforts bore fruit. Défense de la France did eventually have a few members in the South, but it remained an essentially North-based movement. Nothing more was heard about the merger between the two Libération movements. Most Combat leaders in the North were arrested at the start of 1942. One of the survivors, Jacques Lecompte-Boinet, did succeed in rebuilding a resistance organization in 1943, but he called it Ceux de la Résistance and avoided links with the South.

Apart from the practical obstacles imposed by the demarcation line, the dif-

[38] J. Sainclivier, La Résistance en Ille-et-Vilaine 1940–1944 (Rennes, 1993), 33–4.
[39] Wieviorka, Une certaine idée, 63–7.
[40] Douzou, La Désobéissance, 85–100.
[41] Michel and Granet, Combat, 37–48; Wieviorka, Une certaine idée, 56–8; Douzou, La Désobéissance, 317–26.

ferent conditions in the two zones complicated efforts to create any common organization. The North was more dangerous: the German presence rendered the survival of any group precarious. The Musée de l'homme group was decimated by arrests at the end of 1940; by March 1941 it had been destroyed, and its newspaper with it. Almost none of the first papers set up in the North survived: *Arc* disappeared after twenty issues in January 1941; *Pantagruel* after sixteen issues when its founder, Raymond Deiss, was arrested in October 1941; *L'Homme libre* in June 1941, after the arrest of Lebas; and *Valmy* in April 1942, after the arrest of Raymond Burgard. Sometimes the fleeting existence of a newspaper is only known to us after a group was disbanded. No copy survives of the six numbers (up to 5,000 per copy) of *La Bretagne enchaînée* which apparently appeared between November 1941 and February 1942.[42]

In the South, which was free of Germans, conditions were more relaxed. One visitor to Edmond Michelet, a member of Liberté, had the impression Michelet's activities were so well known that it would have been possible to ask in the streets of Brive for the 'head of the Resistance'. So notorious were the sympathies of the journalists Yves Farge and Georges Altman, who worked on the newspaper *Progrès de Lyon* as well as on the clandestine *Franc-Tireur*, that visitors to the *Progrès de Lyon* had been known to ask the receptionist for the offices of the Resistance.[43] The safety of the South should not be exaggerated—Michelet was arrested in February 1943, and resisters like Frenay and d'Astier had started to live entirely clandestine lives—but some indication of the difference between the two zones is provided by the fact that the 'historic' founders of the three main Southern movements—d'Astier, Lévy, Frenay—as well as the second generation of leaders who replaced them after they went to London or Algiers—respectively Copeau, Claudius Petit, and Bourdet—all survived the war in their posts (apart from Bourdet who was finally arrested in March 1944), whereas the three successive leaders of the northern movement Ceux de la libération were all arrested: Maurice Ripoche in October 1942, Roger Coquoin (Lenormand) in December 1943, and Gilbert Védy (Médéric) in March 1944. Of the movement's first leaders, only one—André Mutter—survived the war.[44]

By 1942, then, separate movements existed in either main zone. In the South, three organizations predominated: Libération-Sud, Franc-Tireur, and Combat. Although Frenay put most emphasis on building up a military organization, while d'Astier placed great store on his links with the unions, in practice all three movements developed a similar kind of organization. After the introduction of the *relève*, Combat created a special Workers' Action section (AO). At about the same time it also created a section to infiltrate the administration (NAP). Libération-Sud followed with a similar section specializing in infiltrating the highest reaches of the administration. Each

---

[42] Sainclivier, *La Résistance en Ille-et-Vilaine*, 33–4.
[43] Bourdet, *L'Aventure incertaine*, 109; Veillon, *Le Franc-Tireur*, 80.
[44] Michel, *Histoire de la Résistance*, 27.

movement had a section to manufacture false papers (Libération-Sud had twelve people fully employed on this by the end of 1942); a social service section to help the families of resisters who had been arrested; a section responsible for gathering intelligence; and embryonic paramilitary units.[45] This specialization of operations showed that the movements were becoming increasingly complex and sophisticated. But propaganda—essentially the newspapers—remained by far the most important activity. In 1942, Libération-Sud spent about 300,000 francs per month—three-quarters of its budget—on producing and distributing its newspaper.[46]

In the North, the consolidation of the Resistance was less advanced than in the South. This does not mean that the Northern resistance was less important than the Southern. On the contrary, Frenay, visiting the North in April 1941, came to the conclusion it was ahead of the South. The greater fragmentation of the Northern Resistance was a result of the greater danger—in secrecy lay security—and also of the geographical divisions between the various zones (Alsace-Lorraine, the Reserved Zone, the Nord/Pas-de-Calais). There were Resistance papers with a specifically regional appeal like *La Voix du Nord*, founded in Lille in April 1941 and calling itself the 'Resistance organ of French Flanders', or *Lorraine*, founded at Nancy in August 1942.

If in the South the three main movements all had newspapers and developed similar structures, in the North there was more diversity. There were papers without movements; movements with papers; and movements without papers. In the first category were several papers which appeared after the disappearance in 1941 of the titles which had emerged at the start of the Occupation. These new newspapers included *La IVe République*, created in December 1941 by some Socialists to replace the defunct *L'Homme libre*; the short-lived *La France continue*, of which thirteen issues appeared in Paris between June 1941 and January 1942; and *Résistance*, created in October 1942, in Paris, by Marcel Renet (Destrée), to replace *Valmy*. When Renet chose the title *Résistance* he did not know there had already been a paper of the same name—a salutary reminder of how isolated these early efforts were.[47]

In the end, *Résistance* did develop a movement around its newspaper, and this brought it closer to the second category of organizations in the North: movements with papers. The most important of these were Défense de la France and Libération-Nord. *Défense de la France* eventually became the most widely distributed of all Resistance newspapers. Although the movement did develop other branches—especially the forging of identity cards—producing the newspaper remained its most important activity. Libération-Nord's newspaper never took off to the same degree, and as the movement grew, the newspaper became less important to it. The distinctiveness of Libération-Nord lay in its close links to

---

[45] Douzou, *La Désobéissance*, 181–223; Veillon, *Franc-Tireur*, 136–48.

[46] Douzou, *La Désobéissance*, 172.

[47] Bellanger, *Presse clandestine 1940–1944*; Bruneau, *Essai historique*.

the Socialist and trade-union movement, and this may have been one of the reasons why, unlike most other movements, which were dominated by one or two charismatic leaders, it was run on more collegial lines.

The third category comprised movements without papers. The biggest of these was the Civil and Military Organization (OCM) which emerged in December 1940 out of the merger of two groups: one headed by the industrialist Jacques Arthuys and two professional officers, Colonel Alfred Heurtaux and Colonel Alfred Touny, and the other headed by Maxime Blocq-Mascart, an economic consultant and lobbyist. After the arrest of Arthuys and Heurtaux at the end of 1941, OCM was run by Blocq-Mascart and Touny. Recruiting its cadres among industrialists, top civil servants, and professionals, it gave priority to military action—the collection of intelligence, building up fighting units—but it also organized groups to reflect on post-war economic and political problems. The fruits of these discussions were published in a series of *Cahiers* which gave the movement the reputation of being technocratic and elitist. Up to a point this was true, but OCM also contained intellectuals of left-wing origin, including former members of the *cabinet* of Jean Zay under the Popular Front.[48]

The two other important northern movements without newspapers were Ceux de la Résistance (CDLR) and Ceux de la Libération (CDLL), both of which confined themselves to military objectives: collecting intelligence, helping Allied aviators to escape, sabotage, and so on. They were indeed more like networks than they were like the Southern movements. CDLL developed out of the efforts of the engineer Maurice Ripoche to organize resistance in the intelligence service of Vichy's air forces. Initially, he recruited in the air force and among former members of La Rocque's PSF. CDLR was founded in 1943 by Lecompte-Boinet, son-in-law of the famous First World War general Mangin, out of the remnants of Frenay's organization in the Occupied Zone after the arrests of 1942.[49]

Towards Ideology

If some important Northern movements did not have newspapers, this was because propaganda seemed less urgent than in the South. As one Northern resister put it, 'the Germans looked after that'.[50] In the South, where there were no Germans before November 1942, the priority was to shatter complacency, reminding people that half the country was occupied. Unlike the Northern movements, those in the South had to situate themselves in relation to Vichy: what was Vichy's real attitude to the Germans? Did resistance to Germany mean resistance to Vichy? Ultimately this led to another difference between the two zones: in the South, resistance became increasingly ideological.

[48] Calmette, *L'OCM: Histoire d'un mouvement*; Muracciole, *Les Enfants de la défaite*, 46–7.
[49] Granet, *Ceux de la Résistance*, 13–33.
[50] Calmette, *L'OCM: Histoire d'un mouvement*, 24.

The Resistance only discovered politics gradually. The situation after the defeat was unprecedented, rendering previous political alignments redundant. Socialists and Cagoulards, monarchists and Freemasons, Catholics and anti-clericals were to be found on all sides. Many resisters acted out of instinct more than ideology. Yves Farge, the Lyons journalist, described his feelings in June 1940 as follows:

> The trolley bus from Tassin stopped to let a German motorised column pass, and some character on the bus dared to say in a loud voice 'the French are at last going to learn what order really is'. I nearly hit him. Then in front of the Grand Hotel there were women waiting to see the German officers emerge. To one of them I said 'Too old for prostitution'. It all began in ways like that.[51]

A similar knee-jerk revulsion had prompted Texcier to write his *Conseils à l'oc-cupé*. But even if the trigger was emotional, subsequent responses were bound to be shaped by political conviction. The group which formed around Menthon was influenced by shared Christian Democratic values: its members opposed Nazism not Germany, and *Liberté* was not chosen as the title of their paper by chance.[52] Many of the students involved in Défense de France were members of the student section of Catholic Action (JEC), which had been anti-Munich and anti-Nazi before 1940.

Such general principles did not, however, offer clear guidance how to respond to Vichy, especially while Pétain's attitude to collaboration was open to inter-pretation. Vichy initially turned a blind eye to many of the anti-German activ-ities developing in its shadow. General Cochet, whose resistance tracts were signed in his own name, was left in peace by the regime until the spring of 1941. How could resisters not be encouraged by Vichy's attitude to the *passeurs* who smuggled people across the demarcation line? For the Germans this was an illegal activity punishable by death; for Vichy, which claimed that the Armistice did not justify turning the line into an internal frontier, it was entirely legitimate. When Paul Kepfler, a *passeur* from Poligny in the Jura, who was captured by the Germans and sentenced to death, escaped to Lyons, he was sent a cheque by Ménétrel accompanied by a note expressing Pétain's admiration for his 'admirable conduct'.[53] Such gestures heartened those wishing to believe that Vichy was playing a double game.

In this context, it is not so surprising to find the first issue of *Liberté* con-taining quotations from Pétain as well as Foch. The paper was initially ready to credit Vichy with good faith, distinguishing between Pétain and his advisers.[54] Frenay was even more prepared to give Vichy the benefit of the doubt. In 1941, he vigorously attacked the Armistice, but took no stand on Vichy and avoided attacks on Pétain. Having worked at Vichy at the end of 1940, he knew about the anti-German sentiments of people like Paillolle or Groussard. Even after

---

[51] Kedward, *Resistance in Vichy*, 186.   [52] Ibid. 31–3.
[53] Marcot, 'Résistance et population', 42–3.   [54] Kedward, *Resistance in Vichy*, 31–3, 124–5.

Frenay resigned from the army, the 2ème Bureau continued to provide him with information which he exploited for his Resistance activities.[55] When at the end of 1941 some members of Combat were arrested, the informer who had betrayed them to the Gestapo was apprehended thanks to Paillole.[56] In such circumstances it was understandable that Frenay could be open-minded about Vichy. His most controversial involvement with the regime occurred at the start of 1942, after further arrests of Combat members. Frenay was informed that they might be released if he would agree to meet Pucheu, the Interior Minister. He had two meetings (on 28 January and 6 February 1942) with Pucheu who tried, unsuccessfully, to get him to moderate his activities.[57]

Frenay's indulgence towards Vichy was reinforced by sympathy with the regime's political objectives. The manifesto he drafted in the autumn of 1940 was favourable to the spirit of the National Revolution.[58] In August 1941, his paper *Vérités* continued to approve Vichy's internal policies: 'we are on [Pétain's] side when he attacks the power of money, Freemasonry and bureaucracy'.[59] This stance was not unusual. It was shared by General Cochet who declared Vichy's reforms to be 'absolutely in accordance with what I have wanted from the bottom of my heart'. He called for loyalty to Pétain even after Montoire: 'let us keep the most complete confidence in the Marshal whom no other Frenchman could replace in his task of internal recovery'.[60] When Cochet republished his tracts after the war, he omitted such passages and erased the ambiguities of the early Resistance.

We have already noted that the Resistance was slow to condemn anti-Semitism. In fact, some resisters even sympathized with Vichy policy towards the Jews. In January 1942, Viannay in *Défense de la France* condemned the 'invasion of Israel or any other invasion' and proclaimed that there 'is a French way of dealing with these problems which is not the German way'. Vichy would not have dissented from this. In June 1942, the OCM produced a *cahier* on post-war reform which expressed doubts if Jews could ever assimilate into France. Of course, there were other voices as well. *Pantagruel* condemned anti-Semitism in October 1941; so did all thirteen issues of *La France continue* between June and December 1941; *Franc-Tireur* published an article condemning racism in December 1941.[61]

---

[55] Frenay, *La Nuit finira*; Michel and Granet, *Combat*, 86–9.

[56] Bourdet, *L'Aventure incertaine*, 118; Frenay, *La Nuit finira*, 167–8.

[57] Bourdet, *L'Aventure incertaine*, 120–1; Michel and Granet, *Combat*, 91–4; Frenay, *La Nuit finira*, 153–61.

[58] See above, Introduction (section: Ambiguities).

[59] Kedward, *Resistance in Vichy*, 131–2; L. Douzou and D. Veillon, 'Les Premiers Résistants face à l'hypothèque Vichy', in Douzou et al. (eds.), *La Résistance: Villes*, 427–46: 434–6. In general F. Marcot, 'Réflexion sur les valeurs de la Résistance', in Guillon and Laborie (eds.), *Mémoire et histoire*, 81–90.

[60] Cordier, *Jean Moulin*, iii. 194, 231–2, 1366–7.

[61] On this issue see Kaspi, Wellers, and Klarsfeld, *La France et la question juive*, 265–406; Laborie, 'La Résistance et le sort des juifs: 1940–1942', in Guillon and Laborie (eds.), *Mémoire et histoire*, 247–60; Kaspi, *Les Juifs pendant l'Occupation*, 304–7; Cohen, *Persécutions et sauvetages*, 204–8, 234–5.

In the early days resisters did not spend much time discussing political reforms since they all agreed that no meaningful reform was possible until Germany's defeat, but the point is that they did not necessarily contest the kind of reforms Vichy wished to carry out. The *Liberté* group was in close contact with Emmanuel Mounier, and when *Esprit* was banned Mounier did not have to seek out resistance circles: he was already part of them.[62] All that had separated him from them previously was not the values in which they believed, but whether those values stood any chance of being realized while France was occupied. Not many resisters unequivocally condemned Vichy from the beginning. The exceptions included *Libération-Sud* whose first issue in July 1941 directly criticized Pétain. The second issue in August attacked Vichy's anti-Republican measures, criticized the Jewish Statute, and proclaimed it stood for 'Liberty, Equality, Fraternity'. *Franc-Tireur*'s first issue in December 1941 was also hostile to Pétain whom it called a 'conscious traitor'.[63] This was not surprising given the republican sympathies of the movement's leaders, but it was also explained by the late date. At the end of 1941, even those well disposed to Vichy were losing their illusions.

Liberté offered its first personal criticism of Pétain in October, quoting Clemenceau's remark that he had preferred the madness of Foch to the sanity of Pétain in 1918.[64] *Combat* was the last Southern movement to break with Pétain, which it did after Laval's return to power in April 1942. In the next month *Combat* declared; 'All is clear now. The Pétain myth is over . . . All France is now against you.' By October 1942, Pétain had become the 'sinister old man of Vichy'. *Combat*'s condemnation of Vichy now extended beyond collaboration to the regime's internal policies: 'the suppression of our liberties . . . the odious anti-Semitic legislation . . . the omnipotence of the monopoly trusts'. At the end of the year *Combat* was invoking 'Liberty, Equality, Fraternity'.[65]

This ideological radicalization of the Resistance did not occur in the Occupied Zone. Northern resisters were condescending about the South where they saw too little danger and too much politics. After a visit to the South, Pineau claimed that the Southern resisters 'might as well have had visiting cards printed with their clandestine names'; he concluded that they needed some Germans in the street.[66] This was why Lecompte-Boinet decided, after Combat's collapse in the Occupied Zone, that he would create a new movement, CDLR, rather than rejoin Frenay in the South. When an envoy from London tried to discover CDLR's views on a post-liberation regime, he was told that the only purpose of the Resistance was to 'make war'.[67] Some Northern resisters did express politi-

[62] Kedward, *Resistance in Vichy*, 203.
[63] Douzou, *La Désobéissance*, 265–88; Veillon, *Le Franc-Tireur*, 275.
[64] Kedward, *Resistance in Vichy*, 141.
[65] Michel and Granet, *Combat*, 86, 96; Kedward, *Resistance in Vichy*, 238–9.
[66] *La Simple Vérité*, 99.
[67] Granet, *Ceux de la Résistance*, 53–4.

cal views, but of the most diverse kinds. In October 1940, Maurice Ripoche proclaimed that the task of freeing France of Germans must be followed by that of freeing her of 'garrulous and incompetent politicians . . . [and] . . . Jews without *patrie*' in order to create an authoritarian 'New order'; *Pantagruel* recalled the Popular Front of 'lugubrious memory'. On the other hand, *L'Homme libre*, from its first issue in October 1940, wanted a 'democratic Republic where the words Liberty-Equality-Fraternity will not be empty ones'; *Libération-Nord*, hostile to Vichy from the start, was among the first papers to attack Pétain directly; and *La France continue*'s first issue (June 1941) announced that Vichy was the 'anti-France'.[68]

It is wrong therefore to see all the Northern movements as more conservative than those in the South. The real difference was that, being directly confronted with Vichy, the Southern movements evolved in response to it, while the Northern ones did not. In the North, those starting hostile to Vichy remained so; others were slow to rethink their position. *Défense de la France* remained indulgent towards Vichy until November 1942, long after the regime had been discredited among every Southern movement. Viannay later admitted that he had continued to believe in a 'hidden face of Vichy'.[69] In the North, then, no common resistance ideology emerged. There was a world of difference between the technocratic elitism of OCM's *Cahiers*, the Socialist Republicanism of *Libération-Nord*, and the democratic Catholicism of *La France continue*. The difference between the Northern movements and the Southern ones was that the former were still reacting to the republican past while the latter were reacting to the Vichy present.

In the South, however, ideology became central to the self-definition of the Resistance. As Kedward writes: 'the realisation that the underground war against Germany involved a form of civil war against Vichy is the central development in Resistance history in 1941'.[70] The Resistance started to develop a common rhetoric, drawing on the traditions of French Republicanism. In 1942, some members of Franc-Tireur in Lyons resurrected the revolutionary newspaper *Le Père Duchêne* which had been founded in 1793 and revived in 1848 and 1871. Although only four issues appeared, the main purpose was to establish a lineage for the Resistance. This was also the ambition of a paper founded at Saint-Étienne in May 1942, calling itself the 'Newspaper of the Inheritors of the French Revolution'. It took the title 93 in reference to the Second Republic of 1793. Even *Combat* now talked of the 'Fourth Republic', and frequently mentioned revolution.[71]

---

[68] Cordier, *Jean Moulin*, iii. 1122–4, 1116–18; Aglan, 'Le Mouvement Libération-Nord'; R. Bédarida, '1940–1941: Catholiques résistants en zone occupée', in Guillon et Laborie (eds.), *Mémoire et histoire*, 170–81.

[69] Wieviorka, *Une certaine idée*, 43–4, 156–7; Viannay, *Du bon usage de la France* (1988), 31.

[70] *Resistance in Vichy*, 137.

[71] Ibid. 152–4; Michel and Granet, *Combat*, 119–26.

Other Voices I: Catholics and Socialists

The politicization of the Southern Resistance did not occur in a void. In 1940, most political organizations had been stunned into silence, their leaders too discredited to raise their heads. But towards the end of 1941, their voices— Catholic, Socialist, Communist—started to be heard again.

Catholics, especially those with Christian Democratic backgrounds, were prominent in resistance from the start: in the *Voix du Nord*, in *Valmy*, in *Résistance*, in *Liberté*, and in *Défense de la France*. There were also Catholics like Mounier who inhabited a twilight zone between support for Vichy and criticism of it. A similar position was held by Stanislas Fumet, who had been an important Christian Democrat presence before 1940 through his periodical *Temps présent*. Its network of subscribers, the 'Amis du temps présent', was part of the infrastructure of French Christian Democracy. In December 1940, Fumet revived his periodical with the new title *Temps nouveau*. It pushed criticism of Vichy and Nazism as far as legally possible until being banned by the government in August 1941, along with *Esprit*. Mounier and Fumet had helped to create a space through which it was possible to glide almost imperceptibly from Pétainism to Resistance—and not only metaphorically: many future resisters met in their Lyons apartment.

The contribution of these individual Catholic voices to the Resistance as a whole was reinforced by the appearance of a specifically Christian presence in the Resistance in the form of the newspaper *Cahiers du témoignage chrétien*. Its founder was the Jesuit Pierre Chaillet whose role in rescuing Jews through the organization Amitié chrétienne we have already seen. Chaillet had met Frenay in Lyons, and he began contributing to his paper, *Les Petites Ailes*. The first issue of *Témoignage chrétien* appeared in November 1941 with an article by the Jesuit Gaston Fessard entitled: 'France, be careful not to lose your soul.' This was a closely argued critique of the values of Nazism which concluded unequivocally: 'Collaboration in the government of the Marshal = Collaboration in the New Order = Collaboration in the triumph of Nazi principles.' The first issue of *Témoignage chrétien* was printed on the presses of *Combat*, and distributed through Combat's network of contacts. Five thousand copies were produced. Soon the journal established its own presses and distribution networks thanks to the efforts of Louis Cruvillier, who had worked for *Temps nouveau* until its prohibition in 1941. Cruvillier was eventually forced to escape the police by taking refuge in Switzerland in May 1942, but by this time *Témoignage chrétien* had established itself within the French Resistance. No other Resistance publication did more to condemn racism and anti-Semitism.[72]

As well as Catholics, there were many Socialists among the first resisters, but the Socialist Party itself was discredited by its pre-war divisions. Blum had been imprisoned by the Vichy regime while Faure was a discreet supporter of it. In

---

[72] R. Bédarida, *Les Armes de l'esprit: Témoignage chrétien 1941–1944* (1977).

the South the rebuilding of the Party began with a meeting at Nîmes in March 1941. The nine Socialists present christened themselves the Committee of Socialist Action (CAS). To break with the past, they decided to exclude Socialists who had voted for Pétain. The moving force behind the CAS was Daniel Mayer, who had been a journalist on the Party newspaper *Le Populaire*, and was devoted to Blum. In the North, a separate CAS was set up, under Henri Ribière, but progress was slower both because of the need for secrecy and because Libération-Nord assumed the character of an unofficial Socialist resistance movement. Mayer's ambition in the South was not to found a resistance movement, but to ensure that the Socialists would be ready to play a political role at the liberation. In the meantime, he allowed Socialists to join whatever movement they wished.

The turning point in the reputation of the Socialists was the Riom trial which opened on 20 February 1942. Blum, the most prominent defendant, deployed all his dialectical skill and moral passion, and succeeded in turning the tables on his prosecutors. The trial developed into a public relations disaster for Vichy, and was terminated on 11 April. What Vichy had planned as an indictment of the Popular Front was transformed by Blum into a resounding defence of socialism and the Republic. From this point the Socialists felt less obliged to apologize for their past. One sign of this confidence was the (clandestine) reappearance in May 1942 of *Le Populaire*. The newspaper announced that it did not represent 'the party of yesterday' and had repudiated those 'Socialists who have betrayed'. But it called itself the 'Central Organ of the Socialist Party (SFIO)' and was numbered 'New series, No. 1, 26th Year, No. 6329'. This was an assertion of continuity, and Socialists now had a voice that could not be ignored. By the end of 1942 the combined forces of the CAS in the two zones were probably about 28,000 (about a quarter of the pre-war membership). In the South, the Party was strong in Marseilles where it had able organizers in the persons of Félix Gouin and Gaston Defferre.[73]

Other Voices II: The Communists

The Communists also had to live down a compromised past, but there is still much controversy about just how compromised that past was. Non-Communist historians argue that the Party came close to collaboration in the summer of 1940 by negotiating with the Germans to legalize *L'Humanité*.[74] Until the 1960s Communist historians denied the existence of the negotiations, and when this position was no longer sustainable they blamed them on junior officials. The official line was that the Party had been the pioneer of resistance. The Party's Appeal of 10 July was presented as the first call for resistance in France, parallel to de Gaulle's call from London. Non-Communist historians contested

[73] Kedward, *Resistance in Vichy*, 95–104; Sadoun, *Les Socialistes sous l'Occupation*, 109–32.
[74] D. Peschanski, 'La Demande de parution légale de "l'Humanité" (17 juin 1940–27 août 1940)', *MS* 113 (1980), 67–89.

the alleged date of the Appeal and cast doubt on its resistance credentials. It certainly is a curious document, attacking Pétain's government and calling for 'a free and independent' France, but without mentioning the Germans.

Some light has been shed on these mysteries by the recently opened Soviet archives.[75] It emerges from these that the Comintern in Moscow was caught unawares by the German victory. It was initially unsure how to respond, and its directives were slow to reach Paris. The situation was further complicated by the dispersal of the French Communist leaders. Maurice Thorez, their chief, was in Moscow; his deputies, Jacques Duclos and Maurice Tréand, were in Brussels; the remaining leaders left in Paris headed south during the Exodus. Arriving back in Paris on 15 June, Duclos and Tréand saw the power vacuum in France as an opportunity to see if the German presence might allow the Communists to recover influence after the repression they had suffered during the Phoney War. Given the Nazi-Soviet non-aggression pact it was reasonable to assume that such a policy would be approved in Moscow. But everything would depend on the attitude of the Germans.

When some Communist mayors in the Paris region tried to re-enter the town halls from which they had been ousted during the Phoney War, the Germans would not support them.[76] The Communists received more encouragement in the negotiations over the possible legalization of *L'Humanité*. On the French side, the negotiators included Tréand and Jean Catelas, who were, after Duclos, the two most senior Communists in Paris; on the German side, they included Abetz and representatives of the German military authorities. When two of the French negotiators were arrested by the French authorities, the Germans got them released on 25 June. During the negotiations, Tréand and Catelas promised that if *L'Humanité* were allowed to reappear, it would 'pursue a policy of European pacification' and 'denounce the activities of the agents of British imperialism'. *L'Humanité* (which had been appearing underground since September 1939) printed three articles praising fraternization between French workers and the Germans, the last on 27 July.

On 3 July, Duclos received a telegram from Moscow instructing him to organize the 'resistance of the masses against the aggressor'. This directive probably originated during the last stages of the battle of France and was Comintern's reaction to the unexpectedly rapid German advance. But by the time the directive had passed the bureaucratic procedures and reached Duclos, the Armistice had been signed.[77] Nonetheless Duclos felt obliged to take account of it, while not

---

[75] S. Courtois, 'Un été 1940: Les Négociations entre le PCF et l'occupant allemand à la lumière des archives de l'Internationale communiste', *Communisme*, 32–4 (1992–3), 85–112; M. Narinski, 'Le Komintern et le Parti communiste français, 1939–1941', *Communisme*, 32–4 (1992–3), 11–40; V. Smirnov, 'L'Union soviétique, le Komintern et la Résistance française en 1940–1941', in Douzou et al. (eds.), *La Résistance: Villes*, 499–510.

[76] J. Clesse and S. Zaidman, *La Résistance en Seine Saint-Denis 1940–1944* (1994), 39–42.

[77] This at least is the interpretation of Courtois, 'Un été 40'; Smirnov, 'L'Union soviétique', 502, does interpret it as a Resistance text.

abandoning negotiations with the Germans. This resulted in the Appeal of 10 July (probably drafted towards the end of July) whose contradictions appear less baffling once this background is understood: Duclos was trying to respect the Comintern's redundant instructions while also trying to formulate a policy appropriate to the present context. How little importance Duclos attached to the Appeal was clear from the report he sent to Moscow a few days later. He devoted only one sentence to it, and spent more time discussing the negotiations with the Germans, even commenting favourably on the humane treatment of French prisoners by German soldiers.

When Duclos's reports on the negotiations arrived in Moscow in mid-July, they were a complete surprise. Comintern's response was confused. While not totally condemning the attempt to get *L'Humanité* legalized, it cautioned against the meetings with Abetz. Duclos was told to refrain from attacking the British, but also to avoid provoking the Germans. Thorez, however, was alarmed by what he heard from Paris, and, partly under his influence, Comintern toughened its stance. Duclos was sent another message telling him to end the negotiations and warning against 'any manifestation of solidarity' with the Germans. In reply, Duclos defended himself from any suspicion that he might have become a 'plaything of the occupier'. The Communists broke off the negotiations in the third week of August. Robert Foissin, one of the negotiators, was made a scapegoat and excluded from the Party. Almost simultaneously, Abetz decided against the legalization of any Communist newspaper. How close Abetz had come to allowing this is not clear, but the German military authorities had never been keen. The flirtation between the Communist Party and the Germans ended just as the Germans were about to end it anyway. Fortunately for the future reputation of the Party, the Germans had never allowed the relationship to go beyond a flirtation.

From September 1940 the PCF's stance towards the Germans mirrored the fluctuations in the relationship between Hitler and Stalin. A Gestapo report in January 1941 noted that since September 1940 the Party had embarked upon anti-German propaganda.[78] The extent of this should not be exaggerated: it was no more than a change of tone. *L'Humanité* started referring to the 'occupying authorities' rather than, more neutrally, the 'authorities'. In Moscow, Thorez, who had not approved of Duclos's flirtations with the Germans, was pushing to accentuate this more anti-German orientation.[79] A document prepared by the PCF leaders in Moscow in April, and approved by the Kremlin, stressed that the 'main task is not the overthrow of capitalism . . . but the defence of national interests . . . national liberation from the yoke of the foreigner'.[80] The Party did not prevent the activities of a group of its intellectuals in Paris who founded the

---

[78] S. Courtois and D. Peschanski, 'La Dominante de l'Internationale et les tournants du PCF', in Azéma et al., *Le Parti communiste français des années sombres*, 250–73: 262–3.

[79] A. Kriegel, 'Le PCF, Thorez et la France', *MS* 172 (1995), 95–9.

[80] Narinski, 'Le Komintern et le Parti communiste', 25.

clandestine periodical *L'Université libre* in November 1940, and then its successor *La Pensée libre* in February 1941. *La Pensée libre* was easily the most substantial clandestine publication which had so far appeared in France, and could not have appeared without help from the Party's underground publishing networks. Its first issue denounced 'German imperialism and its vassal Marshal Pétain'. The choice of the word 'imperialism' in preference to 'Nazism' shows, however, that a class analysis still prevailed over a patriotic or anti-fascist one.[81]

In May 1941 the patriotic orientation became more pronounced with the call for a 'National Front of Struggle for the Independence and Freedom of France' and a condemnation of the 'barbaric methods of Nazism'. This later enabled the PCF to claim that it had not suddenly become anti-German after Hitler's invasion of the Soviet Union on 21 June 1941, but it cannot disguise the fact that before this date the central axis of Communist policy was neutralist. The war was denounced as an imperialist conflict; the Party's slogan was 'Neither a British Dominion nor a German protectorate'. Only after 21 June did the conflict become a 'War for National Liberation'. Before this date, if it cannot be said that the Communists collaborated, it cannot be said that they resisted either. Although Communist students were involved in the 11 November demonstration in Paris, the Communist press ignored the event.

Any frustration felt by Communist activists about the Party's policy was channelled into uncompromising denunciation of Vichy. Sometimes this permitted an oblique attack on the Germans through phrases such as 'collaboration signifies the domestication of France' even if the identity of the domesticator was not spelled out. In general, however, the attack on Vichy 'traitors' concentrated on domestic issues: Vichy as a regime of capitalist oppression and political reaction. Class not patriotism was the Party's frame of reference at this stage. The Communists tried to organize people's committees (*comités populaires*) to exploit discontent over food shortages; they agitated for higher wages in the factories. This propaganda had little impact, but the violence of the Communists' opposition to Vichy set them apart from any other group in France. Only the Communists could have said about Pétain at this time: 'France hates you for its misfortunes.'[82]

The PCF's attacks on Vichy were a logical response to the repression which the regime had unleashed against it. In the autumn of 1940, French police launched anti-Communist operations throughout the country. The Party was vulnerable because its activists had come out of hiding in the first weeks of the Occupation. Generally the Germans approved Vichy's anti-communism, but some prefects of the Occupied Zone complained of a lack of German co-operation. After June 1941 they had no complaints. This date appears in retrospect as a turning point in the history of the Communists under the Occupation, but this is not how it appeared at the time to Communist activists in the South

[81] N. Racine-Furland, '*L'Université libre*, novembre 1940 à décembre 1941' in Azéma et al. (eds.), *Les Communistes français de Munich à Chateaubriant*, 133–44; Sapiro, *La Guerre des écrivains*, 474–8.
[82] Kedward, *Resistance in Vichy*, 56.

who were still reeling from the effects of the repression. In the Var, the Party had almost been wiped out, and it showed no signs of life between March and September 1941.[83] Repression was the main experience of the Communists in Vichy France both before and after June 1941.

In July 1941, Comintern instructed the PCF to launch armed struggle. The orders were to disrupt industrial production in factories working for the Germans, carry out acts of sabotage, and organize armed groups.[84] The first objective merely involved giving a patriotic slant to the previous factory agitation for improved pay: disrupting production was now presented as undermining the German war effort.[85] The first act of sabotage was the derailing of a train at Épinay-sur-Seine on 18 July. The first case of armed action was the assassination of a German soldier by the Communist Pierre Georges (Colonel Fabien), in full daylight, at Barbès-Rochechouart metro station on 21 August. Two days later, two German officers were killed in Lille. Most Communist resistance activity occurred initially in the Paris region and the Nord/Pas-de-Calais. The Germans recorded sixty-eight actions in the Paris region between August 1941 and January 1942.[86] From the autumn, Communist resistance spread to other parts of the Occupied Zone. Three incidents occurred on three successive days of October 1942: on 19 October, the derailing of a train between Paris and Rouen; on 20 October, the assassination of a senior German officer in Nantes; on 21 October, another assassination in Bordeaux.

Despite these spectacular operations the Communists did not possess a smooth military machine, ready to leap into action at the first opportunity. Except for those, like Fabien, who had fought in Spain, few Communists had experience of armed action or the stomach for it. Communist 'military resistance' consisted of a handful of determined and desperate individuals armed with a few revolvers. The first actions were carried out by three minuscule groups restricted mainly to the Paris region: the Organisations speciales (OS), teams which had been created in the autumn of 1940 to protect Communists during the distribution of tracts; Young Communists organized into so-called Bataillons de la jeunesse; and the immigrants of the MOI. In total, these represented probably not more than a hundred people, a tiny minority of a party which had itself been decimated by the repression it had suffered. In the autumn of 1941, Charles Tillon was instructed to co-ordinate these groups by setting up a national military committee (CMN). Previously Tillon had been a Communist organizer in the south-west. He was one of the few Party leaders who had openly called for resistance to the Germans as early as the summer of 1940. Normally Communists did not tolerate deviations from the Party line, even—especially—if these

[83] Guillon, 'La Résistance dans le Var', 87–95.
[84] M. Narinski, 'L'URSS, le Komintern et la lutte armée en France', in Marcot (ed.), *La Résistance: Lutte armée et maquis*, 361–72: 361–2.
[85] Courtois, *Le PCF dans la guerre*, 217–20, 242–7.
[86] Courtois et al., *Le Sang de l'étranger*, 126.

anticipated positions subsequently adopted by the Party. But in 1941 the Communists needed all the leaders they could find, especially ones as energetic and able as Tillon who was to become the organizer of the Communists' entire military effort. At first, however, Tillon's CMN had only the most shadowy existence. It is not even clear whether the three operations of mid-October had been co-ordinated.[87] This was a darkly mysterious time in the Communist Party's history.

In February 1942, Moscow ordered the Communists to intensify armed action. After the German failure to take Moscow in 1941, the Soviet leadership believed that the Red Army would soon be ready to undertake a decisive offensive. Stalin wanted the Allies to organize a second front to take the pressure off his forces. The Communists were encouraged to expect victory in 1942. This optimism seemed less well founded after the successful German offensives into the Caucasus, and the Allies' rejection of a second front in Europe during 1942. But such setbacks only increased the demands made of the Communists: they were supposed to take pressure off the Red Army by pinning down German troops in the West. In July, the PCF came close to calling for a national insurrection. Its armed groups were now designated Sharpshooters and Partisans (FTP) which were organized into small groups of three or four men who were supposed to retain their normal jobs, meet when there was an action to carry out, and then disperse. There was also one full-time armed unit operating from the forest of Moret-sur-Long not far from Paris. This group, an anticipation of the rural-based Maquis of 1943, carried out its actions in the city—it shot Doriot's secretary in August 1942—and then retreated back to the countryside.[88]

As the number of Communist actions increased, so did the intensity of repression. The German and French police were now co-operating fully. In Paris the Bataillons de la jeunesse had been completely wiped out by the spring of 1942. In August, a new unit, calling itself the Valmy group (no relation to the defunct *Valmy* newspaper) carried out two spectacular attacks in Paris at the Rex Cinema and the Jean-Bouin Stadium. Several Germans were killed, but the entire Valmy group was arrested. Only the MOI remained operational in Paris. The Communist leader Charles Debarge, who had masterminded daring attacks on the Germans in the Nord, was arrested in September after several close shaves, and a huge police operation almost eliminated the entire Party organization in the *département*.[89] The Moret-sur-Long group was destroyed. In the spring of 1942, the Party came close to disaster when the fourth most important figure in the hierarchy, Raymond Dallidet, was arrested. Had he talked under torture, the entire leadership of the Party would have been at risk.[90]

[87] R. Bourderon, 'Le PCF dans la lutte armée: Conceptions et organisations', in Marcot (ed.), *La Résistance: Lutte armée et maquis*, 131–40.

[88] Narinski, 'L'URSS, le Komintern et la lutte', 363–5; Courtois, *Le PCF dans la guerre*, 257–60, 272; Bourderon, 'Le PCF dans la lutte', 136.

[89] Azéma and Bédarida (eds.), *La France des années noires*, i. 502–3.

[90] Courtois, *Le PCF dans la guerre*, 239–42.

The summer of 1942 was the nadir of Communist fortunes. It was also the period when, in the Occupied Zone, the Party constructed the skeleton of an underground organization which allowed it to survive and eventually develop a highly effective resistance operation. In the long run the Party profited from adversity. At the time, however, the Communists were close to extinction, and they were almost completely isolated. After June 1941, the Party called for national unity. It tried using the 'National Front' idea, launched in the previous month, to rally the entire resistance under its banner. But the other Resistance movements were wary. Frenay's paper *Vérités* attacked the Front national in September 1941; *Franc-Tireur* pointed out in February 1942 that one could not simply forget the behaviour of the Communists before June 1941.[91] Quite apart from this problem, most other resistance movements disapproved of terrorism. Faced with this lack of response, the Communists abandoned the prospect of alliance with other groups and downplayed the Front national theme. *L'Humanité* did not mention it in the first five months of 1942.[92] The Communists seemed entirely alone.

Towards Unity

In May/June 1942, there was another shift in Communist policy. The Front national idea was resurrected and *L'Humanité* now called for the unity of all 'patriots' whether Socialist, Radical, conservative, Catholic, Jewish, or atheist. The Communists started to employ the Republican rhetoric—the language of 1793—which had served them so well during the Popular Front. They launched a major propaganda campaign for the celebration of the battle of Valmy in September 1942. This kind of language offered a possible bridge to the other movements which, especially in the South, were developing similar themes. Despite the other movements' wariness towards the Communists, an objective convergence was occurring between those resisters, like Frenay, whose original sympathy for Vichy's political objectives had been eroded as they lost faith in the regime's foreign policy, and the Communists, who had always contested the political objectives, but ignored the foreign policy until June 1941.[93]

Given the reputation of the Republic by the end of the 1930s, this reassertion of republican values was not self-evident. It was a situation which Vichy itself created by becoming so identifiably a right-wing regime, and linking its fate so irremediably to Germany's. Those like Mounier, who had hoped to opt out of politics and defend spiritual values—in Peguy's words, *mystique* not *politique*—found that politics could not be circumvented after all. The issue was decided for them when Vichy drew a line beyond which criticism could not be expressed: it was Vichy which ensured that the Resistance would be Republican. The

---

[91] Michel, *Les Courants de pensée*, 268; Kedward, *Resistance in Vichy*, 124–31.
[92] Courtois, *Le PCF dans la guerre*, 234–6.   [93] Kedward, *Resistance in Vichy*, 137.

Republic could possess a *mystique* again, and provide the Resistance, especially in the South, with an identity which transcended differences between the movements.

In fact these differences had never meant much to the ordinary members of resistance movements. The movements recruited wherever they could. In Marseilles, Combat had many Socialists in its ranks. When the southern movements eventually united in 1943, it was discovered that the same person was often distributing the papers of several movements.[94] The same was true in the North. In the Pas-de-Calais, the OCM, reputedly a right-wing organisation, recruited many Socialists (including the future Socialist leader Guy Mollet). After the war, some members of Défense de la France turned out not even to know the name of the movement to which they had belonged; 11 per cent of them had worked for other organizations as well.[95]

For these reasons, there was a compelling case for the movements to unite their efforts. The main obstacle came from the susceptibilities of the leaders. There could hardly have been two men more temperamentally mismatched than d'Astier and Frenay who first met in the summer of 1941. Frenay realized that d'Astier's political and trade-union contacts were superior to his own, but wondered how seriously to take him. D'Astier, who tried to dazzle Frenay with his eloquence, realized that Combat was better organized than Libération. This made him wary when Frenay started pushing for a merger: he did not want to be swallowed up by him. During the summer of 1941, there were discussions about a federation between three Southern movements: Libération, Liberté, and Libération nationale. But when Liberté and Libération nationale did merge in December 1941 (to form Combat), d'Astier remained aloof. Frenay's contacts with Vichy worried many resisters including even members of his own movement, and the revelation of his contacts with Pucheu caused genuine shock. D'Astier used this as a pretext to break off talks and exploited Frenay's discomfiture by giving the matter some publicity in *Libération*.[96] At this moment, just when it seemed that the momentum towards unity had stalled, it was reinforced by the arrival of de Gaulle's envoy, Jean Moulin. He had instructions to bring the movements together, and money to offer them, if they were ready to comply.

[94] Guillon, 'La Résistance dans le Var', 73; Bourdet, *L'Aventure incertaine*, 90.

[95] Azéma and Bédarida (eds.), *La France des années noires*, i. 509; Wieviorka, *Une certaine idée*, 180, 188.

[96] Douzou, *La Désobéissance*, 100–4, 324–5; Douzou and Veillon, 'Mouvements de résistance non communiste', in Marcot (ed.), *La Résistance: Lutte armée et maquis*, 88–9; Cordier, *Jean Moulin*, iii. 136.

18

De Gaulle and the Resistance 1942

Moulin's Plan

Jean Moulin's resistance began on 17 June 1940 when he tried to cut his throat rather than sign a document dishonouring French colonial troops. This was one of those actions which reveals an individual's inner resources of courage, but the political convictions which inspired it had long been evident. Moulin came from a family where republicanism was lived like a religion. In 1939, as prefect of Chartres, it fell to him to attend the annual banquet in memory of a hero of the First Republic, General Marceau. Moulin's speech made clear that as 'the great grandson of a soldier of the Republic, grandson of a man who knew the prisons of the Second Empire for daring to declare his attachment to the Republic', the occasion was no mere formality for him.[1]

Moulin's father, a teacher at Perpignan, had Radical and Masonic connections which helped Moulin in the first stages of his career. By 1925, he was the youngest sub-prefect in France. Around this time, Moulin met the left-wing Radical Pierre Cot who was a passionate advocate of a Franco-Soviet alliance. Cot became a close friend and patron, and in 1936 when he became Air Minister in the Popular Front government, he made Moulin his *chef de cabinet*. Moulin's experience of underground activity dated not from 1940, but from this experience of working for Cot when he helped to organize secret shipments of arms to the Spanish Republicans. One of Moulin's associates later dubbed this his period of 'archeo-Resistance'. These shipments occurred with Blum's secret approval, and involved other members of Cot's entourage—Pierre Meunier, Robert Chambeiron, and Henri Manhès—and also brought Moulin into contact with a number of Comintern agents: Maurice Panier, André Labarthe, and Louis Dolivet. Despite subsequent insinuations that Moulin was a crypto-Communist, even a Soviet agent, there was nothing sinister about these contacts in the context of the interna-

---

[1] Cordier, *Jean Moulin*, ii. 198–200.

tional movement of solidarity with Spain. Moulin was strongly pro-Soviet at this time—Cot later said that Moulin was 'the most left-wing' of those around him—but this did not make him a Soviet agent.[2]

After being dismissed by the Vichy government in November 1940, Moulin went to Paris and sought out his associates from the Cot team. Cot himself had left for America, where Dolivet, who broke with Comintern after the Russo-German Pact, joined him in December 1940. Meunier, who was working at the Ministry of Finance, had made some contacts with early resisters including Raymond Deiss, who produced the newspaper *Pantagruel*, and Maurice Ripoche, who was later to found CDLL. Manhès was organizing his own network, called Frédéric, which included Meunier and Chambeiron among its members.[3] Moulin's aim at this stage seems to have been to collect information about anti-German activities. He also learnt a lot from his close friend Antoinette Sachs who had an extensive network of relationships. She informed him about the anti-German sentiments of the former Cagoulards around Colonel Groussard, whose mistress was her sister.[4]

Having prospected in the North, Moulin returned to the Unoccupied Zone in December 1940. It seems that he hoped to head for America from where Cot and Dolivet had plans to mastermind a resistance network in France. Owing to difficulties in obtaining a Portuguese visa, Moulin's departure was postponed for nine months. This delay was important because, at some point during it, Moulin decided to go to London instead of America. It also allowed him to make the contacts in the South which were crucial in establishing his credibility with de Gaulle. His most important meeting was with Henri Frenay in the summer of 1941. Frenay provided information on the Resistance and told Moulin that he desperately lacked money and arms.[5]

Moulin finally left France on 9 September, and for six weeks he was stuck in Lisbon. From there he wrote to Cot, who still seems to have expected Moulin to join him, that he had decided he could be more useful 'in following another path and being closer to our English friends'. The absence of any reference to de Gaulle in this letter may have been to reassure Cot, who shared the widely held view of the general as a fascist. It may also have reflected genuine doubt in Moulin's mind about whether to offer his services to the British or Free French. The report which Moulin drafted in Lisbon was calibrated to appeal both to de Gaulle and the British.[6] It said nothing about Moulin's contacts with the former members of the Cot entourage, possibly because such company was unlikely to endear him to the Gaullists or the British. When the British asked why Dolivet

---

[2] On Moulin's early career see Cordier, *Jean Moulin*, ii. 198–200; P. Péan, *Vies et morts de Jean Moulin* (1998), 7–172.

[3] Péan, *Vies et morts*, 275–305; J. Baynac, *Les Secrets de l'affaire Jean Moulin* (1998), 77–84.

[4] Péan, *Vies et morts*, 307–33.

[5] Ibid. 347–50.

[6] Cordier, *Jean Moulin*, iii. 793–4. For the various drafts of the report, see ibid. 1210–26.

was so keen that Moulin should come to America, Moulin lied directly, claiming that they had had no contact for two years.[7] When he arrived in London, Moulin had not revealed his whole hand.

Moulin's most important information concerned the Resistance in the South although his information was not entirely accurate. He reported the existence of three movements—Liberté, Frenay's Libération nationale movement (this was just before their merger), and Libération—but he had not heard of Franc-Tireur and had no idea that d'Astier, whose existence he knew about, was the leader of Libération. Moulin knew much less about the Resistance than he let on, but the important fact was that no one else in London knew any more.

Moulin first met de Gaulle on 25 October 1941. Whatever reservations Moulin might have harboured quickly evaporated. To François de Menthon, he later remarked: 'De Gaulle is a very great man . . . What does he think, in his heart, about the Republic? I could not tell you. I know his official positions, but . . . is he really a democrat? I don't know.'[8] He wrote to Cot in America: 'for the moment one has to be with de Gaulle. Afterwards we'll see.'[9] De Gaulle's private thoughts are not known, but he was certainly delighted by the arrival of someone of Moulin's stature—the first prefect to come to London—and impressed by his personality. One of Moulin's British interrogators noted that he had 'the sort of natural authority and experience which his past history brings him'.[10] Moulin also managed to inflate his knowledge of the Resistance and his relationship to it. He claimed not only to have met the leaders of all the main movements—in fact he had not met d'Astier—but also to be bearing instructions from them. This idea that Moulin had some kind of mandate from the Resistance would certainly have surprised the resisters whom he had met.[11]

Moulin not only provided information about the Resistance, he also proposed a strategy to exploit it, arguing that it could make a military contribution to the war. Its forces could assist the allies at the liberation, and maintain order in the transition from the Vichy regime to its successor (this was the ex-prefect speaking). Moulin also warned that if the Resistance was not taken in hand by the Free French, it could fall under Communist influence. These arguments impressed de Gaulle who sent Moulin back to France as official 'Delegate of the French National Committee to the Unoccupied Zone'. His mission was to persuade the Southern movements to recognize de Gaulle and co-ordinate their meagre military forces which would be placed under Free French authority. In return, the Resistance would receive the material aid it desperately needed.[12] On

---

[7] Péan, *Vies et morts*, 366.   [8] Ibid. 383.
[9] Cordier, *Jean Moulin*, i. 55, 761.   [10] Ibid. iii. 1418 n. 11.
[11] Id., *Jean Moulin: La République des catacombes*, 128.
[12] Id., *Jean Moulin*, iii. 50–6; id., *Jean Moulin: La République des catacombes*, 139–53; Crémieux-Brilhac, *La France libre*, 249–53.

1 January 1942, Moulin was parachuted back into France where he remained until 15 February 1943.

The Resistance and London: First Contacts

Moulin had concluded his report by saying that the movements looked 'above all' to the Free French to help them. This may have been what he surmised de Gaulle would want to hear, but it was probably not what Frenay had told him. There is no contemporary record of the meeting between Frenay and Moulin in 1941, but there is one of a meeting at about the same time between Frenay and Howard Brooks, an American Unitarian pastor. Brooks was visiting France ostensibly for humanitarian purposes, but in reality to glean information about the Resistance. Frenay told Brooks that he was 'very distrustful of the De Gaullists' and did 'not wish to work with them'. Quite apart from 'bad blunders' like Dakar, de Gaulle was 'not sympathetic to democracy, without a social plan, and seriously handicapped by his political ineptitude'.[13]

Resistance leaders were certainly interested in obtaining help from de Gaulle, but they were interested in any sources of funds. SOE received a report from d'Astier in December 1941 saying that the movements sought above all a direct agreement with the British government.[14] From July 1941, Frenay was receiving funds from General de Laurencie who had in 1940 been Pétain's representative in the Unoccupied Zone before breaking with Vichy. De Laurencie's money came from the Americans who were hoping to build him up as a counterweight to de Gaulle. In December 1941, there was a meeting between de Laurencie, Frenay, and d'Astier. The stumbling block to an agreement proved to be de Laurencie's attitude to de Gaulle. Like many in the army, de Laurencie could not forgive de Gaulle his defiance of Pétain in 1940. 'I'll amnesty him', he told one resister; another was told de Gaulle could become military governor of Strasbourg.[15] D'Astier and Frenay insisted that de Laurencie reach an accommodation with de Gaulle. His refusal to do so ended their connection with him.[16] The de Laurencie affair showed that, whatever reservations Resistance leaders harboured towards de Gaulle, they were starting to incorporate him into their vision of the world. The term 'Gaullist' had become a synonym for opponents of the Germans or Vichy; his name itself functioned as an effective recruiter for the Resistance organizations. This smoothed Moulin's task, but his most powerful means of persuasion was money. Having resumed contact with Frenay, and having soon afterwards met d'Astier and Lévy, he provided them with funds from the 1.5 million francs he had brought over from London. Moulin also had the prestige of being the first officially accredited representative of de Gaulle whom the Resistance

---

[13] Brooks's report is in Baynac, *Les Secrets*, 420–6.
[14] Cordier, *Jean Moulin*, iii. 906–10.
[15] Bourdet, *L'Aventure incertaine*, 85; Pineau, *La Simple Vérité*, 99.
[16] Michel and Granet, *Combat*, 55–7; Cordier, *Jean Moulin*, iii. 60–2.

leaders had ever met. The matchbox in which he carried the microfilm of his instructions from de Gaulle had an almost talismanic quality to these resisters starved of contact with the outside world.[17]

Moulin's position as sole intermediary between de Gaulle and the Resistance was short-lived, however. Even while Moulin was still in London, Yvon Morandat had, on 7 November 1941, left for France on his much-delayed mission. Having contacted trade-union circles, as he was instructed to do, Morandat encountered Libération-Sud. He got on so well with d'Astier that he was invited to join the movement's executive committee. Meanwhile in 1942 Resistance leaders started to visit London. The first, in March, was Christian Pineau of Libération-Nord. After several meetings with de Gaulle, Pineau returned to France with orders from BCRAM to set up a new network. Pineau's visit to London had important political consequences. Before leaving France, he had consulted a number of Resistance leaders, including d'Astier and Frenay. They deputed him to request de Gaulle to provide a statement of his position on democracy. Reluctantly, de Gaulle agreed to do this, and he drafted a 'Declaration to the Resistance Movements', which Pineau took to France. The Declaration contained an unequivocal commitment to democracy, but also a condemnation of the Third Republic. It promised that at the liberation the French would be allowed to elect a national assembly to decide their future. Finally, it affirmed de Gaulle's support for the principles of liberty, equality, and fraternity, announcing that while 'the people of France are uniting for victory . . . they are preparing for a revolution'. The Declaration merely expressed more solemnly what de Gaulle had been saying for several months, but it was this solemnity which made it so important.[18]

The next visitor to London, between April and July 1942, was d'Astier de la Vigerie. He got on remarkably well with de Gaulle, and badly with Passy.[19] May saw the arrival of Philippe Roques who had been instructed in the previous year to sound out French politicians. He brought the names of fifty-six politicians favourable to the Resistance and reported that Mandel and other politicians were considering the idea of a sort of underground parliament which would accept de Gaulle as the symbolic leader of France. It is not known what de Gaulle thought of this, but Roques was sent back to develop his contacts.[20]

The most important French arrival was Pierre Brossolette. Before 1940, Brossolette had been a rising star of the Socialist Party and a brilliant journalist opposed to Munich. After defeat, he was involved in various Parisian resistance groups, including the Musée de l'homme group and OCM. As a cover, he ran a bookshop which became a meeting point for resisters. Having been contacted by Rémy's CND network, he began producing reports on French opinion which

[17] Frenay, *La Nuit finira*, 143.
[18] Pineau, *La Simple Vérité*, 157–91; Aglan, 'Le Mouvement Libération-Nord', 215–21; Crémieux-Brilhac, *La France libre*, 369–72.
[19] Passy, *10 Duke Street*, 81–3.   [20] Crémieux-Brilhac, *La France libre*, 344–5, 506–7.

were highly appreciated in London.[21] Brossolette arrived in London in April 1942, with precious information about the Resistance in the Occupied Zone. He made a deep impression on Passy who became a devoted admirer. Brossolette argued strongly against the separation of responsibility for political and military operations between the Interior Commissariat and BCRAM. Passy had been saying the same for a long time, but since Brossolette spoke with the authority of someone directly arrived from France, his views carried great weight. As a result, BCRAM was renamed BCRA in July 1942. The dropping of the final 'M' (Militaire) signalled that BCRA was now authorized to carry out political missions, although overall political strategy still rested with the Commissariat.[22] In fact the distinction was hazy, and the rivalry between the two bodies continued.

Besides inspiring these organizational reforms, Brossolette offered a strategic vision of the Resistance comparable in its breadth to Moulin's. He argued that the discrediting of the old political parties opened the way for the creation of a unitary 'Gaullist' movement to link the new forces which had emerged in the Resistance with what could be salvaged from the parties, extending from Socialists on the left to La Rocque's PSF on the right. Brossolette was as committed to de Gaulle as Moulin was, but where Moulin, the prefect, thought in terms of administration, Brossolette thought in terms of politics. Moulin saw de Gaulle as the provisional incarnation of the Republic; Brossolette saw him as a symbol of political renewal. Moulin wanted the Resistance to serve the State; Brossolette wanted it to regenerate the nation.[23] As a step towards this end, Brossolette returned to France in June in order to bring back two leading personalities, representing diametrically opposed positions: André Philip, a Socialist who was involved in Libération-Sud, and Charles Vallin, a leader of the PSF.

Philip, who arrived in London in July 1942, was the most important politician to have joined de Gaulle so far. He was immediately appointed to head the Interior Commissariat. In September, Brossolette returned from France with Vallin. They gave a joint news conference, and Brossolette wrote an article in the Free French newspaper La Marseillaise, arguing that the association between a Socialist like himself and a member of the extreme right like Vallin, showed that former political conflicts were moribund: one was either for Vichy or against it, 'Gaullist' or 'anti-Gaullist'. This article aroused criticism from the Socialists in London, and from liberal British newspapers like the Observer, who portrayed Brossolette as a proto-fascist. This scotched any idea of bringing Vallin into the National Committee and for the moment Brossolette shelved his idea of creating a Gaullist movement. Instead he began to prepare another mission to France—to organize the Resistance in the North, as Moulin was doing in the South.[24]

[21] G. Piketty, Pierre Brossoloette: Un héros de la Résistance (1998), 157–76.
[22] Passy, 10 Duke Street, 86–95.
[23] Piketty, Pierre Brossolette, 177–204; Cordier, Jean Moulin: La République des catacombes, 229–39.
[24] Piketty, Pierre Brossolette, 205–28.

Moulin and the Resistance

Up to a point this proliferation of contacts between London and France complicated Moulin's task. It increased the likelihood of crossed wires, especially given the rivalry between the Interior Commissariat and BCRA. Moulin, who had not even known about the Morandat and Roques missions which were the responsibility of the Interior Commissariat, was jealous of any potential rivals to his authority.[25] He and Morandat did succeed in working together, but their relationship was uneasy. Moulin, arguing that Free French envoys should remain independent of the Resistance movements, criticized Morandat for having become too involved with Libération. Morandat believed that Moulin wanted to control everything and was scheming to have him recalled to London.[26] There was also friction between Moulin and Pineau who had returned to France with a mission from BCRA. Moulin claimed Pineau was interfering in matters beyond his brief; Pineau retorted to London that one person could not expect to have 'exclusive control over all possible contacts'.[27]

The arrival of Resistance leaders in London also threatened Moulin's position. Having established independent contact with London, they might become tempted to undermine his authority by operating behind his back. This did occur eventually, but it took time for resisters to discover the complexities of the rivalries existing in London. At first the burgeoning contacts between France and London did more to help Moulin than hinder him: Resistance leaders were reassured about de Gaulle the more they learnt about him. Morandat's contacts with Libération-Sud made it the first Southern movement to rally formally to de Gaulle. In 1941, the newspaper *Libération* had not mentioned him; in the first four months of 1942, he became a 'symbol of recovery'; from May, the commitment to de Gaulle was unconditional. *Combat* was not far behind and rarely appeared after the middle of 1942 without the phrase: 'Un seul chef de Gaulle'.[28] De Gaulle's Declaration of June 1942 was published by *Combat*, *Libération-Sud* and *Franc-Tireur*. On 22 June, Maurice Schumann read extracts from the Declaration on the BBC, claiming that the Resistance movements had rallied to it 'without reserve'. In fact this anticipated events. *Franc-Tireur* was still worried about de Gaulle's attitude to the Third Republic—it printed de Gaulle's Declaration with the warning that 'we would no more tolerate the dictatorship of a General than of a Marshal'—as were several politicians. Schumann's broadcast aroused some antagonism by seeming to take the Resistance for granted.[29] Nonetheless, on 13 July the British agreed that the Free French could henceforth

---

[25] Passy, *2ᵉ Bureau*, 228; id., *10 Duke Street*, 88.
[26] In his fragmentary memoir of the period, *Souvenirs inédits d'Yvon Morandat*, ed. L. Douzou (1994), Morandat is discreet on the subject of his differences with Moulin, but Douzou's introduction gives more information, 19–21.
[27] Aglan, 'Le Mouvement Libération-Nord', 255–6, 261–2.
[28] Douzou, *La Désobéissance*, 292–8; Michel and Granet, *Combat*, 76.
[29] Aglan, 'Le Mouvement Libération-Nord', 231–42; Lévy, *Mémoires d'un franc-tireur*, 76.

be called France combattante (Fighting France) to signify that it now represented all French citizens opposed to the Armistice—inside France as well as outside it.[30]

Although the Southern movements had rallied to de Gaulle by the middle of 1942, Moulin never had sufficient funds to meet their needs, and one of his problems was to prevent them looking elsewhere for more generous benefactors. The British had money available for movements or networks prepared to work directly with them. The most important of these was the Carte network near Nice, founded in September 1941 by the painter André Girard. He claimed to have some 300,000 men at his disposal. In fact it emerged that he was a total fantasist and SOE broke its connection with him at the end of 1942. But for a time the funds at his disposal had provided a temptation to members of other movements. Some members of Franc-Tireur defected to Carte; others formed a splinter group with their own paper, *Le Coq enchaîné*, funded by the British. But these defections did not spread far: Lévy, the movement's leader, refused Girard's requirement that he break with de Gaulle.[31]

Moulin's task of rallying the movements to de Gaulle proved easier than bringing them to work with each other. When he had left for London, a union between Libération-Sud, Liberté, and Libération nationale seemed imminent. On his return, he discovered that only Liberté and Libération nationale had merged, and that there was another movement—Franc-Tireur—he had not known about. The first joint meeting between Moulin and the three Southern leaders took place in Lyons in May. Moulin found Lévy less jealous of his independence than the other two, and came to use him as a mediator between them. Lévy felt that d'Astier and Frenay both viewed him with slight condescension as the leader of a smaller movement, but this made them less inclined to see him as a threat.[32] The legacy of Frenay's meetings with Pucheu still poisoned his relations with d'Astier. No negotiations about unity were possible during the four months of d'Astier's visit to London. The circumstances of this caused further acrimony. D'Astier had obtained transport to London by misleading an SOE agent into believing that he was the official representative of all the movements. Frenay resented this attempt by d'Astier to steal a march on him in establishing direct relations with de Gaulle.[33]

In the absence of high-level negotiations between Resistance leaders, Moulin created two centralized Resistance agencies staffed by members of all three movements. The first of these was the Press and Information Bureau (BIP), a sort of resistance press service, set up in April 1942, to publicize themes of Free French propaganda and pass on suggestions for propaganda to London. The second was the General Study Committee (CGE), a sort of brains trust, set up in July, to discuss post-Liberation reforms. Moulin also organized services to facilitate

---

[30] Crémieux-Brilhac, *La France libre*, 335–8, 369–77.

[31] Veillon, *Le Franc-Tireur*, 326, 330, 336–7.

[32] Lévy, *Mémoires d'un franc-tireur*, 68, 74, III.   [33] Douzou, *La Désobéissance*, 106–7.

contact between London and France: one to organize radio contact (WT) and another one to organize parachute drops and transport between Britain and France (SOAM).[34] The SOAM was the lifeline of contact between London and France. Lysanders or Hudson bombers arriving from Britain with money, supplies, and visitors would usually return carrying resisters or distinguished Frenchmen ready to rally to de Gaulle. Each of these landings had to be meticulously prepared.

The CGE and the BIP were based in Lyons which was the centre of Moulin's resistance activities. Here he lived an undercover existence with a series of pseudonyms. Moulin adapted to clandestine life with remarkable facility. Although someone capable of close friendships with both men and women, he was also highly secretive by nature, and was used to compartmentalizing his life. During this period, he succeeded in conducting separate relationships with three different women. He divided his time, under his real name, between his family property at Saint-Andiol in Provence, where he had moved after being sacked from his prefectoral post; Montpellier, where his mother lived; or Nice, where he had opened an art gallery. The gallery provided a pretext for travelling, but it also reflected a genuine passion: Moulin was an amateur artist who had published many drawings before the war.[35]

Moulin tried to accustom the movements to work together. He and Morandat encouraged them to co-operate in preparing demonstrations on 1 May and 14 July 1942. The first of these was organized by trade-union leaders, publicized on the London radio, and supported by the movements. It was the most significant public expression of resistance since 1940 and its success encouraged the movements to co-operate even more closely for 14 July. For this occasion the three movements signed a joint manifesto for the first time. As Moulin reported to London, these demonstrations were an opportunity for resisters to experience the benefits of 'synchronization between London and their local leaders'.[36] This also helped create a dynamic of unity at the base. One Resistance leader in Saint-Étienne wrote to Jean-Pierre Lévy that the preparation of the July demonstration had revealed the need for co-ordination: 'it is regrettable that Combat, Franc-Tireur and Libération disperse their activities and give the impression of trying to compete with each other'. Morandat, Pineau, and Moulin all reported to London that the movement leaders were under pressure from their activists to work together.[37]

D'Astier's return from London at the end of July allowed unity negotiations to resume. Frenay remained most enthusiastic about a merger because he believed that Combat would be strong enough to absorb the other movements. Since Combat had the largest military forces, Frenay also assumed that if the move-

[34] Cordier, *Jean Moulin*, i. 72–84.
[35] Id., *Jean Moulin: La République des catacombes*, 179–81.
[36] Douzou, *La Désobéissance*, 327.
[37] Luirard, *La Région stéphanoise*, 488; Cordier, *Jean Moulin*, i. 80.

ments combined their forces, he would effectively be in charge of them. For this reason, d'Astier and Lévy would only agree to a 'single army' if Frenay was not given command of it. The final stage of the negotiations occurred in London between Frenay and d'Astier (Moulin and Lévy having been unable to leave France) in the presence of de Gaulle. An agreement was signed on 2 October 1942. It provided for the movements to pool their paramilitary forces into a single organization known as the Secret Army (AS) which would act under the orders of London. The head of the AS was to be the 65-year-old retired general Charles Delestraint. Because Delestraint had no resistance experience, no Resistance leader could complain that a rival was being favoured. Frenay probably hoped that he would be purely a figurehead. Apart from the AS, the movements were to retain their autonomy, but they also agreed to set up a Co-ordinating Committee composed of their three leaders and chaired by Moulin.[38]

This agreement was a compromise between Frenay (who had wanted a full merger) and d'Astier (who had not). But at the first meeting of the Co-ordinating Committee in France on 27 November Frenay, supported by Moulin, resumed the argument for unity. D'Astier dragged his feet, and at the end of the year he started merger negotiations with two Northern movements—Libération-Nord and La Voix du Nord—hoping to maximize his strength. These efforts came to nothing, and d'Astier bowed to the inevitable. On 27 January 1943, the three movements agreed to form a single organization—the United Movements of the Resistance (MUR)—although retaining their separate newspapers.[39]

The Resistance: Geography and Sociology

In the North, there was still little co-ordination between Resistance organizations, but it can be said that by the end of 1942 a resistance existed throughout France. How influential was it at this stage? This question is difficult to answer because Resistance movements were not like political parties. It is problematic even to define membership of a movement. There were full-time activists and occasional sympathizers, people working for one organization and others participating in several. In 1943 *Libération-Nord* declared: 'all the readers of the newspaper who feel themselves to be in agreement with its spirit must even if they have not been "contacted" by one of our organizers . . . consider themselves incorporated into the Libération movement'.[40] This conception of membership was too broad to be quantifiable.

The relative importance attributed to the Southern movements was reflected in Moulin's distribution of funds between them. In September 1942, Combat

---

[38] Cordier, *Jean Moulin*, i. 89–95; Douzou, *La Désobéissance*, 329–30.
[39] Douzou, *La Désobéissance*, 331–45. The original name was in fact Mouvements de Résistance unis, but soon MUR was preferred to MRU.
[40] Aglan, 'Le Mouvement Libération-Nord', 338.

received 1.2 million francs, Libération-Sud 438,000, and Franc-Tireur 120,000.[41] How many people did these movements represent? After the decision to set up the Secret Army, attempts were made to evaluate the potential numbers available for it. Passy estimated the total at 30,000, of which three-quarters belonged to Combat. But Frenay himself claimed 30,000 for Combat alone, and d'Astier, in November 1942, claimed 19,000 for Libération. The movements inflated their own figures, but this was all that London had to go on. By January 1943, Passy estimated the available forces at 65,000: 16,000 for Franc-Tireur, 23,000 for Libération, 26,000 for Combat. But this overall figure seems high, and if it is correct, the proportion attributed to Combat seems low.[42] Since these 'paramilitary forces' had almost no arms, the figures cannot be taken too seriously. They represented the movements' most optimistic assessment of the numbers at their disposal when arms became available. And the distinction between military and non-military forces, crucial in the eyes of London, was somewhat artificial. Most resisters performed several tasks indiscriminately. A BCRA representative, sent to help Libération-Sud organize its military forces, found that the names he was given frequently cropped up performing non-military activities: newspaper distribution, recruitment, and propaganda.[43]

Who were these rank-and-file resisters? At this stage the Resistance recruited primarily from the middle and lower middle classes; there were few manual workers. The seven founders of Libération-Sud consisted of two journalists, two teachers, two businessmen, and one engineer. The initial core of Franc-Tireur was made up of teachers, small businessmen, and engineers. Défense de la France had the highest proportion of students (25 per cent); Libération-Nord was well represented among teachers (45 per cent).[44] The Resistance was also overwhelmingly urban. It is often said that Lyons was its capital, but the view from the North was different. Pineau commented of d'Astier: 'His only defect was to believe that the heart of the Resistance was at Lyons and that our activities, under the rod of the occupier, were only of secondary interest.'[45] Lecompte-Boinet was equally caustic about Southern resisters who took themselves so seriously and exaggerated their risks: 'not for anything would they cross to our side of the line and they treated me as someone of no importance . . . Their view was that one would never be able to set up anything serious in the Occupied Zone . . . And the restaurants are so good in Lyons!'[46] In fact there were more movements based in Paris than anywhere else. Even in the South, Lyons was not the only significant Resistance centre. At the beginning, Marseilles was more important owing

[41] Douzou, La Désobéissance, 172.

[42] Passy, 10 Duke Street, 261; id., Missions secrètes, 23; Michel and Granet, Combat, 162, 226; Douzou, La Désobéissance, 200; Veillon, Le Franc-Tireur, 145–8.

[43] Douzou, La Désobéissance, 206.

[44] Ibid.; Veillon, Le Franc-Tireur, 45–60; Wieviorka, Une certaine idée, 188–92; Aglan, 'Le Mouvement Libération-Nord', 343–7.

[45] Pineau, La Simple Vérité, 104.

[46] Quoted in Sapiro, La Guerre des écrivains, 482.

to the presence of so many refugees. It was there that Frenay found his first support.[47] In Toulouse, resistance was encouraged by the presence of political refugees attracted by the city's left-wing tradition. The bookshop run by Silvio Trentin, an Italian anti-fascist refugee, became a meeting point for resisters some of whom were involved in producing, from July 1942, the left-wing Resistance newspaper, *Libérer et fédérer*.[48]

Several factors combined to explain why Lyons eventually became the most important site of resistance in the South. Its reputation as a centre for Catholic theology, centred on the abbey at Fourvière, made it a crucible of Catholic resistance. As the press capital of the Unoccupied Zone, it had a high concentration of journalists, printers, and typesetters, as well as facilities for the production of newspapers. Possibly it also helped that Lyons apartment blocks did not have concierges: there was no one to watch when tracts or messages were left in letter boxes. Perhaps also Lyons's famous network of covered passages, the *traboules*, proved useful to the Resistance. They hardly figure in the memoirs of resisters, but it might have been reassuring to know they existed.[49] Above all, Lyons owed its reputation as the Resistance capital to Moulin's decision to centralize his operations there. This is the sense in which Lyons really was a capital. In the North, greater fragmentation meant greater decentralization: Paris may have had more resisters than Lyons, but it had no influence over the resistance in Roubaix.[50]

Resistance and the Population: How to Resist?

If it is difficult to estimate the size of the Resistance at the end of 1942, it is even harder to estimate its impact on the population. One measure of visibility is offered by the distribution of the underground press. At the end of 1941, the combined production of the Southern Resistance press was probably not above 30,000. A year later, the figures were much higher:[51]

SOUTH

Libération-Sud
    July 1941–October 1942: 20,000 per issue
    December 1942: 60,000
Franc-Tireur
    December 1941: 6,000
    November 1942: 30,000

---

[47] Mencherini, 'Naissance de la Résistance à Marseille', in Guillon and Laborie (eds.), *Mémoire et histoire*, 137–47.

[48] C. d'Aragon, *La Résistance sans héroïsme* (1977), 38–44.

[49] S. Ravanel, *L'Esprit de la Résistance* (1995), 57.

[50] Douzou et al. (eds.), *La Résistance: Villes*, 227.

[51] Douzou, *La Désobéissance*, 165; Wieviorka, *Une certaine idée*, 36, 104; Veillon, *Le Franc-Tireur*, 97; Michel and Granet, *Combat*, 141; Aglan, 'Le Mouvement Libération-Nord', 138–9; Bédarida, *Les Armes de l'esprit*, 288.

Combat
   1941: a few 100 per issue
   1942: about 10,000 per issue
Cahiers du témoignage chrétien
   1941: 5,000–10,000
   1942: 20,000–30,000

NORTH

Défense de la France
   1941: 5,000 per issue on average
   1942: 10,000 rising to 30,000 per issue
Libération-Nord
   End of 1941: 100
   End of 1942: 1000

It is impossible to know how many people read these newspapers. Before the end of 1942 few people had probably ever seen one or heard of the organizations they represented. This was certainly the case of the historian Henri Drouot who set out in his diary to chronicle in detail every aspect of life under occupation in his native city of Dijon. He collected tracts and ephemera, noted the graffiti on walls, listened to conversations, and scrutinized the behaviour of his fellow citizens. From the start of the Occupation he observed various examples of resistance—Vs and crosses of Lorraine daubed on walls, the odd Communist tract—but of 'the Resistance' there is no sign until the summer of 1942. The first stray mention of a Resistance newspaper occurs in July 1942 when he comes across a copy of the first issue of *Cahiers du témoignage chrétien*.[52]

It is in the second half of 1942 that one finds the first signs that the Resistance was making some impact on the population. There was an impressive response to the joint appeal from the Southern movements for people to demonstrate on 14 July wearing the national colours. Sixty-six demonstrations took place, two-thirds of them in the Southern Zone. In Lyons and Marseilles, the crowds numbered 15,000.[53] For the first time, the growing disaffection from Vichy had been translated into collective action. In many places, these demonstrations tapped into local political traditions and exploited local symbols of republicanism. In Crest, in the Drôme, there was a demonstration in front of the monument commemorating the anti-Bonapartist rebels of 1851; in Grenoble, there was a procession headed by a woman dressed as the Republic.[54] In Béziers the demonstration occurred on the spot where the statue of the nineteenth-century Republican hero Armand Barbès had once stood. This was

---

[52] *Notes d'un Dijonnais*, 232.
[53] Crémieux-Brilhac, *La France libre*, 222–3; Tartakowsky, *Les Manifestations de rue*, 469–74.
[54] Kedward, *Resistance in Vichy*, 152; J.-M. Guillon, 'La France du Sud-Est', in Azéma and Bédarida (eds.), *La France des années noires*, ii. 159–76: 174.

a symbolically contested site: the statue had been vandalized by the right in January 1936; on 11 November 1940, a group of resisters had organized a small demonstration around it; in March 1942, Vichy had the statue melted down for its bronze, causing local resisters to write on the base where the statue had rested, 'See where collaboration leads; Barbès you will be avenged.'[55]

For Resistance leaders, the evidence that they were acquiring an audience created a novel situation. The first resisters justifiably saw themselves as a tiny elite, a Freemasonry of virtue, like the Carbonari groups in the nineteenth century. When Henri Michel and a group of Socialists called on the population of Toulon to appear at the War Memorial on 11 November 1940, they had expected at least fifty people; only six appeared.[56] The first Resistance newspapers were a bottle thrown into the sea; it was impossible to know what happened to them next. When Mauriac's resistance text, the *Cahier noir*, pilloried the 'disgusting spectacle' offered by the French people, or Frenay castigated their 'apathetic fatalism' and 'despicable cowardice', they were expressing a common view among resisters.[57]

Once this fatalism started to lift, Resistance leaders were caught off guard. As Philippe Viannay said:

> We were looking for people similar to ourselves more than we were trying to convince the masses. We were nomads in a sedentary world. We did not care too much what went on around us. We haughtily ignored the immense troop of cowards and the numerous profiteers . . . We could forget these sad specimens of the French people, for they did not count for us.[58]

Now the Resistance had an audience, its leaders had to decide what they expected this audience to do. Their first propaganda had cautioned people against taking excessive risks. In October 1940, one tract in the North advised:

> In your contacts with the Germans be proud, show the minimum of politeness . . . Ignore them . . . Delay when you are asked to carry out their orders . . . Above all no isolated violent action: the moment has not come. No destruction of electric cables . . . No sabotage of military *matériel*.[59]

Cochet's first tract warned people against doing anything premature; they were urged to practise only a 'spiritual resistance'. Some people considered this to be inadequate. Guillain de Bénouville, eventually a member of Combat, originally got involved with a network not a movement because he considered it less important 'to preach the truth that I already knew than to begin fighting for it'.[60]

---

[55] Cazals, 'Une lecture de la Résistance audoise', in Guillon and Laborie (eds.), *Mémoire et histoire*, 61–70: 64–5.
[56] Guillon, 'La Résistance dans le Var', 62.
[57] J. Steel, *Littératures de l'ombre: Récits et nouvelles de la Résistance* (1991), 128.
[58] Viannay, *Du bon usage*, 105.
[59] Cordier, *Jean Moulin*, iii. 1122–4.
[60] G. de Bénouville, *Le Sacrifice du matin* (1946), 150.

One practical course of action was offered by Jacques Renouvin, a former member of Action française. Renouvin achieved notoriety in 1938 by publicly slapping Flandin for his telegram congratulating Hitler after Munich. In 1941 he conceived the idea of *corps francs*, action groups which would carry out propaganda stunts: daubing statues, bombing newspaper kiosks which sold collaborationist papers, setting off laughing gas in lectures given by collaborators. These operations were little more than pranks, but their purpose was to combat fatalism. Renouvin himself was a colourful figure, immensely tall, and the subject of legends which became part of Resistance mythology. On one occasion, when delivering a time bomb, he disguised himself as a priest and was seen striding down the street with his cassock reaching only his knees. Renouvin was based in Montpellier, and the *corps francs* were initially attached to Liberté, but by 1942 all Southern movements had them. In July 1942, they launched simultaneous attacks on ten recruitment offices for the *relève*.[61]

The *corps francs* were only a minority within the Resistance, and their activities were not suitable for everyone. What guidance did the Resistance offer the mass of the population? In November 1941, *Libération-Nord* exhorted its readers to 'carry out yourself the struggle to deliver the *patrie* from an invader who is pillaging it', but did not explain how. *Liberté* in May 1941 called on people to distribute its newspaper, prepare demonstrations, and boycott the collaborationist press. In August, *Libération* offered a much more extensive list of boycott actions including sabotage of any industry working for the Germans.[62] At this stage, however, most Resistance movements opposed violence. Resistance was defined as an individual moral stance. *Défense de la France* urged each person to 'become in himself a centre of resistance . . . a rock capable of putting up with isolation'.[63]

This was similar to the notion of resistance offered by the most celebrated work of resistance fiction, *Le Silence de la mer*, published by the 'Midnight Press' in August 1942. During the Occupation, the true identity of its author, 'Vercors', was a secret, even in literary circles ('the best-kept secret of the war', said Aragon). In fact Vercors was Jean Bruller, a satirical cartoonist and engraver, who had never written a book before. Quite apart from the message it contained, publishing *Le Silence de la mer* was itself an act of resistance: it was the first book to appear in occupied France without the stamp of the German censor. Although the first edition ran to only 300–400 copies, organizing the printing, binding, stocking, and distribution of a beautifully produced book was a major feat in itself. By the autumn of 1942 a copy had reached London (taken back by Morandat) where it was reprinted and given worldwide publicity.[64]

[61] Kedward, *Resistance in Vichy*, 143–4; Frenay, *La Nuit finira*, 210.

[62] A. Aglan, 'Libération-Nord et la lutte armée', in Marcot (ed.), *La Résistance: Lutte armée et maquis*, 107–16: 110; Kedward, *Resistance in Vichy*, 125–6, 138–9.

[63] Wieviorka, *Une certaine idée*, 47.

[64] A. Simonin, *Les Éditions de minuit 1942–1955* (1994), 14–99. The bilingual edn. of 1991 contains a useful historical introduction: J. Brown and L. Stokes (eds.), *The Silence of the Sea/Le Silence de la mer: A Novel of French Resistance during World War II by 'Vercors'* (1991) (the trans. is Cyril Connolly's of 1944).

In *Le Silence de la mer*, Bruller, writing for a Briandist generation brought up on folk memories of the black propaganda of the First World War, chose not to portray a Nazi. The German protagonist is a musician, a cultured man, more representative of Goethe's Germany than Hitler's. Containing few references to contemporary conditions in France, the book has the timeless quality of a parable. It defends the notion of resistance as an assertion of moral dignity. But by the time that the book appeared in August 1942, this vision had begun to seem outdated: timelessness no longer appropriate. Vercors was criticized from London by Arthur Koestler who claimed that the book was 'psychologically phoney' and its idea of resistance inadequate to a situation in which people were being massacred. Vercors was criticized for the same reason by the Communists. But he had conceived his book while the Germans were still trying to portray themselves as benevolent occupiers, and writers like Chardonne were happy to take them at their word. If one reads Ernst Jünger's diary entry for 5 June 1940 (some believed Jünger to be a model for Bruller's honourable German)—'I chat for a long time every day with my hostess'—one sees the sense of Vercors's notion of resistance as a form of moral hygiene.[65]

Vercors later recalled a conversation with the writer Jean Cassou in 1940 when they both agreed that the Occupation might last a hundred years. In such circumstances, the role of intellectuals was 'similar to that of the monks who in the long night of the Middle Ages secretly and obstinately passed on the flame of the ancient world, keeping it alight almost 1000 years till the Renaissance'. Once it was clear that this was not to be the case, and other forms of protest presented themselves, Vercors himself accepted that the time for silence had passed.[66]

Vercors's silent resistance could not have been more different from the terrorist tactics adopted by the Communist FTP in 1941. This policy was condemned by de Gaulle and criticized by the Resistance, but it also caused problems for the Communists themselves. Isolated terrorist acts were alien to Communist thinking and had been condemned by Lenin. In September 1941, the French Communist leaders in Moscow believed armed action was premature.[67] The first terrorist attacks in France were possibly the initiative of individuals. The Communist press initially said nothing about the attacks, and then claimed them to be a German provocation.[68] Not until February 1942 did the Party start to claim responsibility for the attacks. Even then there were dissenters, including the veteran Marcel Cachin, who made a statement opposing attacks on individual Germans. The Party made sure he never spoke out again.[69]

[65] Steel, *Littératures de l'ombre*, 65–7, 130; Simonin, *Les Éditions de minuit*, 84–7.

[66] J. King, 'Language and Silence: Some Aspects of Writing and the French Resistance', *European Studies Review* (1972), 227–38: 230–3.

[67] Narinski, 'L'URSS, le Komintern et la lutte armée en France', in Marcot (ed.), *La Résistance: Lutte armée et maquis*, 361–72: 363.

[68] P. Laborie, 'A propos de la Résistance et de l'opinion française devant la lutte armée', in Marcot (ed.), *La Résistance: Lutte armée et maquis*, 143–6: 142–3; Bourderon, 'Le PCF dans la lutte armée', ibid. 132–4.

[69] Courtois, *Le PCF dans la guerre*, 272; D. Peschanski, 'Marcel Cachin face à la Gestapo', *Communisme*, 3 (1983), 85–102.

Once terrorism had been adopted by the Communists, it had to be given a theoretical justification. One possible defence was that terrorism would unleash German reprisals, dispelling any lingering notions of German correctness and transforming the Communists into martyrs. In fact, this argument was not the one preferred by the Party. In theory, the Communists never separated armed action from their propaganda for mass action: armed struggle was presented as the vanguard of a mass movement which would culminate in national insurrection. To mobilize mass support the Communists tried to build up their Front national movement and revive their trade-union organizations. In factories, the social themes of Communist propaganda were replaced in 1942 by calls for sabotage: 'it is better to blow factories up than let them work for the Germans'. With such slogans, it is not surprising that the Communists had little audience among workers in 1942.[70] They were more successful in exploiting the food shortages. Many food demonstrations in the Occupied Zone were organized by them. Two such demonstrations in Paris, at the rue de Buci market on 31 May 1942 and the rue Daguerre market on 1 August, led to violence and police intervention. These demonstrations had been supposedly protected by the FTP. This was what the Communists meant by linking the activist vanguard and mass social protest.

Most food demonstrations, however, occurred spontaneously. The forty demonstrations in the Var, in the first half of 1942, had nothing to do with the Communists. When the Communists in the *département* exploited the issue by trying to organize a march of women on Vichy on 11 November, they were unsuccessful.[71] Nor did the Communists get much response to their call in 1942 for demonstrations on the anniversary of the battle of Valmy: there were only three demonstrations important enough to have left any trace.[72] In 1942, therefore, the FTP was certainly not the activist tip of a massive Communist iceberg. Like other Resistance movements, it was a tiny elite largely cut off from the population. But the Communists were unique in having a theory about the relationship between political resistance and social mobilization, between elite and mass; this would serve them well in the future.

Nonetheless, the Communists were as surprised as anyone else when a wave of protests broke out in the Lyons region in October 1942. This was sparked off by the 4 September law authorizing the government to draft workers for labour service. Employers had to prepare lists of those who would be sent to Germany, and when the first names were posted up in the Oullins railway works at Lyons on 13 October, a strike broke out. Over the next few days, strikes spread throughout the area, affecting about 12,000 workers. The resistance movements were unsure how to react. The leaders of Libération-Sud divided between those who

---

[70] Courtois, *Le PCF dans la guerre*, 259, 272.

[71] Guillon, 'La Résistance dans le Var', 121–4, 129–34.

[72] Marcot, 'Résistance et population', 68; D. Virieux, 'Le Front national de la lutte pour la liberté et l'indépendance de la France: Un mouvement de Résistance. Période clandestine (mai 1941–août 1944)' (unpublished thesis, University of Paris-VIII), 225–31; Tartakowsky, *Les Manifestations de rue*, 444.

believed that these strikes were dangerously premature, and those, like Pascal Copeau and Raymond Aubrac, who wanted to exploit and encourage them.[73] The strikes were soon crushed by the police, but they were to be followed by more extensive protest movements in Februrary 1943, after the introduction of STO. From this point, the Resistance really started to count as a force in French society.

Competitors

Paradoxically, the very success of resistance started to cause problems for the Resistance leaders at the end of 1942. As resistance became a wider social phenomenon, it became more difficult for them to control. They were faced with competitors in their ambition to mobilize the French population, most importantly the Socialists and Communists.

Having no Resistance movement of their own, the Socialists had joined various movements, especially Libération, on a purely individual basis. As the Socialists' confidence revived after Riom, they became increasingly frustrated by the absence of any recognition of their specific contribution to the Resistance. When they suggested the possibility of the CAS being accorded separate representation on the Co-ordinating Committee set up in October 1942, the Resistance leaders would have none of it. They judged all political parties to be tainted by their past, and despite the contribution of individual Socialists, they would not accept the CAS on equal terms with the Resistance movements. Léon Blum, who had urged his comrades in London to rally to de Gaulle, wrote to the general from prison in November 1942 with warn against such ostracism: 'there is no democratic state without parties. They must be moralized, renewed, but not eliminated.'[74] What turned this Socialist dissatisfaction into mutiny was the impression that their traditional rivals the Communists were receiving different treatment.

The distinctiveness of the Communists was that besides being a political party, they also had their own resistance organizations: the FTP and the Front national (FN). They presented the FN as an independent organization, offering a unitary framework for the Resistance as a whole. The Communists scored a success in the Lyons strikes in October when tracts defending the strikers appeared in the name of the three Southern movements, the PCF, and the FN. For the Communists, this was a double victory: it placed the Party on a footing of equality with the Resistance movements and recognized the FN, by implication, as an independent movement. It is unclear who was behind these tracts which were probably the result of a local initiative. But their political implication was immediately obvious to the leaders of the movements, to London, and

---

[73] Douzou, *La Désobéissance*, 124–5.
[74] *L'Œuvre de Léon Blum 1940–1945* (1955), 379–81.

to the Socialists.[75] This was not all. On 11 January 1943, Fernand Grenier, a member of the PCF Central Committee, arrived in London to bring de Gaulle the Party's official support. This was a major boost to de Gaulle's prestige, and he replied to the Central Committee in friendly terms a month later. Increasingly the Socialists feared that the Communists were stealing a march on them. Blum warned de Gaulle: 'it would be a terrible mistake to stretch a hand to the Communists over the head of the Socialists'.[76]

The Socialists began to develop their counter-strategy. As early as June 1942, a number of Socialists had floated the idea of a sort of umbrella resistance committee to include representatives of parties and resistance movements. From November, this idea was taken up officially by Daniel Mayer and other Socialist leaders as a way of giving the Socialists an independent voice in the Resistance. They threatened that otherwise Socialists who had joined Resistance movements would withdraw from them.[77] Defferre complained to Moulin that the Resistance leaders talked about political parties in terms suspiciously reminiscent of Vichy.[78]

This challenge to the Resistance leaders from within France occurred just as they were also beginning to wake up to the challenge from outside France in the form of de Gaulle. Had they forfeited too much of their independence to him? Moulin had never harboured any illusions that the movements would lightly give up their independence. Before leaving for France, he remarked that 'money would be a powerful lever of command in relation to the Resistance organizations'; he would use it 'to keep them in line [*tenir la dragée haute*]'.[79] Frenay recalls in his memoirs that his delight at meeting an accredited representative of de Gaulle was clouded by the realization that Moulin came armed with instructions: 'he showed us several more pages of microfilm that contained precise instructions covering everything down to the tiniest detail of out operations. In fact, they were *orders*.'[80]

Even if Frenay was reading later resentments back into this first meeting, it did not take long for the Resistance leaders to realize that de Gaulle intended to be more than a symbol: Moulin's money came with strings attached. In theory, the decision to set up the AS represented a considerable loss of independence by the movements. In return, however, de Gaulle had agreed to recognize the three movements on the Co-ordinating Committee as representing the Resistance in the South: all people who wished to resist were to be told to join one of these movements. This clause in the agreement was a negotiating success for Frenay and d'Astier, but almost immediately it started to look increasingly out of touch

[75] Aglan, 'Le Mouvement Libération-Nord', 681–2; Noguères, *Histoire de la Résistance*, ii. 622–3; the tract is printed in Passy, *Missions secrètes*, 301–2.

[76] *L'Œuvre de Léon Blum*, 381.

[77] D. Cordier, *Jean Moulin et le Conseil national de la Résistance* (1983), 90–100.

[78] Noguères, *Histoire de la Résistance*, iii. 198–9; Cordier, *Jean Moulin: La République des catacombes*, 253; D. Mayer, *Les Socialistes dans la Résistance* (1968), 62–73.

[79] Cordier, *Jean Moulin*, iii. 914.   [80] *La Nuit finira*, 144.

with reality, as other political forces in France claimed their right to be heard. Could de Gaulle ignore them? And if he decided to listen to them, how would the Resistance react?

As more Resistance leaders visited London, they came to see that de Gaulle's authority was more contested than they had realized. This emboldened them to become less deferential towards him. BCRA's head of counter-espionage, Roger Wybot, commented of a conversation with Frenay in November 1942: 'he seems less firm in his support for de Gaulle than he is in his writings . . . Losing his calm for the second time, he even shouted "never will anyone make me swear an oath to de Gaulle".'[81] Before he left London in November 1942, Frenay had a revealing dialogue with de Gaulle. What, asked Frenay, would happen if conflict arose between Moulin and the Resistance? 'You will come to London and try and find a solution.' 'And if we can't find one?' 'In that case', replied de Gaulle, 'France will choose between you and me.'[82] The question in 1943 was what 'France' would decide.

[81] Cordier, *Jean Moulin: La République des catacombes*, 211.
[82] Quoted by Passy, *10 Duke Street*, 248; and, slightly differently, by Frenay, *La Nuit finira*, 256–7.

19

Power Struggles 1943

De Gaulle's relationship with the Resistance in 1943 was intimately linked to his conflicts with the British and Americans. These had worsened significantly after the Allied landings in North Africa in November 1942. De Gaulle was given only three hours' notice of the landings because Roosevelt still harboured the belief that Vichy could be more useful to him than the Free French. Darlan's slowness in rallying to the Allies did nothing to shake this conviction. Roosevelt told André Philip: 'Darlan gave me Algiers, long live Darlan! If Laval gives me Paris, long live Laval! I am not like Wilson, I am a realist.'[1] Such 'realism' so shocked Allied public opinion that on 17 November Roosevelt tried to defuse criticism by announcing that Darlan was only a 'temporary expedient'. This did not stop Darlan installing himself at the head of a committee of imperial proconsuls—including Boisson and Noguès—who had been loyal to Vichy. Pétainist legislation remained intact and North Africa became a sort of Vichy across the sea under the patronage of America. There were now three claimants to French sovereignty: the Vichy regime in France; Darlan in North Africa; de Gaulle in London.

Churchill, anxious not to antagonize Roosevelt, forbade de Gaulle from criticizing Darlan publicly. Public opinion, however, remained hostile to Darlan, and this assisted de Gaulle's evolution into a symbol of democracy, even for those on the British left who had previously been suspicious of him. The choice of Darlan also alarmed the Foreign Office on the grounds that de Gaulle had now acquired legitimacy and that it would not be in Britain's long-term interests to abandon him. In 1940 Churchill had backed de Gaulle in the teeth of Foreign Office reluctance; now Foreign Office officials frequently shielded de Gaulle from Churchill's increasing animus against him.[2]

On 24 December 1942, Darlan was shot dead by a 22-year-old royalist, Fernand Bonnier de la Chapelle. Because this was a crime for which everyone had a motive—even the Americans who were increasingly embarrassed by their deal with Darlan—speculation about who ordered the assassination has kept conspiracy theorists happy for fifty years. The finger has often been pointed at

---

[1] Crémieux-Brilhac, *La France libre*, 442. [2] Thomas, *Britain and Vichy*, 157–70.

the Gaullists, but in fact Darlan's disappearance was not an unmixed blessing for de Gaulle. Roosevelt replaced him by General Giraud, America's original choice for the North African operation. Giraud, who was not tainted by collaboration, did not arouse the same opprobrium as Darlan. This meant that if he refused a deal with de Gaulle, he might prove harder to dislodge than Darlan. De Gaulle hoped that, in return for being offered the position of Commander-in-Chief of the army, Giraud would recognize his political authority. But Giraud, a man of reactionary views and no political sense, viewed de Gaulle merely as a dissident general, junior to himself. He rejected de Gaulle's approaches, and far from relaxing the Vichyite legislation in North Africa, he gave a post to Marcel Peyrouton, who had been Pétain's Interior Minister in 1940.

A meeting between de Gaulle and Giraud at Casablanca in January 1943, in the presence of Roosevelt and Churchill, solved nothing. They shook hands for the cameras, but de Gaulle returned to London empty-handed. His relations with Churchill sank to a new low; on 3 March, he was refused permission to leave England. In retaliation, he retreated to Hampstead, declaring himself a prisoner; Churchill instructed that the 'monster of Hampstead' must not be allowed to escape.[3] Giraud retained the support of Roosevelt, who argued that until elections were held in liberated France, de Gaulle had no exclusive authority to speak for the French. De Gaulle's future depended on proving him wrong.

The Resistance had been shocked by the Darlan affair. On 17 November, Moulin sent a telegram from the Southern movements to London, calling for de Gaulle, their 'uncontested leader', to be installed in North Africa. The message was also signed by representatives of political parties, including the Radicals, the PDP, and the Republican Federation. In addition, Blum wrote to Roosevelt and Churchill in support of de Gaulle.[4] All this was a sign to de Gaulle that besides the recognition he had already received from the Resistance, he could also tap the support of the traditional political forces in France. At the same time, the Socialists were clamouring for fuller recognition of their role in the Resistance through the creation of a council of the Resistance. If de Gaulle wanted the backing of the Socialists, concessions would have to be made to them.

De Gaulle's envoys in France were also beginning to see the advantages of a Resistance council. When this idea was first mooted in June 1942, Morandat had been favourable, but he was overruled by Moulin and Pineau. But by the end of the year, both Pineau and Moulin, alarmed by the increasing dissatisfaction of the Socialists, had changed their minds.[5] On 14 December 1942 Moulin wrote that the 'movements are not the whole Resistance . . . there are moral forces, trade-union forces and political forces'; the newly created Co-ordinating Committee could not pretend to control the whole Resistance. In a similar vein,

---

[3] Kersaudy, *Churchill and de Gaulle*, 262.   [4] *L'Œuvre de Léon Blum*, 382–3.
[5] Aglan, 'Le Mouvement Libération-Nord', 682–5.

Pineau criticized the movements' tendency to 'exclude systematically' all potential competitors.[6] This converging advice found a receptive audience in de Gaulle who needed to prove that he, not Giraud, represented French political opinion. On 10 February, de Gaulle wrote to Blum, supporting the idea of a Resistance council. Such a body would, he said, undermine the 'attempts at division and confusion attempted by some among the Allies [i.e. America] with the assistance of their French clients [i.e. Giraud].'[7] Five days later, Moulin arrived back in London, after fourteen months in France. On 21 February he drafted a set of 'new instructions' specifying the role and form of the proposed Resistance council. It was to be a single body, encompassing both zones, and comprising representatives of Resistance movements and political parties. The council's role would be to enunciate general principles, whose execution would fall to a smaller permanent committee comprised exclusively of representatives of the Resistance movements.[8]

Moulin, Brossolette, and the Movements

Moulin set off for France again on 19 March. His new mission was to set up the Resistance council and get it to declare support for de Gaulle. He was now 'sole representative of de Gaulle and the National Committee' for all France where previously he had only had responsibility for the South. In fact he had made one visit to Paris in July 1942, and his former associates Manhès and Meunier were in contact with Northern movements on his behalf, but little co-ordination had so far occurred in the North. On behalf of BCRA Rémy had made contact with OCM in April 1942, and in May with the FTP, but this link was severed almost immediately afterwards when his network was disrupted by a wave of arrests. Rémy returned to France in October 1942 with instructions to investigate the possibilities of co-ordinating the Resistance's military forces in the North. Having concluded that OCM was the only organization which counted militarily, he proposed to put one of its leaders, Colonel Touny, in charge. London rejected this solution on the grounds that no single movement should be accorded such a preponderant role. OCM had many enemies: the elitist tone of its publications raised many hackles, and movements like Libération-Nord were suspicious of 'OCM imperialism'.[9]

Not only did the Northern movements have little contact with each other, they had no single response to de Gaulle. Although Pineau was the first resister to visit London, when he returned to France enthusiastic about his meeting with

---

[6] Cordier, *Jean Moulin: La République des catacombes*, 219, 253–4.
[7] Id., *Jean Moulin*, i. 138–9.
[8] Id., *Jean Moulin: La République des catacombes*, 302–14.
[9] Aglan, 'Le Mouvement Libération-Nord', 284; Noguères, *Histoire de la Résistance*, ii. 649 ff., iii. 233 ff.; Passy, *Missions secrètes*, 53.

the general, his colleagues had given him a 'glacial' reception. Their trade-union traditions made them wary of any political allegiances. Not until December 1942 did *Libération-Nord* rally to London with a series of articles on 'Our leader de Gaulle'. *Défense de la France*, which had been Pétainist until November 1942, remained ambivalent about de Gaulle as late as March 1943.[10] A lot therefore remained to be done in the North.

Moulin's task was complicated by the fact that on 26 January, six weeks before he set off on his second mission to France, Brossolette had already been sent to the North as de Gaulle's representative. It was certainly no coincidence that at this very moment Moulin, who was imminently expected in London, had chosen to send over his aide Manhès. Passy commented: 'Never before had Moulin signalled his existence . . . We were amazed to discover that Moulin had entrusted him, since 1942, with organizing action in the North. If Moulin himself had not sent him, we would have taken him for an impostor or agent provocateur.'[11] If Passy somewhat exaggerated his surprise in retrospect—Moulin had never hidden the fact that he had contacts in the North even if he had not said much about them[12]—it was because, as an ally of Brossolette, he suspected that Manhès's arrival was Moulin's attempt to stake his own claim to the North. Equally Brossolette's eagerness to leave for France before Moulin's return to London suggests he wanted to begin work without Moulin's interference. If Brossolette were to fulfil his ambition of playing the same role in the North as Moulin had in the South, he had to act fast.[13]

On 26 February Passy himself joined Brossolette, and for the next month they enjoyed an almost entirely free hand. Manhès came out to join them, but he was almost immediately arrested. The purpose of their mission, code-named 'Brumaire-Arquebuse', was to co-ordinate the Northern movements, and set up a unified military organization like the AS in the South. Given the previous lack of co-ordination between the Northern movements, they achieved a remarkable amount in six weeks. By the start of April, Passy had centralized the gathering of intelligence information in the North, and set up a military co-ordinating committee to begin the process of creating a secret army. The Northern movements, including the FTP, agreed to contribute their forces to it.[14]

Brossolette, meanwhile, set about creating a co-ordinating committee of the movements similar to that existing in the South since October 1942. This objective was consistent with his original instructions, but not with Moulin's 'new instructions' which Passy brought over in February. Although Moulin envisaged only a single organism for both zones, Brossolette took no notice, believing that

[10] Aglan, 'Le Mouvement Libération-Nord', 177, 236; Wieviorka, *Une certaine idée*, 201–3.
[11] *Missions secrètes*, 54.
[12] Cordier, *Jean Moulin: La République des catacombes*, 275–6.
[13] Crémieux-Brilhac, *La France libre*, 341–4, 382–5; Passy, *Missions secrètes*, 30; Noguères, *Histoire de la Résistance*, ii. 575–83; Piketty, *Pierre Brossolette*, 231–57; Cordier, *Jean Moulin: La République des catacombes*, 301–3.
[14] Noguères, *Histoire de la Résistance*, iii. 222–45.

he understood the North better than Moulin. His view was that the idea of a single Resistance council was premature until preliminary co-ordination had occurred in the North and he played on the apprehensions of Northern Resistance leaders that their organizations might be annexed by the more developed ones in the South. Brossolette also ignored what the 'new instructions' said about the political parties. He found the Northern Resistance leaders hostile to any 'rehabilitation' of the parties. Since this coincided with his own views, Brossolette suggested that, instead of including parties, the proposed Resistance council should contain only representatives of France's 'spiritual families'. When London reprimanded him for 'exceeding the limits' of his mission, Brossolette was unrepentant. On 12 March he communicated his disagreement with the 'new instructions': 'Yes, to the Republic . . . but not that of yesterday . . . The fact that you are resigned to admitting the political parties into the running of the Resistance is unanimously opposed in this zone.'[15]

As soon as Moulin had returned to Lyons from London, he sent Brossolette a message announcing his imminent arrival in Paris and instructing him to postpone any definitive decisions until then. This only spurred Brossolette to move faster. On 26 March, four days before Moulin's arrival, he held the first meeting of the Co-ordinating Committee of the Occupied Zone. Five movements were represented: OCM, CDLR, CDLL, FN, and Libération-Nord. The Committee declared itself ready to accept a Resistance council which might include representatives of 'currents of opinion', but not representatives of political parties. It also rejected the idea of a permanent committee with executive powers: the Resistance council was acceptable only if it remained symbolic.[16]

Before he could turn his attention to the North, Moulin, on returning to France, had had to confront a challenge to his authority in the South where the movements were no less antagonistic to political parties than their comrades in the North. Claude Bourdet was scandalized that Moulin wished to give a 'Resistance certificate' to these 'ghosts about whom no one had spoken since 1940'; Frenay accused Moulin of being the 'gravedigger of the Resistance'.[17] The Resistance leaders, especially Frenay, were also regretting that they had ceded control of their meagre military forces to the AS. Once it was clear that Delestraint intended to be more than a figurehead, Frenay began to attack him violently in the meetings of the Southern Co-ordinating Committee.[18]

The conflict with Delestraint was not only about the command of the AS, but also about the strategy it should pursue. London wanted the military and political operations of the Resistance to be separate: the AS was required to wait in reserve for the liberation and then play its prescribed role in the Allied strategic plans, under de Gaulle's authority. Resistance leaders viewed this distinction between political and military activity as artificial. They refused to accept that

[15] Piketty, *Pierre Brossolette*, 257–82.   [16] Ibid. 284–8.
[17] Frenay, *La Nuit finira*, 290; Bourdet, *L'Aventure incertaine*, 215–19.
[18] Cordier, *Jean Moulin*, i. 156–7.

their paramilitary forces could be treated like regular soldiers or that the AS had no role until the liberation: there might be circumstances in which immediate action was possible. This disagreement might have remained purely theoretical because apart from the Communists the Resistance had hardly undertaken any military operations, unless the stunts of the *corps francs* were viewed in this light. But the introduction of STO in February 1943 suddenly opened up new possibilities, as thousands of young men, some of them eager to fight, fled the labour draft. Soon the first so-called Maquis groups were forming in the foothills of the Alps. To exploit this potential, money and arms were urgently needed and the Resistance leaders inundated London with pleas for help. D'Astier wired on 5 March: 'Grave situation. Country quickly emptied of men. Only salvation total resistance . . . Country ripe, I repeat ripe, for violent resistance if supported by clear instructions.'[19]

At this moment Moulin was still in London, trying to persuade British service chiefs that if they armed the AS, it could make a military contribution to the war. His arguments made a favourable impression, but the British view was that premature military action would be suicidal. The impatience of the Resistance leaders therefore jeopardized Moulin's attempt to prove the seriousness of the AS. Moulin tried to calm the Resistance leaders; they felt betrayed. Even if he had wanted to meet their demands, Moulin's ability to do so was compromised by the deteriorating relationship between de Gaulle and Churchill. Fearing that British funding might be curtailed at any moment, Moulin had felt it necessary to cut back the funds he transferred to the Resistance in March.[20]

All these issues faced Moulin on his return to Lyons where he found the Southern Resistance leaders in a state of 'considerable over-excitement'. Although Moulin managed to win grudging acceptance of the idea of a Resistance council, by arguing that de Gaulle needed political support in his battle against Giraud, no other issues had been resolved when he left for Paris on 30 March.[21] On his arrival in Paris, Moulin had two furious altercations with Brossolette. The 'cold hatred' he displayed to Brossolette, in Passy's words, was fuelled by Meunier, who alleged that Brossolette had been criticizing Moulin's 'devouring ambition'.[22] Moulin was also upset by the arrest of Manhès, and the fact that this event had obviously not displeased Brossolette and Passy unduly.

Nonetheless Moulin had to accept the fait accompli of Brossolette's Co-ordinating Committee, but the choice of the five movements represented on it caused him problems. These were the movements which Brossolette and Passy had judged to have the best military potential, and not those, like Défense de la France, Voix du Nord, Lorraine, and Résistance, whose main activity was pro-

---

[19] Cordier, *Jean Moulin,* i. 143.
[20] Ibid. 140–6, 150–6, 210–12; Crémieux-Brilhac, *La France libre,* 519–22.
[21] Cordier, *Jean Moulin,* i. 165–8.
[22] Passy, *Missions secrètes,* 86, 180–2; see Meunier's testimony in Cordier, *Jean Moulin et le Conseil,* 66–8.

ducing newspapers. The exclusion of Défense de la France was particularly anomalous since its newspaper had the largest circulation of any resistance publication in France. Moulin informed London that he had spent much time mollifying these excluded movements.[23] Probably Moulin dwelt upon these difficulties in order to discredit Brossolette who had returned to London on 15 April and was launching an offensive against him.

Returning to the Unoccupied Zone, Moulin found that Frenay was also conducting a campaign against him and Delestraint. Frenay accused Moulin of 'bureaucratizing the Resistance'. He complained that Moulin was trying to control everything, even the Resistance 'think-tank', the CGE. Delestraint was blamed for choosing too many professional officers without experience of the Resistance to command the AS. 'Liberation and revolution are inseparable', Frenay wrote to Moulin: 'a revolutionary army names its leaders . . . they are not imposed upon it . . . It is not an army we have forged . . . [but] . . . a band of partisans who want to fight for their liberties in France even more than they want to fight against the invader.' Behind these arguments lay Frenay's agony at relinquishing control over his own forces:

> Throughout 1942, the Movements developed entirely independently . . . Just to talk of Combat . . . I developed a real ascendancy over my comrades and subordinates . . . I am the person in whom they placed their confidence . . . We cannot forget that we are responsible for the men whom we have placed in your hands, whom we recruited and trained . . . You have harvested the fruit of two years' work, and you can understand that we cannot so easily disinterest ourselves in their fate.[24]

Frenay found a way to fight back when the first Maquis groups appeared in the spring. He was quick to see their military potential, and at his instigation the Southern Resistance movements set up a new section—the National Maquis Service (SNM)—to organize the Maquis and provide it with logistical support. Moulin understood the implications of this: 'the leaders of the Movements, seeing the AS to a certain extent escaping from their control, have tried to reconstitute another AS with the Maquis.'[25]

While Frenay was attacking Moulin within France, on 15 April d'Astier left

---

[23] See Moulin's report of 7 May 1943, reprod. in F.-L. Closon, *Le Temps des passions: De Jean Moulin à la Libération* (1974), 80–96; Wieviorka, *Une certaine idée*, 214–19; Cordier, *Jean Moulin*, i. 182–96; Noguères, *Histoire de la Résistance*, iii. 271–4; Piketty, *Pierre Brossolette*, 257–85. The large movements had given the erroneous impression that they spoke for the smaller ones: see Passy, *Missions secrètes*, 173; Bruneau, *Essai historique du mouvement*, 44–7; L. Pardieu, 'Un journal clandestin de la zone interdite: "Lorraine" 1942–1944' (unpublished mémoire de maîtrise, University of Nancy-II, 1991), 43–7.

[24] Frenay's two letters of 8 Apr. to Moulin and Delestraint are reprod. in Noguères, *Histoire de la Résistance*, iii. 277–82. See also Bourdet, *L'Aventure incertaine*, 187–8; D. de Bellescize, *Les Neuf Sages de la résistance: Le Comité général d'études dans la clandestinité* (1979), 96–114; P.-H. Teitgen, 'Faites entrer le témoin suivant' 1940–1958: De la Résistance à la Vème République* (Rennes, 1988), 62–76, 82.

[25] F. Marcot, 'Le Service national maquis: Structures, pouvoirs et stratégies', in id. (ed.), *La Résistance: Lutte armée et maquis*, 211–23: 211–14.

for London, where he drafted a ferocious report demanding Moulin's dismissal. Criticizing Moulin's rehabilitation of political parties and Delestraint's choices of AS commanders, d'Astier described Moulin as a 'civil functionary . . . whose only aim has been to destroy the leadership of the Movements and to incorporate them into his system for the sole purpose of his power'. Even the more conciliatory Lévy, usually ready to mediate between his comrades and Moulin, signed a letter with d'Astier blaming Moulin for the 'bureaucratization and sterilization' of the Resistance.[26] Moulin realized how isolated he had become. When he drafted his report criticizing Brossolette, he sent it directly to de Gaulle, circumventing BCRA, to ensure that his version of events got through.[27]

The attacks on Moulin had some effect. On 10 May André Philip of the Interior Commissariat warned him not to proceed too fast with the centralization of the Resistance. On the AS, de Gaulle even conceded some ground to the Resistance. In an Instruction of 21 May, he accepted the principle of 'immediate action', leaving its execution to the initiative of the movements.[28] Whether this was partly a disavowal of Moulin is not clear but even if it was, its significance should not be exaggerated.[29] De Gaulle's Instruction also reaffirmed that, after D-Day, Delestraint's authority over the AS must be uncontested. Equally, the gap between Moulin and the Resistance over immediate action was not as wide as it appeared. Since the AS was a force existing largely on paper—it was like a reserve army which had no arms and had never seen service—when the Resistance leaders spoke of immediate action, they had never envisaged major operations. As Bourdet said, the purpose of immediate action was primarily psychological: to prevent the enthusiasm of resisters 'rusting' in enforced passivity.[30]

Moulin's Victory: The CNR

Despite the campaigns against Moulin, by the middle of May he had succeeded in the primary objective of his mission: to persuade the Resistance movements to accept a Resistance council. He did, however, abandon the idea of capping this body with a permanent committee. The movements would be less hostile to the council if they believed, in Passy's words, that it would only be a 'puppet body'.[31]

---

[26] Cordier, *Jean Moulin*, i. 223–6; id., *Jean Moulin: La République des catacombes*, 402–8.

[27] Passy, *Missions secrètes*, 195; Closon, *Le Temps des passions*, 71.

[28] Passy gives the full text in *Missions secrètes*, 189–91. See also Noguères, *Histoire de la Résistance*, iii. 351–4.

[29] F.-Y. Guillin, *Le Général Delestraint: Le Premier Chef de l'Armée secrète* (1995), 200–1 underplays its significance; Baynac, *Les Secrets de l'affaire*, 204 and Péan, *Vies et morts*, 498, see it as more important.

[30] Bourdet, *L'Aventure incertaine*, 185; see also his remarks in Cordier, *Jean Moulin et le Conseil national*, 42–3.

[31] *Missions secrètes*, 184.

Moulin triumphed because he was able to exploit the rivalries between the movements. He had already done this in 1942—during the merger negotiations he had backed Frenay against d'Astier; during the negotiations to choose a commander for the AS, he had backed d'Astier and Lévy against Frenay—but paradoxically the rivalries increased after the movements decided in January 1943 to amalgamate into the MUR. In this new unitary organization each region was to be headed by one leader chosen from the three movements. Bargaining over the allocation of these posts caused months of friction. Guillain de Bénouville, conducting the negotiations for Combat, complained in June 1943 of the 'perfidious manifestations of hostility' displayed by the other movements.[32] Pascal Copeau, acting for Libération during d'Astier's absence in London, was equally acerbic about Combat. He reported that, although there were no major differences between the rank and file of the movements, Combat's cadres were 'latent fascists . . . or reactionary bourgeois who . . . never pronounce the word Republic except through gritted teeth'; and Frenay ran the movement like a Führer. According to Copeau, some Libération leaders felt that Frenay's removal was the 'greatest service one could render the Resistance at the moment'. After the war, Copeau admitted to finding Frenay 'impossible', claiming to have 'schemed with Moulin . . . to eliminate the "historic" leaders in order to make way for the leaders of the second wave who did not carry all the baggage of their memories of the early days'.[33]

Moulin had the opportunity to go on the offensive when it was revealed that, in the hope of increasing his funding, Frenay had contacted American secret service representatives (OSS) in Switzerland. He had obtained an initial payment of 1 million francs. In return for further payments, the Americans wanted to obtain intelligence information from the French. Hearing about these negotiations in late April, Moulin accused Frenay of stabbing de Gaulle in the back, and ordered the Southern movements to summon their executive committees to discuss the matter. Even those who did not contest the principle of Frenay's action were alarmed that he had acted unilaterally. It did not help that Frenay's representatives in Switzerland, General Jules Davet and Guillain de Bénouville, were very right-wing. Copeau feared that in such 'dangerous' hands, the Swiss negotiations took on the appearance of a 'fascist plot'.[34] There were reservations about Frenay even within Combat. In calling the movements to summon their executive committees, Moulin hoped to exploit tensions within the movements as well as between them. He knew that the leaders of the former Liberté movement, who had joined Frenay in December 1941, felt that they had too little influence within Combat. Some of them had become involved in the CGE as a

[32] Cordier, *Jean Moulin*, i. 64–5.

[33] Douzou, *La Désobéissance*, 349–61, 239–42; Noguères, *Histoire de la Résistance*, ii. 549.

[34] Cordier, *Jean Moulin*, i. 210–14; id., *Jean Moulin: La République des catacombes*, 350–7; Noguères, *Histoire de la Résistance*, iii. 283–7; Bourdet, *L'Aventure incertaine*, 197–200.

sort of refuge from Combat, and Frenay had been right in detecting an emerging axis between the CGE and Moulin.[35]

In short, the truth was that the movements were even more suspicious of each other than of London. On 4 June, Copeau wrote to d'Astier:

> It is historically established that Gervais [Frenay] has lost the contest with Max [Moulin]. We must not lose it with him. After all, Max inspires greater confidence than Gervais . . . Certainly Max has taken over things that he should have left to the Resistance. But are we going to continue opposing him over organizational questions?[36]

Moulin's victory was consummated when the long-awaited Resistance council, which came to be called the National Council of the Resistance (CNR) held its inaugural meeting on 27 May. As a final gesture of protest, Frenay refused to attend, as did Blocq-Mascart of OCM. They were represented respectively by Claude Bourdet and Jacques-Henri Simon. The Council had sixteen members, eight for the Resistance (representing the five movements on the Northern Co-ordinating Committee and the three movements in MUR), five for the political parties (Socialists, Communists, Radicals, Fédération républicaine, PDP, Alliance démocratique) and two for the trade unions (CGT, CFTC). In the case of the conservative parties, like the Fédération républicaine and Alliance démocratique, which had sunk without trace in 1940, the choices of representative were somewhat arbitrary. Indeed, there was a last-minute delay while someone was found to represent the former.

The first meeting of the CNR took place in the Parisian flat of a former associate of Pierre Cot. It was not a particularly cordial occasion: the Resistance representatives eyed the politicians warily. Moulin, having reassured the participants that the presence of politicians did not signify any commitment to the existence of the same parties after the liberation, read out a message from de Gaulle. Then the Council voted a motion calling for de Gaulle to be recognized as the single head of a French provisional government.[37]

De Gaulle and Giraud

Moulin's telegram announcing the imminent formation of the CNR arrived in London on 14 May. The next day the Free French published the news, giving the impression that the CNR already existed and had expressed its loyalty to de Gaulle. This premature announcement—the CNR was not to meet for another ten days—annoyed Moulin who was worried about offending the sus-

---

[35] Michel and Granet, *Combat*, 104–5, 167; Bellescize, *Les Neuf Sages*, 91; Teitgen, *Faites entrer le témoin*, 51; Frenay, *La Nuit finira*, 312–13.

[36] Cordier, *Jean Moulin*, i. 240–2. See also Hervé's views on Frenay quoted in Virieux, 'Le Front national', 308.

[37] Crémieux-Brilhac, *La France libre*, 537–9; Cordier, *Jean Moulin*, i. 197–202.

ceptibilities of the movements.[38] London's precipitation occurred because the negotiations between de Gaulle and Giraud had reached a critical juncture, and de Gaulle needed all the support he could muster.

After the inconclusive encounter at Casablanca in January, de Gaulle had returned to London, and Giraud to Algiers, but negotiations between their representatives continued for the next five months.[39] Behind the struggle for power lay differences of principle. Giraud's sole concern was to secure American arms so that the French army in North Africa could re-enter the war. His indifference to political questions suited Roosevelt whose policy was to negotiate with local French authorities on an ad hoc basis without offering any political guarantees for the future. For Roosevelt no one had the authority to speak for France: 'France', he said, no longer existed. For de Gaulle, the political issue was central. He set out his negotiating position on 23 February 1943 in a memorandum calling for a single political authority to represent French interests in negotiations with Allied governments. Without such an authority, the French would be at the mercy of their eventual Allied liberators, and 'France' would not be among the victorious nation-states. De Gaulle also insisted on the repeal of Vichyite legislation still prevailing in North Africa, and the dismissal of those former Pétainists—Boisson, Noguès, Peyrouton—who still held power there.

On 14 March, Giraud took a step in the direction of de Gaulle by declaring all Vichy's legislation to be null and void, and committing himself to republicanism. This speech, which Giraud later called the first democratic speech of his life, was the work of Jean Monnet whom Roosevelt had despatched to act as Giraud's political adviser. It eased the path towards an agreement with de Gaulle, and Catroux left for Algiers to negotiate with Giraud on de Gaulle's behalf. Harold Macmillan, Churchill's representative in North Africa, tried to act as a mediator. By the start of April, de Gaulle declared himself ready to leave for Algiers to discuss the final details of an agreement. But on 4 April, Eisenhower informed de Gaulle that his presence would not be opportune during the final stages of the Tunisian campaign. De Gaulle saw the hand of the British behind this attempt to exclude him from Algeria. In fact, the real culprit was Catroux who felt that de Gaulle's presence would do more harm than good. De Gaulle knew nothing about this, but he was suspicious of Catroux's 'inclination to concession'.[40] Catroux himself was driven to distraction by de Gaulle's intransigence, and frequently came close to resigning. His frustration was so evident that the Americans, perpetually in search of an acceptable alternative to de Gaulle, had hopes of weaning Catroux away from him. This was probably wishful thinking: despite his bouts of irritation with de

[38] Crémieux-Brilhac, *La France libre*, 541–2; Cordier, *Jean Moulin*, i. 202–3.
[39] Levisse-Touzé, 'L'Afrique du Nord', 763–860; A. Kaspi, *La Mission de Jean Moulin à Alger, mars–octobre 1943* (1971).
[40] De Gaulle, *Lettres, notes et carnets: juillet 1941–mi-1943* (1982), 587.

Gaulle, there is no evidence that Catroux contemplated playing an independent role.[41]

By 27 April, Catroux had secured a compromise agreement for the creation of a single North African body, jointly headed by de Gaulle and Giraud. The next problem was where the first meeting between the two generals would take place. Giraud wanted it out of the limelight, in Biskra; de Gaulle insisted on Algiers. He asked an aide: 'can you imagine Clovis or Joan of Arc going to Biskra?'[42] On 5 May, de Gaulle delivered a violent speech in London, denouncing the French administration in North Africa for the hypocrisy of its 'Republican declarations under the portrait of the Marshal'. Monnet said he was reminded of the negotiating tactics of Hitler; Catroux cabled that the speech had destroyed the 'web I have patiently constructed'.[43] De Gaulle sounded a more conciliatory note in a message on 7 May. The final obstacles were overcome by Macmillan and Monnet who pushed Giraud to give more ground. He agreed to the setting up of a committee jointly chaired by de Gaulle and himself, with seven members, two named by de Gaulle and two by himself, and the other three to be decided subsequently. On 17 May, Giraud handed Catroux a letter confirming that he was ready to allow de Gaulle to come to Algiers. De Gaulle accepted the terms, and left for Algiers on 30 May.

Because Giraud's final retreat occurred immediately after the (premature) announcement of the CNR, it is tempting to assume, as Gaullist mythology asserts, that this was the clinching factor.[44] In fact, what really brought Giraud round was the diplomacy of Catroux, Macmillan, and Monnet. The letter which Giraud handed to Catroux had been worked on by Macmillan for several days before the CNR announcement. Macmillan barely mentions the CNR in his account of the negotiations, suggesting only that it threatened to complicate matters at the last moment.[45] Given Giraud's poor view of the Resistance, it seems unlikely that the CNR would have impressed him unduly, especially since there was uncertainty about the authenticity of the message announcing it.[46] This uncertainty was substantial enough for de Gaulle himself to send Catroux his 'word of honour' that the telegram announcing the CNR was authentic.[47]

If Giraud allowed himself to be swayed by Macmillan and Monnet, it was because even he was not so obtuse that he could not recognize de Gaulle's posi-

---

[41] Kaspi, *La Mission*, 134, 145.   [42] Crémieux-Brilhac, *La France libre*, 471.

[43] J. Charmley, 'Harold Macmillan and the Making of the French Committee of Liberation', *International History Review*, 4/4 (1982), 553–67: 563.

[44] Cordier, *Jean Moulin*, i. 202–3.

[45] *The Blast of War 1939–1945* (1967), 326. For a similar view see M. Thomas, 'The Discarded Leader: General Henri Giraud and the Foundation of the French Committee of National Liberation', *French History*, 10/1 (1996), 86–111; Crémieux-Brilhac, *La France libre*, 540–5; but Kaspi, *La Mission*, 176, sees the foundation of the CNR as vital.

[46] See Allen Dulles's scepticism cited by Péan, *Vies et morts*, 497; and that of Comert in London: E. Roussel, *Jean Moulin 1888–1979* (1996), 353.

[47] *Lettres, notes et carnets: juillet 1941–mi-1943*, 593.

tion was improving all the time. There were defections to the Free French from the North African army. More and more figures in France were rallying to de Gaulle. In March 1943, the important Radical politician Henri Queuille arrived in London; in April, he was followed by the Socialist Pierre Viénot. This does not mean, however, that the CNR was entirely irrelevant to de Gaulle's success. The knowledge that it was in gestation had encouraged de Gaulle to be even more than usually intransigent in his negotiations with Giraud. He told an envoy from Catroux in May: 'important things are happening in France about which I will inform you when the time comes; you will have to explain them to General Catroux; he will understand, I hope, the reasons why I have been so firm'.[48]

De Gaulle's arrival in Algiers was far from the end of Giraud. In theory he and de Gaulle were now joint heads of the single National Committee of French Liberation (CFLN). In North Africa, Giraud remained more popular than de Gaulle, and he had the support of the Americans. De Gaulle, on the other hand, was close to losing the support of the British. As he was preparing to leave for Algiers, de Gaulle did not know that Churchill, who was in Washington, had finally succumbed to Roosevelt's anti-Gaullist barrage. On 21 May, Churchill sent a telegram to Eden, suggesting that it was time to break with de Gaulle. Although the British cabinet rejected this idea two days later, Roosevelt had not given up. On 17 June, while de Gaulle was engaged on the next round of his contest with Giraud, Roosevelt informed Eisenhower, in North Africa, that a break with de Gaulle was likely in the coming days.[49]

The break never came, and within six months de Gaulle was sole head of the CFLN. This occurred partly because, although Roosevelt's animus against de Gaulle remained undiminished, the American military commanders on the ground quickly realized Giraud's inadequacies. Politically Giraud was no match for de Gaulle, and made the fatal mistake of spending most of July in America to discuss the rearmament of France's troops. On the CFLN, several of Giraud's nominees shifted their allegiance to de Gaulle. One of the most important defectors was Jean Monnet, whom the Americans later accused of having betrayed de Gaulle. But Monnet, who found de Gaulle's personal style antipathetic, had merely bowed to reality. The problem was that by trying to make Giraud more politically acceptable, Monnet had undermined his support among Pétainist loyalists, without winning him corresponding support on the left: once he had become a republican, however unconvincingly, Giraud had no raison d'être.

The CFLN increasingly took on the appearance of a provisional government. On 26 August, it was recognized by the British as 'administering those French overseas territories which acknowledge its authority'. The Americans employed a more restrictive form of words. In September 1943, de Gaulle decided to set up a consultative assembly, made up of former politicians and prominent

[48] Crémieux-Brilhac, La France libre, 481.   [49] Kersaudy, Churchill and de Gaulle, 273–89.

resisters. This body, which met for the first time on 3 November 1943, further increased de Gaulle's democratic credentials. On 9 November, the CFLN was reshuffled, and Giraud lost his place on it. It was now headed by de Gaulle alone. Giraud retained command of the army, until this too was taken from him in April 1944. Harold Macmillan commented at the end of 1943: 'I would suppose that never in the whole history of politics has any man frittered away so large a capital in so short a time.'[50]

After Caluire: The Resistance Fights Back

One result of de Gaulle's absorption in Algerian affairs was that he had less time to devote to the Resistance, and less need of it. Resistance leaders saw an opportunity to recover some independence. Frenay had not lost hope of getting Moulin replaced. He was anxious to go to London and defend his contacts with the OSS in Berne. When Moulin's revelation of these had reached London, Passy intervened with the Americans to secure an assurance that future funds for the Resistance would be channelled through a representative of de Gaulle not through Frenay's emissaries. Hearing this news, Frenay wrote on 24 May to his representatives in Berne that if he could not get the decision rescinded, he would 'take back my full liberty, which would not of course affect my unconditional rallying to de Gaulle as a symbol'. Meanwhile he asked them to sound out whether the Americans would be ready to continue providing funds in the event of a rupture with de Gaulle.[51]

There is still dispute today over how serious Frenay was about the possibility of breaking with de Gaulle.[52] Not aware of the extent of Washington's hostility to de Gaulle, Frenay may well have believed that his attempt to secure extra American funding from the Resistance did not necessarily imply disloyalty to de Gaulle. Impulsive and confrontational at the best of times, Frenay was deeply hurt by what he saw as de Gaulle's bid to take over the Resistance. This made him liable to violent swings of mood, and his political beliefs remained wayward. Although he had evolved politically since 1940, he was still capable of telling one Northern resister at the end of 1942 that he mistrusted the 'British, Jewish, and Masonic' influences around de Gaulle.[53] On the other hand, he firmly told the Americans in March that their attempt to build up Giraud as an alternative to de Gaulle was unacceptable because only de Gaulle represented the political aspirations of the Resistance.[54] Nonetheless, once the two generals had reached an agreement, Frenay saw an opening for himself. Was it not possible that de

[50] Thomas, 'Discarded Leader', 86.

[51] Cordier, *Jean Moulin: La République des catacombes*, 358–60.

[52] For the former view, see Cordier, *Jean Moulin*, i. 214–20; Péan, *Vies et morts*, 443–4; for the latter, Baynac, *Les Secrets*, 183–94.

[53] Cordier, *Jean Moulin: La République des catacombes*, 167.

[54] See the report by Frenay reprod. in Baynac, *Les Secrets*, 432–9. Even Cordier, *Jean Moulin*, i. 242, has to accept that Frenay was suspicious of Giraud.

Gaulle, forced into cohabitation with Giraud on the CFLN, might have to cede some ground to the Resistance? Frenay suggested to Claude Bourdet that Combat's slogan should be changed from 'One sole leader, de Gaulle' to 'One sole authority, the CFLN'. He hoped to replace Moulin as intermediary between the Resistance and the new French authority in North Africa.[55]

Frenay arrived in London on 18 June to pursue his campaign against Moulin. He was not helped by the antipathy his abrasive personality aroused among other resisters. Copeau reported to d'Astier from France that everyone was relieved by the 'absence of this poor captain who has put everyone's back up'. While Frenay was in London plotting the elimination of Moulin, Copeau was plotting the elimination of Frenay with Moulin. Claudius-Petit of Franc-Tireur asked Moulin to do what he could to prevent Frenay ever returning to France.[56] In fact, within days of Frenay's arrival in London, his mission became redundant when news arrived that first Delestraint, and then Moulin himself, had been arrested by the Germans.

Moulin was arrested on 21 June 1943 at a meeting of resisters at Caluire in the suburbs of Lyons. Within three weeks, he was dead after undergoing terrible torture. Moulin's arrest is one of the unsolved mysteries of the Resistance, but certainly the conditions which made his betrayal possible were not unrelated to the internal rivalries within the Resistance. The trail which led to Moulin's arrest went back to March when the Germans obtained Resistance documents about the AS. These documents, which were considered sufficiently important for a summary to be sent to Hitler in person, vastly inflated the forces of the AS. On 28 April, the Gestapo arrested a Combat member called Multon who agreed to work for them. Multon's treachery resulted in the arrest of 120 resisters, among them Bertie Albrecht on 28 May and Delestraint on 6 June. The arrest of the head of the AS was a terrible blow, and it was to discuss the consequences that Moulin called the Caluire meeting.

Those present at Caluire included René Hardy, a member of Combat. Hardy had been arrested by the Lyons Gestapo chief Klaus Barbie on 7 June, thanks to information provided by Multon. He was quickly released after interrogation; at Caluire, he managed to escape arrest. This luck seemed too good, and several resisters were convinced that Hardy had betrayed Moulin. Some even tried to kill Hardy by sending him a packet of poisoned jam, which he did not open. After the war, Hardy was tried twice (January 1947 and May 1950), and both times acquitted. The presumption of guilt nonetheless remains strong. Two German reports in the summer of 1943 imply that he was working for the Gestapo, although he may have been playing some double game that backfired. The interesting question, however, is why Hardy was present at Caluire at all. Believing that the purpose of the meeting was to designate a replacement for

---

[55] Cordier, *Jean Moulin*, i. 232–8; id., *Jean Moulin: La République des catacombes*, 417–22.
[56] Id., *Jean Moulin*, i. 239–43; id., *Jean Moulin: La République des catacombes*, 423–4.

Delestraint, the Combat leaders wanted to be fully represented in the discussions. For this reason, Hardy was sent (without Moulin's knowledge) to reinforce the other Combat representative, Henri Aubry. The presence of someone who had been in the hands of the Germans was a breach of elementary security, but the rivalries between the movements, and between the movements and Moulin, caused such precautions to be ignored.[57]

When the news of these events reached London, Frenay hoped he might be appointed to replace Delestraint. This was never likely. 'The ructions he could cause in France surpass the imagination', commented Georges Boris of the Interior Commissariat.[58] Frenay was also denied facilities to leave for Algiers to prevent him causing mischief between de Gaulle and Giraud.[59] When he did eventually reach Algiers in August, de Gaulle had consolidated his position. Frenay had little choice but to accept a place on the CFLN four months later, as did d'Astier at the same time.[60]

The departure of d'Astier and Frenay from France alleviated tension between the Resistance and de Gaulle. Their replacements, Copeau and Bourdet, were less touchy than the founding fathers. At the same time, they had less reason to complain about outside interference because Moulin's death had changed the balance of power between the Resistance and London/Algiers. Moulin turned out to be almost irreplaceable. On 7 May, he had warned London that he needed more help: 'If I were to die, I shall not have had the time to prepare my successors.' This remark was only too prescient. Moulin's role was filled provisionally by Claude Bouchinet-Serreulles, who had been sent from London to assist him, and arrived just before his arrest. For two months Serreulles did his best to hold the fort. In August, he was joined by Jacques Bingen of BCRA: Serreulles became interim delegate for the North, and Bingen for the South. Others were sent out to assist them, and instead of Moulin's almost single-handed operation, a team was taking shape. Moulin had been de Gaulle's single delegate; now there was 'the Delegation'. Eventually this was a source of strength, but not in the short term: Bingen and Serreulles only enjoyed provisional status and could not match Moulin's detailed knowledge of the Resistance.

The most obvious candidate to fill Moulin's shoes was Brossolette, and there was discussion in London whether he should be appointed to replace him. Brossolette's candidature was supported by Passy, but opposed by Boris and Philip of the Interior Commissariat, who argued that it would needlessly antagonize the Resistance. Although Brossolette had posed as the champion

[57] Azéma and Veillon, 'Le Point sur Caluire', in Azéma et al. (eds.), *Jean Moulin et la Résistance en 1943* (1994); Cordier, *Jean Moulin: La République des catacombes*, 430–76.

[58] Crémieux-Brilhac, *La France libre*, 748; Cordier, *Jean Moulin*, i. 242.

[59] Cordier, *Jean Moulin*, i. 232–6; Michel and Granet, *Combat*, 310–11; Crémieux-Brilhac, *La France libre*, 534.

[60] D'Astier returned to France from London on 25 July, and then left on 18 Oct. for Algiers.

of the Resistance against Moulin on the matter of political parties, many leading resisters had reservations about him. He was an alarmingly energetic personality, and, as de Menthon remarked, 'the movements need a period of calm'.[61] The quarrel over Moulin's replacement raged throughout the summer until in September the decision was taken to appoint the former prefect Émile Bollaert.[62] Prefectoral rank was all that Bollaert shared with Moulin. He had been chosen largely as a compromise candidate and had little inside knowledge of the Resistance. Having spent the war in France, he had never met de Gaulle. Brossolette, although having lost the battle to replace Moulin, was instructed to return to France and help Bollaert settle into his new position.

Brossolette now hoped to become the power behind the throne, and this immediately brought him into conflict with Serreulles and Bingen who had been minding the shop. He had a chance to undermine their position only three days after his return to France when Serreulles's offices in Paris were raided by the Gestapo. Blaming lax security, Brossolette got Passy to instruct his agents to break off contact with Serreulles and Bingen. The feud between the Interior Commissariat and BCRA was now transposed to France itself. In their reports to London, Bingen and Serreulles described Brossolette as 'mean, cowardly and discredited', and his influence as 'unhealthy, if not indeed nefarious'; Brossolette countered by describing Serreulles as a 'feeble nullity'.[63] The situation became so fraught that both Serreulles and Brossolette were ordered back to London at the end of the year.

Behind these power struggles, one must never forget that these were people living on their nerves, with the prospect of arrest never far away. Pineau wrote of his second visit to London in January 1943: 'underground life was exhausting for one's nerves . . . One became obsessed by the idea of enjoying for a few weeks a real sensation of liberty.'[64] Pineau himself was arrested in May 1943; Brossolette was arrested in February 1944, before he could return to London, and he threw himself from a balcony to avoid succumbing to torture; Bingen was arrested in May 1944, and swallowed cyanide. Bollaert was also arrested, in February 1944, before he had had time to consolidate his authority. The conflicts between de Gaulle's envoys had not assisted his task, but the view of most Resistance leaders was that he lacked the experience to replace Moulin: 'a functionary for normal times' was how one described him.[65] After Bollaert's arrest, Bingen again took over as interim delegate until another permanent replacement, Alexandre Parodi, was named at the end of March 1944. For almost nine months, however, there had been no clear authority at the centre.[66]

Serreulles, Bingen, and Bollaert suffered from the additional handicap that

[61] Piketty, *Pierre Brossolette*, 304–9.
[62] Cordier, *Jean Moulin: La République des catacombes*, 487–95.   [63] Ibid. 508–28.
[64] *La Simple Vérité*, 273.   [65] Cordier, *Jean Moulin: La République des catacombes*, 550–64.
[66] Hostache, *Le Conseil national*, 183–215; Bellescize, *Les Neuf Sages*, 158–9.

they went several months without guidance from Algiers or London. Innumerable telegrams asking for instructions went unanswered. They felt isolated, ignored, and forgotten.[67] Communication was slow because correspondence with Algiers had to go via London. But it was not only that decisions were not reaching France; they were not being made at all. Decision-making was complicated by the split between Algiers and London. Although the centre of de Gaulle's operations was now Algiers, there was still a Free French operation in London. The Interior Commissariat was headed in Algiers by André Philip (and then by d'Astier) and in London by Georges Boris; BCRA was headed in Algiers by Passy, and in London by his deputy, André Manuel. This caused much confusion and made it easy to sabotage decisions one did not like. D'Astier discovered that twenty telegrams sent by Bingen and Serreulles to London had never been passed on to him.[68]

If de Gaulle had intervened decisively, he could doubtless have imposed his will, but he now had other priorities besides the Resistance. The CNR had provided democratic legitimacy at a delicate moment, but now this function was performed by the Algiers Consultative Assembly. He told d'Astier: 'Your [*sic*] CNR is getting a bit above itself.'[69] De Gaulle was also absorbed by the struggle with Giraud in Algiers. Brossolette, seeing him in August, found him '95% preoccupied by governmental problems . . . and only intermittently thinking about action in France'.[70] Similarly, Passy, although doing his best to further Brossolette's interests, was much preoccupied by his power struggle with the former Vichyite intelligence services in Algiers whose primary loyalty was to Giraud. Not until the end of November was this conflict resolved when the two services were merged to become a single intelligence service (DGSS).

For a variety of reasons, then, de Gaulle's authority over the Resistance was weakened after Moulin's death. One of de Gaulle's envoys talked of a dangerous 'void at the centre', Bingen of 'total stagnation'.[71] The Resistance leaders were quick to seize their opportunity. In the North, control of the AS was taken over by a military committee of the movements headed by Colonel Touny; in the South, the movements appointed General Pierre Dejussieu (Pontcarral), a career officer from Combat, to head the general staff of the AS. Meanwhile the CNR moved to elect a new chairman to replace Moulin. At the end of August, the choice fell upon Georges Bidault, who before 1940 had been a journalist for the Christian Democratic newspaper *L'Aube*. Bidault was a member of both Combat and the FN, but he had also been close to Moulin, having been appointed by him to run the BIP. These many contacts made him an obvious candidate to

---

[67] Noguères, *Histoire de la Résistance*, iii. 503–6; Cordier, *Jean Moulin: La République des catacombes*, 569–70.
[68] Cordier, *Jean Moulin: La République des catacombes*, 540.
[69] Crémieux-Brilhac, *La France libre*, 756.
[70] Cordier, *Jean Moulin: La République des catacombes*, 496–7.
[71] Bellescize, *Les Neuf Sages*, 212; Cordier, *Jean Moulin: La République des catacombes*, 545–7.

head the CNR, acceptable both to the Resistance and the Delegation.[72] It was dangerous for the CNR to meet regularly, and after its inaugural meeting it only met twice in plenary session before the Liberation. Decisions like the election of Bidault were taken after a protracted process of consultation of individual members. To circumvent this problem, it was decided in September to set up a permanent CNR Bureau empowered to take executive action between meetings. The Bureau had five members representing respectively the MUR (Copeau), the Northern Co-ordinating Committee (Blocq-Mascart), the unions (Louis Saillant), the FN-PCF (Pierre Villon), and the other political parties (Bidault).

Neither the creation of thd Bureau nor the election of Bidault were in themselves challenges to de Gaulle's authority. After all, the Bureau somewhat resembled the permanent committee Moulin had wanted for the CNR in the first place and Serreulles had supported Bidault's election because he thought, lacking any firm instructions, that Bidault might eventually be de Gaulle's candidate to replace Moulin as delegate.[73] There was, however, a direct challenge to the Delegation's authority only four days after Moulin's death when Resistance leaders met to form a Central Committee of the Movements (CCDM). This body was composed of five representatives of the Northern Co-ordinating Committee and three from the MUR. In other words, it consisted of the CNR minus representatives of the parties or unions. Although recognizing de Gaulle's authority, the CCDM proclaimed itself the executive authority of the Resistance, setting up subcommittees to run the increasingly specialized services of the Resistance. Serreulles had not even been informed of the setting-up of the CCDM. Although he subsequently obtained the right to chair its meetings, there was no doubt that the CCDM was a potential rival to the CNR, which had been Moulin's creation.

In the end, however, this threat never materialized. By failing to admit movements like Défense de la France, which had not been included in the CNR and were keen to acquire 'official' recognition, the CCDM missed an opportunity to make itself more genuinely representative of the Resistance than was the case of the CNR.[74] Another weakness of the CCDM was the under-representation of the Communist Party. On the CCDM, the Communists only had one place (as the FN-FTP) out of eight, on the CNR they had two (as the PCF and as the FTP-FN) out of sixteen, and on the CNR Bureau they had one out of five. For this reason, Villon, who represented the FN on both the CNR and the CCDM, stopped attending the latter. The CNR Bureau became the real centre of power: in February 1944, the CCDM ceased to exist, and its subcommittees were attached to the CNR.[75] All this occurred to the chagrin of Brossolette who

---

[72] Noguères, *Histoire de la Résistance*, iii. 498–501; Hostache, *Le Conseil national*, 158–60.
[73] Cordier, *Jean Moulin: La République des catacombes*, 638–41.
[74] Wieviorka, *Une certaine idée*, 236–7; Bourdet, *L'Aventure incertaine*, 222–3.
[75] Hostache, *Le Conseil national*, 216–19; Wieviorka, *Une certaine idée*, 235–9; Virieux, 'Le Front national', 447.

saw the CNR Bureau as similar to the permanent committee of the CNR which he had succeeded in preventing.[76]

Communist Policy

The eclipse of the CCDM in favour of the CNR was one illustration of the most striking development in the Resistance during the second half of 1943: the growing influence of the Communists. This was important because the Communists had their own strategy which set them apart both from de Gaulle and from the rest of the Resistance. There were three distinctive features of this Communist strategy: their ambivalence towards de Gaulle; their hegemonic ambitions over the internal Resistance; and their denunciation of *attentisme*.

Although the PCF had rallied to de Gaulle at the end of 1942, it did not offer him unconditional support against Giraud. The Party treated the two generals equally: having sent Fernand Grenier as a representative to de Gaulle, it also sent one to Giraud. At the inaugural meeting of the CNR the Communists unsuccessfully proposed a motion calling upon the two generals to reach an agreement rather than for Giraud to submit to de Gaulle. Possibly the Communists believed that Giraud would be easier to manipulate than de Gaulle, but their position was primarily determined by Soviet policy: in his eagerness to obtain a second front in Europe, Stalin would happily have sacrificed de Gaulle to win Allied goodwill.[77]

The Communists' instrument for hegemony over the Resistance was the Front national. Throughout France, they aimed to create FN committees open to resisters of all allegiances. The idea was to absorb members of the other movements into the FN from below and eventually enable the FN to claim to be the single representative organization of the Resistance. The extent of Communist ambitions for the FN emerged during Rémy's mission to Paris in October 1942. Having been instructed to extend his contacts with the FTP, Rémy, to his surprise, found himself negotiating directly with a representative of the Communist Central Committee itself. On 28 November, he signed a joint document registering a significant community of views between the Communists and the Free French. Rémy, who was politically naive, congratulated himself on having brought the Communists to rally de Gaulle. He did not see that the document he had signed put the FN on the same footing as the Free French: de Gaulle was presented as the defender of French interests outside France, and the Communists, through the allegedly independent FN, as his equal within France.[78]

At first, little was known in London about the FN, but BCRA soon realized

---

[76] Cordier, *Jean Moulin et le Conseil national*, 169 n. 227; Virieux, 'Le Front national', 641, 652.

[77] Courtois, *Le PCF dans la guerre*, 327–8; P. Buton, *Les Lendemains qui déchantent: Le Parti communiste français à la Libération* (1993), 18–19, 24–6.

[78] Cordier, *Jean Moulin*, i. 170–8, iii. 24–5, 34–5; Noguères, *Histoire de la Résistance*, iii. 643–53; Courtois, *Le PCF dans la guerre*, 304–7.

that it was not a genuinely independent organization.[79] In France, Moulin had refused to negotiate with the FN as a separate resistance organization. The Communists did, however, get the FN included by Brossolette in the Northern Coordinating Committee. This decision, which later enabled the Communists to obtain double representation on the CNR, as both Resistance movement and political party, was another of Moulin's grievances against Brossolette. But Brossolette had merely bowed to the fact that in the North the Communists did have a significant resistance presence, whether via the FTP or the FN, which could not be ignored. He believed it was safer to have the FN on the Committee than outside it. The irony was that Brossolette, by facilitating the Communists' double representation on the CNR, unwittingly strengthened an institution which he opposed.[80]

The potential offered by the FN committees was revealed in Corsica in the summer of 1943. In July, the Allies landed in Sicily. It was clearly only a matter of time before Italy left the war, and this meant that Corsica, which was occupied by Italy, could soon be liberated. The FN leaders on the island prepared for an uprising. On 9 September, the day after the Italian surrender, demonstrations occurred throughout the island. FN groups assembled the population in village squares to 'elect' selected 'patriots' to municipal councils by popular acclaim. Free French forces arrived a few days later, but the FN already controlled 200 municipal councils, including Ajaccio.[81]

In mainland France, however, the FN committees did not take off, especially in the South where the Resistance movements were highly developed, had a head start over the Communists, and knew that the FN was merely an emanation of the PCF. In May, therefore, the Party changed tack. Since the other Resistance movements had no intention of being absorbed into the FN, the FN declared itself ready to co-operate with them. Instead of inviting individuals to join FN committees, the Communists now invited other movements to form local committees with the FN. In other words, these were to be pluralistic not unitary committees. The Communists proposed calling them 'Fighting France committees', to lure the unwary into believing they enjoyed official status.[82]

By the autumn, the Communists claimed that Fighting France committees existed in eleven *départements*. Frequently, however, their members represented only fictitious Communist front organizations. The Fighting France committee of the Languedoc announced that it contained representatives of the FN, the FTP, the MUR, and numerous other groups representing women, wine-growers, war veterans, and unions. These supposedly independent groups were mostly emanations of the Communist Party. This manoeuvre was too transparent, and

[79] Cordier, *Jean Moulin*, i. 178–81.
[80] Virieux, 'Le Front national', 300–1; Piketty, *Pierre Brossolette*, 260, 279, 295; Cordier, *Jean Moulin*, i. 193–4.
[81] Buton, *Les Lendemains qui déchantent*, 27–9; Crémieux-Brilhac, *La France libre*, 577–8.
[82] Buton, *Les Lendemains qui déchantent*, 30–1; Virieux, 'Le Front national', 342–7.

the MUR ordered its representative to resign.[83] The Communist Party reprimanded its local organizers for applying Party policy in such a crude manner. One of the more subtle Communists wrote that the Party should avoid establishing 'puppet committees' consisting only of Communists disguised in different forms: 'Better to create a real committee which is not necessarily easy to "handle", which might even rebel, but which genuinely contributes to widening the movement.'[84]

Having accepted the idea of pluralistic committees at the base, the Communists were now ready to participate in them at every level. Thus having originally been sceptical about the idea of the CNR, on the grounds that the Front national was the only valid representative of the Resistance in France, the Communists in the end agreed to join it. At its first meeting, they proposed to recognize it as the 'provisional organ of national sovereignty'. This would have given the CNR the status of a provisional government until de Gaulle's arrival. Moulin had the motion rejected, but in July, after his death, the CNR passed an Appeal to the Nation which was drafted in similar terms. The Communists had decided to develop the CNR as a possible counterweight to de Gaulle.[85]

The third distinctive feature of the Communists was their denunciation of what they called *attentisme*. Condemning the idea that the Resistance should delay military action until an Allied landing, they contrasted the activist strategy of the FTP with the waiting strategy of the AS. This was an oversimplification since many non-Communist resisters were just as impatient as the Communists about waiting for D-Day, and de Gaulle's Instruction of 21 May had allowed the non-Communist Resistance to undertake immediate action. Nonetheless, the primary objective of the AS was to prepare for the liberation, and it was not entirely untrue for the Communists to assert that no other organization was as ready as the FTP to act immediately.[86]

Responding to the Communists

In the second half of 1943, the rivalry between the Communist and non-Communist movements transformed the dynamics of the conflict between de Gaulle and the Resistance. Some were quicker than others to appreciate the challenge posed by the Communists. No one had been quicker than Moulin. One of the arguments of his report of October 1941 was that the Resistance risked being thrown into the arms of the Communists if de Gaulle did not act first.[87] At the first meeting of the Northern Military Co-ordination Committee in

---

[83] Buton, *Les Lendemains qui déchantent*, 30–3; Virieux, 'Le Front national', 568.

[84] Hervé, quoted in Virieux, 'Le Front national', 405.

[85] Virieux, 'Le Front national', 1497–9, reproduces Villon's report on the first meeting of the CNR. On the Appeal to the Nation see Cordier, *Jean Moulin*, i. 269–70; Passy, *Missions secrètes*, 257–8, 453–6.

[86] Courtois, *Le PCF dans la guerre*, 336–8, 377–8; Virieux, 'Le Front national', 342–7, 358–70.

[87] Cordier, *Jean Moulin*, iii. 826, 856.

April 1943, Moulin clashed with the FTP representative over the issue of immediate action. Immediately afterwards, he cut funding to the FTP. He told the FTP representatives they should click their heels ('claquer les talons') and obey.[88]

De Gaulle treated the Communists with wary respect. Grenier's arrival in London had been a major boost to his prestige, but the Corsican events alerted him to the threat the Communists could pose at the Liberation. He wanted the support of the Communists, but on his terms. On 25 August, he invited them to join the CFLN, but the Party delayed its response. De Gaulle's relations with the Communists were not helped by the arrival in Algiers, from Moscow, of André Marty to sit on the Consultative Assembly. Marty, with a reputation for ruthlessness acquired during the Spanish civil war, was exceptionally abrasive. In October, the Communists finally accepted de Gaulle's offer of a place on the CFLN, but only if they could decide who would be selected. De Gaulle refused to accept any restrictions on his choice, and stalemate ensued. Having now eliminated Giraud, de Gaulle had less need of Communist support.[89] He was also becoming more suspicious of the Communist Party in the light of reports from his representatives in France. Initially they had got on well with the Communists. When it came to asserting the CNR's primacy over the CCDM, their policy converged with the Communists', even if for different reasons.[90] But from the autumn, the Communists started to cause concern. Bingen in November described them as a 'dynamic and mysterious force'. Another of de Gaulle's representatives, Francis-Louis Closon, thought they were planning to take power: 'the Communists are powerful, well organized, in possession of a general doctrine . . . Do we have anything constructive to set against them?'[91]

The MUR leaders were slowest to take the measure of the Communists. The highly developed structure of the Resistance in the South made them confident that the Communists did not pose a serious threat. But the Languedoc Fighting France committee was a worrying portent of Communist methods. An MUR organizer in the Toulouse region in November observed correctly that the Party was using these committees to 'win itself at our expense . . . the troops which it lacks without having to resort to direct recruitment in the name of the party'.[92] The FN was also trying to obtain a seat on the Executive Committee of the MUR, placing itself on an equal footing with the other three component movements. This was refused on the grounds that the FN was predominantly a

[88] Ibid. i. 153–4; Piketty, *Pierre Brossolette*, 291.

[89] Buton, *Les Lendemains qui déchantent*, 37–8; Crémieux-Brilhac, *La France libre*, 620–2.

[90] Virieux, 'Le Front national', 453–6, 635–8. Virieux notes that Serreulles was not unhappy about the text voted by the CNR on 14 July despite its being close to that rejected by Moulin two months earlier. Since then the Movements had formed the CCDM, and it was important to assert the primacy of the CNR.

[91] Crémieux-Brilhac, *La France libre*, 758.

[92] Virieux, 'Le Front national', 569.

northern organization which already enjoyed representation on the central organisms of the Resistance. Instead the MUR leaders offered the FN the prospect of a merger, something the Communists refused because they knew that the MUR was stronger than them in the South.[93]

Within the MUR, the rivalry between Combat and Libération resurfaced around their attitude towards the Communists. The Combat leaders were deeply suspicious of the Communists, and the Libération leaders more sympathetic. All the tactical realignments occurring in the Resistance at this time were dominated by this problem of responding to the Communists. From the autumn of 1943, proposals were being floated to extend Resistance unity further by forming a single umbrella organization: the National Union of the Resistance (UNR). But the FN was hostile, suspecting a ploy to absorb it into a body controlled by the other movements.[94] For this reason, the UNR proved abortive, and instead, in February 1944, the MUR and some Northern movements which had originally been excluded from the CNR and the CCDM—among them Défense de la France, Résistance, Lorraine—formed themselves into the Movement of National Liberation (MLN).

The participants in the MLN each had their own agenda. Défense de la France wanted an 'official' recognition which had so far eluded it. For MUR, the objective was to lay the foundations of a political force which would carry the ideal of the Resistance into the post-war world, and replace the discredited parties. But the MUR leaders held different views about the political identity of this new movement. Those from Combat, like Bourdet, wanted it to be non-Communist, even anti-Communist. Bourdet hoped to involve other Northern movements, like OCM, CDLR, and CDLL, in order to counterbalance the influence of Communist sympathizers within MUR. The Libération leaders, like Copeau, wanted the MLN to be a grouping of the progressive non-Communist Resistance which the FN would want to join. The aim was to tame the Communists not oppose them: a merger between the MLN and the FN would anchor the Communists in the Resistance mainstream and anchor the Resistance on the left.[95]

Neither MUR faction got exactly what it wanted from the MLN. Copeau failed to entice the Communists, but as a result he blocked Bourdet's attempt to bring in other Northern movements. He wrote to d'Astier: 'I succeeded in keeping out OCM, CDLR and CLL in order not to create a bloc which would be predominantly bourgeois where I would not be able to prevent anti-Communist plots of the Bourdet variety.'[96] There was another attempt at full unity in March 1944 when all the non-Communist movements—CDLR, CDLL, Libération-Nord, OCM, MLN—signed a Charter intended to be the foundation of a future union of the entire Resistance. But when in April

[93] Virieux, 'Le Front national', 441, 490, 643–5.   [94] Ibid. 629–34.
[95] Wieviorka, *Une certaine idée*, 245–52.   [96] Virieux, 'Le Front national', 721–2.

the FN confirmed that it was not interested in joining, the whole idea fizzled out.[97]

These attempts to create a single resistance movement—with or without the Communists—were complicated by other conflicts cutting across the division between Communists and non-Communists. There was the conflict between the 'official movements'—those admitted to the CNR or CCDM—and those still lobbying for recognition.[98] Merger negotiations between Libération-Nord and the smaller La Voix du Nord foundered because the latter refused to give up its independence. Serreulles agreed to continue funding La Voix du Nord as a separate organization: 'We must do our best', he wrote in July 1943, 'to avoid the emergence of a distinction between recognized and non-recognized movements.'[99]

Another important conflict was that between the South and the North: movements like OCM amd CDLR remained suspicious of 'politics' and feared that in the MLN they would lose their independence to the Southern movements.[100] There were also conflicts of generation: Maurice Chevance-Bertin, one of Frenay's first recruits, nostalgically recalling 'the heroic improvised Resistance of the beginning', felt that 'the historic leaders' like himself irritated the second generation like Copeau.[101] He was right about Copeau who later mocked the 'war veteran mentality' of the first wave of leaders: 'their stories of the early days when for the first time, all alone, with only 3 fr. 25 in their pocket they had produced the first mimeographed tract . . . all that appeared quite outmoded to us'.[102] The Resistance was changing so fast that when Jean-Pierre Lévy returned to France, after having been in London between April and July 1943, he felt almost a stranger within his own movement.[103]

The most important conflict was between resistance movements and political parties. Resisters could not overcome their contempt for the parties. 'Parties' really meant the Socialists, since the others did not count, despite a token presence on the CNR. All the disdain of the resister for the politician is contained in Bourdet's recollection of meeting a group of Socialists: 'they had the air of solid bourgeois from the Midi, dark overcoats, hats the same. If I wasn't worried that my imagination was getting the better of my memory, I would say that they were probably a bit pot-bellied.'[104] Having no resistance movement, the

[97] C. Andrieu, *Le Programme commun de la Résistance: Des idées dans la guerre* (1984), 84–5; Granet, *Ceux de la Résistance*, 305–7; Wieviorka, *Une certaine idée*, 259–60; Noguères, *Histoire de la Résistance*, iv. 192–5; Pierre Hervé, quoted in Michel and Granet, *Les Idées*, 107–9.

[98] Bruneau, *Essai historique*, 46–7.

[99] Aglan, 'Le Mouvement Libération-Nord', 329.

[100] Granet, *Ceux de la Résistance*, 140–1; Aglan, 'Le Mouvement Libération-Nord', 282.

[101] *Vingt mille heures d'angoisse* (1990), 139–40.

[102] Noguères, *Histoire de la Résistance*, ii. 548–9.

[103] Lévy, *Mémoires d'un franc-tireur*, 118. The same was true of Lecompte-Boinet in 1944, see Granet, *Ceux de la Résistance*, 138.

[104] Sadoun, *Les Socialistes sous l'Occupation*, 113.

Socialists tended to spend time planning post-war policy or navel-gazing. *Le Populaire* of February 1944 devoted its front page to the anniversary of the Riom trial rather than to the increasingly bloody battles taking place in France.[105] Resisters saw this as typical of the politicians' mentality.

Socialists in Marseilles and the south-west did form their own military resistance units, called Groupes Veni (the pseudonym of their leader Colonel Lefevre) in imitation of the FTP. When Daniel Mayer warned that these groups, totalling 20,000 men, might secede from the MUR if the Socialists were not treated properly, resistance leaders accused him of being a traitor. The Socialists could not win: if they threatened to form their own resistance organization they were accused of jeopardizing Resistance unity; if they confined themselves to being a party they were accused of being politicians who could not understand the Resistance. In fact the threat to secede was hollow since the Veni groups probably had no more than 6,000–10,000 members. An agreement was signed in November 1943 integrating them fully into the MUR.[106]

Resistance leaders never overcame their reservations about the Socialists—Mayer failed to get the Socialists a separate seat on the CNR Bureau—but their hostility softened as they became more apprehensive of the Communists. The Resistance was torn between contempt for the Socialists and awe of the Communists. Even Frenay, who despised politicians, wanted the Socialists to be given a place on the CNR Bureau: his main concern was now to weaken the Communists who were planning, in his view, to turn de Gaulle into a French Kerensky.[107] As for the Socialists, they remained wary of the Resistance. They were attracted to the MLN as a weapon against the Communists, but suspicious of it as a weapon against the parties—an entirely logical response since the MLN had been conceived to fulfil both objectives. Following the Socialist lead, Libération-Nord refused to join the MLN.[108] The Socialists blew hot and cold, and were still deliberating whether to join the MLN at the Liberation. In the end, then, the MLN was never more than the MUR plus some Northern movements.

Communist Infiltration?

Those resisters who wanted the MLN as a barrier against the Communists soon started to fear that the MLN itself had fallen under Communist influence. This was the latest version of a persistent rumour that Communist moles were playing on the naivety of non-Communist resisters and colonizing the Resistance.[109] There was the example of Marcel Degliame, a Communist tradeunion

---

[105] Sadoun, *Les Socialistes sous l'Occupation*, 115.
[106] Ibid. 173–6; 218; Passy, *Missions secrètes*, 31–3; Laborie, *Résistants, Vichyssois*, 290.
[107] Virieux, 'Le Front national', 482, 638; Sweets, *Politics of Resistance*, 137.
[108] Wieviorka, *Une certaine idée*, 249, 254–5; Sadoun, *Les Socialistes sous l'Occupation*, 222.
[109] Noguères, *Histoire de la Résistance*, iv. 555–8. Douzou, *La Désobéissance*, 365–92, offers a critique of this view. In the light of material presented by Virieux, his account underplays the degree of Communist organization. See also Buton, *Les Lendemains qui déchantent*, 67–71.

activist, who had joined Combat after escaping from a prisoner of war camp, and ended up running its Workers' Action division (AO). Degliame was unusual since most of the alleged moles were in Libération not Combat. Libération acquired the reputation of being the Trojan horse through which the Communists hoped to dominate the MLN. Suspicion centred on several possible culprits: Lucie and Raymond Aubrac, founding members of Libération, who had been student Communist activists before the war; Pierre Hervé, another former Communist student activist, who joined in July 1942; Maurice Kriegel, a Communist trade unionist, who joined in the summer of 1942 and became Aubrac's deputy as commander of the movement's paramilitary forces; and Alfred Malleret, another trade unionist, who joined in the autumn of 1942 and headed the Lyons region until 1944.

One problem with viewing the presence of these Communists as an entryist conspiracy is that some of them were only in Libération in the first place because they had lost contact with their Party in 1940–1. But did the Party subsequently use them as moles once it had reorganized in the South? Certainly they kept their Communist affiliations secret: as late as May 1944, Morandat scoffed at allegations that Degliame, Kriegel, and Hervé were Communists.[110] Hervé later denied suggestions that the Communists in Libération had secretly formed themselves into a separate section,[111] but his own reports to the Party certainly showed that they saw themselves as working in Communist interests. On 9 May, he wrote: 'now that we have two heads of region and one deputy head who are Communists—and if you provide us with the men we will have one or two others—we can influence the political line taken by the Resistance'.[112] But one must not exaggerate the effectiveness of the Party's control. Degliame complained in January 1944 at 'having to act without Party advice since we cannot wait when there are decisions to take'.[113] In April, Kriegel wrote to the Party, on behalf of Degliame, Hervé, Malleret, and himself, to say that if their relations with the Party had been more 'normal' it might have been able to avoid 'hesitations' on their part. This presumably meant that they had awaited instructions, but that the mechanisms of communication did not work well.[114]

Another alleged Communist tactic was the manipulation of sympathizers who were not full members. It was claimed after the war that this had enabled the Communists to control the Bureau of the CNR. But of the five members of the Bureau, only Pierre Villon was a Communist. Blocq-Mascart was anti-Communist. Of the other three, Bidault, although in the FN and for this reason seen by some as a tool of the Communists, also had other affiliations, and was considered an ally by the Delegation. So too was Saillant, a non-Communist trade unionist of whom the Communists were at this time suspicious (although

[110] Sadoun, *Les Socialistes sous l'Occupation*, 218.
[111] Noguères, *Histoire de la Résistance*, iii. 95.
[112] Virieux, 'Le Front national', 338–9.   [113] Ibid. 707.   [114] Ibid. 337, 407.

after the war he did join the Party).[115] Finally, there was Copeau whom many saw as a fellow-traveller. Although this may have been true after the war, Copeau's position at this time was more complex. In December 1943, he even complained to d'Astier that Bidault was too subservient to the FN. Copeau's ambition for the MLN, as he expressed it in February 1944, was 'to counteract the policy of the Communist party and Front National . . . by proving . . . that we are as capable as them at meeting events and acting'.[116] These are hardly the words of a complaisant fellow-traveller. By promoting the MLN, Copeau was certainly not doing what the Communists wanted.

Only if Copeau and Bidault are both put in the Communist camp, which would be wrong, did the Communists enjoy a majority on the CNR Bureau. If the Communists frequently got their way in the Bureau, it was partly because Villon was an exceptionally effective political operator, and Blocq-Mascart an inept one. It was also because the themes of their propaganda were attractive to many people who were neither Communist nor even fellow-travellers. Copeau was far from alone in becoming increasingly fascinated by the Communists in this period: they were admired for the heroic role of the Red Army, for their FTP martyrs, for their uncompromising language of action. The Communists' increasing influence within the Resistance in 1943 is therefore explained less by their infiltration of the leadership of the Resistance than their ability to voice the aspirations of many ordinary resisters. To understand the Communists' success, it is necessary to leave the leaders and return to the base.

[115] Andrieu, *Le Programme commun*, 59.
[116] Douzou, *La Désobéissance*, 365–86, 388, 392.

20

Resistance in Society

Chapter 19 described the history of the Resistance in 1943 in terms of power struggles: between London and France, BCRA and the Interior Commissariat, Communists and non-Communists, North and South, politicians and resisters, first- and second-generation resisters. These conflicts were, however, accompanied by a parallel process of consolidation. Through the creation of such organizations as the AS, the CNR, the MUR, and the MLN, the Resistance was moving towards greater integration and unification: controlling this process was what lay behind the power struggles. Consolidation was accompanied by centralization. From the spring of 1943, even the main resistance organizations in the South—the BIP, the CGE, and the MUR—moved their headquarters to Paris. Lyons had become too dangerous and too small. The former 'capital of the Resistance' was now also the regional capital of the Gestapo. Serreulles reported in August that resistance leaders had been forced increasingly to 'confine themselves to the outskirts of Lyons in premises which were each day harder to find, and which they could not leave once they had taken refuge in them'.[1] Paris offered greater anonymity. The move to Paris also signalled that the Resistance was looking to the day when it would be called upon to govern.

Diversification and Radicalization

Consolidation and centralization did not mean uniformity. The Resistance was not just a series of acronyms. Centralization at the summit was accompanied by diversification at the base. This diversification was partly a result of size. Resistance never became a mass movement, but 1943 was the year of fastest expansion. Défense de la France never had more than about 2,500 members, but three-quarters of them joined between February and December 1943; just over half Libération-Nord's members joined in 1943. Of the 3,658 members of resistance organizations in the Alpes-Maritimes, 52 per cent joined in 1943 (19 per

---

[1] Quoted in L. Douzou, 'La Constitution du mythe de la Résistance', in C. Franck (ed.), *La France de 1945: Résistances retours renaissances* (Caen, 1996), 73–83: 75.

475

cent in 1944).[2] Estimates of the size of the AS fluctuated enormously. Libération-Nord claimed to have 4,900 men available to it in April 1943, and 31,000 in September. BCRA estimated in March that the AS could count on 126,000 men (51,000 in the North and 75,000 in the South); two months later, it put the figure at 208,000. In October, another report suggested 128,250 in the North alone.[3] Even if such figures are correct, only a tiny proportion of these potential forces were armed—10,000 at the most—and even fewer knew how to use the arms they possessed.

The increasing professionalization and militarization of the Resistance, symbolized by the growing importance of the AS, might have militated against a rapid increase in numbers. In 1942, Pineau distinguished two kinds of Resistance: 'military Resistance can only be performed by a real Secret Army . . . composed of men ready, outside their daily tasks, to undertake a specific mission . . . Political Resistance, on the other hand, is performed by each Frenchman in the framework of his normal activities.' The former required 'a hierarchy, a discipline, a discretion incompatible with the idea of a mass movement'; the latter 'leaves a lot to individual initiative'.[4] In fact, both these kinds of resistance developed in 1943: the Resistance started to undertake an increasing variety of operations which created opportunities for more and more people. This allowed it to tap the anti-Vichy mood which had existed for at least a year. The population's amorphous resentment was channelled into action. In 1940–1, a few resisters had struggled to create a 'Resistance'; in 1943, the Resistance began to create 'resisters': it offered tasks to people who wanted to act.[5]

Many of these people had already carried out individual acts of protest like tearing down posters or scrawling graffiti: they had already been, as it were, in a state of latent resistance. A quarter of those who eventually joined Défense de la France had performed some resistance activities before January 1943, but at this stage only 12 per cent of them were already members of the movement. In only 55 per cent of cases did the decision to join the movement represent their 'entry into resistance'.[6] This phrase should, however, be used cautiously. There were certainly people whose participation in the Resistance was a sudden moment of rupture. One resister remembered his engagement in the following way:

> After the debacle I knew a period of apathy. Then on one spring day, having thought for a long time about it, hesitated for several weeks, it seemed to me absolutely clear and ineluctable. It was destiny. There was no longer any hesita-

[2] Wieviorka, *Une certaine idée*, 177; Aglan, 'Le Mouvement Libération-Nord', 371 (in fact this percentage refers only to those who were arrested).

[3] Aglan, 'Le Mouvement Libération-Nord', 300, 540; Michel and Granet, *Combat*, 169–70, 226–7; Calmette, *L' "O.C.M."*, 137.

[4] Aglan, 'Le Mouvement Libération-Nord', 296.

[5] Guillon, 'La Résistance dans le Var', 341.

[6] Wieviorka, *Une certaine idée*, 174–7.

tion . . . It was from that moment that I started looking for a group and it was not very easy to find one.[7]

In this case, the decision was sudden, although there was a delay before it could be acted upon. But for many people, 'joining' the Resistance was a chain of small actions cumulatively acquiring the form of an engagement: the quantitative became qualitative.[8]

After the war, official recognition of participation in the Resistance was conferred through the possession of a card attesting that its recipient had been a Voluntary Resistance Fighter (CVR). By 1994, 260,919 of these cards had been issued. They provide much information on the social background of the 'foot soldiers' of the Resistance, but this information must be treated critically. The rules governing the attribution of CVR cards were quite restrictive. The cards reveal more about the associations of former resisters after the war than about the Resistance itself.[9] Many people did not bother to acquire a card; others with incontrovertible Resistance credentials were refused one for technical reasons. In the two Normandy *départements* of Calvados and Manche, 1,336 cards were distributed, but subsequent research suggests that at least another 1,350 people could have been included.[10]

Attempting to quantify the Resistance fails to grasp its true character in 1943. As more people came into the orbit of the Resistance, it lost the quality of a Freemasonry to which one belonged, permeating society in ever more complex ways. Ripples of complicity extended into communities previously untouched. Even people who only played an intermittent role could make a significant contribution. Take the example of an FTP fighter wounded by gendarmes in the village of Barjols in the Var, and given refuge by a peasant also working for the FTP. After his wounded finger went gangrenous, this resister was looked after by two doctors, both of whom kept silent. The whole operation was organized by the wife of a local agent of the Azur-F2 network. In total, ten people participated in saving this one resister.[11] Without such help, invisible except under the microscope of local histories, the activities of the more visible Resistance leaders would have been impossible.

The expansion of the Resistance occurred at a time when it seemed increasingly likely Germany would lose the war. This does not mean that these comparatively late arrivals should be written off as opportunists. As the Germans became weaker, they became more dangerous: the growth of resistance was a function of opportunities more than opportunism. Although many resisters

---

[7] Ibid. 174.

[8] Marcot, 'Résistance et population', 18–20.

[9] Guillon, 'La Résistance dans le Var', 335–6; J. Sainclivier, 'Sociologie de la Résistance: Quelques aspects méthodologiques et leur application en Ille-et-Vilaine', *RHDGM* 179 (1980), 34–74: 33–5.

[10] Boivin and Quellien, 'La Résistance en Basse-Normandie: Définition et sociologie', in Sainclivier and Bougeard (eds.), *Enjeux stratégiques*, 163–73: 164–6.

[11] Guillon, 'La Résistance dans le Var', 355.

themselves believed the contrary, there was no hierarchy of virtue attaching to the moment of entry into Resistance. The strata of resistance generations reveal not different levels of courage or patriotism, rather, they reflect how the combination of background, conviction, and experience caused people to respond in different ways, and at different times. Every group had its own moment of truth. Even the Jews only gradually became aware of the threat facing them. The Jewish resistance fighters of the MOI have been tellingly described as the 'generation of the Vel d'Hiver round-up'.

The expansion in the size of the Resistance also widened its sociological and geographical base: it spread from towns to countryside, from plains to mountains. It embraced workers and peasants, Catholics and Protestants, men and women, French and foreigners. The social composition of the Resistance changed as new tasks presented themselves. Or, as one historian puts it, the 'sociology of the Resistance was first of all a reflection of the sociology of the needs of resistance'.[12] In 1941–2 it required people to write for newspapers and produce them; it needed people whose jobs allowed them to move around. Within the working class, there were early opportunities for rail and postal workers to disrupt communications and transport. For the peasantry, opportunities only presented themselves in 1943.

As people discovered in the Resistance an outlet for their desire to act, they also offered it new forms of action: the needs of the Resistance also developed in relation to the sociology of the Resistance. Resistance was a constant process of self-creation. Sabotage and terror attacks on Germans and collaborators became increasingly common. Abetz counted 3,800 sabotage operations between January and September 1943.[13] In Marseilles, there were four 'terrorist' actions in January 1943, eight in February, twenty-one in April, nineteen in November. These included several assassinations: of a police commissioner on 22 March 1943; a German soldier on 29 March; the head of the Milice of the *département* on 24 April; two *miliciens* on 29 May. In Britanny, sabotage and terror attacks increased sixfold between July and December. In the Haute-Saône, there were ten such actions in August 1943, twenty-two in September, sixty-four in October (including five assassinations); seventy-four in November (four assassinations).[14] Such actions were no longer carried out only by the Communist FTP, but also by the *corps francs* of the non-Communist movements which had moved beyond publicity stunts.

This radicalization of Resistance affected even a movement like Défense de la France which had originally privileged the idea of spiritual resistance. The

---

[12] F. Marcot, 'Les Paysans et la Résistance: Problèmes d'une approche sociologique', in Sainclivier and Bougeard (eds.), *Enjeux stratégiques*, 245–55: 250.

[13] Azéma, *De Munich à la Libération*, 254.

[14] Kitson, 'Marseilles Police', 166–7; Jankowski, *Communism and Collaboration*, 96; J.-C. Grandhay, 'Le Maquis haut-saônais dans son environnement social', in Marcot (ed.), *La Résistance: Lutte armée et maquis*, 279–89: 282.

Catholic convictions of its leaders made them suspicious of violence. But in November 1942 the movement's newspaper declared that everyone's duty was to bear arms; a year later, it approved FTP assassinations of individuals; and in March 1944, Viannay wrote an article entitled 'The Duty to Kill' (which did cause some dissent within the movement):

> Kill the German to purify our territory, kill him because he kills our people . . . Kill those who denounce, those who have aided the enemy . . . Kill the police-man who has in any way contributed to the arrest of patriots . . . Kill the *miliciens*, exterminate them . . . strike them down like mad dogs . . . destroy them as you would vermin.[15]

As violent action became more important in the Resistance, words became less so. People no longer needed to be persuaded. In the Var, propaganda took up three-quarters of resistance activity before November 1942, and 38 per cent after it.[16] From the middle of 1943, Libération-Nord, whose newspaper had appeared regularly since December 1940, put more and more emphasis on military action. The newspaper, which had helped recruit members in 1941–2, now became more of an information sheet for people who were already members.[17] The circulation of *Défense de la France* continued to expand, but there was a change in the relationship between the newspaper and its readers. In 1941–2, the production of the newspaper had involved finding people to distribute it; in 1943, the production of the newspaper was unable to keep up with the demand from people eager to distribute it.[18]

The relative importance of propaganda may have diminished, but in absolute terms the clandestine press continued to expand. It acquired a real presence in French society. The diary of Henri Drouot, which barely registered the existence of the resistance press in 1942, is full of references to it in 1943. In August he noted that resistance newspapers circulated easily and in large numbers. He mentions seven titles by name.[19] The Bibliothèque nationale catalogue of resistance publications, which is not exhaustive, lists 1,015 titles for the Occupation as a whole (not all existing at one time). The publication figures of some papers became enormous:

Libération-Sud
  December 1942–July 1943: 60,000–100,000
  July 1943–March 1944: 120,000–150,000
  March 1943–August 1944: 120,000–200,000

---

[15] Wieviorka, 'Défense de la France et la lutte armée', in Marcot (ed.), *La Résistance: Lutte armée et maquis*, 97–105. See also *Combat* in Aug. 1943: 'For a long time we have given counsels of caution . . . Caution not fear. The hour of total resistance is now upon us', cited by Marcot, 'Résistance et population', 126.
[16] Guillon, 'La Résistance dans le Var', 355.
[17] Aglan, 'Le Mouvement Libération-Nord', 151–2.
[18] Wieviorka, *Une certaine idée*, 106–8.   [19] Drouot, *Notes d'un Dijonnais*, 686.

Franc-Tireur
 January 1943: 50,000
 September 1943: 100,000
 August 1944: 150,000
Combat
 1942: 10,000
 November 1943: 50,000
 1944: 100,000–200,000
Défense de la France
 1943: 100,000–250,000
 January 1944: 450,000
Cahiers du témoignage chrétien
 July 1943: 75,000
 September 1943: 80,000
 December 1943: 100,000[20]

The Disintegration of Vichy

The growth of the Resistance was accelerated by the introduction of STO in February 1943. STO not only helped the Resistance win new recruits, it also discredited Vichy even among its hard-core supporters. The regime could no longer convincingly claim to be protecting the population and guaranteeing order and justice. Traditionally law-abiding citizens were now ready to help young people evading the labour draft (*réfractaires*) who seemed to have natural justice on their side. Doctors forged medical certificates; mayors resigned or pursued a tactic of non-cooperation. The STO had become, in Kedward's words, a 'dissolvent of Vichy authority'.[21]

The law was flouted so blatantly that Vichy came to look ridiculous. At the town of Mende, in May 1943, eighty-three people were supposed to turn up for the labour draft, but only seventeen did so; the bus transporting them broke down, allowing all but two passengers to disappear; on arrival at the destination, the last two escaped as well.[22] After Bichelonne's agreement with Speer in September, Laval announced that there would be no more departures for Germany that year. He offered to amnesty *réfractaires* who were ready to regularize their position. But STO had already had turned law-abiding citizens into outlaws, and it was too late to win back their allegiance. France in 1943 had become a 'society in resistance', which is not quite the same as saying that it was a 'society of resisters'.

---

[20] Douzou, *La Désobéissance*, 165; Veillon, *Le Franc-Tireur*, 97; Michel et Granet, *Combat*, 140–1; Wieviorka, *Une certaine idée*, 104; Bédarida, *Les Armes de l'esprit*, 288–9.
[21] *In Search of the Maquis*, 41.
[22] Id., 'The Maquis and the Culture of the Outlaw', in id. and Austin, *Vichy France and the Resistance*, 232–51: 243.

The Vichy State crumbled away at the top and the bottom. Public servants were drawn into NAP, the organization which infiltrated the administration. It had six sections: telecommunications, the police, the prefectoral administration (vital to forge papers), the ministry of supply (vital to obtain ration cards), electricity, the railways (so important that it eventually became an entirely autonomous organization: Résistance-Fer). There was also Super-NAP which recruited amongst the administrative elite. In the summer of 1943, NAP was extended to the North, although in fact many of the Northern movements already had their own infiltration services (OCM in the higher administration, Libération-Nord and the FN in the police).[23] The numbers in NAP were not huge, perhaps a total of about 1,500, but for security reasons the Resistance did not want the numbers to be too large. The quality of the recruits, who included a member of Pétain's *cabinet* and of Laval's, was more important than the quantity. Those formally involved in NAP were only the tip of the iceberg of public employees considered favourable to the Resistance.[24] In the Var, in the first half of 1943, NAP counted six 'resisters' and ten 'lukewarm friends [*amis mous*]' among the twenty-four magistrates of Draguignan and Toulon; and eighty-one 'friends' and thirty-five 'enemies' in the Toulon police. In the prefecture of Creuse, in December 1943, twenty-nine employees were described as 'good', thirty as 'neutral', and three as 'doubtful'.[25]

The increasing volume of resistance propaganda directed towards the police also found a receptive audience. Tracking down *réfractaires* who were protected by the complicity of the communities around them was a thankless task. In many cases, the police were themselves sympathetic to the *réfractaires*.[26] The extension of the Bousquet-Oberg agreement to the South in April 1943 caused problems of conscience for police officers who, unlike their Northern colleagues, had no previous experience of working with the Germans. In March 1943, a Communist, Jacques Cardonne, was arrested in Marseilles for attempting to sabotage a train. The Germans asked for him to be handed over, but the French authorities temporized, claiming that he had targeted the French railways not German soldiers. In the end, the French had to back down, but the police chief reported that this had caused dismay among some of his employees. One police commissioner did resign. In June 1943, a specialized resistance network, Ajax, was founded within the police. It passed on information, provided false identity papers, and warned the targets of potential raids. By September 1943, the prefect in Marseilles estimated 90 per cent of the city's police to be loyal to the underground Socialist Party. At the end of the year, Bousquet felt that even the GMR, which Vichy itself had created, could no longer be relied upon.[27]

Vichy not only suffered the defection of its public servants but even of those people who staffed institutions closely associated with the National Revolu-

[23] Baruch, *Servir l'État*, 493–7.   [24] Ibid. 511–13.
[25] Guillon, 'La Résistance dans le Var', 301; Baruch, *Servir l'État*, 508–9.
[26] Kedward, *In Search of the Maquis*, 58–9.   [27] Kitson, 'Marseilles Police', 172–88.

tion—such as Uriage, the Compagnons, and the Chantiers de la jeunesse. The loyalty of the Chantiers was severely tested by the introduction of STO. The Germans insisted that when members of the Chantiers reached the end of their period of service, they should immediately be sent to work in Germany. De la Porte du Theil, head of the Chantiers, felt compelled to accept, with great reluctance, fearing that otherwise the Chantiers would be closed down. The first draft of former Chantier members left for Germany in May 1943. The consequences were predictable. Many young men now decided to escape the Chantiers, often with the complicity of the staff. All this increased the mood of disaffection, demoralization, and indiscipline which had long been evident in the Chantier camps. De la Porte du Theil commented: 'the French State is bordering on total collapse. If we do not check its downhill course, we shall be lost.' He was himself arrested and deported to Germany in January 1944. This proved the death knell to whatever residual loyalty the Chantiers staff felt towards Vichy.[28]

Even that bastion of conservatism the Académie française began to distance itself from the regime. One sign was the election of Georges Duhamel to be its perpetual secretary in 1942; another was the bestowal of its annual literary prize on the writer Jean Schlumberger, a founder of the *NRF* who had refused to have anything to do with it under Drieu's editorship. For the prudent members of the Académie, this was certainly equivalent to an act of resistance.[29] Of all the institutions supporting Vichy, none found find it harder to break with the regime than the Church. In March 1943, Cardinal Liénart of Lille (who had remained silent about the fate of the Jews) declared that it was not a duty for a Christian to submit to STO. This position was officially adopted by the ACA in April. But the Church did not go as far as to advise disobedience, and in October 1943 it condemned the 'theologians without mandate' of Témoignage chrétien, who were doing so. In February 1944, the Church condemned the extension of STO to married women, because of the effect this would have on families, but the same declaration also attacked 'terrorism', which was the word used by Vichy to describe the Resistance.[30] As Church leaders inched towards a more hostile stance, always stopping short of condemnation, they became less and less representative of the lower clergy or the Catholic laity. In the Catholic Haute-Savoie, the parish clergy actively helped *réfractaires*.[31] The strongest resistance to STO came from the Catholic Action (ACJF) youth organizations whose members were the most directly affected by it. At a meeting at Avignon in March 1943, the ACJF protested against STO. The Bishop of Avignon who attended and spoke in favour of the regime was greeted with glacial silence. In November, the ACJF moved from dissidence to resistance by creating the Équipes chrétiennes

[28] Halls, *Youth of Vichy France*, 386–94.   [29] Sapiro, *La Guerre des écrivains*, 304–15.
[30] Duquesne, *Les Catholiques*, 301–16, 335–8.
[31] Kedward, *In Search of the Maquis*, 401; Abrahams, 'Haute-Savoie at War', 166–7.

to bring together those of its members who had been acting on an individual basis in different resistance movements.[32]

Vichy was powerless to staunch the haemorrhaging of its support. The public now saw little of Pétain who came to seem almost irrelevant: in 1941, he had made forty public declarations, in 1942 thirty-seven, in 1943 only eleven. People no longer talked about Pétain in their letters: of 90,000 letters read in the Var by the censors in December 1943 and January 1944, only 151 mentioned him, a quarter in critical terms.[33] Pétain's age was often commented upon. If he inspired any sentiment, it was pity rather than hatred.[34] A planned visit to the Auvergne in August 1943 was cancelled, despite preparatory fanfares, because it was felt Pétain was unlikely to be accorded a sufficiently enthusiastic reception.[35]

The Legion of Veterans meetings were sparsely attended and it now confined itself largely to charitable work. Laval's attempt win back support through a cosmetic republicanization of Vichy's institutions had no impact: the new *conseils départementaux* were hardly noticed.[36] In the Hérault, the reports on public opinion in the summer of 1943 were 'little more than a catalogue of the issues which were driving the public further and further from the regime'.[37] One Propaganda Delegate noted in September 1943: 'the population hangs upon every word of the radio, believes every false rumour and awaits with impatience the landing of the Anglo-Americans. As for the young they prefer anything to going to work in Germany. This opinion is well established and all efforts to modify it are absolutely fruitless.'[38]

The Maquis

Against this background, it was easy for *réfractaires* to find help. Their first objective was to secure a hiding place. Some took refuge in the countryside, hiding out with relatives, or in deserted farm buildings and forestry camps in the mountains. It was in the mountains that the first Maquis camps were formed, the word *maquis* coming from the local word for the scrubland countryside of Corsica. By April the term *maquisard* was in general use. At first, many who went into the hills were soon driven down again for lack of food or protective clothing. Once the MUR had set up the SNM in April to provide logistical support, the Maquis became less of a leap into the unknown. Even so, most *réfractaires* did not join any Maquis group. Instead they chose individual forms

[32] Duquesne, *Les Catholiques*, 316–26, 349–50.
[33] Guillon, 'La Résistance dans le Var', 309.
[34] Laborie, *Résistants*, 251.
[35] E. Martres, *Le Cantal de 1939 à 1945: Les Troupes allemandes à travers le massif central* (Courdon d'Auvergne, 1994), 164–5.
[36] Guillon, 'La Résistance dans le Var', 304–5.
[37] Austin, 'Propaganda and Public Opinion', 474.
[38] Marcot, 'Résistance et population', 81.

of escape, using personal connections. Of the 2,000 *réfractaires* in the Isère, only about 300–400 were in Maquis groups; in Tarn, only 19 per cent; in the Doubs, 5 per cent. In the three Britanny *départements* of Ille-et-Vilaine, Côtes-du-Nord, and Morbihan, almost 10,000 *réfractaires* took refuge in the summer of 1943 on thousands of scattered farms; the Maquis was almost non-existent at this stage.[39]

The number of *réfractaires* swelled enormously during the summer of 1943. In Ariège, *réfractaires* represented only 13 per cent of those liable for STO in March but 81 per cent by July; in the Lot, 11 per cent in March, 95 per cent in July. Churchill's speeches encouraged *réfractaires* to believe that an Allied landing was imminent. But with the onset of winter—the greatest enemy of the Maquis—and no sign of the Allies, many took advantage of the amnesty. Almost two-thirds of the 2,844 *réfractaires* in the Alpes-Maritimes had returned to normal society by April 1944.[40] There was a constant process of coming and going, but overall numbers certainly declined from the autumn.

In October 1943, the SNM estimated the numbers of *maquisards* in the Southern Zone at approximately 15,000. But just as not all *réfractaires* were *maquisards*, so not all *maquisards* were 'resisters'. Hiding was not the same as fighting. The first Maquis camps were mostly not intended as bases for military operations: there were both *maquis-refuges* and *maquis-combats*.[41] The myth of the fighting Maquis was first popularized by Schumann's BBC broadcast in March 1943, claiming that there was a 'rising in the Haute-Savoie'.[42] Such a rising did not yet exist, but in the popular imagination the idea of it transformed the *maquisard* from passive fugitive to activist hero. The heroic image was further elaborated in a series of directives issued by the SMN in the summer. Those submitting to the 'tough discipline of the Maquis' were summoned to renounce links with friends and family until the end of the war. They were depicted as rugged fighters of the countryside, pure and uncorrupted by the city: 'the men of the Maquis are the elite of the country'.[43]

What military support could the Maquis offer the Resistance? The answer to this question became caught up in the debate between advocates of immediate action and advocates of a waiting strategy. Moulin had feared that the Maquis might upset the careful planning of the AS. His resolution of this dilemma was to accept the so-called Montagnards Plan which envisaged the creation of a sort of Resistance fortress on the Vercors plateau, in the Alps. The objective was to concentrate large numbers of men able to attack the Germans at the opportune

[39] Rousso, 'Où en est l'histoire de la Résistance', in *Études sur la France de 1939 à nos jours*, 122; Kedward, 'STO et Maquis', in Azéma and Bédarida (eds.), *La France des années noires*, ii. 270–94: 281; C. Bougeard, 'Les Maquis de Bretagne dans leur environnement social', in Marcot (ed.), *La Résistance: Lutte armée et maquis*, 291–301: 292.

[40] P. Mermet, 'Du service du travail obligatoire au maquis', in Institut d'Histoire des Conflits Contemporains (IHCC) (ed.), *Colloque sur le maquis* (1986), 59–64: 60.

[41] Kedward, 'STO et Maquis', 280–3.

[42] J.-L. Crémieux-Brilhac, *Les Voix de la liberté; Ici Londres 1940–1944* (1975), 115–16.

[43] Kedward, *In Search of the Maquis*, 25–35; Noguères, *Histoire de la Résistance*, iii. 657–70.

moment. This offered the Maquis a military role which slotted into the long-term strategy of the AS. The SNM, on the other hand, favoured immediate Maquis operations. But from the autumn, when the likelihood of an imminent Allied landing receded, it became more cautious, and gradually lost its autonomy to the AS.[44] As for the Communists, their opposition to *attentisme* made them initially suspicious of the Maquis, fearing it would drain the towns of potential fighters and immobilize them in the countryside. They talked derisively of 'Maquis camping'.[45] When the FTP formed its first Maquis groups it designated them 'combat groups', thereby making no distinction, apart from location, between them and its town-based groups. Both were supposedly partisan fighters committed to immediate action.[46]

Sometimes there were conflicts between FTP and AS Maquis. In the Haute-Savoie, a member of the AS reported an FTP Maquis to the police; in Tulle, in March 1944, when the FTP Maquis freed resisters from the town prison, two of the prisoners gave themselves up because their rescuers had been Communists.[47] Such incidents were exceptional, and when rivalries did exist, they had little to do with ideology. Proximity or chance usually determined an individual's choice of group. Some groups were run by charismatic leaders who were a law unto themselves, and inspired fierce personal loyalty. In the Lot, the leader of the Maquis was a trade unionist called Jean-Jacques Chapou, who was admired on all sides. Suddenly, in February 1944, he announced that he was changing his allegiance from the AS to the FTP, but his groups remained loyal to him. His Maquis remained the same except for its name.[48] The Limousin Maquis of the Communist Georges Guingouin was commonly known as 'Guingouin's Maquis'.[49] Some Maquis leaders were flamboyant and romantic figures, like the leader in the Drôme who wore a black cape embroidered with a coat of arms and his resistance pseudonym, L'Hermine.[50] As Vichy's authority disintegrated, there was a risk that parts of the countryside would break up into warring fiefdoms.

The theoretical debates over strategy had little relevance to the problems facing most *maquisards*. Immediate military action was not feasible because they lacked arms, but total inactivity made no sense either. Quite apart from the need to stave off boredom, Maquis groups were forced to prey on the local

[44] F. Marcot, 'Les Maquis dans la Résistance', in IHCC (ed.), *Colloque sur les maquis*, 13–31: 36; id., 'Le Service national maquis' in id. (ed.), *La Résistance: Lutte armée et maquis*, 211–23: 218–20.

[45] Id., 'Villes et pouvoirs de commandement' in Douzou et al. (eds.), *La Résistance: Villes*, 215–28: 225.

[46] Kedward, *In Search of the Maquis*, 36–7; R. Bourderon, 'Les Maquis FTP', in IHCC (ed.), *Colloque sur le maquis*, 87–98.

[47] Abrahams, 'Haute-Savoie at War', 184; P. Trouillé, *Journal d'un préfet pendant l'Occupation* (1965), 9.

[48] Laborie, *Résistants, Vichyssois*, 288–91; Kedward, *In Search of the Maquis*, 128–30.

[49] S. Farmer, 'The Communist Resistance in the Haute-Vienne', *FHS* 14/1 (1985),

[50] A. Funk, *Hidden Ally: The French Resistance, Special Operations and the Landings in Southern France* (New York, 1992), 18.

countryside in order to feed and clothe themselves. It was a short step from this kind of activity to small acts of sabotage or punitive acts against collaborators. Maquis leaders developed guerrilla tactics to maximize their limited resources and exploit the local terrain. No one did this more effectively than the former army officer Henri Romans-Petit, leader of the AS Maquis in the Ain. Organizing a network of camps in the densely forested hills, he taught his Maquis to be highly mobile in order to convey an impression of strength: unexpected small-scale raids were followed by a rapid retreat.[51]

Despite the inventiveness of leaders like Romans-Petit, the military contribution of the Maquis was infinitesimal in 1943. Maquis military actions were less important than those carried out by the Groupes francs of the MUR, by Résistance-Fer, and by the urban FTP forces. In the Côtes du Nord, where the number of resistance attacks increased from 70 in the first half of the year to 182 in the second half, there was as yet no Maquis in existence. The operations were carried out by FTP groups, whose members then dispersed and returned to their families and jobs. Only later, when the police had discovered their identities, did they form into a Maquis.[52] Most Maquis actions were about survival: raids on Chantiers de jeunesse to seize provisions, thefts of ration cards from town halls. Neither Vichy nor the Germans viewed the Maquis as a military threat at this stage. When General Jodl provided Himmler with a summary of the military situation facing the Germans in November 1943, the only guerrilla groups he saw fit to mention were the Yugoslav partisans.[53] Nonetheless, having lost faith in the Vichy police, the Germans did start to launch direct attacks on Maquis camps from the autumn: in the Corrèze (September 1943), on Mont Ventoux (October), and in the Cantal (January 1944).

Although the Maquis had little military significance, it did contribute to undermining Vichy's authority in the countryside. The *maquisards* assumed the romantic aura of bandit heroes, outlawed and persecuted by an unjust society, descending periodically into the towns to dispense a 'people's justice'. One such occasion was the 'occupation' of the little town of Oyonnax in the Jura by the Ain Maquis, on 11 November 1943. Three hundred *maquisards*, dressed in uniforms, arrived in the town at midday. Watched by an enthusiastic crowd, they paraded to the war memorial, deposited a wreath, and then slipped back into the countryside. The operation, which had been meticulously planned by Romans-Petit, was publicized by the clandestine press throughout France, and by de Gaulle on the radio.[54]

There were no Germans in Oyonnax, but this did not matter. The objective

---

[51] G. Goupil, 'Débats stratégiques autour des maquis de l'Ain', in Marcot (ed.), *La Résistance: Lutte armée et maquis*, 235–47; Kedward, *In Search of the Maquis*, 61, 50.

[52] C. Bougeard, 'Les Maquis de Bretagne', in Marcot (ed.), *La Résistance: Lutte armée et maquis*, 291–2.

[53] E. Martres, 'Points de vue allemands sur résistance et maquis', in Marcot (ed.), *La Résistance: Lutte armée et maquis*, 193–210: 195–7.

[54] Kedward, *In Search of the Maquis*, 65–6. There were other such 'descents' e.g. at Bagnac and at Marcilhac-sur-Cele in the Lot: see Laborie, *Résistants, Vichyssois*, 297.

of the operation was to demonstrate symbolically the power and discipline of the Maquis, staking a claim to supplant Vichy's legitimacy in the countryside. When the *maquisards* robbed shops they sometimes provided receipts to show that these were not thefts, but requisitions, even taxes, carried out in the name of the future Republic.[55] In the Lot, the theft of ration cards became almost a routine: secretaries at the town halls waited at the end of each month for them to occur. The Maquis imposed its authority over the local countryside, fixing prices for the black market: Guingouin posted up lists of approved prices which he signed 'Prefect of the Maquis'. Sometimes individuals were 'fined' for making excessive profits on the black market. In the Cévennes, a Maquis 'police' punished acts of pillage, and warned the population to beware of 'false' *maquisards.*[56]

The Peasantry and the Resistance

The descent into Oyonnax was a symbolic representation of the extent to which the Resistance had moved from town to countryside. In the Var, the Resistance initially spread up the coastline and along railway lines; in 1943, it moved into the rural hinterland. This does not mean that many peasants joined the Maquis. Peasant *réfractaires* could usually fall back on their own resources to find refuge in the countryside. The Maquis was largely made up of urban workers: in the Aude, the peasantry accounted for half the *réfractaires* and only 6 per cent of the *maquisards.*[57] But the Maquis brought the Resistance into contact with a peasant population that had so far largely ignored its existence. This was no longer possible. As the mayor of one village said: 'they were there in our countryside face to face with us . . . We could not be neutral.'[58]

The peasantry's increasing disaffection from Vichy changed into active complicity with the Resistance.[59] Until 1943 resisters, largely urban-based, had paid little attention to the peasantry. In the Franche-Comté, none of the resistance tracts produced in 1941, and only 4 per cent of those produced in 1942, addressed the peasantry.[60] Resisters were suspicious of a group so assiduously courted by the regime: one OCM *cahier* denounced the egotism of the 'hard and wily' peasants.[61] The 'ruralization' of the Resistance transformed such attitudes: in 1943, 43 per cent of Resistance tracts in the Franche-Comté addressed the peasantry.

---

[55] Bougeard, 'Les Maquis de Bretagne', 297–8; J. Sweets, 'Clermont-Ferrand et les Maquis', in Marcot (ed.), *La Résistance: Lutte armée et maquis*, 315–25: 317.

[56] Kedward, *In Search of the Maquis*, 85, 96; G. Guingouin, *Quatre années de lutte sur le sol limousin* (1991), 106; Wieviorka, *Une certaine idée*, 298–9; Kedward, 'Culture of the Outlaw', 246.

[57] Mermet, 'Du service obligatoire au maquis', 61.

[58] Cited in Marcot, 'Les Maquis dans la Résistance', 24.

[59] H. R. Kedward, 'Le Monde rural face au maquis', in Marcot (ed.), *La Résistance: Lutte armée et maquis*, 339–50: 344.

[60] Marcot, 'Les Paysans et la Résistance', 250.

[61] Steel, *Littératures de l'ombre*, 104.

This propaganda did not fall on deaf ears. Whereas the demonstrations of 14 July 1942—the first important expression of collective opposition to Vichy—had mainly taken place in towns, in July 1943 they occurred in villages as well.[62]

The peasantry, however, never played a large role in the organized Resistance. In the two Normandy *départements* of the Manche and Calvados, the peasantry comprised 35 per cent of the population, but they only received 10 per cent of CVR cards after the Liberation.[63] The picture was the same throughout France. In the spring of 1944, there were members of organized resistance movements in only a third of villages in the Var.[64] If one adopts a less restrictive definition of Resistance, however, the contribution of the peasantry seems immeasurably larger. Peasants provided the infrastructure on which the Maquis depended: they supplied food and clothing; they indicated hiding places; they passed on local knowledge; they warned against denunciations. The peasants often talked about 'nos maquis' with pride.[65] Léon Werth, whose jaundiced opinions of the Jura peasantry in 1941–2 have been quoted above, had changed his view by 1943:

> The peasants' vision of the Maquis is too strong to be affected by the German or Hitlero-Vichyite propaganda. One could say without exaggeration that the Maquis for them is France, is their liberty (in the most material sense of the word). Whatever the Maquis is, it is theirs. If they talk about it, it is with affection.[66]

It would be as wrong, however, to represent the peasantry as united behind the Resistance in 1943–4 as to represent it as united behind Vichy in 1941–2. The relationship between the peasantry and the Resistance was ambivalent, increasingly so as time went on. It became harder to feel sympathy for young men fleeing STO once they had started stealing crops or inviting German reprisals. The peasantry of the Limousin must have had mixed feelings when Guingouin's Maquis destroyed baling machines to prevent the Germans requisitioning hay.[67] At a local level, the Maquis could degenerate into an 'occupation' as irksome as the German one. Relations between the local population and the Resistance became even more strained in the winter when *maquisards* who had taken refuge in mountain chalets had to move closer to areas of habitation and prey on them for survival.

Government propaganda exploited such tensions by depicting the *maquisards* as criminals. In one valley of the Haute-Savoie, sympathy for the Maquis was reported to be 'in serious decline' as early as July 1943. The peasantry distinguished between local *réfractaires* and 'terrorists from outside'.[68] *Instituteurs*, who were active in many Maquis groups (Guingouin was one), used their position as

---

[62] Marcot, 'Les Paysans et la Résistance', 251.
[63] Boivin and Quellien, 'La Résistance en Basse-Normandie', 163–6.
[64] Guillon, 'La Résistance dans le Var', 328.   [65] Kedward, *In Search of the Maquis*, 88.
[66] *Déposition*, 553.   [67] Farmer, 'Communist Resistance in the Haute-Vienne', 98–9.
[68] Abrahams, 'Haute-Savoie at War', 194.

local figures of authority to act as intermediaries with the peasantry. Sometimes this role was played by priests. Where intermediaries did not exist, it was vital for Maquis leaders to stamp out cases of criminality which could lose them popular sympathy. In the Morbihan, the Resistance executed about twenty people for supposed acts of banditry.[69]

The importance of local support can be shown by the fate of a small Maquis in the Haute-Saône, in October 1943. Made up of fifteen young men (the average age was 20), the group alienated the local population by its uncontrolled behaviour. This included killing a cheese seller who refused to hand over his produce, and killing a young girl who had a baby by a German soldier. As a result, the local population was only too ready to help the authorities, and the culprits were quickly arrested. The group had lasted about forty days. The prefect reported:

> When the terrorist wave started it found a sympathetic ear among people misled by foreign propaganda . . . But the pillage of farms which could have had no political motive discredited terrorism in the countryside . . . Thus the police were able to obtain information necessary to carry out their duty, whereas, at the end of September, after each incident, they met with total silence.[70]

The relationship between the Maquis and the rural population also reflected local political traditions. In conservative and Catholic Aveyron—the 'Britanny of the Midi'—where the isolated peasantry viewed outsiders with suspicion, resistance was slow to emerge. Here the peasants' formal participation in the Resistance was exceptionally low—they held 7.5 per cent of CVR cards although comprising 56 per cent of the population—and the news of the Allied landings in 1944 aroused alarm more than hope. Quite different was the Var with its traditions of sociability and its long-standing Republicanism. In the small town of Salernes the whole community turned out in September 1943 for the funeral of a local *maquisard*; cafés closed and the local informer for the Germans described the occasion as resembling a state funeral.[71] In the Lozère there was a marked difference between the attitude of the Catholic north of the *département*, where the local clergy were obsessed with communism, and the Protestant Cévennes which displayed the same solidarity towards *maquisards* as towards the Jews. The prefect noted that tracking down resisters was impossible: 'no local inhabitant, not even the local authorities, will give the slightest information'.[72]

The Cévennes may have been an extreme example, but there are few examples anywhere of Maquis groups being denounced to the police. In general, the peasantry's attitude towards the Maquis was one of solidarity tempered by prudence, respect tempered by apprehension. Whether one stresses the prudence or

---

[69] Kedward, *In Search of the Maquis*, 102–4; Bougeard, 'Les Maquis de Bretagne', 297.

[70] Grandhay, 'Le Maquis haut-saônais', 279–85.

[71] C. Font, 'Les Paysans et la Résistance, le modèle aveyronnais', in Sainclivier and Bougeard (eds.), *Enjeux stratégiques*, 175–89; Guillon, 'La Résistance dans le Var', 326.

[72] P. Cabanel, 'L'Église, les paysans et la Résistance', in Sainclivier and Bougeard (eds.), *Enjeux stratégiques*, 221–31.

the solidarity, there is no doubt that the Maquis could not have survived without the peasantry. In that sense, the small number of peasants 'officially' registered in the Resistance underestimates their contribution to it.

Women in the Resistance

The participation of women in the Resistance is also grossly under-represented in the official figures. Of the 1,036 people decorated with the Order of the Liberation—very much a Free French decoration—6 were women. There is no breakdown of the total distribution of CVR cards between men and women, but figures from *départements* where such a calculation has been made, suggest that on average about 11 per cent of cards were held by women. The formal participation of women in different movements and networks shows some variation:

Libération-Sud	12 per cent
Franc-Tireur	10 per cent
Témoignage chrétien	24 per cent
Défense de la France	17 per cent
Jade-Fitzroy	14 per cent
Zéro-France	14 per cent

The higher female participation in Défense de la France and Témoignage chrétien probably reflects their Catholic nature, and the lower one in Franc-Tireur its recruitment among Radicals and Freemasons.[73]

Just as women are under-represented in the official statistics of the Resistance, so also were they not a target of the first Resistance propaganda. For many early resisters, it was the sight of women with Germans which crystallized their decision to act.[74] When Jean Texcier drafted his *Conseils à l'occupé* (it was not the 'occupée') in August 1940, he addressed himself to men. He denounced women who consorted with Germans, and exhorted men witnessing such behaviour to administer a salutary whipping: 'look her up and down, locate the tender spot and savour your pleasure in advance'.[75] Texcier did not think to advise women themselves to avoid contact with Germans. In much Resistance fiction, women are frequently depicted as treacherous or frivolous. Even when portrayed favourably, their contribution to Resistance is conceived in passive terms. In *Le Silence de la mer*, the narrator's niece is a figure of nobility, but her resistance consists of sewing in a corner and preserving an attitude of dignified silence. In Aragon's resistance poem *La Rose et le réséda*, France is depicted as a beautiful female prisoner who will be rescued by a chivalric male. The moral in both cases is the same: show dignity and wait on events.[76]

---

[73] C. Andrieu, 'Les Résistantes, perspectives de recherche', *MS* 180 (1987), 69–96: 73–5.
[74] Pineau, *La Simple Vérité*, 72; Frenay, *La Nuit finira*, 80.
[75] Texcier, *Écrits dans la nuit*, 11–12, 20.   [76] Steel, *Littératures de l'ombre*, 150–3.

In fact, from the beginning women were prominent both in opposition to Vichy—notably in food demonstrations—and in the formal Resistance. Women were among the founding members of Franc-Tireur, the Musée de l'homme group (Germaine Tillion), Défense de la France (Helène Viannay), Libération-Sud (Lucie Aubrac), and Combat (Bertie Albrecht). Madeleine Fourcade, who headed the Noah's Ark network, had 3,000 agents under her command. Nonetheless, women did not usually rise to these heights. Among the ninety-two leading members of Libération-Sud, there were twenty women (20 per cent)—a higher proportion than in other movements for which such figures are available—and only two of these held top positions.[77]

Women had to overcome male reservations about their suitability for Resistance work. One member of Défense de la France was 'almost scandalized to find so many women: war is not for women'.[78] Even Helène Mordkovitch, one of the founders of Défense de la France with Philippe Viannay (whom she married in 1942), was reticent about imposing herself. Unlike Viannay, she never harboured any illusions about Pétain, but it never occurred to her, or to him, that her views on politics should be taken into account on the newspaper, which remained a male preserve. It took her husband two years to reach views she had held from the start.[79] Reticence in putting themselves forward after the Liberation probably explains why women held so few CVR cards.

Some women overcame male prejudice by converting themselves almost into honorary men. Fourcade hid from British Intelligence the fact she was a woman. One woman wrote of her entry into the Resistance: 'we embarked on our life as men'.[80] Juliette Plissonnier, a regional leader of the Communist Resistance, sometimes encountered men who were startled to find a woman in such a position. On one occasion, a male resister who expressed his surprise by uttering the words 'What! A woman here?', provoked the response from another male resister present: 'she's not a woman, she's the boss'.[81] Lucie Aubrac, however, writes about her resistance experience as inseparable from her femininity. She recounts her life as 'resister, wife, and mother'. It was during her second pregnancy in 1943 that she masterminded an operation to rescue her husband from prison (something she had already done twice before). The preparation for this involved her playing the role of innocent fiancée on a visit to the Gestapo chief Klaus Barbie.[82] Aubrac was not unusual in being both a mother and a resister. Marie-Madeleine Fourcade was mother of two children; Margueritte Gonnet, a departmental head of Libération-Sud, was a mother of eight and pregnant with a ninth baby which was lost in prison.[83] The information available from CVR cards is that, whereas the age group 15 to 25 provided the highest proportion of male resisters, among

---

[77] Andrieu, 'Les Résistantes', 91, 94; Douzou, *La Désobéissance*, 149.

[78] Wieviorka, *Une certaine idée*, 74.   [79] Ibid. 45–6.

[80] Andrieu, 'Les Résistantes', 70.

[81] P. Schwartz, ' "Partisanes" and Gender Politics in Vichy France', *FHS* 16/1 (1989), 126–51: 136.

[82] L. Aubrac, *Ils partiront dans l'ivresse: Lyon, mai 1943, Londres, février 44* (1984).

[83] Andrieu, 'Les Résistantes', 80–1; Guillon, 'La Résistance dans le Var', 341–3.

women there was no significant age differentiation (apart from a decline after the age of 50).

The functions performed by the few women Resistance leaders were no different from those performed by men. But lower down the scale some resistance tasks came to be considered as the speciality of women. Women ran the Resistance social-service sections which had originally been the brainchild of Bertie Albrecht in Combat. The 21-year-old Ségolène Manceron, who worked for the Social Service of Libération-Sud in 1942 insisted on being moved to another section, in protest against the assumption that women were good for nothing else.[84] In all Resistance movements, women acted as liaison agents—carrying instructions and arranging rendezvous—and as couriers of arms and supplies. Women could move around without exciting the same suspicion as men, flirt their way through security checks, and hide compromising material in shopping bags, 'pregnant' pouches, prams, even nappies. Often the identities of liaison agents are only known today through their Christian names or their code names—but they were the lifeblood of the Resistance.[85]

The activities of many women resisters were no less dangerous than those of men, even if less spectacular. History has remembered that, by the end of the war, Albert Camus was an editor of Combat. Less celebrated is the story of Jacqueline Bernard who effectively acted as the editorial secretary of Combat from its inception until her arrest in the spring of 1944. She was, in Frenay's phrase, the 'sinew' of the movement.[86] History has remembered the resistance exploits of André Malraux who spent most of the Occupation writing on the Côte d'Azur, joined the Maquis in March 1944, and ended the war as the flamboyant 'Colonel Berger' at the head of the Alsace-Lorraine Brigade. Less well known is the story of Malraux's estranged wife Clara who, although a Jew and mother of a young daughter, was involved in the most dangerous variety of Resistance work from the very beginning. Using her perfect German, she worked for a network which sounded out German soldiers who might be liable to desert, and then arranged false papers for them to do so. This went on until the funding of the network was stopped because its activities were judged too dangerous.[87]

Women also contributed to Resistance in more informal ways. As one woman recalled about her childhood in the Toulouse region:

My father was a resister and Communist . . . so he received a lot of men and women in the house. People might say that my mother was not a resister. But who got up in the morning to look after the resister who had to depart before dawn? Who mended the socks and washed the clothes of the resister while he was asleep? Who prepared the food he took away with him? Who received the police

[84] Douzou, La Désobéissance, 183.

[85] Michel and Granet, Combat, 173; Schwartz, ' "Partisanes" and Gender Politics', 131–2.

[86] M. Weitz, Sisters in the Resistance: How Women fought to free France 1940–1945 (New York, 1995), 70.

[87] I. de Courtivron, 'The Resistance of Clara Malraux', Contemporary French Civilization 18/1 (1994) 23–32.

when there was an alert? I think therefore that my mother resisted quite as much as my father.[88]

It could of course be argued that this was not a choice for resistance, merely the continuation of normal life which the context transformed into acts of resistance. But there is no reason to assume that this wider context was not perceived, and welcomed, by the women involved. Christian Pineau, who regularly took refuge with a family in Lyons, remembered that the mother of the household looked after all his needs. One night he came upon her ironing his clothes at two in the morning. When he reprimanded her for exhausting herself on his behalf, she replied: 'It is for France.'[89]

Often women in the household were highly exposed to danger while fielding the police to allow a resister the time to escape. It has been remarked that the image of the 'woman at the doorway' is a recurring image of the period.[90] There is a striking scene in *The Sorrow and the Pity* where two former peasant resisters— both male—are interviewed around a dinner table. A woman observes the scene from the doorway without ever crossing into the room although she intervenes three times in the discussion to set the record straight. By 1968, when the film was made, the doorway had receded into the background because it fitted less easily into dominant narratives of the Resistance; in 1943 it was very much to the fore.[91] This version of Resistance as an extension of running the home and protecting the household, went beyond the immediate family. Women provided much of the support structure on which the Maquis depended. Maquis groups were adopted by 'Godmothers', who provided food and medical help, and organized shelter. Odette Belot, a hotelier in Saint-Pons (Hérault), was known as the 'Patronne de la Résistance locale'.[92]

It was rare, however, for women to participate in the Maquis. Unlike Yugoslavia and Greece, women in France did not generally perform combat roles in the Resistance. When they did, like Madeleine Baudoin who carried out commando raids with the *corps francs* in Marseilles, it tended to be in the urban Resistance where resisters lived in 'normal' society. Here the presence of women was not unusual and even added an appearance of normality to the life of resisters. In the male community of the Maquis, however, women were seen as a complicating intrusion.[93] This was not only true of the Maquis. The leader of the Phalanx network was summoned to London in May 1944 because he was suspected of having affairs with his agents. One of his critics told the British: 'If

---

[88] Diamond, 'Women's Experience', 151.   [89] *La Simple Vérité*, 293.

[90] Kedward, *In Search of the Maquis*, 89.

[91] L. Douzou, 'La Résistance, une affaire d'hommes', in F. Rouquet and D. Voldman (eds.), *Identités féminines et violences politiques 1936–1946* (IHTP Cahier 31; 1995), 11–24.

[92] P. Schwartz, 'Redefining Resistance: Women's Activism in Wartime France', in M. Higonnet et al. (eds.), *Behind the Lines: Gender and the Two World Wars* (New Haven, 1987), 141–53: 146; Kedward, *In Search of the Maquis*, 93.

[93] Schwartz, ' "Partisanes" and Gender Politics', 139–45; ead., 'Women, Resistance and Communism', 196–9.

women must be used, then it is preferable to use older women . . . less likely to be a source of temptation to colleagues . . . Sentimental complications are always to be feared.'[94] In late 1943, there was an order for women to be phased out of the Maquis.[95] In short, if women did not fight much in the French Resistance, it was partly because men did not want them to.

Foreigners in the Resistance

If the participation of women in the Resistance was undervalued at the Liberation, the same was true of the participation of another category of resisters: foreigners and immigrants. The dominant rhetoric of the Resistance was patriotic.[96] Foreigners who settled in France were not keen to stress their foreignness after the war: for them, the Resistance was an initiation into Frenchness. On the other hand, many political refugees from Eastern Europe or Italy participated in the Resistance as part of the fight against fascism, returning to their own countries immediately after the Liberation. For these reasons, the role of foreigners in the Resistance was largely ignored at the Liberation—although as a proportion of their total number in France, the active involvement of foreigners in the Resistance was certainly greater than that of the French. Foreigners participated in most aspects of resistance, but they also had specific skills to offer. Political refugees who had been in the International Brigades provided much-needed combat experience in 1943–4. Refugees who spoke German were used to test out or undermine the morale of German soldiers. The Communists had a 'German Work' (TA) section entirely devoted to this purpose. It also ran a German language newspaper, *Der Soldat im Westen*, which spread defeatist propaganda.[97]

There were regional variations in the participation of immigrants in the Resistance, reflecting their distribution within the population as a whole. In the southeast, Italians predominated. After June 1940, Italians were much resented in the Italian Zone, for strutting around as if they were conquerors, and this did not initially facilitate contact with the Resistance. Despite such obstacles, 7 per cent of the officially counted resisters in the Alpes-Maritimes were foreigners, mainly Italian.[98] In the Nord, the main role was played by Poles who had two movements of their own: the Communist PKWN which had about 10,000 members by June 1944 and the non-Communist POWN which had about 8,000. Their

---

[94] Aglan, 'Le Mouvement Libération-Nord', 412–13.

[95] Schwartz, '"Partisanes" and Gender politics', 146–7.

[96] For an overview, see D. Peschanski, 'La Résistance immigrée', in Laborie and Guillon (eds.), *Mémoire et histoire*, 201–15.

[97] Courtois et al., *Le Sang de l'étranger*, 128–32.

[98] J.-M. Guillon, 'Italiens et Résistance dans le Sud-Est', in P. Milza and D. Peschanski (eds.), *Exils et migration: Italiens et Espagnols en France 1938–1946* (1994), 651–9; Guillon, 'Les Étrangers dans la Résistance provençale', *RHMC* 36 (1989), 658–71.

combined total represented about 4 per cent of the entire Polish population of France. The POWN had been founded in the Southern Zone in 1941 by Polish army officers loyal to the Polish government in London. In 1942, it spread to the Nord and built up a considerable working-class base in the mining basin, recruited through Polish community organizations. Although an agreement was signed with the French military resistance in 1944, the movement kept its distance from the French Resistance. Its ultimate objective was to free Poland: one of its tracts read 'All for Poland. Only for Poland.' The POWN carried out about 300 sabotage operations, the most successful being to cut the cables of a Vi launching ramp in August 1944.[99]

In the south-west, there were about 120,000–150,000 Spanish Republican refugees (quite apart from the 250,000 Spaniards already living in France).[100] They were among the earliest victims of the Vichy regime, liable to be forced into immigrant labour camps or sent to work in Germany. They were also suspected for their political sympathies: 8,000 Spaniards were deported to Mauthausen. For many Spaniards, resistance was a necessity as much as a choice. For two years, however, Spanish émigré groups were still riven by squabbles dating from the Spanish civil war. The turning point occurred in November 1942 when the Spanish Communist Party, like its French counterpart, converted to a unitary policy, forming its own version of the National Front (UNE). The Spanish Communists threw themselves into the new line with vigour. Up to 30 Spanish clandestine newspapers were produced in France under the aegis of the UNE. The Spanish Communists also formed a guerrilla unit, the XIV Corps, which had about 3,400 fighters in the south-west by June 1944. This represented a considerable local presence: in the Gers *département*, there were about 800 French FTP fighters and 520 Spanish *guérillas*. The XIV Corps was supposedly integrated into the FTP in the autumn of 1943, but this did not alter the fact that its ultimate objective was the liberation of Spain from Franco.

Although the Poles and Spaniards had their own organizations, many immigrants also participated in French resistance organizations. It was Poles who ran the important intelligence network R2, which was largely staffed by French agents; it was the Spaniard Francisco Ponzan who, as a member of the Pat O'Leary network, helped Jews, Allied aviators, and French resisters to cross over to Spain; it was a group of Spaniards, threatened with deportation to Germany in the spring of 1942, who were among the first *maquisards* in the Ardèche; it was German refugees in the Gard and Lozère, hiding in the forests, who joined

---

[99] *Revue du Nord*, 226 (1975), 397–474 is entirely devoted to the Poles in France during the Occupation.

[100] G. Dreyfus-Armand, 'Les Espagnols dans la Résistance: Incertitudes et spécificités', in Laborie and Guillon (eds.), *Histoire et mémoire*, 217–26; id. and D. Peschanski, 'Les Espagnols dans la Résistance', in Milza (eds.), *Exils et migrations*, 593–626; R. Trempé, 'Le Rôle des Étrangers: MOI et guérillas', in Trempé (ed.), *La Libération dans le Midi*, 63–78.

the 'Montaigne' Maquis at La Fare in December 1943.[101] One SOE agent sent to instruct the Maquis of Villefranche-du-Périgord in the use of plastic explosives found that his French was of no use to him because all its members were Spanish refugees and understood only Spanish and Catalan.[102]

There were numerous comparable examples of this kind, but in general those immigrants who did not resist through their own separate national organizations, did so through the Communist FTP-MOI. Although the FTP-MOI was small, it played a role out of all proportion to its size. After the decimation of the Communist Party in Paris in 1942, the four 'detachments' (Romanian, 'Jewish', Italian, 'mixed') of the FTP-MOI were all that remained of the Party's urban guerrilla organization in the city. In 1943, Communist military resistance in Paris was the work of about sixty immigrants, who carried out an astonishing number of operations. There were ninety-two attacks of various kinds in the first six months of that year, seventeen in August, and fourteen in September. These included:

> 3 September: the derailing of the Paris–Reims train; the killing of two German policemen in the suburb of Argenteuil, two German soldiers at the Porte d'Ivry, and two German soldiers in the Rue de la Harpe.
> 8 September: a grenade attack on a German lorry at Saint-Ouen; an attack on a German convoy at Stains.
> 10 September: a grenade attack on a PPF meeting in the Rue Lamarck.
> 10 September: the shooting of a German soldier.
> 13 September: the derailing of a German train between Paris and Troyes.

The most spectacular exploit was the assassination on 28 September 1943 of Julius Ritter, Sauckel's deputy in France. Only after carrying out the attack did the group learn the identity of their victim, whom they had been tailing for several days.[103]

During the summer, there were a series of arrests. The military head of the FTP-MOI in the Paris region, Boris Holban, asked permission to transfer his men out of the city, where their existence had become so perilous. Instead he was told to intensify military action.[104] Those who had not been arrested were consolidated into a single detachment under the command of the Armenian Missak Manouchian. Finally, the 'Manouchian group' was itself arrested in November 1943. A lot of ink has been spilled over this affair. Some believe that Manouchian was betrayed by an informer, but this was probably not true. The French police had a special unit (BS2) just to track down immigrant Communist resisters. Thanks to an elaborate system of tailing, they gradually identi-

---

[101] G. Garrier, 'Montagnes en Résistance: Réflexions sur des exemples en Rhône-Alpes', in Sainclivier and Bougeard (eds.), *Enjeux stratégiques*, 207–20.
[102] *The Special Operations Executive: Sound Archive and Oral History Readings* (1998), 132.
[103] B. Holban, *Testament* (1989), 306–7.
[104] Ibid. 177–9.

fied most members of the group. By the end so many French policemen—possibly 100—were involved in the full-time activity of tracking down a tiny handful of resisters that no traitor was required.[105]

Paris was not the only city with FTP-MOI groups. In Lyons, there was the Carmagnole group which comprised about thirty members at the start of 1944, a quarter of them Jewish. The nationalities included Poles (a third of the total), Spaniards, Italians, Hungarians, Austrians, Romanians, Germans, and French. They carried out 241 actions, including thirty-four attacks on Germans in broad daylight.[106] In Grenoble, there was the Liberté group, founded in March 1943 by four Polish Jews. Between September 1943 and March 1944, this group was responsible for almost all the Resistance actions in the city, including fifty-four out of fifty-nine sabotage operations.[107] In Toulouse, there was the Marcel Langer group, also known as the 35th Brigade of the FTP-MOI. Langer was a Polish Jew who came to Toulouse after fighting in the International Brigades in Spain. Even after his arrest in March 1943, the group, which included Poles, Italians, Spaniards, Romanian Jews, and Brazilians, continued to wage sporadic guerrilla warfare. In March 1944, it planted a bomb in a cinema notorious for showing German films. This operation miscarried when the bomb detonated earlier than intended, killing a spectator (and two members of the group). The Communists, not wishing to be associated with the killing of innocent French citizens, even in the name of France, disavowed the action of the Langer group. It has even been suggested that when resisters working in the *préfecture* informed the Communist Party that the police was on the group's trail, the Party did not pass on this information.[108]

Whether this allegation is correct—and in resistance history allegations of betrayal are commonplace—it reveals that there were problems in the relationship between the 'French' Resistance and the foreigners within it. There was a danger of offering a flank to Vichy propaganda depicting the Resistance as a hotbed of Communists, Jews, and foreigners. In Paris in 1943 this allegation was not far from the truth. Twenty-three of the Manouchian group were given a highly publicized show trial, before being executed in February 1944. A poster was produced—the notorious 'Affiche rouge'—displaying the supposedly sinister faces of the group with their unpronounceable names—Szlama Gryzwacz, Wolf Wasybrot, and so on—printed underneath. Nine of the people on the poster were Jews; half of them were under 25; three had seen their entire families arrested in the Vel d'Hiver round-up. There has been controversy whether, as Manouchian's widow believed, the PCF deliberately sacrificed the Manouchian

[105] Courtois et al., *Le Sang de l'étranger*, 274–370, dissects the police operation in detail.
[106] J. C. Simmonds, 'Immigrant Fighters for the Liberation of France: A Local Profile of Carmagnole-Liberté in Lyon', in R. Kedward and N. Wood (eds.), *The Liberation: Image and Event* (Oxford, 1995), 29–41.
[107] Wieviorka, *Ils étaient juifs, résistants*, 267.
[108] M. Goubet, 'La Résistance étrangère à Toulouse 1940–1944', in Douzou et al. (eds.), *La Résistance: Villes*, 74–81; C. Lévy, *Les Parias de la Résistance* (1970), 206–11.

group in order to rid itself of resisters with embarrassingly foreign names.[109] Why else did the Party reject Holban's request to be transferred from the capital? But there is no evidence that the Party leadership was motivated by any consideration other than the fact that it had no one left in Paris to replace the MOI whose exploits were vital to boost the Party's reputation for daring activism.[110]

'Twenty three who cried the name of France', was how a poem by Aragon described those on the Affiche rouge. After the war the plaques to the immigrant Jews killed in the Resistance read 'Fallen for France'. Was this how the immigrants who fought in the FTP-MOI saw their action? Certainly they were expected to celebrate the patriotic themes of French history which dominated Communist propaganda. But the Party was successful at offering multiple identities to those who fought with it. One Party directive to the MOI insisted it must 'popularize to the largest possible extent the tradition of the old Italian, Polish, Hungarian patriots who came to defend the liberty of France because they considered it as their second homeland . . . It is necessary to strengthen the sense of double patriotism of the immigrant workers.'[111] Only the Communist press gave much coverage to the execution of the Manouchian group. It was the Communists on the CNR who pushed for the publication of a manifesto denouncing xenophobia and proclaiming that the Resistance welcomed immigrants who fought in its ranks: 'whether Jews, Poles, Italians, Spaniards . . . they are dear to the French, worthy of the names . . . united to them by the bond of blood shed in the same cause'. This was certainly a more ringing embrace of the immigrant contribution than was to be found in most resistance propaganda, and it marked a different approach from Maurice Schumann's denial on the radio in April that the Resistance was made up of Jews and bandits.[112]

Recruiting the Professions: Communists and Writers

The ability to offer multiple identities was one key to the Communist success in the Resistance. Communist propaganda was, as Guillon remarks, 'homogeneous in thought but diversified in form'.[113] Although the Communists insistently repeated the same themes at every level from the Central Committee to the tiniest local paper, at the same time they also addressed specific interest groups in order at appeal to the widest spectrum of opinion. They had organizations recruiting specifically among women and immigrants, and a press targeted at all varieties of regional, local, or class identity. In the Var alone their newspapers included *La Lutte patriotique de Draguignan, Le Cri du Haut-Var,*

[109] For the betrayal theory, see P. Raymond, *L'Affiche rouge* (1975); P. Robrieux, *L'Affaire Manouchian: Vie et mort d'un héros communiste* (1986).

[110] S. Courtois, *Le Monde*, 2/3 June 1985; *L'Affiche rouge*, documentary by Christophe Muel, 1994.

[111] P. Joutard and F. Marcot (eds.), *Les Étrangers dans la Résistance en France* (Besançon, 1992), 108.

[112] R. Bourderon, 'PCF, FTP, MOI: Le PCF, le FTP et le MOI automne–hiver 1943–1944', *Cahiers d'histoire de l'Institut Maurice Thorez*, 22 (1985), 11–12; C. Lévy, 'L'Affiche rouge', *L'Histoire* 18 (1989), 22–30.

[113] Guillon, 'La Résistance dans le Var', 502.

La Défense paysanne du Var, and *Le Cri des mineurs du Var*.[114] Sometimes these front organizations were very thinly disguised: in the Jura in 1942 the tracts of the 'Committee of Housewives', the 'United Forces of Patriotic Youth', and the 'Front national' were all written by the same hand.[115]

Another distinctive feature of the Communists was that they targeted not only individuals but also specific professional groups. The FN was organized into sections of architects, teachers, university professors, journalists, lawyers, and doctors. Of course most resisting doctors, journalists, lawyers, and so on were in other movements. Once these other movements also decided to create professional sections comprising those doctors or journalists or lawyers who had joined them, the Communists had to decide how to react.[116] This dilemma arose in September 1943, with a proposal to create a single resistance medical committee (CMR) of all doctors in the Resistance. The FN doctors' section elected to join the Committee, despite being in a minority on it. This was in line with the Communist tactic of accepting a presence on 'pluralist' committees (i.e. sitting alongside representatives of other organizations) if they could not establish 'unitary' ones (i.e. where everyone was in the FN). Eventually the tactic paid off, and the FN doctors managed to increase their influence on the Committee by winning the support of the distinguished paediatrician Robert Debré who had his own scores to settle with other participants.[117]

The one professional group which the Communists succeeded in organizing almost exclusively under their aegis were writers. This was done by the National Writers' Committee (CNE) whose origins went back to the summer of 1941 when the Communists were starting to build the FN.[118] The Communist writer Jacques Decour was instructed to get writers to participate in a clandestine literary review to be called *Les Lettres françaises*. Decour secured the co-operation of Jean Paulhan, not himself a Communist, who had an unrivalled address book of literary contacts, based upon fifteen years as editor of the *NRF*. From his office next door to Drieu in the Gallimard offices, Paulhan worked at setting up an underground network of resistance writers. By the end of 1941, a small group of writers had been assembled, and enough articles had been collected for the first issue of *Les Lettres françaises*. Before it could appear, Decour was arrested in February 1942, and shot three months later. With him perished most of the contents of the first issue of *Les Lettres françaises*.

Another Communist writer, Claude Morgan, who had assisted Decour in 1941, was designated to replace him. Everything had to start again from scratch

---

[114] Ibid. 356–8.
[115] Marcot, 'Résistance et population', 53.
[116] D. Virieux, 'Résistance—professions: un rapport sans histoire(s)', *MS* 180 (1997), 113–46.
[117] A. Simonin, 'Le Comité médical de la Résistance: Un succès différé', *MS* 180 (1997), 159–78.
[118] See in general, Thomas, *Le Témoin compromis*; C. Morgan, *Les 'Don Quichotte' et les autres* (1979); G. Sapiro, 'Les Conditions professionnelles d'une mobilisation réussie: Le Comité national des écrivains', *MS* 180 (1997), 179–91; M. Atack, *Literature and the French Resistance: Cutural Politics and Narrative Forms, 1940–1950* (Manchester and New York, 1989), 30–54.

because, for security reasons, Morgan had not been told the names on Decour's list. He was also one of the few writers in France not to know Paulhan. From what he had salvaged of Decour's efforts, Morgan managed to produce an issue of *Les Lettres françaises* in September 1942. Its four scrappy typed pages, on cheap brown paper, were a solo effort; they were not the mouthpiece of a 'writers' committee' since no such committee existed. In the autumn of 1942, through another Communist writer, Edith Thomas, herself a Gallimard author, Morgan met Paulhan. The work of forming a writers' committee was resumed.

By the summer of 1943, Morgan had gathered about fifteen members including Jean Guéhenno, François Mauriac (who had already offered a piece for Decour's abortive review), Michel Leiris, and Jean-Paul Sartre. Edith Thomas's flat became their meeting place. Their main activity was the production of *Les Lettres françaises* which appeared monthly until the Liberation. From October 1943, it was properly printed, with about 12,000 copies produced monthly. It also incorporated a clandestine journal for French film-makers, *L'Écran français*, and another one for the theatre, *La Scène française*. The CNE's success occurred as much for professional as political reasons. As an underground reconstitution of the writers in the Gallimard stable, it also allowed aspiring writers to gain access to that powerful network without passing through the *NRF*, which was now tainted by Drieu's editorship. Writers actively involved in the Resistance tended to be younger and less well established than those who supported Vichy.[119]

In the South, the organization of writers developed in a slightly different way.[120] Until 1942, writers like Aragon had exploited the possibilities of legal expression offered in reviews like *Confluences*, *Poésie*, and *Fontaine*. Once these avenues were closed off, it was Aragon, himself a Gallimard author, who played Paulhan's role of literary impresario. The poetry which Aragon had published in the first two years of the Occupation had given him the stature, in Claudel's words after the Liberation, of a 'national poet', somewhat on the model of Victor Hugo exiled in Guernsey under the Second Empire. He was quoted by de Gaulle in a speech at Algiers in October 1943. Aragon's achievement was not only to give expression to French patriotism in his poetry, but also to confront the language of collaborationism on its own territory. Where Montherlant in the *NRF* celebrated the masculine and warrior civilization represented by medieval chivalry—the contemporary analogy was clear—Aragon riposted that medieval chivalry was also about 'courtesy', justice, and 'the defence of the weak'. Aragon's essay 'La Leçon de Riberac', suggesting that the traditions of troubadour poetry could be revived to convey covert messages when open expression was impossible, was attacked by Drieu in the *NRF* in October 1941. That Drieu should feel it necessary to use the full weight of the NRF's authority to attack someone who

---

[119] Sapiro, *La Guerre des écrivains*, 432–45, 534–48; id., 'Complicités et anathèmes', 339.
[120] Id., *La Guerre des écrivains*, 512–28.

was writing in the small literary reviews of the Southern Zone showed how literary 'legitimacy' had shifted to the opponents of collaboration.

It was these small reviews which provided the network of contacts around which Aragon began to construct an underground literary resistance in the South. Because intellectuals in the South were more dispersed than in the North, he organized them into so-called 'stars', groups with five branches which would eventually interconnect with each other. Out of this developed a journal, *Les Étoiles*, and a committee of writers. About twenty writers eventually sat on this Southern committee, but allegedly as many as 300 had offered their support. It included Communists like Aragon and Georges Sadoul, Catholics like Stanislas Fumet and Louis Martin-Chauffier, and writers without specific affiliation like Albert Camus. Some of the names claimed by the committee had only the most tenuous connection with it. Roger Martin du Gard, who spent the Occupation in Nice, cut off from politics, received a visit in 1943 from Georges Sadoul, who introduced himself as a friend of Paulhan. Sadoul informed du Gard that a committee of intellectual resistance was being set up, including figures such as Paulhan and Mauriac. Despite his rule of avoiding all political commitments, du Gard, reassured by the presence of such names, agreed to be associated with them. This is as far as his commitment went despite subsequent visits by Sadoul. At the Liberation, du Gard was surprised to find himself proclaimed by the Communists as a member of a committee which he had never attended.[121]

The only rival to the Communists for influence among writers were the Éditions de Minuit which had published *Le Silence de la mer*. This had been followed by other books: *A Travers le désastre* by Jacques Maritain (from his American exile) in November 1942; *L'Honneur des poètes*, a collection of pieces by twenty-one poets, published in July 1943; *Le Cahier noir* by Mauriac in August 1943. The output steadily increased, and in the first seven months of 1944 thirteen books were published, all under pseudonyms. Originally the Éditions had been entirely independent of the Communists, but they gradually became more entwined with each other, if only because several contributors to the Éditions were also involved in the CNE. From June 1943, the poet Paul Éluard, who had recently rejoined the Communist Party, was in charge of the publications list of the Éditions. A quarter of the members of the publications committee were Communists. But the Éditions never entirely lost their autonomy. Aiming not to publish 'resistance' literature but 'clandestine' literature, not politics but art, their publications did not espouse the activist line of the Communists. While the Communists popularized the slogan 'everyone get a Boche', the Éditions held on to the idea of the 'good German' until the very end.[122]

The Éditions sounded a different note from the Communists—complementing them rather than competing with them—but in all other respects the

---

[121] Verdès-Leroux, *Refus et violences*, 386–7.
[122] Simonin, *Les Éditions de minuit*, 145–87.

cultural influence of the CNE was unchallenged. When in September 1943 d'Astier set up *Cahiers de la Libération*, a publication intended to appeal to intellectuals, the Communists detected an attempt to compete with them on the cultural terrain. But the *Cahiers* never got off the ground. Villon reassured the Party that its rivals had been 'disappointed in their efforts to recruit intellectuals . . . Continually they receive the response: "we are in the FN".'[123]

Of the fifty writers on the executive committees of the CNEs of the two zones, under a third were members of the Party; half had been associated in the 1930s with left-wing anti-fascism; the rest had no previous left-wing affiliations. This was a testimony to the Communists' success in projecting an ecumenical image. In 1941, Decour had refused to accept Sartre on the CNE because the Communists viewed him as a degenerate writer steeped in Heidegger; a year later, such reservations were cast aside. But the Communists hesitated as to how far their ecumenism should be extended. They had hesitated even about the designation of their writers' committee. Originally it was conceived as the writers' section of the FN and called the FNE (National Front of Writers), a name which prevailed until July 1943 in the North. But in the South, Aragon chose the name CNE to show that the committee was entirely independent even of the FN. This would, in Aragon's words, 'permit us to attract people who don't want to be in the FN'. To make this explicit, he announced that the CNE would attach itself to both the FN and the MUR. This was going too far for the Party hierarchy who refused to allow other professional organizations under its influence to do the same. But in the case of writers, Aragon's suggestion prevailed in both zones. In this way, the Party created a gamut of organizations which offered a sliding scale of commitment: writers could join the Party, the FN, or the CNE.[124]

Bringing in the Workers: National Insurrection

The attraction of the Communists lay in their uncompromisingly activist rhetoric. Up to a point, this was a matter of rhetoric only. It might once have been fair to accuse the non-Communist Resistance of *attentisme*, but not in 1943. The *corps francs* now carried out executions and sabotage operations every bit as spectacular as the FTP's; Résistance-Fer carried out railway sabotage; daring operations were also carried out by the Maquis and the AO. In July 1943, all these branches of the MUR involved in direct action were grouped together in a single Immediate Action section (AI) under the overall command of Degliame.

Immediate Action designated all operations undertaken before the Allied landings; the AS remained responsible for military action after that. In Septem-

---

[123] Virieux, 'Le Front national', 426, 610, 619.
[124] Sapiro, 'Les Conditions professionnelles', 188–91.

ber 1943, the Executive Committee of MUR ordered that $\frac{3}{7}$ of all arms received should go to the Maquis, $\frac{2}{7}$ to the AO, and $\frac{2}{7}$ to the AS. Thus $\frac{5}{7}$ of all arms were to go to Immediate Action—a sign of the importance that this had assumed even for the non-Communist Resistance.[125] For the Communists, of course, the very existence of a distinction between the AI and the AS was proof of *attentisme*, but in reality, even among Communist resisters, the FTP were only a tiny minority: most Communist resisters were not throwing bombs or shooting Germans.

The Communists' distinctiveness lay not in the fact that they were the only people carrying out direct action, nor in the fact that all Communists were doing this—neither proposition was true—but in their conception of the relationship between the activist minority and the rest of the population. In 1943, the Communists started calling insistently for a 'National Insurrection'. They did not use this term to mean the suicidal uprising of an unarmed population against heavily armed Germans. For the Communists, the call for an insurrection was a way of democratizing the idea of resistance. One tract read: 'Every petition, every demonstration, every strike is a step in the practical preparation of the National Insurrection.'[126] Another proclaimed: 'Acting does not only mean armed action . . . From the most heroic to the tiniest . . . there is a whole gamut of activities which correspond to the feelings and attitudes of each person.'[127] Whether a woman knitting socks for the FTP or a peasant hiding his grain—all were participating in the 'daily action' which was the 'best school for the National Insurrection'.[128] For the Communists, this insurrection was a constant process of self-creation. They did not deny that the other Resistance movements now practised Immediate Action, but they claimed that these movements had too elitist a notion of what this meant. By linking patriotic protest to the tiniest manifestation of social protest, the Communists offered everyone the opportunity to participate in—or the illusion of participating in—the final liberation of France. Immediate Action was open to all.[129]

Thanks to this open-ended notion of resistance and insurrection the Communists were uniquely placed to exploit the developing militancy of the working class in the second half of 1943. STO had shaken France's industrial workers out of the apathy affecting them since 1940. Even if for many workers the sticking point was not so much working for Germany as working in Germany, even if many *réfractaires* regularized their positions after the amnesty and worked in German-protected factories in France, nothing was to be the same again.[130] In the autumn of 1943, industrial unrest reached a peak not witnessed since the days of the Popular Front. In September, there were strikes in the shipyards of Marseilles; in October, another major coal strike broke out in the Nord/Pas-de-Calais,

---

[125] Marcot, 'Le Service national maquis', 219.   [126] Michel, *Les Courants de pensée*, 647.
[127] Virieux, 'Le Front national', 370–1.   [128] Ibid. 382.   [129] Ibid. 372–3.
[130] Guillon, 'Y-a-t-il un comportement ouvrier?', 471–2.

and also among the miners of Montceau les Mines in Saône-et-Loire. Throughout France, there were strikes on the symbolic date of 11 November.[131] Membership of the clandestine CGT union also increased dramatically in the last four months of the year. In the Rhône, membership rose to 50,000, having fallen to 20,000 in 1940; in the Haute-Pyrénées, there was an increase from 934 to 2,664.[132]

As in 1936, trade-union membership increased after a successful strike. At Toulon, there was a strike in the Arsenal for the first time since 1938. It took place in an atmosphere of highly charged patriotism. Singing the Marseillaise, strikers marched to demonstrate in the Place de la Liberté. By the end of the month, trade-union membership had reached the levels of 1936; union meetings were massively attended; and the fear prevailing in the factories since 1938 had disappeared.[133] Everywhere the mood was volatile. In the Peugeot factory, in the Jura, a strike broke out on 16 December after the Germans had forbidden anyone to travel by bicycle in reprisal for the shooting of a German customs officer in Montbéliard.[134] In general, the strikes were sparked off by social demands, but the political and the social had now become inextricably intertwined.

The Communists were best at exploiting this working-class radicalism. In the Var, 36.4 per cent of the Communist resistance cadres but only 6.4 per cent of the MUR cadres were workers. The non-Communist movements never successfully adapted to the idea of Resistance as a mass phenomenon. This was particularly true in the North where movements like CDLR, CDLL, and OCM conceived it as the specialized activity of an elite. But it was true even in the South where the Resistance movements never fully overcame their contempt for the initial passivity of the population. In May 1944, a local paper produced by *Combat* in the Franche-Comté called on people not involved directly in the Resistance not to compromise its activity by idle gossip: 'You who do not participate directly in action for whatever reason (age, family situation, lack of courage) . . . the Resistance does not concern you, it is our business.'[135] This was clearly an extreme example—and one could find many counter-examples where the population was called upon to act—but it was inconceivable that such a quotation could have emanated from the Communists.

At the base, then, the MUR did not have the dynamism of the Communists. In the Var, it had only one local paper to rival the plethora of specialized Communist publications.[136] One member of Libération wrote in January 1944: 'Instead of developing propaganda our leaders are more concerned to close the entry of our movement to new members . . . to hold on to entrenched positions

[131] E. Dejonghe, 'Les Départements du Nord et du Pas-de-Calais', in Azéma and Bédarida (eds.), *La France des années noires*, ii. 490–514: 510; Madjarian, *Conflits, pouvoirs et société*, 44; Chapman, *State Capitalism and Working Class Radicalism*, 251; Marcot, 'Résistance et population', 89.
[132] Le Crom, *Syndicats nous voilà*, 206.
[133] Guillon, 'La Résistance dans le Var', 526–37.
[134] Marcot, 'Résistance et population', 89.
[135] Ibid. 124.   [136] Guillon, 'La Résistance dans le Var', 389–90.

or court some prefectoral official.'[137] One problem was that the MUR was becoming integrated into the structures created by London. Frenay had not been entirely wrong to accuse Moulin of bureaucratizing the Resistance. The MUR leaders, planning for the future Allied landings when the AS would spring into action, were part of a military structure which they did not control.

The compensation might have been that, as D-Day approached, the MUR would find itself treated as indispensable by the Allied planners. In fact, the opposite was happening. At the end of 1943, the MUR found itself competing for the favour of London with a late arrival in the Resistance, but one enjoying the advantage of professional military expertise. It was at the beginning of 1943 that the professional officers from the former Armistice army, disbanded in November 1942, began to reorganize themselves secretly into an organization which eventually took the name of the Resistance Organization of the Army (ORA). ORA was viewed with suspicion by many resisters, who saw it as a late convert from Pétainism. Serreulles was unhappy at using such people in a 'revolutionary war'. He consoled himself with the thought that Danton had made use of the services of the *ancien régime* soldier Marshal Soubise, and Lenin of the Tsarist General Kuropatkin, without compromising the purity of the cause.[138] ORA officers played an increasingly important role as the military objectives of the Resistance began to take precedence over others. BCRA was happier dealing with ORA professionals than with well-meaning AS amateurs.[139] In December 1943, a major step towards the military unity of the Resistance was taken with the decision to unite all its military forces, including the FTP, into a single organization—the French Forces of the Interior (FFI)—with a single command structure. In the allocation of command positions within the FFI, ORA, which had started out as a group of cadres without troops, found itself playing a role disproportionate to its size.

The impact of ORA was also felt at the base. People who had joined the AS because they wanted to make a real military contribution to the liberation were tempted to join the professionals; people who thirsted for immediate action were more tempted by the FTP. At the end of 1943, then, the MUR remained the most important resistance force in the South, but it found itself being outflanked on one side by the Communists, and on the other by the ORA: it could offer neither the dynamism of the one nor the professionalism of the other.[140] Some of its leaders took refuge instead in political discussions about the post-war future. The liberation was in sight: but what would happen then?

---

[137] Michel and Mirkine-Guetzévitch, *Les Idées*, 108–9. The author of these words was the Communist Pierre Hervé.

[138] Cordier, *Jean Moulin: La République des catacombes*, 588.

[139] J.-M. Guillon, 'La Lutte armée et ses interprétations', in Marcot (ed.), *La Résistance: Lutte armée et maquis*, 147–57, 152–3; Foottit and Simmonds, *France 1934–1945*, 56.

[140] J.-M. Guillon, 'Le Midi', in Azéma et al., *Jean Moulin et la Résistance*, 103–22: 108–11.

21

Remaking France

In January 1944, Raymond Aubrac was waiting for the Resistance to organize the transport that would take him and his wife Lucie to safety. Having escaped twice from prison in the previous year, Aubrac was too well known to the Germans to be able to stay in France. Although the Aubracs had been founding members of Libération-Sud, the joy of being in France for the denouement was to be denied them. Aubrac's sadness at this knowledge was deepened by the news that his (Jewish) parents had been recently arrested by the Germans.

While preparing to take his leave of France, Aubrac wrote a long reflective letter to d'Astier in Algiers. After recounting his own adventures, he gave vent to the frustrations that many resisters in France felt towards London and Algiers: the excessive influence of veteran politicians, the lack of consideration for the sacrifices of the Resistance. He even wondered if d'Astier was not succumbing to the poisonous atmosphere of Algiers. But Aubrac ended his letter on a more upbeat note: 'This is the last news I have to send you, with a certain melancholy, to which I add my good wishes for the new year which will I hope become Year I.'[1] Year I: these two words encapsulated the almost Messianic self-perception of the Resistance that it was struggling not only to remove the Germans from France, but also to inaugurate a new political order. What was the nature of that order to be?

Vichy and the Resistance: Shared Values

'Pernod, sports stadia, brothels: are these reasons for living?' This is not Pétain speaking, nor Brasillach. It is François Mauriac in *Le Cahier noir*.[2] Such echoes of Vichy moralism were not unusual in the language of the Resistance. We have seen this in the reception accorded to *Le Corbeau* and *Le Ciel est à vous*. Similar ambiguities emerge from another film, Louis Daquin's *Premier de cordée* (1943). The title refers to the leader of a group of mountain climbers, and the

---

[1] Douzou, *La Désobéissance*, 151–4.   [2] Steel, *Littératures de l'ombre*, 176.

film illustrates how mountain climbing instils qualities of leadership and solidarity. Daquin, a Communist and resister, subsequently remarked that his film reflected Vichy's values more than he had realized at the time.[3]

The Maquis in particular helped the Resistance to reclaim those rural and regional values which Vichy had tried to appropriate. Maquis rhetoric celebrated the cleansing purity of mountain life away from the corruptions of the city. The writer Jean-Pierre Chabrol observed: 'I thought of myself as Cévenol by birth, but only the Maquis taught me to know my Cévennes.'[4] The Éditions de Minuit authors took the names of French regions as their pseudonyms: Mauriac was Forez, Edith Thomas was Auxois, Claude Morgan was Mortagne, and so on. One historian has noted that the images of tranquil rural France celebrated in the London-based publication *France libre* are interchangeable with those to be found in Vichyite publications.[5] No one more skilfully turned Vichy's rhetoric against itself than Aragon. His poem 'Le Conscrit des cent villages', composed out of the 'beloved names' of French villages, gloried in the diversity of rural France:

> Adieu Forléans Marimbault
> Vollore-Ville Volmerange
> Avize Avoine Vallerange
> Ainval-Septoutre Mongibaud
>
> Fains-la-Folie Aumur Andance
> Guillaume-Peyrouse Escarmin
> Dancevoir Parmilieu Parmain
> Linthes-Pelurs Caresse Abondance[6]

If the Resistance often sounded a common note with Vichy, this was not only a strategy to reappropriate a language which Vichy had tried to confiscate. By 1943, the Resistance was no longer an isolated elite standing outside society, but a complex micro-society enmeshed in the wider society outside it. Inevitably it became increasingly freighted with the assumptions and values of that society. Thus it would be wrong to view Resistance history as a process of continuous radicalization. For example, it was in the first days of Occupation, when everything was in flux, that women seized opportunities to acquire the kind of leadership roles not previously available to them in French society. Almost all women who occupied leading positions in the Resistance had been there from the start. Those who joined later did not rise to the top: the Resistance became more institutionalized and gender boundaries reasserted themselves.

As the Resistance gave increasing priority to military organization, its rhetoric

---

[3] Ehrlich, *Cinema of Paradox*, 112.

[4] G. Garrier, 'Montagnes en Résistance: Réflexions sur des exemples en Rhône-Alpes', in Sainclivier and Bougeard (eds.), *Enjeux stratégiques*, 210–20: 210–11, 219.

[5] H. R. Kedward, 'Rural France and the Resistance', in Fishman et al. (eds.), *France at War*, 125–43: 136–40.

[6] *La Diane française* (1946), 54–8.

became more 'masculine'. Its cult of virility was no less insistent than Vichy's. It was after all Sartre who identified collaboration with passivity and homosexuality, and, by implication, resistance with virility. In his novel *Iron in the Soul* this idea is embodied in the homosexual Daniel who is stunned by the beauty of the Germans arriving in Paris: 'longing to be a women so that he could load them with flowers'.[7] Resistance polemics against the Minister of Education Abel Bonnard often highlighted his notorious homosexuality: 'active collaboration and passive pederasty' as one publication put it.[8] Jean Guéhenno wondered in his wartime diary why so many homosexual writers were collaborators. He deplored the influence of 'these writers almost exclusively turned in on themselves, so weak, so vain'; the young lacked virile models.[9] There were of course homosexuals in the Resistance—for example, Pascal Copeau, Denis Rake, the SOE agent who appears in *The Sorrow and the Pity*, the young Jewish writer Roger Stéphane, the future novelist and critic Jean-Louis Bory—but, like women, they do not fit into the dominant narrative of the Resistance.[10]

Of the approximately 1,000 Resistance newspapers, seventy-six directly targeted women. Eighty-eight per cent of these were inspired by the Communist Party which created an organization exclusively for women, revealingly entitled the Union of French Women for the Defence of the Family and the Liberation of France (UFF). Despite some references to the Soviet *partisanes*, and to Louise Michel, a heroine of the Commune, the Communists addressed women primarily as housewives and mothers. They accused Vichy of betraying the promises it had made to women, but they did not offer women a different role. The same was true of the Resistance in general—to the limited extent that it discussed the issue.[11]

Anti-Semitism was another area where the frontiers between Vichy and the Resistance were not as sharply defined as might be supposed. The ambivalence towards the Jews which had surfaced in some Resistance publications before 1942 did not entirely disappear. A BCRA report in January 1943 noted that people who helped the Jews after the round-ups acted out of 'compassion' not 'esteem'. To resolve the Jewish problem 'in a way satisfactory to both justice and public opinion', the opposition to Germany should be separated from any commitment to restore the Jews to an excessive role. Further BCRA reports later in the year observed that however much sympathy people felt for Jews, 'one cannot deny that there is a Jewish question'. The French were not anti-Semitic but they 'cursed the banks of Israel'.[12] In October 1943, the CFLN drafted a questionnaire to

---

[7] In Roger Vailland's novel *Un jeune homme seul* (1951) homosexuality is also associated with treason and collaboration.

[8] J.-M. Muracciole, *Les Enfants de la défaite: La Résistance, l'éducation et la culture* (1998), 180.

[9] *Journal des années noires*, 152.

[10] P. Leenhardt, *Pascal Copeau 1908–1982* (1994).

[11] K. Adler, 'Idealizing France 1942–1948: The Place of Gender and Race' (D.Phil. thesis, Sussex, 1998), 60–73.

[12] Poznanski, *Être juif en France*, 555–6.

evaluate the political attitudes of the Resistance. One respondent wanted Jews 'kept out of all governmental and public functions'; another demanded the 'relegation of all Jews, Freemasons . . . and former politicians'.[13] When the staff of Uriage entered the Resistance, they took the decision to create an order to defend the principles in which they believed. One rule read: 'Israelites are not admitted as members of the Order or as novices. If we are resolutely hostile to anti-semitism, particularly as practised since the armistice, we ought not to underestimate the danger of a Jewish revenge nor ignore the existence of a Jewish international whose interests are opposed to those of France.'[14]

The entry of Uriage into the Resistance reminds us that the Resistance was composed of many generations, including people who had been loyal to Vichy. The Resistance was created by a process of sedimentation: a Mounier or a Beuve-Méry could move into it without making fundamental ideological adjustments.[15] One area of common ground between all these resistance generations was contempt for the Third Republic. *Combat* in December 1943 attacked the rehabilitation of former Third Republic politicians in terms which Vichy could easily have used: 'Why not Josephine Baker? There is no reason why the tide of Republican continuity should be allowed to wash up detritus of this kind.'[16] Like Vichy in 1940, the Resistance wanted to engender a new elite. The Uriage team, which had started out building an elite for Vichy, ended up hoping to do the same for the Resistance.

Pétaino-Resisters: An Abortive Third Way

One fervently Pétainist organization which moved into resistance in 1943 was the prisoner-of-war movement. No group was more assiduously courted by Vichy than the prisoners of war. There was a Prisoner of War Commissariat to assist the reinsertion of prisoners into society, and under its aegis, a Centre d'action des prisonniers, headed by Jean de Fabrègues. The Centre d'action aimed to harness the spirit of fraternity which had existed in the prisoner-of-war camps to the cause of the National Revolution. As well as being pro-Pétainist, the Centre d'action was anti-German, and it was involved with a semi-clandestine organization called the Chaîne. The Chaîne acquired the Château de Montmaur in the Alps, ostensibly as a refuge for former prisoners, but also to prepare a future resistance organization. After the occupation of the Southern Zone, the Commissariat's loyalty to Vichy became more strained. In January 1943, Laval replaced its head, Maurice Pinot, with someone more committed to collaboration. Several of Pinot's aides resigned in solidarity, and members of the Centre

---

[13] A. Shennan, *Rethinking France: Plans for Renewal 1940–1946* (Oxford, 1989), 43–4.

[14] Hellman, *The Knight-Monks of Vichy France*, 197–8; Comte, *Une utopie combattante*, 530.

[15] M. Kelly, 'Humanism and National Unity: The Ideological Reconstruction of France', in N. Hewitt (ed.), *The Culture of Reconstruction. European Literature, Thought and Film, 1945–1950* (1989), 103–19.

[16] Michel, *Les Courants de pensée*, 363.

d'action and the Chaîne met at Montmaur to form an underground prisoners' movement. Suspended initially between loyalty to Pétain and determination to act against the Germans, they entered fully into resistance in the spring of 1943. Here was a movement, as Pétainist as it was possible to be, pulled by the force of circumstances from loyalty to dissidence and from dissidence to resistance.[17]

The figure who came to dominate this movement was not the former head of the Commissariat, Maurice Pinot, but his younger aide, François Mitterrand. In the 1930s, Mitterrand had been a conservative student, sharing the distaste for republican politics so characteristic of his generation. Taken prisoner in 1940, he escaped at his third attempt. After returning to France, he acquired employment as a Vichy functionary, first as a documentarist for the Legion (January to April 1942) and then as a press officer for the board of rehabilitation of prisoners of war (May 1942 to January 1943). His sympathy with the values of the National Revolution emerged in two articles he published in 1942. The first, in April, approved the formation of the SOL and lamented the Legion's lack of 'fanaticism'; the other, in December 1942, criticized France for '150 years of mistakes' (i.e. since 1789). This article appeared in the Vichyist periodical *France*, alongside one by a leader of the Legion denouncing Jews, Masons, and Gaullists. For his services to Vichy, Mitterrand was awarded Vichy's decoration, the *francisque*, in the spring of 1943.[18]

Mitterrand's move into resistance was sinuous. While building contacts with Resistance leaders and with ORA, he did not burn his bridges with those members of Pétain's entourage who were hostile to Laval. He probably looked more to Giraud than de Gaulle. Mitterrand's first public act of resistance occurred on 10 July 1943 when he disrupted a public meeting addressed by André Masson, the man Laval had put in charge of the Prisoner of War Commissariat. This was a courageous act, and it was celebrated some months later on the BBC by Maurice Schumann—but it was also discreetly approved by Mitterrand's contacts at Vichy. Mitterrand had a rival in Michel Caillau who had in 1942 started to organize a resistance movement from a group of prisoners with whom he had been in captivity. Caillau had never had any relations with the Vichy regime, and he also happened to be de Gaulle's nephew. Mitterrand and Caillau discussed the possibility of unifying their efforts until Caillau realized that he risked being absorbed by Mitterrand's larger organization. His response was to go to Algiers in July to secure the backing of de Gaulle, playing not so much on his family connection as the fact that he had no Vichy past. Caillau returned to France in October, believing that he had prevailed. But Mitterrand himself set off for Algiers in November. Arriving with a reputation as a Giraudist, his first meeting with de Gaulle on 3 December 1943 was frosty even by de Gaulle's

[17] P. Péan, *Une jeunesse française, François Mitterrand, 1934–1947* (1994), 231–84; D. Peschanski and L. Douzou, 'La Résistance française face à l'hypothèque Vichy', in Bidussa and Peschanski (eds.), *La France de Vichy*, 3–42: 27–33.
[18] Péan, *Une jeunesse française*, 111–295.

standards. In the end, however, de Gaulle, came down on the side of Mitterrand who returned to France with the mission to unite the prisoner-of-war movements. Caillau had lost, and in March 1944 Mitterrand became head of a single resistance movement of prisoners (MNRPDG).

Mitterrand prevailed partly because his movement was larger than Caillau's. He was also politically more skilful than Caillau: Mitterrand, the former Giraudist, outwitted the Gaullist Caillau as ruthlessly as de Gaulle had outwitted Giraud. But victory had its price. Mitterrand had to jettison his previous ideological baggage. Caillau had warned de Gaulle in December 1943 that Mitterrand remained 'Maurrassian at heart'.[19] Whether or not this was still true about Mitterrand 'at heart'—as late as June 1943 he certainly had told a leader of Franc-Tireur that there were things worth salvaging in the National Revolution, especially corporatism[20]—it was no longer something he publicly said. In August 1944, the MNRPDG produced a tract whose rhetoric was indistinguishable from that of the Resistance as a whole. It called for a 'total revolution in the economic and social structure' to complete what had been started in 1789; and poured scorn on the 'enterprise called the National Revolution' which it described as a means by which capitalists had tried to exploit France's misfortunes.[21]

Mitterrand, whose politics had been entirely in tune with the National Revolution, understood that it was too late to create a conservative resistance grounded in Pétainist values. Giraud had represented the last chance of achieving this, but his political demise was the death knell of any ideological third way.

The New Elite

Mitterrand's evolution shows that it would be wrong to overstate the common ground between Vichy and the Resistance. The Resistance may have talked about Jews in a tone which jars with modern sensibilities, but it opposed Vichy's anti-Semitism. It might have despised the Third Republic, but it was committed to Republican democracy. Its gender assumptions might have been traditional, but it was not obsessed with the family in the same way as Vichy.[22]

The ideology of the Resistance is summed up in the title of a book by André Hauriou, an academic lawyer who was a member of Combat before sitting on the Algiers Consultative Assembly: 'Towards a Doctrine of the Resistance: Humanist Socialism.'[23] This humanist socialism was conceived within the framework of a reinvigorated Republic. In 1944, Défense de la France sent a letter to de Gaulle defining its objectives as 'the idea of the Republic, the idea of

---

[19] Ibid. 403.   [20] Ibid. 311.   [21] Ibid. 427–31.
[22] Shennan, *Rethinking France*, 208–10.
[23] *Vers une doctrine de la Résistance: Le Socialisme humaniste* (Algiers, 1944).

socialism, the idea of nation'. The founding charter of MLN took the slogan: 'The Republic, Socialism, the Nation.'[24] Socialism, broadly defined, was probably the most important strand in the ideology of the Resistance. Even a movement like CDLR, which distrusted politics, was talking in the spring of 1943 of the need for a Fourth Republic and a new social system.[25] The socialism of the Resistance was mixed with the Catholic humanism of Mounier, *Esprit*, and Uriage. Resistance ideology owed much to the nonconformists of the 1930s, but within a Republican tradition to which they had been indifferent or hostile: Georges Zérapha, a founding member of Libération-Sud, had been involved in *Esprit*, Arthyus of OCM in Ordre nouveau.[26]

The Resistance squared its contempt for the Third Republic with its rediscovery of Republicanism by demanding a Fourth Republic that would be saved from the sins of its predecessor by a new elite.[27] The first step was to purge France of those who had betrayed her after 1940. Reprisals against alleged collaborators became increasingly common in 1943. In August 1943, de Gaulle spoke for the first time of the need to purge the guilty—'France will know that she has been avenged'—but he also insisted that the purge must be carried out by the State.

By what criteria were collaborators to be judged? How could they be punished without recourse to retroactive laws offensive to the Resistance's commitment to justice and its repudiation of the methods of Vichy? The CGE discussed this problem in 1943, and concluded that Article 75 of the Penal Code, condemning treason and intelligence with the enemy, would cover most cases. As for those whose did not merit the harsh penalties applicable under Article 75, the CGE proposed the new offence of national indignity. This was not categorized as a crime—hence avoiding the problem of retroactivity—and was punishable by the loss of civic rights for a specified period. These recommendations were adopted by the CFLN in June 1944.[28]

Even before the Liberation of mainland France, the CFLN had to decide how to handle the purge in North Africa. Pétainism had been strong in North Africa, especially in the army, but an excessive purge of the army conflicted with de Gaulle's desire to bring France back into the war militarily at the earliest opportunity. Some resisters wanted General Juin to be punished for his hesitations in November 1942; de Gaulle, aware of Juin's popularity in the North African army, wished him to command the French forces in the Italian campaign. The case for pragmatism and reconciliation conflicted with the call for justice and revenge. In January 1944 the Consultative Assembly unanimously voted a motion condemning the 'delays in the punishment of traitors'.

---

[24] Shennan, *Rethinking France*, 37.   [25] Granet, *Ceux de la Résistance*, 56–7.
[26] Muracciole, *Les Enfants de la défaite*, 77–8.
[27] Shennan, *Rethinking France*, 40–1; Muracciole, *Les Enfants de la défaite*, 74–9.
[28] P. Novick, *The Resistance versus Vichy: The Purge of Collaborators in Liberated France* (1968), 140–56; Bellescize, *Les Neuf Sages*, 171–8.

De Gaulle parried this move by making an example of some prominent figures: Flandin, Buisson, and Peyrouton were arrested in December. Three months later, Pierre Pucheu was tried by a military court in Algiers. Pucheu had arrived in North Africa in May 1943, having been promised a safe-conduct by Giraud, whose failure to respect this commitment further discredited him among conservatives. Pucheu was especially hated by the Communists for his alleged role in selecting hostages for execution in 1941. Although his trial failed to prove that he had done this, he was found guilty, and sentenced to death. De Gaulle refused to commute the sentence, and Pucheu was shot on 20 March 1944. After the war, former Vichy supporters never forgave de Gaulle for this. They claimed that Pucheu's life was the price that de Gaulle had paid for Communist support. In fact, almost the entire Resistance was clamouring for Pucheu's death.[29]

In the eyes of the Resistance, the objective of the purges was not only to punish the guilty, but also to make way for France's new elite. *Franc-Tireur* declared in 1944: 'France will not allow the remaking of the country to be entrusted to the "well-born", to the "notables", to the grand bourgeois, to the members of the Conseil d'État, the Finance Inspectors . . . it was not the Conseil d'État which set up the Maquis . . . or in the École des sciences politiques that the FTP groups were recruited.'[30] In fact, Resistance leaders came from the same social strata as the pre-war governing elites.[31] The only novelty about them was their relative youth. The Resistance did not respect hierarchies of age, and offered opportunities for the young to seize their chances: in Libération-Sud, the average age of the central leaders was 33; the average age of the regional leaders to whom they gave orders was 39.[32] In Franc-Tireur the 55-year-old Marc Bloch took orders from the 31-year-old Jean-Pierre Lévy. Lévy looked so young for a resistance leader that BCRA even experimented with dying his temples grey.[33]

All resisters would have agreed with OCM that the 'Resistance is a comradeship that we hope will be indissoluble.'[34] But how to ensure that they would not be pushed aside at the Liberation? For most resisters this required the disappearance of the pre-war political parties. Frenay wrote in October 1943:

> It would be puerile to suggest that in this great test of France, men died for the Radical Party or the Alliance démocratique, but there are certainly men of the Radical Party and the Alliance démocratique who died for France in the

---

[29] Novick, *Resistance*, 56–9; Crémieux-Brilhac, *La France libre*, 604; Douzou, *La Désobéissance*, 153.

[30] Michel and Mirkine-Guetzévitch, *Les Idées*, 261–2. The same sort of language could also be found among collaborationists. In May 1942 one of them wrote that it was not 'on the benches of the École des sciences politiques that one will recruit revolutionaries': see Baruch, 'Les Revues de l'État français', 40.

[31] Sainclivier, 'Essai de prosopographie comparée des dirigeants de la Résistance', in Douzou et al. (eds.), *La Résistance: Villes*, 321–36.

[32] Douzou, *La Désobéissance*, 256–7.

[33] Lévy, *Mémoires d'un franc-tireur*, 66, 107.   [34] Michel, *Les Courants de pensée*, 369.

Resistance. Thus the reconstitution of the political parties, as they existed before the war, would be a grave error.[35]

Frenay wanted the MLN to form the basis of a new party perpetuating the ideals of the Resistance. Even those sceptical about a resistance party hoped that the MLN would become a moral force in post-war France offering a progressive alternative to communism. Fusing socialism and progressive Catholicism, it would represent a socialism cleansed of the doctrinaire Marxism and anti-clericalism of the Socialist Party.[36] The problem with this idea of a Third Force between conservatism and communism—a French *travaillisme* as it was dubbed—was that it required the Socialists to offer themselves up for sacrifice. But their refusal to join the MLN in 1944 showed that they were not ready to do this. Another obstacle was that various Christian Democrats in the Resistance were discussing the possibility of creating a new confessional party.[37] This was the origin of the post-war MRP. A resistance party without the Socialists or pro-gressive Catholics was clearly doomed to insignificance.

Nor was the Resistance, despite its rhetoric of unity, able to transcend the conflicts that had existed in French politics before 1940. On education, for example, most strands of the Resistance, from OCM to the Communists, agreed on the need for greater democratization through the removal of the barriers between the primary and secondary systems. But they had no common view about Vichy's policy of subsidizing Catholic schools.[38] Although the issue was tacitly shelved in order to preserve the façade of unity, dissension lay only just beneath the surface. Only five days after the Normandy landings, Maurice Schu-mann attended a lunch at Bayeux in honour of the Resistance. As one historian describes the scene: 'for the first time the members of the various movements discovered that they included Catholics, atheists, Freemasons, and even priests. By the end of the meal the assembled company were already quarrelling over subsidies to the confessional schools.'[39]

Making Plans

The Resistance avoided the intractable issue of religion and education with good reason, but many other issues were debated in great detail. An extraordi-nary amount of time was devoted to drafting plans for the post-war world. This had not been true at the beginning. The first issue of *Libération-Sud* proclaimed in July 1941: 'Tomorrow will be the time for political doctrines. Today our object-ive must be to escape the wretched condition of a conquered people.'[40] But pri-

[35] Michel and Mirkine-Guetzévitch, *Les Idées*, 114.
[36] Michel, *Les Courants de pensée*, 369–73.   [37] Sweets, *Politics of Resistance*, 180.
[38] Muracciole, *Les Enfants de la défaite*, 93–127.
[39] Halls, *Youth of Vichy France*, 101–2.   [40] Shennan, *Rethinking France*, 35.

orities began to change when the question became not if, but when, France would be liberated. In November 1942, *Défense de la France* asked: 'What do we want to do after the country is liberated?' A year later, another publication observed: 'in the heat of battle . . . essays, political theses, draft constitutions are springing up almost everywhere, circulating, being discussed.'[41] The journalist Jean-François Revel recalls that his own role as a messenger boy for the Resistance involved carrying around elaborate plans for the future of France with no relevance to the struggle against the Germans. After the war, he made himself unpopular by writing a satirical story in which a resister is arrested and found to be carrying not plans for sabotage, but a study of the oil resources of Central Anatolia.[42]

The pioneer of reflection about the political future was OCM. Although no other movement matched the detail of the OCM *Cahiers*, others also created specialized publications to discuss reforms: Défense de la France started producing its *Cahiers* in the spring of 1943, and Libération-Sud in September 1943.[43] But post-war planning was not confined to these publications: between November 1942 and August 1944, a fifth of the content of the newspaper *Défense de la France* concerned the post-Liberation political future.[44] The most detailed planning was done by the CGE, set up for this purpose in 1942. Although its members were recruited from the Resistance, the CGE began to work closely with the Delegation, and its outlook became increasingly governmental. For this reason, it needs to be distinguished, as a centre of reflection, from the rest of the Resistance. D'Astier complained that the CGE was 'a circle too closed to the wishes of the most activist part of the Resistance'.[45] Originally the CGE had six members recruited from the Southern movements. There were three jurists (de Menthon, Paul-Henri Teitgen, and the former Radical *député* Paul Bastid), a trade unionist (Robert Lacoste), a high-ranking civil servant (Alexandre Parodi), and a professor of economics (René Courtin). In 1943, Moulin added three members from the North: Michel Debré, a young civil servant; Pierre Lefaucheux, an engineer; Jacques Charpentier, a lawyer. They were a homogeneous group, all (except Lacoste) members of the liberal upper bourgeoisie, most with legal backgrounds—exactly the kind of people *Franc-Tireur* had said should not be in charge of the post-war destinies of France. Thinking governmentally was what these mandarins had been trained to do.

The Socialists also spent much time discussing post-war reforms. In 1942, the CAS set up study commissions to examine post-war policies, and by March 1944 it had produced four different draft programmes.[46] The Communists, however, devoted little attention to post-Liberation arrangements. They avoided detailed commitments, wanting the situation at the Liberation to be as open-ended as possible. Communist propaganda concentrated on the present: the denunciation

[41] Ibid. 36.   [42] J.-F. Revel, *Le Voleur dans la maison vide* (1997), 77.
[43] Douzou, *La Désobéissance*, 306–10.   [44] Wieviorka, *Une certaine idée*, 261.
[45] Bellescize, *Les Neufs Sages*, 203.   [46] Shennan, *Rethinking France*, 85–9.

of *attentisme* and the call for an insurrection. To the extent that the Party did start discussing post-war reforms in the second half of 1943, it was in order not to leave the initiative entirely to the Socialists.[47] In 1943, the Socialists and CGT had both presented draft programmes to the CNR. Not to be outdone, Pierre Villon proposed an alternative draft on behalf of the Communists. This formed the basis of a programme that was adopted by the CNR in March 1944. This CNR Charter, as it came to be called, demanded the punishment of traitors, the reestablishment of the freedom of the press, the introduction of a system of social security, and the implementation of a 'directed economy'. The Charter was vague on details, and designed to be as consensual as possible. Its most radical proposal was for the 'return to the nation' of various key economic sectors including mining, energy, banking, and insurance. The vague term 'return to the nation' was a compromise between the Socialists, who wanted a commitment to full-blooded nationalization, and the Communists, who wanted to avoid antagonizing conservatives.[48] The CNR Charter was the nearest that the Resistance came to producing a single programmatic statement about the future. At the time, however, it was not seen as particularly important. It was only after the Liberation, when people feared that the Resistance was being betrayed, that the Charter acquired legendary status.

Planning for the future also occurred outside France. As early as December 1941, de Gaulle set up four commissions in London to study post-war reforms. After the move to Algiers, committees were set up to examine reforms in four areas: the Empire, the constitution, education, and the economy.[49] No single view about reform emerged from these discussions. The CFLN represented an increasingly wide spectrum of opinion as de Gaulle broadened its base. In November 1943, he brought in historic Resistance leaders who had arrived from France (Frenay, d'Astier, Menthon), former Third Republic politicians who had rallied to de Gaulle (Pierre Mendès France, Henri Queuille, André Philip), and veterans of the Free French (Catroux, Diethelm, Pleven, Tixier).

The two policy areas most intensely discussed were the economy and constitutional reform. On the economy, there were several broadly shared assumptions—hostility to the bourgeoisie which had supposedly let France down in 1940, rejection of laissez-faire capitalism and support for dirigisme, repudiation of the allegedly Malthusian attitudes of the pre-war period and an embrace of modernization—but there was little agreement on details. The main conflict centred upon the degree of dirigisme. The difference between the more and less dirigiste positions did not run between the Resistance and the Free French. In November 1943, René Courtin of the CGE produced an economic policy document which most Resistance leaders considered to be too laissez-faire. Within the Free French, most points of view were represented. A Free French commission, chaired by the civil servant Hervé Alphand, had in 1942 produced a report which pleased neither the Socialists and the Resistance, nor the more laissez-faire camp, represented in London by the businessman Étienne Hirsch. After the move to Algiers, the balance within the CFLN swung towards the left. Pierre Mendès France, who was given the economic portfolio, was an ardent advocate of planning. But no decisions were taken, and the case remained to be fought out in the post-Liberation government.[50]

On constitutional reform, the CNR Charter demanded a democratic system combining efficiency with 'effective accountability before the representatives of the people'. This answered none of the difficult questions, and the constitution was something about which everyone had an opinion. When Sartre tried setting up an abortive resistance group in 1941, the first thing he did was to draft a new constitution—which has not survived. The first *cahiers* of OCM (June 1942) and Défense de la France (March 1943) were devoted to the constitution. In January 1944, the CFLN set up a committee to co-ordinate all the proposals that were proliferating on this subject. It was said, with some exaggeration, that there were almost as many constitutional projects as resisters.[51] A recent study has reprinted nineteen separate constitutional projects.[52]

The central problem was how to avoid the weakness of the Third Republic without falling into the authoritarianism of Vichy. Was it possible satisfactorily to reconcile liberty and authority? In constitutional terms, this revolved around the difference between a presidential and a parliamentary republic. Advocates of a more presidential system looked to ways of widening the franchise of presidential elections or allowing the President to dissolve parliament as Tardieu advocated in the 1930s. Those who rejected presidentialism argued that the Third Republic's weakness resided in the lack of parliamentary majorities. The solution lay in encouraging the emergence of two or three organized parties on the British model. OCM and Défense de France were the firmest supporters of some form of presidentialism, and the Socialists of reformed parliamentarianism. In between, lay the detailed CGE blueprint (September 1943) which was seen as 'timid' by OCM and as too presidential by the Socialists.[53]

De Gaulle expressed no detailed public views about post-Liberation reforms. From the summer of 1943, his main rival was no longer Giraud but the Communists, and his speeches stopped talking about revolution.[54] De Gaulle was always pragmatic about details. On economic matters, his immediate

[50] Margairaz, *L'État, les finances et l'économie*, 721–51; Kuisel, *Capitalism and the State*, 157–86; Bellescize, *Les Neuf Sages*, 185–8.

[51] Michel, *Les Courants de pensée*, 376.

[52] J.-E. Callon (ed.), *Les Projets constitutionnels de la Résistance* (1998).

[53] Shennan, *Rethinking France*, 37–9, 112–27; Michel, *Les Courants de pensée*, 376–84.

[54] Andrieu, 'Charles de Gaulle, héritier de la Révolution', 62–3.

priority was not to adjudicate between the finer points of liberalism or planning, but to ensure that the French people were fed after liberation. For this purpose, he sent Monnet to Washington to co-ordinate relief programmes with the Americans. On constitutional matters, de Gaulle committed himself in no way. His view was probably that no amount of planning would matter if the CFLN did not immediately impose its authority on liberated France. The most urgent objective was not to produce ever more finely tuned constitutions, but to ensure that there was no administrative void after Vichy had gone.

Building a Clandestine State

In the summer of 1943, the CFLN started the process of selecting the prefects who would take over from Vichy. It also devised two new organizational structures for the Liberation: the *commissaires de la République* and the Departmental Liberation Committees (CDL). The eighteen *commissaires* were to be 'super-prefects'—like Vichy's regional prefects—who would maintain order until central authority had been restored. The CDLs, containing members of Resistance movements and political parties, were to organize formal representation of the Resistance in each *département* at the Liberation. Since the Resistance was likely to be a significant local presence, it had to be brought into the process of re-establishing order. In July 1943, Émile Laffon was sent from London to supervise the selection of *commissaires* and prefects, and a month later Francis-Louis Closon to do the same for the CDLs.

The problem was to define the relationship between the CDLs, on the one hand, and the *commissaires* and prefects, on the other. The CNR wanted the CDLs to exercise real power; it proposed that the prefects be responsible to them. But the CFLN, worried that the CDLs might become like local soviets, wanted to restrict them to a consultative role. The compromise reached in March 1944 gave the CDLs the authority to prepare the liberation uprisings—they were described as the 'soul of the *département* which under their leadership struggles for its liberation'—but required them to accept the authority of the *commissaire* once liberation had occurred.[55]

These arrangements left much room for conflict. A lot would depend on the skill of the prefects and *commissaires*. According to what criteria should they be chosen? What should be done about able administrators who had compromised themselves with Vichy? Had the Resistance generated new elites to replace them? In deference to resistance susceptibilities, Laffon made his choices in collaboration with a nominations subcommittee (Comité des Désignations) of the CNR, chaired by Debré of the CGE, and staffed by members of the Resistance move-

---

[55] Closon, *Le Temps des passions*, 239–45; H. Footitt and J. Simmonds, *France 1943–1945* (Leicester, 1988), 44–50; Hostache, *Le Conseil national*, 293–5, 465–70.

ments. In September, he took a preliminary list of nominations back to Algiers. They were largely approved by the CFLN, and he returned with decrees naming one hundred prefects and ten *commissaires*. But the Southern movements complained that the Resistance was insufficiently represented, and the negotiations dragged on into 1944. By March, all but fifteen prefects had been chosen, but there were still four *commissaires* to find on the eve of liberation. All the designated *commissaires* had administrative or political experience: there were eight members of the liberal professions, six former civil servants, three former parliamentarians. Although this was hardly the elite formed in the Maquis of which *Franc-Tireur* had dreamed, most of the appointees had genuine links to the Resistance: the competing claims of political virtue and administrative competence were satisfactorily met.[56]

Like Laffon, Closon, whose job it was to select the members of the CDLs, worked in co-operation with a subcommittee of the CNR. Each CDL was to have about ten members, but it was decided that there would also be a smaller 'active core' (*noyau actif*) to prepare the insurrection which was planned for the liberation. The *noyau actif* would comprise only members of the movements, to reassure Resistance leaders who feared that the CDLs might fall into the hands of politicians.[57] Especially in the South, where the Resistance was more politicized, there was tough bargaining over the composition of the CDLs. One point of contention was the number of places allocated to the political parties. Another problem was the attitude of the Communists. Initially they showed limited interest in the CDLs since these contradicted the Communist desire that the situation at the liberation should be as fluid as possible. Then the Communists decided that the CDLs offered them a way of consolidating their power locally. Where possible, they tried to get their Committees of Fighting France recognized as CDLs. This succeeded in a few cases, like the Isère, where they secured three out of five places on the *noyau actif*. But generally, in the South, the MUR tended to prevail, partly because it was accorded places for each of its three component movements, and partly because, however dynamic the Communists were becoming, their institutional presence lagged behind those movements which had been around longer.[58]

The Communists did score a major success in September 1943, by setting up a Parisian Liberation Committee (CPL), a kind of CDL for the capital. Of the eighteen members, which included the main Northern movements, like Défense de France, OCM, Libération-Nord, CDLR, and CDLL, seven were Communists or members of Communist front organizations. Closon reluctantly accepted

---

[56] Bellescize, *Les Neuf Sages*, 189–208; C.-L. Foulon, *Le Pouvoir en province à la libération: Les Commissaires de la République 1943–1946* (1975), 70–84.

[57] Closon, *Le Temps des passions*, 138–60.

[58] Buton, *Les Lendemains qui déchantent*, 50; Virieux, 'Le Front national', 573–8; Hostache, *Le Conseil national*, 289–316; Closon, *Le Temps des passions*, 138–40.

this fait accompli: 'we cannot hope to get the help of the Communists if we eliminate them from the Paris scene. We know the methods of our comrades, and realise that it is better to give them an official position than allow them to create organisations in the shadows to spread disorder.'[59]

As well as preparing the transfer of power at local level, the CFLN also set about organizing a team to take over central government in the period between liberation and the arrival of de Gaulle. This was to be the task of so-called provisional secretary-generals who were in effect to act as a pre-provisional government. The CGE drew up a list of nominations mostly drawn from its own ranks, and this excited the ire of the CNR which had not been consulted. In the end, most of the CGE's original choices were accepted, but the CNR gained an important concession when it obtained the right to appoint a ministerial commission to advise the secretary-generals.[60]

Closon and Laffon played an important role in this period, in co-operation with Bingen, Serreulles, and the CGE. This was the period when de Gaulle's delegates, operating with little guidance from Algiers, were thrown on to their own resources. Although no individual had acquired authority comparable to Moulin's, the Delegation as a whole was assuming the appearance of a provisional government in waiting. What it now required was a more formal recognition of its importance by de Gaulle after months of neglect. This finally occurred on 10 March 1944 when de Gaulle appointed Alexandre Parodi as his single Delegate to France. Parodi's appointment was accompanied by detailed instructions formalizing the hierarchy among de Gaulle's representatives in France. At the apex was Parodi himself, the Delegate-General, with two seconds-in-command, Teitgen and Lacoste (both, like him, members of the CGE), and a number of deputies with specific duties, including Laffon and Closon. In each zone, there was also a deputy delegate: Bingen for the South and Roland Pré for the North.[61]

The 10 March instructions also clarified the military organization of the Resistance, which had undergone several changes since the summer of 1943. The disruption which followed the arrests of Moulin and Delestraint had demonstrated the dangers of excessive centralization and BCRA had devised a more decentralized system which would allow the regions to function autonomously, even if cut off from the centre. Each military region was allocated a 'Regional Military Delegate' (DMR) whose role was to liaise directly with London. The only central co-ordination was provided by two zonal military delegates (DMZs), one for the North and one for the South. The DMRs, who were parachuted into France from September, had no hierarchical authority over regional AS commanders. But their possession of radio contact with London, and their responsibility for distributing material, gave them considerable power.[62]

[59] Footitt and Simmonds, *France 1943–1945*, 49; Closon, *Le Temps des passions*, 176–9. On the CPL, see H. Denis, *Le Comité parisien de libération* (1963).

[60] Bellescize, *Les Neuf Sages*, 214–31; Teitgen, '*Faites entrer le témoin*', 88–102.

[61] Hostache, *Le Conseil national*, 192–7.   [62] Crémieux-Brilhac, *La France libre*, 766–70.

The only problem with this system, as Brossolette noted in the autumn of 1943, was that some regions, especially in the North, had barely begun building a command structure for the AS. It was impossible to decentralize power which had never existed in the first place.[63] It was therefore decided to reintroduce some degree of centralization, especially since all the military forces of the Resistance were now to be incorporated into a single FFI with a central general staff. The 10 March instructions created the post of National Military Delegate (DMN), crowning the hierarchy of zonal delegates and DMRs. The role of the DMN was to liaise between London/Algiers and the FFI general staff in France. This post was given to Jacques Chaban-Delmas, making him the military equivalent to Parodi, although ultimately subordinate to him since Parodi was representative of the civil authority of the CFLN. It was also necessary to establish unambiguously who commanded the military forces of the Resistance. This had been a grey area since the death of Delestraint. In February 1944, the Resistance had set up a Military Action Committee—eventually known as COMAC—to oversee the creation of the FFI. Although COMAC was an emanation of the Resistance movements, it had been encouraged by the Delegation on the grounds that it would speed up the military integration of the Resistance. But de Gaulle wanted to ensure that the Resistance did not use COMAC to claim a military authority which he insisted should rest with the CFLN: this had been the major bone of contention between Moulin and Frenay. On 10 March, de Gaulle therefore underlined that COMAC did not have right of command over the FFI; its role was only one of inspection and co-ordination. On 4 April, he appointed General Koenig as overall commander of the FFI from London. Thus the structure of the clandestine State and its secret army was organized as shown in Fig. 1.

Neat diagrams, however, fail to capture the constantly shifting dynamics of the Resistance. For a start, the steady haemorrhage of Resistance leaders always threatened to disrupt these painfully constructed hierarchies. After Bingen's death in May, it took time for Parodi to find a successor who could win the trust of the MLN leaders. In the Resistance, authority had to be earned: the personality of individuals was more important than the labels they wore.[64] The potential for conflict went deeper than personalities. It revolved around the thorny problem of the relationship between the Resistance and de Gaulle. The compromise between the CNR and the CFLN on the powers of the CDLs left much scope for interpretation. The CNR announced in April 1944 that CDLs had the right to appoint provisional municipal councils at the Liberation.[65] This was certainly a breach of the agreement that had been reached, and conflicted with a CFLN ordinance of 21 April 1944 on the organization of local power after liberation. This document curtailed the powers of the CDLs by requiring them to

---

[63] Cordier, *La République des catacombes*, 585–6.
[64] Hostache, *Le Conseil national*, 198–9.
[65] Ibid. 300–5, 465–70; Debû-Bridel, *De Gaulle et le Conseil national de la Résistance*, 137–8, 262–4.

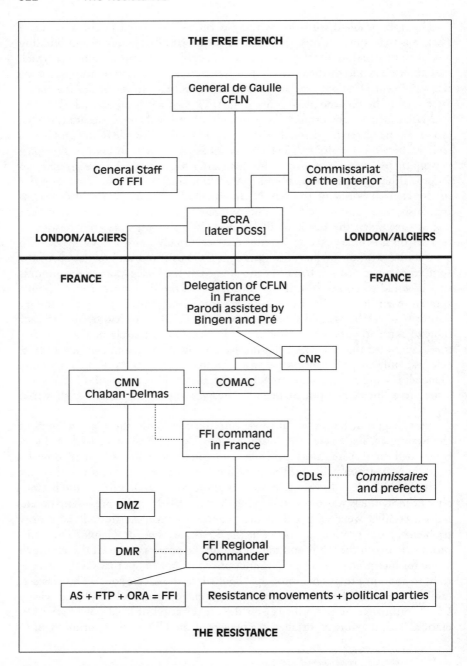

Fig. 1 The Organization of the Resistance and Free French at the end of 1943

reinstate the municipalities which had existed in 1939, purged of their collaborating elements. De Gaulle wanted no repetition of the Corsican situation.[66]

Thus the parallel set of structures which had been created for the liberation —CDLs and *commissaires*, secretary-generals and ministerial commissions, COMAC and DMN—left many questions unresolved. The heart of the problem was the relationship between those bodies representing the CFLN, the embryonic government of the future, and those representing the Resistance. Was the CNR simply a representative of the Resistance in France—standing in the same relationship to the Delegation as the Algiers Consultative Assembly to the CFLN—or did it have executive powers of its own? Was it like a pre-provisional government or a pre-provisional legislature? In practice, the CNR and the Delegation worked together fairly harmoniously, but the CNR and its dependencies offered an alternative power base, and an alternative source of legitimacy, in any rivalry with the CFLN. Many people feared that the Communists intended to make full use of these possibilities.

[66] Closon, *Le Temps des passions*, 239–34.

Part V

Liberation and After

Introduction to Part V

At the end of February 1944 Walter Stucki, the Swiss Minister at Vichy, reported on a meeting with Laval:

> He tried first to prove to me that Germany could never lose the war. According to him the fall back in the East was intended to lengthen and weaken the Russian lines of communication. In the summer a powerful German counter-offensive would result in the annihilation of Russia . . . There was no question of a breach of the Atlantic Wall. I repeated this conversation to one of his close collaborators who said to me: 'what do you expect! Laval has played banco and he knows he has lost. But he wants neither to believe nor admit it.'[1]

It is hard to believe that Laval did not realize at the beginning of 1944 that the game was up. On two occasions, in February and May, he offered himself to Abetz as a possible peace mediator between Germany and the West, at the expense of the Soviets. There was no response.[2] This did not mean Laval had no more cards to play. Germany's defeat was now inevitable, but what would follow it was not yet clear. There were at least four possibilities.

1. That by exploiting Roosevelt's distrust of de Gaulle, Laval or Pétain might succeed in presiding over the transition to liberation. This solution, which might be called the 'Badoglio scenario', had no chance of success unless the Americans were persuaded that Vichy was still able to keep order in France. It also required giving the regime a last-minute democratic facelift, as had already been tried in the autumn of 1943.

2. That the Allies would administer France directly on the model of the Italian AMGOT (Allied Military Government of Occupied Territories). Certainly this was one of the options being considered by Roosevelt. At Charlottesville, Virginia, a team of Americans was being trained to be ready to administer liberated France.

3. That liberation would spark off a descent into anarchy or at least a total disintegration of central power, leaving the field open to a much-feared Communist attempt to seize power. Whether or not the Communists had any

---

[1] Cointet, *Pierre Laval*, 473.   [2] Warner, *Pierre Laval*, 392.

intention of trying to do this, the Allies and de Gaulle certainly liked to pretend that there was a real danger. The Corsican precedent was a reminder of how effective the Communists could be at furthering their interests.

4. That the plans which the CFLN had devised would ensure a smooth assumption of power by de Gaulle. But quite apart from any ambitions which the Communists might have had, these plans left much scope for conflict between the Resistance—Communist or otherwise—and the CFLN.

Which of these outcomes came about would depend partly on the rapidity with which France was liberated. It would also depend on the attitude of a population whose total alienation from the Vichy regime did not necessarily imply that it was ready to fall into the arms of de Gaulle, or that it would not turn to a saviour ready to offer it not only liberation but also peace and order, and save it from the civil war which threatened. The end of the war was in sight, but the future of France remained an open question.

22

Towards Liberation:
January to June 1944

By the spring of 1944, much of southern rural France could be more appropriately described as 'Resistance France' than 'Vichy France'. In many areas the Resistance now had more impact on people's lives than the Vichy government.[1] In March, the new prefect of the Corrèze, Pierre Trouillé, described his *département* as experiencing two occupations: seventeen cantons were controlled by the Maquis, and nine, mainly in the urban areas, by the Germans. Without resistance approval, a prefect could no longer operate, and Trouillé quickly made contact with the Maquis.[2] A similar situation existed in the neighbouring Dordogne where the prefect reported that he had lost control over his *département*. The Germans stuck to the towns, emerging only on brief and bloody forays.[3] They now viewed the Maquis as a genuine military threat in the eventuality of a landing.[4] After a meeting with d'Astier in January 1944, Churchill too was persuaded of the potential of the Maquis, and he ordered an intensification of arms drops to the Resistance.

The Milice State: Darnand and Henriot

Enfeebled from above by the Germans, from within by the collaborationists, from below by the Resistance, and from outside by de Gaulle, the Vichy government existed in only the most nominal sense. Since December 1943, Pétain was constantly shadowed by his German minder, Cecil Renthe-Fink, whom he called his gaoler. Laval hardly had more power than Pétain. In January Sauckel, whose influence was now eclipsing Speer's, demanded a further million workers, at a rate of 91,000 per month, and threatened to comb the protected 'Sperr-Betriebe'. Laval was forced to extend STO liability to every man aged between

[1] Kedward, *In Search of the Maquis*, 116.
[2] P. Trouillé, *Journal d'un préfet sous l'Occupation* (1965), 8, 19.
[3] M.-T. Viaud, 'Problèmes stratégiques et tactiques des maquis de Dordogne', in Marcot (ed.), *La Résistance: Lutte armée et maquis*, 261.
[4] Jäckel, *La France dans l'Europe*, 438.

16 and 60, and even to married (but childless) women between 21 and 35. Laval did, however, secure the concession that these women would not be sent to work in Germany. In March, he was forced to appoint Marcel Déat as Minister of Labour, with the task of overseeing labour conscription. Déat's entry into the government, in the wake of Joseph Darnand and Philippe Henriot, signalled the final victory of the Paris collaborationists: he did not even bother to come to Vichy. Having preached the gospel of collaboration for four years, Déat was now confronted with its realities, in the form of Sauckel screaming at him for more workers. All this was somewhat academic: in the first four months of the year, fewer than 20,000 workers left for Germany.[5]

As the Vichy regime lost control, it became more violent and unpredictable. The strong man was now Darnand, who had total authority over internal security. On 20 January, summary courts were instituted to judge 'terrorists' expeditiously. Bousquet's delimitations between French and German spheres of authority were now redundant, and the French police were required to work directly with the Germans.[6] In fact the police were no longer reliable and Darnand resorted more to the Milice, stuffing its members into key positions. The new director of prisons, Jocelyn Maret, was a *milicien* who dressed as a Nazi and gave the Nazi salute.[7] There was an administrative purge: thirty-one prefects or sub-prefects were sacked or moved, nine at the direct behest of the Germans. In May, the existence of the Resistance infiltration network Super-Nap was uncovered, and this sparked off another purge of thirty-six prefects or sub-prefects. Most were deported to Germany.[8] A few prefects, like Chiappe in Orléans or Pujes in the Pas-de-Calais, remained unquestioningly devoted to the regime, but most tried to mitigate the effects of the irruption of these thuggish elements into the administration.

The Milice became ever more unrestrained. On 2 December 1943, the respected Radical newspaper editor, Maurice Sarraut, was assassinated; on 10 January 1944, it was the turn of the 81-year-old Victor Basch and his 82-year-old wife. Basch's crime was to have been president of the League of the Rights of Man and also a Jew. Apart from carrying out such killings and pursuing resisters, the Milice also participated enthusiastically, along with the PPF, in rounding up Jews. Milice violence spiralled further out of control after Pétain's broadcast on 28 April condemning resistance terrorism.[9] Collaborationist organizations like the Milice and the PPF were now attracting increasingly marginal, even criminal, elements of society. Many of them were young men who had joined to escape from STO. This was true of about a third of the *miliciens* in Marseilles in 1944. By this time 55 per cent of PPF members in Marseilles were under 28 as opposed to 15 per cent in 1940–2.[10]

[5] Milward, *French Economy*, 169–70.   [6] Baruch, *Servir l'État*, 538.
[7] Ibid. 537.   [8] Ibid. 544–60.   [9] *Discours aux Français*, 324–6.
[10] Jankowski, *Communism and Collaboration*, 92–130.

In its last stages Vichy has been described as a fascist regime. But there was no longer a grand project, no illusion of winning mass appeal. The regime had become a police state—or Milice state—which existed only to crush its enemies. In 1940, Vichy's rhetoric had oscillated between three themes: regenerating France, protecting the population from the consequences of the war, and preserving order. In 1944 only the last theme remained: Vichy presented itself as the last bulwark against revolution and anarchy. The regime lived on fear. The executant of this policy was Darnand; its orchestrator was Philippe Henriot, the French Goebbels.

In the inter-war years Henriot had moved from the National Catholic Federation to the right wing of the Fédération républicaine. After 1940, his anticommunism drove him inexorably rightwards. His fanatical Catholicism makes it difficult to describe him as a fascist, but by 1943 he was certainly an unconditional collaborationist. After taking over responsibility for propaganda in 1944, he spoke twice daily on the radio. Playing on the fear of civil war, he depicted the Resistance as a horde of terrorists and Communists. He was a mesmerizing orator and his broadcasts had an extraordinary impact. One observer noted that the streets were deserted when he spoke; Trouillé reported that everyone found Henriot compelling, even those who were not persuaded by him. A case in point was François Mauriac who, according to his son Claude, started switching from the BBC to tune in to Henriot: 'he cannot, despite everything, stop himself listening . . . refuting the arguments as he goes along, as if he needed to persuade himself'.[11] For Maurice Schumann on the BBC, Henriot was an adversary not to be underestimated.

Glières: 'Defeat of arms, victory of souls'

The climax of their duel over the airwaves occurred during the battle of the Glières Maquis in March 1943. Glières was a plateau, 1,500 metres high, in the Haute-Savoie. In the summer of 1943, a military mission was sent from London to assess if it could be used as an operational base for a secret Alpine army. The conclusion was positive, and Romans-Petit was instructed to organize the local Maquis. Once Churchill decided to arm the Maquis, Glières was chosen as a site for parachute drops. Romains-Petit, forced to return to the Ain, where his own Maquis was under pressure, appointed Lieutenant Théodose ('Tom') Morel to replace him. At the end of January, Morel took a detachment of *maquisards* to Glières to receive the first parachute drops. These events occurred just when Darnand needed to prove to Germany that he was ready to act vigorously

---

[11] Martin du Gard, *Chronique de Vichy*, 311–13; Trouillé, *Journal d'un préfet*, 82; C. Mauriac, *Les Espaces imaginaires* (1975), 71. On Henriot, see R. Kedward, 'The Vichy of the other Philippe', in G. Hirschfeld and P. Marsh (eds.), *Collaboration in France: Politics and Culture during the Nazi Occupation* (Oxford, 1989), 32–46.

against the Resistance. Deciding to make an example of the Haute-Savoie, he despatched a force of *miliciens* and GMR. Schumann broadast to the Haute-Savoie, warning of an imminent attack, and virtually calling for an insurrection. Although, at the behest of BCRA which opposed premature action, he followed this broadcast with counsels of caution, Schumann's words had already had their effect.

This combination of these circumstances—the imminence of arms drops, the fear of an attack by Darnand, the eloquence of Schumann—caused the numbers on the Glières plateau to swell to almost 500. Three parachute drops occurred, and there were sporadic skirmishes between the *maquisards* and the Vichy forces. In one of these, on 9 March, Morel, whose charismatic leadership had contributed to the reputation of the Maquis, was killed. Although the noose was tightening around the *maquisards*, Morel's replacement, Captain Anjot, decided to fight on. Darnand visited Annecy on several occasions to supervise operations, but the *maquisards* held out. The Milice was better at torturing than fighting, and the GMR were unhappy about fighting not only 'terrorists' but also regular officers like Morel and Anjot. Eventually the Germans lost patience. After a preliminary air bombardment of the plateau, 6,000–7,000 German troops, aided by the Milice, moved in for the kill on 24 March. Two days later, Anjot gave the order to disperse, but too late to prevent the deaths of about 150 *maquisards* in the retreat. Another 200 *maquisards* and local civilians were hunted down and killed by the Milice in the following weeks.

There was much controversy about what had gone wrong. Was it a mistake, as the Communists alleged after the war, to have encouraged a static concentration of forces—a kind of Alpine army—instead of small mobile units? In fact, Glières had not been conceived as the site of an Alpine army, but as the destination for parachute drops to supply what might eventually become one. But once the supplies had been dropped, the *maquisards* were reluctant to abandon the site; and it also took time to unload the containers and store their contents. Thus the *maquisards* became prisoners of the parachute drops. At the same time, the sheer numbers of *maquisards* congregating on the plateau led some to believe that an army was forming under their eyes. Even Jean Rosenthal, one of the London envoys who had been sent out in 1943, succumbed to this excitement. He appealed to London for troops to be parachuted to relieve the *maquisards* and allow Glières to hold out until D-Day. The tragedy of Glières was not so much a misconceived strategy as confusion about what the strategy should be.

As the first fully-fledged battle between the Maquis and the Germans, Glières became a myth which transcended the defeat. Romans-Petit called it 'defeat of arms but a victory of souls'. For almost a month, a mixed bunch of AS and FTP *maquisards* (including fifty-six Spanish Republicans) had sunk their differences and lived out the image of purity, heroism, and camaraderie which constituted the Maquis legend. They had sworn an oath to 'Live in freedom or die'. It was because he realized that a myth was being born that Anjot delayed the order to disperse. Schumann, in constant radio contact with Rosenthal, broadcast the epic adventure to the world. The BBC announced that three countries in Europe were resisting the Germans: Greece, Yugoslavia, and the Haute-Savoie. On the other side, Henriot, who rushed down to the Haute-Savoie when the battle was over, depicted the *maquisards* as a criminal rabble.[12]

Who won this propaganda war? The prefect of the Haute-Savoie, although not favourable to the Resistance, reported that the local population had not swallowed Henriot's version of events. A secret poll undertaken by the CFLN found that 94 per cent of respondents admitted to listening to Henriot's broadcasts, but 84 per cent also said that his words had no effect on them.[13]

Springtime of Fear

Henriot did not convince, but he did instil fear in his listeners. People had waited so long for liberation that lassitude and anxiety had replaced hope. As Morandat described the state of France to London on the eve of D-Day: 'the population is feeling the effects of four years of nervous tension, emotion and hopes raised then dashed . . . People believed in the landings in January then February . . . and this will go on until it arrives. It is no longer the long-awaited miracle but a mathematical certainty, and it has in the process lost its wondrous quality.'[14] Resentment was growing towards the Anglo-Americans who seemed more capable of bombing France than liberating her. Four bombing raids on Paris in March and April left 1,113 dead. On 26–7 May, ten major cities were hit, causing almost 6,000 deaths.

At the same time, the Germans inspired increasing terror as they resorted to random reprisals in the hope of cutting off the Maquis from the population. An operation against the dispersed Maquis groups of the Cévennes between 26 February and 4 March was accompanied by atrocities like the burning of the village of Ardailles and the massacre of sixteen inhabitants of the village of Les Crottes.[15] On 1 April, the SS Division Adolf Hitler massacred eighty-six inhabitants of the town of Ascq a few miles from Lille. Early April, in the Corrèze, witnessed what Trouillé called the 'bloody week': houses burned, 3,000 arrests, fifty-five executions.[16] The combination of Allied bombing and German massacres had made France a battlefield again.

On top of this came the violence of the Milice. In most communities, the *miliciens* were pariahs. Their families were sent miniature coffins to show the

[12] M. Germain, *Glières: Vivre libre ou mourir* (1994); J.-L. Crémieux-Brilhac, 'La Bataille de Glières et la guerre psychologique', *RHDGM* 99 (1975), 45–72; Kedward, *In Search of the Maquis*, 132–41; Crémieux-Brilhac, *La France libre*, 796–811; Noguères, *Histoire de la Résistance*, iv. 422–36.

[13] Kedward, *In Search of the Maquis*, 138; Eck and Crémieux-Brilhac, *La Guerre des ondes*, 126.

[14] Veillon, *Vivre et survivre*, 275–6.

[15] Kedward, *In Search of the Maquis*, 122–3.

[16] Trouillé, *Journal d'un préfet*, 33–46.

fate in store for them. Many *miliciens* defected, but those who did not resorted to ever more desperate acts of violence, knowing that they had burnt their bridges. One report to the CFLN in 1944 described the country as in a 'state of pre-civil war': 'the Milice assassinate daily and arrests by the Germans and the Vichy police are common currency. No one, strictly no one knows if they will sleep the night in their bed, if they will be executed or shot the next morning. We live in a dreadful atmosphere, stifling and agonizing, above all in the big cities.'[17]

Resistance attacks increasingly targeted the Milice. One tract read: 'From today every member of the Milice must be thought of as a mad dog and treated as such. Fire on the Milice.'[18] In the Haute-Savoie two *miliciens* were killed in September 1943, three in October, nine in November.[19] In the countryside, these Resistance attacks caused almost as much fear as the depredations of the Milice. Only 20 per cent of letters opened by the postal censors approved of Maquis 'terrorism' in the first six months of 1944. A typical comment was: 'The Maquis act in the name of patriotism, but fortunately the police are getting tough and I hope with all my heart that these youths are soon destroyed, for they commit all kinds of atrocities on innocent people.'[20] People were understandably cautious in their letters, but other evidence exists that Maquis violence was widely condemned. In the Jura, where there was terrible German repression in April, the FFI encountered people three months later who refused to shelter them, doctors who refused to tend the wounded, priests who refused to say prayers for the dead.[21] In the neighbouring Haute-Saône, the prefect noted: 'less and less do the terrorists enjoy the complicity of the rural population'.[22] Jacques Bingen reported to London on 'the great emotion now felt by the average Frenchman— that is the Frenchman who hates the Germans and awaits the liberation from his balcony or his cellar. The most fantastical stories are circulating; people talk of hold-ups and attacks on isolated people.'[23] There were also many examples of solidarity between the population and the Maquis, but it would be wrong to assume that these increased in the last months before the Liberation: reasons to fear the Maquis grew alongside the rejection of Vichy.

This does not mean, however, that France was divided into two equal camps. Only a tiny number of people were actively involved in either the Resistance or collaborationism, and among those who were not, sympathy lay, as it had for a long time, with the Resistance. In that sense there could not be said to have been

---

[17] A. Kaspi, *La Libération de la France* (1995), 24.
[18] Sweets, *Politics of Resistance*, 188.
[19] Abrahams, 'Haute-Savoie at War', 205–9.
[20] Laborie, *Opinion publique*, 311–26; Kedward, *In Search of the Maquis*, 113–14.
[21] F. Marcot, 'La Résistance et la population: Relation d'une avant-garde et des masses', *GMCC* 146 (1987), 3–22.
[22] Marcot, 'Résistance et population', 113; see also Laborie in *Colloque sur le maquis*, 39.
[23] Quoted in Cordier, *Jean Moulin: La République des catacombes*, 600.

a civil war in France as there was in Italy.[24] In civil war there must be two sides. But in France, if the Maquis was feared, the Milice was both feared and detested. One observer reported of the Hérault in April: 'The public is completely disorientated and ready to throw itself, like a lost child, into the arms of those who will bring peace.'[25]

April 1944: Pétain in Paris

This background explains a surprising recovery in the popularity of Pétain at the start of 1944.[26] The Allied bombing raids enabled Pétain to resume his role as the father of the nation, sharing its grief and shielding it from war. On 20 April, a bombing raid in Paris left 651 dead and 461 wounded. Six days later, Pétain visited the city, his first trip to the Northern Zone since the Armistice. He attended a ceremony in memory of the dead at Notre-Dame, and went to the Hôtel de Ville where he addressed a crowd from the balcony. Because large crowds turned out to cheer de Gaulle only four months later, this occasion has generated much sarcastic commentary on the fickleness of the French: how many who acclaimed de Gaulle in August had done the same for Pétain in April?

In fact, the crowds cheering de Gaulle were immeasurably larger, and although the newsreels of Pétain's visit depict an ecstatic population, this was only achieved by a certain degree of cheating. In the version that appeared once the visit had been memorialized in a documentary, the sad and tired face of an old lady, which appeared in the first version of the newsreels, had been replaced by a more suitable image.[27] Even then, the documentary cannot disguise the fact that the crowd's reaction was far from the adulation of 1940. The applause for Pétain reflected the ambiguity of the situation more than the inconstancy of the French. During Pétain's visit, the Germans kept in the background, and allowed French flags to be displayed for the first time since the Armistice. In this context, cheering Pétain was a way of showing patriotism.

The complex emotions aroused by Pétain's visit are recorded in the contemporary account written by Claude Mauriac. His attitude towards Pétain had been similar to that of most of his countrymen: hostility to collaboration from the outset; faith in Pétain turning to disillusion; increasing sympathy for the Resistance. It was no unconditional Pétainist who wrote the following words:

> At last, after at least two hours, the Marshal's car appeared, preceded by helmeted motorcyclists, as we had often seen in the newsreels, and it was exactly what I

---

[24] On the idea of a civil war in Italy, C. Pavone, 'The General Problems of the Continuity of the State and the Legacy of Fascism', in J. Dunnage (ed.), *After the War: Violence, Justice, Continuity and Renewal in Italian Society* (Hull, 1999), 5–20.

[25] Austin, 'Education and Youth Policies', 321.

[26] Flonneau, 'L'Évolution de l'opinion', in *VEF*, 510, 512; Laborie, *Opinion publique*, 296–7.

[27] See the documentary film *Les Voyages du Maréchal*.

had expected. What I had not expected was the emotion which suddenly took hold of me, at the sight, under the gold braid of his kepi gleaming in the sun . . . of Marshal Pétain . . . slumped between the Prefect of the Seine and the Prefect of Police, both also in full uniform . . . I was so moved that I failed to observe the reactions of the spectators (which had been the supposed pretext of my long wait), and was even incapable of saying if they had shouted 'Long Live Pétain' or 'Long Live France' or anything else. This was the miracle of the 'presence': on the radio the sparse acclamations which greeted Pétain when he left Notre-Dame had seemed to me ridiculous. But now I was overcome, and although I did not go as far as to shout, I was filled with a feeling of love and gratitude. 'If he does two tours of Paris like this, he will re-conquer France', I thought to myself . . . This morning, with a bit more distance from the event, I was even more amazed, and humiliated, by my reaction, which I have only noted down in my great desire to be always as truthful as possible.

Mauriac reported his reactions to a friend who had another version of the event: 'what overwhelmed me today was not the sight of the old man, it was a mother showing her 5- or 6-year-old child the French flag which was flying at the Hôtel de Ville for the first time since the start of the Occupation . . . For the child had never yet seen the French flag.'[28] The Paris visit was followed by others to bombed cities of the Northern Zone. In Normandy, Pétain found himself in deserted streets with closed shutters.[29] Visits to Orléans and Nancy were more successful. Overall, this evidence that the Pétain myth was not entirely discredited encouraged those at Vichy who hoped for a smooth transition to the post-Liberation regime. For de Gaulle, such a solution was out of the question—he did not wish to receive his legitimacy from Vichy—but it might appear attractive to the French if the alternative was a descent into anarchy or the threat of a Communist seizure of power. Everything depended on the Communists' intentions, and on de Gaulle's capacity to control events.

The Communists

The Communist Party was viewed by its opponents as a monolithic organization. But in 1944 the Party leadership was still scattered in three places: Thorez had been in Moscow since November 1939; Duclos and Tillon were in Paris; Marty was in Algiers. Contact between these leaders was difficult, and there were differences of tone, if not policy, between them. Thorez, who had disapproved of Duclos's overtures to the Germans in 1940, now believed that Marty was being excessively intransigent towards de Gaulle and missing the opportunity to increase Communist influence. He resented being stuck in Moscow at such a crucial moment. On the other hand, it was in Moscow that important decisions were taken. Thorez did not write an article without first securing Soviet

[28] Mauriac, *Terrasse de Malagar*, 164–8.
[29] Baudot, *L'Opinion publique sous l'occupation*, 115.

approval; Marty sent Moscow every scrap of information he could glean in Algiers.[30]

At the end of 1943, the Communists realized they had overplayed their hand in trying to impose conditions on their participation in the CFLN. On 4 April 1944, a compromise was reached, and two Communists joined the CFLN: Fernand Grenier and François Billoux. Nonetheless Communists remained extremely suspicious of de Gaulle. Marty told Moscow in April that the CFLN was stuffed with *attentistes* and de Gaulle was an enemy. Four months later, he described de Gaulle's government as a 'ragbag of agents of the Allies and the trusts and also elements linked to the enemy (Frenay)'. Johanny Berlioz told the Central Committee: 'we are entering the government as into battle for it is impossible to believe in the peaceful coexistence of two systems, either between capitalist and Socialist states, or between the parties within France'.[31]

The Communists relentlessly attacked the Delegation and the Resistance. They claimed they were being discriminated against in arms drops to the Resistance and that the exploits of the FTP were ignored by Gaullist spokesmen on the BBC.[32] Such was the ferocity of these attacks that the Delegation thought the Communists might break entirely with the CFLN. But they had no intention of doing this, and even when calling for an insurrection they were careful to declare that it was to be in the name of the CFLN.[33]

The Communists' strategy was to exploit every source of influence in order to maximize their options at the liberation. As well as consolidating their position within the Resistance institutions like the CNR, they tried to develop competing centres of power. At the end of 1943, they began promoting the formation of 'Patriotic Militias' to create the embryo of a sort of people's army. The Communists wanted these militias to be independent of the existing Resistance organizations, but the CNR would only accept them if they were integrated into the FFI. On 26 March, the Communists flouted this instruction by announcing they had set up a Central Council of the Patriotic Militias. In effect, this would have brought the Patriotic Militias under exclusive Communist control. In the face of protests by Copeau and Bidault (further evidence that Copeau was no Communist stooge), Villon backed down and accepted the dissolution of the Council. In fact, at this stage the issue was somewhat theoretical because the militias hardly existed except on paper.[34]

The Communists also pressed for the creation of Local Liberation Com-

---

[30] Buton, *Les Lendemains qui déchantent*, 38–48; M. Agulhon, 'Les Communistes et la Libération de la France', in Comité d'histoire de la Deuxième Guerre mondiale (CHDGM) (ed.), *La Libération de la France: Actes du colloque international tenu à Paris du 28 octobre au 31 octobre 1974* (1976), 67–90.

[31] Buton, *Les Lendemains qui déchantent*, 62–5, 73, 83; Courtois, *Le PCF dans la guerre*, 431–4.

[32] Courtois, *Le PCF dans la guerre*, 409–18.

[33] Sweets, *Politics of Resistance*, 133; Agulhon, 'Les Communistes', 76; C. Andrieu, 'Le Conseil national de la Résistance: Les Logiques de l'insurrection', in Fondation Charles de Gaulle (ed.), *Le Rétablissement de la légalité républicaine* (Brussels, 1995), 310.

[34] Buton, *Les Lendemains qui déchantent*, 61–2, 72, 89–90; Andrieu, *Le Programme commun*, 72–5.

mittees (CLL) in factories and villages, below the CDLs. These Committees would organize an insurrection at grass-roots level, and allow local leaders to emerge 'spontaneously'—as in Corsica. The aim was to fragment power as much as possible at the Liberation. In February 1944, the Communist dominated Parisian Liberation Committee (CPL) went ahead and set up CLLs in the Paris region. Closon worried that these could become like local Soviets, but rather than opposing this tendency outright, he tried to neutralize it by proposing to subordinate CLLs to the authority of the CDLs. When the CNR agreed to the creation of CLLs in March, the Communists had to concede this point. But they continued to harbour greater ambitions for the CLLs. In June, Party cadres were instructed that after the Liberation, they should nominate new municipal councils, taking account of the 'desire of the masses'. This contravened the CFLN ordinance of 21 April stipulating that in most cases pre-war municipalities would be restored, and that where they were not, the prefect would select a new one in consultation with the CDL.[35]

The Communists invented the idea of CLLs partly because they felt they were under-represented in the CDLs. They now demanded that this injustice be remedied. In the Alpes-Maritimes, for example, the CDL set up in December 1943 comprised eight members: three MLN, one Catholic trade unionist (CFTC), one non-Communist trade-unionist, one Christian Democrat (PDP), one Communist, and one 'Catholic'. The Communists successfully lobbied for two more seats, one for the FN and one for a Communist trade unionist. But this still gave them only three out of ten seats. In the spring of 1944, the Communists demanded seats for their various front organizations such as the UFF or the 'Committees of Wives of Resistance Martyrs'. The conflict became increasingly acrimonious until in June the CDL split when the Socialists and MLN refused to have any more to do with the Communists.[36] In the Var for similar reasons, the CDL was close to splitting by April.[37]

By now the MLN's fear of the Communists had prevailed over its suspicion of the Socialists. In April, it officially supported the Socialists' desire for representation on the *noyaux actif* of the CDLs.[38] Awareness of the political ambitions of the Communists should not obscure the fact that the Socialists were hardly less determined to maximize their political influence at the Liberation. In July 1944, Morandat reported that Libération-Nord had become essentially a movement of 'cadres placing its men in municipalities, in administrative posts and in CDLs'.[39]

By the Liberation, the Communists had about a quarter of the places on the

[35] Buton, *Les Lendemains qui déchantent*, 48–9, 73–4; Andrieu, *Le Programme commun*, 72–5.
[36] Girard, 'La Résistance dans les Alpes-Maritimes' (3ème cycle thesis, Nice, 1973), 94–8, 353–5.
[37] Guillon, 'La Résistance dans le Var', 587–604.
[38] Sadoun, *Les Socialistes sous l'Occupation*, 218–19.
[39] Aglan, 'Le Mouvement Libération-Nord', 589.

CDLs of the North and 35 per cent of those in the South.[40] Their greatest achievement, however, was to succeed, by a mixture of luck, subterfuge, and determination, in acquiring significant control over the military organization of the Resistance, starting with COMAC at the top. Originally COMAC had three members: one from the North (Jean de Vogüé of CDLR), one from the South (Maurice Chevance of MLN-Combat), and one from the FN (Pierre Villon). The Communists, therefore, had one out of three seats. The Delegation tried to reduce this to one out of four, by arguing that General Revers should be allowed to sit on behalf of ORA. But Revers's Pétainist past aroused hostility from more than just the Communists. After he had formally repudiated Vichy, he was granted a seat on COMAC in February, but only in a consultative capacity.[41]

At this point, the Communists had several pieces of luck. On 24 March, Claude Bourdet, Combat's representative on the Executive Committee of the MLN, was arrested. He was replaced by Marcel Degliame who proceeded to form a powerful axis with Libération-Sud's representative, Pascal Copeau. Now that the two dominant figures on the MLN were both sympathetic to the Communists, when Chevance, the MLN's representative on COMAC, left on a mission to Algiers, he was replaced by the Communist Maurice Kriegel. This meant that two of the three full members of COMAC were now Communists. On 5 May, Pontcarral-Jussieu, head of the AS, was arrested, and in his place COMAC appointed Alfred Malleret (Joinville), another undeclared Communist. Malleret in turn appointed the Communist Rol-Tanguy to command the FFI in the crucial Paris region. By the spring of 1944, the Communists held some twenty-two of the thirty-eight top military posts in the Resistance, although, owing to arrests, this figure fluctuated.[42]

COMAC now began to assert its independence. On 13 May, it declared that it had the right to issue operational orders to the FFI in France. A COMAC directive of 24 May called for 'mass resistance of an insurrectional nature'. Although COMAC accepted theoretically that the FFI would act within the framework of Allied plans, the role it was claiming for itself was bound to result in conflict with the CFLN. De Gaulle had, after all, only just appointed General Koenig to command the FFI from London.[43]

This was not simply a conflict between the Communists and de Gaulle. The non-Communist member of COMAC, de Vogüé, often sided with the Communists. Like many non-Communist resisters, he resented outside

[40] Foulon, 'Prise et exercise du pouvoir à la Libération', in CHDGM (ed.), *La Libération de la France*, 501–26: 511.

[41] Crémieux-Brilhac, *La France libre*, 769–70; Buton, *Les Lendemains qui déchantent*, 60–1.

[42] Buton, *Les Lendemains qui déchantent*, 68–9.

[43] M. Kriegel-Valrimont, *La Libération: Les Archives du COMAC mai–août 1944* (1964), 11–30; J. Delmas, 'Conceptions et préparations de l'insurrection nationale', in CHDGM (ed.), *La Libération de la France*, 433–59: 438–9.

interference in the affairs of the Resistance.[44] When the Communists complained that the CFLN had discriminated against them in the choice of provisional secretary-generals, they played on the touchiness of the Resistance at attempts to exclude it from decision making. When it came to working out the balance of power between the provisional secretary-generals, chosen by the CFLN, and the ministerial commissions to advise them, chosen by the CNR, the anti-Communist Blocq-Mascart was among those in favour of strengthening the latter.[45] The attitude of the Resistance to the CFLN was tellingly illustrated by Laffon's warning in July that the Resistance was unhappy at a new replacement for the post of Commissaire de la République in Rouen: 'if they reject any idea of a foreign AMGOT, they are also irritated by the idea of a French AMGOT'.[46]

The distinction between the 'activist' FTP and the '*attentiste*' AS was increasingly blurred when in April 1944 the AI (Immediate Action) division of the MLN was merged with the AS to form a single organization: the Free Corps of the Liberation (CFL). By eliminating the distinction between immediate action and action after D-Day, the CFL undercut Communist accusations of *attentisme*: the CFL was to the MLN what the FTP was to the FN.[47] Staking out a position between the CFLN and the Communists, the MLN moved closer to the latter.

In reality, the creation of the CFL made little difference on the ground. Where local Resistance leaders had accustomed themselves to waiting for orders from London before acting, the invention of a new abbreviation did not change anything. Madeleine Baudouin, a member of the MLN's Groupes francs (part of the AI) in Marseilles, remembered that her group, which carried out daring actions with minimal resources, found the AS excessively cautious. Despite being formally linked with it in the CFL, they felt more affinity with the FTP. The same was true of the saboteurs in the Workers' Action (AO) section of the MLN who were also now formally part of the CFL.[48] In other words, the line between immediate action and *attentisme* passed not between the non-Communist Resistance and the Communists, but through the non-Communist Resistance. The attraction of the Communists was that they were unambiguously in favour of immediate action, and this won them support from members of non-Communist movements who found their leaders too timid. The lure of military action was so compelling that even Philippe Viannay asked to be given an FFI command in the spring of 1944, although his resistance comrades felt it was absurd for him to stop doing what he had done brilliantly for three years—

---

[44] Granet, *Ceux de la Résistance*, 160–3; Wieviorka, *Une certaine idée*, 289.
[45] Andrieu, 'Le Conseil national', 313.   [46] Bellescize, *Les Neuf Sages*, 201.
[47] Guillon, 'La Lutte armée et ses interprétations', 152–4.
[48] M. Baudoin, *Histoire des groupes francs (MUR) des Bouches-du-Rhône de septembre 1943 à la Libération* (1962), 65, 84–5, 142; Guillon, 'La Résistance dans le Var', 619–23; Bourderon, *Libération du Languedoc méditerranéen*, 53.

produce a newspaper—in favour of something for which he had neither training nor experience.[49]

What Kind of Insurrection?

How was the military action of the Resistance supposed to fit into Allied plans? The truth was that the French Resistance had hardly figured in Allied planning before D-Day. The priority for arms drops in 1943 were Greece and Yugoslavia where genuine guerrilla war was occurring. Churchill's sudden decision to arm the Maquis was a typically impulsive gesture, but not part of any strategic reconsideration of the Resistance.[50] The Allies did not expect more from the Resistance than to disrupt German communications after D-Day. The same view was held by BCRA which drafted an 'Instruction on the military action of the French Resistance'. This was approved by the Allied General Staff, and communicated to FFI regional commanders in March 1944.

The Instruction anticipated a three-stage liberation battle: the coastal region (five days), the bridgehead (four to six weeks), and finally the Liberation of the rest of the country (four to six months). The Resistance would be provided with specific objectives: preventing the movement of German reinforcements to the coast (Tortoise Plan), sabotaging rail transport (Green Plan), disrupting radio communications (Violet Plan), targeting electricity lines (Blue Plan). The Instruction also envisaged the possibility of mobile operations by Maquis guerrilla groups based in secure mountain bases, but there was to be no insurrection. One BCRA official wrote in May: 'it is important for the success of our plans that there is in France no general insurrection, nor partial uprising, nor general strike'.[51] The only concession to the possibility of an insurrection was the idea that, in some mountainous areas of the south-east, military action might lead progressively to an insurrection, within the framework of Allied military planning, and assisted by an Allied airlift. This was dubbed the Caiman Plan.

Nothing could have been more different from the views of the Communists who were ever more feverishly calling for an insurrection. In the Communist scenario of liberation, strikes and demonstrations would lead on to the construction of barricades and the seizure of arms, and in the final stages, the masses, led by the Patriotic Militia, would join the armed action of the FTP. Such insurrectionary rhetoric was not confined to the Communists. *Lorraine* declared in February 1944: 'It is no longer the time to wait for D-Day. Fire on the Milice and the Boches. Forward towards direct action, towards the national insurrection.'[52] The word 'insurrection' summoned up romantic images of

[49] Wieviorka, *Défense de la France*, 278–9.   [50] Funk, *Hidden Ally*, 9.
[51] Delmas, 'Conceptions et préparations', 442–6; Crémieux-Brilhac, *La France libre*, 779–82.
[52] Pardieu, 'Un journal clandestin', 107.

nineteenth-century barricades. In October 1943, a manifesto of the resistance movements in the CCDM declared:

> There is no liberation without insurrection. This could take diverse forms, but what the Resistance owes to itself and to its martyrs is something more than a palace revolution or a coup d'état. As a manifestation of the strength of the masses the Insurrection will give a popular and democratic base to the provisional Government . . . and immediately impose on it revolutionary economic and social measures.[53]

Such language sounded similar to that used by the Communists, but in fact it lay somewhere between the BCRA/Allied conception of liberation as an operation carried out by trained fighters, witnessed by a non-participating but supportive population, and the Communist idea of liberation as an insurrection involving the whole population.[54] The Communists saw insurrection as a continuous process moving from civil disobedience to a *levée en masse*, and occurring independently of Allied operations; the manifesto confined it to the 'short space of time . . . between the departure of the Germans . . . and the arrival of the Anglo-Saxons'. The Communists wanted the insurrection to be as open-ended as possible; the manifesto wanted it to consolidate the legitimacy of de Gaulle's provisional government. The Communists wanted it to be as spontaneous as possible; the manifesto warned that it must not be 'left to fantasy or improvisation'. D'Astier telegraphed to Parodi in May that he hoped for a 'short insurrection' of three to four days, ideally forty-eight hours. This restrictive notion of insurrection as the culmination of liberation rather than the means by which it occurred, was acceptable even to the cautious officers of ORA.[55]

The Communists never missed an opportunity to remind people that de Gaulle himself had declared in a speech on 18 April 1942: 'Liberation is inseparable from national insurrection.' At that time, de Gaulle was in his most radical phase, and although he used the term insurrection on other occasions,[56] he was never again so unequivocal. In a document produced on 16 May 1944, specifying the military role of the Resistance during liberation, de Gaulle personally changed the words 'generalized insurrection' to 'generalized actions of force'.[57] Exactly what de Gaulle wanted is not certain, but his sense of the political dimension of the Resistance, and the profit he could draw from it, suggests that he was not averse to the idea of a short-lived insurrection—in a speech on 25 July 1944

[53] Vistel, *La Nuit sans ombre*, 624–32.

[54] 'Pour une inscription de la lutte armée dans les stratégies de Résistance', in Marcot (ed.), *La Résistance: Lutte armée et maquis*, 506–11; J. Delmas, 'Libération avec ou sans insurrection?', in C. Levisse-Touzé (ed.), *Paris 1944: Les Enjeux de la Libération* (1994), 28–40.

[55] Delmas, 'Conceptions et préparations', 440–1.

[56] 13 June and 14 July 1942; 18 Mar. 1943.

[57] Crémieux-Brilhac, *La France libre*, 782–4; Delmas, 'Conceptions et préparations', 449–51; C. Bachelier, 'L'Organisation de Résistance de l'armée et la lutte armée', in Marcot (ed.), *La Résistance: Lutte armée et maquis*, 117–28: 123–4.

he preferred the term 'national uprising [*soulèvement*]'—providing the moment was right, and order was quickly restored.

How quickly order was restored would depend on the effectiveness of the administrative structures prepared by the CFLN. But it was unclear how much influence the Allies were prepared to allow the CFLN in the liberated areas. In September 1943, the CFLN submitted a draft memorandum to the Allies distinguishing between a combat zone, where the military would have full control, and an interior zone, where the 'competent French authority' would be in charge. This document received no acknowledgement because the British and Americans had different views. Roosevelt was unrelenting in his hostility to de Gaulle. In fact, even many Americans were starting to find Roosevelt's attitude increasingly unsustainable, among them Eisenhower, who arrived in London, in January 1944, to take up his post as Supreme Allied Commander. Taking matters into his own hands, Eisenhower authorized discussions with Koenig. He was tartly reminded by Roosevelt that all arrangements worked out with the CFLN were tentative, and told that he should feel free to consult with other authorities. In fact, the Eisenhower-Koenig talks were ended on 4 May by de Gaulle, who was furious that the British had, for security reasons, imposed a ban on communications between London and Algiers.[58]

De Gaulle further annoyed Roosevelt by announcing on 26 May that the CFLN was now to be known as the Provisional Government of the French Republic (GPRF). Eisenhower, however, remained anxious for de Gaulle's cooperation after the landings, and Roosevelt agreed that de Gaulle could be invited to London on the eve of D-Day. De Gaulle arrived on 4 June, but a furious row broke out over the wording of the proclamation which Eisenhower intended to make on D-Day. This made no allusion to any French authority, and invited the French people to 'execute his orders'. De Gaulle was also enraged that his own message was to be broadcast last, after those of Eisenhower and the heads of state of the other countries of occupied Europe.

De Gaulle riposted that he would broadcast at an entirely different time from everyone else and that he would not allow Free French liaison officers to land with the Allied troops. This threw Churchill into such a fury that on 6 June he fumed that de Gaulle should be sent back to Algiers, 'in chains if necessary'. Cadogan commented on 5 June: 'we always start by putting ourselves in the wrong and then de Gaulle puts himself *more* in the wrong. He deserves to lose the rubber.' In the end, a compromise was reached: 20 liaison officers would depart out of the full quota of 120. Even so, on the eve of the landings, relations between de Gaulle and his allies could hardly have been worse and it still remained to be seen who would win the rubber.[59]

---

[58] Footitt and Simmonds, *France 1943–1945*, 16–28, 58–64; Crémieux-Brilhac, *La France libre*, 686–93.
[59] Crémieux-Brilhac, *La France libre*, 832–41; Footitt and Simmonds, *France 1943–1945*, 64–70.

23

Liberations

On 6 June 1944 at 5.30 p.m., eight hours after Eisenhower, General de Gaulle broadcast to the French people. Ordering them to obey the orders given by the 'French government', and making no mention of the American troops, he proclaimed: 'the supreme battle is engaged . . . it is France's battle and it is the battle for France . . . It is a battle which the French will fight with fury.' He knew of course that there were no French troops among the forces landing in France on D-Day.

On the same day Pétain broadcast a message which had been recorded three months earlier, following tough negotiations with the Germans. He summoned the French people not to obstruct the Germans in their defensive preparations or take any action that might invite German reprisals. To the end, Pétain clung on to French neutrality. In a subsequent message to the Legion, he appealed to the French to avoid 'fratricidal warfare': 'the French must not rise up against each other, their blood is too precious for the future of France and hatred can only compromise the unity of the country'.[1] As he spoke these words, the French conflict was entering its final and bloodiest stages.

Uprisings and Massacres

De Gaulle's D-Day message warned against 'premature insurrection'. But on the previous day the BBC had broadcast coded messages instructing the Resistance to implement all the prearranged colour-coded plans. This break with caution, which took Koenig by surprise, was decided by SOE in order to confuse the Germans about where the real attack would come.[2] During the first week after D-Day, the colour-coded plans were implemented with great success: 960 out of 1,055 planned operations of railway sabotage took place. Every train leaving Marseilles for Lyons after D-Day was derailed at least once during its journey; in the *département* of Indre, site of the railway line from

---

[1] Ferro, *Pétain*, 562–4.   [2] Crémieux-Brilhac, *La France libre*, 856–7.

Paris to Toulouse, there were eight hundred cases of railway sabotage in June alone.[3]

The BBC's call to action, however, had consequences which went beyond these careful plans. Thousands of new recruits flocked to the Maquis: in the Jura, the number of *maquisards* rose from about 1,000 in May to 8,000 in mid-June, in the Doubs from 100 to 5,000.[4] Often there were insufficient arms to go around, and volunteers had to be turned away.[5] In two cantons of Haute-Garonne, over 900 people, 'sent into a frenzy by the Allied landings', left their villages to join the Maquis in the woods. But they were so unprepared for the existence awaiting them that they were soon all sent home.[6]

Sometimes these new recruits are dismissed as 'resisters of the last hour' or 'mothball resisters'—referring to those who had got their uniforms out of four-year storage. But people who joined the Maquis in June 1944 did not know how soon the end would come: three months, remarks François Marcot, passes faster for a historian than it will have done for the *maquisards*.[7] Joining the Maquis in 1944 was more dangerous than ever before. These sudden concentrations of men excited German attention, often with tragic consequences. On the night of 6 June, seventy volunteers from Capestang, in the Languedoc, west of Béziers, set off in two lorries to join the Maquis. On the road, they fortuitously met a German lorry. Five were killed, and eighteen others arrested and shot the next day. A few days later, the Germans arrested 183 people in Capestang as a reprisal.[8]

The dangers of overconfidence were illustrated on a vaster scale in the forest of Mont Mouchet in the Auvergne. On 20 May, the regional AS commander, Émile Coulaudon (Gaspard), had ordered a mobilization of all able-bodied men of the region. Up to 6,000 volunteers answered the call, creating the largest-ever concentration of resisters. The Germans attacked on 10 June, and after four days the Maquis dispersed, at the cost of high casualties among fighters and local civilians. Coulaudon's motives in launching this operation are unclear. He may have been influenced by the 'Caiman plan' in which the Auvergne was given the role of a liberated enclave, pinning down German troops. He had announced, 'The Liberation Army is now constituted in the Auvergne.' One village erected a banner proclaiming 'Here begins Free France'. If Coulaudon had consciously provoked a military confrontation with the Germans, he gravely miscalculated. Mont Mouchet was both a tactical failure—the 350 French deaths vastly out-numbered German ones—and a strategic one—the troops who suppressed the

[3] M. R. D. Foot, *SOE in France* (1966), 389; S. Weiss, 'The Resistance as Part of Anglo-American Planning', in Sainclivier and Bougeard (eds.), *Enjeux stratégiques*, 53–66: 63.

[4] Marcot, 'Résistance et population', 152.

[5] Viaud, 'Problemes stratégiques et tactiques', in Marcot (ed.), *La Résistance: Lutte armée et maquis*, 264, 266.

[6] Kedward, *In Search of the Maquis*, 187.

[7] Marcot, 'Résistance et population', 153.

[8] Noguères, *Histoire de la Résistance*, v. 114; Kedward, *In Search of the Maquis*, 186.

rising had never been intended for the Normandy front. At best, Mont Mouchet was, like Glières, a sort of symbolic victory: the Resistance had challenged the Germans in the heart of Vichy France.[9]

There was no symbolic victory in the events at Tulle in the Corrèze. On 7 June, the FTP arrived. The small German garrison surrendered, and for fifteen hours Tulle was liberated. When the prefect expressed his fear that the Germans might return, he was told: 'Rest assured M. le Préfet, you won't see any more Boches in the Corrèze. France is in revolt.' This confidence did not last long. Hearing that a contingent from the heavily armed SS Division Das Reich was making its way to Tulle, the FTP withdrew on 9 June, following its orders not to engage in set battle with the Germans. On the next day, the Germans inflicted terrible reprisals on the civilian population: ninety-nine men were hanged from balconies, trees, and lamp-posts in the main square.[10]

In neighbouring Creuse, the town of Guéret also enjoyed a two-day liberation. In that case, however, there was no massacre after the Germans arrived. The difference in the treatment meted out to the two towns lay in the fact that in Tulle the resisters had executed some German prisoners alleged to belong to the Gestapo. At this stage of the war, the Germans were not usually so discriminating. On 10 June, the day after the Tulle massacre, the Das Reich Division descended on the town of Oradour-sur-Glane in the Haute-Vienne and massacred everyone they found: 642 people were killed. The men were machine-gunned; the women and children were burnt alive in the church; then the town was razed to the ground.

COMAC v. London

To prevent further carnage, on 10 June Koenig called for a 'maximum brake on guerrilla activity'. This provoked an immediate protest from COMAC which declared on 14 June: 'the national insurrection is a vital necessity for the country'.[11] Koenig's message caused a lot of confusion, and he backtracked on 17 June, calling on the Resistance to 'continue elusive guerrilla action to the maximum' while avoiding excessive concentrations of force. In practice, Koenig's revised message was not so different from COMAC's order on 21 June, to 'intensify everywhere mobile guerrilla action'.[12] But this was the beginning of two and a half months of acrimonious wrangling between COMAC and London. In COMAC's view, Koenig was in no position to give orders from London because the situation on the ground was changing so rapidly. It also rejected the idea of

---

[9] Martres, *Le Cantal de 1939 à 1945*, 347–498; Kedward, *In Search of the Maquis*, 164–70.

[10] Noguères, *Histoire de la Résistance*, v. 122–6; Kedward, *In Search of the Maquis*, 172; Amouroux, *La Grande Histoire des Français*, viii. 123–56.

[11] Kriegel-Valrimont, *La Libération*, 41–8.   [12] Ibid. 53–6.

confining the FFI to a purely military role: the political (the insurrection) and the military were inseparable. COMAC pushed for full command authority; in telegram after telegram, Koenig repeated that only he could issue orders to the FFI; Chaban-Delmas, de Gaulle's national military delegate (DMN), was caught in the middle. Koenig's own authority within the Allied camp was precarious because the Americans had been slow to recognize him as commander of the FFI. Only towards the end of June was Koenig's status confirmed with the setting up of a tripartite Franco-Anglo-American general staff (ÉMFFI), but this did not acquire real authority until August.[13]

The CNR was divided. The two Communists supported COMAC, and so did Pierre Hervé, representing the MLN. Given Hervé's Communist affiliations, it is tempting, but once again misleading, to see this simply as a conflict between the Communists and de Gaulle. Among the members of COMAC, de Vogüé sided with the Communists, although he was quite capable of opposing them on other matters like the Patriotic Militias. On the other hand, CDLL, CDLR, OCM, and Libération-Nord, which had always been readier than the Southern movements to view resistance in purely military terms, supported Koenig. Vogüé was much criticized by his own movement, the CDLR. A compromise was finally reached in mid-August. This conceded much ground to COMAC.[14]

In fact, the conflict was academic because neither COMAC nor London controlled the situation on the ground. Nor, in many cases, did the regional and departmental FFI commanders. The truth was that the integration of the military forces of the Resistance into the FFI was often very notional. After the arrest of Delestraint in June 1943, the organization of the AS had proceeded very slowly. When the first DMRs arrived from London in September, they found no accredited military leaders with whom they could work. As Serreulles reported to London in March 1944:

> It took the DMRs several months to make contact in their respective regions with the military leaders of the Movements who often didn't know each other . . . When the DMRs wanted to carry out the orders they received from London, they had to address the regional leaders of the different movements present in the region; these regional leaders then turned to their respective central leaders to ask for orders; some received an answer and others did not . . . The result was a situation of total anarchy . . . In some regions the DMRs tried to contact independent elements who might be willing to work directly for them . . . but that caused vehement protests from the other movements who claimed that the DMRs were suborning their members.[15]

[13] Funk, *Hidden Ally*, 11.
[14] Andrieu, 'Le Conseil national de la Résistance', in Douzou et al. (eds.), *La Résistance*: *Villes*, 285–98: 288–92; Crémieux-Brilhac, *La France libre*, 870–5; Buton, *Les Lendemains qui déchantent*, 87.
[15] Aglan, 'Le Mouvement Libération-Nord', 548–9.

Many of these organizational deficiencies had been overcome in the early months of 1944, but in many places the FTP and ORA jealously guarded their independence.[16] They continued to resent the DMRs, who had no hierarchical authority over the FFI commanders but enjoyed direct radio contact with London, and the SAP officers who had responsibility for parachute drops and controlled the arrival of precious supplies from London. Resistance leaders saw the DMRs and SAPs as outsiders imposed on them by London, 'local tyrants' who took too little account of the Resistance.[17] But Coulaudon in the Auvergne recalled that in his case the DMR had played almost no role: 'He had no importance; I hardly remember anything about him.'[18]

Although resented by the Resistance, the DMRs themselves frequently felt that their own position was undermined by other BCRA envoys or British agents who had been sent to France on specific missions. The various agents parachuted directly into France by the Allies included members of the SAS (Special Air Services), of the American Operational Groups (OG) and the 'Jedburgh teams'. The last were three-man units—British, American, and French—parachuted behind German lines to make contact with the Resistance, locate landing spots for parachute drops, and instruct the Maquis in the use of arms: 82 of them were dropped into France in June, July, and August 1944. Their ability to order arms directly from London enabled them to arbitrate between FTP, ORA, and AS leaders. Technically the Jedburgh teams were under the authority of the ÉMFFI, but in practice they acted on their own initiative, to Koenig's irritation.[19]

COMAC complained that these Allied missions were stealing forces from the Resistance,[20] and the Communists complained they were being discriminated against. But although the Jedburgh teams were wary of the Communists' political ambitions, they were not systematically anti-Communist; their main priority was military effectiveness. FFI commanders who had been in place for a long time could suddenly find their authority undercut. For example, an SAS unit of 175 men, commanded by the one-armed Commandant Bourgoin, was parachuted into Britanny on 5 June. The number of *maquisards* grew too large, and after a German attack on the Maquis camps at Saint-Marcel in the Morbihan, Bourgoin decided on 18 June to disperse his men to avoid a repetition of the events of Mont Mouchet. The regional FFI commander, Jaeger (Michelin), trying to pursue the COMAC policy of insurrection, reported his inability to

---

[16] For some examples, see Buton, *Les Lendemains qui déchantent*, 84; Abrahams, 'Haute-Savoie at War', 221; Luirard, *La Région stéphanoise*, 536; Bachelier, 'L'Organisation de Résistance de l'armée', 125–7.

[17] Wieviorka, *Une certaine idée*, 286.

[18] Martres, *Le Cantal de 1939 à 1945*, 362.

[19] A. Brown,'Les Jedburghs: Un coup de maître ou une occasion manquée?', *GMCC* 174 (1994), 127–42; A. Calmette, 'Les Équipes Jedburgh dans la bataille de France', *RHDGM* 61 (1966), 35–48; R. Frank, 'Les Missions interalliées et les enjeux de la lutte armée', in Marcot (ed.), *La Résistance: Lutte armée et maquis*, 353–60; Footitt and Simmonds, *France 1943–1945*, 85–6; Foot, *SOE in France*, 400–4.

[20] Kriegel-Valrimont, *La Libération*, 106–10.

impose his authority on the local FFI leaders who had welcomed Bourgoin like the Messiah.

Micro-Histories

The resolution of these conflicts depended on the local balance of forces between resistance organizations, on the authority of individual leaders, on chance arrests, and on the proximity of Allied forces. The situation was so fragmented that it is as difficult for the historian to tell a coherent national story as it was for COMAC or Koenig to control events—even to know what was going on. The General Staff of the FFI noted on 14 July: 'For many regions we are almost totally ignorant of not only the numbers and movements of the enemy, but even the state of our own forces and the operations they have undertaken.'[21] COMAC controlled less of France than the early Capetians. The military history of the Liberation can only be written as a series of micro-histories, different from *département* to *département*, valley to valley, village to village.

In the Seine-et-Oise, for example, Philippe Viannay the departmental FFI commander was in conflict with the DMR, Pierre Sonneville, a former naval officer. Sonneville had strictly military priorities: to win time for the Allies. Viannay had political priorities: 'to solder the country to the Resistance . . . and bring the mass of the population to participate in the struggle'. Sonneville complained to COMAC that Viannay was too reckless. In July, however, Viannay's relations with Sonneville improved when they both came under fire from the Communists. Viannay could not get the FTP to obey his orders, and far from being backed up by the regional FFI commander, Rol-Tanguy, he was the target of an unsuccessful attempt by Tanguy to have him replaced by a Communist. Tanguy also tried to remove Sonneville, and COMAC would have supported him but for the intervention of Chaban-Delmas. The situation was summed up by a letter to Viannay from one of his comrades in Défense de la France which speaks volumes about the conflicts within the Resistance:

> I am absolutely in agreement with you about defending the rights of the metropolitan Resistance against the Anglo-Saxons and the émigrés of Algiers [*a revealing indicator of how the CFLN was perceived*] . . . If COMAC was differently composed, there would only be one policy to follow. But unfortunately there are the facts which distort everything . . . COMAC is today purely and simply an instrument of the Communists. The real conflict is not France against Algiers or France against the Allies, for in that case how could one hesitate? The real conflict is a struggle between the Communists and de Gaulle . . . To take a stand against de Gaulle's National Military Delegate is to take a stand against de Gaulle.[22]

---

[21] Delmas, 'Conceptions et préparations', 457.   [22] Wieviorka, *Une certain idée*, 285–95.

In Provence, there were conflicts between the regional military commanders of the Resistance. The regional ORA commander, Jacques Lécuyer, was unhappy about Koenig's countermanding order of 10 June because his men had successfully liberated the lower Alps. He moved his headquarters into the mountains in order to build an Alpine retreat able to hold out against the Germans. Lecuyer's superior, the regional FFI commander, Robert Rossi [Levallois], also contested Koenig's view, but from an FTP perspective. He opposed the idea of a static Alpine redoubt and wanted to encourage resisters not to head for the mountains but to stay in the cities and launch insurrectional strikes. The regional CFL/AS commander Juvenal opposed both views, and wanted to postpone action until the Allies had landed in the south.

How these conflicts in the Provence region were resolved at departmental level depended on the allegiances of the departmental commanders. In the Alpes-Maritimes, the departmental FFI commander, Chatel, wanted to hold his guerrilla forces in reserve for the landings, but his chief of staff, Malherbe, who was from ORA, obeyed Lecuyer, and tried to bring the Maquis over to him. Chatel gave orders that Malherbe was not to be obeyed, but many ORA officers ignored him. As for Rossi, his orders had little effect on the ground, even on the FTP, and in the Basses-Alpes many FTP troops fought with the ORA. This situation was further complicated by Rossi's arrest on 17 July, and then almost immediately afterwards by that of his replacement Renard. When the Allies did land in the South in August, the Provençal Resistance had no functioning regional command. In such circumstances, it was remarkable that the Resistance was able to make any contribution at all.[23]

In general, the fate of FFI operations, in the seven weeks between D-Day and the moment when the Allies broke out of the Normandy bridgehead, depended on the Germans. Where the Germans decided to crush the Resistance, they could always do so. Where this was not worth their while, the innumerable local Maquis operations, especially in the South, helped destroy what was left of Vichy's authority. In the Aveyron, high in the Massif Central, the prefect reported on 12 June that the 'the Maquis had reduced prefectoral authority to impotence'; all the *département* of the Lot was in the hands of the Maquis except for the town of Cahors; in the Haute-Savoie, the FTP were in total control of Thonon and Bonneville, where 'they make their own laws'; the situation was similar in much of the Ain, Savoie, Gard, and Lozère.[24]

Nowhere did the Resistance enjoy greater success than in the small town of Mauriac in the Cantal, away from all major communication axes. The Resistance took control of Mauriac on 6 June. The *commissaire de la République* arrived; the CDL came out into the open and began to run the town; and the MLN installed its Southern headquarters there. Vichy and the Germans were fully aware of the

---

[23] J.-M. Guillon, 'La Résistance provençale', *Provence historique*, 178 (1994), 429–40; Noguères, *Histoire de la Résistance*, v. 107–11; Guillon, 'La Résistance dans le Var', 656–60.

[24] Kedward, *In Search of the Maquis*, 195–200.

situation, but given Mauriac's lack of strategic importance, the Germans did nothing, allowing it to become a sort of free enclave in occupied France. While the inhabitants of Oradour were being massacred, those of Mauriac could read, from 9 June, the first openly produced Resistance paper in France, *L'Homme libre*.[25]

Entirely different was the fate of the plateau of Vercors, south-west of Grenoble. This huge natural fortress had been designated by the Montagnards Plan of 1943 as the site of a Resistance army big enough to hold down substantial numbers of German troops. After Glières and Mont Mouchet, it proved to be the third, and bloodiest, proof that the Resistance could never win a pitched battle with the Germans. After D-Day, the number of *maquisards* on the plateau swelled to almost 4,000. On 3 July, they declared the re-establishment of the Republic. The Allies dropped large quantities of supplies, but no weapons. Nor was there any sign of an Allied landing in the South. German attacks intensified during July. On 21 July, the Maquis leaders sent a desperate telegram to London begging one last time for help. It ended by saying that if no help arrived, the defenders of Vercors would conclude that the leaders in London and Algiers were 'criminals and cowards'. On the same day, forty gliders appeared in the sky. The *maquisards* cheered until they realized the planes were German. By 23 July, the Germans had eliminated the Maquis. Some 640 *maquisards* and 201 local inhabitants were killed.[26]

De Gaulle in Bayeux

While sporadic fighting was occurring throughout France, where liberated pockets, like Mauriac, coexisted with pitched battlefields, like Vercors, or scenes of carnage, like Oradour, the Allies remained penned up in Normandy, unable to break through the German lines. It was in Normandy, therefore, that de Gaulle was obliged to test his popularity for the first time, although he might have preferred to choose another area for such an exercise. Normandy had suffered so badly from bombing that the Allies were far from popular. The Normandy peasantry anyway had the reputation of being prudent and conservative. The DMR reported at the end of 1943 that he found an apathetic population of black marketeers terrified of 'terrorists'.[27] The official report on the Tortoise Plan stated: 'Everywhere we came up against inertia and the feeling that we threatened the interests of the Norman peasant . . . Even after the invasion, the peasants preferred to sell their butter to the retreating Germans than to our men who were considered suspect.'[28] In their bridgehead, the Allies found no popular demand for a purge of the Vichy authorities. In Bayeux,

[25] Martres, *Le Cantal de 1939 à 1945*, 512–16.
[26] P. Dreyfus, *Vercors: Citadelle de la liberté* (1969); Noguères, *Histoire de la Résistance*, v. 336–85.
[27] Baudot, *Libération de la Normandie* (1974), 79–80.
[28] Porch, *French Secret Services*, 564 n. 118.

liberated on 7 June, Allied commanders met with co-operation from the Vichy sub-prefect.

De Gaulle decided to intervene before this became a pattern for the future. On 14 June, he landed at Courselles in Normandy, with a small entourage. Having paid his respects to General Montgomery, he set off for Bayeux. Two policemen met en route were told to go ahead and announce the arrival of General de Gaulle—whom they had not recognized. De Gaulle commented to an aide: 'see the State is restored; they have obeyed me when they didn't even know they were going to meet me'.[29] Having allowed long enough for people to gather, de Gaulle arrived in Bayeux where, in his words, he was greeted with 'extraordinary emotion'. Having visited the sub-prefect, who scrambled on to a chair to remove the portrait of Pétain which he had forgotten to take down, he spoke to a crowd of about 2,000. The Bishop of Bayeux, who expected to see de Gaulle surrounded by red scarved bandits, was reassured to find that his entourage included Thierry d'Argenlieu who had been at the same seminary with him, and Colonel de Boislambert, who was the nephew of a major benefactor to the Catholic Church in Normandy.[30]

Having visited two other localities, de Gaulle returned to England at the end of the day, leaving behind François Coulet as *commissaire de la République*. Coulet promptly dismissed the Vichyite mayor and sub-prefect. But his authority was not officially recognized by the Allies: visiting Normandy on 20 June and 11 July Churchill avoided meeting him.[31] The Allied administrators on the ground, however, although finding the Gaullist nominees less accommodating than their Pétainist predecessors, were happy to co-operate with them once it was clear that the population was ready to accept their authority. This de facto recognition of Gaullist power, which suited Eisenhower and Montgomery, made it increasingly difficult for Roosevelt to persist in ignoring de Gaulle. On 11 July, after de Gaulle had paid a visit to the United States, Roosevelt finally recognized the GPRF as 'the working authority for civilian administration in the liberated areas of France'.[32]

De Gaulle had successfully presented the Allies with a fait accompli, and his bluff had paid off. Although the crowds had cheered him, Allied intelligence reports described a population without strong political preferences, and in some areas even anti-Gaullist.[33] Jacques Kayser, a journalist travelling around liberated Normandy, and hoping to find Gaullist enthusiasm, was struck by the indiffer-

---

[29] D. Mauss, 'Rapport introductif', in Fondation Charles de Gaulle (ed.), *Le Rétablissement de la légalité républicaine* (1996), 184.

[30] Abrahams, 'Haute-Savoie at War', 301.

[31] J.-P. Benamou, 'L'Écho de l'arrivée du Général de Gaulle dans le Calvados', in Fondation Charles de Gaulle (ed.), *Le Rétablissement de la légalité républicaine*, 223–32: 226.

[32] Crémieux-Brilhac, *La France libre*, 843–54; R. Hostache, 'Bayeux, 14 juin 1944', in Fondation Charles de Gaulle (ed.), *Le Rétablissement de la légalité républicaine*, 231–42; Footitt and Simmonds, *France 1943–1945*, 70–95.

[33] Footitt and Simmonds, *France 1943–1945*, 79–82; Benamou, 'L'Écho de l'arrivée', 228.

ence of the population to politics in general and de Gaulle in particular. After one week he noted that no one had asked him any questions about de Gaulle. He was also amazed at the lavish meals he was served compared to his experience of wartime London: the Norman peasants were faithful to their reputation.[34] But Kayser was also struck by the fact that it seemed as if Vichy had never existed. De Gaulle had not arrived as a long-awaited Messiah; he had simply inserted himself into a void. The same was observed by the American historian Crane Brinton, reporting to the OSS. Having noted 'little spontaneous enthusiasm' for de Gaulle—no one had even mentioned de Gaulle's name to him in four days—Brinton went on: 'Vichy has faded away like Lewis Carroll's Cheshire cat, but not even the leer has remained . . . I need hardly tell you that the question as to whether the de Gaulle government is accepted simply does not exist.'[35]

The Last Days of Vichy

At the top, however, the Vichy government continued to go through the motions. In June, Admiral Fernet was still working on the powers to be exercised by the governors of the regions. Bonnard, who had been told by a medium in April that there would be no Allied landings, was worrying whether the baccalaureate examinations could go ahead as normal. As France spiralled into violence, he sent a memorandum to the examiners asking them to be generous in their marking so as to demonstrate 'the spirit of friendship which should govern the relations between the French'. He also quarrelled with Bichelonne over whether those who had spent more than a year in prisoner-of-war camps should be exempted from the entry exams to the civil service.[36]

Despite this serene indifference to reality, the final manoeuvring of the Vichy factions became ever more acrimonious. On 28 June Philippe Henriot was assassinated by the Resistance. He was given a near State funeral in Notre-Dame, conducted by Cardinal Suhard. The ultra-collaborationists felt that Laval had not paid sufficient respect to Henriot's memory, and they launched a final attack on him. Admiral Platon went to see Pétain on 9 July bearing a manifesto signed by, *inter alia*, Déat, Bichelonne, de Brinon, Bonnard, Benoist-Méchin, Drieu, Luchaire, Rebatet, and Chateaubriant. It called for Laval to be replaced by a head of government fully committed to the German war effort. The instigator of this plot was Déat who had visited Pétain in May, and came away convinced that he had won the Marshal over. Pétain's faculties may have been failing, but he was still sharp enough to outwit the incorrigibly credulous Déat. Hearing of the plot against him, Laval called a cabinet meeting on 12 July, the last to be held at Vichy.

[34] J. Kayser, *Un journaliste sur le front de Normandie: Carnet de route juillet–août 1944* (1991), 54, 62.
[35] C. Brinton, 'Letters from Liberated France', *French Historical Studies*, II/I (1961), 2–27: 4, 12.
[36] Baruch, *Servir l'État*, 562.

He rounded on his critics, and accused them of wanting to plunge France into civil war.[37]

If Laval clung to power, it was in the hope of presiding over the transition between Vichy and the post-Liberation regime. Pétain harboured the same ambition, and the two of them tried to outflank each other in the race to be in at the end. First, they tried to distance themselves from the ultra-collaborationists. Laval did so by publishing the minutes of the 12 July cabinet meeting. Pétain did so on 6 August in a long letter to Laval, belatedly condemning the excesses of the Milice.[38] In August, Laval conceived the idea of reconvening parliament. His idea was to win its support for the formation of a government which would present the Americans with an alternative to de Gaulle when they arrived in Paris. The key to this plan was Édouard Herriot, president of the lower house of parliament in 1940, whom the Germans had interned in Lorraine. With Abetz's approval, Laval had Herriot released and brought to Paris. Herriot did not entirely rule out Laval's proposition, and the two men resumed the camaraderie of two old parliamentary stagers of the Third Republic. Herriot, who was not without suspicions of de Gaulle, procrastinated, possibly in the hope of ensuring that such an arrangement would profit him not Laval. In the end, the whole scheme was sabotaged by the Germans themselves. On 17 August, three days after Herriot's release, Himmler ordered him to be reinterned. This was the history of collaboration in a nutshell: Abetz misreading the intentions of his masters, and Laval believing him.

During the negotiations Laval rang Pétain urging him to come to Paris and back the Herriot plan. Pétain refused to leave Vichy, not because he opposed the idea of organizing a smooth transition of power to the Allies, but because he wanted to be the beneficiary of such a plan. To this end, on 11 August, Pétain sent Admiral Auphan to Paris to represent 'the principle of legitimacy I embody', and be ready to negotiate on his behalf with the Allies or de Gaulle. But on 20 August the Germans arrived in Vichy and took Pétain forcibly to Belfort where he joined Laval who had been taken there two days earlier. Pétain had two messages ready. In the first, he protested against his abduction, and declared that he was no longer ready to continue as head of State; in the second, drafted by Henri Massis, he defended his actions since 1940, and expressed the hope that his sacrifice had paved the way towards 'the sacred union for the renaissance of the patrie'.[39]

Liberation and Insurrection

By now the Liberation of France was well under way. On 31 July, the Allies finally broke out of Normandy. The Third Army under General Patton swept

---

[37] Cointet, *Pierre Laval*, 479–82; Warner, *Pierre Laval*, 397–401; Ferro, *Pétain*, 549–50.
[38] Ferro, *Pétain*, 567–73.   [39] Pétain, *Discours aux Français*, 340–42.

through Brittany while the rest of the Allied forces headed eastwards towards the Seine. On 15 August, the Allies landed on the Riviera coast. Operation Anvil, as this was called, included seven divisions of the First French army under General de Lattre de Tassigny. The Allied advance along the south coast was extraordinarily rapid: troops arrived at Toulon on 23 August, twelve days earlier than planned; Marseilles fell on 28 August, twenty-six days earlier than planned. Moving up the Rhône valley, troops from de Lattre's army joined up with troops from Leclerc's Second Armoured Division, coming from the north, at Langres on 13 September.

The military contribution of the Resistance to this stage of the Liberation was more important than during the period immediately after D-Day. In Brittany, the Allies had planned for the Maquis to intervene when the Americans broke through from Normandy. The ground was prepared in July when eleven Jedburgh teams were sent to join Bourgoin's SAS groups. Substantial arms drops occurred, and by the end of the month there were 30,000 armed FFI fighters poised to act. Their contribution was so effective that when the Americans marched west to the naval bases of Lorient, Brest, and Saint-Nazaire, they encountered little German opposition.

This success encouraged Allied planners to upgrade the role of the Resistance in the Anvil operation. Fifty-two more Jedburgh missions were despatched in August. Originally the Allies had not intended to pursue the Germans up the Rhône valley before establishing a secure bridgehead on the Riviera coast. But the strength of the Resistance in the lower Alps led to a modification of these plans: a force was sent immediately to Grenoble in the hope of cutting off the German retreat in the lower Rhône valley. This plan worked so well that Allied troops reached Grenoble on 22 August, seven days after the landings, instead of three months as originally intended. The clearing of the road to Grenoble was one of the major strategic achievements of the Resistance although the size of the force sent to Grenoble was too small for the encirclement operation to succeed entirely.[40] In the Rhône valley itself, the Resistance helped to disrupt communications. The destruction of the bridge at Livron on 16 August, at the confluence of the Drôme and Rhône rivers, allowed the Allies to inflict terrible damage on the German troops escaping north. Had the Allies been able to arrive in greater numbers before the Germans restored a crossing over the Drôme, the entire German Nineteenth Army might have been destroyed.[41]

In the south-west, the role of the Resistance was less important because the Germans had spontaneously started to withdraw on 16 August in order to avoid being cut off by the armies advancing up the Rhone.[42] As they retreated, the Germans had to face the Resistance groups 'yapping at their heels like angry

---

[40] Funk, *Hidden Ally*, 123–8; Foot, *SOE in France*, 412; Crémieux-Brilhac, *La France libre*, 882–3.

[41] Funk, *Hidden Ally*, 153–5, 171–2.

[42] D. Pike, 'La Retraite des forces allemandes du sud-ouest de la France (août 1944)', *GMCC* 164 (1991), 49–73.

terriers closing on a fox', as M. R. D. Foot puts it. One hundred thousand Germans were cornered near Limoges and forced to surrender.[43]

Quantifying the contribution of the Resistance to France's liberation is difficult. One historian of French intelligence is sceptical about the importance of the Resistance, as is the economic historian Alan Milward. When Milward interrogated Speer about the effects of the Resistance on German war production, the reply was: 'What French Resistance?'[44] Certainly there were few Resistance operations which had any strategic impact on the outcome of the war. One exception might be the extraordinary exploits of André Jarrot and Raymond Basset (the 'Armada' team) working for BCRA and the RF section of SOE. Their sabotage operations caused major damage to the canal network of north-eastern France at a time when the Germans were desperately trying to send small craft down to Italy to prevent the Allied landings.[45]

In the period immediately after D-Day, the colour-coded plans were successfully implemented, but their impact has often been exaggerated. It is possible that the 11th German Armoured Division, which took twenty-three days to get from Strasbourg to Caen, was delayed by the disruption to communications, but more important was the fact that the German High Command had hesitated when and where to send the troops.[46] It is certainly not true, as was once alleged, that the Maquis delayed the progress of the Das Reich Division from Toulouse to Normandy, prolonging a journey of three days to two weeks. German sources show that the Division's orders were to terrorize the Maquis of the south-west as it moved north. The victims of Oradour could not even have the posthumous satisfaction of having diverted this force from its real mission; they were its real mission.[47]

In many cases, however, the Allies reported that the FFI's contribution to the Liberation had been greater than expected, and could have been greater still if it had been adequately armed.[48] Eisenhower later paid fulsome tribute to the role of the Resistance after the Allies broke out of Normandy:

> Great assistance was given us by the FFI in liberating Brittany . . . As the allied columns advanced, these French forces ambushed the retreating enemy, attacked isolated groups and strong-points, and protected bridges from destruction. When our armour had swept past them, they were given the task of clearing up the localities where pockets of Germans remained, and of keeping open Allied lines

---

[43] *SOE in France*, 413.

[44] Porch, *French Secret Services*, 225–64; A. Milward, 'The Economic and Strategic Effectiveness of Resistance', in S. Hawes and R. White (eds.), *Resistance in Europe 1939–1945* (1976), 186–203: 197.

[45] Foot, *SOE in France*, 147.

[46] Crémieux-Brilhac, *La France libre*, 858.

[47] Jäckel, *La France dans l'Europe*, 458–60.

[48] Weiss, 'The Resistance as Part of Anglo-American Planning', 60. For a specific example of the strategic contribution of the Resistance see A. Debon, *La Mission Helmsman: Un combat décisif de la Résistance au succès de l'opération Overlord* (juin–juillet 1944) (1997).

of communication . . . Not least in importance, they had, by their ceaseless harassing activities, surrounded the Germans with a terrible atmosphere of danger and hatred which ate into the confidence of the leaders and the courage of the soldiers.[49]

In his memoirs, Eisenhower concluded, probably over-generously, that the total contribution of the Resistance to the Liberation was the equivalent of fifteen divisions. In the end, such estimates can only be speculative, but one can offer three incontrovertible propositions about the military role of the Resistance: if there had been no Resistance, France would still have been liberated; if there had been no Resistance, the Liberation would have cost the Allies significantly higher casualties; if the Allies had had more faith in the potential of the Resistance, its contribution to saving Allied lives could have been greater. The Resistance was always desperately short of arms, and despite Churchill's order to increase arms drops to southern France at the start of 1944, France never received the quantities of supplies which went to Yugoslavia or Italy. Between 1943 and 1945, the Yugoslav Resistance received 16,470 tons of supplies, Italy 5,907 tons, and southern France 2,878.[50]

It is ultimately misleading to dwell excessively on the military contribution of the Resistance. Probably more has been written on these two months of military operations than on the rest of the history of the Resistance, but for most of the Resistance's existence, military activity comprised only a tiny part of its experience. The Liberation fighting is the least characteristic moment by which to judge what resistance had represented for most of its protagonists most of the time. The resisters whom Viannay led into action in June had no idea how to use the few arms they had. One of them said: '[the deputy DMR] was supposed to show us how to use our equipment. But he never deigned to do so. I had a rocket-thrower. I carried the thing about with me two or three times, but each time I left it in a field because I had no idea what to do with it.'[51] Equally, the arms dropped on Mont Mouchet were only of limited value because the younger men lacked experience in how to use their weapons.

The importance of the Resistance to the Liberation was political and moral rather than military. By August, the FFI forces, which had been approximately 50,000 in January 1944 and 100,000 in June, approached 500,000.[52] The case for the Resistance—if a case needs to be made—is not that liberation could not have occurred without it, but precisely that it could have done. Those who joined the FFI towards the end chose to enlist in a battle that would have been won without them—which does not mean that they were running no risk. About 24,000 FFI combatants were killed in the Liberation fighting. Those who fought

[49] Foot, *SOE in France*, 408.
[50] Funk, *Hidden Ally*, 258; Foot, *SOE in France*, 472–4.
[51] Wieviorka, *Une certaine idée*, 301.
[52] Buton, 'La France atomisée', in Azéma and Bédarida (eds.), *La France des années noires*, ii. 382–5.

at the Liberation did so voluntarily, contradicting the truism that no soldier wants to risk his life at the end of a war that is already won.[53] The FFI, of course, did not include all the French people. To what extent did the population as whole participate in the Liberation? Was there a national insurrection in 1944?

Even the GPRF started to back this idea of an insurrection as the battle moved to its final stages. On 5 August, Algiers radio called on the people of Brittany to join in a 'national uprising', as the Americans moved west. Two days later, de Gaulle broadcast that it was everyone's duty 'to participate in the supreme effort'—although the BBC refused to broadcast the word 'uprising'.[54] It was, of course, the Communists who did most to whip the population into a pre-insurrectionary fever. Numerous strikes occurred in the spring of 1944, most of them short-lived. The biggest was a general strike in Marseilles on 25 May which started with a demonstration by women protesting against food shortages. But the strikers were stopped in their tracks after an Allied bombing raid on 27 May which left 1,700 dead. From 6 June, the Communists called for a general strike in the Nord/Pas-de-Calais. Everywhere they used their front organizations to organize food demonstrations and push for the formation of Patriotic Militias. Where they could not get the CDLs to proclaim an insurrection they set up their own insurrectional committees.[55] Under Communist pressure, the CNR issued a strike call for 14 July. The Communists worked tirelessly for this strike which was billed as a preparation for the National Insurrection: in the Var, they produced forty-five tracts in two weeks, full of references to 1792.[56]

What were the results of this frenetic activity? The Communists got nowhere in forming Patriotic Militias. In most places, these were tiny or non-existent.[57] In Marseilles, working-class morale had not recovered from the Allied raid, and when the Communists tried to prepare a demonstration on 14 July, they had to bring in FTP members from Aix.[58] In Toulon also, the Communist strike was undermined by Allied bombing raids: the workforce of the Arsenal fell to half its normal strength as people fled the city to escape the bombs.[59] Elsewhere the 14 July strikes were successful, but they were not usually the prelude to a generalized insurrection.

Liberation assumed many different forms. The Haute-Savoie was the first *département* to be liberated without Allied help. The Resistance fighters, numbering about 55,000, faced 2,500 ill-equipped and low-grade German troops. In four towns, there was a semi-insurrectionary situation.[60] In the south-west, the

[53] Kedward, *In Search of the Maquis*, 209.

[54] Crémieux-Brilhac, 'Ici Londres: L'Arme radiophonique et l'insurrection nationale', in Levisse-Touzé (ed.), *Paris 1944*, 152–63.

[55] Buton, *Les Lendemains qui déchantent*, 93.   [56] Guillon, 'La Résistance dans le Var', 700.

[57] Buton, *Les Lendemains qui déchantent*, 102–3.

[58] J.-M. Guillon, 'Les Rapports de force dans la Résistance provençale', *Cahiers d'histoire de l'Institut des recherches marxistes* 34/5 (1988), 61–6: 64.

[59] Guillon, 'La Resistance dans le Var', 663.   [60] Abrahams, 'Haute-Savoie at War', 251–2.

rapid German retreat meant that there was no enemy against whom to stage an insurrection. In Limoges, for example, a general strike was called on 19 August, and the Maquis surrounded the city. On the next day, the Maquis leader Guingouin, working with SOE and OSS representatives, got the German commander to surrender without firing a shot. In Provence, there were some urban insurrections before the Allies arrived. In Marseilles, which had a German garrison of 17,000 men, a general strike broke out on 19 August. The Groupes francs built barricades, shots were fired at German lorries, and the Liberation Committee took over the prefecture on 21 August. By the time the Allied troops arrived on 24 August, much of the city had been in Resistance hands for several days. The Germans finally surrendered on 28 August. The insurrection, which lasted ten days, had resulted in 5,500 German deaths. Among the resisters, an important role had been played by the MOI. The same was true in Nice, where of the hundred resisters who sparked off the insurrection, about sixty were in the MOI.[61]

In Lyons, most Resistance leaders had been arrested in the spring, leaving only the immigrant Communists of the 'Carmagnole' group. By 20 August, the Germans were retreating northwards through the city. On 24 August, members of the Carmagnole group set off to liberate the two prisons near the central station. On arrival, they discovered that most of the inmates had already been released. They were fired upon by the Germans, and retreated to the suburb of Villeurbanne where people were gathering on the streets. The leader of the Carmagnole group tried to disperse the crowds, but instead they started to build barricades around the Villeurbanne town hall. The Carmagnole group found itself at the head of an insurrection that it had not planned. Setting itself up in the town hall, it appealed for help from the Resistance outside the city. No help arrived because the regional FFI leaders felt that the insurrection was premature. So when the Germans arrived in Villeurbanne, on 26 August, with heavy arms to clear the barricades, the crowds melted away, and the resisters defending the barricades were too poorly armed to hold out. By the end of the day, the insurrection was over, and the Resistance leaders had dispersed to join the Maquis outside the city. The liberation of Lyons was delayed until the first week of September when Allied troops arrived. By then, the Germans had evacuated the city: it was too late for an insurrection.[62]

It is impossible to consider every case in detail. Philippe Buton, examining local studies of the Liberation, has tried to quantify the number of insurrections which took place in 212 urban centres. He distinguishes three models of liberation. First, the 'ideal type' insurrection which involved the FFI fighting the

---

[61] P. Guiral, *La Libération de Marseille* (1974); Guillon, 'Les Étrangers dans la Résistance provençale', 669.

[62] C. Collin, *L'Insurrection de Villeurbanne a-t-elle eu lieu?* (1994); J. Simmonds, 'Immigrant Fighters for the Liberation of France: A Local Profile of Carmagnole-Liberté in Lyon', in Kedward and Wood (eds.), *Liberation*, 29–41; G. Chauvy, *Lyon des années bleues: Libération, épuration* (1987), 240–1.

Germans, and the general population participating through strikes and the erection of barricades. Secondly, liberation by 'partial insurrection', where the FFI's contribution was important, but the population remained passive. Thirdly, liberation without any form of insurrection, carried out by the Allies alone or occurring thanks to the spontaneous departure of the Germans. In the first category, Buton finds only five localities (2 per cent of the total), but these include the major cities of Marseilles, Lille, and Paris; in the second, he finds twenty-eight localities (13 per cent); in the third, he finds 179 (85 per cent).[63]

Inevitably, these categorizations are open to debate. In Toulouse, three eyewitness accounts suggest that the city was liberated by the Resistance. This seems to vindicate Buton's decision to put the city in his second category. But another eyewitness, Philippe Bertaux, the government's *commissaire* in Toulouse, claimed that the Resistance had not genuinely liberated the city because the Germans left so precipitately. On this reading, Toulouse fits Buton's third category. Appeals for an insurrection in the city had been posted up on 17 August. In the next two days, there were skirmishes with the Germans, but when the Germans left on 19 August, they were observed passively by most of the population. Four days *after* the liberation of the city, the local MLN paper called on the population to build barricades: 'as in 1793 our people must conquer their liberty'. The justification for this 'posthumous' insurrection was that the Germans were still not far away, but symbolic considerations were probably more important: the German evacuation had cheated the population of its insurrection. On the other hand, 335 people were killed during the fighting that did take place.[64]

In many rural areas the population played no part at all in the Liberation. After the war the government organized an investigation into the experience of different *départements* before and during the Liberation. In the Breton *département* of Finistère 134 mainly rural localities answered the survey. In ninety cases (70 per cent) 'liberation' had simply involved the departure of the Germans; in twenty-two cases (16 per cent) it had been carried out by the Allies often accompanied by the FFI; and in fourteen by the FFI alone. In forty-six localities (34 per cent) there had not even been an FFI or Maquis group. And Finistère was a *département* with quite a high level of resistance.[65] Often it is impossible to say whether a locality was liberated as a result of the arrival of the Allies, the departure of the Germans, or the action of the FFI. Indeed these possibilities were not mutually exclusive. In many cases liberation did consist of *maquisards* marching into towns from which the Germans had recently departed to the cheers of the local population, but this does not necessarily make such liberations phoney. Often, as in Limoges, the peaceful arrival of the Maquis followed sporadic clashes between Maquis and Germans in the surrounding countryside: in such cases,

---

[63] Buton, *Les Lendemains qui déchantent*, 104–6.

[64] P. Bertaux, *Libération de Toulouse et de sa région* (1973), 17–31, 70; Kedward, *In Search of the Maquis*, 214–15.

[65] L. Capdevila, *Les Bretons au lendemain de l'Occupation* (Rennes, 1999), 20–4.

the Maquis can be said to have earned its victory.[66] Nonetheless, it is undeniable that the summer of 1944 did not witness a national insurrection of the kind envisaged by the Communists. If the image of insurrection remains an enduring one, the reason lies in the Paris insurrection whose symbolic resonance was enormous—but whose insurrection was it?

The Liberation of Paris

Careful plans had been made for the takeover of power in Paris.[67] De Gaulle's Delegate, Alexandre Parodi, had full authority to act for the GPRF. The provisional secretary-generals had been selected, and they were in contact with the NAP members in the relevant ministries. The role of NAP was to neutralize opposition at the designated moment, and ensure a smooth transfer of power. But the situation was complicated by the strong presence of the Communists in the CPL (and many CLLs in the suburbs), in the trade unions, and in the FFI, whose regional commander was Rol-Tanguy. The Delegation had initially agreed that while it would occupy government offices at the Liberation, the CPL could take over other buildings. But de Gaulle sharply reminded Parodi that no sector should escape the authority of the GPRF.[68] De Gaulle made clear what he expected of Parodi in a telegram of 31 July: 'Always speak loud and clear in the name of the State. The numerous acts of our glorious Resistance are the means by which the nation fights for its salvation. The State is above all these manifestations and actions.'

From early July, the Communists were exerting every effort to create a pre-insurrectionary climate. Some 100,000 people participated in strikes and demonstrations on 14 July. On 10 August, the unions called a railway strike which quickly spread to other industries. On the same day Charles Tillon, in the name of the FTP, issued a call for insurrection. This was not followed by any immediate flare-up, and the next stage towards the insurrection came from an unexpected quarter: the police. Having become increasingly mistrustful of the reliability of the police, the Germans started to disarm them. In response, the three police Resistance organizations went on strike from 15 August. Two of these organizations were non-Communist—the Gaullist Honneur de la Patrie and the Socialist Police et Patrie—but it was the Communist Front national which took the lead. The police were warned that those not obeying the strike call would be considered as traitors after Liberation.

From 15 August, there were almost no police to be seen on the streets of Paris. This emboldened the FTP fighters in their skirmishes with the Germans. They were also encouraged by being able to hear the battle raging between the Allies

---

[66] Kedward, *In Search of the Maquis*, 215.
[67] In general, see A. Dansette, *Histoire de la Libération de Paris* (1946)
[68] O. Wieviorka, 'La Résistance intérieure et la Libération de Paris', in Levisse-Touzé (ed.), *Paris 1944*, 137–51: 143.

and the Germans to the west of the capital. On 17 August, for the first time since the start of the Occupation, Parisians woke up to hear no Radio Paris. Its best-known voice, Jean-Hérold Paquis, had left Paris in a convoy of other collabora-tionists. The end seemed near.

The escalation of violence worried Parodi whose instructions were to avoid a premature insurrection which might become a bloodbath without Allied inter-vention. Such intervention seemed unlikely because Eisenhower, fearing that the capture of Paris would delay the Allied advance, had decided to by pass the city and only return once the Germans had been fatally weakened. Chaban-Delmas returned from a visit to London on 16 August, with the news that the Ameri-cans did not intend to reach Paris before early September. Parodi sent telegrams to London urging that the Americans change their plans, or, if this was impos-sible, that the BBC appeal for the Paris population to stay calm. On 17 August, at a meeting of the CNR Bureau, Parodi argued against Villon who wanted to call for an insurrection. Even Bidault, usually a reliable ally of the Delegation, felt that events were developing a momentum which could not be stopped. The CPL also met on 17 August, and was split between the Communists, arguing for an insurrection, and Léo Hamon, the representative of CDLR, arguing against. A decision was deferred until the CNR had taken a formal decision.

On the next day (18 August) three posters appeared, summoning the popu-lation to action: one from the unions, calling for a general strike; one from Rol-Tanguy, in the name of the FFI, calling for a mobilization of all resistance forces; one from the Communist Party, calling for an immediate insurrection. By the evening of 18 August, the FTP had seized a number of town halls in the suburbs, and it seemed as if an insurrection was underway. It was the occupation of the Prefecture of Police on the next morning (19 August), which finally overcame Parodi's opposition to an insurrection. The Prefecture was a building of central symbolic importance, as well as being in the geographical heart of Paris, oppo-site Notre-Dame. The decision to occupy it had been taken by the three police Resistance organizations, but on this occasion the initiative came not from the FN, but the Gaullist Honneur et Patrie.[69] The building was occupied without a shot being fired, and at 11 a.m. the GPRF's appointee as Prefect of Police, Charles Luizet, arrived to take up his post. Neither Parodi, who was trying to slow things down, nor Tanguy, who was trying to speed them up, had any prior knowledge of the seizure of the Prefecture. In the light of this event, at a meeting of the CNR Bureau on 19 August, Parodi decided to ignore his orders from London. He later said that to have opposed the insurrection any longer would have com-promised his authority over the Resistance, and jeopardized his chance of exer-cising any control over events. As it was, Parodi at least ensured that the CNR's

---

[69] Footitt and Simmonds, *France 1943–1945*, 124; S. Kitson, 'The Police in the Liberation of Paris', in Kedward and Wood (eds.), *Liberation of France*, 43–56: 47 claims all three police movements were involved.

call to insurrection occurred in the name of the GPRF. On the same morning, the CPL published its call for action. The insurrection which had started the day before was now official.

During the rest of the day, the plans for the occupation of key buildings were put into effect. The provisional secretary-generals moved into several ministries without opposition; a group of security guards took control of the Élysée Palace; post offices and telephone exchanges were seized. In the district town halls of Paris and the suburbs, CLL representatives, often Communist, took over the local administration. Although supposedly under the control of the CPL, this process occurred in a very haphazard way, sometimes resulting in skirmishes with the Germans.

The Germans were far from beaten. The 15,000–20,000 German troops armed with tanks were still a match for 35,000 poorly armed FFI fighters without anti-tank weapons. There was serious fighting in the Latin Quarter and around the Gare de la Villette in the north-east. In the afternoon of 19 August, the Germans started attacking the Prefecture whose defenders had insufficient ammunition to hold out beyond the next morning. At this point, the Swedish consul Raoul Nordling, who was in touch with the German commander General Dietrich von Choltitz, proposed an hour-long truce to allow the wounded on both sides to be evacuated. Hearing of this, Hamon, the most prominent non-Communist member of the CPL, contacted Nordling and got the truce at the Prefecture extended until 6 a.m. the next morning.

At the same time, Hamon conceived the bold stroke of seizing the Hôtel de Ville, ostensibly on behalf of the CPL. But since he did not inform the other members, it is likely that his intention was to pre-empt a similar action by the Communists. Early the next morning (20 August), Hamon arrived at the Hôtel de Ville, with a small group representing different resistance factions. The Vichy prefect was arrested, and later that morning, Marcel Flouret, whom the GPRF had selected as the new prefect, arrived to assume his post without any problem. Hamon then went to see Nordling. Claiming to speak for the CPL, he got him to agree to negotiate an extension of the truce to cover all the fighting in Paris, not just around the Prefecture. Hamon took this proposal to the CNR Bureau (of which he was not a member) to secure official approval for it. Parodi was enthusiastic, arguing that the German willingness to concede a truce, leaving most public buildings in Resistance hands, was recognition that the insurrection had succeeded. Villon, who argued that the truce would cheat the people of their insurrection, was overruled. The text of the truce was taken to Choltitz who agreed to sign it. He had chosen to ignore Hitler's order to destroy Paris rather than surrender.

Loudspeaker cars were soon informing the population of the truce. People were told to remain at home and allow the Germans to evacuate Paris. This had little effect: no one really controlled the situation on the ground. Rol-Tanguy refused to accept the truce, and so did his subordinate Colonel Lizé, not a

Communist. While loudspeakers were announcing the truce, it was denounced by an FFI poster. On the face of it, the FFI was defying CNR instructions, but the validity of these instructions was open to question. The CNR Bureau which decided on the truce that morning had not been regularly constituted. Bidault therefore called the CNR into full session for the afternoon (20 August). This meeting was acrimonious, but because Parodi could not attend—having fallen into the hands of a German patrol, he was a prisoner until Choltitz released him in the evening—a decision was postponed until the next day.

The situation on 20 August was therefore highly confused. The CNR and the CPL were divided about the truce; the Delegation (Parodi/Chaban-Delmas) was in favour; the leaders of the FFI and FTP were against. COMAC prepared a memorandum opposing the truce to be presented to the CNR on the following day. But what was the status of the truce in the meantime? The Communists argued that the CNR had not backed a truce since the plenary meeting (in the afternoon) had reserved its decision until the next day. The Delegation argued that since a truce had been decided by the Bureau (in the morning), it was operative until a plenary meeting decided otherwise. Meanwhile the street fighting continued, as did the stealthy takeover of ministries by the provisional secretary-generals. Morandat, arriving to take over the Matignon Palace, residence of the French prime minister, not only met with no opposition, but found himself greeted deferentially by the official guard.[70]

On the next morning (21 August), the CPL, despite Hamon, decided to oppose the truce and call for immediate insurrection. All now depended on the meeting of the CNR in the afternoon. This was to be the stormiest meeting in its history. It took place in a small apartment near the Port d'Orléans with the noise of fighting not far away. The heat was stifling and the participants exhausted. Villon, who called for the CNR to align itself with the CPL, accused Chaban-Delmas of being a traitor for defending the truce. The two men came near to blows. Laniel, one of the more conservative members of the CNR, felt that the atmosphere was worryingly reminiscent of the Commune. In the end, Parodi, feeling he could not hold out any longer, supported a compromise to win more time: he secured an agreement that the end of the truce would not be announced until the following afternoon.[71]

In fact, this deadline was never respected. From the morning of 22 August, barricades went up around the city. Over 600 barricades were constructed, mainly in the working-class areas of the north and east. Less romantically, while the barricades were going up, Parodi held the first meeting of provisional secretary-generals at the Matignon Palace: in effect, this was the first meeting of the interim Liberation government. For the first time, the Resistance press appeared openly, and Parisians were given learned explanations of the confusing

---

[70] Noguères, *Histoire de la Résistance*, v. 495–8, 523.
[71] Debû-Bridel, *De Gaulle et le Conseil national,* 162–4.

acronyms—CNR, GPRF—which many heard for the first time. Fighting continued during the next two days (23 and 24 August). The Germans set fire to the Grand Palais, and the situation could still have become catastrophic if Eisenhower had not changed his plans.

Up to 23 August, the Americans remained deaf to French entreaties that they should make for Paris. Eisenhower had long agreed that the privilege of entering Paris would fall to French troops—the Second Armoured Division of General Leclerc—but he was unwilling to revise his schedule. An envoy sent by Rol-Tanguy to appeal for help was killed before reaching the American lines. On 20 August, de Gaulle arrived from Algiers to increase the pressure on Eisenhower, even threatening to withdraw Leclerc from American command and send him in alone. On the evening of 22 August, Colonel Cocteau (Gallois), another envoy from Rol-Tanguy, finally succeeded in getting through the German lines. He was summoned to Patton's headquarters, but told that the plans could not be changed. The next morning he saw Leclerc and some more American officers. At 6 p.m. on 23 August, Leclerc finally received the order to march on Paris.

In the mythology of the Liberation of Paris, Gallois's arrival is seen as decisive in causing the Americans to change their plans. In fact it seems that they had been about to do so anyway in the light of their own intelligence information.[72] At 5 p.m. on 24 August, a message was dropped from a plane, close to the besieged Prefecture, announcing that help was on its way. Later that evening, a small unit of Leclerc's Armoured Division under Captain Dronne appeared at the Hôtel de Ville. The bulk of Leclerc's forces arrived on the next day (25 August), accompanied by American troops. In the afternoon von Choltitz signed the German surrender at the Gare Montparnasse where Leclerc had installed his headquarters. De Gaulle arrived there at 4.30 p.m. Having established himself in his old office at the Ministry of Defence, and visited the Prefecture, he went to the Hôtel de Ville to meet representatives of the CPL and the CNR. There he made his first speech since his arrival: 'Paris! Paris humiliated! Paris broken! Paris martyrized! But now Paris liberated! Liberated by herself, by her own people with the help of the armies of France, with the support and aid of France as a whole, of fighting France, of the only France, of the true France, of eternal France.'[73]

If de Gaulle was able to pronounce these words with any semblance of conviction, it was thanks to the insurrection—which his representatives, faithful to his wishes, had opposed until the last moment. But it would be wrong to see the argument over the insurrection as one dividing the Communists from everyone else. The truce had been opposed by many non-Communists: by de Vogüé on COMAC; by Lizé, a career officer who was in most other respects extremely

[72] A. Kaspi, 'Les États-Unis et la Libération de Paris' in Levisse-Touzé (ed.), *Paris 1944*, 41–8: 46.
[73] *Discours et Messages*, 439–40.

hostile to the Communists; by Marie-Hélène Lechaufeux, the OCM representative on the CPL. On the other hand, de Gaulle's representatives were not alone
in fearing the consequences of an insurrection without Allied help. It was the
Communist Rol-Tanguy who took the initiative of sending an envoy to hurry
the Allied advance. Did the truce benefit the Germans or win valuable time for
the Resistance? In theory, the full truce (as opposed to the short truce affecting
the Prefecture) had lasted for only about forty-eight hours (from midday on 20
August to midday of 22 August), but in practice its impact had been negligible.
Even if he had wanted to implement the truce, which he did not, Rol-Tanguy
would have been powerless to do so.[74]

It is true that the Communists were the driving force behind the insurrection, but this does not mean they had a strategy to seize power. It was not the
Communists who took the decision to occupy the Prefecture on 19 August or
the Hôtel de Ville on the next day; nor did they try to interfere in the takeover
of ministries. If there was a strategy for the seizure of power, it came from the
Gaullist Delegation. The Communists were more interested in using the insurrection to build up their grass-roots influence—setting up Patriotic Militias in
factories and taking over town halls.[75] But the insurrection never became the
popular uprising the Communists had imagined. The Patriotic Militias were tiny,
and there was never an insurrectional general strike. By the middle of August,
most workers were no longer at work, but this was because their employers had
decided that it would be easiest to send them on holiday. On 14 August, one
Communist trade unionist noted of the railway workers, among whom he found
little enthusiasm for action: 'the "strike" is effective because most of the workers
are on leave'. The Communist activists had problems involving the workers once
they were no longer collected together in the workplace. For many workers, the
'insurrectional strike' was a matter of going home for two weeks and trying to
get enough food to survive until the radio told them on 27 August that they
could return to work. Many workers did participate in the Liberation as individual members of the FFI, but not collectively as a class.[76]

A sceptical Polish observer of the Liberation of Paris was disgusted at the
self-satisfied boasting of the first papers announcing that Paris had liberated
herself:

> In a week people won't even mention the Americans and British . . . All these
> French cocks preening themselves in cafes and under porches . . . waiting for the
> Americans, jam, and chocolate. But as soon as one of them hears the distant noise
> of a German motorcycle the street is deserted in seconds, doors close and people
> fight to look through keyholes.[77]

---

[74] Wieviorka, 'La Résistance intérieure', 146.
[75] Buton, Les Lendemains qui déchantent, 99.
[76] Courtois, Le PCF dans la guerre, 453–5.
[77] A. Bobkowski, En Guerre et en paix: Journal 1940–1944 (1991), 611.

Galtier-Boissière was hardly less acerbic: 'fighting in the streets is less risky and more picturesque than open campaigning; one comes home to lunch carrying one's rifle; the whole neighbourhood is at the windows to watch and applaud. If only the cameras were clicking, glory would be absolute.'[78]

It would be wrong, however, to reduce the Paris insurrection to a charade. It is true that many of the barricades served no useful military purpose; it is true also that while the fighting raged there were painters or fishermen on the banks of the Seine, seemingly oblivious to the events around them. But the people who built or manned the barricades had not been forced to do so. And what else could be done by people without weapons? Those who participated in the fighting ran considerable risks: 901 members of the FFI and 582 civilians were killed; another 2,000 were wounded; German casualties numbered 3,200. The insurrection allowed the people of Paris to become participants in, and not merely spectators of, their own deliverance.

The greatest irony of the Paris insurrection was that the Communists had willed it, but it profited de Gaulle. In his Memoirs, de Gaulle commented that the news of the truce had made a 'disagreeable impression' on him. This was because by the time the news of the truce reached him, he knew that Leclerc had been authorized to advance, and in these circumstances a popular insurrection, carried out in the name of the GPRF and strictly limited in time, could help consolidate his legitimacy as France's leader. To underline this point, on 26 August, the day after his arrival in Paris, de Gaulle organized a triumphal procession down the Champs-Élysées where massive crowds turned out to cheer him.

Vichy-Sigmaringen: From One Spa to Another

While de Gaulle was enjoying his apotheosis on 26 August, the Vichy State was on its final journey into exile.[79] The site chosen by the Germans for Vichy to act out its denouement was the small German town of Sigmaringen. Its castle, overlooking the Danube, became the seat of the government. In fact technically there was no longer a government because Pétain and Laval, in protest against their forcible abduction, both refused to carry out their duties. But the Germans were reluctant to abandon the semblance of legality since an aura still surrounded Pétain's name, especially for the prisoners of war on German soil. The impasse created by Pétain's refusal to name a government was overcome by persuading him to allow Fernand de Brinon, who had been Vichy's official Delegate in the Occupied Zone, to continue to exercise this authority on behalf of the French citizens on German soil (POWs and workers). With this legal cover, Brinon became head of the 'French Governmental Delegation' at Sigmaringen. Brinon's

---

[78] Quoted in Pryce-Jones, *Paris in the Third Reich*, 204.
[79] For this section see Rousso, *Pétain et la fin de la collaboration*.

'government' consisted of a handful of ultra-collaborationists: Darnand was head of police; Déat responsible for looking after the interests of French workers in Germany; Luchaire in charge of propaganda. Doriot, still harbouring ambitions of his own, remained aloof.

If Vichy itself had often seemed like the parody of a government, its reincarnation at Sigmaringen was a parody of a parody. Pétain inhabited the top floor of the castle, still accompanied by the faithful Ménétrel. Regretting his agreement to delegate authority to de Brinon, Pétain started to send him notes, via Ménétrel, claiming that he had no right to act in his name. Brinon retaliated by having Ménétrel arrested, thus depriving Pétain of his main comfort and support. The floor below Pétain was occupied by Laval and those members of his government who had followed him to Sigmaringen. Since they were no longer carrying out their duties, they wandered round the castle like ghosts while Abel Bonnard, the court jester, kept up his endless stream of bons mots and malicious stories. Laval worked into the small hours preparing his post-war defence. Céline, who was the doctor at Sigmaringen, visited him regularly to treat his ulcer, and was the recipient of endless self-justificatory monologues. These proved more useful to him as copy for the book he eventually published on his experiences at Sigmaringen than they did for Laval when he appeared before the High Court in 1945.

The third floor of the castle was the seat of Brinon's Delegation. Luchaire ran a newspaper called *France* and a radio station called *Ici la France*. Since the Delegation had nothing to govern and no foreign policy to conduct—it enjoyed diplomatic relations with Mussolini's rump 'Republic of Salò'—its members spent much time squabbling. They lived in the desperate hope of a sudden reversal of the Allied advance. The brief success of the German offensive through the Ardennes in the winter of 1944 aroused a flurry of optimism. After this they fell back on the fantasy that Hitler was about to unleash a secret weapon capable of destroying London at a stroke. In another parody of the situation prevailing at Vichy, Doriot set himself up away from Sigmaringen at the town of Neustadt-an-der-Weinstrasse. He created a Committee for the Liberation of France—this time the parody was of de Gaulle—with its own radio station, Radio-Patrie, and its own newspaper, *Le Petit Parisien*. Doriot's intention was that his Committee would eventually supplant Brinon's Delegation. In this ambition he enjoyed the support of the Germans who believed that he was the most capable French leader. But before Doriot could prevail, he was killed by Allied aircraft fire on 22 February 1945. Déat now created his own 'liberation' committee to undermine de Brinon.

While the Brinon Delegation pursued its futile existence, a small band of Frenchmen found themselves fighting alongside the German armies in the newly formed Charlemagne Division of the Waffen-SS. A French division of the SS had first been set up in 1943. Now it was reconstituted to include about a third of the *miliciens* who had come to Germany, and the remnants of the LVF. In

February 1945, the Charlemagne Division, which totalled about 10,000 men, was sent into action against the Red Army in Pomerania. By March it had been destroyed. About 100 survivors ended up defending the Reich Chancellery in the final battle for Berlin.

As this handful of fanatics, adventurers, criminals, and lost souls met its fate in the rubble of Berlin, the French in Sigmaringen prepared their escapes. Déat, who published his last article in the newspaper *France* on 15 April, made his way across the Dolomites with his wife, and sought refuge in a monastery. Céline managed to make his way to Denmark, Bonnard to Spain; Châteaubriant took refuge in the Austrian Tyrol. Pétain, however, wanted to render his account to the people of France. His last letter to Hitler, on 5 April 1945, was to ask if he could be allowed to go to Paris to defend himself before the High Court. There was no answer.

24

A New France?

It was the sea. A huge crowd was jammed together on either side of the street. Perhaps two million people. The roofs too were black with many more. Small groups were clustered at every window, with flags all around. . . . As far as the eye could see, there was nothing but this living tide of humanity, in the sunshine, beneath the tricolour . . . I went on, touched and yet tranquil, amid the inexpressible exultation of the crowd, under the storm of voices echoing my name . . . This moment was one of those miracles of the national consciousness, one of those gestures which sometimes through the centuries illuminate the history of France. In this community, with only a single thought, a single enthusiasm, a single cry, all differences vanished, all individuals disappeared.[1]

This was how de Gaulle described his triumphal procession down the Champs-Élysées on 26 August 1944. Watching the newsreels of this even a few days later, the young Stanley Hoffmann, free at last from the threat of arrest and deportation, did not dissent. He felt that the 'euphoria of a national general will was palpable—fleetingly'.[2]

De Gaulle's moment of apotheosis, however, was not the 'Liberation of France'. It occurred halfway through a process which had begun in Corsica in September 1943 and was finally complete only in April 1945 when the last German pockets in Saint-Nazaire and Lorient were liberated. Each locality had its own moment of liberation. Some, like Tulle or Guéret, had more than one. The Liberation, therefore, was an intense experience of national communion at a moment when French national territory had never been more fragmented.[3] The Liberation was a rite of passage between the old regime and the new, an unreal moment suspended between past and future. But it was also a moment dense with historical symbolism: in Paris the barricades were a conscious re-enactment of 1848 and 1871. Léon Werth, in Paris on 24 August, wrote: 'I didn't believe in history. And now everything is resonant with history. My chest is swelling with history.'[4] Each liberation was a compression into one day of all the

---

[1] De Gaulle, *Mémoires*, 573.   [2] 'To be or not to be French', 16.
[3] See Kedward's reflections in Kedward and Wood (eds.), *Liberation of France*, 1–9.
[4] *Déposition*, 723.

14 July fêtes which had not been celebrated under the Occupation.[5] Flags were omnipresent, especially in the former Occupied Zone, because they were the simplest way in which communities could take back their streets, reclaim a public space which had been confiscated for four years. In one village in the Aisne, women were feverishly sewing flags out of any available material in the days before the Liberation. One commented: 'I was keeping these shirts for the return of my POW husband but I'm happy to make them into a flag.'[6]

As in 1848 when the priests blessed liberty trees, the Church was not absent from the celebration. In each liberated community church bells rang out. One witness in Paris wrote: 'On the evening of 24 August, as the night fell, the bells, all the bells of Paris, began to ring. With an almost religious emotion and tears, real tears, I went to the balcony with my family: what grandeur, what fullness, what gravity, what joy in this formidable concert of over a hundred church bells in the dark warmth of this immense city.'[7] Throughout France Te Deums were sung, often by bishops who had remained Pétainist almost until the end.[8] But the Cardinal Archbishop of Paris, Suhard, who had unwisely been present at Henriot's funeral two months earlier, was excluded from the thanksgiving ceremony attended by de Gaulle in Notre-Dame on 26 August.

If the Liberation was a moment of national communion it was only, as Hoffmann observed, 'fleetingly' so. De Gaulle may only have heard a 'single cry' as he proceeded down the Champs-Élysées, but in reality the celebrations concealed very different interpretations of the past and very different visions of the future. The Resistance looked to a political and moral regeneration of France; the mass of the population wanted food and a return to peace; de Gaulle wanted order and France's re-entry into the war before it was too late.

Restoring Order

From the moment he entered Paris on 24 August, de Gaulle's every action had been calculated to bring the Resistance to heel and reassert the supremacy of the State. It was not by coincidence that he had immediately installed himself at the Ministry of War and then paid a visit to the Prefecture of Police: these were symbols of state power. Only reluctantly had he been prevailed upon to visit the Hôtel de Ville where the CNR was waiting to receive him. The Hôtel de Ville was the symbol of revolution in the nineteenth century: from its balcony, the Second and Third Republics had been proclaimed. De Gaulle, who was only too aware of these historical associations, refused Bidault's request that he proclaim the restoration of the Republic. He replied that the Republic had never

---

[5] A. Brossat, *Libération, fête folle. 6 juin 1944–8 mai 1945: Mythes et rites ou le grand théâtre des passions populaires* (1994), 98–100.

[6] Ibid. 100.   [7] Ibid. 107.

[8] J.-M. Guillon, 'La Libération du Var: Résistance et nouveaux pouvoirs', *Cahiers de l'IHTP*, 15 (1990), 18–19.

ceased to exist. Having made a short speech, and treated the Resistance leaders with formality, de Gaulle departed.

Paying this visit to the CNR was the only symbolic concession de Gaulle was ready to make to the Resistance. On 27 August, he wrote to the CNR thanking it for its services to the nation, and emphasizing that its role was now over. Its members were now to be integrated into the government or into the Consultative Assembly which had previously sat in Algiers and was now transplanted to France. On 28 August de Gaulle ordered the dissolution of the FFI: members of the FFI who wished to go on fighting were to be incorporated into the regular army. On the same day, de Gaulle received leaders of the FFI and the members of COMAC. On entering the room, he declared, 'there are rather a lot of colonels here!' As de Gaulle shook each officer's hand in turn, he asked what they had done in civilian life, and made it clear that their duty was now to return to the factories, schools, or offices where they had worked before. On leaving the meeting, one of the participants remarked: 'I have already witnessed human ingratitude in my life, but never on this scale.'[9] The provisional secretary-generals, who were no firebrands needing to be summoned to discipline, encountered the same icy formality when de Gaulle received them on 29 August.[10]

Outside Paris it was the role of the *commissaires de la République* and newly appointed prefects to ensure that de Gaulle's orders were carried out. Owing to the fragmentation of the country, the local situation varied enormously. In areas like Normandy, where the Resistance had been comparatively weak, and the Allies were present in force, de Gaulle's representatives had little difficulty in imposing their authority. Often the outgoing Vichy authorities eased the process of transition. In Rambouillet, Maurice Schumann was surprised on 21 August to see a Rue Ferdinand Dreyfus. The sub-prefect told him that during the war it had been changed to Rue Jeanne d'Arc, but on the day before he had 'thought it right to give it back its old name'.[11] In Normandy, by the end of August, the *commissaire* was already writing his official correspondence on paper headed 'La République française' (his colleague in Brittany was still having to use the old Vichy notepaper and cross out the heading 'État français').[12] In the South the situation was more volatile.

When it came to restoring State authority a lot depended on how quickly a *département* had been liberated. Because liberation was such a gradual process, by the time prefects were able to take possession of their offices in the main city (*chef-lieu*) of the *département*, other localities had often been liberated for several days already, and the Resistance forces had taken over: Pamiers in the Ariège was liberated by the FTP on 18 August, but the prefect was not able to install himself in the *chef-lieu* Foix until 25 August. In other cases, communications difficulties

---

[9] P. Villon, *Résistant de la première heure* (1983), 116–17.
[10] Teitgen, '*Faites entrer le témoin*', 156.   [11] Kayser, *Un journaliste sur le front*, 176–7.
[12] Capdevila, *Les Bretons*, 68.

delayed the arrival of the prefect. In the Var the prefect was held up at Hyères until 24 August although the *chef-lieu*, Draguignan, was liberated on 17 August.[13] Owing to the highly fragmented situation, the Liberation process did not go entirely as planned. The CFLN decree of 21 April 1944 prescribed that local councils elected before 1939 be restored. If the councils had been retained by Vichy and were judged to have 'favoured the designs of the enemy', the decree stipulated that the prefect would nominate a new council in consultation with the CDL. Every *département* had a CDL which had been secretly constituted in the months before liberation but, immediately after the Liberation, Local Liberation Committees (CLLs) also constituted themselves—in the Côtes-du-Nord 93 per cent of localities had them, in the Var 28 per cent[14]—and in many places they immediately moved to replace or purge the existing local councils. The extent of this grass-roots municipal revolution should not be exaggerated—even in a fairly radical *département* like the Côtes-du-Nord in Brittany, out of 387 councils 86 (22 per cent of the total) were unchanged and 206 (53 per cent) retained the majority of those elected in 1935[15]—but nonetheless the CLLs, originally a proposal of the Communists, ended up playing a much more significant role than had been originally planned.

The Soviet chargé d'affaires reported back to Moscow in mid-September that 'especially in the provinces' there was a 'duality of power' between the representatives of de Gaulle's government—*commissaires* and prefects—and the Resistance—CDLs and CLLs.[16] This was possibly wishful thinking; it was certainly an oversimplification of the complicated and varied relationships between the prefects and the Resistance. In most cases the prefects and CDLs worked together, especially where, as in the Var, the prefect had been a respected local Resistance leader.[17] Sometimes the CDL, while not challenging the prefect's authority, did act as a sort of pressure group to represent Resistance interests. Finally, in a small minority of cases, the CDLs did figure as competitors and rivals to the prefect.[18]

Even where this third situation existed, it did not necessarily represent the threat to order so feared by the central authorities. For example, in the Côtes-du-Nord the prefect complained in November 1944 of the 'constant attempt' by the CDL to 'install a duality of powers'. But the real problem was that the prefect was hardly known to the local Resistance whereas the head of the CDL, Henri Avril, enjoyed a good Resistance reputation. The prefect felt aggrieved because Avril had greater local legitimacy than he did. There was a situation of dual power, but this did not mean that the CDL was pushing for more radical policies or contesting the authority of the government. Sharing the prefect's

---

[13] Guillon, 'La Libération du Var', 15–16; P. Buton and J.-M. Guillon, *Les Pouvoirs en France à la Libération* (1994), 28–9.

[14] Capdevila, *Les Bretons*, 85; Guillon, 'La Libération du Var', 54–6.

[15] Capdevila, *Les Bretons*, 95. [16] Buton, *Les Lendemains qui déchantent*, 142.

[17] Guillon, 'La Libération du Var', 26. [18] Buton and Guillon, *Les Pouvoirs*, 31–4.

objective of restoring order, Avril was better placed to achieve it. Recognizing this, the government in June 1945 appointed Avril as prefect instead. In neighbouring Finistère the situation was very different. The prefect reported in November that his relations with the CDL 'were marked by the most extreme cordiality' while the CDL publicly proclaimed its task as 'assisting the prefect in his difficult task'. Many documents were co-signed by the two of them. In another Breton *département*, the Morbihan, the co-operation between prefect and CDL was so seamless that the CDL risked cutting itself off from the local Resistance represented in the CLLs. When delegates from the CLLs assembled at a congress in Vanves in November 1944 there was violent criticism of the CDL.[19]

The most explosive situation existed in the south-west, where the Maquis was strong, Allied troops were absent, and German atrocities had been particularly violent. In Limoges, one Communist leader talked of gathering sufficient forces to march on Paris and replace the government of 'Kerensky-de Gaulle' by that of 'Lenin-Thorez'.[20] In the Hérault, the CDL and the prefect worked well together, but they were unable to control the situation in the town of Béziers. Here, in an atmosphere of exalted rhetoric reminiscent of 1793, the CLL, presided over by a socialist lawyer, tried to implement some of the more radical ideas of the Resistance, taxing profiteers and requisitioning goods. In mid-November, however, the CLL president was forced out of office, having lost the support of the Communists. Béziers's revolutionary days were now over.[21]

In Toulouse, instability was exacerbated by the fact that the *commissaire*, Pierre Bertaux, was a last-minute replacement for the original nominee, Jean Cassou, who was thought to have been killed in an accident. The region was swarming with armed resisters, many of whom contested Bertaux's authority. This subsequently gave rise to the idea that Toulouse had been on the verge of anarchy or a Communist revolution. It was true that the local Resistance, and not just the Communist Resistance, was highly politicized. But the myth of Red Toulouse was largely created by the alarmist reports of BCRA agents who transposed their own fears of communism on to a situation which was confused but not revolutionary. The myth, however, proved useful to de Gaulle's fledgling government in proving the necessity for firm policies to restore order. In his memoirs, de Gaulle claimed that the local Resistance had formed itself into a Soviet. The moral was that he had saved France from revolution.[22]

The case of Béziers, however, demonstrated that challenges to the authority of the Provisional Government did not necessarily come only from the Communists. Some of the most radical elements were to be found rather, among left-

[19] Capdevila, *Les Bretons*, 71–82.

[20] Buton, *Les Lendemains qui déchantent*, 123.

[21] J.-A. Bailly, *La Libération confisquée: Le Languedoc 1944–1945* (1993), 208, 288; H. Chaubin, 'L'Hérault', in Buton and Guillon (eds.), *Les Pouvoirs*, 508–17.

[22] P. Laborie, 'La Libération de Toulouse vue par le pouvoir central', in Trempé (ed.), *La Libération dans le Midi*, 149–73; M. Goubet, 'Une "République rouge" à Toulouse à la Libération: Mythe ou réalité?', *RHDGM* 131 (1983), 25–40.

wing Socialists like the Libérer et Fédérer group in Toulouse. Nonetheless only the Communists, who represented easily the most powerful political force in France at the Liberation, could have posed a serious threat to de Gaulle. The Party's membership stood at 205,000 in September and 384,000 by the end of the year. Newspapers run by the Communists or their satellites accounted for 21 per cent of the national press, and *L'Humanité*, selling 289,000 copies per day in September, was the most popular newspaper in France. The FTP had about 200,000 members and the FN 530,00. The Patriotic Militias, which had hardly got off the ground before the Liberation, swelled massively after it, acquiring 40,000 members in the Paris region alone. Finally, the Communists held about 30 per cent of the seats in the CDLs, and in some areas, like the south-east, up to 50 per cent.

What use would the Party make of its massive potential power? As before and during the Liberation, the Party continued its dual strategy of participating in, and supporting, the government while building up its strength in competing sources of power associated with the Resistance, and using these to challenge the government. From the start of September to the end of November the Communists blew hot and cold, and the possibility of a formal rupture with the government had probably not been ruled out.[23] There were certainly signs that the Communists hoped to exploit the CDLs as a counterweight to the government. In the south-east, some CDLs tried, with Communist support, to co-ordinate their activities. Delegates from six CDLs gathered at Vizille on 5 September 1941; and delegates from thirty-seven of them assembled at Avignon on 8 October. They protested against any attempt to phase them out, and called for a national Estates General of CDLs in Paris. One Communist leader wired to Thorez in Moscow that the Avignon meeting opened up great possibilities. The Communists envisaged a pyramidal structure of committees which would represent, in their words, a 'direct and active democracy'. It was interesting in this context that the Party opposed any premature holding of municipal elections since these would obviously have led to the supplanting of the organisms which had emerged out of the Resistance. Duclos declared at the end of October that the 'Resistance represents the legal basis of the Provisional Government'. This was certainly not de Gaulle's view.

The Communists had at first done all they could to obstruct the incorporation of the FFI into the regular army. But by the middle of September they abandoned this strategy and fell back on arguing for the creation of a new army in which the cadres who had been formed by the Resistance would prevail over the professional career officers. They drew analogies with the Revolutionary army of 1792–3, the Red Army, and the Spanish Republican army of 1936. The real moment of truth in the relationship between de Gaulle and the Communists

---

[23] The best analysis of Communist policy in this period is Buton, *Les Lendemains qui déchantent*, 107–94.

came at the end of October when the government decreed the dissolution of the Patriotic Militias. The Communists protested vigorously and refused to implement the measure. On Armistice Day 1944 the Communists paraded their militias and other armed groups—allegedly 100,000 of them—through the streets of Paris. For the next month the Party kept up its campaign of protest, but without going as far as to withdraw its two ministers from the government.[24]

On the day de Gaulle announced the dissolution of the militias, he had also declared his readiness to amnesty Maurice Thorez who had been condemned as a deserter in 1939 and was still languishing in Moscow. Whether this was meant to sugar the pill or whether de Gaulle had information that Thorez would be likely to support a more moderate Party line, Thorez's return to France at the end of November brought the Party's dual strategy to an end. In his first speech on 30 November Thorez pointedly omitted any reference to the militias. At a meeting of the Central Committee between 21 and 23 January 1945, he was more explicit. The Party's policy was now 'one state, one army, one police'. There was no place for competing forces like the militias. On the CDLs Thorez could not have been clearer: 'the local and departmental Committees of Liber-ation must not act as a substitute for the municipal and departmental adminis-trations, any more than the CNR must act instead of the government'.[25] Although there are signs that some local activists were disorientated and per-plexed by this change of policy, it was applied rapidly and without difficulty. One *commissaire* reported to the government in mid-February 1945 that there had been 'a complete reversal . . . in the policy of the CDL since M. Thorez's speech at Ivry'.[26]

There were doubtless many reasons for the new Communist line. First, if the Party had adopted a more confrontational—even insurrectionary—line, it could not necessarily have counted upon the reliability of many new recruits who had joined the Party because of its role in the Resistance. Secondly, in any direct con-frontation with the government, the Communists would have found themselves taking on the large number of Allied troops on French soil. But perhaps most important of all, a disruption of the war effort against Germany would not have served the interests of the Soviet Union. Germany was still not defeated, and Stalin was haunted by the possibility of a reversal of alliances and an Anglo-American peace with Germany. The last thing that he needed was an attempted revolution in France which might put a strain on his relations with his allies. As the venerable Communist Marcel Cachin wrote in his diary in February 1945: 'many thought that we were heading to power as in February 1917. But in 1917 the Bolsheviks wanted peace, while peace today would be to save Hitlerism.'[27]

[24] Footitt and Simmonds, *France 1943–1945*, 155–63; Buton, *Les Lendemains qui déchantent*, 157–64.
[25] Footitt and Simmonds, *France 1943–1945*, 194.
[26] Ibid. 197.   [27] Buton, *Les Lendemains qui déchantent*, 172.

The Purges I: Myth and Reality

One issue on which the Communist kept up a constant barrage of criticism against the government was the need for a thorough purge of collaborators. They claimed that the purges—the *épuration*—were being carried out in a half-hearted manner. But even today the *épuration* is so encrusted with myths that it is difficult to know exactly how many people were punished. After the Liberation, Vichy apologists depicted the purges as a bloodbath—a new Terror—with up to 100,000 victims. Even if this exaggerated figure never gained general credence, it was widely felt in the early 1950s that terrible excesses had been committed. Robert Aron followed his indulgent history of Vichy with a non-indulgent history of the Liberation which suggested that between 30,000 and 40,000 people had been killed, a figure which seemed to have been reached by splitting the difference between the largest estimates and the smallest ones.[28] In the 1950s, the Comité d'histoire de la Deuxième Guerre mondiale launched a study of the purges on a *département* by *département* basis, reaching the conclusion that about 9,000 suspected collaborators were killed in the period before and immediately after the Liberation, mostly without any form of trial. This *épuration sauvage* ('wild purge'), as it is often called, preceded the setting up of the special Liberation courts in early September. From this point, the State took in hand the process of carrying out the purges.

Four different kinds of courts were set up to judge alleged collaborators. First, there was a High Court to judge the cases of Vichy ministers and secretary-generals. It consisted of three presiding magistrates, and twenty-four jurors selected by the Consultative Assembly. Secondly, Courts of Justice (*cours de justice*) dealt with other cases of collaboration. They consisted of one magistrate and four jurors chosen by CDLs from citizens who had 'proved their patriotic sentiments'. Thirdly, Civic Courts (*chambres civiques*) dealt with less serious cases of unpatriotic behaviour which were not technically crimes, but could be punished by *dégradation nationale*, the loss of civic rights. Finally, there were military tribunals which were particularly important in the early days before the other courts had started to operate.

The High Court pronounced eighteen death sentences, ten *in absentia*. Of the eight death sentences pronounced in the presence of the accused, three were carried out (Laval, Darnand, de Brinon). The Courts of Justice pronounced about 6,760 death sentences, 3,910 *in absentia* and 2,853 in the presence of the accused. Of these 2,853, 73 per cent were commuted by de Gaulle, and 767 carried out. In addition, about 770 executions were ordered by the military tribunals. Thus the total number of people executed before and after the Liberation was approximately 10,500, including those killed in the *épuration sauvage*.[29]

---

[28] *Histoire de l'épuration*, i. (1967), 556–7.

[29] 'Approximately' because the number of people who died in the *épuration sauvage* cannot be established precisely, and because there are considerable variations even in the numbers of those estimated to have been sentenced by the courts.

A total of 311,263 alleged cases of collaboration were sent for consideration to the courts. Given that these cases sometimes involved several people, it is possible that some 350,000 people had at some time a threat of legal action hanging over them. In 60 per cent of these cases the courts eventually decided that there were no grounds to proceed further. In total, 171,252 cases were judged and in three-quarters of them sentences were pronounced: over 40,000 people were sentenced to prison or detention of some kind, and some 50,000 to *dégradation nationale*. In addition, most professional organizations set up their own purge committees, as did the state administration. Many people not convicted by a court might find themselves subject to a professional sanction ranging from a reprimand to dismissal. For a long time it was generally accepted by historians that 11,343 public servants suffered some kind of sanction at the Liberation. But this figure has recently been revised upwards since it excludes the police and employees of the local administration. The true figure lies between 20,000 and 28,000.[30]

It is clear therefore that although the wilder accusations of the extreme right were unfounded, the purges were far from a cosmetic exercise. But the intense and continuing debate about the *épuration* is not only about figures. There are many different criteria for judging the effectiveness or success of the purges. In recent years, as attention has focused on the fate of the Jews during the Occupation, and on the fact that those responsible for implementing the Final Solution in France were not punished for this after the war, it has become widely believed that the purges did not go far enough. It is true that the issue of anti-Semitism did not figure as prominently after the war as in recent years—although it was not entirely ignored—but retrospective criticisms of this kind are anachronistic. The interesting question is how contemporaries viewed the purges and what they expected from them. The recent experiences of countries like Argentina, Chile, East Germany, and South Africa show how difficult it is to carry out a transition from one regime to another after a period of intense political polarization. Each of these countries has dealt with the problem differently, and in no case has the process been judged entirely satisfactory. The *épuration* is interesting because it allows us to observe the French people, whether from below in the *épuration sauvage*, or from above in the courts, constructing their first representations of the Occupation.

The single term *épuration sauvage* to describe what occurred before the courts started functioning is unsatisfactory because there were various distinct phases in the killings which took place in this period. First, about 2,400 killings occurred before June 1944. There may well have been some wild acts of criminality or serious excesses, but they belong to the period of resistance during the Occupation not to the Liberation. Secondly, about 5,000 people were killed

[30] Novick, *The Resistance versus Vichy* is the classic account; it needs to be supplemented by H. Rousso, 'L'Épuration en France: Une histoire inachevée', *VSRH* 33 (1992), 78–105.

during the fighting which occurred between D-Day and the Liberation. These were acts of war rather than examples of 'people's justice'. Thirdly, there was the purge itself when about 1,600 people were killed immediately after the Liberation for their alleged behaviour during the Occupation.

This explosion of post-Liberation violence must, however, be placed in the context of the dramatic intensification of German repression in the summer of 1944. On a smaller scale there were Oradours all over France. In Brittany, for example, atrocities were committed by the SS, the Wehrmacht, and by Ukrainian and Georgian troops working for the Germans. On 13 June, thirty-one hostages were executed in Boudan wood near Saint-Brieuc; on 25 July, twenty people were tortured and then executed in Colpo wood in the Morbihan; on 4 August eleven people were shot in Saint-Pol-de-Léon; on 8 August, fourteen people, including a 78-year-old man and a child of 5, were shot in Plounévez-Lochrist. Often the Milice, PPF, or extremist Breton nationalists in the Perrot group were also involved in these atrocities.[31] After D-day, the violence of the Milice had become ever more unrestrained. This was the chance for a final settling of scores. On 20 June, Jean Zay, who had been Popular Front Education Minister, was taken from his prison by three *miliciens* on the pretext that he was being transferred to another prison. On the journey he was shot dead. Exactly the same happened to Georges Mandel on 7 July. Mandel's killing was a reprisal for the assassination of Henriot which had sparked off revenge killings all over France. On 29 June, Paul Touvier, the local Milice leader in the Savoy, rounded up and shot seven Jews.

The events occurring in the little town of Saint-Amand near Bourges, in the centre of France, were not untypical. The Maquis had entered the town immediately after D-day in the absence of the Germans. This liberation was short-lived because the Germans were known not to be far away. The Maquis therefore withdrew, having taken a number of hostages. The Germans and Milice arrived two days later, and seized anyone suspected of links to the Resistance. Some were shot on the spot; others were taken to Vichy and tortured. After several weeks of negotiations, the Maquis leader agreed to give up a number of his hostages, but thirteen remaining ones were considered too guilty to be released. On the other hand, their presence was impeding the mobility of the Maquis and increasing the risk that the Germans would discover its location. The Maquis leader therefore decided to kill the hostages on 20 July, hanging them in case the sound of gunfire was heard by the Germans. On hearing the news, the Milice leader Joseph Lécussan, who had a particularly gruesome reputation—in his wallet he carried a Star of David made from the skin of a Jew—rounded up seventy-six Jews in Saint-Amand, twenty-eight men, thirty-eight women, and ten children. The men were taken to an abandoned farm, pushed into a well, and buried alive under bags of cement and boulders. After the

---

[31] Capdevila, *Les Bretons*, 32–4.

shooting of a *milicien* in Bourges on 7 August, nine of the women were also killed and thrown into a well.[32] This was the kind of atmosphere in which the immediate post-Liberation purges took place. And it must also be remembered that because the Liberation was not simultaneous throughout the country, one community might not be far away from another which was still occupied. The fear of a 'fifth column' was always present. The 'wild' purge shootings sometimes took the form of summary executions without any trial, but in most places, immediately after a community was liberated, the FFI quickly set up their own 'courts' which dispensed a rudimentary form of rough justice. The fact that these tribunals genuinely saw themselves as meting out justice is suggested by the fact that the executions were sometimes carried out in public in the presence of a large crowd.[33] The severity of these courts varied considerably. In Montpellier some seventy-two executions were ordered before the official courts began to operate.[34]

One tribunal which acquired a particularly ferocious reputation was that of Pamiers in the Ariège which sat from 19 August to 31 August 1944. It seems that about fifty people were executed, a large number for such a small community. Before their execution the guilty had to cross the town under a hail of insults from the population; some had to dig their own graves. The last four executions occurred on the morning of 31 August, fifteen minutes before the time fixed by the prefect for the transfer of prisoners to the authorities in the departmental capital of Foix. Undoubtedly Pamiers witnessed some scenes of public cruelty and violence which could hardly be characterized as justice, but as in many cases where such excesses occurred, this was a region where the Milice had been particularly ferocious in the months before the Liberation.[35] Violence engendered violence. The explosion of popular justice was almost certainly inevitable after four years of occupation and latent civil war. Judgements about whether it was excessive are meaningless: against what measure is it to be judged?

The Purges II: Cleansing the Community

Another feature of the *épuration sauvage* was the shaving of women's heads.[36] Almost all these shavings occurred in August and September although

---

[32] T. Todorov, *Une tragédie française: Été 44, scènes de guerre civile* (1994).

[33] Capdevila, *Les Bretons*, 136.

[34] Bailly, *La Libération confisquée*, 268–78.

[35] A. Laurens, 'Le Phénomène milicien en Ariège et l'évolution de ses représentations dans l'opinion', *RHDGM* 131 (1983), 3–23: 21–3; P. Laborie, 'Entre histoire et mémoire, un épisode de l'épuration: Le Tribunal du peuple de Pamiers', in M. Brunet et al. (eds.), *Pays pyrénéens et pouvoirs centraux XVIᵉ–XXᵉ siècle*, ii. (n.p., 1995), 267–83.

[36] In general see C. Laurens, ' "La Femme au turban": Les Femmes tondues', in Kedward and Wood (eds.), *Liberation of France*, 155–79 (with many photographs); ead., 'La Femme au turban: Images of Women in France at the Liberation, 1944–1949' (unpublished Ph.D. thesis, University of Southampton, 1995); F. Virgili, 'Les Tondues à la Libération: Les Corps des femmes, enjeu d'un réappropriation', *Clio: Histoire, femmes et sociétés*, 1 (1995), 111–27; 'Les Tontes de la Libération en France', *Cahiers de l'IHTP*, 31 (1995), 53–64; A. Brossat, *Les Tondues: Un carnaval moche* (1992).

there was a second wave in May and June 1945 after the shock caused by the
return of deportees from the German camps. Shavings were carried out all over
the country, in cities as well as villages. Frequently they were made into a public
spectacle: the women were paraded down the street, sometimes naked; then they
were shaved in front of an audience on a hastily erected platform or a balcony;
swastikas were daubed on their faces or their shaven skulls. There is no way
of knowing how many shavings occurred, but a figure of between 10,000
and 30,000 seems plausible. Sometimes they were the result of personal
vendettas masquerading as people's justice. Sometimes angry crowds searched
for scapegoats in a random and sadistic manner. One witness in Toulouse
remembered:

> I knew a woman in this area who made funeral wreaths. She worked near to the
> window for the light. Not far from her house there was a German post which
> patrolled the crossroads. One of these men went to speak to her in the evening;
> he stayed outside talking to her; he never went indoors. At the Liberation there
> was a furious crowd which went to this poor woman's house. They made her come
> out, they hit her, they knocked her down, they undressed her and they shaved
> her head. Then they dragged her round the roads around the area with her daugh-
> ter behind her who must have been about fourteen. Then, when they had had
> enough, she went home and did not dare come out for weeks.[37]

In many cases, however, the shavings were far from spontaneous: they were
ordered, planned, and executed by local Resistance leaders. When the CLL at
Trégastel in Britanny constituted itself on 10 August 1944 its first act was to order
the shaving of ten women on the following Saturday at 4 p.m. This committee
was not composed of young FFI hotheads. Its members, two of whom were
women, included shopkeepers, two primary school teachers, and a retired
sailor.[38] The element of premeditation in the shavings has been underplayed in
many retrospective accounts because the initial enthusiasm was quickly replaced
by a sense of shame. The Liberation Committee of the French Cinema which
produced a film on the Liberation of Paris at the end of August 1944 omitted
any scenes of shavings despite having footage of them.[39] One witness from the
Var claims that 'true resisters' were not happy about the shavings.[40] But although
some contemporary diaries, especially literary ones, do convey disapproval, it is
far from certain that this disapproval was widespread. Father Bruckberger, chaplain of the FFI, wrote: 'these girls could be dipped in tar and it would affect me
no more than a fire in the fireplace of a neighbour's house'.[41]

How can the shavings be explained? Some historians have argued that they
helped to channel the violence of the Liberation. In this view, the shavings

[37] Diamond, *Women and the Second World War*, 135.
[38] Capdevila, *Les Bretons*, 152.
[39] S. Lindeperg, *Les Écrans de l'ombre: La Seconde Guerre mondiale dans le cinéma français (1944–1969)*
(1997), 66.
[40] Guillon, 'La Libération du Var', 13.
[41] Laurens, 'La Femme au turban: Images of Women', 19.

indirectly saved many other men—and women—from execution. But apart from the fact that shaved women were sometimes executed subsequently, the shavings occurred exactly at the time that summary executions were taking place: they were part of the *épuration sauvage* not a substitute for it. Anthropological interpretations of the shavings draw parallels with the early modern customs like carnival and charivari which still persisted in certain parts of the Midi.[42] The carnival-like atmosphere was noted by contemporaries. It was a means by which the community symbolically reappropriated the public space after four years of occupation.

But why were women singled out as expiatory victims?[43] The practice of shaving women for sexual infidelity has a long history. Head shavings had occurred at the end of the Great War in the part of France occupied by the Germans. German women who slept with French soldiers during the French occupation of the Rhineland in 1923 suffered the same fate. In 1944, women were usually singled out for two offences: delation and relations with Germans. The two were often linked in people's minds, and even when it could not be shown that a woman had denounced anybody, it was argued that her relationship with the Germans made this likely.[44] But the shavings also have to be placed in the wider context of what people expected from the *épuration*, and how they constructed their images of collaboration.

The historian Luc Capdevila has suggested that the world-view of the French population at the Liberation was a syncretic one, drawing unconsciously both on the rhetoric of the National Revolution and the Resistance. The years of occupation were seen as the accentuation of a long national decline dating back to the 1930s. Before 'resurrection' and 'renewal' could occur, France had to 'cleanse' herself, cutting out those 'gangrenous' elements which had caused her 'decadence' (very much the language used by Vichy about Jews and Communists). Those elements which needed to be extirpated included those people who had directly aided and co-operated with the Germans, but also those who had profited corruptly from the misfortunes of the country, especially black marketeers. The Occupation had, as one writer put it, engendered a 'crisis of public morality' and a 'taste for lucre and laziness' (very much the language used by Vichy about the Popular Front).[45]

Obviously it was not the case that most people felt themselves to have been corrupted during the Occupation in this way—in that case France's resurrection would be impossible—nor, however, could they convincingly represent themselves as having been active resisters. Instead the majority of the population depicted themselves as *bons Français*, genuine patriots who had kept aloof from the Germans and never doubted France's victory. They may not have been heroes

---

[42] Brossat, *Les Tondues*, 247–56.

[43] Rare cases of male head-shaving have been found in at least four *départements*: Virgili, 'Les Tondues', 65.

[44] Capdevila, *Les Bretons*, 222.   [45] Ibid. 204–18.

but they had participated in a shared community of suffering. Conversely those who had profited from the Occupation or frequented Germans had cut themselves off from the national community. They were no longer fully French, and had become *embochi(e)* ('krautified'). (The word 'collaboration' was sometimes spelt with a 'K' to give it a more German sounding connotation.) Thus, although collaboration in its most extreme form was defined as having offered active help to the Germans, and was punishable by law, it was also represented as a moral category, especially in small communities where people scrutinized each other closely.[46]

It is easy to see why women were singled out when collaboration was constructed in this way. In the first place, those women who consorted with German soldiers were judged to have defiled themselves and their community: like Marianne they had slept with the enemy and must be punished for it. Their punishment was described as a sort of moral disinfecting of the community and even quite literally a physical one as well: sometimes women who had slept with Germans were instructed to go for regular venereal investigations, as if they were prostitutes.[47] Secondly, women who had had any kind of affective relationship with a German were represented as having led a life of debauchery. Whether or not people believed the lurid stories about orgies, such accusations were a way of demonstrating that the women had excluded themselves from the suffering of the community: they had enjoyed themselves at a time when it was the duty of the 'good' citizen to suffer.[48] Thirdly, these women had forfeited their identity as French even more than was the case of men who had mixed with Germans. Women's naturally subordinate status meant that they were presumed to have taken on the identity of their male companions. Many women themselves internalized this assumption by defending themselves on the grounds that they had also had lovers who were in the Resistance. It was rare for them to adopt Arletty's line that their private life was their own affair.[49] Interestingly enough no reprobation seems to have attached to French men who had consorted with German women. In June 1945 a female member of the UFF in Toulouse asked the municipal council what attitude should be taken to male prisoners of war who returned with a German wife and child. The council showed no interest.[50]

The head-shavings were part of what Capdevila has called 'neighbourhood purges' in preference to the term 'wild purges'.[51] Even after the Maquis and FFI tribunals had ceased to operate, resisters continued to take direct action against

[46] Ibid. 197–218, 356–72.
[47] Virgili, 'Les Tondues', 117–19; Capdevila, *Les Bretons*, 215–16.
[48] Virgili, 'Les Tondues', 117–19; Capdevila, *Les Bretons*, 210.
[49] L. Capdevila, 'Les Femmes en Bretagne au lendemain de l'occupation allemande: Une libération inachevée', *Mémoires de la Société d'histoire et d'archéologie de Bretagne*, 77 (1999), 361–83: 380–2.
[50] Diamond, *Women and the Second World War*, 138–9.
[51] In a similar vein, M. Koreman, *The Expectation of Justice: France 1944–1946* (1999), 93–4, talks of 'local purges'.

alleged collaborators, usually with the complicity, even approval, of the local population. These neighbourhood purges from below were not viewed as a challenge to the authority of the courts or the State, but a supplement, or sometimes corrective, to the official purge from above. In Béziers, for example, a group of former FFI fighters penetrated into the prison on 29 December 1944 and shot three suspected collaborators; on 1 January 1945 they shot a *milicien* in hospital. In total, there were eight such killings in the town in the winter of 1944–5. In Alès, in the same area, a crowd of several thousand gathered outside the prison when their former mayor's death sentence was commuted to imprisonment. Hearing that the culprit had been transferred from the prison, the crowd's mood turned ugly, and four other prisoners who had been condemned to death were taken from their cells and shot in the prison courtyard.[52]

This was not just an example of southern extremism. In Brittany too neighbourhood purges went on well into 1945. There were incidents ranging from the breaking of windows of collaborators' houses to the throwing of bombs. In the Finistère there were twenty-one bomb attacks on commercial properties in October and November 1944, and nineteen in the Morbihan between June and August 1945. The main target of these attacks were former black marketeers who had escaped the courts. In general the police encountered a wall of silence when they tried to track down the perpetrators. On 5 March 1945 an ex-police inspector who had been assiduous in hunting down resisters was shot near Quimper. The prefect reported that this had 'provoked neither emotion nor reaction among the population' who felt that 'he had deserved to be killed'. At his funeral a crowd gathered to boo and whistle. On 2 June 1945 in Dinan, a crowd of 4,000–5,000 people—almost half the population—gathered outside the prison to demand the release of five young men who had been accused of carrying out bomb attacks. They stormed the prison and released the men who were carried triumphantly to the war memorial. The police stood by powerless. The prefect was not sure of being able to count on the loyalty of his own men. But in fact the local authorities themselves were not entirely out of sympathy with the perpetrators of such incidents. Despite the fact that there had been thirty-five bomb attacks in May alone, the police chief in the Côtes-du-Nord took a very relaxed attitude to the situation: 'the situation is calm . . . bomb attacks are still going on . . . [but] public security is not threatened. The victims of the various attacks are generally individuals suspected of collaboration against whom no legal action had yet been taken.'[53]

These purges were, then, supported by entire communities. Sometimes they were seen as punishing transgressions which were not within the remit of the courts; sometimes they were seen as redressing what was perceived as the insufficient vigilance, or excessive clemency, of the authorities. In Chambéry, in the

[52] Bailly, *La Libération confisquée*, 279–83. See other examples in Aron, *Histoire de l'épuration*, i. 224–7.
[53] Capdevila, *Les Bretons*, 171–94.

Savoie, vigilantism had been brought under control by the summer of 1945, but this situation changed in the autumn when the government commuted the death sentence of a young *milicien* named Capella. This was an area where the conflict between the Resistance and Milice had been very intense. Capella had been responsible for the burning of local farms, the deaths of resisters, and the deportation of others; and he had worked directly with the Germans. The commutation of his sentence outraged local opinion. There were demonstrations and petitions, and in January 1946 there were ten bomb attacks in seven different towns, one of them targeting Capella's uncle. In Chambéry the archiepiscopal palace was bombed, possibly because the Church was suspected of harbouring former *miliciens*.[54]

Such local outbursts of anger were often linked to national events. The German offensive in the Ardennes in December 1944 stimulated panic about the fifth column, and the return of the deportees in April/May 1945 revived memories of the horrors of the Occupation. Deportees were often involved in vigilante incidents. At the small town of Rambervilliers, in the Vosges, on 31 May 1945 deportees and others set up what was described as a 'people's tribunal' in a local café and shaved the heads of a dozen women. But local vigilantism only retained the support of local communities as long as it was perceived as genuinely redressing injustice. If vigilantes went too far they risked cutting themselves off from the local population. This occurred in the Vosges in August 1945 when two families with young children were found murdered in two adjacent villages. Although both families had been under suspicion of collaboration, public opinion was horrified by the murders. Vigilantism was discredited, and when at the end of the year two local *miliciens* were pardoned, the local reaction was muted: imperfect official justice was now seen as preferable to lawless violence. By March 1946 the same was true even in Chambéry where emotions had run so high a few weeks earlier. Opinion was shocked by the murder in broad daylight of two naturalized Italians who were alleged to be collaborators. On another occasion five men broke into the farm of a widow, shaved her head, and beat up her nephew. The interesting fact is that the perpetrators of these acts felt it necessary to wear masks: they could no longer rely on the complicity of the local population.[55]

The Purges III: The Trials

The variable intensity of the purges from below was intimately linked to the progress of the official purge from above. From the beginning there was frustration at the slowness with which the courts carried out their task. There were so many cases to consider that massive bottlenecks developed. By the beginning

---

[54] Koreman, *Expectation of Justice*, 139–46.   [55] Ibid. 127–9, 146–7.

of December the Paris Court of Justice alone faced a backlog of 4,200 cases; in Lyons the court started work on 26 October 1944 but by 1 February 1945 it had only heard forty-four cases.[56] The first important cases to come before the courts were those of journalists and propagandists. This was because the evidence against them was easiest to assemble: they had convicted themselves through their own writings. The first of these trials concerned the journalist Georges Suarez who had run the pro-German newspaper *Aujourd'hui*. He was sentenced to death and shot on 9 November. Next came the turn of Henri Béraud, one of the leading journalists of *Gringoire*. He too was sentenced to death on 30 December 1944. This decision provoked an article from François Mauriac calling for clemency on the specific grounds that Béraud, despite his violent Anglophobia and anti-Semitism, had never written a single article in support of the Germans or indeed set foot in Paris (*Gringoire* was published in the Unoccupied Zone), and on the general grounds that writers should be allowed to make mistakes. On 13 January de Gaulle commuted Béraud's sentence to twenty years' hard labour.[57]

Mauriac spoke out again to appeal for clemency for Robert Brasillach who was sentenced to death by the Paris court in January 1945. Although, unlike Béraud, Brasillach certainly had written pro-German articles, fifty-nine intellectuals (including Mauriac, Valéry, Claudel, and Paulhan) signed a petition calling for clemency. This was taken to de Gaulle by Mauriac in person. On this occasion de Gaulle decided to let the sentence stand and Brasillach was shot on 6 February 1945. The case of Brasillach aroused disquiet even among intellectuals who had not signed the petition. Simone de Beauvoir worried that his death had transformed him from a villain to a martyr; Vercors claimed in his memoirs to have been shocked by the arbitrariness of singling out one writer to assume the sins of so many others who escaped more lightly.

Mauriac's plea for mercy—one paper dubbed him 'St Francis of the Assizes'—led to a debate in the press between him and Albert Camus. Camus argued that although the purges must be carried out without hatred, justice had to prevail over charity: 'every time I talk of justice, M. Mauriac talks of charity'. Nonetheless Camus did in the end sign the petition in favour of Brasillach, and although he claimed to have done this because he opposed the principle of the death penalty, he had not applied this principle in the case of Suarez whose execution he had approved. It seems likely therefore that Camus, despite his public stance, was himself beginning to have doubts. By August he had begun to find the purges 'odious' and retrospectively he judged Mauriac to have been right.[58] Whatever the rights and wrongs of the individual cases, there was undoubtedly considerable arbitrariness in the sentences meted out to writers. As passions calmed, the

---

[56] H. Lottman, *The People's Anger: Justice and Revenge in Post-Liberation France* (1986); Novick, *Resistance versus Vichy*, 160.

[57] In general see P. Assouline, *L'Épuration des intellectuels* (Brussels, 1985).

[58] Sapiro, *La Guerre des écrivains*, 601–11; Assouline, *L'Épuration*, 44–56.

sentences tended to become more lenient irrespective of the merits of the case: the date of the trial mattered more than the gravity of the crime. Rebatet, whose trial was not held until November 1946, was sentenced to death but had his sentence commuted; Céline who was tried *in absentia* in February 1950 was sentenced to one year in prison and a fine. As Jouhandeau remarked, 'If Drieu agrees to remain hidden two years in a cellar, he'll end up as a minister.'[59] But Drieu was already dead.

The work of the High Court began in March 1945 with the trial of Admiral Estéva who, as resident-general of Tunisia, had helped the Germans in November 1942. Estéva, who had obeyed orders without ever being particularly pro-German, was sentenced to life imprisonment. He was definitely a second-rank figure, and what people were really waiting for was the trial of Pétain. De Gaulle's hope that Pétain could be tried *in absentia* as quickly as possible was dashed when Pétain appeared at the Franco-Swiss border on 26 April. Although he had been offered asylum in Switzerland, Pétain was determined to render his account to the French people. For former resisters, the trial was to have a pedagogic purpose. Mauriac wrote: 'it is precisely because so many people are still under the spell of this great figure that nothing must be left in the shadows . . . the sentence must be delivered in the full light of day'.[60]

Pétain's trial opened on 23 July 1945. His defence strategy was devised by the young lawyer Jacques Isorni who had made his reputation defending Brasillach. Pétain began by reading out a prepared statement. It declared that the Armistice had contributed to the Allied victory by keeping North Africa free of German troops, and that Vichy had acted as a shield to protect the French: 'every day, a dagger to my throat, I struggled against the enemy's demands'. The statement ended with Pétain refusing to accept the jurisdiction of the court and announcing that he would participate no further in its proceedings. Although he did speak out on one or two occasions, for most of the rest of the trial Pétain was silent, sometimes asleep, sometimes seemingly unaware of what was going on.

The prosecution began by trying to prove that Pétain's arrival in power was part of a long-laid plot to bring down the Republic. The problem with this strategy was that most people were much more concerned with what had happened during the Occupation than with going over events of 1940 which seemed almost like ancient history. Ageing Third Republic politicians—Daladier, Herriot, Reynaud, Lebrun—emerged like ghosts to testify about Pétain's behaviour in 1940. Reynaud and Weygand clashed in an undignified slanging match. No one emerged from this with much dignity except Léon Blum, and the Third Republic did not appear in its best colours.

Suddenly, on the ninth day of the trial, the prosecutor announced that he did

[59] Assouline, *L'Épuration*, 26.
[60] F. Kupferman, *Le Procès de Vichy: Pucheu, Pétain, Laval* (Brussels, 1980), 53.

not after all have the evidence to prove any culpability on Pétain's part before the Armistice, and that the trial would now concentrate on the Vichy government. The defence used the argument that Pétain had been playing a double game. Much was made of supposed secret contacts between Britain and Vichy in 1940, and of the secret telegrams to Darlan in 1942. Most of these claims were false, or did not bear the construction put on them, but this was not so easy to prove, and the defence's strategy did sow doubts. The defence was not, however, helped by the sudden and unexpected appearance of Laval who had arrived from Spain on 1 August after failing to obtain political asylum from Franco. Shrunken and haggard, Laval had aged dramatically, but his mental faculties were intact. Appearing in court on 3 August, he was unstoppably eloquent, arguing that all his actions had met with Pétain's full approval. On 15 August the jury delivered their verdict. Pétain was condemned to death, but with the recommendation— which de Gaulle accepted—that owing to his age the sentence should be commuted to imprisonment.

Next the High Court had to deal with the case of Darnand. He presented himself as an honest soldier who had obeyed the Marshal and preformed what he believed to be his patriotic duty. If he had made mistakes, he had always acted in good faith. Although Darnand was sentenced to death and executed, his performance had won grudging admiration even from his enemies.[61] Quite different was the case of Laval who had been feverishly preparing his defence ever since Sigmaringen. Confident of his abilities until the end, Laval seems to have been half convinced that his eloquence would enable him to persuade the jury that he had acted in France's best interests. In the end he was never given the chance. His trial opened on 3 October. The president of the Court was incapable of keeping order and jurors shouted abuse at Laval. On 6 October Laval announced that he would no longer participate in the proceedings. His only hope was that the government would order a new trial given the irregularities which had occurred. Although the conditions of the trial caused widespread unease, there was no reprieve, and Laval was sentenced to death. His end was as sordid as his trial. Hours before he was due to be shot he swallowed a cyanide capsule. His stomach was pumped out seventeen times, and he was dragged, half-dead, to be executed on 15 October.[62]

The High Court continued to operate, but its proceeedings attracted decreasing attention. The trial of de Brinon in March 1947 was sparsely attended although he was sentenced to death; Benoist-Mechin was sentenced to death in May 1947 but the verdict was commuted; Vallat got a ten-year prison sentence in December 1947.[63] The last case was heard in July 1949. The Civic Courts went on until December 1949; by October 1948 there were only four Courts of Justice

---

[61] Aron, *Histoire de l'épuration*, ii. 534–42; *Les Procès de la collaboration: Fernand de Brinon, Joseph Darnand, Jean Luchaire* (1948), 243–347.

[62] Kupferman, *Le Procès de Vichy*, 128–54.

[63] *Les Procès de la Collaboration: Fernand de Brinon*, 7–240.

still working, and the last one, in Paris, was wound up in January 1951.[64] The sentences were increasingly lenient—although Luchaire was condemned to death and executed in December 1946—but what caused most public disquiet was a feeling that the punishments were mostly affecting the poor and defenceless while the bigger fish were getting off free. This was not entirely untrue. For example, of those appearing before the court at Valenciennes, one-third of employers and a quarter of artisans, shopkeepers, and professionals were acquitted, but only one-tenth of peasants and workers.[65]

The purge, however, went beyond the courts. In both the public administration and the professions, purge committees were set up to judge and punish collaborators. Among public servants the purge of the police was particularly severe. In the Paris Prefecture of Police 3,939 cases were considered—20 per cent of the total force—and 1,906 policemen were sanctioned in some way, half of them with dismissal. Four hundred cases were sent to the courts, resulting in 196 condemnations (twenty death sentences). In the rest of the police force there were 1,162 dismissals, and 857 lesser sanctions.[66] The purge was also severe in the Ministry of Information, but less so in posts and telecommunications and the railways.[67]

In the private sector, the cases that attracted most public attention were those of film stars and entertainers. Those who had been arrested at the Liberation included Arletty, Sacha Guitry, Tino Rossi, Maurice Chevalier, Pierre Fresnay, and Ginette Leclerc (the last two both stars of *Le Corbeau*). Most of them were soon released while their cases were considered. Arletty spent about four months in prison and then eighteen under house arrest. Finally in November 1946 the cinema purge committee allowed her to resume her career, having pronounced a formal sentence of 'blame'. Carné too was 'blamed' for having signed a contract with the Continental although he had never made a film with them. Clouzot, the director of *Le Corbeau*, received a sanction, as did almost anyone involved in the film. Guitry was soon released but not until August 1947 did the Paris Court of Justice decide that there was no case for him to answer. In his memoirs of these tribulations, he seemed impervious to the fact that if he had indeed never betrayed his country he had hardly brought great honour upon it either.[68] Undoubtedly in the cases of Guitry, and others like him, what aroused such resentment—a poll in September 1944 showed 56 per cent approval of Guitry's arrest—was that they had so palpably *enjoyed* themselves under the Occupation. Guitry had certainly not been part of any community of suffering.

[64] Aron, *Histoire de l'épuration*, ii. 218.

[65] J.-P. Rioux, 'L'Épuration en France', in *Études sur la France de 1939 à nos jours* (1985), 162–77: 169–70.

[66] Berlière, *Le Monde des policiers en France*, 207–18.

[67] F. Rouquet, 'L'Épuration administrative en France après la Libération', *VSRH* 33 (1992), 106–17, and id., *L'Épuration dans l'administration française* (1993).

[68] Guitry, *Quatre ans d'occupations* (1947).

More serious than socializing with the Germans was doing business with them. At the Liberation the mood had been strongly anti-capitalist. In the south of France, in places like Marseilles, Toulouse, and Nice, a total of about 100 factories had been taken over by workers' management committees.[69] Louis Renault was arrested but died in October 1944 before he could be tried (in fact his mind had almost completely gone). There was a national purge committee (CNIE), and also regional ones, representing workers, employers, and the State. But working through company accounts to establish guilt—even if it could be agreed what constituted guilt in the first place—was more complicated than exhuming the articles of journalists or establishing membership of the Milice. Once the purge commissions had got around to assembling the evidence, the mood had shifted towards leniency. The regional commission of Paris examined 4,889 cases and pronounced 2,596 sanctions. The CNIE considered 1,538 cases but pronounced only 191 sanctions. In the end few employers lost control of their businesses.[70]

Intellectuals in the Dock

Even if public interest in the purges was waning by 1946, there was a widespread feeling that of all social categories industrialists had escaped most lightly. This was elegantly expressed by Jean Paulhan in June 1946:

> The purge has been hard on writers. The engineers, entrepreneurs, and builders who constructed the Atlantic Wall live peacefully among us. They are building new walls. They are building the walls of the new prisons where we lock up the journalists who made the mistake of writing that the Atlantic Wall had been well built.[71]

The impression that the purges had affected writers disproportionately harshly was probably a slight distortion caused by the fact that the first high-profile trials, when interest in the *épuration* was at its height, had concerned writers, and that those who were tried earliest suffered the severest penalties.[72] Paulhan's remark, however, was not only about numbers. It was a contribution to a wider debate about the responsibility of the intellectual. This debate divided former Resistance allies from each other, and called into question the entire basis of the *épuration* of writers and intellectuals.

Two bodies assumed responsibility for the purge of intellectuals: the National Purge Committee of Writers and Composers and the CNE. The former, created by a formal government *ordonnance*, had the right to prevent writers publishing or republishing their works for up to two years. Sitting intermittently between mid-1945 and mid-1949 it considered ninety-one cases, and pronounced sanc-

[69] Madjarian, *Conflits et pouvoirs*, 165–83.   [70] Rousso, 'L'Épuration', 101.
[71] Sapiro, *La Guerre des écrivains*, 613.
[72] Ibid. 587; Novick, *Resistance versus Vichy*, 163–4.

tions in fifty-two cases. The CNE's role was less well defined. In September 1944 it drew up its notorious 'black list' of writers who had collaborated. The ninety-four names included Chardonne, Drieu, Giono, Maurras, Montherlant, Céline, Brasillach, Jouhandeau, Guitry, Rebatet, Benjamin, and Fabre-Luce. Two subsequent lists in October and November increased the total number of names to 160. But what was the purpose of this list? The original intention was to communicate the names on it to the Ministry of Justice, but this idea was abandoned after protests from Mauriac and Paulhan. Mauriac commented to Paulhan that writers should not have the 'soul of cops'. Paulhan wrote: 'that the first public act of the CNE is to demand the arrests of other writers seems to me to be nothing less than *horrible*. His principle was that writers should be 'neither judges nor informers'.[73] In the end it was decided that the CNE would restrict itself to a kind of moral sanction: its members would refuse to write in publications alongside anyone on the list.

Nonetheless the existence of the list continued to cause disquiet. One problem was its arbitrariness: Morand was on the first list, absent from the second, and back on the third; Cocteau was on none. There was clearly bargaining behind the scenes as to who should be included. There were differences of opinion as to whether support for Pétain was in itself sufficient to merit inclusion, or was some sign of sympathy with Germany also required?[74] Another problem was that while writers were finding themselves sanctioned and vilified, publishers were more lightly treated. Most of them had at least one Resistance writer on their books ready to speak out in their defence. Denoël, one of the most compromised, was assassinated in mysterious circumstances in December 1945 before he could stand trial. Gallimard, the publisher of the *NRF*, was able to assemble a stellar list of witnesses to testify in his favour, including Malraux, Sartre, Éluard, and Camus. The *NRF* for the second time served as a useful lightning conductor. Having continued the *NRF* during the war to save the rest of his publishing house from the Germans, Gallimard wound it up in 1945 to preserve the rest of his publishing house from reprisals at the Liberation. Pierre Seghers and Vercors resigned from the Publishing Purge Commission as early as the winter of 1944, disgusted that the mutual back-scratching between authors and publishers had saved so many skins.[75]

For Paulhan, however, the problems of the purge went far beyond the cases of injustice and arbitrariness. At the very first post-Liberation meeting of the CNE on 4 September, he argued that to make a mistake, to take intellectual risks, was the writer's 'first prerogative'. As early as October 1944 he had to be dissuaded from resigning from the CNE. But not everybody shared Paulhan's view. Taking up Paulhan's comparison between the treatment of industrialists and that of writers, Vercors wrote: 'to compare the industrialist to the writer is

[73] *Choix de lettres*, 374–7.   [74] Sapiro, *La Guerre des écrivains*, 565–90.
[75] Ibid. 591–2; Fouché, *L'édition française*, i, 152–257.

to compare Cain to the devil. Cain's crime ends with Abel. The devil's is without limit.' Or as Sartre put it: 'we ought to rejoice that our profession involves some dangers'.[76]

Behind these abstract debates about the responsibility of writers lay more specific concerns that the CNE, from being the mouthpiece of the intellectual Resistance, was becoming an instrument of the Communist Party. There were signs that the Communists were ready to use their power to settle scores rather than advance the wider agenda of the Resistance. The most blatant example of this was an article by Aragon in the CNE's review *Lettres françaises* in November 1944 criticizing Gide for his ambivalent attitude in the early days of the Occupation. Quite apart for the fact that the Communists had little to boast about where their attitude in 1940 was concerned, many people assumed that Gide was being singled out because of the critical book he had written in 1937 about his visit to the Soviet Union. The Communists had never forgiven him for this. Aragon, whose reputation as France's 'national poet' gave him enormous influence at the Liberation, seemed now to want to play the role of communist Grand Inquisitor of letters.[77] In November 1946 Paulhan finally resigned from the CNE, and was followed by several other writers who had long shared his doubts. Among them was the Catholic philosopher Gabriel Marcel who claimed that the CNE had become 'an instrument of political sectarianism'.[78] The unity of the literary Resistance was in ruins.

The Resistance Betrayed?

Looking back on the Occupation in 1946 François Mauriac wrote:

Do you not sometimes think . . . of those sombre days with a secret nostalgia? Who would have said then that in liberated France we would be tempted to say: 'Those were the good old days . . . ?' Certainly those days of horror were not good days. But they were days of friendship and confidence . . . We were not unhappy because we were over-brimming with hope, because we had confidence in each other, because we felt that we were brothers, as indeed we were.[79]

This sense of nostalgia was common among former resisters by 1946. The Resistance had excited almost millenarian expectations; its rhetoric was rich with images of revolution and renewal. 'From Liberation to Revolution' was the slogan of *Combat* after the Liberation. But well before 1946 the mood had started to change. For some local resisters the moment of disillusion was their first meeting with de Gaulle. From the autumn of 1944, de Gaulle had embarked on a tour of the country to establish his authority in person. He visited Lyons on 14 September, Marseilles on 15 September, and Toulouse on 16 September. Everywhere he received the local Resistance leaders with calculated coldness verging on rude-

---

[76] Sapiro, *La Guerre des écrivains*, 611–21.
[77] Ibid. 592–9.   [78] Ibid. 654–62.   [79] Ibid. 692.

ness. This came naturally to de Gaulle, but it was also part of his strategy of bringing the Resistance to heel. In Toulouse, the regional Resistance leader Serge Ravanel remembered the day of de Gaulle's visit, which should have been so glorious, as one of the saddest of his life: 'Our interview lasted an hour. De Gaulle asked me no questions. I discovered the existence of an immense abyss between this man who had lived all of the war outside France, and the metropolitan Resistance which had had such a different experience.'[80]

More and more Resistance leaders began at the end of 1944 to experience a sense of frustration and disappointment. At the beginning of 1945, Pierre Hervé published *La Libération trahie* (The Liberation Betrayed), a book whose title speaks for itself. Soon afterwards appeared Philip Viannay's *Nous sommes tous des rebelles* (We are All Rebels) whose theme was similar. A year later Frenay published an article entitled 'The Gravediggers of the Resistance'.

It was convenient to blame de Gaulle for this sense that things had not turned out as expected, but in truth the problems of the Resistance after the Liberation went much deeper. Ravanel's account of de Gaulle's visit does not hide the fact that deliriously enthusiastic crowds had turned out to cheer the general. Ravanel's sadness, then, was not only about the treatment meted out to him by de Gaulle, but also about the isolation which many resisters soon came to feel in liberated France—an isolation almost as great as in Pétainist France four years earlier.

The ambivalence with which the Resistance had always viewed the mass of the population, and the population had viewed the Resistance, was provisionally masked by the euphoria of the Liberation. In this fête of unanimity, those who had resisted suspended their contempt for those who had not, and those who had not, bathed in the glory of those who had. But as early as the end of 1944 the Resistance was beginning to lose credit with the population. The prefect of Calvados reported in December 1944: 'the Resistance which immediately after the Liberation enjoyed great prestige has lost the population's esteem'.[81] Perhaps this was not surprising in an area where the Resistance had never been strong, but the same was reported throughout France.[82] It must be remembered that the Liberation had not ended the difficulties of daily life. In 1945 and 1946 rations were even smaller than they had been during the Occupation. Food, fuel, and soap were all hard to find, and there was a thriving black market. This situation was less easy to tolerate now that the Occupation was over. What was the point of liberation if the conditions of daily life were no better—even worse—than they had been previously? The joyous dancing of the Liberation seemed like a distant memory, and just to underline the point, even Vichy's ban on dancing was restored in October 1944 on the grounds that it was unseemly to dance while

---

[80] *L'Esprit de la Résistance*, 393–4.

[81] J. Quellien, 'La Resistance dans le Calvados en 1945', in Franck (ed.), *La France de 1945*, 59–71: 62.

[82] P. Laborie, 'Opinion et représentations: La Libération et l'image de la Résistance', *RHDGM* 131 (1983), 65–96; Capdevila, *Les Bretons*, 277–8.

so many prisoners and deportees still languished in Germany. De Gaulle remained extraordinarily popular, but popular discontent turned against his government and those representatives of the Resistance who were now in positions of authority.[83]

In May 1945, municipal elections took place. These gave a massive victory for those political forces associated with the Resistance, especially the Communists, but also the Socialists and the new Christian Democrat party, the MRP. Right-wing parties were decimated. In that sense the elections represented a triumph for the political values of the Resistance. But they also marked the death knell of the specific institutions which had emerged from the Resistance: what was the point in the CDLs and CLLs now that genuine local democracy had been restored?[84] The final flourish of the CDLs occurred in Paris between 10 and 14 July 1945 with the holding of the 'Estates General of the French Renaissance' at which delegates chosen from all the CDLs of France assembled to present, as in 1789, *cahiers de doléances* expressing the aspirations of the French population. The preparation of this event aroused almost no interest despite Communist attempts to whip up enthusiasm for it.[85]

As for the hope that a single movement or party might emerge to embody the 'ethical maximalism' of the Resistance, this never materialized.[86] The first post-war congress of the MLN in January 1944 was divided over whether or not to merge with the Communist FN. Six months later the MLN split over this issue. Those who joined the Communists soon found that there was no space for a specific Resistance voice within the Communist monolith. Those who refused to join the Communists formed themselves into a new party called the Democratic and Social Union of the Resistance (UDSR). Despite its grandiose name, this party, small in size, was a far cry from the expectations which resisters had harboured during the Occupation.

The disappointment experienced by many resisters was inevitable because their vision of the new France was a moral and spiritual one as much as it was political. They were rediscovering the truth of Péguy's famous aphorism: 'Everything begins as *mystique* and ends as *politique*.' When resisters tried to offer a more concrete account of the nature of their 'betrayal', they fastened on to the CNR Charter which gradually acquired a talismanic status. In fact even the CNR Charter was vague on details, and in many respects the measures carried out by de Gaulle's provisional government between August 1944 and October 1945— when the first post-war national elections occurred—were faithful to its spirit. These measures included extensive nationalizations (there were more of these in 1946), the setting up of a national social security system, the creation of a new

[83] Koreman, *Expectation of Justice*, 56–63, 68–71, 148–88.

[84] Guillon, 'Parti de l'ordre et parti de mouvement', in id. and Buton, *Les Pouvoirs en France*, 38–59: 52–4.

[85] Ibid. 53; Capdevila, *Les Bretons*, 305–13.

[86] For the phrase 'ethical maximalism' see Pavone, 'Continuity of the State', 17.

training school for top civil servants (ENA), and the institution of consultative committees (*comités d'entreprise*) in factories to represent the views of workers and other employees. This represented a major programme of social and economic reform, comparable to that undertaken after 1945 by the British Labour government.

Yet many resisters believed that the government could have gone further. Some wanted greater power to be given to the *comités d'enterprise*; others wanted the government to undertake Socialist-style economic planning. Such issues were debated within de Gaulle's government between René Pleven, the Finance Minister, and Pierre Mendès France, the Economics Minister. Mendès France argued for a temporary policy of financial austerity to avert inflation, and a long-term policy of economic planning. When de Gaulle finally came down in favour of Pleven, Mendès France resigned in April 1945. This has in retrospect been seen as a missed opportunity to carry out structural economic reforms—and Mendès France was certainly right about the danger of inflation—but it would be wrong to see his resignation as a betrayal of the Resistance. The conflict between Pleven and Mendès-France had involved two former members of the Free French, neither of whom had been in the internal French Resistance. And when it came to the *comités d'entreprise*, the 'radical' Mendès France had been in favour of limiting their powers rather than allowing them to become genuine experiments in worker participation.[87]

When resisters expressed their disappointment that more radical changes had not occurred at the Liberation—Claude Bourdet subtitled his memoirs 'From Resistance to Restoration'—they both underestimated the extent of the changes which had occurred, and implied misleadingly that there was a single radical Resistance project which the government had failed to carry out. Moreover, those areas in which the Liberation did represent continuity more than change were not always evident to resisters themselves, who shared the prevailing values of French society more than they realized. To what extent, for example, did 1944–5 see a liberation for French women? The question might seem surprising given that for the first time French women had acquired the right to vote. De Gaulle had implicitly promised this as early as June 1942 although it was hardly a major concern of his. Nor had it been a major preoccupation of the Resistance—it was not mentioned in the CNR Charter—but there was almost no objection to it either (except from the Radicals). Female suffrage was officially promulgated in a CFLN decree of 21 April 1944, and women voted for the first time in the municipal elections of May 1945. At the first post-war legislative elections in October, thirty-three women were elected to parliament.[88]

Despite the political emancipation of women, however, the Liberation also witnessed an attempt to redraw traditional gender boundaries. As we have already

[87] Shennan, *Rethinking France*, 193.
[88] H. Footitt, 'The First Women *députés*: "Les Trente Glorieuses"', in Kedward and Wood (eds.), *Liberation*, 129–41.

noted, the self-image of the Resistance became increasingly masculine even as more women were participating in it. Sartre's 1945 essay identifying collaboration with feminine passivity fits into this model. Similarly the head-shavings can be interpreted partly as a ritualized punishment of women for the independence which many of them had enjoyed, even flaunted, during the Occupation. In the Côtes-du-Nord, one woman who had had her head shaved and a swastika tattooed on her cheek complained to the prefect. Having investigated the case, the prefect was reassured by the mayor of her town that no injustice had been committed although there was no evidence she had collaborated:

> To the best of my knowledge she has never denounced anyone to the enemy or caused any harm to patriots. She has a reputation for loose morals. She is separated from her husband. She was shaved like many other women from the locality for having probably had sexual relations with German soldiers during the Occupation, and in my view she does not deserve to be rehabilitated.[89]

In this case it was clearly a style of life which was being punished as much as any crime, rather as the female abortionist executed by Vichy was punished as much for who she was as what she had done. Abortion could also be an aggravating circumstance at the Liberation. Of one woman who had her head shaved in the Charente-Maritime it was said: 'she is rumoured to have had an abortion. It is well known that she frequented Germans.'[90]

The punishment of women at the Liberation for having transgressed traditional boundaries of respectability occurred within the context of continuing concern about the birth rate. Natalism remained omnipresent in public discourse even if reference to the family tended to be less pervasive than under Vichy.[91] In a speech in March 1945 de Gaulle called for 'twelve million beautiful babies'; the Communist UFF declared in June that 'France needs children'. In May 1945 the Ministry of the Interior exhorted prefects to give prominence to Mother's Day. Although the death penalty for abortion was removed, the 1920 anti-abortion law continued to be rigorously enforced. Prosecutions for abortion increased, and magistrates often meted out sentences of up to four years' imprisonment. In short, women after 1944 continued to be viewed as reproducers not producers.[92] In that respect little had changed.

Attitudes towards race and immigration also changed less than might have been expected. Immigration was one of the subjects discussed by the new Committee on Population and the Family set up in April 1945 to study the demographic problem. Its secretary, Georges Mauco, was recognized as an expert on immigration, and had acted as an adviser on immigration to Daladier's govern-

---

[89] Capdevila, *Les Bretons*, 215.
[90] Virgili, 'Les Tondues', 118.
[91] Muracciole, *Les Enfants de la défaite*, 320–3.
[92] C. Duchen, 'Occupation Housewife: The Domestic Ideal in 1950s France', *French Cultural Studies*, 24 (1991), 1–11; J. Jenson, 'The Liberation and New Rights for French Women', in Higonnet et al., *Behind the Lines*, 272–84.

ment in 1938. A member of the PPF from 1940, Mauco was one of the relatively small band of French racial theorists. During the Occupation he had published two articles in Montandon's *Ethnie française*, arguing that Jews were the least desirable of all immigrant groups. Their 'servile and obsequious' nature had contributed to 'devirilizing' France. Somehow Mauco, who resigned from the PPF in November 1942, succeeded in dissociating himself from Montandon (who was assassinated by the Resistance in August 1944) and even invented a Resistance reputation for himself in the nick of time.[93] Other members of the post-Liberation Committee on Population included the irrepressible natalist Fernand Boverat, and the statistician and demographer Alfred Sauvy. Sauvy was head of the newly created National Institute for the Study of Demography (INED) which was in fact a continuation, under a new name, of the Fondation Carrel.[94]

On the Committee, Mauco argued for a selective immigration policy operating according to strictly ethnic criteria. Sauvy, whose priority was to increase France's population at any cost, opposed this. Even if in the end Mauco's line did not prevail, Sauvy's racial assumptions were not so different. In 1946 Sauvy published a book on the population problem with the paediatrician and former resister Robert Debré. Their chapter on immigration acknowledged its debt to the work of Mauco. While accepting the need for large-scale immigration they wanted priority to be given to those most likely to assimilate easily into French civilization. This meant preferring northerners to 'credulous and fatalistic Arabs or . . . crafty Levantines'. Immigrants should be dispersed so as to avoid any replica of the 'little Israelo-Oriental' ghetto in central Paris.[95] This was closer to the tone of Giraudoux's *Pleins pouvoirs* in 1939 than one might expect from two leading spokesmen of the spirit of the 'New France'. Similarly, the new legislation codifying the rules for French nationality was very much in line with the discriminatory legislation of the late 1930s. Newly naturalized citizens were excluded from elective office for ten years and from full civic rights for five. Naturalization was only possible for those who had demonstrated their 'assimilation into the French community'—the first time this had been explicitly written into the law—providing it was clear that their 'state of physical health' meant that they would not be a 'burden or a danger for the collectivity'.[96]

Thus although the post-Liberation government abolished all Vichy's discriminatory legislation against Jews, the terms in which nationality was discussed did not represent a total break with the past. Little was said after 1944 about the

[93] On Mauco see Adler, 'Idealising France', 166–220; P. Weil, 'Georges Mauco: Un itinéraire camouflé', in Taguieff, *L'Antisémitisme de plume*, 267–76.

[94] This is one of the themes of H. le Bras's polemic against INED, *Marianne et les lapins: L'Obsession démographique* (1991).

[95] R. Debré and A. Sauvy, *Des Français pour la France: Le Problème de la population* (1946), 93, 230–1. P. Weil, 'Racisme et discrimination dans la politique française de l'immigration: 1938–1945/1974–1995', *VSRH* 47 (1995), 74–99.

[96] Noiriel, *Les Origines républicaines*, 275–8; Adler, 'Idealising France', 130–64.

important role which foreigners had played in the Resistance. But to the extent that this was a betrayal of the pluralistic identity of the Resistance, it was a betrayal in which resisters were themselves complicit. The rhetoric of the Resistance had always tended to stress unity over diversity. The most open acknowledgement of the role of immigrants had come from the Communists, but they retreated from this position after 1945 in their attempt to portray themselves as France's truly national party. Writing in *L'Humanité* in August 1945 after the liberation of the camp of Majdanek, Maurice Thorez declared of the victims that their names were 'redolent of the old French countryside . . . names of Bretons and Alsatians, Flemish and Corsican names, Norman and Provençal names . . . French names'.[97] In 1946, the FTP published a collection of letters from martyred Communists, *Lettres de fusillés*, which included some written by members of the FTP-MOI. Another edition of the same work in 1951, under the slightly different title *Lettres de communistes fusillés*, with a preface by Aragon, no longer contained any FTP-MOI names. Foreigners disappeared posthumously from the Resistance.

It is not surprising that liberation was accompanied by a discourse of national unity which privileged unity over diversity, but this made the Liberation in some respects, if not a 'restoration', to use Bourdet's term, at least a moment of closure, as much as one of renewal. The Resistance had celebrated France's regional diversity, but this did not result in any questioning of the centralized traditions of the republican State. Regionalism was too discredited by its Vichyite associations. The issue of decentralization did come to the fore in 1947 after the publication of the influential book 'Paris and the French Desert' by Jean-François Gravier.[98] It is often forgotten that during the Occupation Gravier had run Marion's school for training propaganda delegates, and he had already written a book on the issue of regionalism in 1942.[99] Although the word regionalism was taboo after 1944, cultural decentralization was viewed positively. It was inspired by the idea that French education was too narrowly intellectual and too elitist: it must be democratized and broadened.[100] These ideas were embodied in the organization Peuple et culture (People and Culture) which attracted the support of many intellectuals. Such initiatives were inspired by the Popular Front, but also by Jeune France and Uriage. Jean Vilar, founder of the Avignon festival in 1947 and presiding influence over the decentralization of French theatre after the Liberation, had worked for Jeune France.[101] Joffre Dumazadier, the founder of Peuple et culture, had taught at Uriage.

[97] Wieviorka, *Déportation et génocide*, 52.   [98] J.-F. Gravier, *Paris et le désert français* (1947).
[99] Gravier, *Région et nation* (1942).
[100] B. Rigby, 'Intellectuals, Education and Culture at the Liberation: The Opposition to "la culture scolaire"', *French Cultural Studies*, 5/15 (1994), 241–52.
[101] S. Added, 'Les Premiers Pas de la décentralisation dans les années Vichy', in R. Abirached (ed.), *La Décentralisation théâtrale: Le Premier Âge 1945–1951* (Avignon, 1992), 43–51; D. Lindenberg, 'Révolution culturelle dans la Révolution nationale: De Jacques Copeau à Jeune France: Une archéologie de la décentralisation théâtrale', *Révoltes logiques*, 12 (1980), 2–18.

Many of those who had worked at Uriage enjoyed greater intellectual influence, especially in journalism and publishing, after the Liberation than they had ever done under Vichy. Of no one was this more true than of Hubert Beuve-Méry, founding editor of the new newspaper *Le Monde* in 1945. Under Beuve-Méry's austere leadership, *Le Monde*'s editorial team in the early days was inhabited by the same exalted sense of mission which had inspired Uriage. But it was also true that while most of the former Resistance press eventually succumbed to internal squabbles or financial difficulties, *Le Monde* became probably the post-war institution which most perfectly embodied the rigorous ethical values of the Resistance. That it took a former Pétainist to prolong the mystique of the Resistance into the post-war world is not the least of the paradoxes of this period. It is the existence of such contradictions and cross-currents which makes the memory and the inheritance of the Dark Years so complex, and so difficult to confront even in the France of today.

Epilogue: Remembering the Occupation

In January 1945, the conservative newspaper *Le Figaro* launched a campaign for the remains of Charles Péguy to be transferred to the Panthéon. This idea was a response to a Communist campaign for the 'pantheonization' of the recently deceased writer Romain Rolland who had been France's most famous fellow-travelling intellectual and an opponent of appeasement in the 1930s. Another proposal, from the Christian Democrat newspaper *L'Aube*, was that both Péguy and Rolland should be pantheonized, along with the philosopher Henri Bergson, who had been one of the *maîtres à penser* of Péguy.

What did these three figures symbolize? Péguy represented a link between the patriotism of 1914 and that of 1944; Rolland a link between the anti-fascism of the 1930s and that of the Resistance; Bergson a reminder of the contribution of Jews to French culture. But other messages could also be read into their lives: Péguy's name had been exploited by Vichy; Rolland had been a pacifist during the First World War; Bergson had moved towards Catholicism at the end of his life.[1] In the end, no one was transferred to the Panthéon in 1945, but these debates were only the first skirmishes in what was to be a long battle to claim the inheritance of the Resistance, a battle which was itself only the beginning of a longer war of memory over the Occupation.

Constructing Memory

No one was quicker off the mark to claim the inheritance of the Resistance than the Communists. Dubbing themselves the Party of the 75,000 martyrs, the Communists presented themselves as the true inheritors of the patriotic tradition of the French Revolution. In fact, the total number of French shot by the Germans was nearer 35,000, and not all of these were Communists. But by force of repetition, the figure of 75,000 attained a sort of poetic truth—and it was undeniable that the Communists had suffered higher casualties than any

---

[1] G. Namer, *La Commémoration en France de 1945 à nos jours* (1987), 25–45.

other Resistance group. Within weeks of the Liberation, the Communists were orchestrating ceremonies in memory of their martyrs. There was one at the cemetery of Ivry on 6 October 1944 and another at Père-Lachaise two days later. Eighteen squares or streets in Paris were almost immediately renamed after Communist martyrs.[2] The Resistance has remained central to the mythology of the Party ever since.

It is no less central to the mythology of Gaullism. De Gaulle's aim in 1944 was to reunite the nation and restore its self-respect. This involved the construction of the myth that, despite a few traitors, the French nation, united behind de Gaulle, had liberated itself. On 14 June 1944, in his first speech on liberated French territory, de Gaulle assured the peaceable and bemused inhabitants of Bayeux of his confidence that they would 'continue the struggle today, as you have not ceased to do since June 1940'.[3] In this interpretation of history, Vichy was an episode best forgotten once the necessary trials had taken place. This was the logic of the CFLN Ordinance of 9 August 1944 declaring all legislation enacted in France since 16 June 1940 null and void. What occurred between 1939 and 1944 was represented not as a French civil war, but as an episode in a longer struggle against Germany. On 2 April 1945, de Gaulle talked of a 'thirty years' war' which had started in 1914. A plaque unveiled in memory of Mandel in 1946 proclaimed that he had been 'murdered by the enemies of France'—without specifying that those enemies had been French.[4]

It would be wrong to see this emerging resistance mythology as having been constructed entirely from above. Many local communities quickly developed their own Resistance liturgies, celebrated their own heroes, and mourned their own martyrs. This was the case, for example, of the small market town of Saint-Flour, in the Cantal, which was one of the localities where the Germans had exacted reprisals after the failed Maquis uprising at Mont Mouchet. Twenty-five men were shot in the back on 14 June on a bridge near the town. After the Liberation the road leading to the bridge was renamed the Avenue des Martyrs, and a memorial was built in their memory. Among the victims was Pierre Mallet, son of the local doctor, Louis Mallet, who was in the Resistance. Shortly afterwards Louis Mallet himself was captured by the Germans, and he and another of his sons were shot along with other resisters on 24 June. After the Liberation, Mallet became the object of an intense local Resistance cult. The avenue Maréchal Pétain was renamed avenue Dr Louis Mallet and a local Day of Remembrance was instituted on the anniversary of his death. When de Gaulle visited the region on 1 July 1945 he spent fifteen minutes in Saint-Flour and presented Mallet's widow with a posthumous Croix de Guerre for her husband. In June 1946 she was chosen to unveil the Monument to the Glory of the French

[2] Namer, *La Commémoration en France*, 18–19.
[3] *Lettres, notes et carnets, juin 1943–mai 1945* (1983), 245–6.
[4] Rousso, *Vichy Syndrome*, 17–22.

maquisards at Mont Mouchet. In such ways did small towns like Saint-Flour insert themselves into the grand national narrative of the Resistance.[5]

At the national level the Resistance myth was orchestrated separately by de Gaulle and by the Communists. For all their differences, they both agreed on one thing: the Resistance had represented the real France and incarnated the true feelings of the French people throughout the Occupation. This reassuring myth did, however, cause some problems to both of them, especially in its early stages. For the Communists it was important to prevent the Resistance generation claiming superiority over those leaders who had been in place before 1939—not least Maurice Thorez, who had spent the war in Moscow, and played no part in the Resistance. At the Party's XIIth Congress in 1950, fourteen major resisters were dropped from the Central Committee; 1952 saw the demotion of the former head of the FTP, Charles Tillon. Tillon's long-awaited history of the FTP, which was ready in 1952, did not appear until 1962 because the Party insisted on amendments. In short, the Party preferred its Resistance heroes dead to alive.[6]

De Gaulle's problem was slightly different. In the late 1940s and early 1950s he had adopted an increasingly right-wing political stance at the head of the violently anti-Communist movement the RPF. Inevitably many members of this movement were Pétainists and de Gaulle did not want to alienate them by harping endlessly on the past. He even made some favourable references at this time to the services Pétain had once rendered to France, and intimated his belief that it was cruel for the old man to languish in prison. But there were limits to how far he was prepared to go down this road. In 1950 the Resistance hero Colonel Rémy, himself a founding member of the RPF, published an article claiming that de Gaulle had confided to him that in June 1940 France had needed two strings to her bow, the Pétain string and the de Gaulle string. This was too much for de Gaulle and he wrote to Rémy expressing his outrage, but interestingly enough he never publicly denied Rémy's allegation.[7]

After de Gaulle's return to power in 1958, there was no obstacle to the full development of the myth of the Resistance, officially consecrated by the transfer of Moulin's remains to the Panthéon. In the immediate post-war years, Brossolette's memory had been more celebrated than Moulin's, but as representative in 1942–3 of the embryonic Gaullist State, Moulin ultimately turned out a more suitable symbol for the Gaullist regime.[8] The high priest of the pantheonization ceremony for Moulin was André Malraux, de Gaulle's Minister of Culture. As Henry Rousso writes, Malraux's speech offered a simple syllogism:

[5] Koreman, *Expectation of Justice*, 200–12.

[6] S. Courtois, 'Luttes politiques et élaboration d' une histoire: Le PCF historien du PCF dans la Deuxième Guerre mondiale', *Communisme*, 4 (1983), 5–26.

[7] Rousso, *Vichy Syndrome*, 32–40.

[8] L. Douzou, 'La Résistance française en quête d'un héros éponyme (1942–1996)', in Charle et al., *La France démocratique*, 431–40.

the Resistance equals de Gaulle; de Gaulle equals France; France equals the Resistance. Even Communist resisters like Rol-Tanguy participated in the ceremony. *L'Humanité* was not without criticisms of the occasion, but in the end its reaction was positive: 'Honour to Jean Moulin! Honour to those who, following his example, died for their country! Honour to the French Resistance!'[9]

The way that the myth of the Resistance squeezed out alternative readings of the Occupation emerges particularly clearly in the cinema.[10] Films in the immediate post-war period had offered no unified image of the Occupation. At the Liberation, there was a flurry of films celebrating the Resistance: *La Bataille du rail* (1946) depicted the heroism of the working class, in the form of railway workers, and *Le Père tranquille* (1946) the heroism of the *Français moyen*, in the form of a peaceable insurance agent who is also secretly a resister. But the Resistance passed from fashion on the screen in the early 1950s, and the public was soon offered more complex images of the Occupation. Rene Clément's *Jeux inderdits* (1952) was an unsettling story about two small children traumatized by the war. André Cayatte's *Nous sommes tous des assassins* (1951) was about a young man who, having started killing for the Resistance, is unable to stop after the war. What made the film especially disturbing was that his original commitment to the Resistance had no political or patriotic motives: he could just as easily have killed for the other side. Not surprisingly, the film was disliked by the Communists and by former resisters like the historian Henri Michel. Another far from heroic vision of the Occupation was portrayed in *La Traversée de Paris* (1956) based on a story by Marcel Aymé. Starring two of the most famous actors of the period, Jean Gabin and Bourvil, the film depicts the adventures of two men transporting a black-market pig across Paris.

Censorship intervened if depictions of the Occupation too dramatically contradicted the official myth. The film *La Neige était sale* (1954), based on a novel by Simenon, presented such a bleak view that the censors insisted it be set in an imaginary country. Jean Dewever's *Les Honneurs de la guerre* (1962) had to undergo several changes before it could be released: the role of the Milice had to be played down, as did a suggestion that the French police had worked for the Germans. The most blatant example of censorship occurred in 1956 when an image of a French policeman participating in the arrest of Jews had to be cut from Alain Resnais's documentary film about concentration camps, *Night and Fog*. What made this case particularly flagrant was the fact that it concerned not a fictional representation but an authentic photograph from the period.

In the 1960s, the Resistance came back into fashion in the cinema and most films now faithfully echoed the Resistance myth. In 1966, the Resistance was treated in the comedy *La Grande Vadrouille*, one of the most successful French

---

[9] *Vichy Syndrome*, 82–97.

[10] For this and the next three paragraphs, see S. Langlois, 'La Résistance dans le cinéma français de fiction 1944–1994' (unpublished doctorate, McGill University, 1996); Lindeperg, *Les Écrans de l'ombre*.

films of all time. Starring France's two most famous comic actors, Bourvil and Louis de Funès, it tells the story of two 'ordinary' Frenchmen—one a house painter, the other a conductor—who only want to get on with their lives but find themselves helping an English pilot (Terry Thomas) escape to the Southern Zone. The moral is that, when necessary, the ordinary Frenchman will do his duty. Nineteen sixty-seven was the year of René Clément's *Paris brûle-t-il?* in which an all-star international cast presented a Gaullist vision of the Liberation of Paris. Finally, in 1969, Jean-Pierre Melville's *Armée des ombres* offered an epic vision of the internal Resistance united behind de Gaulle. In this film the real Colonel Passy even makes a brief appearance, playing himself; the Communists are barely mentioned.

Dissenting Memories I: The Resistance

It is easy enough to describe the official memory of the war, but difficult to know how universally it was endorsed. The idea that there was ever a consensus around the myth is probably a myth itself. Any society's collective memory is an amalgam of officially constructed memories, specific group memories, individual personal memories, and all the other sources upon which people draw for their images of the past (films, fiction, historical writing).[11] The main problem with the Resistance myth was that it imposed a unitary vision on what had been highly fragmented experience. This fragmentation was vividly demonstrated in 1953 when twenty-one ex-members of the Das Reich Division, which had carried out the Oradour massacre, were tried in Bordeaux. The trial aroused great emotion, not only because Oradour had been elevated into an official monument to Nazi barbarism, but because thirteen of the defendants were Alsatians who had been forcibly drafted into the German army (as 'malgré nous'). Southwest France saw them as war criminals; Alsace saw them as war victims. In the end, the Alsatians were amnestied—to the fury of the survivors of Oradour.[12]

The Oradour trial was a case that did not fit the simple categories of the official myth, but it was far from the only one. What did the non-Communist Resistance feel about the role it was assigned by the Gaullists and Communists? How did the 1.5 million prisoners of war fit into the heroic vision? What about the 650,000 workers who were forced to work in German factories? What about the Jews? What about the varieties of regional memory (of which the Oradour trial was only one example)? What about people who had supported Vichy and were not ashamed of it?

Unlike the Great War, the memory of the Second World War in France is not preserved in single memorials at the heart of local communities; it is dispersed and fragmented. FFI fighters and Free French fighters, those shot as hostages and

[11] R. Frank, in Institut d'histoire du temps présent, *La Mémoire des Français: 40 ans de commémoration de la Seconde Guerre mondiale* (1986), 372–3.
[12] S. Farmer, *Oradour: Arrêt sur Mémoire* (1994).

those exterminated as Jews, prisoners of war and political deportees: all have their own memorials.[13] There was no consensus even about which day should be selected to commemorate France's victory and Liberation. In 1945 the official German surrender on 8 May was not a day of great celebration in France. Despite de Gaulle's success in ensuring a French presence at the surrender of Germany, the victory could not efface memories of 1940. As de Gaulle declared: 'our satisfaction at the outcome of the war still leaves—and will always do so!—a dull pain in the depths of our national consciousness'. Another date to commemorate might have been 18 June, but its associations were too specifically Gaullist. Instead the main celebration organized in 1945 occurred on 11 November, as if the ambiguity which hovered over the victory of 1945 could be subsumed into the victory of 1918. This underscored de Gaulle's theme of continuity between the two conflicts: the thirty years' war.[14]

Resisters, however, wanted a specific commemoration of the Second War, and in 1946 they obtained partial satisfaction when the Sunday following 8 May was declared a national holiday. In 1953 this concession was extended further when 8 May itself became a holiday. After de Gaulle's return to power in 1958, this decision was reversed and the victory was again commemorated on the Sunday nearest to 8 May. This annoyed former resisters who continued to celebrate 8 May, and they got their way in 1968 when 8 May once again became a holiday. Nonetheless 8 May never caught on in the popular imagination in the same way as 11 November.[15]

Former resisters not only resented any attempt to downplay the significance of the period 1940–4 by subsuming it in a 'thirty years' war', they were also uneasy with the idea of associating the majority of the population with the Resistance. They were reluctant to sacrifice their sense of having being an elite in a society initially indifferent, even hostile, to them. As a former resister wrote in 1955: 'it is time to unmask a pious myth which has not really deceived anyone. The great majority of the people of this country played only a small and fleeting part in the events. Their activity was passive, except at the last moments. In these circumstances how can one require them to keep a faithful memory?'[16] Of course de Gaulle was no less aware that the resisters had been a tiny minority, but for him this truth was best overlooked in the cause of healing the divisions of the nation and restoring France's reputation abroad. For the Resistance, whose objectives had been as much moral as political, the renewal of France could not be built on a lie; for de Gaulle, *raison d'état* required nothing less.

Among many resisters the sense of betrayal which had emerged soon after the

---

[13] S. Barcellini and A. Wieviorka, *Passant, souviens-toi! Les Lieux de souvenir de la Seconde Guerre mondiale en France* (1995).

[14] S. Barcellini, 'Les Cérémonies du 11 novembre 1945: Une apothéose commémorative gaulliste', in Franck (ed.), *La France de 1945*, 85–100.

[15] R. Frank 'La Mémoire empoisonnée', in Azéma and Bédarida (ed.), *La France des années noires*, ii. 483–514: 499–501; id., *La Mémoire*, 379–83.

[16] A. Vistel, *L'Héritage spirituel de la Résistance* (1955), 58.

Liberation intensified in the following years. Jean Cassou wrote in 1953 that 'nothing remains of the spirit of the Resistance'.[17] It would be wrong, however, to deduce from such remarks that the Resistance generation had been excluded from positions of influence in post-war France. Former resisters like Bidault, Pineau, Mitterrand, Teitgen, Michelet, Claudius-Petit, Debré, Chaban-Delmas, and Defferre were major players in the politics of the Fourth Republic.[18] Why, then, was there a feeling of betrayal? Whatever the individual role of resisters in politics after 1945, there was no official representation of the Resistance in French society. The UDSR, which had originally hoped to play such a role, soon ended up as a small centrist grouping in parliament, skilled in the arts of compromise, but as removed from the intransigent purity of the Resistance as it was possible to be. It was in this party that François Mitterrand honed the arts of political intrigue and manoeuvre that would serve him so well in the future.

Some resisters were disillusioned by the arbitrariness of the post-war purges and the way in which the Communists tried to monopolize the memory of the Resistance. Jean Paulhan's repudiation of his former Resistance comrades was sealed in his violent polemic *Lettre aux directeurs de la Résistance* (1952). There were self-conscious echoes of Péguy's break with his former Dreyfusard comrades. During the war, Paulhan had worked with Aragon in the literary Resistance; Aragon's wife, Elsa Triolet, denounced him as a Nazi.[19] Even Mauriac felt that Paulhan, whose views he had shared in 1944, had now gone too far: he was giving ammunition to the Rebatets and Célines who remained as full of hatred as they had always been.[20] The truth was that the ideals of the Resistance did not provide unambiguous answers to the problems of the post-war world. Many Resistance newspapers continued after the Liberation, but their existence was increasingly compromised by acrimonious quarrels over the correct editorial line. *Franc-Tireur* folded in 1958. The former editors of *Défense de la France* (which renamed itself *France-Soir*) were hardly on speaking terms by 1945, and the paper, which soon suffered major financial difficulties, was taken over by the press group Hachette in 1950.

Nothing better illustrated the impossibility of defining a single resistance line in the post-war years than the problem of Algeria. Some resisters, like Claude Bourdet, were in the forefront of the anti-colonialist movement; others, like Georges Bidault, were fervently committed to the French Empire in Algeria. Both claimed to be defending the values of the Resistance. Bourdet believed that the French army in Algeria was perpetrating crimes similar to those committed by the Germans in France during the war; Bidault believed that those who wanted to abandon Algeria were no better than those who had abandoned France to the Germans in 1940. Having been president of the National Council of the

---

[17] *La Mémoire courte* (1953), 66.
[18] R. Faligot, *Les Résistants de la guerre de l'ombre aux allées de pouvoir* (1989).
[19] Verdès-Leroux, *Refus et violences*, 385.
[20] Sapiro, *La Guerre des écrivains*, 682–3.

Resistance in 1944–5, Bidault announced in 1961 that he was setting up a new Resistance council—this time to fight for French Algeria.[21]

Dissenting Memories II: Pétainists and Collaborators

These divisions within the Resistance assisted the rehabilitation of former Pétainists or collaborators. Paulhan's denunciation of the excesses of the purges was a balm to the former victims of those purges. Many former Pétainists, who were ardently committed to the defence of French Algeria, suddenly became patriots in the eyes of people who would once have designated them as traitors, and whom they would have designated as terrorists. Now both agreed that the 'terrorists' were to be found in Algeria.

The rehabilitation of former Pétainists had commenced several years earlier. An amnesty law in January 1951 reduced the numbers in prison from 40,000 to 1,570. After a second amnesty in July 1953, only 62 prisoners remained.[22] These two laws had been sponsored by Catholic resisters like Edmond Michelet in a spirit of national reconciliation. At the same time, however, the political pendulum swung towards the right after the onset of the Cold War. This allowed Vichy ghosts to re-emerge. Jean Jardin, who had headed Laval's *cabinet* from April 1942 to October 1943, became an influential behind-the-scenes figure in Fourth Republic politics.[23] So too did Georges Albertini, who had been Marcel Déat's right-hand man at the head of the RNP.[24] In March 1952, the conservative politician Antoine Pinay became prime minister. Pinay had been appointed to sit on Vicky's Conseil national, and his elevation to the premiership breached an important taboo.

Pinay, who cannot be described as a hard-line Pétainist, was interested in putting the past behind him, and playing the game of Fourth Republic politics. There were, however, many Vichy survivors who wanted to profit from the changed political climate to challenge the prevailing Resistance orthodoxy. They began to publish in a number of small circulation extreme-right newspapers which emerged to provide a platform for the defeated of 1944 (*Écrits de Paris*, 1947, *Rivarol*, 1951). Those who set about the task of rehabilitation adopted two strategies. The first was to discredit the alleged excesses of the Liberation by depicting the purges as a bloodbath—a new Terror—with up to 100,000 victims. Instead of attacking the Resistance directly, these writers coined the term 'resistentialism' to describe pseudo-resisters who had profited from the Liberation to unleash class war or carry out personal vendettas. *Les Crimes masqués du résistentialisme* (1948, The Hidden Crimes of Resistentialism), by the conser-

---

[21] Rousso, *Vichy Syndrome*, 75–82.   [22] Ibid. 49–54.
[23] P. Assouline, *Jean Jardin 1904–1976: Une eminence grise* (1986).
[24] L. Lemire, *L'Homme de l'ombre: Georges Albertini 1911–1983* (1990).

vative *député* Abbé Desgranges, was an early example of the genre.[25] A literary representation of this counter-myth was Marcel Aymé's novel *Uranus* (1948), a pitiless depiction of the Liberation in a small town. *Uranus* is populated by corrupt black marketeers, who convert to resistance at the last moment; sanguinary Communists, who exercise arbitrary tyranny over innocent citizens; and disillusioned hypocrites, who accommodate themselves cynically to the prevailing hypocrisy.[26]

A second strategy of rehabilitation was to separate Pétain's reputation from that of Laval. Louis Rougier published a book on his mission to London in which he claimed that Pétain had been playing a double game. The title of Louis-Dominique Girard's *Montoire: Verdun diplomatique* (1948, Montoire: A Diplomatic Verdun) speaks for itself. These authors argued that de Gaulle and Pétain were two sides of the same patriotic coin: the sword and the shield. After Pétain's death in 1951, at the age of 95, his supporters set up the Association to Defend the Memory of Marshal Pétain (ADMP), of which Rémy was a founding member. The ADMP lobbied, and has done ever since, for a judicial review of the Pétain trial, and for the Marshal's remains to be buried at Douaumont, near Verdun. Although never having more than a few thousand members, the ADMP's board of directors has over the years included twenty-two former ministers and twelve members of the Académie française.[27]

The Resistance myths were challenged not only by Vichy survivors, but also by a group of writers, known as the Hussards, who were mostly too young to have been personally implicated in collaboration. Reacting against what they saw as the stifling political correctness of Resistance orthodoxy, they rejected the whole idea of political 'engagement'. In Roger Nimier's *Le Hussard bleu* (1950), one of the characters is a resister who is sent to infiltrate the Milice and discovers that its members share the same values of comradeship and courage as the Resistance. In Antoine Blondin's picaresque *L'Europe buissonière* (1949) the hero lives through the battle of France, the Resistance, STO, and the Liberation. Instead of choices and clear moral values, he finds only absurdity and arbitrariness, rather like the hero of Céline's *Voyage to the End of the Night*. The Hussards aimed to shock by adopting a debunking stance of frivolity and cynicism. They championed compromised writers like Cocteau, Morand, Chardonne, and Drieu.[28]

Writers whose reputations had once seemed irremediably tainted gradually re-emerged from purgatory. Lucien Rebatet who left prison in 1952 resumed writing

---

[25] N. Hewitt, '1944/1793: La Droite intellectuelle et le mythe de la Terreur rouge', *French Cultural Studies*, 5 (1994), 281–92.

[26] On Aymé in general, see N. Hewitt, 'Marcel Aymé and the Dark Night of Occupation', in Hirschfeld and Marsh (eds.), *Collaboration France*, 203–26.

[27] Rousso, *Vichy Syndrome*, 32–49.

[28] N. Hewitt, *Literature and the Right in Post-war France: The Story of the 'Hussards'* (1996).

film criticism which was much admired by the young François Truffaut. Georges Soulès became a successful novelist writing under the pseudonym of Raymond Abellio. Céline, returning to France from his Danish exile in 1951, resumed his novelistic career, and adopted the persona of an irascible and victimized eccentric who had never wished harm to anyone. Paul Morand returned to France in 1954, and embarked on a campaign to get into the Académie française. His election was blocked in 1959 by the combined efforts of former resisters and de Gaulle himself, but he finally succeeded in 1968.[29] Robert Brasillach, who was saved from this fate by his execution, became the object of a tiny cult orchestrated by his brother-in-law, Maurice Bardèche.

Bardèche became France's most articulate defender of fascism. This should remind us that the defeated of 1944 did not all share the same vision of the past. The wartime division between Vichy and Paris continued in the post-war period, separating those who defended Pétain as a French patriot, and those who defended Laval as a European and anti-Communist. Déat, who lived out his days teaching French in Italy, still believed that his day would come.[30] Pierre-André Cousteau, a former member of the *Je suis partout* team, remained unrepentant until the end of his life. In 1958, he wrote: 'if I adopted, in 1941, an attitude of collaboration, it was not to limit the damage . . . or play some kind of double game. It was because I wanted the victory of Germany . . . because it represented . . . the last chance of the white man, while the democracies . . . represented the end of the white man.'[31]

Buried Memories: The Victims

It was only to be expected that the Gaullist myth had little comfort to offer the defeated of 1944, but it had little place either for those who had been persecuted under the Occupation—especially the thousands of civilians who had been deported to Germany. The return of *déportés* from German camps in April 1945 had caused a terrible shock. The sight of these ghostly and emaciated creatures cast a pall over the victory celebrations. Nor was it easy to fit them into the embryonic Gaullist interpretation of the Occupation which required heroes not victims. On 11 November 1945, a solemn ceremony was held at the fort of Mont Valérien outside Paris where many French hostages had been shot by the Germans: fifteen people who had died for France were buried in a crypt there. They consisted of nine soldiers who had fought in 1940 or in 1944, one prisoner of war shot while trying to escape, three resisters, and two *déportés*, both of whom had been resisters. There was no representative of those *déportés* who had simply been victims of the Germans although not involved in the Resistance.

[29] Rousso, *Vichy Syndrome*, 68–9.
[30] J. Algazy, *La Tentation néo-fasciste en France 1944–1965* (1984), 59–94.
[31] Verdès-Leroux, *Refus et violences*, 445.

In the face of this official neglect, various associations of *déportés* kept alive the memory of their experiences. In 1954, they succeeded in getting parliament to vote for an annual National Deportation Day every April. On the first of these occasions, an urn containing the ashes of *déportés* was transferred to Mont Valérien to join the remains of the fifteen people already buried there, and reappropriate the site from the exclusively heroic memory ascribed to it by de Gaulle. But this battle of memory between heroes and victims rumbled on. On 18 June 1960, two years after returning to power, de Gaulle inaugurated a grandiose Monument to Fighting France at Mont Valérien. Two years later, the associations of *déportés* obtained the construction of a specific monument to the Martyrs of Deportation. This monument, situated at the tip of the Île de la Cité in Paris, was inaugurated by de Gaulle on National Deportation Day in 1962.[32]

In the hierarchy of virtue in post-war France, the deportees had come to occupy a central place only just below the resisters. They symbolized the suffering of the French nation in the war, and were depicted as having been spiritually purified by their terrible experiences in the camps.[33] They stood in the same relation to post-war society as the prisoners of war in relation to Vichy. But the community of *déportés* was itself far from homogeneous. In 1948, their status was fixed by law. Two categories were distinguished: the *déportés résistants* who had been deported as a result of their Resistance activities and the *déportés politiques* who had been entirely innocent victims of the Germans, such as civilian hostages taken in reprisal for Resistance operations. Those who had been sent to Germany as STO workers were, however, not granted *déporté* status at all. They were seen as much less deserving of either admiration or sympathy than the *déportés*. When in 1956 it was mooted that former STO workers should be granted *déporté* status, a number of leading personalities—including Vercors, Lucien Febvre, Camus, Fernand Braudel—signed a declaration of protest about honouring these '*transplantés*' in such a way.[34] The former STO workers much resented this implied assumption that they were not victims in the same way as the other *déportés politiques*, especially since during the war it had been common to refer to them as *déportés de travail*. But no amount of lobbying has so far succeeded in winning them back this designation. Over those who had worked in Nazi Germany floats the suspicion that they could—or should—have avoided STO and joined the Resistance.[35]

Another group not accorded any specific recognition among *déportés* were the Jews. When the first Jewish survivors returned from the camps in 1945 their plight was not differentiated in public consciousness from that of other victims

---

[32] S. Barcellini, 'Sur deux journées nationales commémorant la déportation et la persécution des années noires', *VSRH* 45 (1995), 76–98.

[33] P. Lagrou, 'Victims of Genocide and National Memory: Belgium, France, and the Netherlands 1945–1965', *Past and Present*, 154 (1997), 181–222: 204–5.

[34] Ibid. 204–5.

[35] F. Cochet, *Histoire des prisonniers de guerre, déportés et STO (1945–1985)* (1992), 200–2.

of Nazism. In June 1946, the ashes of Auschwitz victims were buried at Père-Lachaise in a ceremony organized by the Communists. The monument erected on this occasion referred to 'men, women and children, deported from France, exterminated at Auschwitz, victims of Nazi barbarism'. Nothing said that almost all the victims had been Jewish. One deportation convoy to Auschwitz, that of 23 January 1943, had in fact contained 119 Communist women, the only non-Jewish women to be sent to Auschwitz. Through the testimony of the survivors of that convoy, Auschwitz merged into the general memory of all the concentration camps with no recognition of its specific character as a centre of extermination. It was appropriated as a Communist memory not a Jewish one.[36] The Jews who returned to France were subsumed into the category of *déportés politiques* and not viewed with particular sympathy. When after her return from Auschwitz the 17-year-old Jewish girl Simone Jacob—now the politician Simone Veil—presented herself for a medical examination at the National Federation of Resistance Deportees, she was sent away as ineligible.[37]

Jewish survivors who tried to speak about their experiences often found that others, including Jews who had survived the war in France, did not wish to listen.[38] As one returning deportee remarked: 'No sooner did we begin to tell our story than we were interrupted, like overexcited or overly talkative children by parents who are themselves burdened down with real problems.'[39] Jewish organizations readily subscribed to this collective amnesia. To admit a special category of 'racial deportees' contradicted the assimilationist tradition of the Republic to which the Jews owed their freedom in France. Most Jews wanted to put the nightmare behind them and fit back into French society.

A memorial to the dead was unveiled in Paris at the synagogue of the rue de la Victoire in 1949 in the presence of the President of the Republic. The ceremony, ending with the Marseillaise, was as much a Republican as a Jewish one reflecting the Jews' desire to avoid difficult questions about France's role in their wartime fate. At a meeting of the Consistory of Paris in 1946, one speaker paid homage to the people of France 'to whom we owe our survival . . . France who liberated us in 1789 liberated us again in 1944'.[40] Speaking on 14 July 1945, the Chief Rabbi Joseph Kaplan declared: 'the government of Vichy which abandoned the Jews and delivered them to their fate did not represent the true France'. As for those non-French Jews who had participated in the Resistance, mainly through the Communist MOI, they were remembered as members of the FTP who died for France. The MOI, which was wound up in 1945, faded from memory.[41]

---

[36] Wieworka, *Déportation et génocide*, 138–40; P. Lagrou, *The Legacy of Nazi Occupation: Patriotic Memory and National Recovery in Western Europe 1945–1965* (Cambridge, 2000), 237–40.

[37] Ibid. 131–2, 141–57.   [38] Ibid. 163, 169–82.

[39] A. Finkielkraut, *Remembering in Vain: The Klaus Barbie trial and Crimes against Humanity* (New York, 1992), 18.

[40] Wieviorka, *Déportation et génocide*, 347–53.   [41] Ibid. 354–8.

Fragmented Memories

In the 1970s, the glacier of official memory began to break up as a result of two developments: the generational revolt of the 1960s and a reawakening of Jewish self-consciousness. The generational revolt had its most violent expression in the events of 1968 when French students challenged the two political forces whose legitimacy was most closely bound up with the memory of the war: Gaullism and communism. They hurled memories of the past against those who portrayed themselves as custodians of that past. Their slogan comparing the French riot police to the Nazis—'CRS = SS'—shocked defenders of the Gaullist regime. When the Communist leader Georges Marchais dismissed one student activist as a 'German Jewish anarchist', the students responded with the slogan 'We are all German Jews'.

This climate of protest explains the impact of the film *The Sorrow and the Pity* (1971) which subverted every aspect of the myth of the Occupation. Not least of its provocations was the almost total absence of de Gaulle. Constructed around interviews with survivors from the period, the film was as much an exploration of the memory of the Occupation as a history of it. In refusing to allow *The Sorrow and the Pity* to be televised, the head of France's State broadcasting organization remarked that 'certain myths are necessary for a people's well-being and tranquillity'. But the ban only fuelled suspicions that there was something to hide. The film was shown in a Paris cinema, and seen by about 600,000 people. After it, nothing was ever the same again.[42]

The awakening of Jewish memory was part of the same generational phenomenon which produced *The Sorrow and the Pity*, but it had other causes as well. The trial of Adolf Eichmann in 1961 revived interest in the Holocaust while the Six-Day War between Israel and the Arab States increased the sense of self-consciousness among Jews in France, especially after the French government distanced itself from the Israeli cause. In 1977, the main organization of French Jewry, the CRIF, modified its charter to embrace the objectives of unconditional support for Israel and the demand that French schools offer instruction on the Holocaust. Claude Lanzmann's eight-hour documentary film on the Holocaust, *Shoah* (1985), played the same role for Jewish memory during the 1980s as *The Sorrow and the Pity* had for the general memory of the Occupation during the 1970s.[43]

No one did more to raise public self-consciousness about war-time anti-Semitism than the lawyer Serge Klarsfeld who was 8 years old when his father was deported to Auschwitz in 1943. With his younger German wife Beate, Klarsfeld devoted himself to hunting down war criminals. In 1968, Beate publicly slapped the German chancellor Kurt Kiesinger to draw attention to his Nazi past. Klarsfeld also became a considerable historian. His *Vichy-Auschwitz* traced the mechanisms of the Final Solution in France; his *Mémorial de la déportation*

---

[42] Rousso, *Vichy Syndrome*, 98–114.   [43] Ibid. 132–8, 239.

des juifs de France published the name of every Jew deported from France. In 1979, he created the Association of Sons and Daughters of Jewish Deportees from France.

As the Resistance was challenged during the 1970s, incidents that might once have passed unnoticed exploded into scandal. This was discovered, to his cost, by de Gaulle's successor President Georges Pompidou. In November 1971, Pompidou quietly (as he had hoped) granted a pardon to the former Milice leader in Lyons, Paul Touvier. After the war, Touvier had been sentenced to death *in absentia*, but successfully evaded arrest. For twenty years, he was hidden by Catholic clergymen, acting out of a mixture of charity and right-wing conviction. In 1967, the death sentence lapsed when the Statute of Limitations took effect. Pompidou's pardon affected various secondary penalties that still carried force.

The pardon caused uproar. After four months of polemics, Pompidou defended his action: 'are we going to keep the wounds of our national discord bleeding eternally? Hasn't the time come to draw a veil over the past, to forget a time when Frenchmen disliked one another, and even killed one another?' Since Pompidou himself had survived the Occupation by keeping out of trouble and devoting himself to producing a critical edition of Racine's play *Britannicus*— 'clearly I lacked an adventurous spirit', he once observed—his desire to forgive and forget appealed to him personally. But drawing a veil over collaboration in a spirit of national reconciliation also conformed to the spirit of the Gaullist myth. Unfortunately for Pompidou, times had changed, and his pardon only contributed further to the unravelling of the myth.[44]

Another scandal erupted in October 1978 when the magazine *L'Express* published an interview with the former head of Vichy's Commissariat for Jewish Affairs, Darquier de Pellepoix, who had taken refuge in Spain after his condemnation to death in 1947. In the interview Darquier poured out his anti-Semitic bile and alleged that the gas chambers were a Jewish hoax. This was not the first time Darquier had made statements to the press or the first article that had been written about him. But once again timing was all, and the ranting of this crazed octogenarian created a furore in France.[45]

By the late 1970s, Vichy was becoming, as Henry Rousso suggests, an obsession. The slightest incident was seized upon and interpreted in the light of Occupation. There was an outcry in 1975 when President Valéry Giscard d'Estaing decided in a spirit of European unity that 8 May would no longer be celebrated as a national holiday. Veiled references were made to the Vichyite past of his parents. Another polemic broke out over the Communist leader Georges Marchais who turned out to have worked in a German factory during the war. Whether he had been there as an involuntary victim of STO

---

[44] Rousso, *Vichy Syndrome*, 114–16.   [45] Ibid. 139–44.

or a volunteer, neither alternative conformed to the image of Communist Resistance heroism. The memory of the Occupation haunted the presidential elections of 1981: the Gaullist Colonel Passy urged people to vote for Mitterrand and was supported by a bevy of former resisters who claimed that Mitterrand was the only candidate 'interested in pursuing the broad programme of the CNR'; de Gaulle's son-in-law reminded electors that Mitterrand had a Vichy past; the Socialist Gaston Defferre responded by alleging that Giscard's family had been 'full of collaborators'.[46]

These polemics took place against a background of increasing aesthetic fascination with the period, a sort of Forties Revival, dubbed the *mode rétro*. It is strikingly illustrated by the novelist Patrick Modiano whose entire output, since his first book *La Place de l'étoile* (1968), has explored the murkiest aspects of the Occupation—the points at which collaboration overlapped with the worlds of criminality and marginality. But the Occupation is not just a background for his novels. Born in 1945, the son of a Jewish father who survived the war thanks to ruse and compromise, and a mother who worked in occupied Paris for a German film company, Modiano's obsession with the Occupation is a personal quest for origins and identity. His novels, impressionistic and fragmented, are meditations on the interplay between memory and history and on the possibility of ascribing coherence to the past. To the general public, Modiano is best known as the author of the screenplay of *Lacombe Lucien*, the film which, after *The Sorrow and the Pity*, most contributed to undermining heroic representations of the Occupation.[47]

Memory on Trial

In the 1970s then, the old mythology shattered, but it proved impossible to put the pieces together and create a new consensus. In the 1980s it fell to the courts, more than to historians, to offer interpretations of the Vichy past. This was a consequence of the French parliament's vote in 1964 to end the Statute of Limitations on crimes against humanity. That decision had been taken to allow the possibility of pursuing Nazi war criminals still at large, but in the 1970s the weapon was turned against French perpetrators of war crimes. Even people who had been tried at the Liberation became vulnerable to retrial on new grounds. After the war no one had been specifically tried for their role in the deportation of the Jews. Now this came to be seen as the central crime of the Occupation, and one which could be pursued as a crime against humanity.

The first Frenchman to be successfully indicted for crimes against humanity

[46] Ibid. 168–90.
[47] C. Nettlebeck, 'Getting the Story Right: Narratives of the Second World War in Post-1968 France', in Hirschfeld and Marsh (eds.), *Collaboration in France*, 252–93: 282–5; A. Morris, *Collaboration and Resistance Reviewed: Writers and the Mode Rétro in Post-Gaullist France* (1992).

was Jean Leguay in March 1979. As René Bousquet's representative in the Occupied Zone until the end of 1943, Leguay had been profoundly implicated in the round-ups of Jews. In January 1983 followed the indictment of Maurice Papon who had organized deportations of Jews in his capacity as an official in the prefecture of the Gironde. Finally, Bousquet himself was indicted in March 1991. Leguay and Bousquet had both been tried at the Liberation but suffered only minor penalties because they were able to show that they had abetted the Resistance. Papon had not been tried at all. Their role in the Jewish deportations had barely been an issue at the Liberation. All of them had gone on to glittering careers in business and politics. Papon had served as Prefect of Police under de Gaulle in from 1958 to 1967, and Budget Minister under Giscard d'Estaing, until the revelations about his past forced him to resign in 1981. Even after the indictments had been issued, preparing the evidence against these highly placed figures was laborious. Leguay died in July 1989 just as the case against him was ready to come before the courts. Bousquet was assassinated by a publicity seeker in 1993 before his case could be tried. Papon's indictment was quashed for procedural reasons in 1987, and he was indicted again in 1988. The preparation of his case dragged on for years. Meanwhile in 1989 Touvier was finally discovered hiding in a priory in Nice. He was arrested and indicted, but it took time to prepare the case against him.

These delays meant that the first trial turned out not to be of a Frenchmen but of the German Klaus Barbie who had been the Gestapo chief in Lyons. Found guilty *in absentia* of war crimes in the 1950s, Barbie escaped to Bolivia where Beate Klarsfeld located him in 1971. After several abortive attempts to secure his extradition, Barbie was eventually brought back to France in February 1983 and indicted for crimes against humanity. The French government intended his trial to serve as a national history lesson and chance for the French to confront the past—but complications soon arose.

The crimes with which Barbie was associated in the popular imagination, in particular the death of Jean Moulin, could not be included in the indictment because they were categorized as 'war crimes', carried out against combatants. 'Crimes against humanity' were those perpetrated against innocent civilians. Thus the central charge against Barbie became the round-up on 6 April 1944 of forty-three Jewish children from the refuge at Izieu. Some former resisters felt aggrieved that the indictment against Barbie had nothing to say about them, but including them would have subverted the claim of the Resistance that its members had been voluntary combatants, a status denied to them by Germany during the Occupation. Before Barbie came to trial these tensions were skilfully exploited by his defence lawyer Jacques Vergès. Vergès was a leftist radical with contempt for bourgeois democracy. He argued that the French had no right to try Barbie when they were unwilling to assume responsibility for their own crimes against humanity in their colonies, especially during the Algerian war. But Vergès's main counter-attack was to claim that the exclusion of resisters from the trial meant the French State had something to hide: it was terrified that Barbie would reveal who had betrayed Moulin. Vergès knew nothing that had not been common knowledge for years, but his insinuations sowed doubts.

In November 1985, the Cour de Cassation, France's highest appeal court, issued a ruling which allowed some crimes against the Resistance to be included in the indictment against Barbie. This was done by redefining crimes against humanity to include acts carried out in 'the name of a state practising a policy of ideological hegemony . . . not only against people by reason of their belonging to a racial or religious group but also against the opponents of this political system'. The definition of crimes against humanity was shifted from the identity of the victims to the motives of the perpetrators. Barbie's trial which lasted from 11 May to 4 July 1987 was not the cathartic event which had been expected. He was tried on forty-one separate counts. Thirty-nine lawyers representing Jewish groups, Resistance groups, and individuals appeared in court to file separate suits against him. He was found guilty and sentenced to life imprisonment. But although Vergès's claim to have revelations about the Resistance proved to be a bluff, the trial uncovered tensions between Resistance memories and Jewish memories. The inclusion of crimes against the Resistance blurred the focus of what some had wished to be a ringing condemnation of the Final Solution.[48] As Simone Veil put it: 'we the victims have never asked to be considered as heroes; so why do the heroes now want . . . at the risk of mixing everything up, to be treated as victims?'[49]

The trial of Paul Touvier, seven years later, was no more successful in providing simple answers about the past. The main crime alleged against Touvier was the round-up and shooting of seven Jews on 29 June 1944 in retaliation for the assassination of Philippe Henriot. There was no doubt about Touvier's responsibility for this crime, but in April 1992 it looked as if the trial would not go ahead after the Paris Court of Appeals decided, to universal amazement, that there was no case against Touvier under the strict definition of crimes against humanity. The court's view was that the Vichy regime, in whose name Touvier acted, could not be said to have been inspired by a policy of 'ideological hegemony' since its ideology was confused, and the Jews were not defined as an enemy of the State as in Nazi Germany. The spectacle of judges, three of them known for their right-wing sympathies, setting themselves up as historians of Vichy caused outrage. Seven months later the judgement was partially overturned by another appeal court. While declaring itself incompetent to contest the assessment of Vichy, this court decided that Touvier had acted on German orders, and therefore on behalf of a State inspired by a policy of ideological hegemony. This judgement made it possible to judge Touvier, but meant that his trial could not consider crimes committed by Vichy. It led to the absurd result that,

---

[48] N. Wood, 'Crimes or Misdemeanours? Memory on Trial in Contemporary France', *French Cultural Studies*, 3 (1994), 1–21: 7–12; Rousso, *Vichy Syndrome*, 199–216.

[49] Finkielkraut, *Remembering in Vain*, 20.

in the words of Tzvetan Todorov, 'the same acts are crimes if they are commit-ted by the Germans or anyone in their service, but cease to be so if their authors are French, acting for the French State or French institutions'. Law was being manipulated 'to meet the political objective of the moment, instead of allowing it to judge individual cases according to unchanging criteria'.[50]

The trial opened on 17 March 1994 and closed on 20 April 1994. Four histor-ians, including Robert Paxton, testified. Touvier was found guilty and sentenced to life imprisonment. Throughout the proceedings, there was a sense of frustra-tion at the banality of the 79-year-old defendant who seemed half absent from the proceedings. The main problem was that evidence which had been painstak-ingly assembled to prove that Touvier had acted for Vichy now had to be mar-shalled to prove the opposite—that he had acted at the instigation of the Germans. What had once been used by Touvier in his defence—that it was the local Gestapo head who had forced him to kill the hostages—now became the basis of the case against him. Witnesses who had previously claimed that Touvier was not acting on German orders now alleged the opposite. These con-tradictions caused a certain embarrassment. To the irritation of his colleagues, one of the prosecution lawyers, Arno Klarsfeld, the son of Serge, refused to accept the theory that Touvier had acted at the behest of the Germans—although he claimed that this did not affect the issue of crimes against humanity. But the truth was that Touvier's conviction could only be secured by distorting the his-torical record.

Obsessive Memory

The trials of Barbie and Touvier, while failing to clarify understanding of the Occupation, had intensified the preoccupation with the persecution of the Jews. The fiftieth anniversary of the Vel d'Hiver round-up on 16 July 1942 was a moment of high emotion. A commemorative ceremony was held on the site of the former Vel d'Hiver in the presence of numerous dignitaries, including the President of the Republic, François Mitterrand. A petition appeared in Le Monde, signed by over two hundred personalities calling themselves the 'Vel d'Hiver 42 Committee'. They demanded that Mitterrand formally acknowledge France's complicity in the Final Solution. Although Mitterrand was unwilling to do this, in February 1993 his government decided to designate 16 July as a national day of commemoration of the persecution of the Jews.

This has recently led the historian Henry Rousso, director of the Institut du temps présent, to warn against the danger of creating a new myth about the Occupation. Rousso argues that concentrating on the persecution of the Jews to the exclusion of almost every other aspect of Vichy—what he calls 'Judaeo-

[50] Todorov, 'The Touvier Trial', in R. Golsan (ed.), *Memory, the Holocaust and French Justice: The Bousquet and Touvier Affairs* (Hanover, NH, 1996), 169–78: 175.

centrism'—neglects other victims of the regime: Communists, Freemasons, resisters. There are now national days to commemorate the end of the war (8 May), the deportees (April), and the Jews (16 July), but there is none to commemorate the Resistance. The contemporary focus on the Jews redresses the previous neglect of their plight, but since, as Rousso reminds us, many Jewish survivors in 1944–5 wanted to be considered as French citizens not as Jews, it would be anachronistic to attribute that neglect only to the existence of anti-Semitic prejudice. Rousso also identifies problems in selecting 16 July to commemorate France's guilt towards the Jews. French complicity in the Vel d'Hiver round-ups is undeniable, but it was primarily a result of Vichy's policy of collaboration rather than Vichy's anti-Semitism. Certainly the two policies cannot, in this instance, be entirely separated, but Vichy's anti-Semitism was one of persecution not extermination. Extermination was a German policy. If France genuinely wished to confront her own anti-Semitic demons, it would, Rousso argues, be more appropriate to commemorate the Jewish Statute of October 1940. Finally, Rousso questions whether it is healthy for a society to become too fixated on the past. There may be a 'duty to remember', but there is also sometimes a need to put the past behind one in order to confront the problems of the present and the future.[51]

However salutary Rousso's call for a sense of proportion in discussing anti-Semitism during the Occupation, there is a danger that he could give ammunition to revisionists with their own political agendas. Rousso himself has no such ulterior motives. On the contrary, born in 1954, he is one of the leading historians of the period, too young to have any personal scores to settle, and he was quick to denounce the pro-Vichy revisionism of a recent book. Indeed one of his points is that if a distorted picture of the Occupation were allowed to gain credence it would be vulnerable to attack from people wishing to rehabilitate Vichy. Having refuted those distortions, they would be able to cast doubt even on the existence of the regime's genuine crimes. Thus Rousso's warning against an obsession with Vichy deserves to be listened to. But in other hands this warning could become apologetic. In this context, one should note that the title of Rousso's book echoes a well-known article by the German historian Ernst Nolte, 'Vergangenheit, die nicht vergehen will'. It is notorious that Nolte's own call for relativization of the Holocaust was serving a contemporary conservative agenda, and leading him into increasingly troubled waters. In this context it is not insignificant that Rousso's book has been commented upon favourably by Jean-Marc Varaut, the defence lawyer of Maurice Papon, the Vichy functionary accused of crimes against humanity, and author of a recent revisionist account of Pétain's trial. Varaut applauds Rousso's rejection of Manichaean explanations and praises his stress on the complexity of events. In short, the dilemma is: how to historicize without becoming Nolte?[52]

---

[51] E. Conan and H. Rousso, *Un passé qui ne passe pas* (1994), 9–30, 267–86.

[52] C. Flood and H. Frey, 'The Vichy Syndrome Revisited', *Modern and Contemporary France* (1995), 244–5.

This dilemma is all the more acute given the strength of the extreme right in contemporary France. Jean-Marie Le Pen's Front national has provided a home to former Pétainists and collaborationists. For example, Paul Malguti, who stood for the FN at elections in 1992, was a former member of Doriot's PPF, involved in a massacre of resisters by the Gestapo at Cannes in August 1944, and condemned to death *in absentia* in 1945.[53] The old Pétainist sage Gustave Thibon emerged from the shadows to give the FN his support. Le Pen himself makes little secret of his loathing for de Gaulle, his indulgence for Pétain, and his dislike of Jews. Asked in 1987 what he thought about negationism—the attempt to deny the existence of the Holocaust—he said that he was not competent to comment on this historical issue, but that in any case the Holocaust was merely a 'detail' in the history of the Second War. In 1988, he attacked a government minister by making a tasteless pun about crematorium ovens.

Negationism has enjoyed remarkable success in France. Indeed it was invented in France by the former Socialist resister Paul Rassinier who had been in Buchenwald. He became convinced after the war that the gas chambers, of which there were indeed none at Buchenwald, had never existed.[54] In 1978 Robert Faurisson, a lecturer at the University of Lyons, announced his support of Darquier de Pellepoix's allegations that the gas chambers had not existed. Faurisson's case acquired notoriety in 1980 when Noam Chomsky foolishly prefaced one of his books in a spirit of defending free speech. Faurisson was in the end required to pay symbolic damages to those whose memory he had insulted. In 1985 another academic, Henri Roques, was awarded a doctorate which contained negationist claims. The degree was revoked a year later.[55]

Negationism is beyond the boundaries of respectability even to most supporters of the Front national, but there are other subtly apologetic accounts of the Occupation on offer. One of the best-selling authors on the period is Henri Amouroux, a journalist whose nine-volume history of the life of the French under Occupation provides a minute chronicle which submerges judgement and analysis in detail. Amouroux's account offers neither heroes nor villains, only an immensely complicated tragedy in which everyone has their reasons. The moral seems to be that to understand everything is to forgive everything. There is no explicitly political agenda, but Amouroux has made it clear that he dislikes what he see as the denigration of France by American historians (that is to say, Robert Paxton).[56]

---

[53] B. Gordon, 'Afterword: Who were the Guilty and should they be tried?', in Golsan, *Memory, the Holocaust and French Justice*, 179–98: 183.

[54] D. Lipstadt, *Denying the Holocaust* (1993); F. Bayard, *Comment l'idée vint à M. Rassinier: Naissance du révisionisme* (1996).

[55] Rousso, *Vichy Syndrome*, 151–8; P. Vidal-Naquet and L. Yagil, *Holocaust Denial in France* (Tel Aviv, 1995).

[56] As he said in an interview on French radio (Europe 1) on 23 Sept. 1997.

Mitterrand's Memories

In short, the line between nuance and apologetics is delicate. When does forgetting become whitewashing, when does reconciliation become rehabilitation? How difficult it has become to construct a consensual interpretation of the French past was demonstrated in the controversy aroused by the publication in 1994 of a book by the journalist Pierre Péan on the Vichyite past of François Mitterrand. The book's cover showed Mitterrand participating in a right-wing demonstration during the 1930s. The story of Mitterrand's past had been told before, but Péan provided an unprecedented wealth of documentation thanks to the co-operation of Mitterrand himself. Mitterrand then allowed himself to be interviewed on television for ninety minutes in September 1994 to appease the uproar excited by Péan's book. This willingness to come clean on his past represented a change of attitude by Mitterrand. In 1969, he had written of his wartime experience: 'Back in France [from the prisoner of war camp] I became a resister after no great agonising.' To say the least, this missed out a lot in between. It was not, however, a direct lie, unlike Mitterrand's claim in the 1970s that he had been an ardent supporter of the Popular Front.[57]

Mitterrand's motive in speaking about his past was possibly a pre-emptive strike against future historians as he approached the end of his life. But he also seems to have seen himself as engaged in a wider pedagogic enterprise of reconciling the French people with their past.[58] In a series of interviews with the historian Olivier Wieviorka in the early 1990s, Mitterrand expressed his distaste for continuing the trials of former servants of Vichy: 'one cannot live the whole time on rancour and memories'.[59] It emerged that Mitterrand had intervened to slow down the preparation of the case against Papon. Péan's most shocking revelation was that Mitterrand had enjoyed friendly relations with René Bousquet into the 1980s. All this came on top of the revelation in 1992 that since 1987 Mitterrand had had a wreath placed on the tomb of Marshal Pétain on each anniversary of the Armistice of 1918. Although the Élysée made clear that this was a homage to the victor of Verdun not the Vichy leader, the news caused outrage.

Mitterrand's response to his critics was to argue implicitly that the past should be embraced in all its complexity. He seemed to be trying to reclaim a place for ambiguous trajectories like his own which had been squeezed out by the vast condescension of Gaullist history.[60] Now that the Gaullist myth was shattered, Mitterrand was suggesting that the alternative was not to assert that the French had all been traitors, but that they had struggled for solutions in a difficult period. For any historian, the most striking feature of Mitterrand's journey from

[57] F. Mitterrand, *Ma part de vérité* (1969), 20, 23–4.
[58] C. Andrieu, 'Managing Memory: National and Personal Identity at Stake in the Mitterrand Affair', *French Cultural Studies*, 142 (1996), 17–31.
[59] O. Wieviorka, *Nous entrerons en carrière: De la Résistance à l'exercice de pouvoir* (1994), 349–50.
[60] Mitterrand, *Mémoires interrompues* (1996),

Pétainism to Resistance is its very ordinariness. In his television interview, Mitterrand made a revealing mistake when asked about the Jewish Statute. He claimed that it was a piece of legislation against foreign Jews about which he had known nothing. That he had known nothing about it seems implausible; that it was directed only against foreign Jews was wrong; and even if it had been, this hardly made it more defensible. The error, odd for someone as steeped in history as Mitterrand, seemed to confirm that he still unconsciously held certain prejudices of the period, distinguishing between French and foreign Jews, and somehow hoping that this distinction would cast Vichy in a more favourable light. As Tony Judt observes, 'he cannot condemn the past root and branch, because he would be condemning himself'.[61]

Even Mitterrand's own supporters found these revelations difficult to accept. The Socialist Lionel Jospin commented that 'one would have liked a clearer and simpler itinerary'. And yet Jospin need only have remembered his own family history to see that simple itineraries were not so common. Jospin's father had been a Socialist supporter of Paul Faure. He accepted municipal responsibilities under the Occupation and was temporarily excluded from the Socialist Party in 1945.

Twice in his television interview Mitterrand said he wished to end France's 'eternal civil wars'. In the end, his attempts to reconcile the French with their past backfired badly, but this was due partly to the contradictions of his own position. When in 1992 the Vel d'Hiver 1942 Committee had tried to obtain an official apology for the role played by Vichy in the extermination of the Jews, Mitterrand refused on the grounds that it was not for the French Republic to apologize for the crimes of Vichy: 'the Resistance, then the government of de Gaulle, then the IVth Republic and the others have been founded on the denial of this "French State"'.[62] Attending the ceremony of remembrance for the Vel d'Hiver on 16 July 1992—the first time a French President had done so—Mitterrand was booed by many of those present. Defending his position subsequently, Mitterrand again refused to link what had happened in the Occupation with the rest of French history. He might, he said, have made an official gesture of repentance, like Willy Brandt in Germany, 'if the French nation had been implicated [*engagé*] in this sad business', but this had not been the case. Even when Mitterrand conceded some ground in the next year with the decision that 16 July was to become a national day of mourning for the Jews, the announcement of this decision was accompanied by the reminder that the anti-Semitic persecutions had been carried out 'under the de facto authority called the "government of the French State"'.[63]

The paradox was that in refusing in 1992 to accept official responsibility for

---

[61] *New York Review of Books*, 3 Nov. 1994. For other reactions to Mitterrand's declarations at this time, see articles in *Le Monde* by T. Judt and Z. Sternhell (21 Sept. 1994), R. Rémond (5 Oct. 1994), P. Birnbaum (21 Oct. 1994).

[62] Conan and Rousso, *Un passé qui ne passe pas*, 42.   [63] Ibid. 44–6.

the French role in the Holocaust, Mitterrand was hiding behind the Gaullist fiction, officially adumbrated in the ordinance of August 1944, that true legitimacy between 1940 and 1944 lay with a French Republic which had never ceased to exist. How did this square with his attempt, in 1994, to rescue Vichy from total obloquy? Perhaps the greatest paradox of all was that the gesture Mitterrand, a lifelong anti-Gaullist, refused to make in 1992 out of fidelity to the Gaullist reading of history, was made on 16 July 1995, by Jacques Chirac, the new Gaullist president. Chirac became the first French leader formally to accept responsibility for France's part in the Holocaust: 'the criminal madness of the occupier was supported by the French people and by the French State . . . France on that day committed an irreparable act . . . It is undeniable that this was a collective fault.' Apart from expressions of outrage by a few die-hard Gaullists— two of them wrote an article in *Le Monde* entitled 'No, Vichy was not France'—it was striking that Chirac's words seemed to meet with general approval.[64] Did this mean that the French had at last reached a consensus about the Occupation? Two years after Chirac's speech of contrition, it became clear that this was far from the case. The trial of Maurice Papon for crimes against humanity in October 1997 caused France's obsession with Vichy to reach a new paroxysm of intensity.

The Papon Trial

Maurice Papon had been the secretary-general of the Gironde prefecture from May 1942 until the Liberation. During this time over 1,500 Jews had been deported from the Bordeaux region, in ten convoys, the last of them in May 1944. Papon was allegedly implicated in eight of these operations, and the civil plaintiffs in the trial represented seventy-two of the victims. What made this trial more controversial than Touvier's was that, unlike Touvier, Papon was no right-wing fanatic. He had been an ambitious young functionary who had owed his rapid promotion before the war to the patronage of Radical-Socialist politicians. In this respect he was similar to René Bousquet, except that despite being only one year younger, he held a much more junior position. In fact, Papon would possibly never have been tried at all if either Bousquet or Leguay had still been alive: his trial acted as a kind of proxy for theirs. In some respects this made the Papon trial unsatisfactory—Bousquet had given the orders, Papon had only obeyed them—but it also gave it greater symbolic resonance: Bousquet's trial would have been that of the Vichy regime while Papon's was that of Vichy France. The trial sparked off an orgy of collective repentance for France's guilt in the Holocaust. For the first time, the Catholic Church performed a public *mea culpa*; so too did the official spokesmen of the French medical profession. More than

---

[64] See the debate on Chirac's speech between Nathalie Heinich and Henry Rousso in *Le Débat*, 89 (1996), 191–207.

ever, Vichy also seemed to haunt the imagination of contemporary French novelists.[65]

Before the trial commenced, the general public had few doubts about Papon's guilt. The trial lasted six months, longer than any other in French legal history. In the end, on 2 April 1998, Papon was convicted of complicity in crimes against humanity and sentenced to ten years' imprisonment. But by the time this verdict was delivered, the certainties with which the trial opened had dissipated. This was partly the result of the many incidents that punctuated the proceedings. Early on there was outrage when the judge agreed that on account of his ill health Papon need not remain in detention during his trial. The civil plaintiffs pointed out that Papon's victims had not enjoyed such privileged treatment. Much time was spent discussing Papon's responsibility for the death of possibly several hundred Algerians in 1961 when as Prefect of Police he banned a demonstration about the Algerian war in Paris. This was clearly a distraction from the real purpose of the trial. Further confusion was caused when the historian Michel Bergès, who had first discovered the documents which led to Papon's prosecution, now made it clear that he was no longer convinced of Papon's guilt. There was also much disagreement among the civil parties as to the degree of Papon's guilt, and the most suitable punishment for it. Arno Klarsfeld annoyed many of his colleagues by demanding a relatively light sentence against Papon on the grounds that, although clearly guilty, he was no Touvier or Barbie.

These incidents and complications added to the daily drama of the proceedings, but the fundamental problem with the trial was fitting Papon's case to a definition of crimes against humanity which had originally been designed, in Nancy Wood's words, 'to catch other and bigger fish'.[66] Papon had been a relatively junior Vichy official obeying orders. To establish that he was complicit in the bid for ideological hegemony by an Axis power—as was required by the 1994 definition of crimes against humanity—it had to be demonstrated that he had had knowledge of the fate awaiting the deportees, and that the constraints on a functionary of his rank did not preclude some freedom of action. Both issues were matters of fine judgement, and difficult to prove. A number of historians, including Robert Paxton and Marc-Olivier Baruch—author of a book on the Vichy administration—testified for the prosecution. One historian, Henri Amouroux, testified for the defence. Henry Rousso refused to testify at all on the grounds that the kinds of truth which historians sought to establish were different from the kinds of truth required by courts of law. Establishing what Papon or anyone else 'knew' about the Holocaust, and what exactly was meant by 'knowing' in such a case, proved almost impossible.

[65] Apart from the latest offering from the inevitable Patrick Modiano, *Dora Bruder* (1996), there is Philippe Dagen, *La Guerre* (1996), Lydie Salvayre, *La Compagnie des spectres* (1997), Marc Lambron, *1941* (1997).
[66] 'Trial of Maurice Papon', 13.

The case against Papon was further muddied by the fact that he had used his position in the Vichy administration to help the Resistance, although it was not clear how early this help had started or what the motivation behind it had been. When Papon had first been accused of crimes against humanity in 1981, a special panel of resisters considered his case and decided that his Resistance credentials were valid, although it also concluded that he should have resigned his post in June 1942. Papon's alleged services to the Resistance had led de Gaulle to appoint him prefect of the Gironde immediately after the Liberation. Papon's glittering career owed as much to de Gaulle as to Vichy.

A number of distinguished former resisters, including Claude Serreulles, now 85 years old, testified at the trial in Papon's favour. But when it came to establishing what Papon might have known about the fate of the Jewish deportees, these former resisters were thrown on to the defensive, finding themselves almost required to apologize for their own belated discovery of the Holocaust. It emerged implicitly from such testimonies that the fate of the Jews had not been an issue of paramount importance for the Resistance. The problem which no one seemed ready to recognize was that whether or not Papon had been, in part at least, a resister was irrelevant to the question whether or not he was guilty of crimes against humanity. In theory, at least, the two facts were not incompatible.[67] Although no-one formulated the issue quite so starkly, many of the resisters who testified were angry that the value of their testimony was not in itself enough to resolve the case. The 88-year-old Jean Jaudel, himself Jewish, and one of the few members of the Musée de l'homme Resistance group to have survived the war, denounced the way in which Papon's trial was turning into a 'trial of the Resistance and of Gaullism'.[68] The writer Maurice Druon, former member of the Free French, denounced the 'insult to the memory' of those resisters who had testified to Papon's Resistance credentials. He worried about the implications of the trial: 'at the Liberation, we made sure that the same aura of heroism surrounded all those who had suffered in the war: the hostages, the deported resisters, the Jewish resisters. Now today we seem to want to create a separate category [ie. the Jews].'[69]

The Resistance Syndrome

To say that the trial of Papon had become the trial of the Resistance was an exaggeration, but the fact that former resisters could interpret it like this revealed how defensive they had become in the years since the myth of the Resistance had lost its hold on the French imagination. What place was there for the Resistance in an account of France's past which seemed only to dwell on the blackest moments? Had France forgotten her debt of gratitude to the Resistance?

---

[67] E. Conan, 'Procès Papon Résistance', *L'Express*, 5 Mar. 1998.
[68] *Le Monde*, 27 Feb. 1998.   [69] Ibid. 24 Oct. 1997.

The relationship between the Resistance and the mass of the population had never been an untroubled one, either during the war or after it. The myth of a nation of resisters flattered the national psyche, but implicitly downgraded the special status of the Resistance. Once that myth had vanished, the Resistance could reclaim its place as an elite standing above the ambient mediocrity, but at the same time, instead of being a source of collective pride, it risked being viewed as irritatingly judgemental and censorious. The Resistance's claim to moral ascendancy sometimes verged on complacent self-satisfaction or even a kind of moral tyranny. When Jean-Melville made his film of *Silence de la mer* in 1949 he had agreed to show the finished product to a jury of resisters, chosen by Vercors, and burn the negative if their verdict was unfavourable.[70] Many ordinary French people probably had sneaking sympathy for Georges Pompidou's remarks to an American journalist about the cult of resistance heroes: ' " I hate all that business", he said with a quick wave of his hand and sharp displeasure in his bright eyes, "I hate medals, I hate decorations of all kinds".'[71] This was the kind of irritation that veterans of the Great War had often aroused in the younger generations after 1918. But at least the veterans had represented most of the population. Unlike the monuments to the fallen of the Great War, many monuments to the Resistance are not in the centre of communities, but outside them. This is a striking spatial representation of the relationship between the Resistance and the population.[72]

It was not surprising, therefore, that the dissipation of the Gaullist myth led not to a positive re-evaluation of the Resistance, but to an erosion of its place in the popular imagination. There seemed no place for heroes any longer. The Resistance disappeared from the cinema. As Michel Foucault wrote in 1974: 'is it possible at the moment to make a positive film on the struggles of the Resistance? One suspects not. One has the impression that people would laugh or that, quite simply, the film would not be seen.'[73] Absent from the cinema in the 1970s, the Resistance became a subject of mockery in it during the 1980s. One of the cinematic successes of the decade was *Papy fait de la résistance* (1983), the story of a family of musicians who refuse to play while the Germans are in France. The film satirized every cliché of Resistance mythology, reworking scenes from classic resistance films like *The Silence of the Sea* or *The Army of Shadows*. But its most subversive moment was the end where the film that has just been seen turns out to have been screened for Les Dossiers de l'Écran, a famous French television series in which a film is used to form the basis of studio debate. In this case the debate is between the resisters who had been depicted in the film and are now shown, thirty years afterwards, as faintly ridiculous figures still quarrelling bitterly about their past, but indignant that anyone else should question it. Thus the film mocks not only the alleged exploits of the resisters, but their claim to

[70] Langlois, 'La Résistance dans le cinéma', 227–39.   [71] Ibid. 458.
[72] Namer, *La Mémoire*, 377.
[73] Langlois, 'La Résistance dans le cinéma', 537.

be the moral custodians of memory and their own history.[74] No less iconoclastic was the cynical *Un héros très discret* (1996) describing how a young man invents for himself an entirely fictitious Resistance past after 1945.

In the face of such attitudes, resisters held on to the idea of themselves as a moral elite. As one of them put it: 'when one meets someone who was a resister, whatever he is doing today, one has the feeling of being part of the same family'.[75] At the Barbie trial one resister declared: 'no schism in the French Resistance will take place here; it is an indissoluble monolith which nothing can destroy'.[76] Such a strategy to defend the memory of the Resistance was undermined during the 1970s as more evidence emerged, much of it from within the Resistance community itself, of the conflicts which had run through the history of the Resistance. The memoirs of Frenay and Bourdet recalled the tensions between de Gaulle and the Resistance. This running sore in the memory of the Resistance was also exploited by François Mitterrand, during the period of his political career when he was saying more about his Resistance past than his Vichy one. In 1969, Mitterrand wrote that de Gaulle had 'confiscated the Resistance's capital of sacrifice, suffering and dignity'.[77]

The many foreigners who had participated in the Resistance through the FTP-MOI might have felt, on the other hand, that the entire French Resistance had confiscated their 'capital of sacrifice'. This was another buried memory to resurface in the 1980s. In 1965–6, when the film-maker Armand Gatti produced a scenario on the Manouchian group, his ten successive versions were rejected by production companies because, he was told, 'a film in which there are only foreigners cannot give us an image of the French Resistance'.[78] When in 1970 the PCF produced a new edition of *Lettres des fusillés*, its collection of letters by Communists who had been shot during the war, the name of Manouchian reappeared, but his Christian name was Gallicized from Misak to Michel. A film was eventually made on Manouchian in 1976—the low-budget production *Affiche rouge*—but the role of foreigners in the Resistance remained a largely unknown story until the screening on television in 1985 of the film *Des terroristes à la retraite*. The film, which suggested that Manouchian had been betrayed by the Communist Party, gave rise to violent polemics in the press. In the long run this had the beneficial effect of bringing the role of foreigners out of the obscurity into which it had fallen—the next edition of the *Lettres des fusillés* restored all the names which had been there in 1946 and there is now a square in Paris named after Marcel Rayman, one of the members of the Manouchian group[79]—but its immediate effect was to cause a feeling that the Resistance, especially the Communist Resistance, had skeletons to hide.

---

[74] Ibid. 523–7; H. Rousso, 'Papy c'est fini', *VSRH* 2 (1984), 77–82.

[75] Douzou, 'L'Entrée en Résistance', 15.

[76] Rousso, *Vichy Syndrome*, 214.

[77] Mitterrand, *Ma part de vérité*, 23–4; see also Mitterrand quoted in Wieviorka, *Nous entrerons*, 343–5.

[78] Langlois, 'La Résistance dans le cinéma', 379–80.

[79] See the C. Muel documentary, *L'Affiche rouge*, 1992.

During the late 1980s, the battles over the memory of the Resistance came to centre on the figure of Jean Moulin. Since 1964, Moulin had become the emblematic hero of the Gaullist Resistance. It was to reclaim Moulin for the Resistance as a whole, as well as situate himself under the symbolic patronage of such a revered figure, that François Mitterrand decided to inaugurate his presidency, on 21 May 1981, by paying a solemn visit to the Panthéon to place a rose on Moulin's tomb. Eight years later, under the general title of 'The Unknown Man of the Panthéon', Daniel Cordier published the first volume of his monumental biography of Moulin. Given Cordier's own background, and his reasons for embarking upon a study of Moulin,[80] it is not surprising that he produced a work which, for all its massive scholarship, sees the Resistance through the eyes of Moulin (and de Gaulle). This alone would explain the irritation which Cordier's work caused among surviving resisters, but they were also offended by his decision to rely exclusively on written archival evidence and exclude memories or oral testimony. Cordier was challenging the position of the Resistance generation as the privileged witnesses to their own history, undermining their aspiration to transmit their memory to future generations.

Nothing, however, caused greater offence to surviving resisters than Cordier's publication of what he claimed to be the Manifesto written by Henri Frenay in the autumn of 1940. The tone of this document, in which Frenay appears as an ardent supporter of the National Revolution and no particular friend of Jews, was not a revelation for any historian of the Resistance, and its authenticity has since been established almost beyond doubt. Nonetheless, numerous surviving resisters wrote to denounce this slur on the reputation of a great Resistance hero. Surviving members of Combat, including Claude Bourdet, met in November 1989 formally to condemn Cordier. As Henry Rousso remarks, surviving resisters reacted to Cordier as if from a bunker under siege.[81]

No one reacted with more violence than Frenay's former lawyer, Charles Benfredj, whose book L'Affaire Jean Moulin, la contre-enquête (1990) moved from a defence of Frenay (and vitriolic denunciation of Cordier) to an attack on Moulin for having been a Soviet agent. He suggested that Moulin had never even been killed but had escaped to Moscow. Allegations about Moulin's alleged Communist sympathies had originated with Frenay as early as 1950 and were repeated in his memoirs and then in a book with the lurid title L'Enigme Jean Moulin (1977). Drawing attention to Moulin's pre-war Comintern and Communist contacts, Frenay argued that Moulin had created the CNR to allow the Communists to gain control over the Resistance. Even Frenay's old comrade Claude Bourdet, himself no friend of the Communists, dismissed these allegations as absurd.[82] Frenay's curious thesis was born out of his own personal grievances. Having lost his battle with Moulin over the future direction of the Resistance, Frenay, as a

---

[80] See above, Introduction.

[81] The controversy over the Manifesto is detailed in Cordier, Jean Moulin, iii. 945–1067, 1286–1335.

[82] Bourdet, L'Aventure incertaine, 219–20.

minister in de Gaulle's post-war Liberation government, was violently attacked by the Communists for his early indulgence towards Vichy. They dubbed him 'Frenay-the-protégé-of-Pucheu'. Frenay expressed his own bitterness at this treatment by creating a conspiracy theory conflating what he saw as his two main enemies: Moulin and the Communists.

Frenay himself had never gone as far as to accuse Moulin of being a Soviet agent. This step was taken most dramatically in 1993 in a book by the journalist Thierry Wolton about the recruitment of Soviet agents by the Comintern in the 1930s. Although Wolton claimed to have read newly released Russian archives, he was coy in revealing his sources, and in the end his argument turned largely on guilt by association. The most disconcerting aspect of the whole affair was that some distinguished historians, like François Furet and Annie Kriegel, lent Wolton an aura of respectability by suggesting his interpretations were worthy of serious consideration.[83]

The role of professional historians was also important in what came to be dubbed the 'Aubrac Affair'. In 1997, Gérard Chauvy, author of a solid history of Lyons under the Occupation, published a book on Raymond Aubrac.[84] With his wife Lucie, Aubrac had been one of the founders of Libération-Sud, and subsequently its main military organizer. Arrested in March 1943, he had been released in May because the police had failed to realize who he was. On 21 June, he was arrested again, with Moulin himself, at the fated Caluire meeting. He escaped in October thanks to an audacious rescue operation organized by his wife. Although not particularly prominent after the war, over the years the Aubrac couple had increasingly taken on the stature of emblematic heroes of the Resistance, thanks to the lively memoir that Lucie wrote on their adventures in 1984. In February 1997, these adventures were romantically depicted in Claude Berri's film *Lucie Aubrac* which received massive publicity. Four months later, Chauvy's book appeared.

Based on genuine new discoveries in the archives, but also on the questionable 'Testament' of Klaus Barbie—a document cobbled together by Barbie and his lawyer Jaques Vergès in order to sow confusion among Barbie's accusers—Chauvy's book cast doubt on the accuracy of the Aubracs' accounts of their Resistance activities. He was at the least able to show implausibilities and contradictions in their writings. Although not going as far as to assert, like Barbie, that after his first arrest Aubrac had become a Gestapo informer and was responsible for the arrest of Moulin, Chauvy insinuated that this was possible. Chauvy's book caused outrage among former resisters of all stripes. Twenty of them, including the Communist Rol-Tanguy, the Gaullist Claude Serreulles, and the conservative de Bénouville, signed a manifesto of protest.[85]

---

[83] See P. Vidal-Naquet, *Le Trait empoisonné: Réflexions sur l'Affaire Moulin* (1993).

[84] G. Chauvy, *Aubrac: Lyon 1943* (1997).

[85] *L'Événement du jeudi*, 3 Apr. 1997. On the Aubrac affair in general, see F. Delpla, *Aubrac: Les Faits et la calomnie* (1997).

The left-wing newspaper *Libération* organized a 'round table' at which the Aubracs could put their case to a group of respected historians of the period, including Henry Rousso and Daniel Cordier. What the Aubracs had expected to be a vindication of their position turned into something quite different. Although all the historians on the panel made it clear that they entirely rejected allegations that Raymond Aubrac had worked for the Gestapo, they launched a merciless dissection of the undoubted discrepancies which existed in the Aubracs' accounts of their past: the round table took on the appearance of a trial. In the face of this assault, the Aubracs defended themselves by arguing that with events occurring so long ago, it was inevitable that inaccuracies should occur. Lucie pointed out that she had written her memoir, entirely from memory, at the age of 73: it was intended to be her history, not a work of history. The historians riposted by claiming that a history of the Resistance based on approximations would not in the long run serve the interests of the Resistance, but only those who wished to denigrate it. Cordier said he was reminded of Zola's remark on Dreyfus's performance at his trial: 'It is enough to make you despair of the innocent.' Another of the historians ended by quoting the inevitable Péguy on the need to tell the truth, however unsettling it might be.[86]

On one hand, it was somewhat unedifying to see these two old and courageous individuals subjected to an examination of this kind. The most distasteful moment came with the suggestion that the Aubracs' imprudence had contributed to the arrest of Raymond's parents, neither of whom was to return from deportation. On the other hand, unless there was to be a crime of *lèse-résistance*, it was not illegitimate for historians to ask searching questions of two people who had, possibly in spite of themselves, become living legends.

In Search of the True France

What is the reason for the recent seemingly endless stream of pseudo-revelations about Moulin and the Resistance? At one level, they are symptomatic of nothing more profound than a predilection for conspiracy theories and a media-generated obsession with historical scoops. The latest theory on Moulin claims that he was killed as he was about to transfer his allegiance from de Gaulle to the Americans. This kind of history will always be written, and, like all conspiracy theories, it remains impervious to reason. Thus for Frenay the fact that Moulin in London avoided contact with the possible Soviet agent André Labarthe, whom he had once known well, was evidence that he had something to hide and was covering his tracks. Of course, if he had had contact with Labarthe, it would have been evidence that he was in contact with the Soviets. In the world of conspiracy theory, one can never win.

There is also an anti-Communist agenda in the attacks on Moulin. The

---

[86] *Libération*, 9 July 1997. See also the comments of H. Rousso, *La Hantise du passé* (1998), 122–38.

historians ready to offer Wolton their support were mostly repentant Stalinists still struggling to overcome their own guilt about their past. In the attack on the Aubracs, latent anti-communism was also present since they had both been close to the Communist Party in the 1950s. But anti-communism has a decreasing hold on contemporary France, and the problem of remembering the Resistance has deeper causes. For the cultural commentator Paul Thibaud, it lies in France's incapacity to acknowledge its debt to the Resistance generation. It is the reverse side of the 'Vichy syndrome'. If the Occupation was such a dark period in France's past, it is more comforting to believe that all were guilty than that the honour of the nation was saved by a tiny minority.[87]

Certainly, the memory of the Resistance seems to oscillate uncontrollably between denigration and celebration with nothing in between. Just as critics of Henry Rousso's attempt to introduce more nuance into the history of Vichy ask whether 'historization' might not become the Trojan Horse of revisionist apologetics, so some Resistance historians have protested against the tone of the interrogation of the Aubracs, asking whether the 'desire to de-mythify is not playing the game of those who have not given up their desire to demolish or undermine' what is valid and important in the legacy of the Resistance.[88]

The continuing political resonance of these debates emerged during the Papon trial. Two years previously President Chirac had acknowledged that 'France' had during the war committed an 'irreparable' act towards the Jews. Many members of Chirac's own party now wondered if he had not gone too far. In an article headed 'Enough, Enough, Enough', the Gaullist leader Philippe Séguin sounded a note of alarm at the ambient mood of self-flagellation, the 'obsession with collective expiation'. De Gaulle had been right to declare Vichy 'null and void'. If Vichy was France, what did that make de Gaulle or the Republic?[89] The former Gaullist prime minister Édouard Balladur asked rhetorically: 'During the Occupation, was France in London or Vichy?'[90] The former president Giscard d'Estaing tried confusingly to distinguish between the Vichy State, France, and the French. He too warned against an obsession with French guilt which would only delight the 'Anglo-Saxon media'.[91] The Socialist Prime Minister Lionel Jospin felt moved to make a statement in parliament:

Is France guilty? I don't think so. Yes, policemen, administrators . . . a French State perpetrated . . . terrifying acts, collaborating with the enemy and with the

---

[87] Thibaud, 'La Culpabilité française', *Esprit*, 168 (Jan. 1991); id., 'La République et ses héros: Le Gaullisme pendant et après la guerre', *Esprit*, 198 (1994), 64–83; id., 'Un temps de mémoire', *Le Débat*, 96 (1996), 166–83.

[88] In Wolwikow, 'Les Images, 23–4; see also J.-M. Guillon, 'L'Affaire Aubrac ou la dérive d'une certaine façon de faire l'histoire', *Modern and Contemporary France*, 7/2 (1999), 89–92. Along with a number of other Resistance historians, including Laborie and Marcot, he signed a letter of protest about the way in which the Aubracs had been treated by certain of his colleagues.

[89] *Le Figaro*, 21 Oct. 1997.

[90] Quoted from *La Croix* in *Le Monde*, 8 Oct. 1997.

[91] *Le Monde*, 28 Oct. 1997.

final solution . . . It is in such terms, it seems to me, that the President of the Republic approached the question in July 1995, even if I myself did not use the same terms, and I myself did not personally use the word France . . . There is no guilt of France because for me France was at London or in the Vercors . . . because Vichy was the negation of France, in any case the negation of the Republic.[92]

Historians alone will never be able to resolve these quarrels of memory which are, at their most fundamental level, debates about national identity. Clearly any attempt to build an identity around the idea that Vichy was not France will be doomed to failure: de Gaulle's assertion that Vichy was null and void no longer serves any purpose in contemporary France. On the other hand, it is no less misleading to repudiate the existence of a Resistance which also represented 'France'. In the end, however, the polarity between these two 'Frances' is itself misleading and sterile. The solution to the problem cannot be to build identity around the utter repudiation of the one or the uncritical embrace of the other. If there is one lesson to be learnt from Péguy, it is that the French past must be faced in all its contradictions and complexity. Only then can it be critically evaluated, and instead of serving to salve the conscience of the present, it can become a usable memory for the future.

[92] *Le Monde*, 23 Oct. 1997.

Appendix
The Camps of Vichy France

It is difficult to provide a full list of camps, and this list is far from exhaustive. The number of camps, and the use which was made of them, fluctuated constantly. In September 1940, not long after the signature of the Armistice, there were no fewer than thirty-one camps in the Unoccupied Zone and about fifteen in the Occupied Zone. A few of these fell into disuse; others were converted to new uses by Vichy; many more were created. Some camps were tiny, with only a score or so of inmates; others had several thousand inmates.

The following list gives the date of the setting up of each camp. Although some camps were restricted to only one category of inmate, most were not. Almost all camps were at some time or other used to intern Jews, and some were used uniquely for this purpose, but other inmates included Communists and other dissidents, Jews, foreigners, gypsies, black-marketeers (from June 1941), abortionists (from February 1942), prostitutes (from August 1943).

There were also several camps in North Africa (Boghari, Colomb-Bechar, Djelfa, etc.), and there was one German concentration camp in Alsace-Lorraine.

1. Rieucros (January 1939): originally for 'foreign undesirables'; became mainly a women's camp.
2. Argelès (February 1939): originally for Spanish refugees.
3. Saint-Cyprien (February 1939): originally for Spanish refugees; in 1940 Jews from the Palatinate sent there.
4. Barcarès (February 1939): originally for Spanish refugees.
5. Gurs (April 1939): originally for Spanish refugees; in 1940 Jews from Baden sent there.
6. Bram (September 1939): originally for nationals of enemy countries.
7. Agde (September 1939): originally for nationals from enemy countries.
8. Septfonds (September 1939): originally for nationals from enemy countries.
9. Casseneuil and Tombebouc (autumn 1939): originally for nationals from enemy countries; later used for foreign workers in GTEs.
10. Le Vernet (October 1939): disciplinary camp originally for foreign 'political suspects'.
11. Milles (May 1940): for German nationals; became a transit camp for those wishing to emigrate from Marseilles.
12. Chibron (June 1940): mainly used to intern Communists.
13. Saint-Sulpice (October 1940): set up to intern Jews after law of 4 October 1940.
14. Brems (October 1940): set up to intern Jews after law of 4 October 1940.
15. Aincourt (October 1940): mainly used to intern Communists from the Paris region.

16. Mérignac (autumn 1940): originally for Communists and other political 'dissidents'.
17. Rivesaltes (December 1940): founded to group internees with their families.
18. Troyes (December 1940): founded to intern foreign Jews living in the Burgundy area.
19. Noé (February 1941): founded as a 'hospital camp'.
20. La Lande-des-Monts (March 1941): founded to intern foreign Jews.
21. Jargeau (March 1941): internment camp for gypsies.
22. Récébédou (April 1940): camp for the sick and old; intended as a 'show camp'.
23. La Morellerie (December 1940): internment camp for gypsies.
24. Nexon (February 1941): in 1942 used to gather Jews prior to deportation.
25. Pithiviers (May 1941): founded to intern Jews recently arrested in Paris.
26. Beaune-la-Rolande (May 1941): founded to intern Jews recently arrested in Paris.
27. Fort-Barraux (July 1941): mainly used to intern Communists.
28. Drancy (August 1941): to intern Jews; in 1942 the main camp used to gather Jews prior to deportation.
29. Rouillé (September 1941): mainly used to intern Communists from the Paris region.
30. La Guiche (October 1941): 'sanatorium camp'.
31. Poitiers (November 1941): internment of Jews.
32. Montreuil-Bellay (November 1941): internment camp for gypsies.
33. Vénissieux (1941): in 1942 used to gather Jews of Lyons area prior to deportation.
34. Compiègne (December 1941): founded to intern Jews.
35. Saliers (June 1942): internment camp for gypsies.

Sources: J. Weill, *Contribution à l'histoire des camps d'internement dans l'anti-France* (1946); Centre de Documentation juive contemporaine, *L'Internement sous Vichy* (1995); A. Grynberg, *Les Camps de la honte* (1991); J. Grandjonc and T. Grundtner, *Zone d'ombres; Exil et internement d'Allemands dans le sud-est de la France* (Aix, 1990); M.-L. Cohen and E. Malo, *Les Camps du sud-ouest de la France* (Toulouse, 1994); D. Peschanski, *Les Tsiganes en France 1939–1946* (1994); K. Bartosek et al., *De l'exil à la résistance: Réfugiés et immigrés de l'Europe central en France 1933–1945* (1989); J.-P. Rioux et al., *Les Communises français de Munich à Châteaubriant* (1987).

Map 3 The Camps of Vichy France

Bibliographical Essay

Full references to the material used in the writing of this book can be found in the footnotes. The purpose of this essay is to provide a guide to the most important studies on the Occupation period. Where an English translation exists I have cited it. Unless otherwise mentioned, the place of publication of books in English is London and of books in French Paris.

Bibliographies

There are two useful bibliographies: H. Michel, *Bibliographie critique de la Résistance* (1964) and D. Evleth, *France under German Occupation 1940–1944: An Annotated Bibliography* (New York, 1991). But so much work has been produced since 1990 that both of these are badly out of date.

For a (not entirely comprehensive) list of clandestine Resistance publications, there is the Bibliothèque nationale's *Catalogue des périodiques clandestins diffusés en France de 1939 à 1945* (1954). For a bibliography of the authorized press see D. Evleth, *The Authorized Press in Vichy and German-Occupied France 1940–1944* (1999).

General Studies

J.-P. Azéma, *From Munich to the Liberation 1938–1944* (Cambridge, 1979) has been the standard textbook for twenty years. J.-P. Azéma and F. Bédarida (eds.), *La France des années noires*, 2 vols. (1993) is a collective work on the entire history of the Occupation with chapters by most leading historians of the period. It is accessible and well illustrated. H. Amouroux, *La Grande Histoire des Français sous l'Occupation*, 8 vols. (1976–91) offers a mass of picturesque detail but no interpretation. At the other extreme, H. R. Kedward, *Occupied France: Collaboration and Resistance* (Oxford, 1985) is very short but has many insights. I. Ousby, *Occupation, the Ordeal of France, 1940–1944* (1997) is a recent study by a non-professional historian. It is readable and perceptive. B. Gordon (ed.), *Historical Dictionary of World War Two France: The Occupation, Vichy and the Resistance, 1938–1946* (Westport, Conn., 1998) is a useful reference book, but the selection of entries is somewhat eccentric and somewhat modish (why *Casablanca* not *Le Corbeau*, why Antoine Blondin not Yves Bouthillier, why Jean Bazaine not Joseph Barthélemy?). For a more conventional approach see M. and J.-P. Cointet, *Dictionnaire historique de la France sous l'Occupation* (2000).

Background

It has been one of the arguments of this book that the Occupation can only be understood in the wider context of French history in the previous forty years, if not indeed longer. Obviously any full list of works on this period would be enormous, but it is worth mentioning some which, directly or indirectly, cast light on France's history after 1940, even if they stop before that date. G. Noriel, *Les Origines républicaines de Vichy* (1999) is a recent attempt to locate Vichy in a longer prehistory. Some parts of the argument are more convincing than others. F. Monnet, *Refaire la République: André Tardieu, une dérive réactionnaire, 1876–1945* (1993), G. Le Béguec, 'L'Entrée au Palais Bourbon: Les Filières privilégiés d'accès à la fonction parlementaire, 1919–1939' (unpublished thesis, University of Paris-X, 1989), and K. Passmore, *From Liberalism to Fascism: The Right in a French Province 1928–1939* (Cambridge, 1997) all have much to say on the crisis of inter-war conservatism. H. Lebovics, *True France: The Wars over Cultural Identity in France 1900–1945* (1992) and S. Peer, *France on Display: Peasants, Provincials and Folklore in the 1937 Paris World's Fair* (Albany, NY, 1998) offer perspectives on French representations of national identity. On interwar gender issues see M. Roberts, *Civilization without Sexes: Reconstructing Gender in Postwar France, 1917–1927* (Chicago, 1994) and S. Reynolds, *France between the Wars: Gender and Politics* (1992). On the impact of the Great War on the arts K. Silver, *Esprit de Corps: The Art of the Parisian Avant-Garde and the First World War, 1914–1925* (Princeton, 1989). R. Golan, *Modernity and Nostalgia: Art and Politics in France between the Wars* (1995) tries to extend Silver's arguments to the whole of the interwar period in a somewhat cruder way. On the legacy of the Great War see A. Prost's monumental history of the war veterans, *Les Anciens Combattants et la société française*, 3 vols. (1977). P. Servent, *Le Mythe Pétain: Verdun ou les tranchées de la mémoire* (1992) is impressionistic but interesting. On anti-liberalism in inter-war French politics Z. Sternhell, *Ni droite ni gauche: L'Idéologie fasciste en France* (1983) is important even if one rejects the central thesis.

On the so-called nonconformists of the 1930s J. Loubet del Bayle, *Les Non-Conformistes des années trente* (1969) is informative, but to get inside the mind of members of that generation there is no substitute for reading the memoirs of some of them, especially J.-P. Maxence, *Histoire de dix ans 1927–1937* (1939), C. Roy, *Moi je* (1969), J. Laurent, *Histoire egoïste* (1976), P. Andreu, *Le Rouge et le blanc, 1940–1944* (1977). Another very vivid memoir of the inter-war years (from the standpoint of a committed fascist) is R. Brasillach, *Notre avant-guerre* (1941). On attitudes towards race, immigration, and demography in the interwar years see G. Noriel, *Le Creuset français: Histoire de l'immigration en France (XIX–XX siècles)* (1988), R. Schor, *L'Antisémitisme en France pendant les années trente* (Brussels, 1992), W. Schneider, *Quality and Quantity: The Quest for Biological Regeneration in Twentieth Century France* (Cambridge, 1990).

The Defeat

J.-L. Crémieux-Brilhac, *Les Français de l'an 40*, 2 vols. (1990) has superseded all previous books on France's defeat although even today M. Bloch's *Strange Defeat* (1953) remains worth reading. The only published book on the Exodus is J. Vidalenc, *L'Exode de mai–juin 1940* (1957) but by far the best study is N. Dombrowski, 'Beyond the Battlefield: The French Civilian Exodus of 1940' (unpublished Ph.D. thesis, New York, 1995).

The Vichy Regime

R. Paxton, *Vichy France 1940–1944: Old Guard and New Order, 1940–1944* (1972) has deservedly become a classic. His first book, *Parades and Politics at Vichy: The French Officer Corps under Marshal Pétain* (Princeton, 1966) is also excellent. S. Hoffmann, 'The Vichy Circle of French Conservatives', in id., *Decline or Renewal? France since the 1930s* (New York, 1974), provides an excellent conceptual framework for understanding the regime. Y. Durand, *Vichy 1940–1944* (1972) is short but full of insights. Fondation nationale des sciences politiques, *Le Gouvernement de Vichy 1940–1942* (1972) remains useful although it ignores the link between the National Revolution and collaboration. Although he is best known for his writing on the Resistance, H. Michel's *Vichy année 40* (1966) is possibly his best book, and provides an excellent account of the first year of the regime. M.-O. Baruch, *Le Régime de Vichy* (1996) is a useful recent short synthesis. On the regime's last days see H. Rousso, *Pétain et la fin de la collaboration: Sigmaringen 1944–1945* (Brussels, 1984).

There is no full-length study of the ideology of the National Revolution, but Pétain's speeches are the obvious starting point: P. Pétain, *Discours aux Français: 17 juin 1940–20 août 1944* (1989). L. Yagil, *'L'Homme nouveau' et la Révolution nationale de Vichy 1940–1944* (1997) tries to analyse Vichy ideology but fails because it takes the discourse of the regime too much at face value. There are now many studies of specific aspects of the regime and its policies. On the working of the administration see M.-O. Baruch, *Servir l'État français: L'Administration en France de 1940 à 1944* (1997). On propaganda D. Peschanski has written a number of articles which are collected in his *Vichy 1940–1944: Contrôle et exclusion* (Brussels, 1997). See also L. Gervereau and D. Peschanski, *La Propagande sous Vichy 1940–1944* (1990). There is also a mass of fascinating information in the two published notebooks of Angelo Tasca who worked for Vichy's propaganda services: *La France de Vichy: Archives inédits d'Angelo Tasca*, ed. D. Bidussa and D. Peschanski (Milan, 1996) and *Vichy 1940–1944: Archives de guerre d'Angelo Tasca*, ed. D. Peschanski (Paris, 1986). On the Legion see J.-P. Cointet, *La Légion française des combattants 1940–1944: La Tentation du fascisme* (1995). On Vichy's attempts to revive folklore see C. Faure, *Le Projet culturel de Vichy: Folklore et Révolution nationale 1940–1944* (1989). On Vichy's economic policy see M. Margairaz, *L'État, les finances et l'économie: Histoire d'une conversion 1932–1952* (1991) and the relevant chapter of R. Kuisel, *Capitalism and the State in Modern France* (Cambridge, 1981). On policy towards women see M. Pollard, *Reign of Virtue: Mobilising Gender in Vichy France* (Chicago, 1998) and F. Muel-Dreyfus, *Vichy et l'éternel féminin* (1996). On youth policy P. Giolitto's recent *Histoire de la jeunesse sous Vichy* (1991) adds nothing to W.-D. Halls's excellent *The Youth of Vichy France* (Oxford, 1981). On policy towards sport see J.-L. Gay-Lescot, *Sport et éducation sous Vichy* (Lyons, 1991). On agricultural policy there is almost nothing except for I. Boussard, *Vichy et la corporation paysanne* (1980), an almost completely unreadable history of the peasant corporation. On the attempt to apply corporatism to industry see J.-P. Le Crom, *Syndicats, nous voilà! Vichy et le corporatisme* (1995).

Another way to approach the regime is through biographies. M. Ferro, *Pétain* (1987) is the best book on Pétain and Vichy, but has little on his career before 1940.

For this see R. Griffiths, *Marshal Pétain* (1970). G. Warner, *Pierre Laval and the Eclipse of France* (1968) is still worth reading but needs to be supplemented by F. Kupferman, *Laval 1883–1945* (1987) or J.-P. Cointet, *Pierre Laval* (1993). H. Coutau-Bégarie and C. Huan, *Darlan* (1989) is definitely the best biography in terms of documentation provided, but its interpretation is apologetic and often unconvincing. The same authors have also usefully published many of Darlan's letters and memoranda in *Lettres et notes de l'Amiral Darlan*, ed. H. Coutau-Bégarie and C. Huan (1992). H. Michel, *François Darlan* (1993) is also worth reading.

Many participants in the regime wrote memoirs. Although these are self-serving and need to be used prudently, they give a good insight into the atmosphere of the regime. For this purpose the most useful are H. du Moulin de Labarthète, *Le Temps des Illusions: Souvenirs (juillet 1940–avril 1942)* (1946), P. Baudouin, *The Private Diaries March 1940–January 1941)* (1948) and J. Barthélemy, *Mémoires, ministre de la justice: Vichy (1941–1943)* (1989 edn.). Y. Bouthillier, *Le Drame de l'armistice*, 2 vols. (1950) is rather drier but full of information.

Collaboration and Collaborationism

P. Burrin's superb *Living with Defeat: France under the German Occupation, 1940–1944* (New York, 1997) is now the essential starting point both for the collaboration of the government and for collaboration in daily life. S. Hoffmann conceptualizes collaboration in 'Self-Ensnared: Collaboration with Nazi Germany' in id., *Decline or Renewal?* (New York, 1974), 26–44. E. Jäckel, *La France dans l'Europe de Hitler* (1968) is an excellent account of the relationship between the Vichy government and the Germans which anticipated many of the conclusions reached by Paxton. J.-B. Duroselle, *L'Abîme 1939–1945* (1982) is a history of French foreign policy during the Occupation which slightly nuances their interpretation. A. Milward, *The New Order and the French Economy* (Oxford, 1970) deals with German economic plans for France and French responses to them. For a local study see E. Papp, *La Collaboration dans l'Eure 1940–1944* (1993).

On collaborationism see P. Ory, *Les Collaborateurs 1940–1945* (1976), B. Gordon, *Collaborationism in France during the Second World War* (Ithaca, NY, 1980), and P. Burrin, *La Dérive fasciste: Doriot, Déat, Bergery 1933–1945* (1986). It is also well worth reading Déat's own memoirs, *Mémoires politiques* (1989), to see how an intelligent man can be so extraordinarily wrong. For an insight into the mind of the collaborationists see P. Drieu la Rochelle, *Journal 1939–1945* (1992) and L. Rebatet, *Les Décombres* (1942). For a more urbane version of collaborationism see A. Fabre-Luce, *Journal de la France 1939–1944* (Geneva, 1946). On literary collaboration J. Verdès-Leroux, *Refus et violences: Politique et littérature de l'extrême droite des années trente aux retombées de la Libération* (1996) has a lot of information, but is weak on analysis. P. Hebey, *'La Nouvelle Revue française' des années sombres: juin 1940 à juin 1941: Des intellectuels à la dérive* (1992) is useful on the *NRF* in the war.

French Society under Occupation

J.-P. Azéma and F. Bédarida (eds.), *Le Régime de Vichy et les Français* (1993) contains numerous contributions on aspects of French society under the Vichy regime. P. Laborie, *L'Opinion publique sous Vichy* (1990) is an excellent account of public opinion. D. Veillon, *Vivre et survivre en France 1939–1947* (1995) gives a clear account of the difficulties of daily life. D. Veillon and J.-M. Flonneau, *Le Temps des restrictions en France 1939–1949* (1996) gives a mass of local detail on prices and food shortages. Enormous insights can be gained from reading diaries and journals of the period. Among the most interesting are J. Bobowski, *En Guerre et en paix: Journal 1940–1941* (1991); *Journal d'un honnête homme pendant l'Occupation (juin 1940–août 1944)*, ed. J. Bourgeon (Thonon-les-Bains, 1990); H. Drouot, *Journal d'un Dijonnais pendant l'occupation allemande 1940–1944* (Dijon, 1998); J. Guéhenno, *Journal des années noires* (1947); C. Rist, *Une saison gâtée: Journal de guerre et de l'occupation* (1983); P. Limagne, *Éphémérides de quatre années*, 3 vols. (Lavilledieu, 1987); L. Werth, *Déposition: Journal 1940–1944* (1992).

Another good approach is through local history. Useful examples include P. Laborie, *Résistants, Vichyssois et autres: L'Évolution de l'opinion et des comportements dans le Lot 1939 à 1944* (1980); M. Luirard, *La Région stéphanoise dans la guerre et dans la paix* (Saint-Étienne, 1980); L. Taylor, *Between Resistance and Collaboration: Popular Protest in Modern France, 1940–1945* (New York, 2000); J. Sweets, *Choices in Vichy France* (New York, 1986); R. Terrisse, *Bordeaux, 1940–1944* (1993); R. Zaretsky, *Nîmes at War: Religion, Politics and Public Opinion in the Gard, 1938–1944* (University Park, Pa., 1995).

On the experiences of women under Occupation see H. Diamond, *Women and the Second World War in France 1939–1948: Choices and Constraints* (1999) and S. Fishman, *We will wait! The Wives of French Prisoners of War 1940–1945* (1991). M. Bood, *Les Années doubles: Journal d'une lycéenne sous l'Occupation* (1974) is the diary of an adolescent girl. On the experience of workers under Occupation there is no adequate single book, but many useful articles in 'Syndicalismes sous Vichy', special issue of *MS* 158 (1993), ed. J.-L. Robert, and in D. Peschanski and J.-L. Robert (eds.), *Les Ouvriers en France pendant la Deuxième Guerre mondiale* (1992). Surprisingly there is no satisfactory study of business during the Occupation. R. de Rochebrune and J.-C. Hazera, *Les Patrons sous l'Occupation* (1995) has lots of information but is too anecdotal. R. Vinen, *The Politics of French Business* (Cambridge, 1991) is ingenious but unconvincing. A. Lacroix-Riz, *Industriels et banquiers sous l'Occupation: La Collaboration économique avec le Reich et Vichy* (1999), is well documented but marred by too schematically Marxist an approach. A. Beltram et al. (ed.), *La Vie des entreprises sous l'Occupation* (1994) contains essays of uneven quality, but Rousso's introductory essay is excellent. C. Andrieu, *La Banque sous l'Occupation: Paradoxes de l'histoire d'une profession (1936–1946)* manages to make the history of banking under the Occupation surprisingly readable. P. Nicolle, *Cinquante mois d'armistice: Journal d'un témoin*, 2 vols. (1947) is the diary of a small business leader which contains a lot of interesting gossip about Vichy.

On the Churches the best two general studies are J. Duquesne, *Les Catholiques français sous l'Occupation* (1996 edn.) which is restricted to Catholics and W. Halls, *Politics, Society and Christianity in Vichy France* (Oxford, 1995) which includes Protestants and Jews. X. de Montclos (ed.), *Églises et Chrétiens dans la Deuxième Guerre mondiale: La Région Rhône-Alpes* (Lyons, 1978) has many useful articles. E. Fouilloux, *Les Chrétiens entre crise et libération 1937–1947* (1997) is too impressionistic and apologetic. The most recent study M. Cointet, *Vichy et l'église* (1999) contains some useful information on Church leaders.

Cultural and Intellectual Life

A good starting point are the essays in J.-P. Rioux (ed.), *La Vie culturelle sous Vichy* (1990). See also G. Hirschfeld and P. Marsh (eds.), *Collboration in Fance: Politics and Culture during the Nazi Occupation* (Oxford, 1989). G. Ragache and J.-R. Ragache, *La Vie quotidienne des écrivains et des artistes sous l'Occupation* (1988) is merely anecdotal. There are many books on cinema. J.-P. Bertin-Maghit, *Le Cinéma sous l'Occupation* (1989) is the best overview. His *Le Cinéma français sous l'Occupation* (1980) is a more narrowly focused study of the themes treated in Vichy cinema. F. Garçon, *De Blum à Pétain: Cinéma et société française 1936–1944* (1984) and E. Ehrlich, *Cinema of Paradox: French Filmmaking under the German Occupation* (New York, 1985) offer interesting interpretations. J. Siclier, *La France de Pétain et son cinéma* (1981) is engagingly personal. On the theatre see S. Added, *Le Théâtre dans les années Vichy 1940–1944* (1992). On the visual arts see L. Bertrand-Dorléac, *L'Art de la défaite 1940–1944* (1993) and M. Cone, *Artists under Vichy: A Case of Prejudice and Persecution* (Princeton, 1992). On publishing see P. Fouché, *L'Édition française sous l'Occupation 1940–1944*, 2 vols. (1987). On writers see G. Sapiro's exhaustive *La Guerre des écrivains 1940–1953* (1999). Sapiro's study is informed by the sociological approach of Pierre Bourdieu, but applies it with subtlety and intelligence. For the Parisian cultural scene through German eyes see E. Jünger, *Premier journal parisien: Journal II, 1941–1943* (1980), *Second journal parisien: Journal III, 1943–1944* (1980) and G. Heller, *Un Allemand à Paris* (1981). For the Parisian scene as witnessed by one of its stars see J. Cocteau, *Journal 1942–1945* (1989).

On universities see A. Guesclin, *Les Facs sous Vichy: Actes du colloque des universités de Clermont Ferrand et de Strasbourg, novembre 1993* (Clermont, 1994). The most comprehensive study of the Uriage school is B. Comte, *Une utopie combattante: L'École des cadres d'Uriage* (1991). For a critical approach see J. Hellman, *The Knight-Monks of Vichy France* (1993). On Mounier and Vichy see M. Winock, *Histoire politique de la revue Esprit 1930–1950* (1975) and M. Bergès, *Vichy contre Mounier: Les Non-Conformistes face aux années 40* (1997). See also some of Mounier's own writings in *Mounier et sa génération: Lettres, carnets et inédits* (1956).

The Jews

There is now a massive bibliography on this subject. S. Zuccotti, *The Holocaust, the French and the Jews* (New York, 1993) and A. Kaspi, *Les Juifs pendant l'Occupation* (1991), offer excellent general accounts. M. Marrus and R. Paxton, *Vichy France and the Jews* (New York, 1981) is the starting point for a study of the policies of the regime towards the Jews. S. Klarsfeld, *Vichy-Auschwitz: Le Rôle de Vichy dans la solution finale en France*, 2 vols. (1983–5) gives the most detailed account of Vichy's role in the Holocaust. On internment camps see A. Grynberg, *Les Camps de la honte: Les Internés juifs des camps français* (1991).

On anti-Jewish propagandists see P.-A. Taguieff (ed.), *L'Antisémitisme de plume*

(1999) and J. Billig's collection of documents on the German sponsored anti-Jewish institute, *L'Institut d'étude des questions juives* (1974). R. Poznanski, *Être juif en France pendant la Deuxième Guerre mondiale* (1994) and A. Cohen, *Persécutions et sauvetages: Juifs et Français sous l'occupation et sous Vichy* (1993) are two excellent books looking at the reactions of French society, Jews and non-Jews, to the persecution of the Jews.

On education and the Jews see C. Singer, *Vichy, l'université et les juifs* (1992) and on lawyers R. Badinter, *Un anti-sémitisme ordinaire: Vichy et les avocats juifs 1940–1944* (1997). Two useful local studies are D. Ryan, *The Holocaust and the Jews of Marseilles* (Champaign, Ill., 1996) and J. Adler, *The Jews of Paris and the Final Solution: Communal Responses and Internal Conflicts, 1940–1944* (New York, 1985). Two poignant and illuminating diaries by Jews are R.-R. Lambert, *Carnet d'un témoin* (1985) and J. Biélinky, *Journal, 1940–1942: Un journaliste juif sous l'occupation* (1992). See also the memoirs of A. Kriegel, *Ce que j'ai cru comprendre* (1991).

Resistance and the Free French

J.-L. Crémieux-Brilhac, *La France libre: De l'appel du 18 juin à la Libération* (1996) surpasses any other histories of the Free French. *The Complete War Memoirs of Charles de Gaulle* (New York, 1967 edn.) are indispensable. The memoirs of de Gaulle's intelligence chief Passy also contain a lot of useful information: Colonel Passy (A. Dewarvin), *2ᵉ Bureau Londres* (1947); *10 Duke Street Londres* (1948); *Missions secrètes en France* (1951). The best biography of de Gaulle for this period is J. Lacouture, *De Gaulle*, i. *The Rebel* (1989).

There is no satisfactory single-volume history of the Resistance. H. Noguères (with M. Degliame-Fouché), *Histoire de la Résistance en France de 1940 à 1945*, 5 vols. (1967–81) provides a detailed month-by-month chronicle but no interpretation. H. R. Kedward, *Resistance in Vichy France* (1978), is the best starting point and offers the most penetrating account of the early days of the Resistance even if it only covers the Southern Zone up to the end of 1942. The series of conferences on the Resistance which took place between 1993 and 1997 have transformed the social history of the Resistance. Their proceedings have been published as J.-M. Guillon and P. Laborie, *Mémoire et histoire: La Résistance* (Toulouse, 1995); J. Sainclivier and C. Bougeard, *La Résistance et les Français: Enjeux stratégiques et environnement social* (Rennes, 1995); R. Frank and J. Gotovitch, *La Résistance et les Européens du Nord*, 2 vols. (1994–6); F. Marcot (ed.), *La Résistance et les Francais: Lutte armée et maquis* (1996); L. Douzou, et al. (eds.), *La Résistance et les Francais: Villes, centres et logiques de décision* (1995); J.-M. Guillon and R. Mencherini, *La Résistance et les Européens du sud* (1999). See also the articles collected in 'Pour une histoire sociale de la Résistance', *MS* 180 (1997).

The best histories of particular Resistance movements are O. Wieviorka, *Une certaine idée de la résistance: Défense de la France 1940–1949* (1995), L. Douzou, *La Désobéissance: Histoire d'un mouvement et d'un journal clandestins: Libération-Sud (1940–1944)* (1995) and A. Aglan, *La Résistance sacrifiée: Le Mouvement Libération-Nord* (1999). But R. Bédarida, *Les Armes de l'esprit: Témoignage chrétien 1941–1944* (1977) and D. Veillon, *Le Franc-Tireur, un journal clandestin un mouvement de résistance, 1940–1944* (1977) also remain valuable. There is urgent need for an updated history of Combat. For a good study of a Resistance network (as opposed to movement) see A. Aglan, *Mémoires résistantes, le réseau Jade-Fitzroy (1940–1944)* (1994).

On the political and social ideas of the Resistance, H. Michel and B. Mirkine-Guetzévitch, *Les Idées politiques et sociales de la Résistance* (1954) and H. Michel, *Les Courants de pensée de la Résistance* (1962) still remain useful. On ideas for post-war reform see A. Shennan, *Rethinking France: Plans for Renewal 1940–1946* (Oxford, 1989). On ideas about education see J.-M. Muracciole, *Les Enfants de la défaite: La Résistance, l'éducation et la culture* (1998). For the CNR Charter see C. Andrieu, *Le Programme commun de la Résistance: Des idées dans la guerre* (1985). For the projects of the CGE see D. de Bellescize, *Les Neuf Sages de la Résistance: Le Comité général d'études dans la clandestinité* (1979).

On what might be called the high politics of the Resistance J. Sweets, *The Politics of Resistance in France 1940–1944: A History of the Mouvements Unis de la Résistance* (De Kalb, Ill., 1976) is good. But the essential book on this subject is now Daniel Cordier, *Jean Moulin: L'Inconnu du Panthéon*, 3 vols. (1989–93). Ostensibly a biography of Moulin, Cordier's massive study is also a minute account of the conflicts between the Free French and the Resistance, and between the Resistance movements themselves. The 300-page preface to the first volume gives the arguments of the seven volumes to follow. In fact only two more appeared, and instead Cordier produced another book *Jean Moulin: La République des catacombes* (1999) which recapitulated the first three volumes and covered the ground which had been projected for the four subsequent volumes. Whatever one thinks of Cordier's angle of approach, his book is now, as the French say, *incontournable*. One effect of the cult of Moulin has been to squeeze out the memory of other important intermediaries between the Free French and the Resistance. One of these, Brossolette is the subject of a good recent biography, G. Piketty, *Pierre Brossolette: Un héros de la Résistance* (1998). Another has left a short memoir recently published by the IHTP: *Souvenirs inédits d'Yvon Morandat*, ed. L. Douzou (1994).

On the Communists and the Resistance see S. Courtois, *Le PCF dans la guerre: De Gaulle, la Résistance, Staline* (1980) and D. Virieux's massive 'Le Front national de la lutte pour la liberté et l'indépendance de la France: Un mouvement de Résistance. Période clandestine (mai 1941–août 1944)' (unpublished thesis, University of Paris-VIII). On the Socialists see M. Sadoun, *Les Socialistes sous l'Occupation: Résistance et collaboration* (1982).

On foreigners in the Resistance see S. Courtois, D. Peschanski, A. Rayski, *Le Sang de l'étranger: Les Immigrés de la MOI dans la Résistance* (1989) and A. Wieviorka, *Ils étaient juifs, résistants, communistes* (1986). On women see M. Weitz, *Sisters in the Resistance: How Women fought to free France 1940–1945* (New York, 1995); P. Schwartz, 'Women, Resistance and Communism in France 1939–1945' (unpublished Ph.D. thesis, New York, 1998). For a memoir by a female resister see L. Aubrac, *Outwitting the Gestapo* (Lincoln, Nebr., 1993). On writers and the Resistance see A. Simonin, *Les Éditions de minuit: Le Devoir d'insoumission* (1994), J. Debû-Bridel, *La Résistance intellectuelle, textes et témoignages* (1970), M. Atack, *Literature and the French Resistance: Cultural Politics and Narrative Forms, 1940–1950* (Manchester, 1989), and J. Steel, *Littératures de l'ombre: Récits et nouvelles de la Résistance* (1991). But Sapiro is best on this subject, as on all matters affecting writers.

One good way to approach the history of the Resistance is through local studies. The best of these is J.-M. Guillon, 'La Résistance dans le Var: Essai d'histoire politique' (Doctorat d'État, Aix, 1989). Although unpublished, this monumental work is one of the most important studies of the Resistance. See also J. Sainclivier, *La Résistance en Ille-et-Vilaine 1940–1944* (Rennes, 1993) and F. Marcot, *La Résistance dans le Jura* (Besançon, 1985). Sensitivity to locality is also one of the most important features of H. R. Kedward, *In Search of the Maquis: Rural Resistance in Southern France* (Oxford, 1993).

Among memoirs of resisters, C. Bourdet, *L'Aventure incertaine: De la Résistance à la restauration* (1975) is in a class of its own because it combines a personal memoir with serious reflection on the nature of the Resistance, and rises above the tendency to anecdote, mythologization, or recrimination which is otherwise common. Other memoirs well worth reading are H. Frenay, *The Night Will End* (1976), C. d'Aragon, *La Résistance sans héroïsme* (1979), C. Pineau, *La Simple Vérité 1940–1945* (1961), G. de Bénouville, *Le Sacrifice du matin* (1946), and J.-P. Lévy, *Mémoires d'un franc-tireur: Itinéraire d'un résistant* (1998).

Liberation

The change in research agendas over the last twenty years is striking if one compares Comité d'histoire de la Deuxième Guerre mondiale, *La Libération de la France: Actes du colloque international tenu à Paris du 28 octobre au 31 octobre 1974* (1976) with H. R. Kedward and N. Wood (eds.), *The Liberation of France: Image and Event* (Oxford, 1995). These are both important collective volumes devoted to the Liberation. The emphasis of the first one is political and military while the second one concentrates on gender and representations. H. Footitt and J. Simmonds, *France 1943–1945* (Leicester, 1988) has a lot to say about liberated France as seen by the Allies. J. Kayser, *Un journaliste sur le front de Normandie: Carnet de route juillet–août 1944* (1991) gives the first impressions of liberated Normandy by a French journalist who had spent the war in London. A. Brossat, *Libération, fête folle. 6 juin 1944–8 mai 1945: Mythes et rites ou le grand théâtre des passions populaires* (1994) gives a good picture of the joyous atmosphere of the Liberation. On the intentions of the Communist Party at the Liberation see P. Buton, *Les Lendemains qui déchantent: Le Parti communiste à la Libération* (1993). P. Buton and J.-M. Guillon (eds.), *Les Pouvoirs en France à la Libération* (1994), studies post-Liberation conflicts in a whole series of *départements*.

There are studies of Liberation for almost every *département* of France. These all contain useful information, but tend to be somewhat descriptive. In a class of its own is L. Capdevila, *Les Bretons au lendemain de l'Occupation: Imaginaire et comportement d'une sortie de guerre 1944–1945* (Rennes, 1999). This is a brilliant study which has some extremely interesting things to say about representations of collaboration and resistance after Liberation. It is also illuminating on the subject of the head-shavings. On these see also F. Virgili, 'Les Tontes de la Libération en France', *Cahiers de l'IHTP*, 31 (1995), 53–64; A. Brossat, *Les Tondues: Un carnaval moche* (1992). On the purges as a whole P. Novick, *The Resistance versus Vichy: The Purge of Collaborators in Liberated France* (New York, 1968) is still worth reading but needs to be supplemented by H. Rousso, 'L'Épuration en France: Une histoire inachevée', *VSRH* 33 (1992), 106–17 and F. Rouquet, *L'Épuration dans l'administration française* (1993).

Memory

H. Rousso, *The Vichy Syndrome* (1991) invented the subject and still remains the essential starting point, to be supplemented by the more polemical H. Rousso and E. Conan, *Vichy: A Past that will not Pass* (1998). Rousso's latest thoughts on the subject are in H. Rousso, *La Hantise du passé* (1998). On commemorating the past see G. Namer, *La Commémoration en France de 1945 à nos jours* (1987) and S. Barcellini and A. Wieviorka, *Passant, souviens-toi! Les Lieux de souvenir de la Seconde Guerre mondiale en France* (1995). On the Occupation remembered in the cinema see S. Lindeperg, *Les Écrans de l'ombre: La Seconde Guerre mondiale dans le cinéma français* (1997). On Jewish memory see A. Wieviorka, *Déportation et génocide: Entre la mémoire et l'oubli* (1992). For reflections on the recent trials for crimes against humanity see R. J. Golsan, *Memory, the Holocaust, and French Justice* (Hanover, NH, 1996), A. Finkielkraut, *Remembering in Vain: The Klaus Barbie Trial and Crimes against Humanity* (New York, 1992), and N. Wood, *Vectors of Memory* (Oxford, 1999).

Index